M000104901

PROPERTIES
OF PROPERTY

EDITORIAL ADVISORS

Vicki Been
Elihu Root Professor of Law
New York University School of Law

Erwin Chemerinsky
Dean and Distinguished Professor of Law
University of California, Irvine, School of Law

Richard A. Epstein
Laurence A. Tisch Professor of Law
New York University School of Law
Peter and Kirsten Bedford Senior Fellow
The Hoover Institution
Senior Lecturer in Law
The University of Chicago

Ronald J. Gilson
Charles J. Meyers Professor of Law and Business
Stanford University
Marc and Eva Stern Professor of Law and Business
Columbia Law School

James E. Krier
Earl Warren DeLano Professor of Law
The University of Michigan Law School

Richard K. Neumann, Jr.
Professor of Law
Hofstra University School of Law

Robert H. Sitkoff
John L. Gray Professor of Law
Harvard Law School

David Alan Sklansky
Yosef Osheawich Professor of Law
University of California at Berkeley School of Law

Kent D. Syverud
Dean and Ethan A. H. Shepley University Professor
Washington University School of Law

Elizabeth Warren
Leo Gottlieb Professor of Law
Harvard Law School

PROPERTIES
OF PROPERTY

GREGORY S. ALEXANDER &
HANOCH DAGAN

Wolters Kluwer
Law & Business

Copyright © 2012 CCH Incorporated.

Published by Wolters Kluwer Law & Business in New York.

Wolters Kluwer Law & Business serves customers worldwide with CCH, Aspen Publishers, and Kluwer Law International products. (www.wolterskluwerlb.com)

No part of this publication may be reproduced or transmitted in any form or by any means, electronic or mechanical, including photocopy, recording, or utilized by any information storage or retrieval system, without written permission from the publisher. For information about permissions or to request permissions online, visit us at www.wolterskluwerlb.com, or a written request may be faxed to our permissions department at 212-771-0803.

To contact Customer Service, e-mail customer.service@wolterskluwer.com, call 1-800-234-1660, fax 1-800-901-9075, or mail correspondence to:

> Wolters Kluwer Law & Business
> Attn: Order Department
> PO Box 990
> Frederick, MD 21705

Printed in the United States of America.

1 2 3 4 5 6 7 8 9 0

ISBN 978-1-4548-1356-9

Library of Congress Cataloging-in-Publication Data

Alexander, Gregory S., 1948-
    Properties of property / Gregory S. Alexander & Hanoch Dagan.
       p. cm.
    Includes index.
    ISBN 978-1-4548-1356-9
1. Property. 2.   Right of property. I. Dagan, Hanokh. II. Title.
    K720.A49 2012
    346.04 — dc23

                                                          2012008716

About Wolters Kluwer Law & Business

Wolters Kluwer Law & Business is a leading global provider of intelligent information and digital solutions for legal and business professionals in key specialty areas, and respected educational resources for professors and law students. Wolters Kluwer Law & Business connects legal and business professionals as well as those in the education market with timely, specialized authoritative content and information-enabled solutions to support success through productivity, accuracy and mobility.

Serving customers worldwide, Wolters Kluwer Law & Business products include those under the Aspen Publishers, CCH, Kluwer Law International, Loislaw, Best Case, ftwilliam.com and MediRegs family of products.

CCH products have been a trusted resource since 1913, and are highly regarded resources for legal, securities, antitrust and trade regulation, government contracting, banking, pension, payroll, employment and labor, and healthcare reimbursement and compliance professionals.

Aspen Publishers products provide essential information to attorneys, business professionals and law students. Written by preeminent authorities, the product line offers analytical and practical information in a range of specialty practice areas from securities law and intellectual property to mergers and acquisitions and pension/benefits. Aspen's trusted legal education resources provide professors and students with high-quality, up-to-date and effective resources for successful instruction and study in all areas of the law.

Kluwer Law International products provide the global business community with reliable international legal information in English. Legal practitioners, corporate counsel and business executives around the world rely on Kluwer Law journals, looseleafs, books, and electronic products for comprehensive information in many areas of international legal practice.

Loislaw is a comprehensive online legal research product providing legal content to law firm practitioners of various specializations. Loislaw provides attorneys with the ability to quickly and efficiently find the necessary legal information they need, when and where they need it, by facilitating access to primary law as well as state-specific law, records, forms and treatises.

Best Case Solutions is the leading bankruptcy software product to the bankruptcy industry. It provides software and workflow tools to flawlessly streamline petition preparation and the electronic filing process, while timely incorporating ever-changing court requirements.

ftwilliam.com offers employee benefits professionals the highest quality plan documents (retirement, welfare and non-qualified) and government forms (5500/PBGC, 1099 and IRS) software at highly competitive prices.

MediRegs products provide integrated health care compliance content and software solutions for professionals in healthcare, higher education and life sciences, including professionals in accounting, law and consulting.

Wolters Kluwer Law & Business, a division of Wolters Kluwer, is headquartered in New York. Wolters Kluwer is a market-leading global information services company focused on professionals.

For Beth and Ted

For Tomer

SUMMARY
OF CONTENTS

Contents   xi
Preface   xvii
Acknowledgements   xix

PART I. WHY PROPERTY?

Chapter 1.   PROPERTY AND LABOR   3
Chapter 2.   PROPERTY AND PERSONHOOD   17
Chapter 3.   PROPERTY AND LIBERTY   29
Chapter 4.   PROPERTY AS A KANTIAN RIGHT   43
Chapter 5.   PROPERTY AND WELL-BEING   57
Chapter 6.   PROPERTY AND CITIZENSHIP   71
Chapter 7.   PROPERTY AND DISTRIBUTIVE JUSTICE   83

Part II. HOW PROPERTY?

Chapter 8.   STRUCTURING OWNERSHIP   97
Chapter 9.   BETWEEN EXCLUSION AND RESPONSIBILITY   123
Chapter 10.   EXIT AND ENTRY   147
Chapter 11.   FOREGROUND VS. BACKGROUND: LAW OR SOCIAL
              NORMS   161
Chapter 12.   COMMON AND PUBLIC PROPERTY   171
Chapter 13.   COMMODITY VS. PROPRIETY   187

Part III. PROPERTY IN CONTEXT

Chapter 14.   THINGS (PROPERTY IN WHAT?)   217
Chapter 15.   FAMILY   269
Chapter 16.   HOME   309
Chapter 17.   TRANSITIONS   361
Chapter 18.   ENVIRONMENTAL LAW AND POLICY   417

Author Index   429
Subject Index   435

CONTENTS

Preface   *xvii*
Acknowledgements   *xix*

PART I.   WHY PROPERTY?   1

CHAPTER 1.   PROPERTY AND LABOR   3

John Locke, Second Treatise on Civil Government   3
Notes and Questions   9
Stephen R. Munzer, A Theory of Property   12
Notes and Questions   13

CHAPTER 2.   PROPERTY AND PERSONHOOD   17

Margaret Jane Radin, Property and Personhood   17
Notes and Questions   24

CHAPTER 3.   PROPERTY AND LIBERTY   29

Robert Nozick, Anarchy, State, and Utopia   29
Notes and Questions   38

CHAPTER 4.   PROPERTY AS A KANTIAN RIGHT   43

Ernest J. Weinrib, Poverty and Property in Kant's System of Rights   43
Notes and Questions   54

CHAPTER 5.   PROPERTY AND WELL-BEING   57

Harold Demsetz, Toward a Theory of Property Rights   57
Notes and Questions   62

Richard A. Posner, Economic Analysis of Law   65
Notes and Questions   68

CHAPTER 6.   PROPERTY AND CITIZENSHIP   71

Gregory S. Alexander, Commodity & Propriety: Competing Visions   71
of Property in American Legal Thought 1776-1970
Notes and Questions   78

CHAPTER 7.   PROPERTY AND DISTRIBUTIVE
JUSTICE   83

Jeremy Waldron, The Right to Private Property   83
Notes and Questions   91

PART II.   HOW PROPERTY?   95

CHAPTER 8.   STRUCTURING OWNERSHIP   97

1. Between Despotic Dominion and Bundle of Rights   97
    William Blackstone, Commentaries on the Laws of England   97
    Wesley Newcomb Hohfeld, Fundamental Legal Conceptions as   97
    Applied in Judicial Reasoning
    Notes and Questions   100
    Hanoch Dagan, The Craft of Property   103
    Notes and Questions   108
2. The *Numerus Clausus* Puzzle   110
    Thomas W. Merrill & Henry E. Smith, Optimal Standardization in   110
    the Law of Property: The *Numerus Clausus* Principle
    Notes and Questions   120

CHAPTER 9.   BETWEEN EXCLUSION
AND RESPONSIBILITY   123

1. Ownership and Exclusion   123
    J.E. Penner, The Idea of Property in Law   123
    Notes and Questions   131
2. Ownership and Responsibility   134
    Gregory S. Alexander, The Social-Obligation Norm in American   134
    Property Law
    Notes and Questions   142

CHAPTER 10.   EXIT AND ENTRY   147

Leslie Green, Rights of Exit   147
Joseph William Singer, Entitlement: The Paradoxes of Property   153
Notes and Questions   158

CHAPTER 11.   FOREGROUND VS. BACKGROUND: LAW OR SOCIAL NORMS   161

Robert C. Ellickson, Order Without Law   161
Notes and Questions   167

CHAPTER 12.   COMMON AND PUBLIC PROPERTY   171

Carol Rose, The Comedy of the Commons: Custom, Commerce,   171
and Inherently Public Property
Elinor Ostrom, Governing the Commons   176
Notes and Questions   182

CHAPTER 13.   COMMODITY VS. PROPRIETY   187

1. Historical   187
    Gregory S. Alexander, Commodity & Propriety: Competing Visions   187
    of Property in American Legal Thought 1776-1970
    Albert O. Hirschman, Rival Views of Market Society   190
    Notes and Questions   199
2. Normative   201
    Elizabeth Anderson, Value in Ethics and Economics   201
    Notes and Questions   212

PART III.   PROPERTY IN CONTEXT   215

CHAPTER 14.   THINGS (PROPERTY IN WHAT?)   217

1. Information   217
    Yochai Benkler, Freedom in the Commons: Towards a Political   217
    Economy of Information
    Notes and Questions   227
2. The Body and Body Parts   229
    Stephen R. Munzer, An Uneasy Case Against Property Rights in   229
    Body Parts
    Notes and Questions   238

3. The "New Property" 243
   Charles A. Reich, The New Property 243
   Notes and Questions 252
4. Artifacts of Cultural Property 256
   John Henry Merryman, The Public Interest in Cultural Property 256
   Notes and Questions 264

CHAPTER 15.   FAMILY **269**

1. Inheritance and Intergenerational Justice 269
   D.W. Haslett, Is Inheritance Justified? 269
   Notes and Questions 274
2. Marriage 279
   Carolyn J. Frantz & Hanoch Dagan, Properties of Marriage 279
   Notes and Questions 290
3. Trusts 293
   Robert H. Sitkoff, An Agency Costs Theory of Trust Law 293
   Notes and Questions 303

CHAPTER 16.   HOME **309**

1. The Home 309
   Stephanie M. Stern, Residential Protectionism and the Legal 309
   Mythology of the Home
   D. Benjamin Barros, Home as a Legal Concept 316
   Notes and Questions 317
2. Homelessness and a Right to Housing 321
   Jeremy Waldron, Homelessness and the Issue of Freedom 321
   Notes and Questions 328
3. Residential Communities 332
   Evan McKenzie, Privatopia: Homeowner Associations and the Rise 332
   of Residential Private Government
   Notes and Questions 337
4. Housing Discrimination 344
   Abraham Bell & Gideon Parchomovsky, The Integration Game 344
   Notes and Questions 355

CHAPTER 17.   TRANSITIONS **361**

1. Takings 361
   Thomas W. Merrill, The Economics of Public Use 361
   Notes and Questions 371
2. Aboriginal Land Regimes and Colonialism 377
   Stuart Banner, Possessing the Pacific 377
   Notes and Questions 388
3. Reparations 393

    Jeremy Waldron, Superseding Historic Injustice   393
    Notes and Questions   401
4. "From Marx to Markets"   407
    Claus Offe, Disqualification, Retribution, Restitution: Dilemmas of   407
    Justice in Post-Communist Transitions
    Notes and Questions   413

CHAPTER 18.   ENVIRONMENTAL LAW
AND POLICY   417

    J.B. Ruhl, Climate Change Adaption and the Structural   417
    Transformation of Environmental Law
    Notes and Questions   424

Author Index   429
Subject Index   435

PREFACE

Properties of Property grew out of our personal experiences as teachers of seminars on property theory as well as courses on property law. It is offered as the main text for the former, and as a theoretical companion to a casebook in the latter. We believe that property theory should be of interest not only in law schools, but also in various other departments, from political science to urban planning. Therefore, this book is both theory-focused and not excessively law-centric.

Properties of Property weaves the thread between theory and the concrete details of everyday life. As lawyers, we want to abstract from law the normative and structural foundations of property, both as an abstract right and as a practical institution or rather a set of such institutions. Hence, we set the necessary groundwork for examining particular property-related institutions by beginning the book with readings that provide a broader theoretical framework. Thus, Part I — *Why Property?* — addresses the major normative accounts of property, focusing on labor, personhood, liberty, rights, welfare, citizenship, and distributive justice. Part II — *How Property?* — shifts from the normative plane to the conceptual, contemplating the question of how ownership and property rights are structured, both legally and in social practice. Here we consider the choice between understanding property as "despotic" dominion or a bundle of rights, the role of the *numerus clausus* principle, the competition between exclusion and social responsibility, the functions of exit and entry, the place of social norms, as well as the features of common and public property and the issue of commodification.

In Part III we consider *Property in Context*. We include materials that cover five grounded topics, namely, things, the family, the home, transitions, and the environment. *Things* include information, body parts, the so-called "new property," and rights to artifacts of cultural heritage. *Family* includes inheritance and intergenerational justice as well as marital property and trusts. *Home*, in addition to the home *strictu sensu*, also covers residential associations as well as the problems of homelessness and of housing discrimination. Finally, *Transitions* touches on property problems that result from shifts to new political and legal regimes. These problems range from eminent domain and regulatory takings to aboriginal land claims, reparations for historic injustices, and the shift from a Marxist political and economic regime to a market-based regime. Throughout Part III our aim is to bring theoretical problems concerning property to life by grounding them in some of the most persistent and contentious problems facing societies around the world. This part thus demonstrates why theory matters and provides some tools for analyzing controversial social phenomena in a theoretically sophisticated way.

We find the selections excerpted as the main text for each chapter very exciting. The materials represent a broad spectrum of the leading forces in property theory from both within and without the legal academic community. These selections provide, in our view, important insights into the topics covered, and raise many issues for deliberation. (We should note that in the interest of space the selections have been significantly edited and that most of the footnotes have been omitted, while the remaining ones have been renumbered.) Following each excerpt, we add a series of notes, comments, and questions, designed both to flesh out the topic and to stimulate discussion. These notes also make some references to other scholarly writings to provide a balanced account of contending approaches to the matter at hand.

The idea of this book started as part of the Cornell Law School — Tel-Aviv University Faculty of Law Exchange Initiative. We are grateful to Robert B. Diener and David S. Litman, the founders of this Initiative, for their financial support, and to Dean Stewart Schwab for his encouragement. We also thank our colleagues Avihay Dorfman, Talia Fisher, Daphna Lewisohn-Zamir, Doug Kysar, Eduardo Peñalver, Jeff Rachlinski, and five anonymous referees for comments and suggestions, Lyndsey Clark, Ziva Lander, and Varda Shmulevich for secretarial support, and Brian Hogue and Catherine Milne, both Cornell Law '12 as well as Sarah Breslow, Cornell Law '13, for research assistance.

Gregory S. Alexander
Hanoch Dagan

March 2012
Ithaca and Tel-Aviv

ACKNOWLEDGMENTS

Alexander, Gregory S., Commodity & Propriety: Competing Visions of Property in American Legal Thought 1776-1970, pp. 1-2, 4-5, Chicago, IL: The University of Chicago Press. Copyright © 1997 by The University of Chicago Press. Reprinted with permission of the University of Chicago Press.

Alexander, Gregory S., The Social Obligation Norm in American Property Law, Cornell Law Review, vol. 94, pp. 745, 747-748, 753-755, 758-759, 760-770, 801-802, 805-807, 809-810. Copyright © 2009 Cornell Law Review. Reprinted by permission.

Anderson, Elizabeth, Value in Ethics and Economics, Cambridge, Mass.: Harvard University Press. Copyright © 1993 by the President and Fellows of Harvard College. Reprinted by permission of the publisher from "The Ethical Limitations of the Market" in Value in Ethics and Economics, pp. 141-146, 150-153, 163-167.

Banner, Stuart, Possessing the Pacific: Land, Settlers, and Indigenous People from Australia to Alaska, pp. 47-63, 68-71, 73, 75-76, 78-89, 91-98, 103, 125-127, Cambridge, Mass.: Harvard University Press, Copyright © 2007 by the President and Fellows of Harvard College. Reprinted by permission of the publisher.

Barros, D. Benjamin, Home as a Legal Concept, 46 Santa Clara Law Review, vol. 46, pp. 255, 277, 278-81. Copyright © 2006 by the Santa Clara Law Review. Reprinted by permission of the Santa Clara Law Review.

Bell, Abraham & Gideon Parchomovsky, The Integration Game, 100 Columbia Law Review, vol. 100, pp. 1965, 1965-70, 1972, 1973, 1974, 1989-96, 2005-08, 2009, 2011, 2014-15. Copyright © 2000 by the Directors of The Columbia Law Review Association, Inc. Reprinted by permission of the Columbia Law Review.

Benkler, Yochai, Freedom in the Commons, Duke Law Journal, vol. 52, pp. 1245, 1245-54, 1260-72. Copyright © 2003 by Yochai Benkler. This article is released under the Public Library of Science Open-Access License and the Creative Commons Attribution License.

Dagan, Hanoch, The Craft of Property, California Law Review, vol. 91, pp. 1517, 1519-20. Copyright © 2003.

Demsetz, Harold, Toward a Theory of Property Rights, American Economic Review, vol. 57 (Papers & Proc. 1967), pp. 347, 348, 350-57. Copyright © 1967 by the American Economic Association.

Ellickson, Robert C., Order Without Law, Cambridge, Mass.: Harvard University Press. Copyright © 1991 by the President and Fellows of Harvard College. Reprinted by permission of the publisher from "Shortcomings of Current Theories of Social Control" in Order Without Law: How Neighbors Settle Disputes, pp. 137-147.

Fennell, Lee Anne, Contracting Communities, University of Illinois Law Review, vol. 2004, pp. 829, 844, 846-848. Copyright © 2005 by the Board of Trustees of the University of Illinois. Reprinted by permission of the University of Illinois Law Review.

Frantz, Carolyn J. & Hanoch Dagan, Properties of Marriage, 104 Columbia Law Review, vol. 104, pp. 75, 81-88, 91-94, 98-112. Copyright © 2004 by the Directors of The Columbia Law Review Association, Inc. Reprinted by permission of the Columbia Law Review.Green, Leslie, Rights of Exit, Legal Theory, vol. 4, pp. 165-167, 170-172, 174-180, 184-185. Copyright © 1998 Cambridge University Press. Reprinted with the permission of Cambridge University Press.

Haslett, D.W., Is Inheritance Justified?, Philosophy & Public Affairs, Vol. 15, pp.123, 137-138, 139, 140, 141-142, 144-148. Copyright © 1986 by Princeton University Press. Reproduced with permission of Blackwell Publishing Ltd.

Hirschman, Albert O., Rival Views of Market Society, from Rival Views of Market Society, pp.105-124 , by Albert Hirschman, copyright © 1986 by Albert O. Hirschman. Used by permission of Viking Penguin, a division of Penguin Group (USA) Inc.

Hohfeld, Wesley N., Some Fundamental Legal Conceptions as Applied in Legal Reasoning, Yale Law Journal, vol. 26, pp.710, 718-723, 733-734, 740, 745-747. Copyright © 1917 by the Yale Law Journal Company, Inc. Reprinted by permission of the Yale Law Journal Company.

Locke, John, Second Treatise on Civil Government, Critical edition, Peter Laslett ed., pp. 303-07, 308-09, 311-14, 317-20. Copyright © Cambridge University Press 1960. Reprinted with the permission of Cambridge University Press.

McKenzie, Evan, Privatopia: Homeowner Associations and the Rise of Residential Private Government, pp. 122-23, 125-128, 140-42, 144-145, 146. New Haven, CT: Yale University Press. Copyright © 1994 by Yale University. Reprinted by permission.

Merrill, Thomas W., The Economics of Public Use, Cornell L. Review, vol. 72, pp. 61, 63-68, 74-78, 80-93. Copyright © 1986 Cornell Law Review. Reprinted with permission.

Merrill, Thomas W. & Henry E. Smith, Optimal Standardization in the Law of Property, Yale Law Journal, vol. 110, pp. 3-8, 9-11, 20, 24, 26-31, 33-35, 38, 40, 42, 58-61, 68-70. Copyright © 2000 by the Yale Law Journal Company, Inc. Reprinted by permission of the Yale Law Journal Company.

Merryman, John Henry, The Public Interest in Cultural Property, California Law Review, vol. 77, pp. 339, 339-341, 343, 344,345-348, 349-352, 353, 355-364. Copyright © 1989 by California Law Review, Inc. Reprinted from California Law Review by permission of California Law Review, Inc.

Munzer, Stephen R., A Theory of Property, pp. 256-60. Copyright © Cambridge University Press 1990. Reprinted with the permission of Cambridge University Press.

Munzer, Stephen R., The Uneasy Case Against Property Rights in Body Parts, Social Philosophy & Policy, volume 11, pp. 259, 260, 266-267, 269-270, 271-274, 284-285. Copyright © Social Philosophy & Policy Foundation 1994. Reprinted with the permission of Cambridge University Press.

Nozick, Robert, Anarchy, State, and Utopia, pp. 150-157, 159-164, 167-172. Copyright © 1977 Perseus Books Group via Copyright Clearance Center, Inc. Reprinted by permission of Perseus Books Group.

Offe, Claus, Disqualification, Retribution, Restitution: Dilemmas of Justice in Post-Communist Transitions, Journal of Political Philosophy, vol. 1, pp. 17, 19-23, 40-44. Copyright © 1993 by John Wiley & Sons. Reprinted with permission of John Wiley & Sons via Copyright Clearance Center.

Ostrom, Elinor, Governing the Commons: The Evolution of Institutions for Collective Action, Copyright © Cambridge University Press 1990. Reprinted with the permission of Cambridge University Press.

Penner, J.E., The Idea of Property in Law (2000), pp. 1-2, 5, 49-50, 68-73, 103-104, 206-207 (4,506 words). Copyright © 1997 J.E. Penner. By permission of the author and Oxford University Press.

Posner, Richard A., Economic Analysis of Law, 7th ed., pp. 31-34, 37-38. Copyright 2007 Richard A. Posner. Reprinted by permission of the author.

Purdy, Jedediah, The Meaning of Property: Freedom, Community, and the Legal Imagination, pp. 16-18. Copyright © 2010 by Yale University. Reprinted by permission.

Radin, Margaret Jane, Property and Personhood, Stanford Law Review, vol. 34, pp. 957, 959-962, 968-973, 975-979, 986-987, 1013-1014. Copyright © 1982 by Stanford Law Review. Reprinted with permission of Stanford Law Review in the format Textbook via Copyright Clearance Center.

Reich, Charles A., The New Property, Yale Law Journal, vol. 73, pp. 733, 734-738, 739-740, 744, 745, 756, 757, 768-779, 785-787. Copyright © 1964 by the Yale Law Journal Company, Inc. Reprinted by permission of the Yale Law Journal Company.

Rose, Carol M., The Comedy of the Commons: Custom, Commerce, and Inherently Public Property, University of Chicago Law Review, vol. 53, pp. 711-714, 718-723, 778-781. Copyright © 1986 The University of Chicago Law Review. Reprinted by permission from The University of Chicago Law Review.

Ruhl, J.B., Climate Change Adaptation and the Structural Transformation of Environmental Law, Environmental Law, vol. 40, pp. 363, 365-66, 392, 394-95, 397, 398, 400-401, 402, 406-07, 408, 409-410, 412, 413, 414-416, 417-18, 423, 425, 426, 427, 428, 429, 431, 432-34. Copyright © 2010 by Environmental Law. Reprinted by permission.

Singer, Joseph William, Entitlement: The Paradoxes of Property, pp. 39-44. Copyright © 2000 by Yale University. Reprinted by permission.

Sitkoff, Robert H., An Agency Cost Theory of Trust Law, Cornell Law Review, vol. 89, pp. 621, 623, 624-625, 638-639, 640, 646-651, 652. Copyright © 2004 Cornell Law Review. Reprinted by permission of the Cornell Law Review.

Stern, Stephanie M., Residential Protectionism and the Legal Mythology of the Home, Michigan Law Review, vol. 107, pp. 1093, 1094-96, 1097-98, 1105-07, 1109-10, 1113, 1114-15, 1127, 1128-29, 1130, 1139-40, 1142-43, 1144. Copyright © 2009 by Stephanie Stern. Reprinted by permission of the author.

Waldron, Jeremy, The Right to Private Property, pp. 115-117, 423, 425-27, 430-39, 444-45. Copyright © Jeremy Waldron 1988. Reprinted by permission of the author and Oxford University Press.

Waldron, Jeremy, Superseding Historical Injustice, Ethics, vol. 103, pp. 4-5, 6-10, 12-16, 20, 24-27. Copyright © 1992 by The University of Chicago Press. Reprinted by permission of The University of Chicago Press.

Waldron, Jeremy, Homelessness and the Issue of Freedom, UCLA Law Review, vol. 39, pp. 295-96, 299-300, 302, 304-07, 308, 310-13, 315, 318, 319-21, 322, 323, 324. Copyright © 1991 Jeremy Waldron. Reprinted by permission of the author.

Weinrib, Ernest, Corrective Justice (forthcoming 2012 with Oxford University Press). Copyright © 2012 Ernest Weinrib. Reprinted by permission of the author.

PROPERTIES
OF PROPERTY

I WHY PROPERTY?

1 | *PROPERTY AND LABOR*

John Locke, Second Treatise on Civil Government[1]

CHAPTER V: OF PROPERTY

25. Whether we consider natural *Reason*, which tells us, that Men, being once born, have a right to their Preservation, and consequently to Meat and Drink, and such other things as Nature affords for their Subsistence: or *Revelation*, which gives us an account of those Grants God made of the World to *Adam*, and to *Noah*, and his Sons, 'tis very clear, that God, as King *David* says, *Psal.* CXV. xvj. *has given the Earth to the Children of Men;* given it to mankind in common. But this being supposed, it seems to some a very great difficulty, how any one should ever come to have a *Property* in any thing: I will not content myself to answer, That if it be difficult to make out *Property*, upon a supposition that God gave the world to *Adam*, and his Posterity in common, it is impossible that any Man, but one universal Monarch, should have any property upon a supposition, that God gave the world to *Adam*, and his Heirs in Succession, exclusive of all the rest of his Posterity. But I shall endeavour to shew, how men might come to have a *property* in several parts of that which God gave to Mankind in common, and that without any express Compact of all the Commoners.

26. God, who hath given the World to Men in common, hath also given them reason to make use of it to the best advantage of Life, and

---

1. John Locke, *Second Treatise on Civil Government, in* TWO TREATISES OF GOVERNMENT 303-307, 308-309, 311-314, 317-320 (Peter Laslett ed., Cambridge Univ. Press 1960) (1690). Peter Laslett took great care to provide a text faithful to the original. Laslett aimed to produce a version that "would have satisfied Locke at the time of his death. . . ." This motivation explains the text's variance with modern English usage, grammar, and spelling. *See id*. at 146-150 (explaining Laslett's methodology in arriving at the textual version reproduced here).

convenience. The Earth, and all that is therein, is given to Men for the Support and Comfort of their being. And though all the Fruits it naturally produces, and Beasts it feeds, belong to Mankind in common, as they are produced by the spontaneous hand of Nature; and no body has originally a private Dominion, exclusive of the rest of Mankind, in any of them, as they are thus in their natural state: yet being given for the use of Men, there must of necessity be a means *to appropriate* them some way or other before they can be of any use, or at all beneficial to any particular Man. The Fruit, or Venison, which nourishes the wild *Indian*, who knows no Inclosure, and is still a Tenant in common, must be his, and so his, *i.e.* a part of him, that another can no longer have any right to it, before it can do him any good for the support of his life.

27. Though the Earth, and all inferior Creatures be common to all Men, yet every Man has a *Property* in his own *Person:* this no Body has any Right to but himself. The *Labour* of his Body, and the *Work* of his Hands, we may say, are properly his. Whatsoever then he removes out of the State that Nature hath provided, and left it in, he hath mixed his *Labour* with, and joined to it something that is his own, and thereby makes it his *Property.* It being by him removed from the common state Nature hath placed it in, it hath by this *labour* something annexed to it, that excludes the common right of other Men. For this *Labour* being the unquestionable Property of the Labourer, no Man but he can have a right to what that is once joyned to, at least where there is enough, and as good, left in common for others.

28. He that is nourished by the Acorns he pickt up under an Oak, or the Apples he gathered from the Trees in the Wood, has certainly appropriated them to himself. No Body can deny but the nourishment is his. I ask then, When did they begin to be his? When he digested? Or when he eat? Or when he boiled? Or when he brought them home? Or when he picked them up? And 'tis plain, if the first gathering made them not his, nothing else could. That *labour* put a distinction between them and common. That added something to them more than Nature, the common Mother of all, had done; and so they became his private right. And will any one say, he had no right to those Acorns or Apples, he thus appropriated, because he had not the consent of all Mankind to make them his? Was it a Robbery thus to assume to himself what belonged to all in Common? If such a consent as that was necessary, Man had starved, notwithstanding the Plenty God had given him. We see in *Commons*, which remain so by Compact, that 'tis the taking any part of what is common, and removing it out of the state Nature leaves it in, which *begins the Property*; without which the Common is of no use. And the taking of this or that part, does not depend on the express consent of all the Commoners. Thus the Grass my Horse has bit; the Turfs my Servant has cut; and the Ore I have digg'd in any place, where I have a right to them in common with others, become my *Property*, without the assignation or consent of any body. The *labour* that

was mine, removing them out of that common state they were in, hath *fixed* my *Property* in them. . . .

31. It will perhaps be objected to this, that if gathering the Acorns, or other Fruits of the Earth, *&c.* makes a right to them, then any one may *ingross* as much as he will. To which I Answer, Not so. The same Law of Nature, that does by this means give us Property, does also *bound* that *property* too. *God has given us all things richly*, I Tim. vi. 17. is the Voice of Reason confirmed by Inspiration. But how far has he given it us? *To enjoy.* As much as any one can make use of to any advantage of life before it spoils; so much he may by his labour fix a Property in: whatever is beyond this, is more than his share, and belongs to others. Nothing was made by God for Man to spoil or destroy. And thus, considering the plenty of natural Provisions there was a long time in the World, and the few spenders; and to how small a part of that provision the industry of one Man could extend it self, and ingross it to the prejudice of others; especially keeping within the *bounds*, set by reason, of what might serve for his *use;* there could be then little room for Quarrels or Contentions about Property so establish'd.

32. But the *chief matter of Property* being now not the Fruits of the Earth, and the Beasts that subsist on it, but the *Earth it self;* as that which takes in and carries with it all the rest: I think it is plain, that *Property* in that too is acquired as the former. *As much Land* as a Man Tills, Plants, Improves, Cultivates, and can use the Product of, so much is his *Property.* He by his Labour does, as it were, inclose it from the Common. Nor will it invalidate his right to say, Every body else has an equal Title to it; and therefore he cannot appropriate, he cannot inclose, without the Consent of all his Fellow-Commoners, all Mankind. God, when he gave the World in common to all Mankind, commanded Man also to labour, and the penury of his Condition required it of him. God and his reason commanded him to subdue the Earth, *i.e.* improve it for the benefit of Life, and therein lay out something upon it that was his own, his labour. He that in Obedience to this Command of God, subdued, tilled and sowed any part of it, thereby annexed to it something that was his *Property,* which another had no Title to, nor could without injury take from him.

33. Nor was this *appropriation* of any parcel of *Land*, by improving it, any prejudice to any other Man, since there was still enough, and as good left; and more than the yet unprovided could use. So that in effect, there was never the less left for others because of his inclosure for himself. For he that leaves as much as another can make use of, does as good as take nothing at all. No Body could think himself injur'd by the drinking of another Man, though he took a good Draught, who had a whole River of the same Water left him to quench his thirst. And the Case of Land and Water, where there is enough of both, is perfectly the same.

34. God gave the World to Men in Common; but since he gave it them for their benefit, and the greatest Conveniencies of Life they were capable to draw from it, it cannot be supposed he meant it should always remain

common and uncultivated. He gave it to the use of the Industrious and Rational, (and *Labour* was to be *his Title* to it;) not to the Fancy or Covetousness of the Quarrelsome and Contentious. He that had as good left for his Improvement, as was already taken up, needed not complain, ought not to meddle with what was already improved by another's Labour: If he did, 'tis plain he desired the benefit of another's Pains, which he had no right to, and not the Ground which God had given him in common with others to labour on, and whereof there was as good left, as that already possessed, and more than he knew what to do with, or his Industry could reach to. . . .

36. [Suppose] a Man, or Family, in the state they were, at first peopling of the World by the Children of *Adam*, or *Noah*; let him plant in some inland, vacant places of *America*, we shall find that the *Possessions* he could make himself upon the *measures* we have given, would not be very large, nor, even to this day, prejudice the rest of Mankind, or give them reason to complain, or think themselves injured by this Man's Incroachment, though the Race of Men have now spread themselves to all the corners of the World, and do infinitely exceed the small number [which] was at the beginning. Nay, the extent of *Ground* is of so little value, *without labour*, that I have heard it affirmed, that in *Spain* it self a Man may be permitted to plough, sow and reap, without being disturbed, upon Land he has no other Title to, but only his making use of it. But, on the contrary, the Inhabitants think themselves beholden to him, who, by his Industry on neglected, and consequently waste Land, has increased the stock of Corn, which they wanted. But be this as it will, which I lay no stress on; This I dare boldly affirm, That the same *Rule of Propriety*, (viz.) that every Man should have as much as he could make use of, would hold still in the World, without straitening any body, since there is Land enough in the World to suffice double the Inhabitants, had not the *Invention of Money*, and the tacit Agreement of Men to put a value on it, introduced (by Consent) larger Possessions, and a Right to them; which, how it has done, I shall by and by, shew more at large.

37. This is certain, That in the beginning, before the desire of having more than Men needed had altered the intrinsick value of things, which depends only on their usefulness to the Life of Man; or [Men] had *agreed, that a little piece of yellow Metal*, which would keep without wasting or decay, should be worth a great piece of Flesh, or a whole heap of Corn; though Men had a Right to appropriate, by their Labour, each one of himself, as much of the things of Nature, as he could use: Yet this could not be much, nor to the Prejudice of others, where the same plenty was still left, to those who would use the same Industry. To which let me add, that he who appropriates land to himself by his labour, does not lessen but increase the common stock of mankind. For the provisions serving to the support of human life, produced by one acre of inclosed and cultivated land, are (to speak much within compasse) ten times more, than those, which are yielded by an acre of Land of an equal richnesse lyeng wast in common.

And therefor he that incloses Land, and has a greater plenty of the con-
veniencys of life from ten acres, than he could have from an hundred left to
Nature, may truly be said, to give ninety acres to Mankind for his labour
now supplies him with provisions out of ten acres, which were but the
product of an hundred lying in common. I have here rated the improved
land very low in making its product but as ten to one, when it is much
nearer an hundred to one: for I aske whether in the wild woods and uncultivated wast of America, left to Nature, without any improvement, tillage or
husbandry, a thousand acres will yield the needy and wretched inhabitants
as many conveniencies of life, as ten acres of equally fertile land doe in
Devonshire where they are well cultivated?

Before the Appropriation of Land, he who gathered as much of the
wild Fruit, killed, caught, or tamed, as many of the Beasts as he could; he
that so employed his Pains about any of the spontaneous Products of
Nature, as any way to alter them, from the state which Nature put them
in, *by* placing any of his *Labour* on them, did thereby *acquire a Propriety in
them*: But if they perished, in his Possession, without their due use; if
the Fruits rotted, or the Venison putrified, before he could spend it, he
offended against the common Law of Nature, and was liable to be punished;
he invaded his Neighbour's share, for he had *no Right, farther than his Use*
called for any of them, and they might serve to afford him Conveniencies
of Life. . . .

39. And thus, without supposing any private Dominion, and property
in *Adam*, over all the World, exclusive of all other Men, which can no way
be proved, nor any one's Property be made out from it; but supposing the
World given as it was to the children of men *in common*, we see how *labour*
could make Men distinct titles to several parcels of it, for their private uses;
wherein there could be no doubt of Right, no room for quarrel.

40. Nor is it so strange, as perhaps before consideration it may appear,
that the *property of labour* should be able to over-balance the community of
land: for it is *labour* indeed that puts the *difference of value* on every thing;
and let any one consider what the difference is between an acre of land
planted with tobacco or sugar, sown with wheat or barley, and an acre of
the same land lying in common, without any husbandry upon it, and he
will find, that the improvement of *labour makes* the far greater part of the
value. I think it will be but a very modest computation to say, that of the
products of the earth useful to the life of man nine tenths are the *effects of
labour*: nay, if we will rightly estimate things as they come to our use, and
cast up the several expences about them, what in them is purely owing to
nature, and what to *labour*, we shall find, that in most of them ninety-nine
hundredths are wholly to be put on the account of *labour*. . . .

44. From all which it is evident, that though the things of Nature are
given in common, yet Man (by being Master of himself, and *Proprietor of his
own Person*, and the Actions or *Labour of it*) had still in himself *the great
Foundation of Property*; and that which made up the great part of what he

applied to the Support or Comfort of his being, when Invention and Arts had improved the conveniencies of Life, was perfectly his own, and did not belong in common to others.

45. Thus *Labour*, in the Beginning, *gave a Right of Property*, where-ever any one was pleased to imploy it, upon what was common, which remained, a long while, the far greater part, and is yet more than Mankind makes use of. Men, at first, for the most part, contented themselves with what un-assisted Nature offered to their Necessities: and though afterwards, in some parts of the World, (where the Increase of People and Stock, with the *Use of Money*) had made land scarce, and so of some Value, the several *Communities* settled the Bounds of their distinct Territories, and by Laws within themselves, regulated the Properties of the private Men of their Society, and so, *by Compact* and Agreement, *settled the Property* which Labour and Industry began; and the Leagues that have been made between several States and Kingdoms, either expressly or tacitly disowning all Claim and Right to the land in the others Possession, have, by common Consent, given up their Pretences to their natural common Right, which originally they had to those Countries, and so have, by *positive agreement, settled a Property* amongst themselves, in distinct Parts and parcels of the Earth. . . .

46. . . . He that *gathered* a Hundred Bushels of Acorns or Apples, had thereby a *Property* in them, they were his Goods as soon as gathered. He was only to look, that he used them before they spoiled; else he took more than his share, and robb'd others. And indeed it was a foolish thing, as well as dishonest, to hoard up more than he could make use of. If he gave away a part to any body else, so that it perished not uselesly in his Possession, these he also made use of. And if he also bartered away Plums that would have rotted in a Week, for Nuts that would last good for his eating a whole Year, he did no injury; he wasted not the common Stock; destroyed no part of the portion of Goods that belonged to others, so long as nothing perished uselesly in his hands. Again, if he would give his Nuts for a piece of Metal, pleased with its colour; or exchange his Sheep for Shells, or Wool for a sparkling Pebble or a Diamond, and keep those by him all his Life he invaded not the Right of others, he might heap up as much of these durable things as he pleased; *the exceeding of the bounds of his* just *property* not lying in the largeness of his Possession, but the perishing of any thing uselesly in it.

47. And thus *came in the use of Money*, some lasting thing that Men might keep without spoiling, and that by mutual consent Men would take in exchange for the truly useful, but perishable supports of Life.

48. And as different degrees of Industry were apt to give Men Possessions in different Proportions, so this *Invention of Money* gave them the opportunity to continue and enlarge them. . . . Where there is not some thing, both lasting and scarce, and so valuable to be hoarded up, there Men will not be apt to enlarge their *Possessions of Land*, were it never so rich, never so free for them to take. For I ask, What would a Man value Ten

Thousand, or an Hundred Thousand Acres of excellent *Land*, ready cultivated, and well stocked too with Cattle, in the middle of the in-land Parts of *America*, where he had no hopes of Commerce with other Parts of the World, to draw *Money* to him by the Sale of the Product? It would not be worth the enclosing, and we should see him give up again to the wild Common of Nature, whatever was more than would supply the Conveniencies of Life to be had there for him and his Family.

49. Thus in the beginning all the World was *America*, and more so than that is now; for no such thing as *Money* was any where known. Find out something that hath the *Use and Value of Money* amongst his Neighbours, you shall see the same man will begin presently to *enlarge* his *Possessions*.

50. But since Gold and Silver, being little useful to the Life of Man in proportion to Food, Rayment, and Carriage, has its *value* only from the consent of Men, whereof Labour yet makes, in great part, *the measure*, it is plain, that Men have agreed to a disproportionate and unequal Possession of the Earth, they having, by a tacit and voluntary consent found out a way, how a man may fairly possess more land than he himself can use the product of, by receiving in exchange for the overplus, Gold and Silver, which may be hoarded up without injury to any one; these metalls not spoileing or decaying in the hands of the possessor. This partage of things, in an inequality of private possessions, men have made practicable out of the bounds of Societie, and without compact, only by putting a value on gold and silver, and tacitly agreeing in the use of Money: for in Governments the Laws regulate the right of property, and the possession of land is determined by positive constitutions.

51. And thus, I think, it is very easie to conceive, without any difficulty, *how Labour could at first begin a title of Property* in the common things of Nature, and how the spending it upon our uses bounded it. So that there could then be no reason of quarrelling about Title, nor any doubt about the largeness of Possession it gave. Right and conveniency went together; for as a Man had a Right to all he could imploy his Labour upon, so he had no temptation to labour for more than he could make use of. This left no room for Controversie about the Title, nor for Incroachment on the Right of others; what Portion a Man carved to himself, was easily seen; and it was useless as well as dishonest to carve himself too much, or take more than he needed.

NOTES AND QUESTIONS

1. *Locke's Heroic Task.* We dedicate this book to contemporary scholarship on property. And yet, we begin our journey with John Locke's classic text, due to its enduring role as the canonical starting point for discussing the legitimacy of private property. This explains why we bypass the historical and theological discussions of Locke and focus instead on the impact of

the text on contemporary property discourse. We, therefore, begin with short historical observations to help appreciate Locke's heroic task.

In line with the natural-law tradition, Locke starts with the natural right to property in common. This right to communal ownership is grounded, as we read in §§25-26, on the natural right to preservation, which entails the corollary right to the means of that preservation. *See* GOPAL SREENIVASAN, THE LIMITS OF LOCKEAN RIGHTS IN PROPERTY 22, 24 (1995). From this initial communal ownership, Locke establishes a regime of unlimited private property rights. These rights are natural in the sense that they do not depend on any pre-existing legal or political framework. Rather, these rights emerge from the legitimate unilateral actions of individual people. Thus, these private property rights are not open for governments to abrogate or reorder. The private property rights limit legitimate governmental power. *See* JEREMY WALDRON, THE RIGHT TO PRIVATE PROPERTY 137-138, 169 (1988).

So, Locke's heroic task was to establish private property on the premise of unilateral appropriation so that private property rights existed independently of any social contract — conceiving private property as a prepolitical right — and without recourse to the mediation of consent. *See* Locke, *supra*, at §44. As Sreenivasan indicates, Locke's argument comes in two parts. One part explains that appropriation (via labor) does not require the consent of others. Here, Locke asserts two provisos: First, appropriation is limited to what the laborer can use before it spoils (the *spoilage* proviso); and second, the laborer ought to leave enough and as good for others (the *sufficiency* proviso). The other part of Locke's argument explains how labor legitimizes the appropriation of particular goods. *See* SREENIVASAN, *supra*, at 24-25, 33-34, 59.

2. *From No-Spoilage to the Money Economy.* We begin with Locke's spoilage proviso. *See* Locke, *supra*, at §§31, 37, 46. How restrictive, in your view, is Locke's concept of legitimate use? Does his critique of spoilage rely on a puritanical credo of strict modesty and simplicity? If not, what are the limits it sets for the amount a person can appropriate? Furthermore, how does Locke allow for accumulation? Are you persuaded by his claim that the use of money is tantamount to consent to the resulting inequality? More generally, is money a neutral medium of exchange, or — put differently — is monetary policy a matter of technical expertise or of politics? *See generally* Christine Desan, *Coin Reconsidered: The Political Alchemy of Commodity Money*, 11 THEORETICAL INQUIRIES. L. 361 (2010) (arguing that money did not spontaneously arise as "commodity," a natural medium of exchange, but as a "constitutional medium" that related the government to its participants).

3. *From Sufficiency to Estoppel.* No one, explains Locke, can object to the laborer's unilateral appropriation if he leaves enough and as good for others. *See* LOCKE, *supra*, at §§33, 36-37. But this proviso can hardly apply if read literally, since one person's appropriation takes the opportunity to appropriate from another. Robert Nozick suggested reading this proviso more broadly: because the appropriator's labor results in prosperity, others

share in a net gain. For example, the industrious use of fallow land results in a net gain of grain (as Locke suggests surplus given away as largess or bartered for gain is not waste). This net gain effectively vitiates the right of others to complain about the appropriation. Robert Nozick, Anarchy State and Utopia 175-176 (1974). Do you agree with the empirical assumption underlying this interpretation? Does it matter whether this accounting applies to land, chattel, or information? For the application of Locke's prescriptions to intellectual property, see William W. Fisher, *Theories of Intellectual Property, in* New Essays in the Legal and Political Theory of Property 168, 184-189 (Stephen R. Munzer ed., 2001). Also, may others legitimately complain where the laborer shows that there is enough and as good of a means of subsistence that remains? Even where there is enough and as good for others, can nonowners nonetheless suffer nonmaterial harms that justify rethinking the laborer's claim to appropriation without consent? *See* Waldron, *supra* Note 1, at 215-216; Will Kymlicka, Contemporary Political Philosophy 107-117, 121 (1990); Alan Ryan, Property and Political Theory 41-42 (1984).

4. *Labor as Mixture.* Consider now the second part of Locke's argument in which he explains why *labor* makes appropriation legitimate. One reading of his claim—firmly established in §27—is that by irretrievably mixing what one obviously owns (labor) with an object that belongs to everyone in common, one is able to obliterate others' rights in that object and establish his own absolute ownership of it. This reading heavily presumes a right of absolute self-ownership, an issue we take up later. See *infra* Chapter 3, Note 4. But even if we take absolute self-ownership for granted, Locke's claim is not straightforward. What aspect of the laborer, in your view, is irretrievably mixed with the object? Why does mixing labor with an object entail the laborer's absolute control over the mixture, rather than just mere expended labor? And why should we not preserve the original ownership in the object by limiting the laborer's entitlement to the value he added? Finally, what about situations in which several individuals mix their labor with a resource (consider workers on an assembly line, each responsible for a discrete task that is necessary for the final product)? For the definitive (critical) analysis of the possible answers to these questions, see Waldron, *supra* Note 1, at 177-191.

5. *Labor as Desert.* Another interpretation based upon Locke's dictum that God gave the world "to the use of the industrious and rational" is that laborers deserve reward because labor fosters human prosperity. *See* Locke, *supra*, at §34. (A related interpretation of Locke is utilitarian: "the need to reward [people] for undertaking the intrinsically disagreeable efforts required to make things serve human purposes." Ryan, *supra* Note 3, at 28. Because Locke "does not say much about questions of efficiency," *id.* at 30, while economic theorists do, we postpone that discussion to Chapter 5.) The desert-for-labor interpretation "rests on a conception of persons as agents who, by their actions in the world, are responsible for

changes in the world and deserve or merit something as a result." Stephen R. Munzer, A Theory of Property 255-256 (1990). For elaboration on the labor-desert theory of property, see the next excerpt.

Stephen R. Munzer, A Theory of Property[2]

This section sketches an argument, based on desert by labor, for rights of private property. Here "labor" means the exertion of effort in order to make or physically appropriate something. "Desert" means worthiness of some recompense because of some personal feature or action. The conclusion of the labor-desert argument is the initial labor theory of property. The argument depends on certain assumptions. They fall into four rough groups: background conditions, features of the laboring situation, physical and psychological effects of laboring, and evaluative or normative features of the effects of laboring. . . .

The background conditions depict a fragment of the state of nature. There is no society or government. The thing sought to be acquired is unowned. Things of that sort (or near replacements), sufficient in both quantity and quality, are available for acquisition by others. The laborer has an exclusive liberty to use his body in the way called for by the work he does.

Certain features of the laboring situation are important. The laborer has no moral duty to work. His intention in working is to acquire enduring control over some thing. He works solely for himself and entirely on his own. His work involves physical contact with the thing he seeks to acquire. The work reflects nothing about how he sees himself in relation to others. All laborers work with equal intensity and effectiveness.

There are, moreover, various physical and psychological effects of laboring. The laborer produces a product, not a service. The "product" is something that he gathers (say, potatoes by digging them up) or makes (say, a table made from wood). The product is not beyond his needs, wasted, or allowed to spoil. Others lose nothing by being excluded from the product. Nor do they experience any adverse sociocultural consequences, such as loss of self-esteem or prestige. No changes in the situation arise after the product is gathered or made.

Finally, there are some evaluative and normative features of the effects of his labor. Its products are good in some general sense. The work done does not benefit anyone besides the laborer. In the event that property rights are justified, there are, subjunctively, certain characteristics that these rights would have. They would not be transferable. They would be exclusive rather than shared. They would last indefinitely. They would be commensurate with the work done and the most fitting benefit

---

2. Stephen M. Munzer, A Theory of Property 256-260 (1990).

for the laborer's work. And they would not infringe any rights held by others.

In outline, the labor-desert argument is this: If the background conditions exist, then the laborer may use his body to gain control over some thing. If, further, there exist the features of the laboring situation and the physical and psychological effects described, then the laborer is responsible for a product that he does not misuse and over which his enduring control has no adverse impact on others. If, finally, the evaluative and normative features are as specified, then recognizing his enduring control is the most fitting benefit for his labor and does not infringe the rights of others. Such recognition is the acknowledgement of property rights.

The initial labor theory is the claim that if all of these assumptions hold, then the laborer deserves property rights in the product. This claim and the conditional sentences in the argument sketched for it express relations of support rather than of entailment. If the laborer digs potatoes or makes a table from wood, then he deserves property rights in the potatoes or the table. Now, following [Joel] Feinberg, the general form of a desert statement is "S deserves X in virtue of F," where S is a person, X is a thing or mode of treatment, and F (the "desert basis") is some feature of or action by S assessed in relation to its surrounding circumstances. Hence, if someone works as described and conforms to the assumptions, then he deserves moral property rights in the product in virtue of his labor. To determine which rights are fitting, one should assess the relative importance of effort, ability, persistence, industriousness, luck, time spent, achievement, the difficulty, unpleasantness, or danger of the work, and other working conditions. These rights can, in turn, serve as a prima facie justification for legal property rights.

NOTES AND QUESTIONS

1. *Labor as Workmanship.* The idea that property is a reward for productive labor is very different from Locke's labor-as-mixture theory. As Munzer intimates at the last sentence of the excerpt, labor, in this account, stands for people's efforts, perseverance, and risk-taking, as well as the application of their innate intelligence and creativity. This means that not any exercise of energy would do — acts of destruction or mere amusement certainly do not qualify. Laborers merit a reward because by engaging in purposeful activities that are directed to useful ends, they contribute to the preservation or comfort of our being. *See* STEPHEN BUCKLE, NATURAL LAW AND THE THEORY OF PROPERTY 149-152 (1991); *see also* Adam Mossoff, *Locke's Labor Lost*, 9 U. CHI. L. SCH. ROUNDTABLE 155 (2002). Should reward for such activity be conditioned upon the actual production of added value, or do unlucky good-faith attempts to add value also merit reward? Also, can this account, which on its face entails a pro-development tilt, nonetheless

coexist with a commitment to environmental conservation? Can the account, in other words, justify rewarding preservation? Finally, what about labors expended — say, by mistake — on someone else's resource? Should such a laborer have a claim against the owner for the value of her labor (or for the title of the improved resource)? *See* HANOCH DAGAN, THE LAW AND ETHICS OF RESTITUTION 82-85 (2004).

   2. *Munzer's Revised Labor Theory.* The assumptions on which this initial theory relies are, as Munzer is the first to admit, unrealistic. Thus, Munzer explores six modifications of this theory that are needed once these assumptions are relaxed. MUNZER, *supra* Note 5, at 266-285. Consider, in particular, the impact of these four complicating factors: (a) Some owners are neither original acquirers nor buyers, but rather beneficiaries of gratuitous transfers; (b) the objective circumstances may change post-acquisition so that the new physical, economic, or demographic conditions make the effect of the laborer's purported entitlement on others much more taxing than it was at the time of acquisition; (c) there are people who are physically or mentally unable to work; and (d) people frequently work with or in relation to others and the prestige of their work is often an important ingredient of their self-esteem, whereas wages are often not commensurate with desert. It seems that taking desert seriously requires the state to correct these (at time significant) gaps from the ideal distribution prescribed by a commitment to desert. Can you see how these corrections may provide a justification for much of what we see in the modern welfare state? Notice that this justification is independent of any commitment to civic solidarity or to distributive justice. For more on civic solidarity and distributive justice, see *infra* Chapters 6 and 7.

   3. *Calibrating Desert.* What should be the appropriate reward for the kind of labor that qualifies as indeed deserving reward? Is it reasonable to award the laborer full and exclusive property rights in the resource on which she has worked? Or, alternatively, should she be limited to the value she added to it, or maybe only to a fraction of that value? *See* MATTHEW H. KRAMER, JOHN LOCKE AND THE ORIGINS OF PRIVATE PROPERTY 170-171 (1997). These questions are particularly poignant considering intellectual property rights. Consider the ways in which the modern artist is not only inspired by culture but also the ways modern artists virtually depend on their cultural heritage. This cultural heritage provides a range of preexisting raw material and previously established methods, practices, or techniques of production. One need only think of Andy Warhol's Campbell's soup cans paintings and the messages he was trying to convey by appropriating commercial images as mass produced art. *See, e.g.,* Edwin C. Hettinger, *Justifying Intellectual Property, in* INTELLECTUAL PROPERTY: MORAL, LEGAL AND INTERNATIONAL DILEMMAS 17, 22-23, 25 (Adam D. Moore ed., 1997). What are the implications of these considerations insofar as the proper entitlements of authors is concerned? For example, should sweat-of-the-brow suffice for copyright protection, or should creativity also be required? *See* Alfred Yen, *Restoring the Natural Law: Copyright as*

Labor and Possession, 51 Oʜɪᴏ Sᴛ. L.J. 517 (1990) (arguing that physical labor suffices for copyright protection).

4. *Back to Locke's Original Communism.* Seana Shiffrin provides an altogether different interpretation of Locke's theory. Her interpretation also challenges the prevailing Lockean justification for intellectual property. Shiffrin claims that we should take seriously Locke's starting point of people's natural right to property *in common.* Private property rights in resources that are useful to all or many can be justified *if, but only if,* they are necessary in order to make adequate use of them (Locke gives the examples of food and land). On this reading, labor comes into play only later, in determining the identity of the proper owners of those property rights, which can indeed be justified. But this means that Locke's theory cannot justify many sorts of intellectual property, such as poems and music, because many uses of intellectual products are nonrivalrous. In other words, because one person's use of these products need not compete with another's, there is no need to shift away from the original regime in which everyone is equally entitled. Quite the contrary: This regime seems best in facilitating full, effective use of intellectual products. *See* Seana Valentine Shiffrin, *Lockean Arguments for Private Intellectual Property, in* Nᴇᴡ Essᴀʏs ɪɴ ᴛʜᴇ Lᴇɢᴀʟ ᴀɴᴅ Pᴏʟɪᴛɪᴄᴀʟ Tʜᴇᴏʀʏ ᴏғ Pʀᴏᴘᴇʀᴛʏ, *supra* Note 3, at 137. Can you think of any qualifications to this analysis? That is, are there intellectual works that require exclusive use for effective use? Are there types of cases in which overuse of intellectual products affects their quality notwithstanding their general characterization as nonrivalrous? Also, can you refine the sense in which Shiffrin's analysis challenges intellectual property regimes that properly calibrate desert along the lines of our previous Note?

2 PROPERTY AND PERSONHOOD

Margaret Jane Radin, Property and Personhood[1]

This article explores the relationship between property and personhood, a relationship that has commonly been both ignored and taken for granted in legal thought. The premise underlying the personhood perspective is that to achieve proper self-development — to be a person — an individual needs some control over resources in the external environment. The necessary assurances of control take the form of property rights. Although explicit elaboration of this perspective is wanting in modern writing on property, the personhood perspective is often implicit in the connections that courts and commentators find between property and privacy or between property and liberty. In addition to its power to explain certain aspects of existing schemes of property entitlement, the personhood perspective can also serve as an explicit source of values for making moral distinctions in property disputes, and hence for either justifying or criticizing current law. . . .

I. PROPERTY FOR PERSONHOOD: AN INTUITIVE VIEW

Most people possess certain objects they feel are almost part of themselves. These objects are closely bound up with personhood because they are part of the way we constitute ourselves as continuing personal entities in the world. They may be as different as people are different, but some common examples might be a wedding ring, a portrait, an heirloom, or a house.

---

1. Margaret Jane Radin, *Property and Personhood*, 34 STAN. L. REV. 957, 957, 959-962, 968-973, 975-979, 986-987, 1013-1015 (1982).

One may gauge the strength or significance of someone's relationship with an object by the kind of pain that would be occasioned by its loss. On this view, an object is closely related to one's personhood if its loss causes pain that cannot be relieved by the object's replacement. If so, that particular object is bound up with the holder. For instance, if a wedding ring is stolen from a jeweler, insurance proceeds can reimburse the jeweler, but if a wedding ring is stolen from a loving wearer, the price of a replacement will not restore the status quo — perhaps no amount of money can do so.

The opposite of holding an object that has become a part of oneself is holding an object that is perfectly replaceable with other goods of equal market value. One holds such an object for purely instrumental reasons. The archetype of such a good is, of course, money, which is almost always held only to buy other things. A dollar is worth no more than what one chooses to buy with it, and one dollar bill is as good as another. Other examples are the wedding ring in the hands of the jeweler, the automobile in the hands of the dealer, the land in the hands of the developer, or the apartment in the hands of the commercial landlord. I shall call these theoretical opposites — property that is bound up with a person and property that is held purely instrumentally — personal property and fungible property respectively. . . .

Once we admit that a person can be bound up with an external "thing" in some constitutive sense, we can argue that by virtue of this connection the person should be accorded broad liberty with respect to control over that "thing." But here liberty follows from property for personhood; personhood is the basic concept, not liberty. Of course, if liberty is viewed not as freedom from interference, or "negative freedom," but rather as some positive will that by acting on the external world is constitutive of the person, then liberty comes closer to capturing the idea of the self being intimately bound up with things in the external world.

It intuitively appears that there is such a thing as property for personhood because people become bound up with "things." But this intuitive view does not compel the conclusion that property for personhood deserves moral recognition or legal protection, because arguably there is bad as well as good in being bound up with external objects. If there is a traditional understanding that a well-developed person must invest herself to some extent in external objects, there is no less a traditional understanding that one should not invest oneself in the wrong way or to too great an extent in external objects. Property is damnation as well as salvation, object-fetishism as well as moral groundwork. In this view, the relationship between the shoe fetishist and his shoe will not be respected like that between the spouse and her wedding ring. At the extreme, anyone who lives only for material objects is considered not to be a well-developed person, but rather to be lacking some important attribute of humanity.

II. THE ROLE OF THE CONCEPT OF PERSON

The intuitive view of property for personhood just stated is wholly subjective: self-identification through objects varies from person to person. But if property for personhood cannot be viewed as other than arbitrary and subjective, then personal objects merely represent strong preferences, and to argue for their recognition by the legal system might collapse to a simple utilitarian preference summing. To avoid this collapse requires objective criteria differentiating good from bad identification with objects in order to identify a realm of personal property deserving recognition. The necessary objective criteria might be sought by appeal to extrinsic moral reality, to scientific truths of psychology, or to the concept of person itself. Taking the latter route, this Part approaches the problem of developing a standard for recognizing claims to personal property by referring to the concept of "person" itself. If that concept necessarily includes certain features, then those features can determine what personal property is while still avoiding ethical subjectivism. . . .

. . . [C]onsider the view that what is important in personhood is a continuing character structure encompassing future projects or plans, as well as past events and feelings. The general idea of expressing one's character through property is quite familiar. It is frequently remarked that dogs resemble their masters; the attributes of many material goods, such as cars and clothes, can proclaim character traits of their owners. Of course, many would say that becoming too enthralled with property takes away time and energy needed to develop other faculties constitutive of personhood. But, for example, if you express your generosity by giving away fruits that grow in your orchard, then if the orchard ceases to be your property, you are no longer able to express your character. This at least suggests that property may have an important relationship to certain character traits that partly constitute a person.

This view of personhood also gives us insight into why protecting people's "expectations" of continuing control over objects seems so important. If an object you now control is bound up in your future plans or in your anticipation of your future self, and it is partly these plans for your own continuity that make you a person, then your personhood depends on the realization of these expectations. This turn to expectations might seem to send property theory back toward Bentham, who declared that "the idea of property consists in an established expectation." But this justification for honoring expectations is far from Benthamite, because it applies only to personal property. In order to conclude that an object figuring into someone's expectations is personal, we must conclude both that the person is bound up with the object to a great enough extent, and that the relationship belongs to the class of "good" rather than "bad" object-relations. Hence we are forced to face the problem of fetishism, or "bad" object-relations. . . .

We must construct sufficiently objective criteria to identify close object relations that should be excluded from recognition as personal property because the particular nature of the relationship works to hinder rather than to support healthy self-constitution. A key to distinguishing these cases is "healthy." We can tell the difference between personal property and fetishism the same way we can tell the difference between a healthy person and a sick person, or between a sane person and an insane person. In fact, the concepts of sanity and personhood are intertwined: At some point we question whether the insane person is a person at all. Using the word "we" here, however, implies that a consensus exists and can be discerned. Because I seek a source of objective judgments about property for personhood, but do not wish to rely on natural law or simple moral realism, consensus must be a sufficient source of objective moral criteria — and I believe it can be, sometimes, without destroying the meaning of objectivity. In the context of property for personhood, then, a "thing" that someone claims to be bound up with nevertheless should not be treated as personal vis-à-vis other people's claimed rights and interests when there is an objective moral consensus that to be bound up with that category of "thing" is inconsistent with personhood or healthy self-constitution. . . .

A broader aspect of the problem of fetishism is suggested by Marx's "fetishism of commodities." Marx attributed power in a market society to the commodities that form the market. He believed that people become subordinate in their relations to these commodities. In other words, under capitalism property itself is anti-personhood.

Even if one does not accept that all capitalist market relations with objects destroy personhood, it is probably true that most people view the caricature capitalist with distaste. Most people might consider her lacking in some essential attribute of personhood, such as the capacity to respect other people or the environment. If there is some moral cut-off point, beyond which one is attached too much or in the wrong way to property, the extent to which someone may emulate the caricature capitalist and still claim property for personhood is not clear, but is not unlimited. Although the caricature capitalist cannot express her nature without control over a vast quantity of things and other people, her need for this control to constitute herself the complete capitalist could not objectively be recognized as personal property because at some point there is an objective moral consensus that such control is destroying personhood rather than fostering it.

III. HEGEL, PROPERTY, AND PERSONHOOD

. . . In postulating persons as rights holders, Hegel . . . initially assumes away those characteristics that render individuals unique beings — particular commitments and character traits, particular memories and future plans, particular relationships with other people and with the world of external objects. . . .

Because the person in Hegel's conception is merely an abstract unit of free will or autonomy, it has no concrete existence until that will acts on the external world. "[T]he person must give its freedom an external sphere in order to exist as Idea."[2] At this level of particularization, the external sphere "capable of embodying the person's freedom" consists of the rest of the world, everything that is distinct from the person.[3]

From the need to embody the person's will to take free will from the abstract realm to the actual, Hegel concludes that the person becomes a real self only by engaging in a property relationship with something external. Such a relationship is the goal of the person. In perhaps the best-known passage from this book, Hegel says:

> The person has for its substantive end the right of placing its will in any and every thing, which thing is thereby mine; [and] because that thing has no such end in itself, its destiny and soul take on my will. [This constitutes] mankind's absolute right of appropriation over all things.[4]

Hence, "property is the first embodiment of freedom and so is in itself a substantive end."[5] . . .

Hegel derives family property from the personhood of the family unit. When personality or "immediate exclusive individuality" enters into marriage, it "surrenders itself to it," and the parties become one person, or a single autonomous unit. It follows that there must be family property wherein "the family, as person, has its real external existence."[6] Family property must therefore be common property by nature. . . .

The intuitive personhood perspective on property is not equivalent to Hegelian personality theory, because that perspective incorporates the attributes of personhood that Hegel initially assumes away. Nevertheless a theory of personal property can build upon some of Hegel's insights. First, the notion that the will is embodied in things suggests that the entity we know as a person cannot come to exist without both differentiating itself from the physical environment and yet maintaining relationships with portions of that environment. The idea of embodied will, cut loose from Hegel's grand scheme of absolute mind, reminds us that people and things have ongoing relationships which have their own ebb and flow, and that these relationships can be very close to a person's center and sanity. If these relationships justify ownership, or at least contribute to its justification, Hegel's notion that ownership requires continuous embodiment of the will is appealing.

---

2. G.W.F. Hegel, The Philosophy of Right §41 (T. Knox trans., 1942). . . .

3. PR §41.

4. PR §44. . . .

5. PR §45R. . . .

6. PR §169.

Second, Hegel's incompletely developed notion that property is held by the unit to which one attributes autonomy has powerful implications for the concept of group development and group rights. Hegel thought that freedom (rational self-determination) was only possible in the context of a group (the properly organized and fully developed state). Without accepting this role for the state, one may still conclude that in a given social context certain groups are likely to be constitutive of their members in the sense that the members find self-determination only within the groups. This might have political consequences for claims of the group on certain resources of the external world (i.e., property).

Third, there may be an echo of Hegel's notion of an objective community morality in the intuition that certain kinds of property relationships can be presumed to bear close bonds to personhood. If property in one's body is not too close to personhood to be considered property at all, then it is the clearest case of property for personhood. The property/privacy nexus of the home is also a relatively clear case in our particular history and culture.

IV.   TWO KINDS OF PROPERTY: THE DICHOTOMY AS CRITIQUE

One element of the intuitive personhood perspective is that property for personhood gives rise to a stronger moral claim than other property. This division of property resembles a recurrent kind of critique of real-world property arrangements. The underlying insight of the many dualist property theories seems to be that some property is accorded more stringent legal protection than other property, or is otherwise deemed more important than other property by social consensus. To the extent these theories are normative, the claim is that some property is worthier of protection than other property.

If the areas of greater and lesser protection under the various dualist theories coincide to any extent, then there is room for a new and more precise theory of the areas of weaker and stronger property. I suggest that the common thread in these theories relates the stronger property claims to recognized indicia of personhood. The personhood perspective can thus provide a dichotomy that captures this critical intuition explicitly and accurately.

The premise of this form of critique is that any dichotomy in property significantly affects the justification of property rights in the real world. Liberal property theories have traditionally justified a property rights scheme by relying on some paradigm case. But if the paradigm case only applies to a subset of all the things called property, then only that subset is justified, and a dichotomy is established between that subset and forms of property that fall outside the purview of the justification. . . .

The personhood dichotomy comes about in the following way: A general justification of property entitlements in terms of their relationship to personhood could hold that the rights that come within the general justification form a continuum from fungible to personal. It then might hold that those rights near one end of the continuum—fungible property rights—can be overridden in some cases in which those near the other—personal property rights—cannot be. This is to argue not that fungible property rights are unrelated to personhood, but simply that distinctions are sometimes warranted depending upon the character or strength of the connection. Thus, the personhood perspective generates a hierarchy of entitlements: The more closely connected with personhood, the stronger the entitlement.

Does it make sense to speak of two levels of property, personal and fungible? I think the answer is yes in many situations, no in many others. Since the personhood perspective depends partly on the subjective nature of the relationships between person and thing, it makes more sense to think of a continuum that ranges from a thing indispensable to someone's being to a thing wholly interchangeable with money. Many relationships between persons and things will fall somewhere in the middle of this continuum. Perhaps the entrepreneur factory owner has ownership of a particular factory and its machines bound up with her being to some degree. If a dichotomy telescoping this continuum to two end points is to be useful, it must be because within a given social context certain types of person-thing relationships are understood to fall close to one end or the other of the continuum, so that decisionmakers within that social context can use the dichotomy as a guide to determine which property is worthier of protection. For example, in our social context a house that is owned by someone who resides there is generally understood to be toward the personal end of the continuum. There is both a positive sense that people are bound up with their homes and a normative sense that this is not fetishistic. . . .

VI. Conclusion

Just as Warren and Brandeis argued long ago that there was a right to privacy that had not yet been named, this article may be understood to argue that there is a right to personal property that should be recognized. Concomitantly, I have preliminarily argued that property rights that are not personal should not necessarily take precedence over stronger claims related to personhood. Our reverence for the sanctity of the home is rooted in the understanding that the home is inextricably part of the individual, the family, and the fabric of society. Where other kinds of object relations attain qualitatively similar individual and social importance, they should be treated similarly.

I have not attempted to use the personhood perspective in property to determine a comprehensive structure specifying both a general justification of property and its detailed institutional working-out. Instead, I have only given a survey of some of its roots, manifestations, and implications. At this stage of knowledge and insight about the roles of the personhood perspective, I suggest, as a starting point for further thought, these propositions:

(1)   At least some conventional property interests in society ought to be recognized and preserved as personal.

(2)   Where we can ascertain that a given property right is personal, there is a prima facie case that that right should be protected to some extent against invasion by government and against cancellation by conflicting fungible property claims of other people. This case is strongest where without the claimed protection of property as personal, the claimants' opportunities to become fully developed persons in the context of our society would be destroyed or significantly lessened, and probably also where the personal property rights are claimed by individuals who are maintaining and expressing their group identity.

(3)   Where we can ascertain that a property right is fungible, there is a prima facie case that that right should yield to some extent in the face of conflicting recognized personhood interests, not embodied in property. This case is strongest where without the claimed personhood interest, the claimants' opportunities to become fully developed persons in the context of our society would be destroyed or significantly lessened.

NOTES AND QUESTIONS

1.   *The Descriptive Claim.* The "intuitive view" with which Radin begins has been empirically verified. *See* HELGA DITTMAR, THE SOCIAL PSYCHOLOGY OF MATERIAL POSSESSIONS: TO HAVE IS TO BE (1992). Dittmar's synthesis of the scientific research confirms that people perceive some of their possessions as symbolically extending their sense of identity beyond the boundaries of their physical bodies: We really express who we are — both to ourselves and to others — through material possessions. Meir Dan-Cohen explores this constitutive aspect of ownership through the analysis of the connection between possessive pronouns and ownership. He concludes that "[o]wnership, as signaled by the application of a possessive pronoun to an object, consists in the permissible inclusion, on a sufficiently enduring, continuous, and exclusive basis, of that object within the scope of the personal pronouns as used by the putative owner." Meir Dan-Cohen, *The Value of Ownership,* 9 J. POL. PHIL. 404, 428-429 (2001).

Radin emphasizes two characteristics of things that belong to this category of constitutive resources: First, people identify their self with such resources because they represent their past experiences; second, loss of, or damage to, this type of resources are experienced as violations of their owner's self, which transcend the financial set-back involved. Notice that the relationship between these features is both explanatory and justificatory: Our attachment to the resources we hold, and thus the sense of personal violation we experience when they are taken from us, is both explicated and justified to the extent that they reflect our identity.

See also Russell W. Belk, *The Ineluctable Mysteries of Possessions, in* To Have Possessions: A Handbook on Ownership and Property 17, 35-37 (F.W. Rudmin ed., 1991), who mentions a few more features of people's attitude towards constitutive resources: unwillingness to sell for market value, willingness to buy with little regard for price, non-substitutability, and unwillingness to discard when utilitarian functions are lost. For a psychological account of these phenomena, based on prospect theory and the endowment effect, see Russell Korobkin, *The Endowment Effect and Legal Analysis*, 97 Nw. U. L. Rev. 1227 (2003). *But see* Charles R. Plott & Kathryn Zeiler, *The Willingness to Pay-Willingness to Accept Gap, the "Endowment Effect," Subject Misconceptions, and Experimental Procedures for Eliciting Valuations*, 95 Am. Econ. Rev. 530 (2005); Charles R. Plott & Kathryn Zeiler, *Asymmetries in Exchange Behavior Incorrectly Interpreted as Evidence of Endowment Effect Theory and Prospect?*, 97 Am. Econ. Rev. 1449 (2007).

2. *Normative Underpinnings.* Describing a human phenomenon does not yet justify its entrenchment in law, especially if we assume that the law has some expressive effect that would thus further reinforce it. *See* Stephen J. Schnably, *Property and Pragmatism: A Critique of Radin's Theory of Property and Personhood*, 45 Stan. L. Rev. 347 (1993). What, then, can justify such an effect? One possible answer is utilitarian, basing our deference to people's attachment to external resources on the respect we owe to their preferences, whatever they may be. But this is clearly not Radin's premise. So what is the non-utilitarian justification of perceiving resources as extension of the self? Jeremy Waldron argues that by making those who change external objects owners we help foster their moral development. *See* Jeremy Waldron, The Right to Private Property 370-377 (1988). Do you see the connection between ownership and moral development for such cases? Is this connection limited to cases of purposefully working to change objects, or does it also apply to other (more prevalent) cases of ownership such as the objects we possess or the places in which we live? *See* Dudley Knowles, *Hegel on Property and Personality*, 33 Phil. Q. 45, 52, 56-57 (1983). Like Radin, Waldron founds his argument on an interpretation of Hegel's personality theory of property. Hegel's argument, in which human freedom necessitates the embodiment of one's personhood in external things, was quite complex and abstract, which may explain why there are quite divergent interpretations thereof. *Compare* Ernest J. Weinrib, *Right and Advantage in Private Law*, 10 Cardozo L. Rev. 1283 (1989), *with* Alan Brudner, The Unity of the Common Law: Studies in Hegelian Jurisprudence 40-85 (1995).

3.   *Examples.* To appreciate the work the personhood justification can do in law, as well as to face some of the challenges it may invoke for those who appreciate the other values property can promote (such as aggregate welfare), consider how this justification plays out in the contexts of rent control, eminent domain, adverse possession, and copyright law. For the first two examples, see MARGARET JANE RADIN, REINTERPRETING PROPERTY 72-190 (1993). As Radin claims, at times the pertinent personhood interest that the law vindicates may be collective, rather than individual. Can you see the implications of this extension of the personhood theory in the areas of marital property, landmarks preservation, and cultural property? For an example of such a discussion with respect to a particularly sensitive issue of national claims to constitutive resources (historical rights and homelands), see CHAIM GANS, THE LIMITS OF NATIONALISM 97-123 (2003). *See also* Kristen A. Carpenter, Sonia K. Katyal & Angela R. Riley, *In Defense of Property*, 118 YALE L.J. 1022 (2009) (exploring stewardship of cultural resources for the peoplehood of indigenous peoples).

4.   *Subjective or Objective?* As Radin argues, explaining our relations to our resources in terms of the personhood theory of property suggests that resources may be classified along a continuum. Radin seems to suggest that respecting people's personhood requires the law to inquire into the specific relations of the holder to the object in question in each and every case. Does this *ad hoc* approach follow the logic of the personhood justification? Is it possible for the law to attach subjective values to resources on a case-by-case basis? What difficulties might such an approach encounter? The law treats different categories of resources (such as land, chattels, copyright, and patents) differently, rather than looking at the particular relationship between particular people and particular resources. Can this practice be justified from within the logic of personhood theory itself? *See* HANOCH DAGAN, UNJUST ENRICHMENT: A STUDY OF PRIVATE LAW AND PUBLIC VALUES 44-47 (1997). Interestingly, in discussing some of the examples mentioned in the previous Note, Radin also follows an objective approach. We return to the choice between subjective and objective approaches in the context of well-being. See Note 4 in Chapter 5.

5.   *Distributive Implications.* One of Radin's purposes in categorizing property between personal (or constitutive) property and fungible property is to argue that only a small fraction of the resources that we categorize as property deserve strong protection, and that the typical resources of modern day capitalism do not belong to this privileged category. *See* REINTERPRETING PROPERTY, *supra* Note 3, at 12. But the distributive implications of the personhood justification go much further than that, because it implies that every person, *qua* person, is entitled to own constitutive resources, namely, resources (such as homes) that are connected to her more important projects and resolutions. *See* WALDRON, *supra* Note 2, at 377-386. Is there a tension between privileging existing owners and facilitating ownership to all? Consider, for example, the protection of *residing* tenants who have a

well-established home, as opposed to "would-be tenants" who have not yet acquired a place of residence.

6. *Transformative or Conservative?* In the last part of our excerpt Radin emphasized the critical edge of the personhood justification. But later she acknowledged its conservative side. While property-as-personhood highlights our need for a stable context in order to constitute and express ourselves as persons, policymakers must realize that an important part of our humanity is the ability to change our surroundings and disrupt our commitments. So law needs to both respect our attachment to context and to facilitate possibilities for detachment from context. *See* REINTERPRETING PROPERTY, *supra* Note 3, at 30-32. Can these prescriptions be reconciled and peacefully coexist in one coherent legal regime? If so, how? And if not, which prescription should prevail?

3 PROPERTY AND LIBERTY

Robert Nozick, Anarchy, State, and Utopia[1]

THE ENTITLEMENT THEORY

The subject of justice in holdings consists of three major topics. The first is the *original acquisition of holdings,* the appropriation of unheld things. This includes the issues of how unheld things may come to be held, the process, or processes, by which unheld things may come to be held, the things that may come to be held by these processes, the extent of what comes to be held by a particular process, and so on. We shall refer to the complicated truth about this topic, which we shall not formulate here, as the principle of justice in acquisition. The second topic concerns the *transfer of holdings* from one person to another. By what processes may a person transfer holdings to another? How may a person acquire a holding from another who holds it? Under this topic come general descriptions of voluntary exchange, and gift and (on the other hand) fraud, as well as reference to particular conventional details fixed upon in a given society. The complicated truth about this subject (with placeholders for conventional details) we shall call the principle of justice in transfer. (And we shall suppose it also includes principles governing how a person may divest himself of a holding, passing it into an unheld state.)

If the world were wholly just, the following inductive definition would exhaustively cover the subject of justice in holdings.

1. A person who acquires a holding in accordance with the principle of justice in acquisition is entitled to that holding.

1. ROBERT NOZICK, ANARCHY, STATE, AND UTOPIA 150-157, 159-164, 167-172 (1974).

2. A person who acquires a holding in accordance with the principle
    of justice in transfer, from someone else entitled to the holding, is
    entitled to the holding.
3. No one is entitled to a holding except by (repeated) applications
    of 1 and 2.

The complete principle of distributive justice would say simply that a distribution is just if everyone is entitled to the holdings they possess under the
distribution.

   A distribution is just if it arises from another just distribution by legitimate means. The legitimate means of moving from one distribution to
another are specified by the principle of justice in transfer. The legitimate
first "moves" are specified by the principle of justice in acquisition. Whatever arises from a just situation by just steps is itself just. The means of
change specified by the principle of justice in transfer preserve justice. As
correct rules of inference are truth-preserving, and any conclusion deduced
via repeated application of such rules from only true premises is itself true,
so the means of transition from one situation to another specified by the
principle of justice in transfer are justice-preserving, and any situation
actually arising from repeated transitions in accordance with the principle
from a just situation is itself just. The parallel between justice-preserving
transformations and truth-preserving transformations illuminates where it
fails as well as where it holds. That a conclusion could have been deduced
by truth-preserving means from premises that are true suffices to show its
truth. That from a just situation a situation *could* have arisen via justice-
preserving means does *not* suffice to show its justice. The fact that a thief's
victims voluntarily *could* have presented him with gifts does not entitle the
thief to his ill-gotten gains. Justice in holdings is historical; it depends upon
what actually has happened. We shall return to this point later.

   Not all actual situations are generated in accordance with the two
principles of justice in holdings: the principle of justice in acquisition and
the principle of justice in transfer. Some people steal from others, or
defraud them, or enslave them, seizing their product and preventing
them from living as they choose, or forcibly exclude others from competing
in exchanges. None of these are permissible modes of transition from one
situation to another. And some persons acquire holdings by means not
sanctioned by the principle of justice in acquisition. The existence of past
injustice (previous violations of the first two principles of justice in holdings) raises the third major topic under justice in holdings: the rectification
of injustice in holdings. If past injustice has shaped present holdings in
various ways, some identifiable and some not, what now, if anything,
ought to be done to rectify these injustices? What obligations do the per-
formers of injustice have toward those whose position is worse than it
would have been had the injustice not been done? Or, than it would
have been had compensation been paid promptly? How, if at all, do things

change if the beneficiaries and those made worse off are not the direct parties in the act of injustice, but, for example, their descendants? Is an injustice done to someone whose holding was itself based upon an unrectified injustice? How far back must one go in wiping clean the historical slate of injustices? What may victims of injustice permissibly do in order to rectify the injustices being done to them, including the many injustices done by persons acting through their government? I do not know of a thorough or theoretically sophisticated treatment of such issues. Idealizing greatly, let us suppose theoretical investigation will produce a principle of rectification. This principle uses historical information about previous situations and injustices done in them (as defined by the first two principles of justice and rights against interference), and information about the actual course of events that flowed from these injustices, until the present, and it yields a description (or descriptions) of holdings in the society. The principle of rectification presumably will make use of its best estimate of subjunctive information about what would have occurred (or a probability distribution over what might have occurred, using the expected value) if the injustice had not taken place. If the actual description of holdings turns out not to be one of the descriptions yielded by the principle, then one of the descriptions yielded must be realized.

The general outlines of the theory of justice in holdings are that the holdings of a person are just if he is entitled to them by the principles of justice in acquisition and transfer, or by the principle of rectification of injustice (as specified by the first two principles). If each person's holdings are just, then the total set (distribution) of holdings is just. To turn these general outlines into a specific theory we would have to specify the details of each of the three principles of justice in holdings: the principle of acquisition of holdings, the principle of transfer of holdings, and the principle of rectification of violations of the first two principles. I shall not attempt that task here. . . .

HISTORICAL PRINCIPLES AND END-RESULT PRINCIPLES

The general outlines of the entitlement theory illuminate the nature and defects of other conceptions of distributive justice. The entitlement theory of justice in distribution is *historical;* whether a distribution is just depends upon how it came about. In contrast, *current time-slice principles* of justice hold that the justice of a distribution is determined by how things are distributed (who has what) as judged by some *structural* principle(s) of just distribution. A utilitarian who judges between any two distributions by seeing which has the greater sum of utility and, if the sums tie, applies some fixed equality criterion to choose the more equal distribution, would hold a current time-slice principle of justice. As would someone who had a fixed schedule of trade-offs between the sum of happiness and equality. According to a current time-slice principle, all that needs to be looked at, in judging the justice of a distribution, is who ends up with what; in comparing any two distributions one need look only at the matrix presenting the distributions. No further information need be fed into a principle of justice. It is a consequence of such principles of justice that any two structurally identical distributions are equally just. (Two distributions are structurally identical if they present the same profile, but perhaps have different persons occupying the particular slots.) . . .

Most persons do not accept current time-slice principles as constituting the whole story about distributive shares. They think it relevant in assessing the justice of a situation to consider not only the distribution it embodies, but also how that distribution came about. . . . [Thus, the] traditional socialist view is that workers are entitled to the product and full fruits of their labor; they have earned it; a distribution is unjust if it does not give the workers what they are entitled to. Such entitlements are based upon some past history. No socialist holding this view would find it comforting to be told that because the actual distribution A happens to coincide structurally with the one he desires D, A therefore is no less just than D; it differs only in that the "parasitic" owners of capital receive under A what the workers are entitled to under D, and the workers receive under A what the owners are entitled to under D, namely very little. This socialist rightly, in my view, holds onto the notions of earning, producing, entitlement, desert, and so forth, and he rejects current time-slice principles that look only to the structure of the resulting set of holdings. . . . His mistake lies in his view of what entitlements arise out of what sorts of productive processes.

We construe the position we discuss too narrowly by speaking of *current* time-slice principles. Nothing is changed if structural principles operate upon a time sequence of current time-slice profiles and, for example, give someone more now to counterbalance the less he has had earlier. A utilitarian or an egalitarian or any mixture of the two over time will inherit the difficulties of his more myopic comrades. He is not helped by the fact that *some* of the information others consider relevant in assessing a distribution is reflected, unrecoverably, in past matrices. Henceforth, we shall refer to such unhistorical principles of distributive justice, including the current time-slice principles, as *end-result principles* or *end-state principles*.

In contrast to end-result principles of justice, *historical principles* of justice hold that past circumstances or actions of people can create differential entitlements or differential deserts to things. An injustice can be worked by moving from one distribution to another structurally identical one, for the second, in profile the same, may violate people's entitlements or deserts; it may not fit the actual history.

PATTERNING

The entitlement principles of justice in holdings that we have sketched are historical principles of justice. To better understand their precise character, we shall distinguish them from another subclass of the historical principles. Consider, as an example, the principle of distribution according to moral merit. This principle requires that total distributive shares vary directly with moral merit; no person should have a greater share than anyone whose moral merit is greater. . . . Or consider the principle that results by substituting "usefulness to society" for "moral merit" in the previous principle. . . . Let us call a principle of distribution *patterned* if it specifies that a distribution is to vary along with some natural dimension, weighted sum of natural dimensions, or lexicographic ordering of natural dimensions. And let us say a distribution is patterned if it accords with some patterned principle. . . . The principle of distribution in accordance with moral merit is a patterned historical principle, which specifies a patterned distribution. . . . The distribution in a society, however, may be composed of such simple patterned distributions, without itself being simply patterned. Different sectors may operate different patterns, or some combination of patterns may operate in different proportions across a society. A distribution composed in this manner, from a small number of patterned distributions, we also shall term "patterned." And we extend the use of "pattern" to include the overall designs put forth by combinations of end-state principles.

Almost every suggested principle of distributive justice is patterned: to each according to his moral merit, or needs, or marginal product, or how hard he tries, or the weighted sum of the foregoing, and so on. The principle of entitlement we have sketched is *not* patterned. There is no one natural dimension or weighted sum or combination of a small number of natural dimensions that yields the distributions generated in accordance with the principle of entitlement. The set of holdings that results when some persons receive their marginal products, others win at gambling, others receive a share of their mate's income, others receive gifts from foundations, others receive interest on loans, others receive gifts from admirers, others receive returns on investment, others make for themselves much of what they have, others find things, and so on, will not be patterned. . . .

To think that the task of a theory of distributive justice is to fill in the blank in "to each according to his _____" is to be predisposed to search for a pattern; and the separate treatment of "from each according to his _____" treats production and distribution as two separate and independent issues. On an entitlement view these are *not* two separate questions. Whoever makes something, having bought or contracted for all other held resources used in the process (transferring some of his holdings for these cooperating factors), is entitled to it. The situation is *not* one of something's getting made, and there being an open question of who is to get it. Things come into the world already attached to people having entitlements over them. From the point of view of the historical entitlement conception of justice in holdings, those who start afresh to complete "to each according to his _____" treat objects as if they appeared from nowhere, out of nothing.

A complete theory of justice might cover this limit case as well; perhaps here is a use for the usual conceptions of distributive justice.

So entrenched are maxims of the usual form that perhaps we should present the entitlement conception as a competitor. Ignoring acquisition and rectification, we might say:

> From each according to what he chooses to do, to each according to what he makes for himself (perhaps with the contracted aid of others) and what others choose to do for him and choose to give him of what they've been given previously (under this maxim) and haven't yet expended or transferred.

This, the discerning reader will have noticed, has its defects as a slogan. So as a summary and great simplification (and not as a maxim with any independent meaning) we have:

> From each as they choose, to each as they are chosen.

How Liberty Upsets Patterns

It is not clear how those holding alternative conceptions of distributive justice can reject the entitlement conception of justice in holdings. For suppose a distribution favored by one of these non-entitlement conceptions is realized. Let us suppose it is your favorite one and let us call this distribution D_1; perhaps everyone has an equal share, perhaps shares vary in accordance with some dimension you treasure. Now suppose that Wilt Chamberlain is greatly in demand by basketball teams, being a great gate attraction. . . . He signs the following sort of contract with a team: In each home game, twenty-five cents from the price of each ticket of admission goes to him. . . . The season starts, and people cheerfully attend his team's games; they buy their tickets, each time dropping a separate twenty-five cents of their admission price into a special box with Chamberlain's name on it. They are excited about seeing him play; it is worth the total admission price to them. Let us suppose that in one season one million persons attend his home games, and Wilt Chamberlain winds up with $250,000, a much larger sum than the average income and larger even than anyone else has. Is he entitled to this income? Is this new distribution D_2, unjust? If so, why? There is *no* question about whether each of the people was entitled to the control over the resources they held in D_1; because that was the distribution (your favorite) that (for the purposes of argument) we assumed was acceptable. Each of these persons *chose* to give twenty-five cents of their money to Chamberlain. They could have spent it on going to the movies, or on candy bars, or on copies of *Dissent* magazine or of *Monthly Review*. But they all, at least one million of them, converged on giving it to Wilt Chamberlain in exchange for watching him play basketball. If D_1 was a just distribution, and people voluntarily moved from it to D_2, transferring parts of their shares they were given under D_1 (what was it for if not to do something with?), isn't D_2 also just? If the people were entitled to dispose of the resources to which they were entitled (under D_1), didn't this include their being entitled to give it to, or exchange it with, Wilt Chamberlain? Can anyone else complain on grounds of justice? Each other person already has his legitimate share under D_1. Under D_1, there is nothing that anyone has that anyone else has a claim of justice against. After someone transfers something to Wilt Chamberlain, third parties *still* have their legitimate shares; *their* shares are not changed. By what process could such a transfer among two persons give rise to a legitimate claim of distributive justice on a portion of what was transferred, by a third party who had no claim of justice on any holding of the others *before* the transfer? . . .

The general point illustrated by the Wilt Chamberlain example . . . is that no end-state principle or distributional patterned principle of justice can be continuously realized without continuous interference with people's lives. Any favored pattern would be transformed into one unfavored by the principle, by people choosing to act in various ways; for example, by people exchanging goods and services with other people, or giving things to other people, things the transferrers are entitled to under the favored distributional pattern. To maintain a pattern one must either continually interfere to stop people from transferring resources as they wish to, or continually (or periodically) interfere to take from some persons resources that others for some reason chose to transfer to them. . . .

It puts things perhaps a bit too strongly to say that every patterned (or end-state) principle is liable to be thwarted by the voluntary actions of the individual parties transferring some of their shares they receive under the principle. For perhaps some *very* weak patterns are not so thwarted. Any distributional pattern with any egalitarian component is overturnable by the voluntary actions of individual persons over time; as is every patterned condition with sufficient content so as actually to have been proposed as presenting the central core of distributive justice. Still, given the possibility that some weak conditions or patterns may not be unstable in this way, it would be better to formulate an explicit description of the kind of interesting and contentful patterns under discussion, and to prove a theorem about their instability. Since the weaker the patterning, the more likely it is that the entitlement system itself satisfies it, a plausible conjecture is that any patterning either is unstable or is satisfied by the entitlement system. . . .

REDISTRIBUTION AND PROPERTY RIGHTS

Apparently, patterned principles allow people to choose to expend upon themselves, but not upon others, those resources they are entitled to (or rather, receive) under some favored distributional pattern D_1. For if each of several persons chooses to expend some of his D_1 resources upon one other person, then that other person will receive more than his D_1 share, disturbing the favored distributional pattern. Maintaining a distributional pattern is individualism with a vengeance! Patterned distributional principles do not give people what entitlement principles do, only better distributed. For they do not give the right to choose what to do with what one has; they do not give the right to choose to pursue an end involving (intrinsically, or as a means) the enhancement of another's position. To such views, families are disturbing; for within a family occur transfers that upset the favored distributional pattern. Either families themselves become units to which distribution takes place, the column occupiers (on what rationale?), or loving behavior is forbidden. . . .

Proponents of patterned principles of distributive justice focus upon criteria for determining who is to receive holdings; they consider the reason for which someone should have something, and also the total picture of holdings. Whether or not it is better to give than to receive, proponents of patterned principles ignore giving altogether. In considering the distribution of goods, income, and so forth, their theories are theories of recipient justice; they completely ignore any right a person might have to give something to someone. Even in exchanges where each party is simultaneously giver and recipient, patterned principles of justice focus only upon the recipient role and its supposed rights. Thus discussions tend to focus on whether people (should) have a right to inherit, rather on whether people (should) have a right to bequeath or on whether persons who have a right to hold also have a right to choose that others hold in their place. I lack a good explanation of why the usual theories of distributive justice are so recipient oriented; ignoring givers and transferrers and their rights is of a piece with ignoring producers and their entitlements. But why is it *all* ignored?

Patterned principles of distributive justice necessitate *re*distributive activities. The likelihood is small that any actual freely-arrived-at set of holdings fits a given pattern; and the likelihood is nil that it will continue to fit the pattern as people exchange and give. From the point of view of an entitlement theory, redistribution is a serious matter indeed, involving, as it does, the violation of people's rights. . . .

Taxation of earnings from labor is on a par with forced labor. Some persons find this claim obviously true: taking the earnings of *n* hours labor is like taking *n* hours from the person; it is like forcing the person to work *n* hours for another's purpose. Others find the claim absurd. But even these, *if* they object to forced labor, would oppose forcing unemployed hippies to work for the benefit of the needy. And they would also object to forcing each person to work five extra hours each week for the benefit of the needy. But a system that takes five hours' wages in taxes does not seem to them like one that forces someone to work five hours, since it offers the person forced a wider range of choice in activities than does taxation in kind with the particular labor specified. (But we can imagine a gradation of systems of forced labor, from one that specifies a particular activity, to one that gives a choice among two activities, to . . . ; and so on up.) Furthermore, people envisage a system with something like a proportional tax on everything above the amount necessary for basic needs. Some think this does not force someone to work extra hours, since there is no fixed number of extra hours he is forced to work, and since he can avoid the tax entirely by earning only enough to cover his basic needs. This is a very uncharacteristic view of forcing for those who *also* think people are forced to do something *whenever* the alternatives they face are considerably worse. However, *neither* view is correct. The fact that others intentionally intervene, in violation of a side constraint against aggression, to threaten force to limit the alternatives, in this case to paying taxes or (presumably the worse alternative) bare subsistence, makes the taxation system one of forced labor and distinguishes it from other cases of limited choices which are not forcings.

The man who chooses to work longer to gain an income more than sufficient for his basic needs prefers some extra goods or services to the leisure and activities he could perform during the possible nonworking hours; whereas the man who chooses not to work the extra time prefers the leisure activities to the extra goods or services he could acquire by working more. Given this, if it would be illegitimate for a tax system to seize some of a man's leisure (forced labor) for the purpose of serving the needy, how can it be legitimate for a tax system to seize some of a man's goods for that purpose? Why should we treat the man whose happiness requires certain material goods or services differently from the man whose preferences and desires make such goods unnecessary for his happiness? Why should the man who prefers seeing a movie (and who has to earn money for a ticket) be open to the required call to aid the needy, while the person who prefers looking at a sunset (and hence need earn no extra money) is not? Indeed, isn't it surprising that redistributionists choose to ignore the man whose pleasures are so easily attainable without extra labor, while adding yet another burden to the poor unfortunate who must work for his pleasures? If anything, one would have expected the reverse. Why is the person with the nonmaterial or nonconsumption desire allowed to proceed unimpeded to his most favored feasible alternative, whereas the man whose pleasures or desires involve material things and who must work for extra money (thereby serving whomever considers his activities valuable enough to pay him) is constrained in what he can realize? . . . In a fuller discussion we would have (and want) to extend our argument to include interest, entrepreneurial profits, and so on. Those who doubt that this extension can be carried through, and who draw the line here at taxation of income from labor, will have to state rather complicated patterned *historical* principles of distributive justice, since end-state principles would not distinguish *sources* of income in any way. It is enough for now to get away from end-state principles and to make clear how various patterned principles are dependent upon particular views about the sources or the illegitimacy or the lesser legitimacy of profits, interest, and so on; which particular views may well be mistaken. . . .

When end-result principles of distributive justice are built into the legal structure of a society, they (as do most patterned principles) give each citizen an enforceable claim to some portion of the total social product; that is, to some portion of the sum total of the individually and jointly made products. This total product is produced by individuals laboring, using means of production others have saved to bring into existence, by people organizing production or creating means to produce new things or things in a new way. It is on this batch of individual activities that patterned distributional principles give each individual an enforceable claim. Each person has a claim to the activities and the products of other persons, independently of whether the other persons enter into particular relationships that give rise to these claims, and independently of whether they voluntarily take these claims upon themselves, in charity or in exchange for something.

Whether it is done through taxation on wages or on wages over a certain amount, or through seizure of profits, or through there being a big *social pot* so that it's not clear what's coming from where and what's going where, patterned principles of distributive justice involve appropriating the actions of other persons. Seizing the results of someone's labor is equivalent to seizing hours from him and directing him to carry on various activities. If people force you to do certain work, or unrewarded work, for a certain period of time, they decide what you are to do and what purposes your work is to serve apart from your decisions. This process whereby they take this decision from you makes them a *part-owner* of you; it gives them a property right in you. Just as having such partial control and power of decision, by right, over an animal or inanimate object would be to have a property right in it.

End-state and most patterned principles of distributive justice institute (partial) ownership by others of people and their actions and labor. These principles involve a shift from the classical liberals' notion of self-ownership to a notion of (partial) property rights in *other* people.

NOTES AND QUESTIONS

1. *The Minimal State.* Nozick's book is the most celebrated libertarian manifesto of recent times. It perceives people's rights—notably their property rights—as side constraints that limit the legitimacy of government, if it is to be guided by Kant's categorical imperative to treat people as ends, rather than means. Hence, it limits the role of government and of its legitimate power to tax to the protection of rights to person and property and criticizes any use of the state's coercive apparatus for either helping the poor, the ill, or the unemployed, or even to supply goods and services that arguably improve the quality of life of everyone. *See* JONATHAN WOLFF, ROBERT NOZICK: PROPERTY, JUSTICE AND THE MINIMAL STATE (1991).

This argument, on which our excerpt is focused, comes from the second part of Nozick's book. (We will not treat here his intriguing discussion of past injustices, a topic we address in Chapter 17.3 below.) In the first part of his book, Nozick defends the legitimacy of the minimal state against the anarchist by claiming that this state can develop from the state of nature without violating anyone's rights. In the third (and last) part of his book, Nozick fortifies his defense of the minimal state by arguing that it is not only right, but also inspiring, because it is the only state that both enables people to be truly benevolent and is truly neutral amongst the divergent lifestyles around which people should be able to organize themselves. Can you try to reconstruct these ambitious arguments?

2. *Nozick's Conception of Property.* Nozick made Wilt Chamberlain[2] a celebrity among political philosophers. But does this example provide a knockout blow to any opponent, as Nozick believes? Does it *analytically* undermine the validity of any competing theory of distributive justice? In order to examine these questions, consider the conception of property underlying Nozick's argument. As Will Kymlicka argues, Nozick allows his interlocutor to specify D_1 only insofar as the initial distribution of holdings is concerned, while assuming that each such holding will accord the owner with unqualified and unconditional rights over the resource at issue. WILL KYMLICKA, CONTEMPORARY POLITICAL PHILOSOPHY 102-103 (1990). Do you see why egalitarians are likely to reject this assumption? Can you think of conceptions of property that avoid it and with it escape the analytical power of the Wilt Chamberlain example? *See generally* JOHN CHRISTMAN, THE MYTH OF PROPERTY: TOWARD AN EGALITARIAN THEORY OF OWNERSHIP (1994). These questions give you some initial reasons for appreciating the significance of the conceptual analysis of property, which is the focus of Part II of this book.

3. *Property and Alienability.* Nozick finds the right to alienate — either by way of entering into a commercial transaction or via a gift or a will — an obvious incident of ownership. What may justify making alienability a typical incident of ownership? To address this question, think about the consequences of a fixed property distribution (one which does not allow any form of alienability) in terms of aggregate welfare (will resources end up with the person in whose hands utility will be maximized?), social mobility, and — our focus in this chapter — personal liberty. For some conflicting reasons, which may justify various limitations on alienability, see Chapter 13.2 below. For an intriguing argument, in which the right to make gifts is a necessary entailment of the right to property, whereas the right to make bargains is emphatically unrelated to property, see JAMES E. PENNER, THE IDEA OF PROPERTY IN LAW 88-92 (1997), discussed *infra* Note 4 in Chapter 15.1.

---

2. Chamberlain is widely considered one of the greatest and most dominant players in the history of the NBA. *See* http://en.wikipedia.org/wiki/Wilt_Chamberlain.

4. *Self-Ownership.* Nozick's discussion of labor taxation underscores his vigorous argument that anything short of full-blown absolute ownership necessarily undermines self-ownership and thus violates the Kantian imperative. To critically examine this argument, think about two main challenges. First, following our discussion of property and labor in Chapter 1, consider whether a laborer can plausibly claim that all the fruits of her work should be attributed to her work or rather necessarily rely also on existing societal goods for which it may well be just to make her pay. *See* MICHAEL OTSUKA, LIBERTARIANISM WITHOUT INEQUALITY 11-40 (2003); Reuven S. Avi-Yonah, *Why Tax The Rich? Efficiency, Equity, and Progressive Taxation,* 111 YALE L.J. 1391, 1404 (2002). A related question involves luck and risk, which obviously affect the fruits people generate from their labor. Nozick implies that each person is responsible for the risks and entitled to such luck. Is this the only possibility? For a taxonomy and a critical examination of other possibilities, see Elizabeth Anderson, *How Should Egalitarians Cope with Market Risks?,* 9 THEORETICAL INQ. L. 61 (2007).

A second, and even more striking, challenge lies in the argument that self-ownership is not an ultimate good, but rather an instrumental good — albeit an important one — to the more fundamental good of autonomy or self-determination. Do you agree with this claim? If you do, do you agree that different limits on people's self-ownership may be treated differently, so that the combination of rights and resources that are most attentive to people's self-determination may both involve more than self-ownership (e.g., access to resources), and allow the state to place some limits on self-ownership? *See* H.L.A. HART, *Between Utility and Rights, in* ESSAYS IN JURISPRUDENCE AND PHILOSOPHY 198, 206-207 (1983); KYMLICKA, *supra* Note 2, at 120, 123-125. For the (surprising?) way in which this conclusion challenges Marxists, see G.A. COHEN, SELF-OWNERSHIP, FREEDOM, AND EQUALITY chs. 5-6 (1995).

One (particularly provocative) possible conclusion from the notion that self-ownership is not an ultimate good is that individuals should be taxed on what they *could* earn irrespective of what they actually do earn. *See* LIAM MURPHY & THOMAS NAGEL, THE MYTH OF OWNERSHIP: TAXES AND JUSTICE 20-23, 121-125 (2002). Murphy and Nagel conclude that this idea of endowment taxation is indefensible, but in considering Nozick's critique of labor taxation they acknowledge that their objection is only due to the *degree* of interference with autonomy it entails. Are there other reasons to object to endowment taxation that suggest it is different in kind from a tax on earning? *See* Tsilly Dagan, *Itemizing Personhood,* 29 VA. TAX REV. 93, 120-125 (2009).

5. *Property as a Bastion of Liberty.* The flip-side of Nozick's insistence that liberty upsets patterns is that a commitment to liberty requires decentralization, or polycentric governance, which only strong property rights provide. Randy Barnett argues along these lines that only a libertarian property regime — a regime of "several property" — provides enough

"diversity of jurisdictions" that guarantees "the effective compartmentalization of partiality." Only several property makes "the jurisdiction of any particular individual or association" bounded or limited, thus enabling "effective checks and balances on partiality" and minimizing the dangers posed by self-interested action, which is imminent whenever power is assigned to human beings. RANDY BARNETT, THE STRUCTURE OF LIBERTY: JUSTICE AND THE RULE OF LAW 139-142, 238 (1998). Indeed, one of the most powerful claims in favor of competitive capitalism is that it preserves freedom by eliminating, or at least dispersing, concentrations of power. *See* MILTON FRIEDMAN, CAPITALISM AND FREEDOM 7-21 (1962).

Many authors who oppose Nozick applaud the role of private property in shielding individuals from claims of other persons and from the power of the public authority, and thus preserving an untouchable private sphere, which is a prerequisite to personal development and autonomy. *See* BRUCE A. ACKERMAN, PRIVATE PROPERTY AND THE CONSTITUTION 1-76 (1977); JOHN RAWLS, POLITICAL LIBERALISM 298 (1993). But does a libertarian property regime guarantee an effective diffusion of power? What about concentrations of private property? *See* CHARLES E. LINDBLOM, POLITICS AND MARKETS: THE WORLD'S POLITICAL-ECONOMIC SYSTEMS 170-188 (1977); C. Edwin Baker, *Property and Its Relation to Constitutionally Protected Liberty*, 134 U. PA. L. REV. 741 (1986); Frank I. Michelman, *Possession vs. Distribution in the Constitutional Idea of Property*, 72 IOWA L. REV. 1319 (1987). Furthermore, while some measure of independence is essential to a meaningful life, doesn't human flourishing require a sense of belonging that is threatened by a libertarian property regime? For a challenging argument along these lines by a particularly competent critic of libertarianism, see ROBERT NOZICK, *The Zigzags of Politics, in* THE EXAMINED LIFE: PHILOSOPHICAL MEDIATIONS 286 (1989).

4

PROPERTY AS A KANTIAN RIGHT

Ernest J. Weinrib, Poverty and Property in Kant's System of Rights[1]

1. KANT ON THE PUBLIC DUTY TO SUPPORT THE POOR

In a passage from the *Doctrine of Right* that is particularly enigmatic even by his own high standards, Kant announces the state's right to tax in order to fulfill a public duty to support the poor. The passage raises fundamental issues about the interpretation of Kant's legal philosophy, about the connection between private law and public law, and about the conceptual resources available to a system of rights for dealing with poverty. . . .

One might suppose that state taxation to support the poor involves a clash between distributive and corrective justice. Whether the state should satisfy the basic needs of its citizens is, of course, a standard issue of distributive justice. This recourse to distributive justice requires the state to use its taxing powers to take something that would otherwise remain within the private resources of those taxed. In a well-ordered state these resources reflect proprietary rights worked out and protected by private law within a conception of corrective justice. Thus, the state's support of the poor, one might think, accomplishes distributive justice at the expense of citizens' corrective justice entitlements.

This supposed clash between distributive and corrective justice leads to the temptation to eliminate one form of justice in favour of the other. Contemporary legal and political thinking shows this temptation operating in both directions. Those opposed to the state's distributive

---

1. Ernest J. Weinrib, *Poverty and Property in Kant's System of Rights, in* CORRECTIVE JUSTICE (forthcoming 2012).

operations claim, in effect, that corrective justice is all the justice that there is. On this view, justice is fully satisfied by the private law notions that recognize entitlements to property and personal integrity, allow for the voluntary transfers through contract and gift, and protect rights through the law of contract, torts, and unjust enrichment. These notions themselves are interpreted as embodying a mode of practical reason distinctive to private law in that it works justice between individual parties without reference to any distributive purposes. "Distributive justice" can be regarded merely as a euphemistic term that camouflages the injustice of the state's treating individuals and their entitlements as means to collective ends. This primacy of corrective justice honours private law entitlements while renouncing the existence of a state obligation to satisfy citizens' basic needs.

On the other hand, those who favour the state's distributive role may be tempted to regard the working of distributive justice as normatively fundamental. The doctrines of private law then become nothing more than special operations of distributive justice. On this view, property can then be seen simply as the residue remaining after the state's distributive activity rather than as a locus of independent normative significance. Liability rules also, whether dealing with contracts, torts, or unjust enrichment are regarded as justified to the extent that they embody distributive moves. State support for the poor is then merely one distributive operation among many. Abandoned or explained away is the distinctive significance of the private law concepts as the legal manifestations of corrective justice.

Kant's remarks on the state's right to tax in order to fulfill a public duty to the poor indicate that he does not share these one-sided views of justice. As a philosopher working within the tradition of natural right—indeed, as perhaps its greatest expositor—Kant gives a detailed non-distributive account of the principal features of private law, especially of property and contract. Developing corrective justice in terms of his own metaphysics of morals, Kant portrays private law as a system of rights whose most general categories give juridical expression to the coexistence of one person's action with another's freedom under a universal law. Yet despite his affirmation that private law entitlements, understood non-distributively, are the necessary components of a free society, Kant nonetheless holds that there is a public obligation (and not merely a liberty) to support the poor. He thus seems to regard this aspect of distributive justice as compatible with corrective justice, with the state being duty-bound to actualize both. Neither of the temptations that characterize certain contemporary approaches to law attracts him.

However, the question that arises is whether Kant is entitled to the view about the alleviation of poverty that he professes. Kant's view of property is at least as extreme as the most extreme of today's libertarians.[2]

---

2. Kant, for instance, has nothing like the Lockean proviso that limits property rights for Nozick. . . .

How on his view can the state function both as the guarantor of purely non-distributive property rights and as the public authority that levies taxes in order to fulfill a public duty to support the poor? This question is all the more serious because Kant is a systematic philosopher for whom obligation signifies necessity, so that the duty to support the poor that he posits must somehow arise out of, and not merely be consistent with, his non-distributive account of rights. Furthermore, for Kant rights are the juridical vindications of freedom that the state coercively protects against infringement; coercion for the benefit of anyone, including the poor, seems inadmissible within the Kantian framework. Kant offers almost nothing resembling an argument in support of the duty he announces. Nor does he explain how this duty is to be integrated into his austere system of rights.

In the crucial passage, appearing in his section on public right in the *Doctrine of Right*, Kant describes the state's right to tax in order to fulfill its duty to the poor in these terms:

> To the supreme commander there belongs *indirectly*, that is, insofar as he has taken over the duty of the people, the right to impose taxes on the people for its own preservation, such as taxes to support organizations providing for the *poor, foundling homes*, and *church organizations*, usually called charitable or pious institutions.[3]

Because for Kant a right is always connected to the authorization to use coercion, Kant goes on to specify that the state's support of the poor should be achieved by coercive public taxation and not merely by voluntary contributions. He explains the basis of the right to tax as follows:

> The general will of the people has united itself into a society that is to maintain itself perpetually; and for this end it has submitted itself to the internal authority of the state in order to maintain those members of the society who are unable to maintain themselves. For reasons of state the government is therefore authorized to constrain the wealthy to provide the means of sustenance for those who are unable to provide for even their most necessary natural needs. The wealthy have acquired an obligation to the commonwealth, since they owe their existence to an act of submitting to its protection and care, which they need in order to live; on this obligation the state now bases its right to contribute what is theirs to maintaining their fellow citizens.[4]

No reader of Kant's legal philosophy can fail to be struck by the apparent oddity of these paragraphs. Kant's legal philosophy is an elucidation of concept of Right, that is, of "the sum of conditions under which the choice of one can be united with the choice of another in accordance with a universal law of freedom."[5] In introducing the concept of Right, Kant

---

3. IMMANUEL KANT, THE METAPHYSICS OF MORALS (Mary Gregor trans.), in The Cambridge Edition of the Works of Immanuel Kant: Practical Philosophy [328]. Numbers in square brackets refer to the pagination found in the standard German edition of this work and reproduced in the margins of The Cambridge Edition.
4. Ibid. [326].
5. Ibid. [230].

notes that "it does not signify the relationship of one's choice to the mere wish (hence also to the mere need) of others, as in actions of benefi-cence. . . ."[6] The consequence of this abstraction from "mere need" is a complex of proprietary, contractual and domestic rights which place others under correlative duties of non-interference, "for anyone can be free as long as I do not impair his freedom by my external action, even though I am quite indifferent to his freedom."[7] Yet when outlining the rights of gov-ernment in the quoted paragraphs, Kant introduces — seemingly out of the blue — a positive duty, which government takes over from the people, to support those "unable to provide for even their most necessary natural needs." . . .

Kant's legal philosophy is so parsimonious and its architecture so aus-tere that little leeway is available in dealing with a perplexity of this sort. Kant's adamantine boundary between right and ethics — the former deal-ing with externally coercible duties, the latter with uncoercible duties done for their own sake — prevents recourse to appealing ideas found in Kant's writings on ethics. For example, because Kant does not formulate the duty to support the poor as the reflex of any correlative right that the poor have, one might be tempted to regard that duty as somehow connected to the personal duty, postulated by Kant elsewhere, to come to another's aid. However, the duty to aid is an ethical rather than a juridical one; it there-fore cannot be associated with the coercive taxation authorized for support of the poor. Kant's own description of the concept of Right, with its contrast between rightful actions and actions of beneficence, confirms that state support of the poor does not fall under the duty to aid. . . .

My contention is that, far from being inconsistent with the internal logic of Kantian right, the state's duty to support the poor is the inexorable outcome of that logic. Kant includes support of the poor as an "effect with regard to rights that follows from the nature of a civil union."[8] The civil union results from the transition to public right from the property regime in the state of nature. Kant's theory of property rights necessitates not only this transition but also — as its consequence — the people's duty to the poor. Just as for Kant the movement from property in the state of nature to the public right of a civil union is obligatory, so the state's support of the poor is an obligatory consequence of that movement. Were the state under no such obligation, the legitimacy of the civil union that replaces the state of nature would itself be impugned.

On this reading of Kant, the very idea of private property implies the state's right to tax property owners in order to discharge a public duty to relieve poverty. Although Kant's notion of property completely conforms to corrective justice, it generates the distributive justice that consists in the alleviation of poverty through taxation. Far from being a self-sufficient and

6. Ibid.
7. Ibid. [231].
8. Ibid. [318].

free-standing institution of justice, property requires redistribution to the poor for its own legitimacy. Thus Kant transcends the categorical difference between corrective and distributive justice while preserving and elucidating the distinct roles that each plays in a free society. In this chapter I attempt to reconstruct the argument, implicit in his theory of law but not articulated by Kant himself, that underlies this remarkable conclusion.

2. KANT'S ACCOUNT OF PROPERTY

Kant's account of property in the *Doctrine of Right* features a conceptual progression that starts from the innate right to freedom and culminates in the establishment of property as an institution of positive law. Kant exhibits the phases of this progression as implicit in the relationship of free persons under the conditions of human existence. Because property is consistent with the freedom of all, it is rightly secured and protected by the law's coercive powers.

This progression has three phases. . . . In the first phase Kant starts with the universal principle of Right, which mandates the coexistence of one person's action with another's freedom under a universal law, and notes the juridical relationship analytically contained within that principle. This juridical relationship does not include property in external things, but it does encompass certain "authorizations" such as equality and non-dependence, which are normative attributes implicit within the universal principle of Right and therefore ascribable to the parties at this phase. In the second phase he extends this initial argument on the ground that having something external as one's own, although not analytically contained in the universal principle of Right, marks a connection to external things that matches the capacity for choice characteristic of self-determining action. This extension, however, is problematic, because although ownership of external things is now permissible, it is not yet put into effect under conditions consonant with the authorizations articulated in the first phase. The second phase, accordingly, is merely provisional. The problems it raises are resolved at the third phase, where the conditions of acquisition take a form that is fully consistent with what was analytically contained in the universal principle of Right. . . .

Although presented in a sequence, these three phases are conceptual, not temporal. Kant is not offering a philosophical reconstruction of the historical evolution of property. Rather, the three phases represent aspects that together are constitutive of property in the juridical relationships of free persons (e.g., that external things can be acquired through acts of will, that property does not require actual possession, that property rights are enforceable, and so on), but presented in an ordering that purports to show property's normative necessity within a system of rights. The three phases comprise an articulated unity. . . . If these phases were considered independently, the argument would not get off the ground or would collapse as soon as it did so. Nor does the third phase stand alone either; its role is to incorporate what is necessary to reconcile the second phase to what is analytically contained in the first one. The result is that the institutions of public law that emerge at the third phase determine and guarantee the property entitlements that are the product of the second phase in a way that expresses the normative significance of the principle of right that initiated the first phase.

The first phase features the innate right to freedom. The innate right to freedom consists in the independence of one's actions from constraint by the actions of another, insofar as such independence is consistent with the freedom of everyone else. This right stands in an analytic relationship with the universal principle of Right, which requires that one person's action be able to coexist with the freedom of everyone under a universal law. . . .

The innate right is "the only original right belonging to every man by virtue of his humanity."[9] This right is innate because every person has it simply by virtue of his or her existence. Similarly, it is original because it arises independently of any act that would establish it. Because my innate right is not mine by virtue of some act of acquisition, it is what is internally mine, in contrast to what is externally mine, which must always be acquired. What is internally mine is my freedom, that is, my capacity to act in the execution of the purposes I form as a self-determining being.

For human beings the paradigmatic manifestation of what is internally mine is the body, the physical organism through which the person expresses his or her freedom as a self-determining being. By mandating actions that can coexist with the freedom of all, the universal principle of Right signals its application to the actions of self-determining agents. In the case of human beings, self-determining activity takes place through the body. Because the body is an "inseparable unity of members in a person,"[10] interference with any part of another's body is a wrong against that person's freedom. This right with respect to one's own body is innate. . . .

In this phase, where one's only right is the innate right of humanity in one's own person, property as the entitlement to something distinct from the person's body does not exist. . . . Property goes beyond innate right by treating the person as entitled to an external thing even when it is not in the person's physical possession. Innate right prohibits another's interference with an external thing only insofar as such interference would simultaneously be an interference with my body as something internally mine. Property, in contrast, entails treating the thing as externally mine, so that . . . the land upon which I was lying remains mine even when I have moved elsewhere. Under a property regime anyone who interferes with what is mine wrongs me despite the fact that my body is not immediately affected.

9. Ibid. [237].
10. Ibid. [278].

The extension of the scope of rights to include what is externally mine is the second phase of Kant's account of property. Kant introduces what he calls "the postulate of practical reason with regard to rights," under which "it is possible to have any external object of my choice as mine."[11] This postulate asserts both the possibility of owning the external objects of a person's will and the existence of a duty of justice to act towards others in recognition of that possibility.

The postulate is based on the notion that external objects of choice have to be conceived in a way that corresponds to the choosing subject. Under the concept of right, what is relevant are not the particular purposes that choosing subjects pursue through their interactions with each other, but rather their purposiveness as choosing subjects whatever their particular purposes. A contract is valid, for instance, because it expresses the purposiveness of both contracting parties, rather than because of the particular purpose that either party has in mind. Thus, from the juridical perspective freedom is a formal concept that refers to the capacity for choice rather than directly to the content of particular choices. It thereby abstracts from the wants and needs that fuel such particular choices. External objects of choice are the objects of choice so conceived. Accordingly, an external object of choice cannot get its juridical status merely from the particular properties that are engaged in particular uses that satisfy particular wants or needs of a particular choosing subject. . . . Rather, it must be possible for an object of choice to lie within the choosing subject's capacity for use even when no particular use is being made of it. . . .

Yet the rights made possible by the postulate are problematic. Although they are consistent with the regime of innate rights in one respect, they are inconsistent with it in another. They are consistent with it by allowing persons to exercise their freedom by controlling external objects of choice, which are not aspects of innate right, in a way that matches the concept of choice operative within innate right. They are, however, inconsistent with it because their actualization does not treat the parties involved as innately equal. Because in the first phase everyone has an innate right that everyone else is obligated to abstain from coercing, the participants in a regime composed exclusively of innate rights have innate equality, which Kant defines as "independence from being bound by others to more than one can in turn bind them."[12] This equality does not obtain in the actualization of the external rights allowed by the postulate of practical reason. Unlike the innate right, external rights are acquired through the performance of an act. In the case of original acquisition, when the proprietor comes to own something not owned by anyone, this act is the exercise of a unilateral will that puts others under an obligation that they would not otherwise have. Despite the fact that innate

11. Ibid. [246]. . . .
12. Ibid. [237].

right authorizes innate equality, the proprietor, by virtue of his or her unilateral act of acquisition, binds others with respect to the acquired thing without being reciprocally bound to them. This should be beyond the rightful power of one person's unilateral will, for it is inconsistent with innate equality of all that the acquirer should be able to subordinate others to his or her purposes.

This inequality has further consequences. Because an acquired right, like all Kantian rights, carries with it the power to coerce others not to violate it, the unilateral act of acquisition that creates the right also gives the right-holder coercive power. Accordingly, although the universal principle of Right forbids an act that does not coexist with the freedom of another, the coercion occasioned by acquisition is precisely such an act, in that it allows the unilateral will to serve as a coercive law for everyone. . . .

Thus, the actualization of the rights made possible by the postulate of practical reason creates a conceptual tension, to be resolved in the subsequent phase, between the unilateralism of the proprietor's conduct and the equality authorized by innate right. The universal principle of Right, in which innate right is analytically contained, forbids one person's coercing the freedom of another. Yet the postulate of practical reason allows one person coercively to restrict another's freedom through unilateral acts that establish proprietary rights to exclude. Because of this tension, such rights are provisional pending an additional move that brings them back into conformity with the equality of innate right. Accordingly, the postulate of practical reason with respect to rights allows us provisionally to hold the notion of external property in place until the thought of it can be completed in a further phase that establishes the conditions under which external property is conclusively rightful.

This transformation of provisional rights into conclusive ones occurs in the third phase of Kant's account of property. Kant introduces a further postulate, the postulate of public Right, which marks the transition from the state of nature to the civil condition of law-governed society. The postulate declares that "[w]hen you cannot avoid living side by side with all others, you ought to leave the state of nature and proceed with them into a rightful condition."[13] In this rightful condition the state provides duly authorized institutions of adjudication and enforcement. These replace the exercise of private judgment about controversial claims with the authoritative judgments of courts that determine the scope of each person's entitlements according to what is laid down as right. Moreover, the coercion that secures each person's rights is no longer private but emanates from a public lawful regime under which rights are secured by adequate power external to the contending parties. The civil condition is the product of a social contract, which is conceived not as an historical occurrence, but as an idea "in terms of which alone we can think of the legitimacy of the

13. Ibid. [257].

state."[14] This notional union of all wills transforms the external acquisition of unowned things from a merely unilateral act on the part of the acquirer to an omnilateral act, to which everyone as possible owners of property implicitly consents and whose rights-creating significance everyone acknowledges. Such acknowledgement follows from the very act of acquisition, because the acquirer cannot claim a right for oneself without recognizing the similar rights of others and requiring that they be effective through the guarantee provided by the state's coercive power. In the civil condition acquisitions are seen not as isolated unilateral acts, but as mutually related through a system of property in which all are reciprocally bound and publicly coerced to respect the property rights of others. . . .

Accordingly, the duty of non-interference with property that makes its appearance in the second phase of Kant's account matures at the transition to the third phase into a duty to leave the state of nature and to enter (and force others to enter) the civil condition.

For Kant, the civil condition is formed through a social contract that unites the will of all. This contract is not an historical event but an idea of reason under which law is legitimate to the extent that it could have arisen from the consent of everyone. The idea of the social contract thereby serves as a norm for the internal constitution of any state. Kant regards the public duty to support the poor as a juridical effect of this move from the state of nature through the social contract into the civil condition. As the passage in the first section of this chapter indicated, he does not explain why he posits such an effect or why he regards support of the poor as a public duty. Given, however, that the civil condition normatively presupposes that all could consent to its laws, he presumably thinks that the laws of a state that failed to legislate in fulfillment of this duty could not enjoy the agreement of all.

3. The Duty of Rightful Honor

[A]lthough innate right does not include a positive right to survival, it imposes both a duty of non-interference on others and, through the duty of rightful honor, a duty on oneself not to put oneself in a position in which one's physical survival becomes dependent on the actions of others. Accordingly, to the extent that the transition to a property-protecting civil condition is inconsistent with the duty of rightful honour, the consent of all would be impossible to attain.

A regime characterized only by innate right systemically maximizes the mutual non-dependence of all. In such a regime, everything is available for use by everyone, except the space that others occupy and whatever is in their physical possession. Accumulation is impossible because no-one has external things as one's own. As long as I occupy a particular space, nobody can push me out of it. But when I move, I can occupy any other space not

14. Ibid. [315].

occupied by someone else, gaining my new space and simultaneously losing the power to prevent others from occupying the old one. . . . This general availability of everything except the space that others occupy and the things that they physically possess means that my survival cannot directly be affected by the actions of others. Whatever external things are available to my neighbours are also available to me. So far as my relationship with others is concerned, I am . . . my own master, able to act on my own and without dependence on others for my continued existence. . . .

The inevitable non-dependence that characterizes innate right disappears with the introduction, first provisional and then conclusive, of external property. Because ownership obtains even in the absence of a physical connection between the owner and what is owned, the accumulation of external things is now permissible. My range of rightful possibilities is now confined to what might be left over from others' efforts at accumulation. The possibility of amassing land makes it conceivable that, given the finitude of the earth's surface, all the land may be appropriated by others, leaving me literally with no place to exist except by leave of someone else. My continued existence may thus become dependent on the goodwill or sufferance of others, to whom I might then have to subordinate myself, making myself into a means for their ends, perhaps becoming their bondsman or slave. Moreover, my inability otherwise to satisfy my basic needs may make me dependent on the generosity of others, that is, on that to which I have no right. The legitimation of the ownership of external things produces a juridical regime in which the survival of one person may be dependent on how others dispose of what is rightfully theirs.

This transformation of one's position relative to others from assured non-dependence to potential dependence renders it impossible to agree to a civil condition in which the law allows the possibility of such dependence. To consent to the possibility of dependence with respect to one's existence would violate one's duty of rightful honor. . . .

Thus, the progression from innate right to the state's guarantee of all property holdings seems to reach an impasse. On the one hand, this progression is a normative necessity in which I am obligated to participate. On the other hand, innate right at least has the advantage that no person or aggregate of persons can engross the world's resources, shut me off from access to what is necessary for my existence, and thereby make the exercise of my freedom dependent on the beneficent or exploitative will of another. Consenting to this possible dependence would be inconsistent with my duty of rightful honor. The civil condition, it seems, is both a fulfilment and an infringement of my duty.

The public duty to support the poor breaks—and indeed is the only thing that can break—this impasse. The requirement allows all persons, consistently with their rightful honor, to consent to the laws of the civil condition. The sovereign's assumption of the duty to support the poor makes up for the possible inaccessibility of the means of sustenance.

The result is that in the civil condition, just as under innate right, no-one's subsistence is dependent on the actions of others. Everyone can now consent to a civil condition that incorporates public support for the poor.

Furthermore, the duty is incumbent on the people (and derivatively on the sovereign) rather than on any particular person. The institution of a regime of external property allows for the accumulation of property; no individual commits a compensable wrong simply by engaging in this process. Moreover, the prospect of impoverishment is created by the systemic legitimacy of acquisition, rather than by the appropriative acts of any particular acquirer. The *systemic* difficulty that property poses for innate right is resolved by the *collective* duty imposed on the people to provide subsistence as needed.

To be sure, individuals pay the tax. This, however, is not because they are duty-bound as individuals to support the poor but because the sovereign is authorized to tax them for a necessary state purpose. The obligation of the taxpayers is to the state, not to the poor directly, because the taxpayers whose property is secured by the state are the beneficiaries of the transition to a civil condition. The incidence of this tax is based on a notion of reciprocity that flows from the state's guarantee of property and, with it, of the proprietors' means of survival: because the wealthy "owe their existence to an act of submitting to the [commonwealth's] protection, which they need in order to live,"[15] they are obligated to contribute what is theirs to sustain the existence of those who, because of the property regime, now lack what they need in order to live. . . .

This does not mean that, for Kant, the poor have a right to subsistence. Since a right is always accompanied by the authorization to coerce and the state is the ultimate repository of legitimate coercive power, Kant can recognize no right against the state. The poor are supported not because they hold a right but because they are the beneficiaries of a duty. The sovereign takes over from the people the duty to support the poor that is an incident of the obligation to make the state conform to the social contract through legislation to which all can consent.

The operation of this duty re-establishes the non-dependence that marked innate right and was threatened by the introduction of private property. In one's relations with another, everyone continues to have the same right to bodily integrity that they had as a matter of innate right. The availability to everyone of everything that was distinct from others' bodies has been superseded by the public duty to support the poor. One's interest in non-dependence with respect to one's continued existence is as well served by the juridical order of the third phase as it was by the juridical order of the first phase. The danger of being reduced to a means for others, present in the second phase, has been eliminated by the public duty to the poor. . . .

15. Ibid. [326].

For Kant, taxation is not theft, and neither is property. On the contrary, taxation and property are jointly necessary for a civil condition to which all can consent. On Kant's view as I have reconstructed it, the public duty to support the poor is latent within private property as a rightful institution. . . .

NOTES AND QUESTIONS

1. *Kant's Theory of Rights.* Kant's theory of property is complex and difficult. In order better to grasp Weinrib's account of Kant's theory of property, it is helpful to get a sense of Kant's conception of the right to independence on which this account relies. Specifically, it is important to appreciate how Kant's conception of personal independence differs from other, more robust conceptions of autonomy, which is understood as the ability to be the author of one's life, choosing among worthwhile life plans and being able to pursue one's choice. As Arthur Ripstein explains, Kantian independence is inherently relational and is exhausted by the requirement that no one gets to tell anyone else what purposes to pursue: "[A]utonomy can be compromised by natural or self-inflicted factors no less than by the deeds of others; Kantian independence can only be compromised by the deeds of others. It is not a good to be promoted; it is a constraint on the conduct of others, imposed by the fact that each person is entitled to be his or her own master." Furthermore, because independence only requires that "nobody else gets to tell you what purposes to pursue," it "is not compromised if others decline to accommodate you." ARTHUR RIPSTEIN, FORCE AND FREEDOM: KANT'S LEGAL AND POLITICAL PHILOSOPHY 14, 34, 45 (2009).

2. *Rejecting the Idea of Pre-Political Property.* The need to rely on the public law of poverty-alleviation as part and parcel of the justification of the private law of property is premised on the notion that outside this full-blown rightful condition the Kantian support for extending innate rights to acquired stuff is only provisional. It is important to realize that by this Kant outright rejects the Lockean idea of pre-political property, implying that "a purely unilateral act of acquisition can only restrict the choice of all other persons against the background of an omnilateral authorization, which is possible only in a condition of public right." RIPSTEIN, *supra* Note 1, at 90. For an elaborate explanation of moral defects of the state of nature, see *id.* at Ch. 6. For a critique, see J.E. Penner, *The State Duty to Support the Poor in Kant's* Doctrine of Right, 12 BRIT. J. POL. & INT'L REL. 88 (2010).

3. *Weinrib as a Private Law Libertarian.* Weinrib argues for near absolute property rights in private law — insofar as people's interpersonal interactions are concerned, property rights in his system are even more robust than those championed by Nozick. Indeed, understood as a Kantian right, property becomes the cornerstone of private law libertarianism: a legal regime with a strict division of labor between public law and private

law. At the same time, Weinrib also defends the welfare state, which Nozick vehemently opposes.

Private law libertarianism attracts quite a few other private law scholars, although there are differences in their normative commitments. Thus, some lawyer-economists claim that only public law should be responsible for other people's well-being because tax-and-transfer mechanisms are always (or at least typically) the most efficient way to redistribute welfare. *See, e.g.,* Louis Kaplow & Steven Shavell, *Why the Legal System Is Less Efficient Than the Income Tax in Redistributing Income*, 23 J. LEGAL STUD. 667 (1994). Can you figure out the basis for this claim? For a fair description and critical analysis of the relevant welfarist arguments, with particular emphasis on their application in property contexts, see Daphna Lewinsohn-Zamir, *In Defense of Redistribution Through Private Law*, 91 MINN. L. REV. 326 (2006). Weinrib's theory is, of course, not grounded in well-being; quite the contrary, it is the most elaborate right-based account of private law libertarianism. But private law libertarianism is not easy to defend. For an early critique, see Anthony T. Kronman, *Contract Law and Distributive Justice*, 89 YALE L.J. 472 (1980) (rules of contract law should be used to implement distributive goals whenever alternative ways of doing so are likely to be more costly or intrusive).

Consider again Weinrib's scheme and notice how much it depends upon the optimistic (some would say unrealistic) assumption that public law can and does supplement private law with rules that sufficiently redistribute resources so as to remedy the distributive distortions of a value-monistic private law. Furthermore, even if such a tax-and-redistribution scheme emerged, do you think that it is likely to ameliorate the distortions of such a private law system in terms of unjustified interpersonal dependence? *See* HANOCH DAGAN, PROPERTY: VALUES AND INSTITUTIONS 63-66 (2011). Weinrib addresses these queries, at least indirectly, by considering the question whether "the public duty to support the poor does not . . . merely replace possible dependency on the actions of others with an equally unsatisfactory dependency on the state?" He takes the view that "dependence involves a relationship with someone who, without breaching a duty, can withhold a benefit necessary for one's survival," so that because the state is under a duty to support the poor and "has no motivation to withhold support," the receipt of state support "does not make the needy subservient to the will of others." WEINRIB, *supra*. Do you agree?

4. *A Competing Right-Based Account of Property.* Alan Brudner argues that because for Kant there is "no pre-civil law validation of right-claims over particular things" — that is, because "the rightness of a contingent and unilateral appropriation depends on its being omnilaterally approved" — the attempt to establish an autonomous private law on Kantian right is doomed to fail. "Private law's autonomy dissolves in the [Kantian] civil condition no matter what the lawgiver does," argues Brudner, because being provisional, the privately acquired rights, in Kant's scheme, "have

no conclusive normative status that a public lawgiver," be it a legislature or a court, "is obliged to respect. Such a lawgiver "is constrained by nothing but omnilaterality," namely: seeking "an optimal accommodation between the common interest in secure possession and competing public interests." Alan Brudner, *Private Law and Kantian Right*, 61 U. Toronto L.J. 279, 288, 295, 298-299, 308 (2011).

For Brudner, the only way to redeem private law's autonomy—to construct an account of property rights that are not contingent upon public goals—is to discard the Kantian system of right in favor of that of Hegel's, which "embraces the distinction between the general will and the particular will of the monadic individual—a will of which the general will is but a constituent element." *Id.*, at 310-311. The private right to property in this view, Brudner insists, remains independent and autonomous, because it already "presuppose[s] the mutual respect of persons." For this to be the case the concept of property cannot undermine other people's "effective autonomy." This means that when the exercise of property rights would amount to oppression—where "an absolute property may become an external power" potentially jeopardizing people's autonomy—property may legitimately be regulated. A regulation of property is legitimate in this view insofar as it is based on reasons that are intrinsic to property, for example, where it is aimed at protecting "the vital interests of persons (e.g., residential tenants, laborers) vulnerable to the exercise of proprietary power," or at preventing "exercises of the right to alienate that deny the human equality on which property rests." Alan Brudner, The Unity of the Common Law: Studies in Hegelian Jurisprudence 68, 74 (1995).

5 PROPERTY AND WELL-BEING

Harold Demsetz, Toward a Theory of Property Rights[1]

Externality is an ambiguous concept. For the purposes of this paper, the concept includes external costs, external benefits, and pecuniary as well as nonpecuniary externalities. No harmful or beneficial effect is external to the world. Some person or persons always suffer or enjoy these effects. What converts a harmful or beneficial effect into an externality is that the cost of bringing the effect to bear on the decisions of one or more of the interacting persons is too high to make it worthwhile, and this is what the term shall mean here. "Internalizing" such effects refers to a process, usually a change in property rights, that enables these effects to bear (in greater degree) on all interacting persons.

A primary function of property rights is that of guiding incentives to achieve a greater internalization of externalities. Every cost and benefit associated with social interdependencies is a potential externality. One condition is necessary to make costs and benefits externalities. The cost of a transaction in the rights between the parties (internalization) must exceed the gains from internalization. . . . Some costs and benefits are not taken into account by users of resources whenever externalities exist, but allowing transactions increases the degree to which internalization takes place. . . .

1. Harold Demsetz, *Toward a Theory of Property Rights*, 57 Am. Econ. Rev. 347, 348, 350-357 (1967).

The Emergence of Property Rights

If the main allocative function of property rights is the internalization of beneficial and harmful effects, then the emergence of property rights can be understood best by their association with the emergence of new or different beneficial and harmful effects.

Changes in knowledge result in changes in production functions, market values, and aspirations. New techniques, new ways of doing the same things, and doing new things—all invoke harmful and beneficial effects to which society has not been accustomed. It is my thesis in this part of the paper that the emergence of new property rights takes place in response to the desires of the interacting persons for adjustment to new benefit-cost possibilities.

The thesis can be restated in a slightly different fashion: property rights develop to internalize externalities when the gains of internalization become larger than the cost of internalization. Increased internalization, in the main, results from changes in economic values, changes which stem from the development of new technology and the opening of new markets, changes to which old property rights are poorly attuned. A proper interpretation of this assertion requires that account be taken of a community's preferences for private ownership. Some communities will have less well-developed private ownership systems and more highly developed state ownership systems. But, given a community's tastes in this regard, the emergence of new private or state-owned property rights will be in response to changes in technology and relative prices.

I do not mean to assert or to deny that the adjustments in property rights which take place need be the result of a conscious endeavor to cope with new externality problems. These adjustments have arisen in Western societies largely as a result of gradual changes in social mores and in common law precedents. At each step of this adjustment process, it is unlikely that externalities per se were consciously related to the issue being resolved. These legal and moral experiments may be hit-and-miss procedures to some extent but in a society that weights the achievement of efficiency heavily, their viability in the long run will depend on how well they modify behavior to accommodate to the externalities associated with important changes in technology or market values.

A rigorous test of this assertion will require extensive and detailed empirical work. . . . In this part of the discussion, I shall present one group of such examples in some detail. They deal with the development of private property rights in land among American Indians. . . .

The question of private ownership of land among aboriginals has held a fascination for anthropologists. . . . What appears to be accepted as a classic treatment and a high point of this debate is Eleanor Leacock's memoir on *The Montagnes "Hunting Territory" and the Fur Trade*.[2] . . .

---

2. Eleanor Leacock, *The Montagnes "Hunting Territory" and the Fur Trade*, 56 Am. Anthropologist, no. 5, 1954.

Leacock clearly established the fact that a close relationship existed, both historically and geographically, between the development of private rights in land and the development of the commercial fur trade. . . . The factual material uncovered by [Frank G.] Speck and Leacock fits the thesis of this paper well, and in doing so, it reveals clearly the role played by property right adjustments in taking account of what economists have often cited as an example of an externality—the overhunting of game.

Because of the lack of control over hunting by others, it is in no person's interest to invest in increasing or maintaining the stock of game. Overly intensive hunting takes place. Thus a successful hunt is viewed as imposing external costs on subsequent hunters—costs that are not taken into account fully in the determination of the extent of hunting and of animal husbandry.

Before the fur trade became established, hunting was carried on primarily for purposes of food and the relatively few furs that were required for the hunter's family. The externality was clearly present. Hunting could be practiced freely and was carried on without assessing its impact on other hunters. But these external effects were of such small significance that it did not pay for anyone to take them into account. There did not exist anything resembling private ownership in land. . . .

We may safely surmise that the advent of the fur trade had two immediate consequences. First, the value of furs to the Indians was increased considerably. Second, and as a result, the scale of hunting activity rose sharply. Both consequences must have increased considerably the importance of the externalities associated with free hunting. The property right system began to change, and it changed specifically in the direction required to take account of the economic effects made important by the fur trade. The geographical or distributional evidence collected by Leacock indicates an unmistakable correlation between early centers of fur trade and the oldest and most complete development of the private hunting territory. . . .

The principle that associates property right changes with the emergence of new and reevaluation of old harmful and beneficial effects suggests in this instance that the fur trade made it economic to encourage the husbanding of fur-bearing animals. Husbanding requires the ability to prevent poaching and this, in turn, suggests that socioeconomic changes in property in hunting land will take place. The chain of reasoning is consistent with the evidence cited above. Is it inconsistent with the absence of similar rights in property among the southwestern Indians?

Two factors suggest that the thesis is consistent with the absence of similar rights among the Indians of the southwestern plains. The first of these is that there were no plains animals of commercial importance comparable to the fur-bearing animals of the forest, at least not until cattle arrived with Europeans. The second factor is that animals of the plains are primarily grazing species whose habit is to wander over wide tracts of land. The value of establishing boundaries to private hunting territories is thus reduced by the relatively high cost of preventing the animals from moving to adjacent parcels. Hence both the value and cost of establishing private hunting lands in the Southwest are such that we would expect little development along these lines. The externality was just not worth taking into account.

The lands of the Labrador Peninsula shelter forest animals whose habits are considerably different from those of the plains. Forest animals confine their territories to relatively small areas, so that the cost of internalizing the effects of husbanding these animals is considerably reduced. This reduced cost, together with the higher commercial value of fur-bearing forest animals, made it productive to establish private hunting lands. Frank G. Speck finds that family proprietorship among the Indians of the Peninsula included retaliation against trespass. Animal resources were husbanded. Sometimes conservation practices were carried on extensively. Family hunting territories were divided into quarters. Each year the family hunted in a different quarter in rotation, leaving a tract in the center as a sort of bank, not to be hunted over unless forced to do so by a shortage in the regular tract. . . .

THE COALESCENCE AND OWNERSHIP OF PROPERTY RIGHTS

I have argued that property rights arise when it becomes economic for those affected by externalities to internalize benefits and costs. . . .

[Consider now] a particularly useful example that focuses our attention on the problem of land ownership. Suppose that land is communally owned. Every person has the right to hunt, till, or mine the land. This form of ownership fails to concentrate the cost associated with any person's exercise of his communal right on that person. If a person seeks to maximize the value of his communal rights, he will tend to overhunt and overwork the land because some of the costs of his doing so are borne by others. The stock of game and the richness of the soil will be diminished too quickly. It is conceivable that those who own these rights, i.e., every member of the community, can agree to curtail the rate at which they work the lands if negotiating and policing costs are zero. Each can agree to abridge his rights. It is obvious that the costs of reaching such an agreement will not be zero. What is not obvious is just how large these costs may be.

Negotiating costs will be large because it is difficult for many persons to reach a mutually satisfactory agreement, especially when each hold-out has the right to work the land as fast as he pleases. But, even if an agreement among all can be reached, we must yet take account of the costs of policing the agreement, and these may be large, also. After such an agreement is reached, no one will privately own the right to work the land; all can work the land but at an agreed upon shorter workweek. Negotiating costs are increased even further because it is not possible under this system to bring the full expected benefits and expected costs of future generations to bear on current users.

If a single person owns land, he will attempt to maximize its present value by taking into account alternative future time streams of benefits and costs and selecting that one which he believes will maximize the present value of his privately-owned land rights. We all know that this means that he will attempt to take into account the supply and demand conditions that he thinks will exist after his death. It is very difficult to see how the existing communal owners can reach an agreement that takes account of these costs.

In effect, an owner of a private right to use land acts as a broker whose wealth depends on how well he takes into account the competing claims of the present and the future. But with communal rights there is no broker, and the claims of the present generation will be given an uneconomically large weight in determining the intensity with which the land is worked. Future generations might desire to pay present generations enough to change the present intensity of land usage. But they have no living agent to place their claims on the market. . . .

The land ownership example confronts us immediately with a great disadvantage of communal property. The effects of a person's activities on his neighbors and on subsequent generations will not be taken into account fully. Communal property results in great externalities. The full costs of the activities of an owner of a communal property right are not borne directly by him, nor can they be called to his attention easily by the willingness of others to pay him an appropriate sum. . . .

The state, the courts, or the leaders of the community could attempt to internalize the external costs resulting from communal property by allowing private parcels owned by small groups of person with similar interests. The logical groups in terms of similar interests, are, of course, the family and the individual. . . .

The resulting private ownership of land will internalize many of the external costs associated with communal ownership, for now an owner, by virtue of his power to exclude others, can generally count on realizing the rewards associated with husbanding the game and increasing the fertility of his land. This concentration of benefits and costs on owners creates incentives to utilize resources more efficiently.

But we have yet to contend with externalities. Under the communal property system the maximization of the value of communal property rights will take place without regard to many costs, because the owner of a communal right cannot exclude others from enjoying the fruits of his efforts and because negotiation costs are too high for all to agree jointly on optimal behavior. The development of private rights permits the owner to economize on the use of those resources from which he has the right to exclude others. Much internalization is accomplished in this way. But the owner of private rights to one parcel does not himself own the rights to the parcel of another private sector. Since he cannot exclude others from their private rights to land, he has no direct incentive (in the absence of negotiations) to economize in the use of his land in a way that takes into account the effects he produces on the land rights of others. If he constructs a dam on his land, he has no direct incentive to take into account the lower water levels produced on his neighbor's land.

This is exactly the same kind of externality that we encountered with communal property rights, but it is present to a lesser degree. Whereas no one had an incentive to store water on any land under the communal system, private owners now can take into account directly those benefits and costs to their land that accompany water storage. But the effects on the land of others will not be taken into account directly.

The partial concentration of benefits and costs that accompany private ownership is only part of the advantage this system offers. The other part, and perhaps the most important, has escaped our notice. The cost of negotiating over the remaining externalities will be reduced greatly. Communal property rights allow anyone to use the land. Under this system it becomes necessary for all to reach an agreement on land use. But the externalities that accompany private ownership of property do not affect all owners, and, generally speaking, it will be necessary for only a few to reach an agreement that takes these effects into account. The cost of negotiating an internalization of these effects is thereby reduced considerably. The point is important enough to elucidate.

Suppose an owner of a communal land right, in the process of plowing a parcel of land, observes a second communal owner constructing a dam on adjacent land. The farmer prefers to have the stream as it is, and so he asks the engineer to stop his construction. The engineer says, "Pay me to stop." The farmer replies, "I will be happy to pay you, but what can you guarantee in return?" The engineer answers, "I can guarantee you that I will not continue constructing the dam, but I cannot guarantee that another engineer will not take up the task because this is communal property; I have no right to exclude him." What would be a simple negotiation between two persons under a private property arrangement turns out to be a rather complex negotiation between the farmer and everyone else. This is the basic explanation, I believe, for the preponderance of single rather than multiple owners of property. Indeed, an increase in the number of owners is an increase in the communality of property and leads, generally, to an increase in the cost of internalizing.

NOTES AND QUESTIONS

1. *Demsetz's Evolutionary Story.* Demsetz's text is the classic modern treatment of private property from the perspective of economics. One aspect of this treatment is an account of the process by which private property rights develop to internalize the externalities when pressure increases on the use of a resource. Notice that Demsetz relies here on cooperative

collective action to undertake this challenge. But this seems to beg the question because it assumes that a community plagued by noncooperation can improve its condition by cooperating. *See* James E. Krier, *The Tragedy of the Commons, Part Two*, 15 HARV. J.L. & PUB. POL'Y 325, 336-338 (1992). *See also* Carol M. Rose, *Property as Storytelling: Prespectives from Game Theory, Narrative Theory, Feminist Theory*, 2 YALE J.L. & HUMAN. 37 (1990) (proposing that after-the-fact narratives are necessary to explain the development of property regimes because these regimes do not always unfold as logic predicts). Krier suggests that a more promising path to solve this evolutionary puzzle is taken by following David Hume's insight that property rights are conventions that arise spontaneously — rather than by deliberate design — from "a general sense of common interest." DAVID HUME, A TREATISE OF HUMAN NATURE 490 (bk. 3, pt. 2, §2) (1965) (1739-1740). Can you see how this path solves the difficulty of the alternative suggested by Demsetz? Do you see problems with Krier's explanation? *See* James E. Krier, *Evolutionary Theory and the Origin of Property Rights*, 95 CORNELL L. REV. 139 (2009) (also discussing the limitations and difficulties of the conventional account). Finally, note that neither alternative seriously considers the political process through which property regimes are formed and thus, among other topics, the effects of interest groups. Do you see why this additional factor should make a difference? For two interesting case studies of the formation of property rights, which highlight this factor, see Daniel Fitzpatrick, *Evolution and Chaos in Property Rights The Third World Tragedy of Contested Access*, 115 YALE L.J. 996 (2006); Katrina Miriam Wyman, *From Fur to Fish: Reconsidering the Evolution of Private Property*, 80 N.Y.U. L. REV. 117 (2005).

2. *The Tragedy of the Commons.* Whatever the merits of his account of the evolution of property rights, Demsetz is rightly credited for being the first theorist to conduct a cost-benefit analysis to establish the long-run superiority of private property over commons property. The famous slogan for this conventional wisdom was coined by Garrett Hardin: *The Tragedy of the Commons*, as the title of his article in 162 SCIENCE 1243 (1968), in which he claimed that rational co-owners are bound to underinvest in the common resource, while overexploiting it. This phenomenon, which derives from the divergence between the aggregate interest in a commons and the individual interest of each of its owners, was already noted by Aristotle. *See* ARISTOTLE, THE POLITICS bk. 2, ch. 1, §10 (H. Rackham trans., 1932). Demsetz's contribution is nonetheless substantial as he crystallized three types of costs from commons property regimes: increased negotiating costs because of holdouts, increased policing or monitoring costs, and the difficulties of too high a discount rate that lead commoners to fail to internalize fully the interests of future generations. Does Demsetz argue that these costs disappear in a private property regime? If not, why does he claim that private property helps solving these problems? Does Demsetz's account apply both to cases of *open access*, in which anyone at all may use a resource and no one may be excluded, and to those of *commons*

ownership, in which a bounded group, such as a group of fishermen, controls access to a valuable resource? Are there possible solutions (excepting privatization) to either form that Demsetz might have overlooked?

   3.   *The Costs of Privatization.* In contrast to the notion of an inevitable tragedy of the commons, political scientists and new institutional economists have supplied a wealth of case studies of well-functioning commons regimes around the globe. The definitive synthesis of these studies, which distills the institutional arrangements that distinguish between cases of long-enduring commons and cases of failures and fragilities, is Elinor Ostrom's book *Governing the Commons* excerpted in Chapter 12. How can one account for this striking phenomenon?

   One possible answer is that at times the costs of establishing and maintaining a private property regime are quite high and its benefits may be limited. As Terry Anderson and P.J. Hill explain, the probability of securing benefits from better-defined private property rights is affected by variables such as the crime rate, population density, cultural and ethical attitudes, and the preexisting "rules of the game" of the institutional structure. On the other hand, anything that reduces the quantity of resources that is necessary for definition-and-enforcement activity or lowers the opportunity cost of such resources—such as changes in technology, in resource endowments, or in the scale of operation—will affect marginal costs. Terry L. Anderson & P.J. Hill, *The Evolution of Property Rights: A Study of the American West*, 18 J.L. & Econ. 163 (1975). Do you understand the effect of each of these factors? Can you see how their contingency explains why we observe varying types of property arrangements covering the spectrum from commons to private? A particularly difficult example for Demsetz's most fundamental claim, that increasing demand requires a move away from commons property toward private property, derives from research in European social history that suggests that communal agricultural property was antedated by a system that was more individualistic and carried out on small, individual fields rather than in communal lots. This means that population growth in one period could produce a shift from individual to common tenures and later produce a shift from commons to individual property. For a discussion of how developmental pressures may encourage greater use of common, rather than individual, property, see Barry C. Field, *The Evolution of Property Rights*, 42 Kyklos 319, 319-320, 328 (1989).

   There are other possible reasons for the prevalence, and possible prosperity, of commons property, which we state here only briefly but consider at some detail in Chapter 12. First, commons property can sometimes be advantageous because of "increasing returns to scale and the desirability of spreading risks." Robert C. Ellickson, *Property in Land*, 102 Yale L.J. 1315, 1332 (1993). Can you see how? Are there other "hidden benefits" to the commons (not necessarily of the economic type)? Second, as a careful account of the success stories reported by Ostrom et al. shows, strong limitations on alienability help facilitate the commoners' cooperation.

See Margaret A. McKean, *Success on the Commons: A Comparative Examination of Institutions for Common Property Resource Management*, 4 J. THEORETICAL POL. 247, 261-262 (1992). Finally, as lawyers know from the numerous contexts in which there are multiple owners to the same set of resources, governance rules may help regulate the use of such resources in a way that ameliorates the costs of common ownership.

   4.   *The Tragedy of the Anticommons.* Michael Heller developed a theory of anticommons property that demonstrates that privatization, which theorists like Demsetz see as a solution to the tragedy of the commons, might actually cause another tragedy. Heller defines an anticommons property as "a property regime in which multiple owners hold effective rights of exclusion in a scarce resource." Michael A. Heller, *The Tragedy of the Anticommons: Property in the Transition from Marx to Markets*, 111 HARV. L. REV. 621, 668 (1998). In an anticommons, too many owners may each exclude others from a resource, the mirror image of a commons with a mirror tragedy: Resources may be prone to waste through underuse rather than from overuse. *See id.* at 633-642 (discussing the consequences of misguided privatization of state property in post-socialist economies). Once an anticommons is in place, rights-assembly turns out to be rather difficult. (Can you see why this is so? Think about the transaction costs, strategic behavior, and cognitive biases that may impede efforts to recombine property.) Therefore, it is particularly important for policymakers to appreciate the potential pitfalls of fragmentation. Thus, for example, Michael Heller and Rebecca Eisenberg demonstrated that efforts to spur private investment in biomedical research by granting property rights may have brought about "[a] proliferation of intellectual property rights upstream," which paradoxically "may be stifling life-saving innovations further downstream in the course of research and product development." Michael A. Heller & Rebecca S. Eisenberg, *Can Patents Deter Innovation? The Anticommons in Biomedical Research*, 280 SCIENCE 698, 698 (1998). Against this unfortunate example, consider Heller's celebration of what he calls property law's "boundary principle that limits the right to subdivide private property into wasteful fragments." *See* Michael A. Heller, *The Boundaries of Private Property*, 108 YALE L.J. 1163, 1165 (1999). Can you think of examples for this principle?

Richard A. Posner, Economic Analysis of Law[3]

THE ECONOMIC THEORY OF PROPERTY RIGHTS: STATIC AND DYNAMIC ASPECTS

To understand the economics of property rights, we must first distinguish between *static* and *dynamic* analysis. Static analysis suppresses the time

---

3. RICHARD A. POSNER, ECONOMIC ANALYSIS OF LAW 31-34, 37-38 (7th ed. 2007).

dimension of economic activity: All adjustments to change are assumed to occur instantaneously. The assumption is unrealistic but often fruitful. . . .

Dynamic analysis, in which the assumption of instantaneous adjustment to change is relaxed, is usually more complex than static analysis. So it is surprising that the economic basis of property rights was first perceived in dynamic terms. Imagine a society in which all property rights have been abolished. A farmer plants corn, fertilizes it, and erects scarecrows, but when the corn is ripe, his neighbor reaps it and takes it away for his own use. The farmer has no legal remedy against his neighbor's conduct because he owns neither the land that he sowed nor the crop, where ownership implies the legal right to exclude. Unless defensive measures are feasible (and let us assume for the moment that they are not), after a few such incidents the cultivation of land will be abandoned and society will shift to methods of subsistence (such as hunting) that involve less preparatory investment.

Although the value of the crop in our example, as measured by consumers' willingness to pay, may have greatly exceeded its cost in labor, materials, and forgone alternative uses of the land, without property rights there is no incentive to incur these costs because there is no reasonably assured reward for incurring them. The proper incentives are created by parceling out mutually exclusive rights to the use of particular resources among the members of society. If every piece of land is owned by someone — if there is always someone who can exclude all others from access to any given area — then individuals will endeavor by cultivation or other improvements to maximize the value of land. Land is just an example. The principle applies to all valuable resources.

All this has been well known for hundreds of years. In contrast, the static analysis of property rights is little more than 80 years old. Imagine that a number of farmers own a pasture in common, meaning that none has the right to exclude any of the others and hence none can charge the others for the use of the pasture. We can abstract from the dynamic aspects of the problem by assuming that the pasture is a natural (uncultivated) one, so that there is no question of improving it by investment. Even so, pasturing additional cows will impose a cost on all the farmers. The cows will have to graze more in order to eat the same amount of grass, and this will reduce their weight. But because none of the farmers pays for the use of the pasture, none will take this cost into account in deciding how many additional cows to pasture, with the result that more cows will be pastured than would be efficient. . . .

The problem would disappear if one person owned the pasture and charged each farmer for its use. The charge to each farmer would include the cost he imposes on the other farmers by pasturing additional cows, because that cost reduces the value of the pasture to the other farmers and hence the price they are willing to pay the owner for the right to graze. . . .

The creation of individual (as distinct from collective) ownership rights is a necessary rather than a sufficient condition for the efficient use of resources. Suppose the farmer in our first example owns the land that he sows but is a bad farmer; his land would be more productive in someone else's hands. Efficiency requires a mechanism by which the farmer can be induced to transfer the property to that someone else. A transferable property right is such a mechanism. . . .

The discussion to this point may seem to imply that if every valuable (meaning scarce as well as desired) resource were owned by someone (call this the criterion of universality), if ownership connoted the unqualified power to exclude everybody else from using the resource (exclusivity) as well as to use it oneself, and if ownership rights were freely transferable or, as lawyers say, alienable (transferability), value would be maximized. This leaves out of account, however, the costs of a property-rights system, both the obvious and the subtle ones. . . .

PROBLEMS IN THE CREATION AND ENFORCEMENT OF PROPERTY RIGHTS

Property rights are not only less exclusive but less universal than they would be if they were costless to enforce. Imagine a primitive society in which the principal use of land is for grazing. The population of the society is small relative to the amount of land, and its flocks are small too. No technology exists for increasing the value of the land by fertilizer, irrigation, or other techniques. The cost of wood or other materials for fencing is very high and, the society being illiterate, a system for publicly recording land ownership is out of the question. In these circumstances the costs of enforcing property rights might well exceed the benefits. The costs would be the costs of fencing to keep out other people's grazing animals, and would be substantial. The benefits might be zero. Since there is no crowding problem, property rights would confer no static benefits, and since there is no way of improving the land, there would be no dynamic benefits either. It is no surprise that property rights are less extensive in primitive than in advanced societies and that the pattern by which property rights emerge and grow in a society is related to increases in the ratio of the benefits of property rights to their costs.

The common law distinction between domestic and wild animals illustrates the general point. Domestic animals are owned like any other personal property; wild animals are not owned until killed or put under actual restraint (as in a zoo). Thus, if your cow wanders off your land, it is still your cow; but if a gopher whose burrow is on your land wanders off, he is not your property, and anyone who wants can capture or kill him, unless he is tame — unless, that is, he has an *animus revertendi* (the habit of returning to your land). . . . It would be difficult to enforce a property right in a wild animal and pretty useless; most wild animals, as in our gopher illustration, are not valuable, so there is nothing to be gained from creating incentives to invest in them. . . .

[T]he *denial* of a property right can be as much an economizing device as the creation of one. [Thus], note that legal protection of a trademark requires actual sales of the product or service that the trademark designates. You cannot just dream up names for products that you or someone else might someday want to sell, and register the names with the Trademark Office and by doing so obtain a right to exclude others from using these names. Allowing such "banking" of trademarks might draw excessive resources into the activity of thinking up trademarks, and also clutter the trademark registry with millions of marks, making it more costly for sellers to search the registry in order to avoid infringing a registered one.

Another illustration of the economizing function of denying a property right is the doctrine of public trust, under which navigable waterways, tidelands, and certain beaches are reserved for public access — no one may establish a property right in them. If a resource is valuable but not scarce (a paradox?), the creation of property rights does not serve an economizing function. All it does is incite rent-seeking and resulting resource dissipation. Another reason for the doctrine of public trust, however, may be to limit rent-seeking by forbidding government to give away valuable public property.

NOTES AND QUESTIONS

1. *The Static Analysis Reconsidered.* In the second half of our excerpt, Posner provides a few examples for the proposition that at times privatization is just too costly or — more generally — that "[t]he relative efficiency of alternative property rights regimes is situation-specific." Thráinn Eggertsson, *Open Access versus Common Property, in* PROPERTY RIGHTS: COOPERATION, CONFLICT, AND LAW 73, 73 (Terry L. Anderson & Fred S. McChesney eds., 2003). Can you analyze Posner's examples using Anderson and Hill's typology of costs and benefits of definition-and-enforcement activity mentioned at the second paragraph of Note 3 above? Do these economic justifications exhaust, in your view, the reasons for avoiding privatization of all of these resources?

The pasture example Posner uses restates Demsetz's main point. It also helps highlight the fact, noted by Lee Anne Fennell, that the misalignment of aggregate and individual well-being, which is the crux of the "tragedy of the commons," is driven by the presence of two "activities that are being pursued at different scales and under different property arrangements" so that the private owner can offload costs onto the commons and use access to the commons for the benefit of his private property. Lee Anne Fennell, *Commons, Anticommons, Semicommons, in* RESEARCH HANDBOOK ON THE ECONOMICS OF PROPERTY LAW 35, 38 (Kenneth Ayotte & Henry E. Smith eds., 2011).

2. *The Dynamic Analysis: Incentives to Work, Improve, Transfer, etc.* The first half of our excerpt summarizes the canonical account of the dynamic case for private property. As Posner explains, without property rights society is likely to incur some deadweight costs in the form of efforts devoted to protect things people possess and to take such things from others. Even more significantly, he emphasizes the welfare-enhancing effects of a property regime in terms of the incentives to maintain and improve things, to transfer, and to work. For a detailed discussion, see STEVEN SHAVELL, FOUNDATIONS OF ECONOMIC ANALYSIS OF LAW 11-20 (2004).

Consider the incentive to work. Posner seems to argue that with no secured right in their output, people have no incentive to work. But is it possible that the reverse is actually the case, namely, that if people know, for example, that half their yield will be taken away they will work twice as hard? In the context of income taxation, the fear that taxes will generate a "substitution effect," inducing people to spend more on leisure and non-market endeavors and less on work and consumption, is countered by an "income effect," which stands for the opposite response of "work[ing] harder in order to achieve a given level of consumption." JOEL SLEMROD & JON BAKIJA, TAXING OURSELVES: A CITIZEN'S GUIDE TO THE GREAT DEBATE OVER TAX REFORM 103-109 (1996). Do you think that a similar indeterminacy applies in our context? *Compare* Frank I. Michelman, *Ethics, Economics, and the Law of Property, in* NOMOS XXIV: ETHICS, ECONOMICS, AND THE LAW 3, 25 (1982) *with* POSNER, at 32 n.1. Also, do you think that non-pecuniary incentives to work significantly affect this analysis?

3. *Property and Stability.* Abraham Bell and Gideon Parchomovsky suggest that all the utility-enhancing features that are characteristic of property can be coherently analyzed around the notion of creating and defending the value inherent in stable ownership. More specifically, they argue that "a property system with stable rights increases the value of assets to users (now owners) and decreases the costs of obtaining and defending those assets." They furthermore insist that "a universally accepted and centrally policed property system provides the most cost-effective means of producing these benefits due to economies of scale" and that "generally, the benefits provided by property systems increase with the stability of the property rights they create." Abraham Bell & Gideon Parchomovsky, *A Theory of Property,* 90 CORNELL L. REV. 531, 552 (2005). Can you see how the stability of ownership (not merely possession) generates the happy utilitarian objectives mentioned above? The injunction of stability prescribes a preference to a property regime of bright-line rules as opposed to vague standards. But is it informative as to the optimal level of property protection or as to the optimal content of property rights?

4. *Preference Satisfaction or Objective Well-Being?* Our discussion thus far followed the customary usage by legal economists of preference satisfaction as the yardstick for well-being. Daphna Lewinsohn-Zamir argues, however, that when property law pursues the goal of maximizing overall well-being

it does not follow the preference-satisfaction understanding of well-being, but rather an objective understanding of this concept. In this rival conception, which she endorses, well-being stands for things that are good for people; things that make their lives better, whether individuals desire them or not, namely: "autonomy and liberty, understanding, accomplishment, deep and meaningful social relationships, and enjoyment." Daphna Lewinsohn-Zamir, *The Objectivity of Well-Being and the Objectives of Property Law*, 78 N.Y.U. L. Rev. 1669, 1702 (2003). She further demonstrates that this conception involves "quality constraints" on property rights, both in terms of the identity of the items of property most conducive to well-being and in terms of the contents of the rights their owners have in them. Lewinsohn-Zamir demonstrates that these constraints help explain a number of otherwise puzzling property rules, such as property exemptions in bankruptcy, the *numerus clausus* principle, the (landlord's) implied warranty of habitability and implied covenant to deliver actual possession, and restrictions on owners' power to control property after death. *See id.* at 1716-1718, 1721-1751. Can you try to reconstruct her argument as per these cases? (We discuss the second example in Chapter 8.2 below.) What do you think of the view that well-being must be analyzed in objective terms?

6   *PROPERTY AND CITIZENSHIP*

Gregory S. Alexander, Commodity &
Propriety: Competing Visions of Property
in American Legal Thought 1776-1970[1]

According to [the "property-as-propriety" view], property is the material
foundation for creating and maintaining the proper social order, the private
basis for the public good. This tradition, whose roots can be traced back to
Aristotle, has continuously understood the individual human as an inherently social being, inevitably dependent on others not only to thrive but
even just to survive. This irreducible interdependency means that individuals owe one another obligations, not by virtue of consent alone but as an
inherent incident of the human condition. This view of human nature
provides the basis for the political-legal principle in proprietarian thought
that when individuals fail to meet their precontractual social obligations,
the state may legitimately compel them to act for the good of the entire
community.

The concept of the common weal, moreover, was understood to have
substantive meaning. The common law maxim *salus populi suprema est
lex* (the welfare of the people is the supreme law) had real content.[2] The
public good was not understood as simply whatever the market produces,
for the market was viewed as a realm in which individuals were too vulnerable to the temptation to act out of narrow self-interest rather than, as

---

1. GREGORY S. ALEXANDER, COMMODITY & PROPRIETY: COMPETING VISIONS OF PROPERTY IN AMERICAN LEGAL
THOUGHT, 1776-1970 1-2, 29-35 (1997).

2. On this maxim and its impact on early nineteenth-century legal regulation, see William J.
Novak, "Public Economy and the Well-Ordered Market: Law and Economic Regulation in the 19th-
century America," *Law & Social Inquiry* 18 (1993): 1.

proprietarian principles required, for the purpose of maintaining the properly ordered society. . . .

THE INTELLECTUAL UNIVERSE OF CIVIC REPUBLICANISM

"Republicanism," as Gordon Wood had explained,[3] "meant more for Americans [of the revolutionary generation] than simply the elimination of a king and the institution of an elective system." The core of American republican thought during the eighteenth century was the idea that private "interests" could and should be subordinated to the common welfare of the polity. This idea originated in classical Greek political writing, particularly that of Aristotle, and underwent periodic revivals and modification in Renaissance Florence and again in seventeenth-century England.[4] By the time of the American Revolution it animated nearly all political and legal writing. "By 1776 the Revolution came to represent a final attempt . . . by many Americans to realize the traditional Commonwealth ideal of a corporate society, in which the common good would be the only objective of government."[5]

The holistic conception of society made the notion of the public good as the central objective of political life intelligible. Society was thought of as a homogeneous body whose members were organically linked together. The common good, then, was not merely what the consensus of society's individual members wished but a substantive conception of the moral good that transcended individual interests. This understanding of society did not exclude the concept of individual liberty, but it did require a public conception of liberty. The central dilemma of American politics was not thought to be the protection of individual freedoms against collective encroachment, but rather, the protection of the public rights of the people against aristocratic privileges and power. Because of society's homogenous character, protecting the political liberty of the collective people necessarily protected individual liberty.

The fundamental challenge to realizing this ideal was maintaining a particular moral character among the citizenry. The republic required citizens to constantly practice "virtue," which may be defined as the willingness of the citizen to subordinate his or her individual wants for the well-being of the entire polity. American republicans were well aware of how extraordinary this demand was and how fragile the requirement of virtue made the republic.

Eighteenth-century American republican discourse was dominated by a dialectic between "virtue" and "corruption." Indeed, virtue was understood as being constantly threatened by "corruption." Political writing was

3. Gordon S. Wood, *The Creation of the American Republic* (New York: W.W. Norton, 1969), 47.
4. See J.G.A. Pocock, *The Machiavellian Moment: Florentine Political Thought and the Atlantic Tradition* (Princeton: Princeton University Press, 1975).
5. Wood, *The Creation of the American Republic*, 54.

preoccupied with the question of the sources of corruption and the necessary social, economic, and political conditions for virtue to thrive. The civic republican ideology posited that virtue, public and private, required the existence of certain social conditions. Jefferson articulated this "sociology of virtue," as J.G.A. Pocock has called it, through an opposition between the "aristocracy of wealth" and the "aristocracy of virtue and talent."[6] That dichotomy was a trope that was in turn part of a cluster of oppositions that characterized the entire structure of civic republican discourse. The most important of these tropic oppositions included:

virtue	vs.	corruption
equality	vs.	privilege
leisure	vs.	luxury
independence	vs.	servility
liberty	vs.	wealth

Property occupied a central place in that discussion. Its role, however, was neither straightforward nor strictly functional. Rather it was dialectical and symbolic.

THE DIALECTICS OF PROPERTY IN CIVIC REPUBLICAN DISCOURSE

The role of property in civic republican discourse differs from the more familiar understanding of the function of property supplied by the political theory that C.B. Macpherson called "possessive individualism."[7] Though property plays a prominent role in both theories, the two ideologies attach strikingly different functions to it. From the perspective of possessive individualism, property is the basis for the categorical separation of private life from the public sphere. It is the central mechanism by which autonomous individuals shield themselves from the potential of collective tyranny. The private realm, in possessive individualist thought, inevitably reduces to property and consolidated ownership.[8]

Civic republicanism, both in revolutionary American thought and in its earlier Harringtonian version, did not categorically separate public and private life. Lacking a categorical opposition between polity and individual, it did not assign a negative role to property. At least protection against governmental action was not the exclusive, or even the primary, role of property in American civil republicanism. Instead, republicans conceived of property as necessary to facilitate a publicly active, self-governing citizenry.

6. See Thomas Jefferson, "Autobiography," in *The Works of Thomas Jefferson*, ed. Paul Leicester Ford (New York: Knickerbocker Press, 1904-5), 1:1.

7. On the theory of possessive individualism, see C.B. Macpherson, *The Political Theory of Possessive Individualism: Hobbes to Locke* (Oxford: Oxford University Press, 1962).

8. For a recent statement of this position, see Richard A. Epstein, *Takings: Private Property and the Power of Eminent Domain* (Cambridge: Harvard University Press, 1985).

Republicans believed that ownership of property provides the necessary foundation for virtue, enabling citizens to pursue the common welfare. J.G.A. Pocock has succinctly stated the republican function of property: "The citizen possessed property in order to be autonomous and autonomy was necessary for him to develop virtue and goodness as an actor within the political, social and natural realm or order. He did not possess it in order to engage in trade, exchange for profit; indeed, these activities were hardly compatible with the activity of citizenship."[9] Property was valued "as a means of anchoring the individual in the structure of power and virtue and liberating him to practice these activities."[10]

Individuals who do not own property are forced to devote their attention to providing for their own personal welfare, exposing them to corrupting influences and distracting them from the public good. John Adams expressed the concern that people who do not own property will be vulnerable to corruption, asking rhetorically, "Is it not . . . true that men in general, in every society, who are wholly destitute of property, are . . . too dependent on other men to have a will of their own? . . . Such is the fraility of the human heart, that very few men who have no property, have any judgment of their own."[11]

American civic republicans, then, understood property within the framework of a conflict between "autonomy" and "dependency." Autonomy is a necessary condition for virtue, while dependency undermines it. Jefferson expressed the civic republican meaning of dependency in his *Notes on the State of Virginia*, stating, "Dependence begets subservience and venality, suffocates the germ of virtue, and prepares fit tools for the designs of ambition."[12]

Static vs. Dynamic Property

The republican image of property as the foundation of political, social and moral order was by itself ambiguous. It failed, for example, to specify what *type* of property was necessary to perform this function, or whether any particular type of property at all was required. Could the republic survive if property were dynamic and continually free to change forms as social and economic conditions changes, or did it have to be static, maintaining a certain type? Related to this question was an uncertainty concerning the character of property as *mobile* or *immobile*. While a dynamic conception of

9. J.G.A. Pocock, "The Mobility of Property and the Rise of Eighteenth-Century Sociology," in *Virtue, Commerce, and History* (Cambridge: Cambridge University Press, 1985), 103.
10. [Joyce] Appleby, *Capitalism and a New Social Order[: The Republican Vision of the 1790s* (New York: NYU Press, 1984)], 9.
11. John Adams to James Sullivan, 26 April 1776, in *The Works of John Adams*, ed. Charles Francis Adams (Boston: Little, Brown, 1854), 9:376.
12. Thomas Jefferson, *Notes on the State of Virginia* (1785; reprint, New York: Harper Torchbooks, 1964), 157.

property would as a practical matter involve a high degree of mobility, in order for property to remain static its mobility would likely have to be restricted. These two meanings of republican property were not simply different, they were contradictory. The static meaning implied an apparently greater degree of control over property to maintain its preferred form and fixity. On the surface the dynamic meaning required little or no social control of property. Only collective restrictions to maintain its fluidity would be necessary.

These two meanings of property were both republican in the sense that they were different readings of the commitments to republic, civic virtue, and the common good. Jefferson's writing on the benefits of cultivated land owned in fee simple and worked by citizen-owners — the republic as constituted by the "fee simple empire" — is often taken to represent the paradigm of republican property. The same interpretation defines the Jeffersonian conflict as one between landed and commercial forms of property. The concept of "commerce" did play, as this interpretation suggests, a crucial role in American republican discourse, just as it did in the discourse of English republicans. But Jefferson's commitment to fee simple ownership of land did not represent a rejection of commerce. The opposition, rather, was between agricultural property and industrial property, i.e., cultivation of land, which he assumed to have a commercial dimension, and manufacturing. "Those who labor in the earth" *were* the "chosen people of God," insofar as they were not exposed to the corrupting influence of manufacturing.[13] As [d]ependence begets subservience," manufacturing begets dependence. "[T]he class of artificers," he observed, "[are] the panders of vice and the instruments by which the liberties of a country are generally overturned."[14] The form property takes in a society thus provides the test for the society's viability as a republic. Reinforcing this view, he stated in the *Notes*:

> [G]enerally speaking, the proportion which the aggregate of the other classes of citizens bears in any State to that of its husbandmen, is the proportion of its unsound to its healthy parts, and is a good enough barometer whereby to measure its degree of

13. Jefferson later revised his general hostility toward manufacturing, limiting his earlier critique that manufacture begets dependence on manufacturing to the "great cities in the old countries," because of the abundance of Western land. This was an early example of the theme of what Henry Nash Smith has called "the West as safety valve." See Henry Nash Smith, *Virgin Land: The American West as Symbol and Myth* (Cambridge: Harvard University Press, 1978), 203.

In this passage Jefferson was also contributing to the greatest symbolic role played by land in eighteenth- and nineteenth-century America — the myth of the Garden of Eden. See generally Leo Marx, *The Machine in the Garden: Technology and the Pastoral Ideal in America* (Oxford: Oxford University Press, 1964). Land's symbolic role within this mythology was to mask "poverty and industrial strife with the pleasing suggestion that a beneficent nature stronger than any human agency, the ancient resource of Americans, the power that had made the country rich and great, would solve the new problems of industrialism." Smith, *Virgin Land*, 206.

14. Thomas Jefferson to John Jay, 23 August 1785, *Jefferson Papers*, 8:426.

corruption. While we have land to labor, then, let us never wish to see our citizens occupied at a workbench, or twirling a distaff.[15]

Later in the *Notes* he stated:

> Our interest will be to throw open the doors of commerce, and to knock off all its shackles, giving perfect freedom to all persons for the vent of whatever they may chose to bring into our parts, and asking the same in theirs. . . . [I]t might be better for us to abandon the ocean altogether, that being the element whereon we shall be principally exposed to jostle with other nations; to leave to others to bring what we shall want, and to carry what we can spare. This would make us invulnerable to Europe, by offering none of our property to their prize, and would turn all our citizens to the cultivation of the earth.[16]

Here, then, we have, not an opposition between land and commerce, but a dialectic between static and dynamic property. On the one hand, the republic may be fatally threatened if property can be transformed from an agricultural into an industrial form. On the other hand, throwing open our doors to commerce represented the embracing of a form of economic dynamism that complemented the political dynamism that he later espoused so forcefully.[17] Moreover, to the extent that Jefferson's thinking remained consistent over the years and that his earlier statements on economic dynamism anticipated the doctrine of political relativism, how could that doctrine be reconciled with the need to maintain property in an agricultural mode, whose very stasis implies intergenerational control? Under the doctrine of political relativism, would not each generation be free to cast off past generations' commitment to any particular form of property and decide for itself what type of property suited its own needs?

The Dilemma of Unequal Distribution

The ambiguity of the meaning of republican property for stasis or change also affected the related questions of the mobility and distribution of property. Jefferson and others viewed the unequal distribution of property, specifically land, as incompatible with republicanism. Writing from Fountainbleau in 1785, Jefferson observed that the high degree of concentration of French land in the hands of the aristocracy was the source of the high degree of unemployment, as French landowners left their lands uncultivated for hunting. He then reiterated a view that he propounded throughout his career:[18]

---

15. Jefferson, *Notes on the State of Virginia*, 157-58.

16. Ibid., 164-65.

17. It also bears mention that Jefferson's suggestion, which his fear of dependence prompted, did not remove that threat altogether. Rather it substituted one form of dependence — on other nations to our trading for us — for another.

18. Thomas Jefferson to Rev. James Madison, 28 October 1785, *Jefferson Papers*, 8:681-82.

I am conscious that an equal degree of property is impracticable. But the consequences of this enormous inequality producing so much misery to the bulk of mankind, legislators cannot invent too many devices for subdividing property, only taking
care to let their subdivisions go hand in hand with the natural affections of the human
mind.

The dilemma he faced was how to prevent the unequal distribution of
land from undermining republican virtue while pragmatically acknowledg-
ing the "natural affections of the human mind" that were embodied in the
concept of individual ownership. John Adams, citing Harrington's dictum
that power always follows property, expressed the recurrent anxiety about
the consequences for republican virtue in terms of a need to maintain a
balance of property in order to maintain a balance of power:

The only possible way . . . of preserving the balance of power on the side of equal
liberty and public virtue is to make the acquisition of land easy to every member of
society; to make a division of land into small quantities, so that the multitude may be
possessed of landed estates.[19]

Jefferson's solution was similar but more complete. He proposed
equal distribution when the state is compelled to distribute land and
when land is inherited, but protection of existing property rights against
governmental *re*distribution.[20] This accommodationist strategy underlay,
for example, his well-known reforms of Virginia inheritance law, including the abolition of primogeniture in favor of partible inheritance and the
abolition of entail.[21] The strategy was for the state to take advantage of the
abundance of uncultivated land in the American West and insure that
every able-bodied citizen be given a relatively small parcel of land.[22] Cultivating this land would make the citizen self-sustaining and independent,
and the state would then protect the personal autonomy secured through
ownership.

But that strategy was incomplete. It failed to insure that autonomous
owners would not exercise their right to transfer land (a right [that is]
clearly part of the extant common-law conception of ownership and
which Jefferson never questioned) in such a way as to undermine the

---

19. James Sullivan to John Adams, 26 April 1776, *The Works of John Adams*, 376-77.

20. See Stanley N. Katz, "Jefferson and the Right to Property," *Journal of Law & Economics* 19
(1976): 467.

21. Stanley Katz has pointed out that "the regulation of inheritance was viewed as a focal point
of scattered, ineffectual statutory efforts to reform the economic structure of society in order to promote
egalitarian ideals and to establish the foundation of a republican polity." Stanley N. Katz, "Republicanism and the Law of Inheritance in the American Revolutionary Era," *Michigan Law Review* 76 (1977): 1.

22. Indicative if this strategy was Jefferson's bill to the Virginia legislature in 1778, proposing
that every freeborn Virginian who marries and resides in that state for one year receive "seventy five
Acres of waster or unappropriated Land." *Jefferson Papers*, 2: 139-40. The proposal, however, was not
enacted. Ibid., 147 n.12.

scheme for maintaining republican virtue treating land as a commodity. The real thrust of the static conception of republican property, which asserted the dependence of the republic upon an ideal type of property (i.e., land) and an ideal form of property holding (i.e., fee simple ownership), was to prevent land from, as these republicans saw it, degenerating into a mere commodity.

It was not the rise of commerce alone but the potential for commerce to transform the sociology of property that aroused the Jeffersonian anxiety. The social transformation would change the meaning of freehold land from that of the stable foundation for republican politics to a fluid item of commerce. Further, property would no longer mean a moral and political component of society, an aspect of virtuous personality, but rather would represent a mere artifact of private life. So transformed, property might become a solvent that dissolves the political bonds of the community.

Restated in modern terms, the anxiety was that property, reduced to mere commodity, would mediate social relations. Individuals would relate to each other as abstract economic actors—buyers or sellers in the marketplace—rather than as concrete, multidimensional human beings. In this respect the civic republican critique of commodified property anticipated the modern theme that connects highly mobile forms of property with the phenomenon of alienation in social relations. Although the concept of alienation did not flower until the next century, its seed was planted well before then. It exists in all theories that define the role of property in terms of self-development and self-governance realized through union with others.[23]

NOTES AND QUESTIONS

1. *The Aristotelian Tradition of Property.* The argument claiming an ethical connection between private property and citizenship traces back to the Classical writers, most notably to Aristotle. In Aristotle's political theory, private ownership of land is a necessary condition of virtuous citizenship. *See* RICHARD KRAUT, ARISTOTLE 359-364 (2002). Civic virtue requires liberty in the positive sense that the citizen is able to bring his own (Aristotle limited citizenship to men) judgment to bear on political issues, and dependence, particularly economic dependence, undermines virtue. The primary function of private ownership of land, then, is to provide this independence without which virtuous citizenship is impossible.

The republican conception of independence differs importantly from that held by libertarians like Robert Nozick, discussed in Chapter 3. Philip Pettit characterizes the conception held by rights-based liberals like Nozick as one of "non-interference." PHILIP PETTIT, REPUBLICANISM: A THEORY OF

---

23. *See generally* ALAN RYAN, PROPERTY AND POLITICAL THEORY (1984).

Freedom and Government 99 (1997). Specifically, it is one whose main concern is protecting the individual from oppression by others, particularly the state. In contrast, Pettit argues, the republican conception of freedom is one of "non-domination." Pettit, *supra*, at 50-79. By "non-domination," Pettit means the personal security that is the result of having no master, or, more specifically, the result of the absence of interference by an arbitrary power. Does this characterization imply, in your view, that the Aristotelian account and the Kantian account (discussed in Chapter 4) converge? If not, what are their distinctive features? And which one do you find more convincing?

2.   *Civic Republicanism and Its Vision of Property.* As the excerpt from Alexander's book indicates, Aristotle's theory of politics, including its vision of property, formed the basis of the political tradition known as civic republicanism. Loosely defined, republicanism understands the purpose of politics to be the realization of the common good of the community, even if this requires sacrificing individual self-interests. Republicans do not think of the common good as the aggregation of the particular interests that make up the community but rather as prior to or distinct from the diverse private interests of individuals and groups throughout society. *See* Gordon S. Wood, The Creation of the American Republic, 1776-1787 53-58 (1969). From the republican perspective, the purpose of land ownership is to secure the citizen's material independence so that he is free from sources of corruption and thereby able to act virtuously for the common good. *See* J.G.A. Pocock, *Civic Humanism and Its Role in Anglo-American Thought, in* Politics, Language and Time 80, 92 (1973).

Are there any possible objections to civic republicanism's conception of the common good? Consider the argument that acting in the interest of the community's common good sometimes involves personal sacrifice and that the ethic of sacrifice has a dark side. "The greater good, on behalf of which calls for sacrifice are made," Hanoch Dagan has argued, "tends to efface individuals." Hanoch Dagan, Property: Values and Institutions 143 (2011). Jean Hampton pushes the point further, contending that those who sacrifice themselves may well harm the very persons for whom they care by teaching them "the permissibility of their own exploitation by submitting to, and even supporting, their subservient role." Jean Hampton, *Selflessness and the Loss of Self, in* Altruism 161 (Ellen Frankel Paul et al. eds., 1993). Is an ethic of sacrifice too risky? (Exactly what are its risks?) Too risky, compared with what?

Another basis of attack on modern republicanism concerns its focus on community. There are many types of communities, and some of these are decidedly unattractive (e.g., the Ku Klux Klan). So, the appeal to community is meaningless in advance of a clear specification of the community to which one refers. *See* Ronald Beiner, Liberalism, Nationalism, Citizenship: Essays on the Problem of Political Community 66-68 (2003). Moreover, to the extent that the communities to which republicans refer are small communities in which genuinely participatory democracy is possible, critics have argued, this notion of community, and the conception of virtue that is premised on it, has become largely irrelevant in the modern nation-state. *See* Jeremy Waldron, *Virtue* en Masse, *in* DEBATING DEMOCRACY'S DIS-CONTENT 32, 35-39 (Anita L. Allen & Milton C. Regan, Jr., eds., 1998). And strong commitment to a small sectarian community may undermine robust citizenship in the broader political community. *See* Michael Walzer, *Sandel's America, in* DEBATING DEMOCRACY'S DISCONTENT, *id.*, at 175-177. What are your reactions to these objections? For what is community an alternative for communitarians? Exactly what work, conceptual or normative, is community supposed to be doing for modern republicans? In this connection, consider Note 5 *infra*.

3. *Contradictory Aspects of Republican Property.* Republicanism's practical implications for property were contradictory. On the one hand, it could and on occasion did lead to egalitarian results. As Alexander notes, republicanism's opposition to feudalism led Thomas Jefferson to successfully propose legislation in Virginia that abolished both primogeniture and the fee tail estate, which he considered aristocratic and unrepublican. *See also* Stanley N. Katz, *Thomas Jefferson and the Right to Property in Revolutionary America*, 19 J.L. & ECON. 467 (1976). Certain nineteenth-century federal land programs, such as the Homestead Act, have also been interpreted as inspired by an egalitarian version of republicanism. *See* Paul Goodman, *The Emergence of the Homestead Exemption in the United States: Accommodation and Resistance to the Market Revolution, 1840-1880*, 80 J. AM. HIST. 470 (1993). Can you think of other egalitarian implications republicanism might have for property? Does it justify or even require substantial efforts at wealth redistribution by the state?

On the other hand, some versions of republicanism have had overtly hierarchical implications. Not only during Aristotle's time but well past the American Revolution, citizenship in the American republic was confined to men. Moreover, not only could slavery coexist with republican ideology, it was integral to some versions of it, such as classical Greece and the slave-holding American South. *See* ALEXANDER, *supra*, at 216-221. Even in non-slaveholding states, the federalist version of republicanism was elitist. For example, citizenship was confined to white males who owned land in fee simple, and federalist republicans generally opposed land redistribution on the ground that it would destabilize the state. *See* JOYCE APPLEBY, CAPITALISM AND A NEW SOCIAL ORDER: THE REPUBLICAN VISION OF THE 1790s 8-19 (1984). Do these objectionable aspects of historical republican property make a republican approach to property entirely unattractive?

4. *The Republican Revival.* Beginning in the 1980s, American legal scholars, inspired by then-recent historiographical rediscovery of America's republican roots, sought to revive aspects of that ideology for purposes of creating a more participatory and deliberative form of democracy. *See, e.g.,* Frank Michelman, *Law's Republic*, 97 YALE L.J. 1493 (1988); Cass R.

Sunstein, *Beyond the Republican Revival*, 97 Yale L.J. 1539 (1988). With respect to property, scholars argued in favor of a conception of property that is, in the words of Frank Michelman, "distributive" as well as "possessive," i.e., not just a matter of private self-interest but also as the requisite foundation of republican self-government. *See* Frank I. Michelman, *Possession vs. Distribution in the Constitutional Idea of Property*, 72 Iowa L. Rev. 1319 (1987). Is such a conception of property, one that simultaneously respects these two visions, feasible?

Consider, for example, rotating credit associations, or informal microfinance groups. These are groups of individuals, usually poor peasants in rural parts of underdeveloped countries, who meet for limited periods of time for the purpose of saving and borrowing money together. Each member contributes the same amount at each meeting, and one member is permitted to take the entire pool of capital once, using it for whatever purpose she wishes. Members of the group select each other. *See* Clifford Geertz, The Rotating Credit Association: A Middle Rung in Development (1956). Are such arrangements a form of republican property? Closer to home, what about tenant interests that are rent controlled? For an argument that such interests do represent a form of republican property, see William H. Simon, *Social-Republican Property*, 38 UCLA L. Rev. 1335, 1359-1361 (1991).

5. *The Various Claims of Communitarianism.* The republican revival is an aspect of a broader intellectual movement: the development of communitarian theory in political and philosophical theory as well as legal theory. "Communitarianism" is really not a single integrated theory in any of these fields, but a group of related claims. In contemporary moral, political, and legal theory at least three claims can be identified in the communitarian literature. The first is ontological: "[T]he community of which an individual is a member is constitutive of that individual's identity and not merely contingent or accidental to it." Stephen A. Gardbaum, *Law, Politics, and the Claims of Community*, 90 Mich. L. Rev. 685, 692 (1992). This claim rejects the view, often labeled "atomism," that views individuals as fully formed and self-sufficient outside of society and who enter into social relationships solely to advance their exogenous preferences. The second claim is metaethical: It argues that values are neither universal nor purely subjective but instead are local and tied to particular communities and traditions. The third claim is political: It is that political association through political communities is intrinsically superior to political association via the liberal state. It is this claim that is at the heart of the republican revival. It rejects value-neutrality. It posits a common good and argues that that good must be pursued through politics and pursued in common and in public. *Id.* at 723-727.

7 PROPERTY AND DISTRIBUTIVE JUSTICE

Jeremy Waldron, The Right to Private Property[1]

SPECIAL- AND GENERAL-RIGHT-BASED ARGUMENTS

... A right-based argument for private property is ... an argument which takes an individual interest to be sufficiently important in itself to justify holding others (especially the government) to be under duties to create, secure, maintain, or respect an institution of private property.

A *special-right-based argument* (or SR-based argument, for short) is an argument which takes an interest to have this importance not in itself but on account of the occurrence of some contingent event or transaction. A *general-right-based argument* (or GR-based argument, for short) is one which does not take the importance of such an interest to depend on the occurrence of some contingent event or transaction, but attributes that importance to the interest itself, in virtue of its qualitative character. ...

It is the thesis of this book that GR-based arguments for private property have quite a different character and quite different implications—particularly distributive implications—from SR-based arguments for private property. ...

PROPERTY FOR ALL

Could private property be the subject of a general right? Is it something we could plausibly provide *for everyone* in the way we try to provide political

1. JEREMY WALDRON, THE RIGHT TO PRIVATE PROPERTY 115-117, 423, 425-427, 430-439, 444-445 (1988).

rights, civil liberty, health, education and welfare? Or—to put it another way—is the ideal of a "property-owning democracy" anything more than a *petit-bourgeois* utopian pipe-dream? . . .

. . . [T]he challenge [was] laid down by Karl Marx in a furious response to bourgeois critics of the socialist programme outlined in *The Communist Manifesto*:

> You are horrified at our intending to do away with private property. But in your existing society, private property is already done away with for nine tenths of the population; its existence for the few is solely due to its non-existence in the hands of these nine-tenths. You reproach us, therefore, with intending to do away with a form of property the necessary condition for whose existence is the nonexistence of any property for the immense majority of society. In one word, you reproach us for intending to do away with your property. Precisely so; that is just what we intend.[2]

Throughout his work, Marx is adamant that the indictment against capitalism is not merely the fact that private property happens to be distributed unequally or in a way that leaves millions without any guaranteed access to the means of production; the problem is that private ownership is a form of property that has this characteristic *necessarily*. No matter how noble your egalitarian intentions, the existence of any distribution of private property rights in the means of production will lead quickly to their concentration in the hands of a few. Thus egalitarian intentions, so far as private property is concerned are hopelessly utopian, for they underestimate the dynamic tendencies of the system they are interested in: "for us the issue cannot be the alteration of private property but its annihilation."[3] GR-based arguments for private property therefore would stand condemned on this approach just to the extent that they have egalitarian or quasi-egalitarian implications.

This is not Marx's only criticism of private property. The main critique throughout his work is [that] private property as a form for productive relations divides man from man, disguises the underlying co-operative nature of production and economic endeavour, and thus prevents the development of conscious and rational freedom in the economic sphere— the only sphere where man can find his true self-realization. If there is a moral basis to Marx's indictment of capitalism, it is not a theory of equality but . . . a theory of freedom.

Nevertheless, according to Marx, it is no accident that *petit-bourgeois* theories of distributive justice are hopelessly impractical. They fly in the face of the logic of the institutions they purport to be dealing with. . . . [because]

2. [Karl] Marx [& Friedrich] Engels, *[The] Communist Manifesto* [(Harmondsworth, Penguin Books, 1967),] 98.
3. See e.g. [Karl] Marx, "Address to the Communist League," [in *Karl Marx: Selected Writings* ed. David McLellan (Oxford, Oxford University Press, 1977),] 280, and *Critique of Gotha Programme* [Moscow, Progress Publishers, 1977] 14ff.

accumulation and the concentration of capital in a few hands, leading to mass propertylessness, is not only "appropriate to" a capitalist mode of production; it is its inevitable result. . . .

Marx's account . . . appeals beyond individual rationality to the historical changes which underlie and condition it. In the modern age, the existence of private property systems is associated with the acquisitive mentality of capitalism, and it is worthless to try and abstract the idea of private property from the historical context and ask what would happen if that mentality were to mysteriously evaporate. Of course, that mentality is not a permanent feature of human psychology. But the possibilities of change are limited and for Marx any change is likely to be associated with the abolition of private property and the institution of collective economic relations rather than with the distribution of private property on an equal or universal basis.

There is also a Marxian argument based on historical materialism against the feasibility of anything like the sort of property-owning democracy that a GR-based argument would require. For Marx the concentration of control of the means of production in fewer and fewer hands is not an accidental feature of modern society, nor even a feature associated exclusively with capitalism. It is, in a contradictory way, an indication that advanced economic production necessarily involves very large-scale control and large-scale decision-making. In this regard . . . the growth of corporate capitalism is seen as an adumbration of the collective control over production that will eventually have to be exercised. It is one of the symptoms of socialism with which capitalism is pregnant. Capitalism is now potentially what socialism will be in practice. As Marx puts it, corporate production

> is a necessary transitional phase towards the reconversion of capital into the property of producers, although no longer as the private property of the individual producers, but rather as the property of associated producers, as outright social property. On the other hand, the stock company is a transition towards the conversion of all functions in the reproductive process which still remain linked with capitalist property, into mere functions of associated producers, into social function. . . .[4]

But to imagine that we could move to or sustain anything like equal or universal private property for individuals is to postulate a move in the *other* direction, against the historical current, from modern capitalism back to its historical forebears. This, then, is the reason why ideas like property-owning democracy are dismissed so scathingly by Marxists as a futile *petit-bourgeois* ideal. From their point of view, a requirement that every individual should have private property in the means of production flies directly in the face of historical experience which tells us that the

---

4. See [Karl] Marx, "Preface to *Critique of Political Economy*," [in *Karl Marx: Selected Writings, supra* note 3,] 390.

development of production, under the conditions of modern industry, is inexorably, necessarily, and desirably in the direction of large-scale collective control.

If Marx is right about this, we can have no reasonable expectation at all under modern conditions that people will voluntarily refrain from exercising the private property rights assigned to them in ways which are non-pattern-disruptive. (Marx's theory has also more radical consequences for GR-based arguments. Since politics is determined at least in the last analysis by class, we can have no reasonable expectation that a government in capitalist society will even attempt to put a general right to private property into effect, still less that it would intervene to prevent subsequent accumulation and concentration of capital. That sort of determinism of course undermines *any* attempt to grapple with problems of justice in capitalist and late-capitalist societies.) . . .

Let us concentrate now on the tighter point posed by the . . . Marxian challenges. Apart from the bare possibility that private property rights could be exercised in a way which fortuitously sustained the pattern required for their distribution, and leaving aside the suggestion that the direction of history is bound to defeat the ideal of a property-owning democracy, is it the case that private property rights *as such* are essentially unamenable to the sort of distributional constraints that would flow, as we saw, from a GR-based argument? If they are, then those arguments are not just utopian but self-contradictory. In calling for something, they are also calling for the conditions that are bound to defeat it.

Proudhon appears to have been convinced on this score. As we have seen, his intention was to show that "every argument which has been invented in behalf of property, *whatever it may be*, always and of necessity leads to equality; that is, to the negation of property."[5] Later he elaborated the indictment:

> They did not foresee, these old founders of the domain of property, that the perpetual and absolute right to retain one's estate, — a right which seemed to them equitable, because it was common, — involves the right to transfer, sell, give, gain, and lose it; that it tends, consequently, to nothing less than the destruction of that equality which they established it to maintain.[6]

The objection we are considering, then, is an embarrassment primarily to those GR-based arguments for private property that lay great importance on individuals' being able to exercise powers of transfer. These arguments cannot avoid deploying a conception of ownership that includes powers whose exercise would generate the embarrassment that Nozick's and Proudhon's arguments predict. Fortunately, as a matter of fact, few of

5. [Pierre-Joseph] Proudhon, *What is Property?*, [trans. Benjamin R. Tucker (New York, Dover Publications, 1970),] pp. 39-40.
6. Ibid. 78.

the arguments we are considering have this feature. Hegel thought it important that individuals should be able to withdraw their will from the objects in which they had "embodied" it; but in our interpretation of his account of the ethical importance of private property, that did not play a significant role. One argument we considered, however, did attribute importance to freedom of trade and contract: it was based on an idea of respect for the individual capacity to enter into arrangements and reach accommodations in the economic sphere with other individuals without the need for overarching direction, and on the view that this required respect for the arrangements and accommodations that were actually entered into. (The underlying notion here is respect for a capacity that is as distinctively human as the capacity to plan on a communal scale.) This argument, then, is prima facie vulnerable to the objection we are considering. It makes it a matter of importance that all individuals should have the wherewithal to enter into arrangements with others on matters of economic significance, but the result of the exercise of that capacity will almost certainly be that some individuals come in time to be deprived of the wherewithal to exercise it.

Moreover, even though Proudhon is wrong in discerning a *logical* connection between private property and powers of transfer, and even though our favourite argument for private property may permit as its upshot a "no-transfer" conception of ownership, still there may be other non-logical but none the less contingently important connections between being a private owner and having the power to transfer one's holding to another. [Thus], most societies that face the problem of allocation will also face the problem of *re*allocation from time to time as individuals' circumstances change. It will tend to be overwhelmingly inconvenient to call in all resources and redistribute them on every occasion when such changes are deemed appropriate, for those occasions are likely to be very numerous indeed. If there is any possibility at all that transfers arranged by individuals between individuals could solve the problem of reallocation, then that will appear the more attractive solution. This then is an independent reason (arising out of the allocation problem) for including a power of transfer in any practicable conception of ownership. . . .

These points suggest that it may not be open to us to adopt a pure "no-transfer" conception of private property. But they suggest also that there may be room for compromise in other directions. Whether or not a conception of private property includes powers of transfer is not an all-or-nothing affair. To begin with, there are several powers to be considered: gift, sale and purchase, abandonment, bequest, inheritance, and so on. It is possible that the points just made could be met by a conception which included some of these powers but not others. Many people have argued that powers of transfer *post mortem*, such as bequest and inheritance, are much more inimical to equality than powers of transfer *inter vivos* such as sale and purchase: the disruption to a favoured distribution of property caused by the latter may be trivial, whereas the former may upset distributional patterns in a more significant way. It is possible that the powers whose exercise threatens the pattern are not those that our argument for property requires. For example, the principle of respecting the arrangements people have entered into may be thought to apply more to arrangements *inter vivos* than to *post mortem* arrangements. Similarly, if the problem of reallocation is the source of our concern that powers of transfer should be included in a conception of ownership, it may be that this concern is much less in the case of the reallocation of deceased estates than it is in the case of goods that somebody is currently holding. As Bentham argued, a general principle of escheat (and redistribution by the state) does not threaten to disrupt expectations in the way that expropriation of living proprietors would.

Further, we should remember that there are a number of different ways in which any given power of transfer may be limited or curtailed. An extreme case is one in which the purported exercise of the power is given no effect in law at all: a man purports to leave his estate to his friend, but because the system does not recognize a power of bequest that exercise is null and void. A much less extreme case is one in which transactions are taxed, either as far as the transferor is concerned (e.g. death and gift duties, payroll taxes, VAT etc.), or as far as the transferee is concerned (e.g. income tax, capital gains tax, etc.). In this case, the transfer is recognized but made subject to certain conditions: for example, no one in New Zealand may make a gift of more than $10,000 without paying a proportion of that sum to the government in gift duty; and no one in Britain may receive income of any sort from another person without paying a (rather large) proportion of that to the state in income tax. When Nozick discusses taxes of this sort, he suggests that their intention is to defeat or partially to defeat the transaction or the point of the transaction. This may be the case but it need not be. Suppose the *point* of my transferring a large sum of money to my son is to disrupt the pattern of the equal distribution of private property. Then it is true that the point of the gift duty we are considering would be to defeat that intention. But that is because the intention, in its content, is explicitly at odds with the ideas of rights, liberty, and justice as we conceive them; it does not seem oppressive in a society committed to those ideals to set out to defeat intentions which are calculated to undermine them. But most transfers will not be motivated in this way. For those that have ordinary commercial or philanthropic motivation, our fiscal experience suggests that taxation is *not* perceived as defeating or undermining the point of a transfer. People adjust their expectations of what they can do in transferring and receiving goods to the exigencies of the fiscal regime, and seem able to carry on transferring goods freely within the constraints it imposes. . . .

So far the argument has concerned the powers of transfer that might be connected with particular conceptions of private ownership. Our response to the objection has been that although many of the conceptions we are dealing with will involve powers of transfer, they will seldom involve any requirement that there should be *unlimited* powers of transfer. If the powers of transfer that we recognize are qualified by a system of taxation, understood to be imposed for the express purpose of maintaining a wide distribution of the property rights in question, then that system can be used to redress any disruption of the distributional patterns favoured by the arguments which have generated the conceptions of private ownership that are giving us this difficulty.

We should note, however, that Proudhon does not rest his argument against private property purely on this putative incompatibility between equality and powers of transfer. At times he seems prepared to make an even stronger claim — that the very element of exclusive and indefinite control that private property involves is incompatible with the demand for equality that the arguments he is considering give rise to. Considering questions of First Occupancy, for example, he writes:

> For, since every man, from the fact of his existence, has the right of occupation, and, in order to live, must have material for cultivation on which he may labor; and since, on the other hand, the number of occupants varies continually with the births and deaths, — it follows that the quantity of material which each laborer may claim varies with the number of occupants; consequently, that occupation is always subordinate to population. Finally, that, inasmuch as possession, in right, can never remain fixed, it is impossible, in fact, that it can ever become property. . . . *All have an equal right of occupancy. The amount occupied being measured, not by the will, but by the variable conditions of space and number, property cannot exist.*[7]

The suggestion is that private property involves the idea of the allocation of a resource to the control of a single individual for an indefinite period (or for a period determined only by his own say-so). But since the population varies, the number of people whose right to property must be satisfied varies with it, and the rightful demands placed on the stock of available resources will change accordingly. An increase in population will mean that the satisfaction of a universal right to property demands a reduction in the amount of resources allocated to individuals before the increase. Since such an increase is always likely, putative proprietors must always hold themselves ready to give up some of their resources in favour of newcomers. But holding resources in this spirit, Proudhon contends, is incompatible with the idea of property as that is usually understood.

Once again, no doubt there are conceptions of private property which make this a plausible objection. On some conceptions, a man cannot be said to be the owner of a resource if his holding is subject continually or even periodically to a redistributive wealth tax. The private property rights of each individual, on these conceptions, are absolutely resistant

7. [Id. at] 39-40.

to redistributive considerations. But it seems unlikely that any of these conceptions will be the upshot of the GR-based arguments we have been considering; that is, it seems unlikely that any of those arguments will establish that private property must be either absolute in this sense or not worth having.

Whether the ethical importance of owning property is undermined significantly by periodic taxation will depend in part on how frequent, how drastic, and how unpredictable such taxation would have to be. If the population varies greatly at irregular intervals, and if the stock of resources available for private holdings remains constant or is liable to diminution, then there is a danger that the redistribution required to ensure that everyone has private property will make it almost impossible for individuals to make medium- or long-term plans about the use of the resources assigned to them. For example, if the population of a small society is periodically increased by the influx of large numbers of refugees, then land redistribution may be so drastic that farmers are unable to follow through on their own plans for development, crop rotation, and so on. In this case, Proudhon's objection is sustained: those to whom land is initially assigned hold it not as owners but, at best, as "usufructuaries," owing a duty to society at large to keep it in a condition where it can be easily transferred to the use of others. In societies not subject to such vicissitudes, however, the effect will be much less drastic. For example, in a society where the birth-rate is not overwhelmingly greater than the death rate, and where the increase in population is matched by economic growth, the need for redistribution in favour of newcomers can possibly be accommodated by a system of taxation on deceased estates, and the owners of property can be confident that their holdings will not normally be subject in their lifetime to compulsory and debilitating transfers.

In all of this, we should bear in mind the possibility of approaching the problem also from the other direction. The GR-based arguments we are considering have important distributive implications, as we have noticed. But . . . they are not implications of strict egalitarianism or anything like it; they are requirements that everyone must have private property in some significant holding, not that everyone must have at most a certain or an equal amount. There is the further point that, though a given argument may require that everyone have property, it may not necessarily require that everyone should continue to be the owner of a significant holding at all times. Indeed, in relation to some arguments, a guarantee of this sort might be counter-productive: for example, it might diminish the contribution that owning property makes to the development of prudence, thrift, and responsibility. This means that the GR-based case for private property may allow for a certain amount of flexibility in distributive patterns. Those concerned for it need not be upset by every fluctuation in the relative wealth and fortunes of individuals. What they will be on the lookout for will be tendencies towards the accumulation of enormous holdings, particularly of capital resources, on the one hand, and the accompanying development of long-term propertylessness, on the other. The danger with these trends is that they give rise to the possibility of what Marxists have called "exploitative" economic relations — relations which are unwelcome in the present context, not because of their injustice or putative coerciveness, but because of the way in which they tend to preclude the autonomous development or occurrence of the sort of transactions and relationships which could shift the distributive balance back in a more egalitarian direction. When these trends become apparent, intervention will be necessary. It does not seem to be unduly optimistic or utopian to suggest that they can be kept in check, at least in a relatively prosperous society, by action which falls considerably short of threatening the very basis of individual ownership. . . .

[To conclude: a] GR-based argument is *radical* in its distributive implications: even if it is not obsessively egalitarian, it generates a requirement that private property, under some conception, is something all men must have. SR-based theories *may* have radical implications: if the procedures by which wealth has been accumulated in a society are not the procedures specified by the theory, then the theory may generate quite radical requirements as a matter of rectification. But the distributional implications inherent in the arguments are not radical: there is no case for distributing private property in resources more widely than those who have legitimately appropriated them choose to do.

These differences of structure and implication are not merely of academic interest. Politicians and theorists alike often try to bring the two strands of argument together in a single case, saying for example, that those who have acquired private property ought to be able to keep it since property is an indispensable condition for the development of a sense of individual responsibility. That juxtaposition needs to be exposed as fraudulent eclecticism, aligning as it does considerations that pull in different directions from utterly different and in fact mutually incompatible theoretical perspectives. Once this has been acknowledged, it may still be the case . . . that the two strands of argument both have contributions to make to the discussion of the moral importance of private property. But that discussion is not merely a matter of *assembling*, on one list, considerations in favour of private property and, on another list, considerations against. It must be informed by an understanding of how different considerations, with different provenances can be related to one another, and by an awareness of the difficulties as well as the possibilities of fitting them together into a single case.

NOTES AND QUESTIONS

1. *GR-based Arguments for Private Property.* Waldron's thesis relies on the unique features of general-rights-based arguments for private property.

These arguments are distinct from two other types of arguments, and we have encountered all three types in the previous chapters. As a right-based argument, a GR-based argument relies on an individual interest, as opposed to a collective interest, as the justification for private property. Thus, neither aggregate well-being nor citizenship qualifies as a GR-based argument. As a *general* right-based argument it is distinct from *special* right-based arguments, which rely not on the importance of an individual interest as such, but rather on a specific event. Thus, while both personhood and liberty qualify as GR-based arguments, labor is a prime example of an SR-based argument. Recall that we have encountered Waldron's claim regarding the intrinsic distributive implications of justifying property from personhood. See Note 5 in Chapter 2. What are the distributive implications of the argument that private property — some private control over the external resources — is necessary for individual liberty? *See* Frank I. Michelman, *Possession vs. Distribution in the Constitutional Idea of Property,* 72 Iowa L. Rev. 1319, 1319 (1987) (private property stands not only for a "possessive proprietary principle" or an "antiredistributive principle"; rather, because it expresses values, such as privacy, security, and independence, property "always involve[s] the distribution as well as the retention of wealth"). See also Waldron's analysis of homelessness in Chapter 16.2.

2. *Waldron and the Realist Legacy.* Waldron is the most important contemporary legal theorist to place questions of distribution at the center-stage of property theory, but he is not the first to take interest in the distributive implications of property. This was, in fact, a major concern of some American legal realists. Thus, Morris Cohen famously stated that "dominion over things is also *imperium* over our fellow human beings." Like Waldron, Cohen was careful not to necessarily condemn private property for having these attributes. But he insists that "the extent of the power over the life of others which the legal order confers on those called owners is not fully appreciated by those who think of the law as merely protecting men in their possession." Property owners "are in fact granted by the law certain powers to tax the future social product. When to this power of taxation there is added the power to command the services of large numbers who are not economically independent, we have the essence of what historically has constituted political sovereignty." Once we recognize that property is a form of government we must "apply to the law of property all those considerations of social ethics and enlightened public policy which ought to be brought to the discussion of any just form of government." Morris Cohen, *Property and Sovereignty,* 13 Cornell L.Q. 8, 11-14 (1927).

A similar argument was made by Robert Hale, who claimed that the law's background rules are partly responsible for the inequalities in the distribution of income and power. *See* Robert L. Hale, *Coercion and Distribution in a Supposedly Non-Coercive State,* 38 Pol. Sci. Q. 470 (1923). Hale can be read as making a stronger argument: that *all* the inequalities in the distribution of income and power are the *direct* result of legal allocation of background rules. But this reading relies on an indefensible "mechanistic image of human agency." Neil Duxbury, *Robert Hale and the Economy of Legal Force*, 53 Mod. L. Rev. 421, 443 (1990). Such economic determinism is particularly inapt for our era of networked information economy, which — *pace* the Marxist conviction that production develops in the direction of large-scale productive control — is characterized by a radical improvement of the practical capacities of individuals to do more for themselves even outside the market sphere. *See* Yochai Benkler, The Wealth of Networks: How Social Production Transforms Markets and Freedom 133-175 (2006).

3.   *Distribution from Within Property.* Waldron does not merely rehash the realist argument. The realist legacy is that the significant distributive ramifications of property law render questions of distributive justice crucial for property theory. Waldron's insight goes further than that. To be sure, Waldron does not place distributive justice on the same footing as the values we considered in the previous chapters: Distributive justice is not an independent justification for private property. And yet, Waldron insists that some commitment to distributive justice derives not only from the distributive impact of instituting rights to private property, but rather internally, so to speak: It is entailed from the very normative infrastructure that justifies property in the first place. In other words, to the extent that we justify law's enforcement of the rights of those who have property by reference to autonomy or to personhood, we must simultaneously guarantee necessary — as well as constitutive — resources to those who do not. This means, of course, that Waldron's approach stands in strong opposition to Weinrib's theory we considered in Chapter 4. Try to imagine the debate between these two authors; whose view do you find more persuasive?

4.   *Why Property?* The astute reader may wonder whether this chapter belongs to the first part of this book, because, as just noted, it does not set forth a theory for the justification of property rights, but rather investigates the implications of prior theories. This is indeed an important difference, which explains why this is the last chapter of this part. In fact, this chapter can serve just as well as an introduction to Part II of this book, because Waldron provides the conceptual tools to integrate distributive justice into property by introducing us to the idea, which motivates much of our discussion in that part, that property is a contested concept that admits of different conceptions.

But we believe that this chapter nonetheless belongs to this part, in which we introduce the major normative accounts of property, because Waldron's argument is importantly about property, rather than about distribution. To see why, we need to understand how his account is distinct from the distributive prescriptions of just distribution more generally. There are two salient differences between Waldron's account and, for example, John Rawls's celebrated theory of distributive justice.

On the one hand, the distributive implications of Rawls's theory are much more demanding than those of Waldron's. Rawls's difference principle prescribes that inequalities in the distribution of income are justified only if they maximize the welfare of the least advantaged representative members of society. Thus, Rawls argues that the strategy of choosing the course that has the least worst outcome follows the dictates of rationality, assuming we can isolate the chooser from his or her natural endowments and social circumstances. *See* JOHN RAWLS, A THEORY OF JUSTICE 78 (1971). But on the other hand, insofar as *property* is concerned, Waldron's prescriptions seem to be more demanding that Rawls's. Rawls had no theory of property; in fact, he believed that private property as such is not an essential part of the constitutional framework of the just liberal state. *See Id.,* at 242. By contrast, Waldron's theory is all about the just property regime. Indeed, Waldron's specific prescription — that law must guarantee both necessary and constitutive resources to everyone — has some ramifications throughout property law, and you should consider what they may be as you go through much of the readings in Part III.

II   *HOW PROPERTY?*

8 STRUCTURING OWNERSHIP

1. BETWEEN DESPOTIC DOMINION AND BUNDLE OF RIGHTS

William Blackstone, Commentaries on the Laws of England[1]

There is nothing which so generally strikes the imagination, and engages the affections of mankind, as the right of property; or that sole and despotic dominion which one man claims and exercises over the external things of the world, in total exclusion of the right of any other individual in the universe.

Wesley Newcomb Hohfeld, Fundamental Legal Conceptions as Applied in Judicial Reasoning[2]

A paucital right, or claim, (right *in personam*) is either a unique right residing in a person (or group of persons) and availing against a single person (or single group of persons); or else it is one of a few fundamentally similar, yet separate, rights availing respectively against a few definite persons. A multital right, or claim, (right *in rem*) is always *one* of a large *class* of *fundamentally similar* yet separate rights, actual and potential, residing in a *single* person (or single group of persons) but availing *respectively* against persons constituting a very large and indefinite class of people.

---

1. 2 WILLIAM BLACKSTONE, COMMENTARIES ON THE LAWS OF ENGLAND *2 (1979) (1765-1769).
2. Wesley Newcomb Hohfeld, *Fundamental Legal Conceptions as Applied in Judicial Reasoning*, 26 YALE L.J. 710, 718-723, 733-734, 740, 745-747, 752-753 (1917).

Probably all would agree substantially on the meaning and significance of a right *in personam,* as just explained; and it is easy to give a few
preliminary examples: If B owes A a thousand dollars, A has an *affirmative*
right *in personam,* or paucital right, that B shall transfer to A the legal ownership of that amount of money. If, to put a contrasting situation, A already
has title to one thousand dollars, his rights against others in relation thereto
are multital rights, or rights *in rem.* In the one case the money is *owed* to A;
in the other case it is *owned* by A. If Y has contracted to work for X during the
ensuing six months, X has an *affirmative* right *in personam* that Y shall render
such service, as agreed. Similarly as regards all other contractual or quasi-
contractual rights of this character. . . .

In contrast to these examples are those relating to rights, or claims,
in rem—i.e., multital rights. If A owns and occupies Whiteacre, not only B
but also a great many other persons—not necessarily all persons—are
under a duty, e.g., not to enter on A's land. A's right against B is a multital
right, or right *in rem,* for it is simply one of A's class of *similar,* though
separate, rights, actual and potential, against *very many* persons. . . .

(a) *A right in rem is not a right "against a thing":* . . . Assuming that the
division represented by *in personam* and *in rem* is intended to be mutually
exclusive, it is plausible enough to assume also that if a right *in personam* is
simply a right against a *person,* a right *in rem* must be a right that is *not against*
a *person,* but *against* a *thing.* That is, the expression right *in personam,*
standing alone, seems to encourage the impression that there must be
rights that are *not* against persons. Then, of course, such a supposed, though
erroneous, contrast is further encouraged by the *prima facie* literal meaning
of the Latin phrase *in rem,* considered *per se.* . . . Such a notion of rights
in rem is . . . crude and fallacious. . . . A man may indeed sustain close
and beneficial *physical* relations to a given *physical thing*: he may *physically*
control and use such thing, and he may *physically* exclude others from
any similar control or enjoyment. But . . . physical relations are wholly
distinct from jural relations. The latter take significance from the law;
and, since the purpose of the law is to regulate the conduct of human
beings, all jural relations must . . . be predicated of such human beings. . . .

What is here insisted on, —i.e., that all rights *in rem* are against persons, —is not to be regarded merely as a matter of taste or preference. . . .
Logical consistency seems to demand such a conception, and nothing less
than that. Some concrete examples may serve to make this plain. Suppose
that A is the owner of Blackacre and X is the owner of Whiteacre. Let it be
assumed, further, that, in consideration of $100 *actually paid* by A to B, the
latter agrees with A never to enter on X's land, Whiteacre. It is clear that A's
right against B concerning Whiteacre is a right *in personam,* or paucital right;
for A has no similar and separate rights concerning Whiteacre availing
respectively against other persons in general. On the other hand, A's
right against B concerning Blackacre is obviously a right *in rem,* or multital
right; for it is but one of a very large number of fundamentally similar

(though separate) rights which A has respectively against B, C, D, E, F, and a great many other persons. It must now be evident, also, that A's Blackacre right against B is, *intrinsically considered*, of the same general character as A's Whiteacre right against B. The Blackacre right differs, so to say, only *extrinsically*, that is, in having many fundamentally similar, though distinct, rights as its "companions." So, in general, we might say that a right *in personam* is one having few, if any, "companions"; whereas a right *in rem* always has many such "companions."

If, then, the Whiteacre right, being a right *in personam*, is recognized as a right against a *person*, must not the Blackacre right also, being, point for point, intrinsically of the same general nature, be conceded to be a right against a *person*? If not that, what is it? How can it be apprehended, or described, or delimited at all? . . .

(b) *A multital right, or claim, (right in rem) is not always one relating to a thing, i.e., a tangible object:* . . . [A]nother important point [is] that a right *in rem* is not necessarily one *relating to*, or *concerning*, a thing, i.e., a tangible object. Such an assumption . . . is clearly erroneous. . . .

[S]ome rights *in rem*, or multital rights, relate fairly directly to *physical objects*; some fairly directly to *persons*; and some fairly directly *neither to tangible objects nor to persons*. . . .

(c) *A single multital right, or claim, (right in rem) correlates with a duty resting on one person alone, not with many duties (or one duty) resting upon all the members of a very large and indefinite class of persons:* . . .

A right *in rem*, or multital right, correctly understood, is simply one of a large number of fundamentally similar rights residing in *one* person; and any one of such rights has as its correlative one, and only one, of a large number of general, or common, duties, — that is, fundamentally similar duties residing respectively in *many* different persons. . . .

(d) *A multital right, or claim, (right in rem) should not be confused with any co-existing privileges or other jural relations that the holder of the multital right or rights may have in respect to the same subject-matter:* . . .

Suppose, for example, that A is fee-simple owner of Blackacre. His "legal interest" or "property" relating to the tangible object that we call *land* consists of a complex aggregate of rights (or claims), privileges, powers, and immunities. *First*: A has multital legal rights, or claims, that *others*, respectively, shall *not* enter on the land, that they shall not cause physical harm to the land, etc., such others being under respective correlative legal duties. *Second*: A has an indefinite number of legal privileges of entering on the land, using the land, harming the land, etc., that is, within limits fixed by law on grounds of social and economic policy, he has privileges of doing on or to the land what he pleases; and correlative to all such legal privileges are the respective legal no-rights of other persons. *Third*: A has the legal power to alienate his legal interest to another, i.e., to extinguish his complex aggregate of jural relations and create a new and similar aggregate in the other person; also the legal power to create a life estate in another and concurrently to create a reversion in himself; also the legal power to create a privilege of entrance in any other person by giving "leave and license"; and so on indefinitely. Correlative to all such legal powers are the legal liabilities in other persons, — this meaning that the latter are subject, *nolens volens*, to the changes of jural relations involved in the exercise of A's powers. *Fourth*: A has an indefinite number of legal immunities, using the term immunity in the very specific sense of non-liability or non-subjection to a power on the part of another person. Thus he has the immunity that no ordinary person can alienate A's legal interest or aggregate of jural relations to another person; the immunity that no ordinary person can extinguish A's own privileges of using the land; the immunity that no ordinary person can extinguish A's right that another person X shall not enter on the land or, in other words, create in X a privilege of entering on the land. Correlative to all these immunities are the respective legal disabilities of other persons in general.

In short, A has vested in himself, as regards Blackacre, multital, or *in rem*, "right-duty" relations, multital, or *in rem*, "privilege-no-right" relations, multital, or *in rem*, "power-liability" relations, and multital, or *in rem*, "immunity-disability" relations. It is important, in order to have an adequate analytical view of property, to see all these various elements in the aggregate. It is equally important, for many reasons, that the different classes of jural relations should not be loosely confused with one another. A's privileges, e.g., are strikingly independent of his rights or claims against any given person, and either might exist without the other. . . .

(e) *A multital primary right, or claim, (right in rem) should, regarding its character as such, be carefully differentiated from the paucital secondary right, or claim, (right in personam) arising from a violation of the former*: Using again the hypothetical case involving A as owner of Blackacre, it is clear that if B commits a destructive trespass on A's land, there arises at that moment a new right, or claim, in favor of A, — i.e., a so-called secondary right that B shall pay him a sum of money as damages; and of course B comes simultaneously under a correlative duty. . . . The entire "right-duty" relation would be one of the class of relations *in personam* designated in Roman law by the term *obligatio*. More specifically, the relation would be known as an *obligatio ex delicto*. . . .

(f) *A multital primary right, or claim, (right in rem) should not, regarding its character as such, be confused with, or thought dependent on, the character of the proceedings by which it (and the secondary right arising from its violation) may be vindicated.*

NOTES AND QUESTIONS

1. *The Substance and Form of Blackstone's Conception of Property*. William Blackstone's dictum, in which he describes property as "sole and despotic

dominion," has become an icon of property theory, even though Blackstone himself did not intend that phrase to be taken literally, as his subsequent discussion of ownership makes clear. *See* Carol M. Rose, *Canons of Property Talk, or, Blackstone's Anxiety*, 108 YALE L.J. 601 (1998); David B. Schorr, *How Blackstone Became a Blackstonian*, 10 THEORETICAL INQUIRIES L. 103 (2009). The key message of Blackstone is that the core of the right to property is the right to exclude. We discuss this aspect in Chapter 9.1. Our concern here is with the structural aspect of Blackstone's conception of property, in which property has one essential meaning throughout its multiple manifestations. The antithesis of this monistic understanding of property comes from Wesley Hohfeld, whose position was by and large followed by the *Restatement of Property*, which explains that property constitutes a set of "legal relations between persons with respect to a thing." RESTATEMENT (FIRST) OF PROP. ch. 1, intro. note (1936).

2. *Hohfeld's Fundamental Legal Conceptions.* Hohfeld's conception of property was popularized under the label of "bundle of rights," although he was not the first to use this term and actually did not mention it. GREGORY S. ALEXANDER, COMMODITY & PROPRIETY 319, 322 (1997). For the most celebrated elaboration of the bundle of rights typical to property in liberal legal contexts, see TONY HONORÉ, *Ownership, in* MAKING LAW BIND: ESSAYS LEGAL AND PHILOSOPHICAL 161 (1987). Hohfeld's version of the notion that property is a bundle appears in the passage that conceptualizes property as "a complex aggregate" of rights (or claims), privileges, powers, and immunities. These terms derive from Hohfeld's prior account of "the lowest common denominators of the law," which includes eight fundamental conceptions that exhaust, in his view, the possible jural interpersonal relations. *See* Wesley Newcomb Hohfeld, *Some Fundamental Legal Conceptions as Applied in Judicial Reasoning*, 23 YALE L.J. 16, 30-35, 58 (1923). Hohfeld suggested expressing all such relations in the scheme of "opposites" and "correlatives." Thus, having a right (or, as he preferred to call it, a "claim") against *Y* entails a correlative (and equivalent) duty of *Y*. A privilege is importantly different from a right; it is just the negation of a duty. The correlative of a privilege is a "no-right." Finally, there are powers and liabilities, and immunities and disabilities. Legal power — one's control over a given legal relation — is the opposite of legal disability and the correlative of legal liability; immunity — one's freedom from the legal power of another — is the correlative of disability and the opposite, or negation, of liability. For an analysis of the liberating potential of this Hohfeldian framework, see Joseph William Singer, *The Legal Rights Debate in Analytical Jurisprudence from Bentham to Hohfeld*, 1982 WIS. L. REV. 975.

3. *Between Rights and Remedies.* In the last paragraphs of our excerpt, Hohfeld suggests that a "multital primary right" should be carefully distinguished from a "paucital secondary right" arising from a violation of the former. A similar distinction underlies the influential account of property rules *vs.* liability rules. *See* Guido Calabresi & A. Douglas Melamed, *Property*

Rules, Liability Rules, and Inalienability: One View of the Cathedral, 85 HARV. L.
REV. 1089 (1972). Do you think that it is correct to analyze remedies merely
as means to protect rights? This is a fundamental question of private law
theory, which we cannot fully address here, but find it important to raise
nonetheless. For a fierce critique of the position that separates the analysis
of rights and remedies, see KARL N. LLEWELLYN, *A Realistic Jurisprudence: The
Next Step, in* JURISPRUDENCE: REALISM IN THEORY AND PRACTICE 3, 8-18, 21-23
(1962), which conceptualizes remedies as constitutive features of rights.
For the opposing position, see Stephen A. Smith, *Rights and Remedies: A
Complex Relationship, in* TAKING REMEDIES SERIOUSLY 31 (Kent Roach & Robert
Sharpe eds., 2010). *See also* Hanoch Dagan, *Remedies, Rights, and Properties*,
4(1) J. TORT. L. art. 3, at 2-9, *available at* http://www.bepress.com/jtl/vol4/
iss1/art3 (2011) (remedies participate in the constitution of the rights they
help enforce, but there may be gaps — due mostly to institutional reasons — between the content of rights and the judicial response to their
infringement).

4. *Liberating or Dismantling.* The bundle-of-sticks understanding of
property is often invoked as part of an effort to examine critically the existing content of property rights. It is helpful for such exercises because —
alongside Hohfeld's other major insight, namely, the dephysicalization of
property rights — this understanding forcefully demonstrates that property
is an artifact, a human creation that can be, and has been, modified in
accordance with human needs and values. *See* JEREMY BENTHAM, THE THEORY
OF LEGISLATION 111-113 (C.K. Ogden ed., 1987) (1802). It reminds us that
there is neither an a priori list of entitlements that the owner of a given
resource inevitably enjoys nor an exhaustive list of resources that enjoy the
status of property. It thus brings home the importance, indeed inevitability,
of the application of normative judgments in property law. Reference to the
concept of property is an invitation to a normative inquiry, rather than a
normative argument in and of itself. *See generally* Kenneth J. Vandevelde,
*The New Property of the Nineteenth Century: The Development of the Modern
Concept of Property*, 29 BUFF. L. REV. 325 (1980).

There is another, more ambitious — and also more controversial —
understanding of Hohfeld's contribution: as the epitome of property's disintegration. In this view, property is conceived of as a "laundry list" of
substantive rights with limitless permutations, so that the legal engineers
can decide — concerning each right separately — who should be its rightful
owner. *See* BRUCE A. ACKERMAN, PRIVATE PROPERTY AND THE CONSTITUTION 9-15,
26-29, 97-100 (1977). This view has been vigorously attacked by neo-
Blackstonians, who revive the "sole and despotic dominion" understanding
of property, insisting that the paradigmatic incidents of property rights
necessarily hang together as they all derive from one coherent legal idea.
Can you reconstruct the argument of this position? *See* J.E. Penner,
The "Bundle of Rights" Picture of Property, 43 UCLA L. REV. 711 (1996) and
Chapter 9.1 below. But even those who resist Blackstone are frequently

troubled by the notion of such a radical disintegration of property. One reason for this uneasiness is that the bundle-of-rights model fails adequately to direct our attention to the ways by which our choices of property rules tend to respond and promote certain cultural visions of social life. *See* Joseph William Singer, Entitlement: The Paradoxes of Property 11 (2000). Another reason given for rejecting the bundle-of-rights conception is that it hides the contents of the bundle. David Lametti argues that the bundle's contents can differ depending upon the particular object of property. *See* David Lametti, *The Concept of Property: Relations Through Objects of Social Wealth*, 53 U. Toronto L.J. 325, 353-355 (2003). Certain objects, Lametti argues, carry with them particular obligations and rights, and a conception of property that fails to focus on the relationships among individuals through objects overlooks these differences. We raise this point again in Chapter 9.2, which discusses the responsibilities of ownership.

A third argument for rejecting a radical disintegration of property is the incongruity between this notion and the fact, which will be the focus of Chapter 8.2, that at any given time property law offers only a limited number of standardized forms of property. Hanoch Dagan's contribution, to which we turn now, can be read as a way to preserve the liberating potential of Hohfeld's theory without falling into this infamous predicament of disintegration.

Hanoch Dagan, The Craft of Property[3]

INTRODUCTION

Property is torn between form and substance. Every student of property remembers—some with joy, others with horror—the system of estates, with its fine distinctions among various forms of present and future interests. Fee simple absolute, fee tail, and life estate are only the beginning of a long repertoire of forms. An intricate taxonomy of various types of defeasible estates, future interests, and concurrent ownerships follows them. This labyrinth of property serves as a nice introduction to the importance and the complexity of form in the life of the law and to the rich catalog of forms for human interaction and organization constituted by law.

But property is also quite obviously about substance. Property is frequently described as a bundle of sticks: that is, a collection of substantive rights, such as the right to exclude, to use, to alienate, and so on. Furthermore, property is—how can it not be?—about values and normative choices. Property is frequently analyzed as a bulwark of individual freedom and independence; some holdings are even regarded as constitutive components of personal identity. Property also concerns the efficient (or

3. Hanoch Dagan, *The Craft of Property*, 91 Cal. L. Rev. 1517, 1519-1520, 1558-1565 (2003).

inefficient) allocation of resources, and is thus a matter of aggregate social welfare (or utility). Finally, because property allocates claims to various scarce resources in society, property must be about distribution, as well as about our conceptions of community and social responsibility.

Is property then a matter of form or of substance? The short answer is that it is both, if we properly understand these classifications. Property is about form because there are a limited number of ways in which the various sticks (rights) are, and should be, bundled together. Each human institution that property law facilitates requires a form: a particular configuration of the bundle of sticks. But prescribing this configuration cannot itself be a matter of form; the forms of property are not free-floating logical entities, each with its own inevitable set of incidents. Rather, property constitutes human institutions, serving human goals and thus involving human values. Their rationale, the raison d'etre of the various configurations of sticks of property as institutions, derives (or at least should derive) from the human values underlying each such property institution. The forms of property are important only if, and insofar as, they help consolidate people's expectations and express law's normative ideals for core types of human interaction.

Property law thus should shape and reshape forms — or, better, institutions — that will optimally promote these human values. This enterprise of institution building requires the application of some contextual judgment, informed by both experience and normative persuasion, as to both the role of legal rules in promoting these values and the values that should be promoted in the context at hand. This ongoing (probably endless) process of reshaping property as institutions does not undermine the importance of the forms of property. To perform successfully their role in consolidating people's expectations and expressing law's ideals for various types of interpersonal interactions, the institutions of property should be limited in number and their reconstitution should be addressed with an appropriate degree of caution. Yet understanding property as institutions does undermine, as it should, any attempt to discuss property as a sheer matter of formal deduction or of counting incidents. ...

THE REALIST APPROACH TO PROPERTY

The realist approach to property neither dismisses nor essentializes the forms of property. Existing property institutions are and should be the starting point of any analysis of property questions. The current forms incorporate valuable — although implicit and sometimes imperfectly executed — normative choices. ... In approaching the forms of property as institutions, one assumes that the existing configurations of rights, privileges, powers, and immunities of any given property institution constitute helpful frameworks for social interaction. This conservative assumption derives not only from the pragmatic reality that existing rules cannot be abandoned completely but also from a recognition that existing property forms represent an accumulated judicial experience that is worthy of respect.

More specifically, our existing repertoire of property forms offers a tentative suggestion to parse the social world into distinct categories of human interaction. People interact in a myriad of ways depending on their relationships to one another. The spectrum of relationships ranges from arm's-length relationships between strangers (or market transactors); through relationships between landlords and tenants, members of the same local community, neighbors, and coowners; to intimate relationships between family members. Accordingly, as Joseph Singer has shown, property is configured in diverse ways.[4] Ideally, the existing property configurations both construct and reflect the optimal interactions among people in given categories of relationships and with respect to given categories of resources. By facilitating such various categories of human interactions, the forms of property can promote important human values.

Some property institutions are structured along the lines of the Blackstonian conception of property as "sole and despotic dominion." These institutions are atomistic and competitive, and they vindicate people's negative liberty. Other property institutions, such as marital property, are dominated by a much more communitarian view of property, in which ownership is a locus of sharing. Many other property institutions—governing relationships between people who are neither strangers nor intimates—lie somewhere along this spectrum between atomistic and communitarian norms. For instance, with the property form of common interest communities, both autonomy and community are of the essence, and thus ownership implies both rights and responsibilities.

To avoid the pitfalls of essentializing the existing repertoire of property forms, however, we must avoid according these forms overwhelming normative authority. If property is understood as institutions, the appeal of these forms need not, and should not, be the end of the legal analysis.

---

4. *See* Joseph William Singer, *The Reliance Interest in Property*, 40 Stan. L. Rev. 611, 655 (1988). Although Singer's spectrum of social relationships is somewhat different from the one I use, it certainly serves as a source of inspiration. Because of this similarity, it may be helpful to describe how my account may differ from Singer's. First, Singer's claim that the reliance interest is an important premise of the entitlements of workers, spouses, adverse possessors, and so forth suggests that reliance can serve as at least part of an argument for property rights. But law never protects reliance *per se*; it protects reliance if and only if there is a good reason to encourage (or at least not discourage) the type and magnitude of the reliance at issue. Therefore, reliance, in and of itself, is a shaky ground for justifying entitlements. Reliance is desirable only when it facilitates some important human good. . . . Moreover, Singer maintains that the legal system may require a sharing or shifting of property interests from the owner to the nonowner to protect the more vulnerable party to the relationship. See Singer, *id.*, at 621, 623, 664-65, 668, 728, 730. Although "sharing" is indeed desirable at times, as the case of marital property . . . shows, I would reject "shifting" of property interests insofar as it legitimates an a posteriori approach to entitlement prescription. Shifting in this sense is undesirable because it generates considerable uncertainty, which might infringe too much on people's liberty and undermine efficiency. Furthermore, such uncertainty might even frustrate the social good, which both Singer and I cherish, of facilitating cooperation and trust: when the rules of the game are uncertain, the parties tend to be suspicious of one another.

Rather, this approach calls for an ongoing (albeit properly cautious) process of identifying the human values underlying the existing property forms and designing governance regimes to promote them. Here, we must rely on the vague notion of promoting optimality to capture the complex ways in which law can facilitate human values. The normative analysis recommended by the realist approach to property must resort to property law's material effect on people's behavior, to its expressive and constitutive impact, and to the intricate interdependence of the two effects.

Property law, like law in general, is a coercive mechanism backed by state-mandated power, and therefore its prescriptions need to be justified in terms of their promotion of human values. Consequently, we must reevaluate the institutions of property in terms of their effectiveness at promoting their accepted values, and the continued validity and desirability of these values. This inquiry requires critical and constructive reexamination of law's existing categorization of relationships (and of resources), as well as the values property law promotes. In the legal realist tradition, this latter inquiry perceives the values of property in an anti-foundationalist spirit, as "pluralistic and multiple, dynamic and changing, hypothetical and not self-evident, problematic rather than determinative." Yet, . . . values are importantly different from sheer preferences: values must be defended with reasons, which must in turn relate to human interests, "and not just anything can count as human interest."[5] Therefore, although property lawyers must not disregard radical alternatives, they can bracket out skeptical doubts and explicitly engage in a normative inquiry.

This ongoing process of reshaping property as institutions is surely antithetical to the understanding of property as free-floating logical forms that can be addressed by means of deductive reasoning or counting incidents. But the conception of property as institutions does not collapse property to a catalog of substantive sticks that are "strikingly independent" (to use Hohfeld's term) and have a limitless number of permutations. The institutions of property are unifying normative ideals for core categories of interpersonal relationships. Therefore, they must be limited in number and standardized.

Each property institution . . . targets, in its own way and with respect to some intended realm of application, a set of human values that can be promoted by its constitutive rules. As such, the institutions of property consolidate people's expectations, so that they know what they are getting into when entering, for example, a joint tenancy, a common interest community, or, for that matter, a marriage. Thus, a set of fairly precise rules must govern each property institution to enable people to predict the consequences of various future contingencies and to plan and structure their lives accordingly. Furthermore, the institutions of property may also

5. Don Herzog, Without Foundations: Justification in Political Theory 232, 237-38 (1985).

affect people's ideals and therefore their preferences with respect to these categories of relationships. In this latter role, property institutions perform a significant expressive and cultural function. Both roles—consolidating expectations and expressing ideal forms of relationships—require some measure of stability: to form effective frameworks of social interaction and cooperation, property law can recognize a necessarily limited number of categories of relationships and resources. This prescription of standardization is particularly acute with regard to the expressive role that mandates limiting the number of property institutions because law can effectively express only so many ideal categories of interpersonal relationships.

Viewing property as institutions in this way is deeply rooted in the realist tradition. . . . [T]his approach rejects deductive reasoning from frozen forms of property. Furthermore, the conception of property as institutions suggests that ownership for one purpose does not necessarily imply ownership for another and that the configuration of property rights is context dependent. However . . . the realist approach to property takes the existing forms of property seriously, using them as tentative suggestions for dividing the social universe into economically and socially differentiated segments. An understanding of property as institutions recognizes that each "transaction of life" has some features that are of sufficient normative importance to justify distinct legal treatment. Finally . . . the realist approach takes the values underlying forms of property, and not only the existing doctrinal content of these forms, as part and parcel of the legal analysis, and thus makes these values an object of ongoing critical and constructive inquiry. In this way, the property as institutions approach is both backward looking and forward looking, constantly challenging the desirability of the normative underpinnings of property institutions, their responsiveness to the social context in which they are situated, and their effectiveness in promoting their contextually examined normative goals.

At times such an account helps fill gaps in the law by prescribing new rules that further bolster and vindicate these goals. At other times it points out "blemishes" in the existing forms: rules that undermine the most illuminating and defensible account of such a property institution that should be reformed so that an institution lives up to its own ideals. This reformist potential may yield—indeed, has yielded throughout the history of property—different types of legal reforms. In some cases, the reform is relatively radical: the abolition of a property form (as was the case, for all practical purposes, with the fee tail form) or an overall reconstruction of its content (as with leaseholds). Sometimes more moderate options are in order, such as restating the doctrine pertaining to a property form in a way that brings its rules closer to its underlying commitments, removing in the process indefensible rules (the best example here is probably the recent *Restatement of Servitudes*), or adjusting one given form—

think here of the fee simple absolute — to the various social contexts in which it may be situated.

The realist approach to property is thus an exercise in legal optimism, an attempt to explain and develop the existing property forms in a way that accentuates their normative desirability while remaining attuned to their social context. This approach reflects a conception of law, introduced by Karl Llewellyn and later popularized (with some important modifications not adopted here) by Ronald Dworkin, as a dynamic practice that evolves along the lines of fit and justification.[6] This conception follows the common law method, described by Llewellyn as "a functioning harmonization of vision with tradition, of continuity with growth, of machinery with purpose, of measure with need," mediating between "the seeming commands of the authorities and the felt demands of justice."[7]

NOTES AND QUESTIONS

1. *The Realist Legacy.* Dagan acknowledges that his conception of property relies on the realist legacy. As he explains, this conception rejects the formalist understanding of legal reasoning as an exercise of classification, induction, and deduction, which, as such, do not involve any normative judgments. *See* NEIL DUXBURY, PATTERNS OF AMERICAN JURISPRUDENCE 10, 15 (1995). It insists that property — like other legal concepts — can be interpreted or elaborated in multiple ways, that the choice among these interpretations involves — as it should — the application of normative judgment, and that obscuring this choice is objectionable because it shields legal prescriptions from empirical and normative critique. *See* Felix S. Cohen, *Transcendental Nonsense and the Functional Approach*, 35 COLUM. L. REV. 809, 811-812, 820 (1935). But, unlike the more ambitious reading of the bundle metaphor, this conception of property also warns us against understanding the incidents of property as a laundry list that permits limitless permutations. (Compare with Note 4 following the Hohfeld excerpt.) "Although we should not treat the common law forms of property as abstract entities with internally untouchable structure and content, we also should not unreflectively dismiss these property forms because they represent our existing default frameworks of interpersonal interaction. To know if and how the existing configuration of a property form should affect the legal outcome, however, we must analyze the forms of property from a normative and contextual (i.e., legal realist) perspective. The forms of property should affect outcomes to the extent that they help constitute property

---

6. *See* RONALD DWORKIN, LAW'S EMPIRE 52-53, 164-258 (1986); KARL N. LLEWELLYN, THE COMMON LAW TRADITION 36-38, 44, 49, 60, 194-95, 222-23 (1960). . . .

7. LLEWELLYN, *supra* note 6, at 37-38. . . .

institutions that serve important human values." Dagan, *supra* footnote 3, at 1534-1535. For an analysis of the legal realist legacy in general, on which this theory of property relies, see Hanoch Dagan, *The Realist Conception of Law*, 57 U. Toronto L.J. 607 (2007).

2. *The Value of Pluralism.* Later on, Dagan characterized his approach to property as "structurally pluralist." Structural pluralism, he argues, is an essential entailment of the liberal commitment to autonomy, understood as people's ability to be the authors of their life (choosing among worthwhile life plans and being able to pursue one's choice). This understanding of autonomy requires an adequate range of significantly divergent options, so that there is enough room for individual choice. Thus, given the diversity of acceptable human goods from which autonomous people should be able to choose and their distinct constitutive values, the state must recognize a sufficiently diverse set of robust frameworks for people to organize their lives. And because many of these plural values cannot be realistically actualized without active support of viable legal institutions, law should facilitate (within limits) the coexistence of various social spheres embodying different modes of valuation. Therefore, despite the ostensible appeal of global coherence, it is reasonable and even desirable for property law to adopt more than one set of principles and, therefore, more than one set of coherent doctrines. *See* Hanoch Dagan, *Pluralism and Perfectionism in Private Law*, available at http://papers.ssrn.com/sol3/papers.cfm?abstract_id=1868198. *See also* Gregory S. Alexander, *Pluralism and Property*, 80 Fordham L. Rev. 1017 (2011) (supporting value pluralism in property theory and arguing that incommensurability of values does not preclude rational choices between competing values).

3. *The Question of Indeterminacy and a Few Other Challenges.* One important challenge for Dagan's theory comes from the critique of value indeterminacy. Crafting property institutions based on more than one foundational value with no agreed-upon formula for measuring and balancing may render property law hopelessly indeterminate. How can Dagan respond to this critique? Is there a real constraint in the requirement, on which he insists, to explicitly apply judgment, which needs to be normatively and contextually justified? For an encouraging answer, see Joseph William Singer, *How Property Norms Construct the Externalities of Ownership, in* Property and Community 57 (Gregory S. Alexander & Eduardo M. Peñalver eds., 2009). One important way to address this challenge is by trying to apply it in real-life contexts, something that Part III of this book allows you to do. When you go through these materials, you will have an opportunity to assess whether addressing the normative infrastructure of these different property institutions yields sufficiently sharp doctrinal teeth or, rather, constantly leads you to a standoff. You can also think about further challenges to this theory, notably regarding institutional and procedural issues, such as who should decide which values should

guide a particular property institution, and how should new institutions evolve or existing ones change.

2.   THE *NUMERUS CLAUSUS* PUZZLE

Thomas W. Merrill & Henry E. Smith, Optimal Standardization in the Law of Property: The *Numerus Clausus* Principle[1]

I.   INTRODUCTION

A central difference between contract and property concerns the freedom to "customize" legally enforceable interests. The law of contract recognizes no inherent limitations on the nature or the duration of the interests that can be the subject of a legally binding contract. Certain types of promises — such as promises to commit a crime — are declared unenforceable as a matter of public policy. But outside these relatively narrow areas of proscription and requirements such as definiteness and (maybe) consideration, there is a potentially infinite range of promises that the law will honor. The parties to a contract are free to be as whimsical or fanciful as they like in describing the promise to be performed, the consideration to be given in return for the promise, and the duration of the agreement.

The law of property is very different in this respect. Generally speaking, the law will enforce as property only those interests that conform to a limited number of standard forms. . . . With respect to interests in land, for example, the basic forms are the fee simple, the defeasible fee simple, the life estate, and the lease. When parties wish to transfer property in land, they must specify which legal form they are using — fee simple, lease, and so forth. If they fail to be clear about which legal interest they are conveying, or if they attempt to customize a new type of interest, the courts will generally recast the conveyance as creating one of the recognized forms. Of course, the law freely allows customization of the more physical, tangible dimensions of ownership rights. Property comes in all sorts of shapes and sizes. But with respect to the legal dimensions of property, the law generally insists on strict standardization.

Every common-law lawyer is schooled in the understanding that property rights exist in a fixed number of forms. The principle is acknowledged — at least by implication — in the "catalogue of estates" or "forms of ownership" familiar to anyone who has survived a first-year property course in

---

1. Thomas W. Merrill & Henry E. Smith, *Optimal Standardization in the Law of Property: The* Numerus Clausus *Principle*, 110 YALE L.J. 1, 3-8, 9-11, 20, 24, 26-31, 33-35, 38, 40, 42, 58-61, 68-70 (2000).

an American law school. The principle, however, is by no means limited to estates in land and future interests; it is also reflected in other areas of property law, including landlord-tenant, easements and servitudes, and intellectual property. Nor is the principle confined to common-law countries; to the contrary, it appears to be a universal feature of all modern property systems. In the common law, the principle that property rights must conform to certain standardized forms has no name. In the civil law, which recognizes the doctrine explicitly, it is called the *numerus clausus* — the number is closed. . . .

. . . The principle that property forms are fixed and limited in number represents an extremely important qualification to the principle of freedom of contract — a principle widely regarded by law-and-economics scholars as promoting the efficient allocation of resources. A willing buyer and a willing seller can create an infinite variety of enforceable contracts for the exchange of recognized property rights, and can describe these property rights along a multitude of physical dimensions and prices. But common-law courts will not enforce an agreement to create a new type of property right. Remarkably, virtually no effort has been made to theorize about whether this critical qualification to freedom of contract is justifiable in economic terms.[2]

. . . Scholars and judges tend to react to manifestations of the *numerus clausus* as if it were nothing more than outmoded formalism. . . . [T]aking this position one step further, Critical Legal Studies (CLS) scholars have portrayed the doctrine of fixed estates as perniciously reinforcing hierarchical social relations. As one CLS-inspired source puts it, the "formalistic, box-like structure" of property law, that is, the *numerus clausus*, reflects a "feudal vision of property relationships designed to channel (force?) people into pre-set social relationships."[3]

A related source of antipathy to the *numerus clausus* may be the perception that it is a trap for the unwary. The menu of recognized property forms is relatively complex, and any attempt to venture beyond simple sales of goods and short-term leases into the arcane worlds of future interests, easements and covenants, or intellectual property requires the advice of a lawyer. When unsophisticated or poorly advised actors enter these worlds, they may find that courts force the transaction into one of the established "boxes," with the result that the actors' intentions are

---

2. A partial exception is [Bernard Rudden, *Economic Theory v. Property Law: The* Numerus Clausus *Problem, in* Oxford Essays in Jurisprudence: Third Series 239, 241 (John Eekelaar & John Bell eds., 1987)], which touches upon several possible economic justifications for the doctrine, including the third-party information-cost theory we develop at length in Part III of this Article. *Id.* at 254-56. Rudden ultimately concludes, however, that the rationale for the doctrine remains a mystery. *Id.* at 261.

3. Curtis J. Berger & Joan C. Williams, Property: Land Ownership and Use 211 (4th ed. 1997). . . . Whatever the merits of such critiques of formalism in other contexts, they are ironic when directed against the *numerus clausus*. Historically, the doctrine is closely associated with efforts in post-revolutionary France to eliminate the proliferation of fragmented rights characteristic of feudal regimes. . . .

frustrated. By contrast, actors who are sophisticated or well-advised can almost always manipulate the menu of options so as to realize their objectives. In this sense, the *numerus clausus* discriminates in favor of those who are well-endowed with legal resources and against those who are poorly endowed. . . .

These casual criticisms of the *numerus clausus* fail to confront what to us are the essential questions. Before condemning standardization of forms and embracing a regime of contractual freedom with respect to the legal dimensions of property, one must first engage in a series of inquiries: What are the costs and benefits of standardization in defining property rights? To what extent should standardization of rights be supplied by the government rather than relying solely on owners' incentives to conform to the most-widely used forms? If the government plays a role in standardizing rights, what is the appropriate division of labor between courts and legislatures in enforcing standardization and in making the inevitable changes to the menu of standard forms that must occur over time? . . .

II. THE *NUMERUS CLAUSUS* IN THE COMMON LAW OF PROPERTY

. . . [N]otwithstanding the absence of logical compulsion behind the *numerus clausus* in common-law systems, it is reasonably clear that common-law courts *behave* toward property rights very much like civil-law courts do: They treat previously-recognized forms of property as a closed list that can be modified only by the legislature. This behavior cannot be attributed to any explicit or implicit command of the legislature. It is best described as a norm of judicial self-governance. Jurisprudentially speaking, the *numerus clausus* functions in the common law much like a canon of interpretation, albeit a canon that applies to common-law decisionmaking rather than statutory or constitutional interpretation, or like a strong default rule in the interpretation of property rights. . . .

The *numerus clausus* appears to function as a deeply entrenched assumption of the common-law system of property rights. There are no significant examples of judicial abolition of existing forms of property. Moreover, courts in the modern era for the most part have declined to create new ones. There are a few prominent exceptions to this latter generalization, such as the judicial creation of the equitable servitude and the recognition in some states of the doctrines of misappropriation of information and the right of publicity. But these exceptions have been confined to nonpossessory property rights and intellectual-property rights, and often, as in the case of the right of publicity, there is great pressure for legislative ratification of judicial innovations when they do occur. Still, recognition of the concept by courts and commentators is remarkably underdeveloped. At the level of doctrinal exposition, the *numerus clausus* is almost — but not quite — invisible. . . .

III. Measurement Costs, Frustration Costs, and the Optimal Standardization of Property Rights

What accounts for the widespread adherence to the *numerus clausus*, not only in the common law but in postfeudal legal systems throughout the world? . . .

. . . In this Part, we develop . . . a theory of the *numerus clausus* based on optimal standardization of property rights.

A. Measurement-Cost Externalities

When individuals encounter property rights, they face a measurement problem. In order to avoid violating another's property rights, they must ascertain what those rights are. In order to acquire property rights, they must measure various attributes, ranging from the physical boundaries of a parcel, to use rights, to the attendant liabilities of the owner to others (such as adjacent owners). Whether the objective is to avoid liability or to acquire rights, an individual will measure the property rights until the marginal costs of additional measurement equal the marginal benefits. When seeking to avoid liability, the actor will seek to minimize the sum of the costs of liability for violations of rights and the costs of avoiding those violations through measurement. In the potential transfer situation, the individual will measure as long as the marginal benefit in reduced error costs exceeds the marginal cost of measurement.

The need for standardization in property law stems from an externality involving measurement costs: Parties who create new property rights will not take into account the full magnitude of the measurement costs they impose on strangers to the title. An example illustrates. Suppose one hundred people own watches. *A* is the sole owner of a watch and wants to transfer some or all of the rights to use the watch to *B*. The law of personal property allows the sale of *A*'s entire interest in the watch, or the sale of a life estate in the watch, or the sale of a joint tenancy or tenancy in common in the watch. But suppose *A* wants to create a "time-share" in the watch, which would allow *B* to use the watch on Mondays but only on Mondays (with *A* retaining for now the rights to the watch on all other days). As a matter of contract law, *A* and *B* are perfectly free to enter into such an idiosyncratic agreement. But *A* and *B* are not permitted by the law of personal property to create a *property right* in the use of the watch on Mondays only and to transfer this property right from *A* to *B*.

Why might the law restrict the freedom of *A* and *B* to create such an unusual property right? Suppose, counterfactually, that such idiosyncratic property rights are permitted. Word spreads that someone has sold a Monday right in a watch, but not which of the one hundred owners did so. If *A* now decides to sell his watch, he will have to explain that it does not include Monday rights, and this will reduce the attractiveness of the watch to potential buyers. Presumably, however, *A* will foresee this when he sells the Monday rights, and is willing to bear the cost of that action in the form of a lower sales price. But consider what will happen now when any of the *other* ninety-nine watch owners try to sell their watches. Given the awareness that someone has created a Monday-only right, anyone else buying a watch must now also investigate whether any particular watch does not include Monday rights. Thus, by allowing even one person to create an idiosyncratic property right, the information processing costs of all persons who have existing or potential interests in this type of property go up. This external cost on other market participants forms the basis of our explanation of the *numerus clausus*.

At this point, it is useful to distinguish three classes of individuals who might be affected by the decision to create idiosyncratic property rights, or fancies, as illustrated by Figure 1. First are the *originating parties*, who are the participants to the transaction creating the fancy; this is *A* and *B* in Figure 1. Second are the *potential successors in interest* to the asset that is being subjected to the fancy. This would be anyone who might purchase *A*'s reserved rights (after the transfer to *B*) as well as anyone who succeeds to the interest acquired by *B*. Potential successors in interest are shown as *C*s and *D*s in Figure 1. Finally, there are the *other market participants*, people who will deal in or with watches other than the one over which *A* and *B* have transacted. Other market participants include those selling and acquiring rights in other watches such as *E* and *F* and *G* and *H* in Figure 1. They also include all who must avoid violating property rights in all watches, rights that are enforced against the world represented by *I* and *J* in Figure 1. In the hypothetical example above, the other market participants are the other ninety-nine watch owners and their successors in title, as well as anyone who potentially might violate a property right in a watch.

FIGURE 1. THE CLASSES OF AFFECTED PARTIES

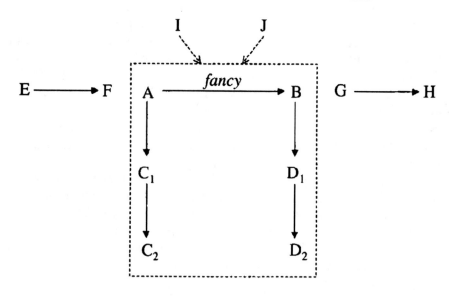

The difference between other possible explanations of the *numerus clausus* and our information-cost theory can be understood in terms of this three-way classification. Other explanations focus on the effect of novel property rights on the originating parties and potential successors in interests — the *A*s, *B*s, *C*s, and *D*s of the world. One may say that these classes of individuals fall within the "zone of privity" designated by the box with the dotted line in Figure 1. Our explanation, in contrast, focuses on the effect of unusual property rights on other market participants — the *E*s, *F*s, *G*s, *H*s, *I*s, and *J*s of the world — classes of individuals who fall outside the zone of privity. As we argue, explanations based on classes of individuals within the zone of privity have difficulty identifying costs that are not impounded into the price facing those who make the decision whether to create the fancy in the first place. An explanation based on costs incurred by classes of individuals outside the zone of privity does not have this difficulty. . . .

[F]ocusing only on the potential detriment to the two original parties to the transaction — *A* and *B* — makes it hard to see that there is any legitimate reason for the law to intervene and prohibit the transaction. The decision to create a time-share in the watch may turn out to be an improvident one. But the law generally does not second-guess mundane mistakes like an improvident sale. . . .

For similar reasons, the costs to potential successors in interest will also be mediated through the price mechanism and so will not require legal intervention. . . .

Again, limited foresight might prevent *A* or *B* from making a completely accurate forecast of the costs to those who deal with the asset in the future. This does not, however, furnish a basis for taking the decision out of the hands of the original transactors, unless officials are in a better position to estimate these costs than are the originating parties, who are closest to the transaction and who face the costs most directly. Generally speaking, this is not likely.

Further, there are less drastic ways to deal with improvident arrangements that cause excessive costs for parties and potential successors in interest than mandating the standardization of rights through the *numerus clausus* principle. For example, the law could adopt a default rule against time-shares in personal property with the opportunity to opt out. . . .

There is, however, a much more straightforward problem of externalities associated with the creation of idiosyncratic property rights as illustrated in the watch hypothetical. These are the effects on the third class of individuals identified above outside the zone of privity — the other market participants. When *A* creates the Monday right, this can raise the information costs of third parties. If the law allows *A* to create a Monday interest, individuals wishing to buy watches or bailees asked to repair watches will have to consider the possibility that any given watch is a Monday-only watch (or a watch for any other proper subset of days of the week) rather than a full-week watch. While *A* and *B* might be expected to take into account the market-value-lowering effect of undesirable idiosyncratic rights when third parties like *C* or *D* consider purchasing property in this watch, they will not take into account the more general effect on processing costs created by the existence of such rights when *F* is considering a purchase of rights in *E*'s watch, or *I* and *J* are worried about violating property rights. . . .

One way to control the external costs of measurement to third parties is through compulsory standardization of property rights. Standardization reduces the costs of measuring the attributes of such rights. Limiting the number of basic property forms allows a market participant or a potential violator to limit his or her inquiry to whether the interest does or does not have the features of the forms on the menu. Fancies not on the closed list need not be considered because they will not be enforced. When it comes to the basic legal dimensions of property, limiting the number of forms thus makes the determination of their nature less costly. The "good" in question here might be considered to be the prevention of error in ascertaining the attributes of property rights. Standardization means less measurement is required to achieve a given amount of error prevention. Alternatively, one can say that standardization increases the productivity of any given level of measurement efforts.

One would expect standardization to have the most value in connection with the dimensions of property rights that are least visible, and hence the most difficult for ordinary observers to measure. The tangible attributes of property, such as its size, shape, color, or texture, are typically readily observable and hence can be relatively easily measured by third parties. . . . These physical attributes, and of course the price, are relatively easy for third parties to process using their senses, and thus there is less to be gained from standardizing them. The legal dimensions of property are less visible and less easy to comprehend, especially when they deviate from the most familiar forms such as the undivided fee simple. Thus, one would expect the effort to lower third-party information costs through standardization to focus on the legal dimension of ownership.

B. Frustration Costs and the Language of Property Rights

If the only concern were in reducing third-party measurement costs, then there should be only one mandatory package of property rights, presumably a simple usufruct or an undivided fee simple. But standardization imposes its own costs. Mandatory rules sometimes prevent the parties from achieving a legitimate goal cost-effectively. Enforcing standardization can therefore frustrate the parties' intentions.

Although the *numerus clausus* sometimes frustrates parties' objectives, often those objectives can be realized by a more complex combination of the standardized building blocks of property. For example, sophisticated parties with good legal advice can create the equivalent of a lease "for the duration of the war" by entering into a long-term lease determinable if the war ends. The fact that the *numerus clausus* is in this sense "avoidable" does not mean that it is trivial: Even if the standardization effected by the *numerus clausus* principle does not absolutely bar the parties from realizing their ends, this standardization comes at a price. The effect is roughly that of price discrimination: Parties willing to pay a great deal for an objective can achieve it by incurring higher planning and implementation costs. Furthermore, the design and implementation costs imposed by the *numerus clausus* function as a sort of "pollution tax" that should deter parties from insisting on overusing hard-to-process property forms, thereby placing higher processing burdens on market participants and especially courts. . . .

C. Optimal Standardization and the *Numerus Clausus*

We are now in a position to see how the *numerus clausus* functions to promote the optimal standardization of property rights. From a social point of view, the objective should be to minimize the sum of measurement (and error) costs, frustration costs, and administrative costs. In other words, what we want is not maximal standardization — or no standardization — but optimal standardization. Fortunately, standardization comes in degrees. There is a spectrum of possible approaches to property rights, ranging from total freedom of customization on the one hand to complete regimentation on the other. Neither of these endpoints on the spectrum is likely to minimize social costs. Extreme standardization would frustrate many of the purposes to which property rights are put. On the other hand, total freedom to customize rights would create large third-party measurement and error costs and high administrative costs. Attention should focus on the middle range of the spectrum. Starting from a position of complete regimentation, permitting additional forms of property rights should reduce frustration costs by more than it increases measurement and error costs to third parties and administrative costs. Conversely, if one starts from a position of complete customization of rights, increasing the degree of standardization should lower measurement and error costs and administrative costs by more than the attendant frustration costs will rise. . . .

The *numerus clausus* principle can be seen from this perspective as a device that moves the system of property rights in the direction of the optimal level of standardization. . . . By creating a strong presumption against judicial recognition of new forms of property rights, the *numerus clausus* imposes a brake on efforts by parties to proliferate new forms of property rights. On the other hand, by grandfathering in existing forms of property, and permitting legislative creation of new forms, the *numerus clausus* permits some positive level of diversification in the recognized forms of property. We do not argue that any particular number of property forms is in fact optimal. Nor do we argue that the forms currently recognized by the common law are ideal and beyond improvement. We do submit, however, that the *numerus clausus* strikes a rough balance between the extremes of complete regimentation and complete freedom of customization, and thus leads to a system of property rights that is closer to being optimal than that which would be produced by either of the extreme positions.

D. Information Costs and the Dynamics of Property

Finally, our explanation of the *numerus clausus* generates some general predictions about the way in which property regimes will change over time: As the costs of standardization to the parties and the government shift, we expect the optimal degree of standardization to rise or fall. Consider the rise of registers of interests in real property, that is, recording acts. This device lowers the costs of notice; it is an alternative method of lowering information costs. . . .

. . . In general, to the extent that technological change allows cheaper notice of relevant interests, the need for standardization by the law will be somewhat diminished. Just as the rise of land registers allowed some loosening of the *numerus clausus*, so too technology that lowers information costs can be expected to weaken the *numerus clausus* further. . . .

V. THE *NUMERUS CLAUSUS* AND INSTITUTIONAL CHOICE

The *numerus clausus* also has important implications for the division of authority between courts and legislatures with respect to changes in the structure of property rights. By limiting courts to enforcing the status quo in terms of recognized property interests, the *numerus clausus* makes the courts an inhospitable forum for modifying existing forms of property or creating new ones. Consequently, parties who wish to secure changes in the pattern of available property rights must look elsewhere—most prominently, to the legislature. . . .

Although the U.S. courts are far more adventuresome than either civil-law courts or English courts, the de facto recognition of the *numerus clausus* has also had a significant impact in channeling reform of property rights to legislatures in this country. . . . The abolition of the fee tail, dower and curtesy, the tenancy by the entirety, and the tenancy in partnership have been accomplished in this country by legislation, not by courts. And the creation of new interests such as condominiums and time-shares has also been accomplished through legislative action rather than judicial rulings. The fact that it is possible to cite counterexamples in the U.S. context, such as the development of the action for misappropriation of information and the right of publicity, simply attests to the reality that the *numerus clausus* is a weaker doctrine in U.S. courts, both in terms of express judicial recognition and in terms of judicial behavior. . . .

Traditional law-and-economics scholars may regard the institutional-choice dimension of the *numerus clausus* as unfortunate. One of the tenets of early law-and-economics literature was that common-law rules are more likely to be efficient than are legislated rules. A central reason for this assumption is that legislatures were regarded as being dominated by interest groups with narrow distributional objectives, whereas common-law courts were regarded as being immune from this type of distortion. Scholars who continue to share these assumptions may regard as pernicious a doctrine that freezes further development of property forms by courts and allocates all legal change to the legislature. The *numerus clausus* from this perspective would appear to consign questions about the design of the property-rights system to the institution least likely to be motivated by concerns with economic efficiency.

Yet if we put aside for the moment concerns about the possible distortions of the legislative process associated with interest-group activity, there are a number of features of legislative decisionmaking that make it relatively more attractive than common-law decisionmaking as a basis for modifying or creating categories of property rights. These features can be summarized under the headings of clarity, universality, comprehensiveness, stability, prospectivity, and implicit compensation. Significantly, each of these features also bears on the explanation for the *numerus clausus* we develop in Part III — that it is designed to reduce the costs to third parties of identifying the legal dimensions of property rights. Because of these features of legislated change, it is possible that the advantages of the *numerus clausus* as a rule of institutional choice may offset or even outweigh the detriments traditionally associated with legislative decisionmaking. . . .

VI. Conclusion

. . . By permitting a significant number of different forms of property but forbidding courts to recognize new ones, the *numerus clausus* strikes a balance between the proliferation of property forms, on the one hand, and excessive rigidity on the other. Proliferation is a problem because third parties must ascertain the legal dimensions of property rights in order to avoid violating the rights of others and to assess whether to acquire the rights of others. Permitting free customization of new forms of property would impose significant external costs on third parties in the form of higher measurement costs. On the other hand, insisting on a "one size fits all" system of property rights would frustrate those legitimate objectives that can be achieved only by using different property rights that fall short of full ownership. Optimal standardization is the solution, and the *numerus clausus* moves the legal system closer to the optimum, although we do not claim it generates a perfect mix of forms.

By insisting that courts respect the status quo in terms of the menu of property rights, the *numerus clausus* also channels legal change in property rights to the legislature. This institutional-choice dimension, we have argued, reinforces the information-cost minimization features of the doctrine, because legislated changes communicate information about the legal dimensions of property more effectively than judicially mandated changes.

The understanding that property rights by their very nature require a significant degree of standardization has a host of potentially valuable applications in assessing particular issues regarding property. These include proposals to expand the list of available intellectual property rights, proposals to use digital technology in conjunction with notice to substitute for standardization, and proposals suggesting that all landlord-tenant issues be resolved in accordance with contract law precepts. It also sheds important light on traditional disputes about the appropriate domain of freedom of contract . . . Similarly, our contention that standardization is advanced by forcing legal change to occur through legislation has important implications for fledgling efforts to devise criteria for comparative institutional analysis of courts and legislatures. . . .

NOTES AND QUESTIONS

1. *Critique of Merrill & Smith's Account.* Is the *numerus clausus* principle fully explained by Merrill and Smith's concern of communication costs? Henry Hansmann and Reinier Kraakman claim that it is not. They argue that limiting the forms of property does not economize on communication costs given parties' ability to tinker with the specific content of each property form. They thus maintain that property's standardization is unjustified and that the only concern of third parties that property law should facilitate is the verification of ownership of rights. Accordingly, for them, the distinguishing feature of property law must be the regulation of notice: providing mechanisms for giving effective notice of the partitioning of property rights in a given asset among multiple people. *See* Henry Hansmann & Reinier Kraakman, *Property, Contract, and Verification: The* Numerus Clausus *Problem and the Divisibility of Rights*, 31 J. LEGAL STUD. S373, S374-375, S380-384, S416-417, S419 (2002). Which side to this debate do you find more persuasive? Consider Merrill and Smith's response: that standardization is nonetheless significant because the way information is structured affects how costly it is for people to process. *See* Merrill & Smith, *supra*, at 33, 43-45. If indeed the relevant concern of third parties is verification, does this response satisfactorily account for the *numerus clausus* principle?

2. *Standardization and Property as Institutions.* Consider how Hanoch Dagan's theory of property, discussed in Chapter 8.1, accounts for the

numerus clausus principle. Dagan argues that "[l]imiting the number of property forms and standardizing their content facilitates the roles of property in consolidating expectations and expressing ideal forms of relationship." Notice that Dagan brackets the debate as to the power of Merrill and Smith's justification insofar as the interests of third parties are concerned because his explanation of the standardization of property "lies . . . within, rather than without, the zone of privity." Hanoch Dagan, *The Craft of Property*, 91 Cal. L. Rev. 1517, 1565-1567 (2003); *see also* Nestor M. Davidson, *Standardization and Pluralism in Property Law*, 61 Vand. L. Rev. 1597, 1653 (2008). To appreciate the difference between these competing accounts, think about how they are likely to differ as to (1) the possibility of contracting around the various incidents of the forms of property and (2) the kind of legal reasoning expected from courts (notably appellate courts). *See* Dagan, *supra*, at 1567-1569. Which of these accounts of standardization do you find more persuasive? What is your view as to the question of freedom of contract in property? And what role, if any, do you think courts should play in the evolution of property law? For opposing views regarding the institutional dimension, see also Avihay Dorfman, *Property and Collective Undertaking: The Principle of* Numerus Clausus, 61 U. Toronto L.J. 123 (2011) (only legislatures should create new property institutions); Hanoch Dagan, *Judges and Property, in* Intellectual Property and the Common Law __ (Shyamkrishna Balganesh ed., forthcoming 2012) (criticizing such property exceptionalism).

3. Numerus Clausus *and Property's Anti-Fragmentation Principle*. Recall that Merrill and Smith argue that "the legal dimensions of property" regulated by the *numerus clausus* principle are distinct from its "more physical, tangible dimensions" because, while the former are generally subject to "strict standardization," with respect to the latter "the law freely allows customization." Merrill & Smith, *supra*, at 3. But is this dichotomy right? Michael Heller thinks it is not. Heller situates the *numerus clausus* principle as part of a larger repertoire of devices throughout property law aimed at preventing excessive fragmentation. Excessive fragmentation of property, whether physical or legal, is detrimental since it "may operate as a one-way ratchet: Because of high transaction costs, strategic behaviors, and cognitive biases, people may find it easier to divide property than to recombine it. If too many people gain rights to use or exclude, then bargaining among owners may break down. With too many owners of property fragments, resources become prone to waste either through overuse in a commons or through underuse in an anticommons." Michael A. Heller, *The Boundaries of Private Property*, 108 Yale L.J. 1163, 1165-1166 (1999). As you may recall from Note 4 of Chapter 5, in an anticommons too many owners may each exclude others from a resource-generating waste through mutual vetoes. Do you understand how the *numerus clausus* can be regarded as an anti-fragmentation device, needed for addressing anticommons difficulties? *See id.* at 1176-1178. *See also* Charles Donahue Jr., *The Future of the*

Concept of Property Predicted from Its Past, in XXII NOMOS: PROPERTY 28 (J.R. Pennock & John W. Chapman eds., 1980), describing the process of categorization in the development of property rules as associated with a fundamental tendency in Western legal systems to agglomerate in a single person, commonly the present possessor of the object in question, all rights, privileges, and powers concerning the object. Merrill and Smith disagree; they argue that the *numerus clausus* principle "does not necessarily lead to less fragmentation" and that "the problem of fragmentation is addressed much more directly through other legal doctrines." Merrill & Smith, *supra,* at 52-53. Which side of this debate strikes you as more persuasive?

4.   Numerus Clausus *and Property Law's Affinity of Bright-Line Rules.* Merrill and Smith's account of the *numerus clausus* principle should be situated in a wider characterization of property law that is more amenable to bright-line rules, which are relatively invariant to context, than to vague standards, which call for contextual judgments. As Smith explains elsewhere, standardization in property through the *numerus clausus* is aimed at making much potential contextual information less relevant. Reducing such reliance on context typifies property, he claims, because property law involves communication with a wide and heterogeneous audience. *See* Henry E. Smith, *The Language of Property: Form, Context, and Audience,* 55 STAN. L. REV. 1105, 1125-1167 (2003). Are there other reasons that can explain—and justify?—the relatively heavy resort of property law to bright-line rules? (Think about the choice between rules and standards in terms of the concerns of liberty, aggregate welfare, and distributive justice, discussed in Part I; we have started addressing this choice as per aggregate welfare in Note 3 of Chapter 5.) Are there any competing normative considerations that may favor vague standards? And is it possible that property law would rather shift from one form of legal norms to the other? *See* Carol M. Rose, *Crystals and Mud in Property Law,* 40 STAN. L. REV. 577 (1988). Finally, Smith argues that the advantages of the relatively context-free rules over the context-rich standards explain and justify the conceptualization of property around the owner's right to exclude. *See* Henry E. Smith, *Mind the Gap: The Indirect Relation between Ends and Means in American Property Law,* 94 CORNELL L. REV. 959 (2009). Do you agree? *Compare* Gregory S. Alexander, *The Complex Core of Property,* 94 CORNELL L. REV. 1063, 1063-1068 (2009); HANOCH DAGAN, PROPERTY: VALUES AND INSTITUTIONS xxiv, 83-84, 148 (2011). We now turn, in Chapter 9.1, to a more general discussion of this conception of property.

9

BETWEEN
EXCLUSION AND
RESPONSIBILITY

1. OWNERSHIP AND EXCLUSION

J.E. Penner, The Idea of Property in Law[1]

. . . In a recent, very long paper I argued that while the idea we call "property" has been with us a long time, it is looking pretty shaky these days, at least in what might be called mainstream Anglo-American legal philosophy. I attributed this to the fact that the generally accepted picture we have of property, that property is a "bundle of rights," treats the idea of property as a kind of deficient concept, whose persistence in the language is to some extent inexplicable. For as I tried to show there, on the "bundle of rights" picture, "property" is not really a useful concept of any kind. It doesn't help judges understand what they're doing when they decide cases, because it doesn't effectively characterize any particular sort of legal relation. Property is pictured as a bundle of different rights, such as the right to possess, the right to use, the right to consume, the right to destroy, the right to manage, the right to give, the right to lend, the right to sell, and so on. Property, it is supposed, is a kind of aggregate or complex composed of more basic elements. One has property when one has some number of these rights, although it has proved exceedingly difficult to say with any certainty whether some rights are essential, or whether a certain critical number are. It is not even clear there is any workable notion of "enough" rights to make up a property bundle. Hence property's identity crisis.

Nevertheless, I think property can be sorted out so that it may once again make a valuable contribution to society. If the paper I have just referred to constituted the negative project of showing why the prevailing

1. J.E. Penner, The Idea of Property in Law 1-2, 5, 49-50, 68-73, 103-104, 206-207 (1997).

picture of property is wrong, this book is the positive project, my attempt to characterize the idea of property to show how vital this idea is to the way we think about the world in moral and legal terms. The view I would like to defend here is that property is what the average citizen, free of the entanglements of legal philosophy, thinks it is: the right to a thing. Without a doubt that idea will require a lot of elaboration, and there are a number of sticky issues. But as it preserves an identity for the notion of property which the "bundle" picture discards, it is surely worth the effort. If successful we may be able to say something interesting about it, and property may be able to tell us something interesting about ourselves. . . .

. . . [P]roperty is the right to determine how particular things will be used, but this right is not to be perceived as the right to live like a hermit and use things on one's own. Nothing in the legal idea of property counsels a retreat from society, so to own includes the right to share one's property and give it to others. This is explained by the fact that persons are capable of treating the interests of others as their own interests. I therefore claim that people can share interests with each other, typically in cases of friendships and family relationships, but elsewhere as well. In consequence, the ownership of property is intimately connected to giving and sharing. By contrast, property is not wedded to contract in any way, so having a right to property does not entail the right to sell what one owns. There is nothing about the right to property which stands *against* contracts, but contract arises from the recognition of a different interest, the interest in forming agreements with others. The way in which parties to contracts conceive their interests is completely different from the way they conceive them when they make gifts, and so bargains with respect to property do not slip into the ambit of property simply because both gifts and sales involve transfers of property. . . .

The interest in property is the interest in exclusively determining the use of things. The precise meanings of "exclusively," "determining the use of," and "things" all have to be elaborated. But first we should remind ourselves that our subject is the *interest* we have in the use of things. We have a critically considered reason for wishing to engage the world of things outside us, in particular the material resources of the world. Not only is occupying some patch of the earth and drawing on its resources for food, shelter, and so on necessary for life itself, much of what humans do culturally depends upon forming our physical environment in ways that appeal to us. . . . [T]he freedom to determine the use of things is an interest of ours in part because of the freedom it provides to shape our lives. If we believe in any fairly robust interest in autonomy, then the interest in determining the use of things is in part an interest in trying to achieve different goals. And we cannot reduce this interest merely to our interest in those determinations of use that turn out actually to be valuable. . . . We can benefit from our failures as well as our successes.

The interest in property is an interest in *exclusively* determining the use of things. This should not be regarded as a requirement that an owner or owners must use things on their own, nor that there cannot be co-owner-ship of property by a few or many people. The claim is that a right to a thing is a property right only to the extent that some others are excluded from the determination of its use. While people speak of "common ownership" or "collective ownership," these can be regarded as ownership only through surreptitiously relying on some notion of exclusion. In the former, though individuals each have equal rights of access to the common property, at the minimum they have the right to exclude others while they are actually using it, if only to the extent that one commoner's cow excludes other cattle from the patch of pasture it is presently grazing. It is clear also that those outside the common ownership are excluded altogether. In "collective ownership," the use is socially determined, that is determined by some mechanism which is intended to reflect the determination of people in general on how the thing in question is to be used. But this is still exclusive: *individuals* are excluded from the determination of the use of the property, although the system is usually justified on the basis that collective determination of use serves their interests better than would a system of private property.

To "determine the use of things" does not mean that one may decide upon any use one fancies, and insist that that use be made of the property, drawing upon any other people, institutions, and resources that are around. . . . The right to property is, in [Isaiah] Berlin's terms, a negative liberty. It is a freedom from constraint, not the provision of a means to act. One's determination of the use of a thing is served only to the extent that freedom from the interference of others does so. . . .

. . . In [what follows] I commence characterizing property from first principles, as it were. I shall approach the task by examining the nature of property rights, or the right to property. This is an exploration of the way in which the law, through imposing duties on others who bear the right kinds of relationship to the owner, protects our interest in things. My contention is that property rights can be fully explained using the concepts of exclusion and use. . . .

The concepts of exclusion and use are more complex than they first appear, because, in general, they are intertwined. One can, of course, have a right to use something without having a right to exclude others, and vice versa. . . .

Yet rights purely to exclude or purely to use interact naturally, as it were, in the sense that use almost always involves some exclusion of others. . . .

So long as we conceive of a right to use in a social situation, in the real world, that is, the implications of that kind of right will raise issues about the rightfulness of excluding others, because the vast majority of the uses that a person will make of a thing are impossible if everyone tries to use the thing at the same time. Because we live in a world of scarcity there is an insufficient quantity of perfect substitutes for everything that people wish to use, and this cannot but give rise to conflict. Now, of course, some things are not scarce, and in some situations commons work (although in the case of commons, too, a large set of people is usually excluded), but this does not detract from the general point. The obvious solution is to link rights of use with rights of exclusion, and so we must look at the different exclusionary rights to which rights of use may be linked.

One can have a right to use so long as no one else was using, or wanted to use, something. This essentially amounts to nothing more than a right not to be excluded from something for no reason at all. This is the sort of right someone at the bottom of a hierarchy might have, who has to relinquish his possession of something whenever a superior person had use to make of it. This right has no exclusionary force over others whatsoever.

A second kind of right to use is the first come, first served version, the right to begin using any unoccupied thing and continue using it until one is finished. This sort of right is exclusionary, preventing others from using or interfering with one's use, but it is limited by the nature of the use one can make of it. Where the thing is generally used for a short time or intermittently, like showers or shoe horns, the exclusionary implications might be minimal. On the other hand, in the case of things which are used more or less continuously to be used properly at all, such as a house or flat, or in the case of things the use of which involves their consumption or destruction, as in the case of food or firewood, this right to use has the implication that the first to use is likely to exclude all others forever.

Finally, one might have the right to use whenever one wants. This is the sort of right the person at the head of a hierarchy might enjoy. With this right, all others must stop using a thing whenever the right-holder decides he wishes to make use of it. The exclusionary implications of this right are patent. . . .

Once these versions of the right to use are laid out, however, it is apparent that they can be framed as corresponding versions of rights to exclude having the same normative effect, so long as we remember that these rights are employed in a social setting. If the link between actual use and exclusion is the factual premise that using something characteristically requires that (at least some) others be excluded from it, the link between rights to exclude and use is that all rightful exclusions can be broadly characterized as serving the interest or purpose of putting a thing to use. . . .

The notion of use, however, must encompass those cases where one excludes others for a purpose without "using" a thing in a narrow sense. Holding land as a natural sanctuary for wildlife, or hoarding gold to drive up the price are examples of a broader sense of "use." The sanctuary is a case of a use, a disposition of land, which accords with the owner's cultural or moral or aesthetic sensibilities. The hoarding of gold is a use of it given that there is a market in gold; it is a meaningful disposition of it. It is no more a use than that, but it is as purposeful and sensible a disposition of one's gold as, say, making jewellery out of it.

We do not normally wear all of our clothes at the same time, nor do we sit on all of the furniture, nor occupy all of the rooms of our house at once. Are they, then, not being used? In an obvious sense, they are not. That is the sense in which "use" means active engagement of some kind. But in a perfectly valid other sense, they are. In this broader sense "use" refers to a disposition one can make of something that is purposeful and can be interfered with by others. On the latter definition, use is still engagement with a thing, but it is simply of a longer term in which there is only intermittent physical interaction. Thus, the natural link of the right to exclude with use is simply that rightful exclusion of someone from a thing will always be purposeful, i.e. having some purpose in respect of the use to which the thing will be put. Were it not for its connotation with "getting rid of," "dispose of" would better describe this purposeful engagement with things.

The right to use something so long as no one else was using it or wanted to use it is equivalent to having no right of exclusion whatsoever. The right to use something so long as one got there first is a right to exclude others while one is using something, and the right to use whenever one wants amounts to a right to exclude others whenever one decides to use something. Yet once we have taken a broad view of use, these last two rights can amount to the right to perpetual exclusion. For example, it is certainly a meaningful disposition of land to hold it as a family seat for oneself and the heirs male of one's body, which use could last forever.

How do the right to use and the right to exclude explain the right to property? The right to property is grounded by the interest we have in using things in the broader sense. No one has any interest in merely excluding others from things, for any reason or no reason at all. The interest that underpins the right to property is the interest we have in purposefully dealing with things. Because we have long-term interests in respect of things, and interests in using them in many different ways the broad definition of use is the appropriate one. But because we are concerned with the *right* to property, we must be concerned with the correlative duties imposed on others. Because of the social setting in which we live, and the ways in which the things of this world are typically used, we see that any meaningful right to use is the opposite side of the coin to a right to exclude. Secondly, the right to use reflects our practical interest in exclusively using things, which correlates to duties *in rem* on everyone else not to interfere with our uses of things. Their not using the property is framed in terms of their duties to exclude themselves from it.

Thus at a theoretical level we understand the right to property equally as a right of exclusion or a right of use, since they are opposite sides of the same coin. Yet we can equally see that only one of these ways of looking at the right might drive the analysis in understanding the shape of the property norms in the legal system. It is my contention that the law of property is driven by an analysis which takes the perspective of exclusion, rather than one which elaborates a right to use. In other words, in order to understand property, we must look to the way that the law contours the duties it imposes on people to exclude themselves from the property of others, rather than regarding the law as instituting a series of positive liberties or powers to use particular things. This can be expressed as follows, in what I shall call the *exclusion thesis: the right to property is a right to exclude others from things which is grounded by the interest we have in the use of things.*

On this formulation use serves a justificatory role for the right, while exclusion is seen as the formal essence of the right. It is our interest in the use of property which grounds the right *in rem* to property and the correlative general duty *in rem*; yet exclusion is the practical means by which that interest is protected, and that makes all the difference to our understanding of property. However, treating the exclusionary aspect of the right to property as a "right to exclude" involves a serious misconception which must be cleared up straight away. The essence of the exclusion thesis is that the duty *in rem* imposed on people generally is what provides the contours to the right. Any true right of an owner to exclude others must be understood to be an auxiliary right which enforces or protects the right to property. The right to property itself is the right that correlates to the duty *in rem* that all others have *to exclude themselves* from the property of others. It is a right of exclusion, certainly, but it is not the right physically or by order or otherwise (say by putting up fences) actually to exclude others from one's property. The fact that we may not have the right to throw trespassers off our land, and must call the police to do so instead, does not mean that we do not have a right to the land, but only that our means of effecting the right are circumscribed. The right to exclude is a right *in rem* like the right of bodily security. One may have various auxiliary rights which make the right to one's bodily security effective, like the right of self-defence, but it is not necessary to have those rights to have a right to bodily security. The essence of the right is that people generally have a duty not physically to harm others, including oneself. I shall hereafter employ the term "the right of exclusive use" to refer to what we normally call a "property right," and to refer to the element of right in "having property" in something.

The exclusion thesis is a statement of the driving analysis of property in legal systems. It characterizes property primarily as a protected sphere of indefinite and undefined activity, in which an owner may do anything with the things he owns. The thesis is not a denial of the fact that an owner's use of property may be circumscribed in various ways, for example by planning restrictions on land use, or by speed limits on highways. What it does deny is that the law defines the right to things in terms of a series of well-enumerated and well-understood uses of things to which individuals have a right. Thus Harris, for example, regards as analytic of the institution of private property that there are "trespassory rules" which provide the legal protection for the legally protected interests of ownership,[2] but says of any enumeration of specifically protected uses:

> The possessory owner has a prima facie privilege to do anything in relation to his land which the dominant culture of his society accords to a landowner. The set of privileges entailed is not a total set, because everywhere some things are excluded. It is, however, an open-ended set, since its present content could never be exhaustively listed; and it is a fluctuating set, because cultural assumptions about what an owner may do vary.[3]

Good reasons lie behind this way of shaping the practice of property. It is difficult in the extreme to quantify the many different uses one can make of one's property, so as to give a workable outline of what the "right to use" property actually is. It is more practical to say simply that one has the *right* to dispose of property any way that one wishes, in the broadest terms, *but only in so far as those dispositions are protected by the specific duties on others to exclude themselves from the property.* The *right* to property is that normatively protected part of our interest in using property, and that part, i.e. that fraction of our uses of property, is determined by the extent to which others must exclude themselves from our property. Thus we are provided with the specific contours of the property right over the many different things that can be objects of property. Nothing in the world is naturally of exclusive interest only to the one most closely associated with it. I can take pleasure in your body simply by seeing it, or in your conversation simply by listening. I can similarly appreciate the beauty of your garden sculpture as a passer-by. I can even have an interest (the exact nature of which is interesting) in your not destroying the Poussin which hangs in your hall, even though I may never actually have the chance to see it. There must, therefore, be defined limits to property rights, that is to the owner's exclusive rights to the things he owns. The driving analysis underlying legal property norms defines these contours in terms of the general duties *in rem* that people have not to interfere in the property of others; it does not specify rights to use or dispose of property. Although I may desire to capture all the benefits of my beautiful garden because it resulted from *my* use of *my* property, even those gained by passers-by that look upon it, the law of property will not help me to do so, for there is no duty on those passers-by not to look. The right to property is thus a right to a liberty, the liberty to dispose of the things one owns as one wishes within a general sphere of protection. It is not the right to any particular use, benefit, or result from the use of property. The duty *in rem* of property correlates with the right to a liberty to dispose of property, not to a specific right in the value of property, or a right to any goal one may set on one's use of it, and so on. And . . . the right to property is not a right that others facilitate or ensure that one is able to use a thing in the particular

2. J.W. HARRIS, PROPERTY & JUSTICE 144-5 (1996).
3. *Ibid.*, 160.

way one would wish. In the same way that having the right to drive a car does not mean that the state is obliged to teach would-be drivers to drive or provide all of them with cars, the right to use is not the right to be given materials to build a house on one's land if that is why one bought it. It is a negative liberty.

Treating the notion of exclusion as underlying the driving analysis of property is also supported by the analysis of norms *in rem* . . . If I am right in my analysis of duties *in rem* as correlatives to the more familiar rights *in rem*, then for these duties to be practical they must be relatively simple. They would not be simple in the right way if they referred to various uses that an owner might make of his property. The general injunction to "keep off" or "leave alone" the property that is not one's own defines the practice of property much better than a series of specific duties which work to facilitate particular uses of others' property. The law does not enquire whether, or to what extent, the trespasser or the thief impinged upon the owner's dispositions in respect of the property in question. The duty *in rem* that correlates with the right to property is the negative duty not to interfere with the property of others, i.e. the duty to exclude oneself from the property of others. The concept of exclusion, not use, dominates the legal analysis. . . .

We can now reformulate the right of property, or the right of exclusive use, to take account of the element of alienability: it is the right to determine the use or disposition of a thing in so far as that can be achieved or aided by others excluding themselves from it, and includes the rights to abandon it, to share it, to license it to others (either exclusively or not), and to give it to others in its entirety.

It is clear that, on this definition, no help will be given to one who wishes to extract some moral about distributive justice from property rights *simpliciter*. . . . [P]roperty rights can be the subject of claims in distributive justice, but only because, like other items of value, property rights can be the subject of different kinds of economic transactions, and therefore they get distributed, sometimes justly, sometimes not. Thus it is also my contention, *pace* Waldron, that recognizing the interest we have as individuals in exclusively determining the disposition of things does not lead to the conclusion that there is a certain minimum amount of property we ought to have, at least in so far as this interest is embodied in the idea of property in law, in so far, that is, as it grounds what we recognize as property rights. The right to property is no more a right to subsistence than it is a right to wealth. This is not to say that our interest in things may not ground a right to own some minimum amount of property, but we may remain sceptical; we must always remember that economies operate on all values, not just property; it is not obvious that to provide a decent minimum of value or wealth, a person need have any property at all especially given the extent to which I have emphasized how owners may share the things they own. . . .

The general point is that concerns about the distribution of property, in which an essential minimum or a constitutive kind are to be given some kind of established basis in the idea of property itself, are generally completely swamped by broader considerations of a person's well-being. ... The legitimacy of property rights *per se* strikes me as well nigh indisputable, for the practice of property protects a liberty, i.e. exclusively to determine the use of things, that has proved marvellously productive in contributing to the good life of many. Determining the justice of any distribution of property, on the other hand, should draw our attention to those distributional mechanisms themselves, such as gifts and contracts and commands, all of which distribute a much broader set of goods than property rights.

NOTES AND QUESTIONS

1. *Exclusion and Simplicity*. Penner emphasizes that duties *in rem* must be simple. Thomas Merrill and Henry Smith, whose views were introduced in Chapter 8.2, also focus on simplicity in developing their claim that exclusion is the core of property. Property rights, they argue, must "be defined in such a way that their attributes can be easily understood by a huge number of people of diverse experience and intellectual skill." Defining property around "the simple right of an owner to exclude the world from the resource" indeed provides "the generality, simplicity, and robustness necessary to coordinate basic expectations of large numbers of interacting members of a community." Therefore, the "broad presumption" of the law is and should be "that owners can dispose of property as they wish," and deviations from this presumption are perceived as peripheral to property. Thomas W. Merrill & Henry E. Smith, *The Morality of Property*, 48 Wm. & Mary L. Rev. 1849, 1851-1857, 1867, 1891-1892 (2007). Do you agree that these propositions follow — as both Penner and Merrill and Smith argue — the ordinary understanding of property? Also, does simplicity entail the exclusion thesis? Both Penner and Merrill and Smith base the exclusion thesis on simplicity where this understanding of property is contrasted with property as the bundle of rights. How well does their argument fare if the alternative to exclusion is Dagan's approach to property as institutions, discussed in Chapter 8.1?

2. *Exclusion, Autonomy, Community, and Distributive Justice*. Unlike Merrill and Smith, Penner's main justification to the exclusion thesis is not its reduced communication costs. Rather, Penner celebrates the happy effects of this understanding of property on people's autonomy, and furthermore believes that only property as exclusion facilitates genuine sharing. These propositions run counter to the republican understanding of property, as described by Alexander in Chapter 6 (see also Alexander's discussion of property and responsibility in Chapter 9.2 below). Who do you think has the upper hand in this debate? Also, at the last two paragraphs of our

excerpt Penner takes issue with Waldron's thesis discussed in Chapter 7. Which side to this debate do you find more convincing?

3. *The Meaning of Property.* Penner argues that "use serves a justificatory role for the right, while exclusion is seen as the formal essence of the right." Do you agree that exclusion and use are, as he puts it, "opposite sides of the same coin"? What do you think of his related claim that "[n]o one has any interest in merely excluding others from things, for any reason or no reason at all"? Does this conception of exclusion conform to what most people mean by exclusion?

Penner's understanding of exclusion is significant because it provides, in his view, the coherence to the other incidents of such rights. Thus, he makes three claims as to the entailed meaning of property rights, which deserve your attention. First, and most significantly, unlike other champions of the right to exclude (and many other property theorists as well), Penner argues that the right to sell — as opposed to the right to make a gift — is not part of the right to property. We return to this point in Note 4 of Chapter 15.1 below. Second, Penner also seems to deny the owner's right to destroy. (For the opposite view, see Lior Jacob Strahilevitz, *The Right to Destroy*, 114 YALE L.J. 781 (2005).) Finally, Penner insists that owners do not have any right to prevent others from using and benefitting from their resources as long as these others keep their duty to exclude themselves from the property. (Consider in this respect the implications for intellectual property; *see* Adam Mossoff, *Exclusion and Exclusive Use in Patent Law*, 22 HARV. J.L. & TECH. 321 (2009).)

4. *Exclusion as the Core of Property.* Felix Cohen demonstrated many years ago that every property right involves *some* power to exclude others from doing something.[4] But as Cohen further emphasized, this is a rather modest truism, which hardly yields any practical implications. Private property is also always subject to limitations and obligations, and thus, Cohen claimed, "the real problems we have to deal with are problems of degree, problems too infinitely intricate for simple panacea solutions." Felix S. Cohen, *Dialogue on Private Property*, 9 RUTGERS L. REV. 357, 362, 370-374, 379 (1954). Indeed, the real debate revolves around the claim of authors like Penner and Merrill and Smith that exclusion is the *core* of property.

Because of the kind of limitations and obligations Cohen observed, even some friends of the idea that property is an exclusive right seek an alternative understanding. Larissa Katz, for example, suggests that the defining feature of ownership — its true "link to freedom" — is the owner's exclusive (or at least supreme) "agenda-setting authority." Larissa Katz, *Exclusion and Exclusivity in Property Law*, 58 U. TORONTO L.J. 275 (2008).

---

4. Interestingly, at times owners apply exclusionary strategies that are not based on the formal law of trespass. *See* Lior Jacob Strahilevitz, *Information Asymmetries and the Rights to Exclude*, 104 MICH. L. REV. 1835 (2006); Lior Jacob Strahilevitz, *Exclusionary Amenities in Residential Communities*, 92 VA. L. REV. 437 (2006).

Does this notion of exclusivity better serve as the core of property in the strong sense suggested by Penner and Merrill and Smith? Dagan claims that neither exclusion nor exclusivity can or should play such a role: "Trying to impose a uniform conception of property on [the] diverse property institutions, which enable diverse forms of association and therefore diverse forms of good to flourish, would be unfortunate, because . . . it would undermine the freedom-enhancing pluralism and the individuality-enhancing multiplicity so crucial to the liberal ideal of justice." HANOCH DAGAN, *Exclusion and Inclusion in Property, in* PROPERTY: VALUES AND INSTITUTIONS 37, 43 (2011). Dagan also warns that essentializing exclusion may marginalize the significance of governance and of inclusion to the idea of property. (We discuss these issues in Chapters 12 and 10, respectively.) What are, in your view, the best responses of Penner, Merrill and Smith, and Katz to these claims?

5. *From Exclusion to a Robust Public Domain?* Jedediah Purdy argues that the right to exclude must be understood not (or at least not only) as an abstract construct, but rather (or also) in a historical context. Accordingly, rather than offering a conceptual analysis (as Penner et al. do), he traces the "vision of social order" on which this right rested for its early proponents. For them, Purdy claims, the idea that owners should enjoy robust powers against all the world was premised on an integration of mutually reinforcing values that defined a whole:

> The paramount feature of ownership in this vision was the power to exclude, which in practice meant the power to decline any proffered relationship or joint venture. . . . The exclusion power tied decisions about resource use ineluctably to interest-based persuasion because that, and that only, was the way to win free consent.
>
> The power of transfer . . . played a similarly important part in this image of social life. The alienability of real property, in particular, subjected it to economic risk, meaning that the wastrels, fools, and unfortunates in each generation stood a fair chance of losing what they began with. Conversely, this implied a greater chance for those who began with modest means to acquire the wealth that traditional restraints on alienability could make difficult to pry from a dynastic heir. Alienability meant risk, risk meant circulation, and circulation meant opportunity and social mobility. . . .
>
> The power to determine the uses of one's property, too, facilitated the development of free personality even as it contributed to social wealth. It made ownership a field for initiative and the affirmative expression of autonomy: not just exclusion of others from one's own space but command over the scope and character of activity there. Such command, in contrast to the subordinate's position of receiving orders and seeking favor, was a major training ground of the free personality.

JEDEDIAH PURDY, THE MEANING OF PROPERTY: FREEDOM, COMMUNITY, AND THE LEGAL IMAGINATION 16-18 (2010). Thus conceived, Purdy's suggestions for implementing this social vision in our times are obviously different from the prescriptions advocated by Penner or the other exclusion theorists. Property law, in Purdy's view, should seek to reconcile the three underlying concerns of reciprocity, responsibility, and self-realization. While he admits that there are no simple ways to achieve such reconciliation, he insists that a partial integration is possible, and is furthermore likely to be reformist. An important example for this relates to the debates over the future of intellectual property law (among the other examples he discusses are microfinance, income support, and global climate change). Purdy believes that the tradition of property he reconstructs supports claims of IP reformers that rather than fortifying owners' entitlements, this field should "empower individuals to influence the technological and social structures that they inhabit." *Id.*, at 112, 146. We return to these issues in some detail in Chapter 14.1.

2. OWNERSHIP AND RESPONSIBILITY

Gregory S. Alexander, The Social-Obligation Norm in American Property Law[1]

[P]roperty owners owe far more responsibilities to others, both owners and non-owners, than the conventional imagery of property rights suggests. Property rights are inherently relational; because of this characteristic, owners necessarily owe obligations to others. But the responsibility dimension of private ownership has been sorely under-theorized in American law. The law has relegated the social obligations of owners to the margins, while individual rights, such as the right to exclude, have occupied the center stage.

The purpose of this Article is to change this picture by drawing attention to the social-obligation norm in American property law. . . . I argue that American property law at times and in some places recognizes something like the social-obligation norm I propose here. . . . I do not contend that American property law widely recognizes this social-obligation norm. I do claim, though, that the social-obligation theory explains and justifies some of the most controversial recent judicial decisions, particularly those concerning the right to exclude. . . .

I. THE SOCIAL-OBLIGATION NORM IN CLASSICAL LIBERAL PROPERTY THEORY[2]

Several conceptions of the social-obligation norm exist, but two ideas are especially notable. The first is based on classical liberalism. This conception provides a strikingly thin understanding of the social obligations of private

---

1. Gregory S. Alexander, *The Social-Obligation Norm in American Property Law*, 94 CORNELL L. REV. 745, 747- 748, 753-755, 758-759, 760-770, 801-802, 805-807, 809-810 (2009).
2. Part I draws heavily from Gregory S. Alexander & Eduardo M. Peñalver, *Properties of Community*, 10 THEORETICAL INQUIRIES IN LAW 127 (2009).

ownership. The classical liberal approach is limited to the negative obligation of the Anglo-American common law to avoid committing nuisance. The approach is captured by the *sic utere tuo* maxim and a weak affirmative obligation to contribute to the provision of public goods, such as national defense, law enforcement, and fire protection.

The law-and-economics version of this view explains which affirmative obligations owners owe to their communities on the basis of the familiar problems of free riders and holdouts. Individual owners are obligated to make contributions to the public fisc because voluntary means of financing public goods founder on the shoals of high transaction costs, free riders, and holdouts. What is conspicuously absent from the list of projects to which the individual owner's social-responsibility obligation must contribute is the redistribution of wealth done for the sake of equality of welfare. Eliminating (or nearly so) wealth-redistribution from the scope of legitimate social-responsibility objectives would cast serious doubt on the viability of, for example, the progressive income tax, the Social Security tax, and the unemployment benefits tax. The thin version of the social-obligation norm requires affirmative action of the owner only for the purpose of providing narrowly defined public goods.

The thin conception of the social-obligation norm is not so much wrong as it is radically incomplete and indeterminate. It is descriptively inaccurate, and its descriptive inaccuracy makes it normatively unappealing as well. As Joseph Singer has pointed out, "It is well understood that owners cannot use their property to harm others, but it is not well understood how difficult it is to define what that means."[3] The problem with using the harm principle as the basis for defining the social obligations of ownership is that it misleads owners into believing that William Blackstone's description of ownership as conferring on owners "sole and despotic dominion"[4] over their property is accurate. That description wasn't accurate in Blackstone's time, and it certainly isn't accurate today. Modern property law imposes a wide range of obligations on owners. For example, landlords must act to maintain their buildings in habitable conditions for their tenants, including, perhaps, keeping air conditioning systems in good repair. Owners of residential real estate must disclose to potential buyers the existence of all known defects in the premises, including, according to one view, neighborhood noise problems. Landowners may not construct buildings on their property in a way that interferes with their neighbors' access to sunlight used for solar power. The list of legally imposed obligations on owners continues to grow.

The thin version of the social-obligation norm underlies what [Frank] Michelman calls the "possessive" conception of constitutional property rights. According to the possessive version of the constitutional right of

---

3. Joseph William Singer, Entitlement: The Paradoxes of Property 16 (2000).
4. William Blackstone, 2 Commentaries *2.

property, Michelman states: "[W]e primarily understand property in its constitutional sense as an antiredistributive principle, opposed to governmental interventions into the extant regime of holdings for the sake of distributive ends."[5] As Michelman points out, the social-obligation norm can thicken even under the aegis of this "possessive" conception of constitutional property. Not only does the conception sometimes accept a surprisingly broad range of regulatory measures undertaken to correct "market failures," but it may also tolerate explicitly redistributive acts of the state as necessary health or safety measures.[6] Still, as Michelman notes, on these occasions we are apt to feel (at least to the extent that we are under the influence of thin social-responsibility thinking), even if we do not admit that the regulation has transgressed the boundary between the owner's zone of personal autonomy and the legitimate need of the state to act in the interest of providing public goods.[7] . . .

II.   THE CONTRACTARIAN VERSION OF THE COMMUNITY-BASED SOCIAL-OBLIGATION NORM

The first conception of the social-obligation norm is premised on a social vision that, in the words of Dean Hanoch Dagan, "underplays the significance of belonging to a community, perceives our membership therein in purely instrumental terms, and insists that our mutual obligations as members of such a community should be derived either from our consent or from their being to our advantage."[8]

The second conception of the social-obligation norm is considerably thicker. It picks up where the first conception leaves off, taking the idea of belonging in a community seriously and building on that idea to develop a social-obligation theory that is liberal even while it focuses on community. In recent years, Dagan has most fully developed this contractarian version of the community-based conception of social obligation in a series of important articles. Dagan is committed to the project of normatively developing the social dimension of property law, both in the private and public legal spheres. The basis for any conception of the social-obligation norm is justice. But obviously many theories of justice compete. The theory of justice that underlies the thin, non-community-based conception of the social-obligation norm is classical liberalism, the same theory that underlies approaches to constitutional protection of property such as [Richard] Epstein's, for example.[9] A community-based conception of the

---

5. Frank I. Michelman, *Possession vs. Distribution in the Constitutional Idea of Property*, 72 IOWA L. REV. 1319, 1319 (1987).
   6. *See id.* at 1319-20.
   7. *See id.*
   8. Hanoch Dagan, *Takings and Distributive Justice*, 85 Va. L. Rev. 741, 771-72 (1999). . . .
   9. *See* RICHARD A. EPSTEIN, TAKINGS: PRIVATE PROPERTY AND THE POWER OF EMINENT DOMAIN 331-34 (1985).

social-obligation norm must be based upon a theory of justice that allows a greater capacity for wealth redistribution. Such a conception seems to underlie the approach to constitutional property that Dagan has developed. His approach appears to be based on a theory of justice that is clearly liberal, but not *classically* so, at least not consistently. The fact that it remains firmly tethered to the liberal political tradition is indicated clearly, I believe, by his understanding of community. . . .

From [Dagan's] perspective . . . , communities can only make demands of their members if those demands are likely to pay back each individual in the community in the long, if not the short, run. That is, membership in a community, political or otherwise, does not ever warrant sacrifices by its members that are highly unlikely to remain uncompensated, even in the long run. Uncompensated involuntary sacrifices violate the basic commitment to personal autonomy and the protection of legitimate individual expectations. To expect individuals to make personal sacrifices for the common good is legitimate just insofar as accounts will even up in the long run, that is, so long as reasonable grounds exist to believe that the total long-term burdens that the individual bears will balance out the total long-term benefits she receives.

III HUMAN FLOURISHING AND THE SOCIAL OBLIGATION OF OWNERSHIP[10]

A second conception of community exists that is more robust. . . . [This conception] might. . . . be called "Aristotelian" for it builds on the Aristotelian notion that the human being is a social and political animal and is not self-sufficient alone. The [Aristotelian] conception stresses the fact that although human beings value and strive for autonomy, dependency and interdependency are inherent aspects of the human condition. . . .

At the core of the Aristotelian [conception] is the belief that a distinctively human life exists toward which all of one's capabilities should be directed. Although many different ways of living such a life are apparent, many of these are also bad ways of living. Actions that contribute to living the distinctively human life are right and to be encouraged. Certain dispositions to do such actions — called virtues — are needed to live such a life. The "Aristotelian conception of human beings as social and political animals operates for us as part of a substantive understanding of what it means to live a distinctively human life and to flourish in a characteristically human way."[11]

Any adequate account of human flourishing must stress two characteristics. First, "human beings develop the capacities necessary for a

---

10. Part III draws heavily from Alexander & Peñalver, *supra* note 2.
11. Alexander & Peñalver, *supra* note 2, at 135, 135-36. . . .

well-lived, and distinctly human life only in society with, indeed, dependent upon, other human beings."[12] Living within a particular sort of society, a particular web of social relationships is a necessary condition for humans to develop the distinctively human capacities that allow us to flourish. Language itself—possibly even the capacity to so much as think—is an artifact of community. Community is constitutive of human flourishing in a very deep sense; perhaps community even comprises humanity (as that term is used by many understandings).

The second characteristic of human flourishing that I must note is that human flourishing must at least include the capacity to make meaningful choices among alternative life horizons, to discern the salient differences among them, and to deliberate deeply about what is valuable within those available alternatives. These two characteristics of human flourishing, developing necessary capabilities and decision-making skills, are deeply interconnected. We cannot develop an adequate capacity to discern among multiple available life horizons by ourselves. Such a capability can only be developed through and with others who teach us discernment both directly and by their examples.

The account of human flourishing on which the thicker conception of community adopted in this Article is based borrows from the "capabilities" approach developed in recent years by Martha Nussbaum and Amartya Sen.[13] That approach measures a person's well-being not by looking at what they have, but by looking at what they are able to do. . . . Social structures, including distributions of property rights and the definition of the rights that go along with the ownership of property, should be judged, at least in part, by the degree to which they foster the participation by human beings in . . . valuable patterns of existence and interaction [and contribute to fostering the capabilities essential for human flourishing]. . . . Among the [capabilities] that are necessary for a well-lived life are *life*, including certain subsidiary values such as health; *freedom*, understood as including the freedom to make deliberate choices among alternative life horizons; *practical reasoning*; and *sociality*. . . .

[T]he crucial point for my purposes is that one cannot acquire these capabilities or secure the resources to acquire them by one's self. This is because the physical process of human development mandates our dependence on others for a great deal of the time during which we are cultivating the necessary capacities. . . .

Life, freedom, practical rationality, sociality, and their attendant [subsidiary values] can meaningfully exist only within a vital matrix

---

12. Alexander & Peñalver, *supra* note 2, at 135; *see also id.* at 134-45.

13. *See, e.g.*, Martha C. Nussbaum, Women and Human Development: The Capabilities Approach (2000); Amartya Sen, Commodities and Capabilities (1985) . . . ; Amartya Sen, Development as Freedom (1999) . . . ; Martha C. Nussbaum, The Supreme Court 2006 Term, Foreword, *Constitutions and Capabilities: "Perception" Against Lofty Formalism*, 121 Harv. L. Rev. 4 (2007); Amartya Sen, *Well-Being, Agency and Freedom: The Dewey Lectures 1984*, 82 J. Phil. 169 (1985). . . .

of social structures and practices. Even the most seemingly solitary and socially threatened of these capabilities, freedom, depends upon a richly social, cultural, and institutional context; the free individual must rely upon others to provide this context. . . .

Precisely because capabilities are essential to flourishing in a distinctively human way, development of one's capabilities is an objective human good, something that we ought (insofar as we accept these particular capabilities as intrinsically valuable) to promote as a good in and of itself. As a matter of human dignity, every person is equally entitled to flourish. This being so, every person must be equally entitled to those things essential for human flourishing, i.e., the capabilities that are the foundation of flourishing and the material resources required to nurture those capabilities. In the absence of these capabilities and supporting resources, recognition of the entitlement to flourish is simply an empty gesture. But not every society will be equally conducive to human flourishing. The cultivation of the capabilities necessary for flourishing depends upon social matrices, and the condition of those matrices varies among societies, sometimes quite widely. A society that fosters those . . . capabilities that are necessary for human flourishing is morally better than one that is either indifferent or (even worse) hostile to their manifestation. . . .

If human capacities such as survival (including physical health), the ability to engage in practical reasoning, and to make reasoned decisions about how to live our lives are components of the well-lived life, then surely we are all obligated to support and nurture the social structures without which those human capabilities cannot be developed. Consequently, from the standpoint of the capabilities necessary for human flourishing, how we participate in political and social communities cannot just be an expression of our preexisting autonomy; our participation cannot be solely a volitional act we commit for instrumental reasons such as preference satisfaction. Our participation in community is also an objectively grounded obligation rooted in our recognition of the value of the capabilities that are necessary for the well-lived life. . . .

. . . The major claim here, in short, is that our (and others') dependence creates, for us (and for them), an obligation to participate in and support the social networks and structures that enable us to develop those human capabilities that make human flourishing possible. . . .

3. The Right to Exclude: Beach Access and Other Controversies

[A] controversial set of recent decisions that one can better explain in terms of social-obligation theory concerns the right to exclude. The right to exclude has never been absolute, of course, but judicial decisions over the past few decades have significantly whittled away at its breadth. One of the most controversial contexts in which this narrowing has occurred is public access to beaches. Although courts have provided the public access to beaches on various doctrinal grounds, the most important—and controversial—of these has been the public trust doctrine.

The controversy surrounding the public trust doctrine has gained steam in recent years as some courts have used it to extend public access to beaches, including privately-owned dry-sand portions of beachfront property, concomitantly reducing the scope of the right to exclude. . . .

A human flourishing-focused social-obligation theorist might attempt to justify the expansion of public access to privately-owned beaches on the basis of the following scenario. Imagine that you are a single parent living in a public housing project in Camden, New Jersey. It is August, and your non-air-conditioned apartment is sweltering. You and your five-year-old daughter would very much like to spend the day at the beach. You take the bus (you have no car) on the long ride to the stop on the New Jersey shore nearest your home. The beach there is privately owned, and the nearest public beach is several miles away, inaccessible by public transportation. The beach in front of you is beautiful. It is also empty because the owner works in New York City and visits his beach home only sporadically. You might try to trespass and perhaps get away with it, but reluctantly (and much to the chagrin of your hot and cranky daughter) you choose to obey the law and take the long bus ride back to Camden.

This is not an invariable scenario for poor city-dwellers, of course. Some of them, at least, can reach public beaches. What the story does illustrate is the subtle and sometimes not-so-subtle ways in which access to recreation is limited or simply unavailable for poor people. Recreation is not a luxury but a necessity, especially for the poor. It is an important aspect of the capabilities of both life and affiliation. With respect to life as a good, ample and growing medical evidence indicates that recreation and relaxation contribute importantly to good health, reducing the risk of diseases ranging from depression to heart disease. Yet some of the very groups who need recreation the most do not, as a practical matter, have access to it. This includes women and especially single mothers. It is no coincidence that the frustrated would-be beachgoer in my story was a single parent. Single mothers are notorious self-sacrificers, literally jeopardizing their health for the sake of their children. I do not suggest that public access to privately-owned beaches is the magic elixir to improve the health of young single mothers. I do suggest, however, that recreation is an important aspect of health, which is itself a vital dimension of the capability of life, and that providing all persons, including poor people, with reasonable access to basic modes of recreation and relaxation would materially contribute to the goal of being capable of living lives worth living.

Recreation also supports affiliation as a good. As a good, affiliation encompasses subsidiary goods such as friendship and social participation. Indeed, affiliation, or sociability, as it might also be called, may explain, or partly explain, many of the circumstances in which courts have recognized some version of a reasonable access rule that limits the common law right to exclude. Affiliation includes the ability "to recognize and show concern for other human beings, to engage in various forms of social interaction; [and] to be able to imagine the situation of another."[14] Affiliation is the indispensable means through which communities create just social relations. By teaching us how to be concerned for others, how to show that concern, and how to place ourselves in their shoes, communities inculcate in us values of equal dignity, equality, respect, and justice, as well as individual autonomy.

No one has written more eloquently about the role of recreation in creating healthy social relationships than Carol Rose. In her justly celebrated article *The Comedy of the Commons*, Rose, paraphrasing the great nineteenth-century landscape designer Frederick Law Olmsted, wrote:

> [R]ecreation can be a socializing and educative influence, particularly helpful for democratic values. Thus rich and poor would mingle in parks, and learn to treat each other as neighbors. Parks would enhance public mental health, with ultimate benefits to sociability; all could revive from the antisocial characteristics of urban life under the refining influence of the park's soothing landscape.[15]

Substitute "beach" for "park," and the point is the same. Rose goes on to point out that these socializing benefits can be maximized only if recreation is "open to all at minimal costs, or at costs . . . borne by the general public, since all of us benefit from the greater sociability of our fellow citizens."[16] As Rose concludes, "[T]his value should not be 'held up' by private owners."[17]

Under the traditional law on beach access, sociability was indeed "held up" by private citizens. Public beaches and parks do exist, of course, but in many parts of the country, they are few and far between. Access to them is often difficult or impractical for the urban poor, the very people who in some ways need recreation the most.

We live in a society characterized by conditions of increasing congestion and social interdependency. The social-obligation theory recognizes that those very conditions, especially our interdependency, create for all property owners an obligation to contribute, in ways that are appropriate to them, to the vitality of the community's material infrastructure that facilitate the cultivation of affiliation, among other essential human capabilities. For private beach owners, this obligation may include providing members of the general public with reasonable access to portions of their beach, depending upon various circumstances. . . . This obligation is not

---

14. Martha Nussbaum, *Human Rights and Human Capabilities*, 20 HARV. HUM. RTS. J. 21, 23 (2007).

15. Carol Rose, *The Comedy of the Commons: Custom, Commerce, and Inherently Public Property*, 53 U. CHI. L. REV. 711, 779 (1986). . . . [The article from which this quote is taken is excerpted in Chapter 12 *infra*. — EDS.]

16. *Id.* at 780.

17. *Id.*

open-ended. Under the social-obligation theory, the issue in beach-access cases is whether the landowner's obligation to contribute to the vitality of capabilities-nurturing aspects of her community includes sharing with members of the general public access to her land, at least at certain times and under certain circumstances. If members of the public wish to use private beach property for recreational purposes and have reasonable means of gaining access to a public beach, as will frequently (perhaps usually) be the case, the owner's right to exclude is preserved. . . .

The question we should ask in these cases is whether the owner's general obligation to contribute to the human flourishing of others includes a specific obligation to promote affiliation by providing some sort of reasonable public access to her land. The answers to that question will not come easily or uniformly. Whether public access to some form of land will promote affiliation in a significant way will not always be clear, warranting even some limited form of public access under the public trust doctrine. Small wonder, then, that courts . . . have struggled to develop some sort of metric by which they may cabin the reasonable access rule and identify its scope of operation. The need to nurture affiliation will not always justify public access. But surely, as social conditions change and make affiliation more difficult, the good of affiliation will justify some version of a reasonable access rule in some circumstances where public access to privately-owned land is sought for recreational purposes.

NOTES AND QUESTIONS

1. *Theoretical Foundations of the Public Right of Beach Access.* Do you agree that private beach owners may, under certain circumstances, owe members of the public an obligation to provide access to their beach property? If you do, do you agree that the strongest theoretical basis for that obligation is the commitment to support those human capabilities necessary to human flourishing? Consider the other conceptions of the social obligation norm described in Note 3 below. Do you think that proponents of those other versions of the social responsibility norm are likely to object to the reasonable-access doctrine? If not, how would their conceptions of the social obligation norm justify the doctrine?

2. *A Right to Roam?* Should the public have a right to roam over privately owned wilderness or similar sorts of undeveloped land? Such a right now exists in England and Wales under the Countryside and Rights of Way Act 2000, ch. 37, and in Scotland under the Land Reform (Scotland) Act 2003. The English statute requires owners of "open land" (defined as land containing mountains, moors, heaths, or downland) to permit members of the public to freely roam across it. This right is qualified in several respects, such as limiting access to foot traffic, prohibiting any commercial activity or camping, swimming, fishing, or hunting. The right does not

apply to cultivated areas, land covered by buildings, garden land, or golf courses. *See* Kevin Gray & Susan Gray, Elements of Land Law 1372 (5th ed. 2009). The Scottish right of access is much broader. It applies to a much greater percentage of the total amount of land in Scotland than its English-Welsh counterpart, including settled suburban land as well as wilderness. Second, the uses that the Scottish statute permits are broader than those allowed under its English counterpart. They include, for example, commercial or for-profit activities so long as these activities are educational or meant to further understanding natural or cultural heritage. Finally, landowners are required to exercise "responsible land management," including not unreasonably interfering with the public right of access. For a good comparison between the two statutory rights, see John A. Lovett, *Progressive Property in Action: The Land Reform (Scotland) Act 2003*, 89 Neb. L. Rev. 301 (2011). Does Alexander's social obligation theory justify either version of a right to roam? What human capabilities might this right implicate?

3. *The Social Obligation Theory and Takings Law.* Another illustration of his theory that Alexander discusses involves the well-known takings case, Penn Central Transportation Co. v. City of New York, 438 U.S. 104 (1978). In that case, the U.S. Supreme Court upheld a denial by the New York City Landmarks Preservation Commission of Penn Central Transportation Co., owners of the famous Grand Central Terminal with its renowned nineteenth-century Beaux Arts era façade, permission to develop the airspace above the terminal for commercial purposes. The owners claimed that the denial amounted to a taking of their property (the air space) without compensation, in violation of the U.S. Constitution's Just Compensation Clause. The Court offered several reasons for its decision, including the fact that the denial did not interfere with the owners' "investment-backed expectations" and that the governmental action still permitted the owners to gain a reasonable return on their investment.

Alexander considers the case in terms of the need to "maintain the kind of culture that enables the development of those [personal] qualities without which no individual can experience meaningful freedom or practice personal responsibility. . . ." Alexander, *supra*, at 149. Alexander argues that maintaining unique architectural sites is necessary for the existence of that type of culture and that the owners of such sites owe the communities within which such sites are located obligations that would not be imposed on owners of ordinary buildings. Hence, the denial of permission to develop Grand Central Terminal, part of New York City's cultural patrimony, without compensation results in no constitutional violation because of the social obligation that is inherent in ownership of that building. Is it likely that as a result of the Grand Central Terminal owners' heavy holdings of other real estate in the vicinity, the owners benefit in the long run directly and proportionately from other public actions by the city? If so, should these benefits be treated as reciprocal to the costs they incurred as a result of the Landmark Preservation Commission's decision? Is this long-term reciprocity theory a more persuasive basis for the decision in *Penn Central* than Alexander's theory? *See* Hanoch Dagan, *Takings and Distributive Justice*, 85 Va. L. Rev. 741 (1999), discussed in Note 5 *infra*.

4. *Other Responsibility-Focused Theories.* Other scholars have also recently developed responsibility-focused approaches to property. Joseph Singer argues that property is a system that is replete with tensions. These tensions exist because ownership involves both granting rights and imposing obligations. This dual aspect of ownership means, Singer says, that inherent in legal property regimes are unavoidable conflicts among different values and that the resolution of these value conflicts depends on some underlying vision of the type of society one wishes to create. Ultimately, according to Singer, because property is a system and not just an entitlement, we all have responsibilities to define property rights in a manner compatible with a free and democratic society, including interests in relatively equal distribution of property and limitations on the power associated with concentrations of property ownership. Singer's theory leads him to support, for example, restrictions on the right to exclude such as recognized by the New Jersey Supreme Court in State v. Shack, 277 A.2d 369 (N.J. 1971), where the court held that a farm owner who employed migrant farm workers did not have the right to exclude from his property government-funded legal and medical service providers who came to assist farmworkers who were housed on the property. *See* Joseph William Singer, Entitlement: The Paradoxes of Property (2000); Joseph William Singer, The Edges of the Field: Lessons on the Obligations of Ownership (2000).

Eric Freyfogle has written extensively about the responsibilities of ownership of land and other natural resources. Freyfogle emphasizes the differences between natural and non-natural resources, particularly the point that all parts of nature are ecologically interconnected. For natural systems to flourish, Freyfogle argues, nature's parts need to fit together and operate as functioning wholes. This leads him to the view that private property rights in nature are permissible only to the extent that the recognition of such rights promotes the common good. He departs from more conventional utilitarian property theorists by arguing that, rather than scrutinizing private ownership generally and testing its legitimacy only once, we should ask, on a right-by-right basis, whether each element of ownership is socially justified. For example, farmland owners owe the community a responsibility not to use their land in ways that erode or degrade topsoil, and their ownership interests should not be understood to include that particular right. Similarly, land owners owe their communities responsibilities not to fill in ecologically significant wetlands or to build on fragile barrier islands, and they should not have the legal rights, as owners, to do so. *See* Eric T. Freyfogle, On Private Property: Finding Common Ground on the

OWNERSHIP OF LAND 131-156 (2007); ERIC T. FREYFOGLE, THE LAND WE SHARE (2003).

Similar to Freyfogle in some respects, Kevin and Susan Gray argue that in a modern environment land ownership can no longer be understood in simple rights terms. Rather, private ownership of land comes infused with a notion of civic responsibility. They state, "Once conceived as a variable aggregation of socially-permitted land uses, property in land comes to consist, not so much in a *fact* or a *right*, but rather a state-directed *responsibility* to contribute toward the ultimate exploitation of all land resources for communal benefit." Kevin Gray & Susan Francis Gray, *The Idea of Property in Land, in* LAND LAW: THEMES AND PERSPECTIVES 15, 40 (Susan Bright & John Dewar eds., 1998).

Along the same lines, David Lametti argues that the dominant bundle-of-rights conception of ownership, discussed in Chapter 8.1, mistakenly hides the responsibilities that are inherent in ownership. Arguing that the nature of ownership varies with the nature of the object in question, Lametti suggests replacing the rights-centered definition of ownership with a definition that focuses attention on the nature of the object in question. David Lametti, *The Concept of Property: Relations Through Objects of Social Wealth*, 53 U. TORONTO L.J. 325 (2003). Can you see how different resources, or objects, would (or might) involve different owner responsibilities? Do you agree with Lametti that the bundle-of-rights conception of ownership hides this point?

More recently, Eduardo Peñalver, in his article *Land Virtues*, 94 CORNELL L. REV. 821 (2009), draws on the Aristotelian tradition of virtue ethics and argues that the principal function of property law is to foster human flourishing. The law accomplishes this both by protecting entitlements and by encouraging, and at times even coercing, owners to meet their obligations to others, particularly the poor, the socially powerless, and future generations, who are not capable of meeting their own needs through market transactions.

5. *Rival Conceptions of Responsibility: Reciprocity or Sacrifice?* Alexander's conception of social responsibility involves sacrifices by the owner. Other conceptions of responsibility, however, do not. For example, in the context of takings law, Hanoch Dagan, who agrees with Alexander that social responsibility is "a constitutive component of the concept of ownership," Dagan, *Takings and Distributive Justice, supra* Note 3, at 772, argues in favor of a conception of social responsibility as long-term reciprocity. *See, e.g., ibid.* Under this conception, a government agency need not pay a property owner compensation for effects of regulatory actions on her property

if, and only if, the disproportionate burden of the public action in question is not overly extreme and is offset, or is likely in all probability to be offset, by benefits of similar magnitude to the landowner's current injury that she gains from other — past, present, or future — public actions (which harm neighboring properties).

Id. at 769-770. Dagan urges this conception over a "naïve version of the social-responsibility [norm that] may lead to the systematic exploitation of weak property owners and to a cynical abuse of social solidarity, subverting the very aims that the social responsibility ideal intends to further." Hanoch Dagan, *The Social Responsibility of Ownership*, 92 CORNELL L. REV. 1255, 1262 (2007). Do you agree with Dagan that Alexander's version of the social responsibility norm is naïve and subject to cynical abuse by powerful interest groups?

6. *Relationships Between Conceptions of the Social Obligation Norm and Basic Normative Theories.* How do these various conceptions of social responsibility relate to some of the basic normative theories explored in Part I of this book? For example, the relationship between Alexander's conception of the social responsibility norm and citizenship is straightforward. Alexander's theory is quite compatible not only with civic republicanism's emphasis on the common good and the notion that property serves the common good but also with its particular understanding of the common good, which may at times require self-sacrifice. Freyfogle's theory would also appear to be consistent with the notion that property must serve the common good. What might Freyfogle say about self-sacrifice for the common good? Does Dagan agree that property must serve the common good? Does he agree that at times self-sacrifice may be required to serve the common good? What might the other writers on responsibility say about citizenship and the common good? Consider other basic moral values, such as freedom and personhood. Think about the implications of the various versions of the social responsibility norm for those values. What are the implications, for example, of Singer's theory for freedom, first as Nozick defines it and then as Singer himself might define it? And, given its focus on *social* responsibility, does a theory like Alexander's overlook (or even undermine) personhood interests?

7. *Structure vs. Substance.* Does Alexander's account suggest that a fixed level of social responsibility should apply across all the various contexts of interpersonal relationships (family, market interactions, friendships, etc.)? If it does, it is structurally monistic and in this respect (and ironically) similar to Blackstone's theory, although substantively, of course, it is very different from it. Compare it with Dagan's structurally pluralistic theory, discussed in Chapter 8.1. *See also* HANOCH DAGAN, *From Independence and Interdependence to the Pluralism of Property, in* PROPERTY: VALUES AND INSTITUTIONS 57 (2011).

10 EXIT AND ENTRY

Leslie Green, Rights of Exit[1]

I. LOVE IT OR LEAVE IT

Social groups claim authority to impose restrictions on their members that the state cannot. Churches, ethnic groups, minority nations, universities, social clubs, and families all regulate belief and behavior in ways that would be obviously unjust in the context of a state and its citizens. All religions impose doctrinal requirements; many also enforce sexist practices and customs. Some universities impose stringent speech and conduct codes on their students and faculty. . . . Those who complain about such internal restrictions on the liberties of members might well be told to "love it or leave it."

Such terms of association would be extortionate if applied to a whole political society. A violation of civil liberties does not become tolerable just because citizens may emigrate. . . . In a free and democratic society, the basic liberties are to be respected, and the right to emigrate is no compensation if they are not.

Why then should smaller social groups be any different? Here, even liberals are inclined to admit that people should, in effect, either love the groups of which they are members or leave them. For example, John Rawls suggests that "particular associations may be freely organized as their members wish, and they may have their own internal life and discipline subject to the restriction that their members have a real choice of whether to continue their affiliation."[2] This may seem obvious. If associations are indeed organized "as their members wish" then how can there be any

---

1. Leslie Green, *Rights of Exit*, 4 LEGAL THEORY 165, 165-167, 170-172, 174-180, 184-185 (1998).
2. JOHN RAWLS, A THEORY OF JUSTICE 212 (1971)

further question about the proper scope of their authority over those members? Indeed, why even require that the members have a "real choice" about whether to remain in the group? Chandran Kukathas suggests that "Cultural communities should . . . be looked on this way: as associations of individuals whose freedom to live according to communal practices each finds acceptable is of fundamental importance."[3] However, the test of acceptability *to each* is extraordinarily exigent. Most cultural communities seek to impose an internal discipline on their members without regard to whether it is approved by each and every one.

The right of exit would be otiose if each member enjoyed a veto against the group. But that strikes squarely at the source of the problem. Few if any of the familiar social groups give individual members a veto over their ways — perhaps no group of any scope or significance could even survive on those terms. No doubt this is why Kukathas is tempted to relax the test and require only acceptability to a majority of the group. . . . This suggests something rather different: a two-stage process according to which the rights of individuals within the group are determined by communal practice while the legitimacy of communal practice is determined by majority rule. This is a pleasantly democratic view of things. Few social groups or cultural communities operate according to majority rule. Universities, churches, professional associations all typically claim legitimacy on other grounds.

So the problem is this: What we call "the wishes of the members" may at best amount to no more than the wishes of a majority of members, or, more typically, even just the wishes of the most powerful members, or the oldest members, that is to say, the wishes of a subgroup sanctioned by some familiar basis of social authority as having the right to speak for the whole. That reality helps explain why there must be what Rawls calls a real choice of whether to continue affiliation. . . .

. . . The hard question is whether such a right of exit is enough to protect internal dissidents. — a person who oppses official policy

In this article I test and reject that idea. I argue that insofar as individual autonomy is the value that grounds rights of exit, this very same consideration also grounds a family of related rights, and thus social groups do not in justice enjoy unlimited sovereignty over their members, not even when the members are perfectly free to leave. Hence, the familiar contrast between the liberties appropriate under a democratic government and those appropriate in special social groups is exaggerated. . . .

III. Entry and Exit

The view just described holds that, as free and purposive associations, particular social groups are entitled to wider control over their members

---

3. Chandran Kukathas, *Are There Any Cultural Rights* in The Rights of Minority Cultures 238 (Will Kymlicka ed., 1995).

provided always that they respect their rights of exit. Clearly, if people were compelled to belong to a group, then we would be less likely to exempt it from the obligation to respect the ordinary principles of political morality. The right to exit is obviously playing a critical role in this reasoning; we need to explore it in more detail.

It is often supposed, especially by those who have in mind the model of a perfectly competitive market, that exit is an unproblematic concept. Albert Hirschman, for example, believes that what he calls "voice" — remaining within a group and striving for change — is a more difficult concept, because trying to change a state of affairs is more complex and difficult than merely leaving it.[4] Voice is a matter of strategy and gradation; exit is an on-off, either-or decision. In fact, however, things are not this simple. The spatial metaphor of an exit has clearest application to territorially bounded groups. To exit the state is to leave its territory and . . . when one permanently crosses the border, that is it. But what does it mean to leave a religion or a nation — to say nothing of an ethnic group or a sexual orientation? In these cases, too, we find kinds, or at least degrees, of belonging and alienation. . . .

The relevant sense of exit is that of *voluntarily* leaving the effective jurisdiction of the group. In the case of groups with a territorial jurisdiction, that means leaving the territory. A group's jurisdiction is given by the scope of the norms that regulate the belief or behavior of its members. What it purports to regulate, and what it in fact does regulate, may, of course, vary, as may the effectiveness of its norms. . . . It seems reasonable to suppose, then, that people must be free to leave not only the *de jure* but also the *de facto* jurisdiction of a group.

What is the point of exit? First and most obviously, it has a protective function. If the group harms the interests of the member as the member sees them, then leaving is a form of self-defense. Of course, it would be wrong to suppose that the protective function is effective only when exit is actually exercised. The possibility of exit may itself make the group responsive to the interests of its members. Second, exit may also have an expressive function, for it is commonly held that leaving is a way to criticize the group, while remaining is to support it. This point is often exaggerated and misunderstood. . . .

. . . [I]t is unlikely that refusal to leave can normally be taken as any kind of *agreement* to obey. Voluntary obligations are belief-dependent: No one agrees unless he believes that he does. But most people do not believe that failure to exit means that they have agreed to obey. Moreover, the option of remaining must be a reasonable one, and as Hume noted, the vast majority of people simply have no choice but to stay out: The costs of uprooting are usually insurmountable and, often enough, no other state

---

4. Albert O. Hirschman, Exit, Voice, and Loyalty: Responses to Decline in Firms, Organizations, and States 15-16, 30 (1970).

will take them in. Is the idea of grounding the authority of groups in tacit consent any more plausible here than it is in the case of political obligation?

It is as difficult to leave many social groups as it is to leave the state, and in some cases it is even impossible. Consider, to begin, that exit from many groups involves taking along a lot of baggage. There are, in the first place, the ordinary consequences of socialization. Those groups that are most important in human life are precisely those in which the mechanical notions of "entry" and "exit" seem less helpful in understanding how people come to be members than do the organic notions of growth and development. For example, save for adult converts, most religious people inherit their faith. . . . They grow up in a family or school with religious outlooks and values that they internalize and adapt. This produces a whole set of profound effects, including—sometimes—the feeling that one is so intimately bound up with the fate of one's religion that it is almost a part of one's personal identity. Abandoning this is so unlike the process of entering or leaving the market for a car or a health club that any similarities seem overwhelmed by the differences. . . .

IV.   AUTONOMY AND EXIT

What then is the relationship between the right of exit and the internal constitution of groups? According to Kukathas, the only fundamental right is that of freedom of association: Provided exit is guaranteed, cultural communities should be free to do with their members as they wish. . . .

. . . Allowing, as we should, that the rights of exit are necessary, is it correct to suppose that they exhaust the fundamental rights of individuals against groups?

There are three powerful reasons to doubt this. First, as I have argued in the previous section, the bare existence of a right of exit does not establish that particular groups are free associations. . . .

There is a second reason to doubt the supremacy and sufficiency of associative freedom. The argument depends on the supposition that if cultural communities *were* free in the relevant sense, then their norms would necessarily command respect or tolerance because of the respect due to agreements or choices. However, it is not plausible to suppose that agreement has unlimited power. Agreements create, vary, and extinguish rights and duties only because there are good reasons to endorse the power-conferring rule that they may do so. But the underlying reasons do not go so far as to validate *every* purported exercise of the power in question. . . .

. . . [For example,] Locke conceded, surprisingly for his time, that there is a right to exit from marriage, at least where it is not prohibited by civil law. Yet he also denied that the marriage contract could ever give husbands despotic power over their wives: The considerations that ground the right to divorce also ground rights to fair treatment during the duration of the marriage.[5] These examples [] illustrate the typical limits to the scope of our normative powers. Similarly, there is no reason to suppose that even willingly created associations have unlimited authority over their members, and that in turn suggests that at least some other rights are as fundamental as the right of exit.

The third reason for doubting the thesis flows from the nature of exit rights themselves. What is the justification for requiring groups to respect a right of exit? It may enhance social stability and perhaps utility by ensuring that only those who are committed to the ways of the group remain. Neither of these, however, would warrant imposing exit as a *necessary* condition of the authority of groups, since either of them might be qualified in any number of circumstances. . . .

Underneath the idea that no one can be required to accept a particular way of life lies, I think, the familiar notion of personal autonomy. The fundamental reason for thinking exit necessary is to fulfill the protective and expressive functions that enhance the capacity for a self-directed life, including the capacity to form, revise, and pursue our ends. Exit is necessary, not for stability, utility, or even tolerance, but to secure individual autonomy. The interest in self-direction is so important and central that it warrants holding others duty-bound to respect it. . . .

If that is correct, however, it also follows that the right of exit is an insufficient safeguard for justice within groups. First, there are conditions necessary for the right of exit to be effective, and these generate further rights. Second, the value of individual autonomy that underlies the right to exit is itself powerful enough to generate other rights independently of any instrumental connection with exit. The following rights can, I think, all be established in the following ways.

A. Freedom of Dissociation

This is the claim right that others not prevent one from leaving the jurisdiction of the group. It is the core right of exit. Because people may be prevented in a variety of ways from leaving, this will in turn give rise to a variety of further rights. . . .

B. Right to Mobility

. . . .

---

5. John Locke, Two Treatises of Government II, ss.80-83 (P. Laslett ed., 1988). . . .

C. *Freedom of Expression*

. . . .

D. *Freedom of [Internal] Association*

. . . .

E. *Fair Share of Common Resources*

People may be prevented from leaving without being forbidden to leave. For example, they may be unjustly deprived of the necessary resources, and this too violates their rights of exit. This is not to say that a church, family, or university must enforce for itself the same principles of distributive justice that are appropriate to a whole society. Rather, it is that it must respect principles of justice in dissolution, conditioned by the legitimate expectations of the members. If there are exit taxes, these must not be punitive. What may be taken on departure will depend on the nature of the goods in question and the understandings of the community. . . . The issue is most difficult in the case of those who leave communal arrangements to which they contributed part of the joint product. It may often be that the product (arable land, buildings, etc.) is indivisible or immovable, and it may be difficult to apportion a proper share to each; but that need not preclude some form of compensation.

I believe it plausible that rights to dissociate, to mobility, to free expression, to freedom of association, and to a fair share of common resources required by any conception of the right to exit are at least necessary to relieve the burden of internal restrictions. Perhaps there are other rights, too. The general point is this: The character and generality of the interest in autonomy means that the duties it is capable of generating cannot be confined to the right of exit. . . .

Hence, certain internal restrictions must be regarded as illegitimate by anyone who endorses the right of exit. And we must therefore reject the view that this right has any special priority over other familiar civil rights. Exit rights are based on a fundamental interest in individual autonomy. That interest both on its own and through various instrumental connections with exit yields a cluster of related rights, all of which are to be respected as much by social groups as by the state. . . .

VI.   THE AUTONOMY OF GROUPS

. . . [T]here is no denying that there are costs to respecting the right of exit. As we have seen, it is but one of a cluster of rights that serve autonomy and, whatever we choose to call it, a "real," "meaningful," or "substantive" right of exit will burden some groups in ways that they would rather avoid. There is also a cost that arises merely from the availability of a right of exit, whether or not it is exercised. The modern world has been a maelstrom of change, but there are other worlds with other values. Certain cultures, including (some say) the aboriginal peoples of North America and Australasia, appear not to place much value on individual autonomy, perhaps because in their more stable social environments they did not need it. . . .

We need to be cautious in supposing that the burden of choice is a uniquely modern phenomenon. In every society people make choices about family and kinship; they make decisions about how to interact with neighboring clans, and there is often some fluidity to group membership. What is surely true, however, is that the scope and significance of these choices have dramatically increased, perhaps nowhere as much as in those pre-industrial cultures and fundamentalist religions that have persisted into the modern era. Choice is an intrusion in such groups. . . . Quite apart from that, however, the right of exit itself works to make certain kinds of group life harder to sustain. An unreflective attachment in which interests of the self and group are not distinguished becomes nearly impossible, and with it at least some forms of communitarian and identity politics. . . .

Joseph William Singer, Entitlement: The Paradoxes of Property[6]

THE RIGHT OF EXCLUSION VERSUS THE RIGHT OF ACCESS

. . . [P]roperty rights are not the only rights protected by the legal system, and nonproperty-based rights sometimes trump property rights.

Consider the right to exclude nonowners from one's property. The Supreme Court has noted that the "power to exclude has traditionally been considered one of the most treasured strands in an owner's bundle of property rights."[7] In many ways, the power that owners have over their property derives from their legally delegated power to call on the aid of the state to exclude nonowners. Any legal rule that limits the owner's right to exclude therefore bears a heavy burden of justification. Or does it?

Think about a shopping center. Can it exclude customers on the basis of race? Of course not. The law prohibits businesses open to the public from discriminating on the basis of race. In addition, federal and state laws now prohibit such businesses from discriminating on the bases of religion, national origin, or disability. Many states prohibit discrimination in such facilities on the basis of sex — although no federal law does so. It is now firmly established that owners who serve the public — such as malls,

---

6. JOSEPH WILLIAM SINGER, ENTITLEMENT: THE PARADOXES OF PROPERTY 39-44 (2000).
7. Loretto v. Teleprompter Manhattan CATV Corp., 458 U.S. 419, 435 (1982). . . .

restaurants, motels, and theaters—have an obligation to allow access to their property and to do business with customers without invidious discrimination. Public accommodation laws are supplemented by other anti-discrimination statutes, such as those requiring business to allow tenants and employees to enter their property even if the owner of the business wishes to exclude them or refuse to deal with them.

Public accommodation laws fit awkwardly with the conventional conception of ownership. The usual statement of the common law is that most owners have the right to exclude nonowners unless that right is limited by a civil rights statute. In this view, the right to exclude is presumptively absolute, and the statutorily created right of equal access to public accommodations is a limited and narrow exception to the basic principle. The traditional formulation of the problem places all property rights on one side, with owners, and suggests that nonowners have a right of access to others' property only in exceptional circumstances. On one side of the dispute is a property claim and on the other side is an equality claim. In this formulation, civil rights laws appear to limit property rights.

This way of conceptualizing the problem ignores the fact that public accommodations laws not only limit the property rights of the owner but *transfer* one of those rights to nonowners. Public accommodations laws grant members of the public a limited right of access to businesses open to the public. The owner's right to exclude is limited by a competing public right of access to the property. A right of access to property possessed by another is a property right. In fact, we have a name for such a right: it is called an *easement.* The most common easement is a right of way for passage, as in a road over another's land. Although we do not ordinarily see public accommodations laws as granting property rights to the public, there is no logical or historical reason to view them as doing anything less.

In *Nollan v. California Coastal Commission*[8] the Supreme Court . . . held that requiring the owner to grant the public the easement . . . was an unconstitutional taking of property from the beachfront owner. A public accommodations law similarly takes away a portion of the owner's right to exclude and creates a public easement of access. In so doing, it takes part of the owner's preexisting property rights and grants countervailing property rights to the public.

I do not mean to argue that we should start talking about the right of access to public accommodations as a property right rather than an equality right, and I certainly do not mean to argue that such laws unconstitutionally take property rights. It may be rhetorically more powerful to use the language of equality than to use the language of property to talk about public accommodation laws. But if we consider the social function of property and ownership, it is crucial to recognize that public accommodations laws dictate significant—even revolutionary—transfers of property rights

8. 483 U.S. 825 (1987).

from business owners to the public and from white persons as a class to African Americans as a class, as well as to other racial and ethnic groups who were historically victimized by discriminatory practices, including Asian Americans, Latinos, Jews, and American Indians.

Public accommodations laws therefore divide ownership rights between store owners and the public. An action that would formerly have constituted a trespass now becomes a privileged entry onto land possessed by another. The tension between the right of exclusion and the right of access relates not only to the question of when a nonowner can enter property possessed by another but also to the question of when an owner can lawfully refuse to transfer her property rights. Public accommodations laws not only grant members of the public a right to enter stores; they also grant a right to purchase goods and services. The owner of an appliance store cannot refuse to sell a refrigerator to a customer because she speaks English with a Mexican accent. A landlord who wants to keep Jews from renting in her building cannot do so legally. An employer who wishes to hire only members of her own race is disempowered from doing so. In all these cases the law requires the owner to engage in a transaction that has the effect to forcibly transferring property rights from the owner to the nonowner.

Property cannot exist as a dynamic social institution if there is no ability to acquire property. If one cannot obtain access to a store in order to purchase property, one cannot become an owner. If an owner can refuse to deal on the basis of race, then the ability of members of that race to become owners has been limited. The Supreme Court has recognized this dilemma in its interpretation of the Civil Rights Act of 1866. That act grants all persons the same rights to contract and to purchase property "as is enjoyed by white citizens."[9] Contracts of sale made between white persons and African Americans became legally enforceable, and testimony about such agreements had to be admitted in court regardless of the race of the claimant — both huge changes from Antebellum law. But the 1866 statute was not originally interpreted as *requiring* owners of public accommodations to contract with customers regardless of their race. In 1986, in *Jones v. Alfred Mayer Co.,*[10] the Supreme Court overturned this long-standing interpretation when it held that the rights to contract and to purchase property enshrined in the Civil Rights Act of 1866 outlawed racially motivated refusals to engage in business dealings. The right to contract and to purchase property, for the first time, meant a correlative duty of private owners not to refuse to sell merely because of the potential buyer's race.

The result of the *Jones* opinion was to acknowledge a fundamental tension within the concepts and social institutions of contract and property. Under one view, ownership entails the right to choose when and to whom

9. 42 U.S.C. §§1981-1982.
10. 392 U.S. 409 (1968).

to sell property, as well as the right to exclude nonowners from one's property. This view suggests that it constitutes a limitation on property rights when the owner of a store who wishes to exclude a customer on the ground of race is forced to admit the customer, or when her right to choose whether and to whom to sell her property is curtailed by law. Under a competing interpretation, however, property rights are only respected if one has the power to acquire property. To do so, the marketplace must be open for anyone to enter and to conduct business. One who is systematically excluded from much of the marketplace has limited opportunities to acquire property. Civil rights laws promote the free flow of property without regards to race, religion, or sex. But to do so they must impose obligations on business owners to deal with anyone who comes through the door.

Allegiance to a system of private property does not automatically entail acceptance of one viewpoint or the other. The ownership idea may appear to favor the position that the one who owns property should have the right to exclude. In this view, ownership must be limited to achieve equal access to property without regards to race, sex, religion, or other irrelevant factors. But the ownership idea also suggests that non-owners are entitled to become owners and that it is unfair to exclude them from doing so by pernicious discriminatory practices. In this alternative view, the refusal to sell because of race denies property rights to the customer; the right to purchase property requires limiting the exclusionary conduct of the store owner. Choosing between these constructions of property entails making judgments about appropriate forms of social life, and the choice is *internal* to the property system.

The conflict between exclusion and access . . . entails a tension — between an absolute right to exclude and the right of access to property to make purchases, obtain employment and housing, and thereby become part of the property system. Public accommodations laws do not represent a wholesale destruction of the right to exclude. In fact, businesses open to the public generally retain the right to exclude individuals who are not there to transact business or who are disruptive or destructive. They therefore draw a line between the store owner's legitimate exclusionary interests and the public's legitimate interests in access.

Public accommodations laws divide property rights in another way, as well. They distinguish between types of property, such as private homes, where rights of exclusion prevail, and types of property open to the public, such as restaurants, motels, and retail stores, where rights of access prevail. Property is not all of a kind; the social context in which the property operates and the types of uses prevalent there affect the assignment of legal rights and obligations.

The idea that property should be open to the public without regard to race cannot reasonably be considered a minor limitation on property rights. Rather, public accommodations laws constitute a revolution in the understanding of ownership and the relation between property and equality. . . .

The idea that property should be open to public without regard to race is wholly foreign to the understanding of the right of exclusion that prevailed in much of the United States before the 1960's. The rights of property owners no longer encompass the right to exclude people from public accommodations on the basis of race. Rather, the general presumption, both in law and in common understanding, is now that owners who use their property to conduct business thereby waive some portion of their property rights, making the property available for public access without regard to race. The effect of this principle is to transfer a large stick in the bundle of property rights from the owner to the public at large. Home owners, on the other hand, retain their right to exclude, as long as they are not renting or selling their property. They are free to act in a racially discriminatory manner in deciding whom to invite into their homes.

One might say that the difference between a home and a business is that the home owners have significant privacy interests in excluding non-owners from their property, while business owners express more limited privacy interests by issuing a general invitation to the public to enter their property for business purposes. Therefore in the home we allow owners to discriminate on the basis of race. Storekeepers, restaurant owners, employers, and landlords, however, are obligated to make their property available without regard to race. In the home, privacy interests outweigh equality interests, whereas in public accommodations, equality interest trumps privacy interests.

Because privacy norms may conflict with equality norms, we identify the types of property where one set of norms prevails over the other. Yet it is an oversimplification and a distortion to declare that property rights prevail in the home and equality rights in places of business. In both cases there is a conflict between two property rights: the right of access and the right to exclude. The owners of private homes retain a general right to exclude nonowners from their premises; the right to exclude prevails over the right of access. However, once an owner opens her property to the public for business purposes, the law requires the property to remain for the public uses to which she has dedicated it; the right of access prevails over the right to exclude.

The rules governing the property system not only must protect the interests of those who already own property, but also must establish legitimate conditions under which nonowners can acquire property rights. The owner of a store that wishes to exclude customers on the basis of race claims a right both to exclude customers from the land and to refuse to sell goods or services to customers as the owner wishes. The customers who claim a right of access seek a right to enter the property as well as a right to purchase goods or services offered to the public. Just as the right to exclude clashes with the right to have access, so the right to purchase property clashes with the right to refuse to sell. The balance between these competing claims is different in the context of the store and the home. Equality norms, as well as privacy and associational norms, all affect how the balance is drawn and which right takes precedence. But in the end we are presented with a conflict among sticks within the property bundle. The tension is not between property rights and equality rights; the tension is *within* our idea of property itself.

NOTES AND QUESTIONS

1. *Exit, Efficiency, and Autonomy.* The concepts of exit and voice were introduced to the literature by Albert Hirschman in his seminal book *Exit, Voice, and Loyalty: Responses to Decline in Firms, Organizations, and States* (1970). As both Hirschman's subtitle and Green's discussion imply, Hirschman discussed these concepts as ideal type ways in which members of organizations could respond to decisions or actions of the organization in order to optimize their performance. Green argues that in addition to this instrumental value of exit, there is also an intrinsic value that is founded on autonomy. Michael Walzer similarly claimed that the commitment to geographical, social, familial, and political mobility is one of the defining features of liberalism. *See* Michael Walzer, *The Communitarian Critique of Liberalism*, 18 Pol. Theory 6, 11-12, 15-16, 21 (1990). As a matter of positive law, this commitment typifies liberal legal regimes and is, for example, an important justification for property law's typical suspicion of restraints on alienation.

2. *Exit's Harms and Costs.* Green is aware of the costs of exit, but is confident that the commitment to exit is nonetheless justified. Eduardo Peñalver is more worried about exit's effects. He encourages us "to reject the notion of the ideal community as one that is freely chosen and just as easily abandoned," and to favor in its stead "a richer, stickier notion of community, one capable of satisfying the human need for stable companionship and sociability." Property law should thus help "tying individuals more closely to their respective social groups," and one of the best ways for doing so is by "[r]aising the cost of exit for individuals." And indeed, "property as entrance" — Peñalver's preferred conception of property — "views the institution of private property as a means of reinforcing community life, by permitting individuals to expose themselves more fully to the values of the particular community in which the property is situated." Facilitating exit, he claims, is detrimental to this goal because it hinders "the ability of communities to employ property as a tool for creating diverse patterns of life." Eduardo M. Peñalver, *Property as Entrance*, 91 Va. L. Rev. 1889, 1894. 1940, 1942-1944, 1962 (2005). Which side of this debate do you favor?

3. *Other Manifestations of the Right to Access.* Most of Singer's discussion revolves around public accommodations. But the right to access — or the

right to entry, as we call it in this chapter—has other manifestations as well. One set of important examples was discussed in Chapter 9.2. Another example, which Singer also mentions, is the prohibition of discrimination in the sale or rental of residential dwellings, which is now prescribed by the Fair Housing Act, 42 U.S.C. §3601. The Act followed the landmark case of *Shelley v. Kraemer*, 344 U.S. 1 (1948), in which the U.S. Supreme Court held that judicial enforcement of racially restrictive covenants is an exercise of state action that violates the Fourteenth Amendment. Carol Rose described *Shelley* as posing "a state action enigma" since the bare potential of judicial enforcement of private arrangements and preferences does not transform them, according to established doctrine, into state action. Rose suggests that this puzzle can be solved by referring to the welfarist commitment of property law to minimize negative externalities on third parties who may not share the preferences of the existing transactors. Carol Rose, *Shelley v. Kraemer, in* Property Stories 169 (Gerald Korngold & Andrew P. Morriss eds., 2004). What do you think of this argument? Can other property values, discussed in Part I of this book, similarly (or better?) justify *Shelley*? If so, should the Supreme Court have declined to intervene due to the institutional concerns highlighted by Merrill and Smith's account in Chapter 8.2?

4. *Entry and the Values of Property.* Singer argues that the right to access is "*internal* to our idea of property itself." He further explains how this right derives from the values of mobility and privacy, which in their turn are aspects of the property values of liberty, personhood, and community discussed in Part I. Hanoch Dagan similarly argues that the right to entry (or to be included) derives from the same values that justify the right to exclude: "Exclusion and exclusivity are typical of many property institutions because *and to the extent that* they serve the property values underlying these institutions." Recall that Dagan distinguishes among property institutions according to their characteristic balance of property values. Hence, "claims by potential entrants" in contexts like public accommodations, fair housing, or fair use of copyrighted works "derive from the pertinent property values" that underlie the pertinent property institutions, "and are thus intrinsic to property rather than external limitations or impositions. Property turns out to be about both exclusion and inclusion. In their different domains, the right to exclude and the right to entry can peacefully cohabit under the heterogeneous, though not formless, umbrella of property." Hanoch Dagan, *Exclusion and Inclusion in Property, in* Property: Values and Institutions 37, 55 (2011). Are these propositions too rosy? What is the likely response of Penner, Merrill and Smith, or Katz, whose views we have discussed in Chapter 9.1?

5. *Exit and Entry.* There are important similarities between the two concepts—exit and entry—discussed in this chapter. Limiting entry, by allowing groups autonomously to determine their own, divergent membership requirements, may serve the same commitment to pluralism and

multiplicity, which Peñalver invokes as the justification for allowing limitations on exit; it can also—as Singer and Dagan insist—raise similar normative concerns. Notice also that exit and entry, or the limitations thereon, may reinforce each other. Severe limits on entry in the form of sweeping restrictions of alienability may be practically tantamount to a substantial limitation on exit. By the same token, the right to entry is almost meaningless for people who do not enjoy free exit. But it is not obvious that the commitments to exit and entry always go hand in hand. Think, for example, about the degree to which each concept fits the market mode of economic organization: Exit is natural to markets, as Hirschman already emphasized. What about entry? In what sense is entry necessary for markets to work? Also, imagine a dialogue between Green and Singer. What, if any, are their likely points of disagreement?

11

FOREGROUND vs. BACKGROUND: LAW OR SOCIAL NORMS

Robert C. Ellickson, Order without Law[1]

BEYOND LEGAL CENTRALISM: A CRITIQUE OF LAW-AND-ECONOMICS THEORY

Law-and-economics scholars and other legal instrumentalists have tended to underappreciate the role that nonlegal systems play in achieving social order. Their articles are full of law-centered discussions of conflicts—such as cattle-trespass disputes between farmer and ranchers—whose resolution is in fact largely beyond the influence of governmental rules. There are, of course, notable exceptions. Law-and-economics stalwarts such as Harold Demsetz and Richard Posner have understood that property rights may evolve in primitive societies without the involvement of a visible sovereign. Several economists have emphasized that promises can enforce express contracts without the help of the state. Nonetheless, many scholars who work in law and economics still seem to regard the state as dominant, perhaps even exclusive, controller.

THE LEGAL-CENTRALIST TRADITION

Oliver Williamson has used the phrase *legal centralism* to describe the belief that governments are the chief sources of rules and enforcement efforts. The quintessential legal centralist was Thomas Hobbes, who thought that in

---

1. ROBERT C. ELLICKSON, ORDER WITHOUT LAW: HOW NEIGHBORS SETTLE DISPUTES 137-147 (1991).

a society without a sovereign, all would be chaos. Without a Leviathan one would observe, in Hobbes's memorable words:

> . . . continual feare, and danger of violent death; And the life of man, solitary, poore, nasty, brutish, and short. . . . To this warre of every man against every man, this is also consequent; that nothing can be Unjust. The notions of Right and Wrong, Justice and Injustice have no place. Where there is no common Power, there is no Law; where no Law, no Injustice. . . . It is consequent also to the same condition, that there be no Propriety, no Dominion, no *Mine* and *Thine* distinct; but only that to be every mans that he can get; and for so long, as he can keep it. . . .[2]

Hobbes apparently saw no possibility that some nonlegal system of social control — such as the decentralized enforcement of norms — might bring about at least a modicum of order even under conditions of anarchy. (The term *anarchy* is used here in its root sense of a lack of government, rather than in its colloquial sense of a state of disorder. Only a legal centralist would equate the two).

The seminal works in law and economics hew to the Hobbesian tradition of legal centralism. Ronald Coase's work is an interesting example. Throughout his scholarly career, Coase has emphasized the capacity of individuals to work out mutually advantageous arrangements without the aid of a central coordinator. Yet in his famous article "The Problem of Social Cost," Coase fell into a line of analysis that was wholly in the Hobbesian tradition. In analyzing the effect the changes in law might have on human interactions, Coase implicitly assumed that governments have a monopoly on rulemaking functions. In a representative passage Coase wrote: "It is always possible to modify by transactions on the market the initial *legal* delimitation of rights. And, of course, if such market transactions are costless, such a rearrangement of rights will always take place if it would lead to an increase in the value of production."[3] . . . Even in the parts of his article where he took transaction costs into account, Coase failed to note that in some contexts initial rights might arise from norms generated through decentralized social processes, rather than from law.

In another of the classic works in law and economics, Guido Calabresi and A. Douglas Melamed similarly regarded "the state" as the sole source of social order:

> The first issue which must be faced by any legal system is one we call the problem of "entitlement." Whenever a state is presented with the conflicting interests of two or more people, or two or more groups of people, it must decide which side to favor. Absent such decision, access to goods, services, and life itself will be decided on the basis of "might makes right" — whoever is stronger or shrewder will win. Hence the fundamental thing that the law does is to decide which of the conflicting parties will be entitled to prevail. . . .

2. Thomas Hobbes, Leviathan 97-98 (Oxford Univ. ed., 1909). . . .
3. Ronald H. Coase, *The Problem of Social Cost*, 3 J.L. & Econ. 1, 15 (1960). . . .

Having made its initial choice, society must enforce that choice. Simply setting the entitlement does not avoid the problem of "might makes right"; a minimum of state intervention is always necessary. Our conventional notions make this easy to comprehend with respect to private property. If Taney owns a cabbage patch and Marshall, who is bigger, wants a cabbage, he will get it unless the state intervenes. . . .[4]

In these passages Calabresi and Melamed lapsed into an extreme legal centralism that denied the possibility that controllers other than "the state" could generate and enforce entitlements.

Economists have hardly been alone in exaggerating the state's role in making and enforcing rules of order. For example, Max Weber and Roscoe Pound both seemingly endorsed the dubious propositions that the state has, and should have, a monopoly on the use of violent force. In fact, as both those scholars recognized elsewhere in their writings, operative rules in human societies often authorize forceful private responses to provocative conduct.[5]

Perhaps because legal centralists overrate the role of law, they seem unduly prone to assume that actors know and honor legal rules. Economists know that information is costly, and a growing number emphasize that humans have cognitive limitations. Yet in making assessments of the instrumental value of alternative legal approaches, respected law-and-economics scholars have assumed that driver and pedestrians are fully aware of the substance of personal-injury law; that when purchasing a home appliance whose use may injure bystanders, consumers know enough products liability law to be able to assess the significance of a manufacturer's warranty provision that disclaims liability to bystanders, and that people who set fires fully understand the rules of causation that courts apply when two fires, one natural and the other man-made, conjoin and do damage.

SOME EVIDENCE THAT REFUTES LEGAL CENTRALISM

As suggested already, many of the Shasta County findings cannot be squared with legal centralism. When adjoining landowners there decide to split the costs of boundary fences, they typically reach their solutions in total ignorance of their substantive legal rights. When resolving cattle-trespass disputes, virtually all rural residents apply a norm that an animal owner is responsible for the behavior of his livestock — even in situations

---

4. Guido Calabresi & A. Douglas Melamed, *Property Rules, Liability Rules, and Inalienability: One View of the Cathedral*, 85 HARV. L. REV. 1089, 1090-91 (1972).

5. Weber regarded the state as the supreme instrument of social control: ". . . [T]he modern state is a compulsory association which organizes domination. It has been successful in seeking to monopolize the legitimate use of physical force as a means of domination within a territory. . . . The right to use physical force is ascribed to other institutions or to individuals only to the extent to which the state permits it." MAX WEBER, ESSAYS ON SOCIOLOGY (H. Gerth & C. Wright trans. 1958). In reality, no state has been able to prevent other controllers from using violence to enforce rules of behavior. . . .

where they know that a cattleman would not be legally liable for trespass damages. Although governmental rules and processes are often important in the resolution of disputes arising out of highway collisions between vehicles and livestock, most Shasta County residents badly misperceive the substantive law that applies to road accidents. Empiricists who have examined other social contexts have come up with analogous findings.

Substantive norms often supplant substantive laws. Law-and-society scholars have long known that in many contexts people look primarily to norms, not to law, to determine substantive entitlements. In a path-breaking study published in 1963, Stewart Macaulay found that norms of fair dealing constrained the behavior of Wisconsin business firms as much as substantive legal rules did.[6] . . .

John Phillip Reid has described how norms brought about order in a virtually Hobbesian environment. In the mid-nineteenth century thousands of pioneers took the Overland Trail from Missouri to the West. Particularly in the mid-1840s, the situation on the trail was nearly anarchic; the identity of the national sovereign over much of the territory was disputed, and no government had law-enforcement agents in the area. According to Reid, travelers on the Overland Trail nonetheless demonstrated a strong respect for conventional norms of property. Those who lacked vital goods typically felt constrained to buy, not to take, what they needed from others.[7]

Laboratory evidence also casts doubt on legal centralism. Elizabeth Hoffman and Matthew Spitzer fortuitously discovered the importance of substantive norms during their laboratory experiments on the dynamics of Coasean bargaining. In an early experiment Hoffman and Spitzer endowed their laboratory-game players with unequal initial monetary entitlements. The game rules allowed the players to negotiate contracts that would increase their joint monetary proceeds from the game. The contracts could include provisions for side payments. Hoffman and Sptizer expected to observe only Pareto superior contracts — that is, ones under which no party to the contract would come out monetarily worse off. In the two-person games, most players (especially those who knew that they would play against each other at least twice) were instead inclined to split equally the gross proceeds from a game, even when an equal split was Pareto inferior for one of them. Intrigued by this result, Hoffman and Spitzer conducted another experiment from which they concluded that a set of informal norms — what they called "Lockean ethics" — helped govern when players were prone to equalize the gross proceeds. In short, Hoffman and

6. Stewart Macaulay, *Non-Contractual Relations in Business: A Preliminary Study*, 28 Am. Soc. Rev. 55 (1963).

7. John Phillip Reid, Law for the Elephant: Property and Social Behavior in the Overland Trail 339-40 (1980).

Spitzer tried to be sovereigns but found that norms (or conceivably personal ethics) often trumped their initial distributions of property rights.[8]

The pervasiveness of self-help enforcement. Legal centralists regard governments as the chief enforcers of entitlements. [But there are] four other enforcement possibilities: self-sanction, personal self-help, vicarious self-help, and organization enforcement. . . . [S]elf-help is rife in Shasta County. Ranchers who refuse to mind their cattle or to bear a proper share of boundary-fence costs risk the sting of negative gossip or some other relatively gentle form of neighbor retaliation, and rural residents are eventually willing to resort to violent self-help against the trespassing livestock of ranchers who have been repeatedly unmindful.

These finding also fit comfortably with what field researches have found elsewhere. Sociologists have long been aware of the important role of gossip and ostracism. Donald Black, who has gathered cross-cultural evidence on violent self-help, has asserted that much of what is ordinarily classified as crime is in fact retaliatory action aimed at achieving social control.

Social scientists working outside of sociology increasingly appreciate the importance of self-help. Albert Hirschman has analyzed how people use the options of "exit," "voice," and "loyalty" to influence others around them. Robert Axelrod has explored the game-theoretic strategy of Tit-for-Tat, a system of measured self-help that a person in a continuing relationship can use to induce cooperation from the other person in the relationship.[9]

The law itself explicitly authorizes self-help in many situations. Both tort and criminal law, for example, authorized a threatened person to use reasonable force to repel an assailant. The legal-centralist assertion that the state monopolizes, or even aspires to monopolize, the use of force is patently false.

The scantiness of legal knowledge. Ordinary people know little of the private substantive law applicable to decisions in everyday life. Motorists may possibly learn that the failure to wear a seat belt is a misdemeanor, but only personal-injury lawyers are likely to know whether the tort law of their state makes an injured motorist's failure to wear a seat belt a defense in a civil action. First-year law students may complain that what they are encountering is boring, but never that it is old hat.

Surveys of popular knowledge of law relevant to ordinary household transactions, such as the leasing of housing or the purchase of consumer goods, invariably show that respondents have scant working knowledge

8. Elizabeth Hoffman & Matthew Spitzer, *The Coase Theorem: Some Experimental Tests*, 25 J.L. & Econ. 73 (1982).

9. Robert Axelrod, The Evolution of Cooperation (1984).

of private law. For example, when interviewers asked some three hundred Austin households thirty yes-or-no questions about Texas civil law, "high income Anglos" answered correctly an average of nineteen out of thirty, and "low-income Mexicans" thirteen out of thirty (a performance worse than chance). Another survey revealed that solid majority of Texas patients in psychotherapy did not know that they were protected by a legal privilege of nondisclosure, perhaps because "[f]or 96% of the patients the therapist's ethics, not the state of the law, provided assurances of confidentiality." . . .

Highly educated specialists might be expected to have a somewhat better grasp of the private-law rules that impinge on their professional practices. Givelber, Bowers, and Blitch conducted a national survey of nearly three thousand therapists to measure knowledge of the California Supreme Court's 1975 *Tarasoff* decision that dealt with the tort duties of therapists when their patients have uttered threats against third parties. They found that although 96 percent of California therapists and 87 percent of therapists in other states knew of the *Tarasoff* decision by name, the great majority wrongly construed it as imposing an absolute duty to warn, rather than a duty to warn only when a warning would be the reasonable response under the circumstances. Many of the therapists were (understandably) confused about whether a California Supreme Court decision could impose duties on therapists in other states. Lest law professors be too quick to gloat, they should ask themselves how well they would perform if closely quizzed about their possible civil liabilities for photocopying copyrighted works for inclusion in class materials.

The infrequent use of attorneys to resolve disputes.   A person ignorant of legal rules can get help from an attorney. Yet even in the allegedly litigious United States, individuals who have nonbusiness problems are highly unlikely to turn to attorneys either to amplify their legal knowledge or to help pursue a claim. In Barbara Curran's nationwide sample of adults, one third had never used an attorney, and almost another third had used an attorney only once. What prompts someone to take the unusual step of consulting an attorney in a nonbusiness context? Curran found that the most common impetus was not an interpersonal dispute but rather the transfer of property — that is, buying real estate, or planning or settling an estate. A solid majority of American adults apparently go through their lives without ever hiring an attorney to help resolve a nonspousal dispute. One of Curran's other survey results may help explain this finding. When asked to appraise the statement "Most lawyers charge more for their services than they are worth," 68 percent of the respondents replied that they agreed with it.

The Civil Liability Research Project (CLRP) is the most ambitious empirical study of dispute-resolution practices in the United States. The CLRP researchers have found that Americans are not reluctant to submit claims for compensation to other parties who they perceive have seriously wronged them. Of these claims, 68 percent result in the payment of some sort of compensation to the claimant. Yet the CLRP data indicate that, even when a claim for over $1000 has been initially rejected, a claimant will employ an attorney to help resolve the dispute in only 10 to 20 percent of cases. If personal-injury and alimony disputes were to be excluded from the sample, the frequency of attorney use would be much lower still.

In short, most people know little private law and are not much bothered by their ignorance. Their experience tells them that the basic rules that govern ordinary interpersonal affairs are not in the law books anyway. This reality need not dispirit scholars who are inclined to use economic analysis to study social order. By shedding the legal-centralist tradition, law-and-economics scholars could make their work more relevant than it has been. By realistically applying game theory, transaction-cost economics, and similar tools, they may well be capable of developing a robust theory of the division of social control labor that is the envy of other social scientists.

NOTES AND QUESTIONS

1. *What Are Norms?* The term *norms* is not self-defining. Elsewhere in his book Ellickson observes that "[n]orm denotes both behavior that *is normal*, and behavior that people *should* mimic to avoid being punished." ELLICKSON, *supra*, at 126. Richard McAdams tells us that most legal scholars use the term *norms* to "refer[] to informal social regularities that individuals feel obligated to follow because of an internalized sense of duty, because of a fear of external non-legal sanctions, or both." Richard H. McAdams, *The Origin, Development, and Regulation of Norms*, 96 MICH. L. REV. 338, 340 (1997). Elsewhere, McAdams and Eric Rasmussen usefully distinguish norms from conventions, which they define as "behavioral regularities that lack such normative attitudes." Richard H. McAdams & Eric B. Rasmussen, *Norms in Law and Economics, in* 2 HANDBOOK OF LAW AND ECONOMICS 1573, 1576 (A. Mitchell Polinsky & Steven Shavell eds., 2005). Legal analysts who study the role of norms exclude conventions from the behavioral phenomena under investigation.

2. *Law, Legal Centralism, and Social Facts.* Ellickson's claim is distinct from the familiar, and rather uncontroversial, claim that law should take account of the social facts pertinent to its intended context of application, in that he argues that quite often law is far less important than the social norms governing these contexts. Indeed, the most provocative aspect of his book *Order without Law*, which is excerpted above, is the relative insignificance of the law of property insofar as disputes in Shasta County are concerned. Norms of neighborliness, rather than formal legal prescriptions, Ellickson argues, determine people's behavior and their expectations from each other.

Ellickson describes legal centralism as the dominant paradigm in the legal academy. (It has become less dominant since the publication of his book, though.) But as he acknowledges, legal centralism was not unchallenged. The most celebrated critique of the twentieth century came from Stewart Macaulay's inquiry of *Non-Contractual Relations in Business*, which Ellickson cites (in footnote 6). As Macaulay claimed, "contract law at best stand[s] at the margin of important long-term continuing business relations," which invoke a set of informal, but highly effective "non-legal sanctions" that render contract and contract law unnecessary. Stewart Macaulay, *An Empirical View of Contract*, 1985 Wis. L. Rev. 465, 467. The same idea of "legal peripheralism" was introduced many years earlier by Underhill Moore, when he argued that "most responses which are thought of as responses to propositions of law . . . actually are responses to stimulus situations which do not include any proposition of law," and that when law fails to follow custom, custom modifies law. *See* Underhill Moore, *My Philosophy of Law, in* My Philosophy of Law: Credos of Sixteen American Scholars 203, 216 (1941). Given that law may, at least to some extent, affect people's preferences, can we really be sure — in cases of such convergence — that law had no effect on the emerging equilibrium?

3. *Order Without Power?* On its face, a grassroots nonlegal regime seems preferable to a legal regime, because it does not rely on the coercive power of the state. But is the former categorically distinct from the latter? Louis Jaffe argues that it isn't: Legal permissions and delegations — using custom or usage as a source of law, granting power to property-holders and promisees, as well as respecting internal decisions of various forms of association — allow specific segments of society to determine "the substance of economic and social arrangement." The fact that this power is covert — that it is obscured by the legal rhetoric of permissions or delegations — should not shield participation in law-making by private groups from an analysis of what it is: a form of law-making. Louis L. Jaffe, *Law Making by Private Groups*, 51 Harv. L. Rev. 212 (1937). *See also* Omri Yadlin, *A Public Choice Approach to Private Ordering*, 98 Mich. L. Rev. 2620 (2000).

4. *Voluntary Cooperation Without Law.* Ellickson's overall message is that the coercive state mechanisms are oftentimes unnecessary in order to produce and sustain peaceable cooperation, which is of course crucial to any viable property regime. For this proposition he cites, among others, Robert Axelrod's famous demonstration that people may cooperate even with prisoner's dilemma incentives. Axelrod defines the Tit-for-Tat cooperative strategy to require "avoidance of unnecessary conflict by cooperating as long as the other player does, provocability in the face of an uncalled for defection by the other, forgiveness after responding to a provocation, and clarity of behavior so that the other player can adapt to your pattern of action." As Axelrod explains, this happy result "requires that the players have a large enough chance of meeting again and that they do not discount the significance of their next meeting too greatly." Robert

Axelrod, The Evolution of Cooperation 20, 174 (1984). The ability to remember and retaliate makes noncooperative moves individually counterproductive, and thus may induce self-interested cooperation, even in a commons. *Id.* at 126-132. But notice that this happy result may collapse in a repeated interaction with a finite ending. Do you understand why? *See* R. Duncan Luce & Howard Raiffa, Games and Decisions 94-102 (1957) (when each participant knows that others will defect on their last move a domino effect is created, so defection becomes the dominant strategy for everyone from the outset). And how does a strong right of exit for each member of the pertinent group affect the likelihood of such voluntary cooperation? *See* Notes 2 & 3 in Chapter 12 below.

5.   *The Limitations of Norms.* Ellickson is a norm-optimist. As he later acknowledged, however, not all legal scholars are sanguine about the contributions of norms analysis to legal theory. Thus, Robert Scott argues that "[t]he introduction of non-falsifiable hypotheses produces an analysis that is rich in content but also speculative and context-dependent." Robert E. Scott, *The Limits of Behavioral Theories of Law and Social Norms*, 86 Va. L. Rev. 1603, 1607-1608 (2000). Other norm-pessimists focus less on the methodological limitations of norm analysis than on its results. Eric Posner, for example, argues that norms are prone to inefficiency owing to pervasive information problems and strategic behavior. *See* Eric Posner, *Law, Economics, and Inefficient Norms*, 144 U. Pa. L. Rev. 1697, 1711-1725 (1996). In what ways do you think norms might be more susceptible to inefficient strategic behavior than legal rules? Ellickson contends that such pessimism reflects less disagreement with norm-optimists "about the nature of norm-making than about the likelihood that government officials can outperform norm-makers." Robert C. Ellickson, *The Evolution of Social Norms: A Perspective from the Legal Academy*, in Social Norms 35, 54 (Michael Hechter & Karl-Dieter Opps eds., 2001). Do you agree with that assessment?

6.   *The Complex Interaction of Law and Social Norms.* The empirical observation Ellickson and others make—that in daily matters law is often ignored—is indeed a truism. But does it mean that law has no role to play in these contexts? Austin Sarat and Thomas Kearns argue that legal peripheralists, such as Macaulay and Ellickson, do not pay enough attention to the extent to which the sheer *availability* of the law may be significant, so that working out arrangements in the shadow of the law is very different from doing so in the total absence of law. Thus, they argue that contract law makes possible reliance on agreements and negotiations that are not explicitly or formally legal. Similarly, Sarat and Kearns suggest that the ways of good neighborliness on which Ellickson focuses might well prevail because both parties know that "if things got ugly" there are clear (and comforting) limits to what either side could gain. Where law functions in this way at the background of the parties' relationship, it is in fact quite effective even when rarely invoked and when agreed-on outcomes are

rarely what the law itself would have prescribed. *See* Austin Sarat & Thomas R. Kearns, *Beyond the Great Divide: Forms of Legal Scholarship in Everyday Life, in* LAW IN EVERYDAY LIFE 21, 45, 47 (Austin Sarat & Thomas R. Kearns eds., 1993). For a review of Ellickson's book, which claims that his ethnography of cattle trespass supports this understanding of law's role as an effective background set of norms, see Barbara Yngvesson, *Beastly Neighbors: Continuing Relations in Cattle Country*, 102 YALE L.J. 1787 (1993).

Suggesting that social norms hardly ever totally supplant the law does not mean that legal rules always, necessarily, and only, take the form of protective background as Sarat and Kearns seem to suggest. Law may interact with social norms in other ways as well, notably on the expressive level. The literature on this matter is divided, with some authors arguing that law tends to crowd out internal motivations making legal intervention potentially backfire, and with others emphasizing the positive effects of law in validating the acceptability of its prescriptions and thus further entrenching them in the relevant population. *See* Yuval Feldman & Tom R. Tyler, *Mandated Justice: The Potential Promise and Possible Pitfalls of Mandating Procedural Justice in the Workplace*, 2012 REGULATION & GOVERNANCE ___ (forthcoming).

7.   *When Law and Norms Conflict: The Case of Custom.* In some instances norms and legal rules conflict with each other. When that occurs in the context of a legal dispute, which should the court apply, the norm or the legal rule? It might seem that at least where both of the parties are members of the same group subject to the norm, the court should apply the norm, but is that necessarily true? Consider the case of custom, itself a form of norms. A well-known debate over the role of custom in law pits famous names like Savigny, Blackstone, and Hayek (pro-norm) against the equally famous Bentham, Austin, and Maine (pro-law). In thinking about when custom should apply and when it should not, what factors seem especially relevant? Should it matter, for example, that the custom in question is one that varies according to community, even though both of the litigants at hand are members of the same group? *See* Henry E. Smith, *Community and Custom in Property*, 10 THEORETICAL INQ. L. 1 (2009) (developing an information-cost theory of custom). Moreover, some of the customs may be normatively unacceptable for the remainder of the society. For example, although the California Gold Rush miners developed apparently efficient norms that eventually became part of California's general mining laws, some of those norms were discriminatory and unconstitutional by today's standards. *See generally* Gavin Wright & Karen Clay, *Order Without Law: Property Rights during the California Gold Rush*, 42 EXPLORATIONS ECON. HIST. 155, 169 (2005). For a balanced analysis of the proper role of custom in intellectual property law, see Jennifer E. Rothman, *Custom, The Common Law, and Intellectual Property, in* INTELLECTUAL PROPERTY AND THE COMMON LAW ___ (Shyam Balganesh ed., forthcoming 2012).

12

COMMON AND PUBLIC PROPERTY

Carol Rose, The Comedy of the Commons: Custom, Commerce, and Inherently Public Property[1]

The right to exclude others has often been cited as the most important characteristic of private property. . . . [E]xclusive private property is thought to foster the well-being of the community, giving its members a medium in which resources are used, conserved and exchanged to their greatest advantage. . . .

[margin note: Right to exclude]

The obverse of this coin is the "tragedy of the commons." When things are left open to the public, they are thought to be wasted by overuse or under-use. No one wishes to invest in something that may be taken from him tomorrow, and no one knows whom to approach to make exchanges. All resort to snatching up what is available for "capture" today, leaving behind a wasteland. From this perspective, "public property" is an oxymoron: things left open to the public are not property at all, but rather its antithesis.

[margin note: downfalls common prop]

Thus it is peculiar to find a longstanding notion of "public property" in the law of the western world. The Romans, whose legal thinking greatly influenced later European law, were sufficiently interested in "public property" to separate it into at least four categories. And despite the power of the classical economic argument for private property, a curious cross-current has continually washed through American law. Our legal doctrine has strongly suggested that some kinds of property should not be held exclusively in private hands, but should be open to the public or at least subject to what Roman law called the "jus publicum": the "public right."

[margin note: Jus publicum]

1. Carol Rose, *The Comedy of the Commons: Custom, Commerce, and Inherently Public Property*, 53 U. CHI. L. REV. 711, 711-714, 717-721, 723, 778-781 (1986).

Moreover, this view is not merely a vestige of premodern thought; there is currently an extensive academic and judicial discussion of the possibility that certain kinds of property ought to be public. In recent years, the most striking version of this "inherent publicness" argument has appeared in a series of cases expanding public access to waterfront property.[2] The land between the low and high tides has traditionally been considered "public property," or at least subject to a public easement for navigational and fishing purposes. But some modern courts have stretched this easement to include a new use — recreation — and have expanded its area from the tidelands to the dry sand areas landward of the high-tide mark.

These new cases extrapolate from older precedents in which the public acquired — or allegedly reasserted — claims to certain types of property, most notably roadways and lands under navigable waters. Like the older precedents, the new beach cases usually employ one of three theoretical bases: (1) a "public trust" theory, to the effect that the public has always had rights of access to the property in question, and that any private rights are subordinate to the public's "trust" rights; (2) a prescriptive or dedicatory theory, by which a period of public usage gives rise to an implied grant or gift from private owners; and (3) a theory of "custom," where the public asserts ownership of property under some claim so ancient that it antedates any memory to the contrary. . . .

Why . . . is any property inherently or even presumptively withdrawn from exclusive private appropriation? What characteristics of the property require it to be open to the public at large, and exempt from the classical economic presumption favoring exclusive control?

Perhaps these doctrines are indeed easily explicable through classical economic thought, and can be subsumed under the well-recognized exceptions to the general principle favoring private and exclusive property rights: "plenteous" goods and "public goods." The first class of exception concerns things that are either so plentiful or so unbounded that it is not worth the effort to create a system of resource management for them, or — stated differently — things for which the difficulty of privatization outweighs the gains in careful resource management. Thus the oceans and air (it used to be said) are at once so plentiful and so difficult to reduce to property that they are left open to the public at large.

The "plenitude" or "boundlessness" exceptions, however, fail to explain the "publicness" of those properties that our traditional doctrines most strongly deemed public property. Roadways, waterways, and submerged lands — not to speak of open squares, which have also sometimes been

---

2. *See, e.g.,* City of Berkeley v. Superior Court, 26 Cal. 3d 515, 606 P.2d 362, 162 Cal. Rptr. 327, *cert. denied,* 449 U.S. 840 (1980); Gion v. Santa Cruz, 2 Cal. 3d 29, 465 P.2d 50, 84 Cal. Rptr. 162 (1970); Borough of Neptune City v. Borough of Avon-by-the-Sea, 61 N.J. 296, 294 A.2d 47 (1972); State *ex rel.* Thornton v. Hay, 254 Or. 584, 462 P.2d 671 (1969); Seaway Co. v. Attorney General, 375 S.W.2d 923 (Tex. Civ. App. 1964).

presumed public—are hardly so copious or so unbounded that they are incapable of privatization. . . .

The second exception to the general rule favoring private property ~~*2nd Exception*~~ may be of more assistance. Since the mid-nineteenth century, economists have told us that there exist predictable instances of "market failure," where Adam Smith's invisible hand fails to guide privately owned resources to their socially optimal uses. These involve "public goods," "natural monopolies," "externalities," and the like. While some of these problems may be solved by collective agreements among the owners of the resources, such agreements are costly and, particularly where a large number of parties must be involved, private collective action is not always possible. Inefficiencies will remain.

Thus a governmental body might be the most useful manager where many persons desire access to or control over a given property, but they are too numerous and their individual stakes too small to express their preferences in market transactions; governmental ownership could broker those preferences. Similarly, a government might be a superior manager (or regulator) of a property whose use involves economies of scale—the railways, bridges, or grain elevators whose monopoly position classically justified governmental ownership or control. Or a government might be a superior manager of those "collective goods" like the broadcast spectrum, wherein some management structure is required to make individual users take account of other users' interests. In a sense, we rely on governmental management of our preeminent system of resource management—private property—and we might view the entire private property regime as a "public property" owned and managed by governmental bodies.

Conventional wisdom instructs that in such cases, the most productive solution would be for government to assume some or all of the rights of ownership and control over the property, and to use its powers to correct *Market Misallocation* the market's misallocation. This conventional conclusion is subject to four conventional caveats: the state must be able correctly to identify instances of market failure; it must be clever enough to exercise its powers so as to 1) reduce the inefficiency; it must avoid errors or political temptations to 2) exercise its powers in ways that create new inefficiencies; and the costs 3) of effective state intervention must not exceed the increase in production 4) it brings about.

This standard paradigm of neoclassical economics and modern microeconomic theory recognizes only two property regimes: either ownership is vested in private parties or it resides with an organized state. The usual economic approach to property law suggests that productive efficiency will be enhanced when private property is the norm, but government intervenes in recognized instances of market failure.

Thus in the conventional lore, markets are based on private rights, or, when markets fail, property may be governmentally managed in the interests of aggregate efficiency. Yet these two options do not logically exhaust all the possible solutions. Neither can they adequately describe all that one finds in the recorded history of property in the Anglo-American universe. In particular, there lies outside purely private property and government-controlled "public property" a distinct class of "inherently public property" which is fully controlled by neither government nor private agents. Since the Middle Ages this category of "inherently public property" has provided each member of some "public" with a bundle of rights, neither entirely alienable by state or other collective action, nor necessarily "managed" in any explicitly organized manner. . . .

Thus our historic doctrines about "inherently public" property in part vested property rights in the "unorganized public" rather than in a governmentally-organized public. For example, the public sometimes had a right of access to property whether or not a governmental body had intervened. Moreover, the "trust" language of public property doctrine, in an echo of natural law thinking, suggested that governments had some enforceable duties to preserve the property of the "unorganized" public. Indeed the "trust" language suggested that even governmental ownership of certain property is only a "qualified," "legal" ownership, for the "use" of public at large, which in classic trust language is the beneficial owner.

Yet property in such an unorganized public would amount to an unlimited commons, which seems not to be property at all, but only a mass or passive "things" awaiting reduction to private property through the rule of capture or, worse yet, their squandering in the usual "tragedy of the commons." Nevertheless, strange though it may seem, precisely this unorganized version of the "public" is strongly suggested in some of the earlier public property doctrine — and in some modern law as well. . . .

[S]ervice to commerce was a central factor in defining as "public" such properties as roads and waterways. Used in commerce, some property had qualities akin to infinite "returns to scale." Thus here, the commons was not tragic, but comedic, in the classical sense of a story with a happy outcome. And customary doctrines suggest that commerce might be thought a "comedy of the commons" not only because it may infinitely expand our wealth, but also, at least in part, because it has been thought to enhance the sociability of the members of an otherwise atomized society. . . .

. . . [S]ome activities . . . require certain places, and perhaps speech is among them. This view might have reinforced the nineteenth-century notion that squares were or could become "inherently public" places.

But what about recreation, and specifically, what about the beach cases . . . with which we began? Certainly the role of recreation is a striking example of historic change in public property doctrine. If recreation now seems to support the "publicness" of some property, this undoubtedly reflects a change in our attitudes toward recreation. We might suspect that this changed attitude relates to an increasing perception of recreation as having something analogous to scale returns, and as a socializing institution.

Recreation is often carried on in a social setting, and therefore it clearly improves with scale to some degree: one must have a partner for chess, two teams for baseball, etc. But in the mid-nineteenth century, Frederick Law Olmsted argued that recreation had scale returns in a much more expansive sense: recreation can be a socializing and educative influence, particularly helpful for democratic values.[3] Thus rich and poor would mingle in parks, and learn to treat each other as neighbors. Parks would enhance public mental health, with ultimate benefits to sociability; all could revive from the antisocial characteristics of urban life under the refining influence of the park's soothing landscape. Later recreation and park advocates, though moving away from Olmsted's more contemplative ethic, also stressed the democratic education that comes with sports and team play.

Insofar as recreation educates and socializes us, it acts as a "social glue" for everyone, not just those immediately engaged; and of course, the more people involved in any socializing activity, the better. Like commerce, then, recreation has social and political overtones. The contemplation of nature elevates our minds above the workaday world, and thus helps us to cope with that very world; recreational play trains us in the democratic give-and-take that makes our regime function. If these arguments are true, we should not worry that people engage in too much recreation, but too little. This again argues that recreation should be open to all at minimal costs, or at costs to be borne by the general public, since all of us benefit from the greater sociability of our fellow citizens. If we accept these arguments, we might believe that unique recreational sites ought not be private property; their greatest value lies in civilizing and socializing all members of the public, and this value should not be "held up" by private owners.[4] . . .

Perhaps the chief lesson from the nineteenth-century doctrines of "inherently public property," then, is that while we may change our minds about which activities are socializing, we always accept that the public requires access to some physical locations for some of these activities. Our law consistently allocates that access to the public, because public access to those locations is as important as the general privatization of property in other spheres of our law. In the absence of the socializing activities that take place on "inherently public property," the public is a shapeless mob, whose members neither trade nor converse nor play, but only fight, in a setting where life is, in Hobbes' all too famous phrase, solitary, poor, nasty, brutish, and short.

---

3. Frederick Law Olmsted, Civilizing American Cities: A Selection of Frederick Law Olmsted's Writings on City Landscapes 74-81 (S. Sutton ed. 1971).

4. [Consult again in this respect Alexander's extended treatment of the beach cases in Chapter 9.2 above. — Eds.]

Elinor Ostrom, Governing the Commons[5]

SIMILARITIES AMONG ENDURING, SELF-GOVERNING CPR INSTITUTIONS

Despite all of the differences among the CPR [common-pool resources] settings . . . all share fundamental similarities. One similarity is that all face uncertain and complex environments. In the mountain commons, the location and timing of rainfall cannot be predicted. In the irrigation systems, erratic rainfall is again a major source of uncertainty. . . .

In contrast to the uncertainty caused by these environments, the populations in these locations have remained stable over long periods of time. Individuals have shared a past and expect to share a future. It is important for individuals to maintain their reputations as reliable members of the community. These individuals live side by side and farm the same plots year after year. They expect their children and their grandchildren to inherit their land. In other words, their discount rates[6] are low. If costly investments in provision are made at one point in time, the proprietors — or their families — are likely to reap the benefits.

Extensive norms have evolved in all of these settings that narrowly define "proper" behavior. Many of these norms make it feasible for individuals to live in close interdependence on many fronts without excessive conflict. Further, a reputation of keeping promises, honest dealings, and reliability in one arena is a valuable asset. Prudent, long-term self-interest reinforces the acceptance of the norms of proper behavior. None of these situations involves participants who vary greatly in regard to ownership of assets, skills, knowledge, ethnicity, race, or other variables that could strongly divide a group of individuals. . . .

The most notable similarity of all, of course, is the sheer perseverance manifested in these resource systems and institutions. The resource systems clearly meet the criterion of sustainability. The institutions meet [the] criterion of intuitional robustness, in that the rules have been devised and modified over time according to a set of collective-choice and constitutional-choice rules. These cases were specifically selected because they have endured while others have failed. Now the task is to begin to explain their sustainability and robustness, given how difficult it must have been to achieve this record in such complex, uncertain, and interdependent environments in which individuals have continuously faced substantial incentives to behave opportunistically. . . .

---

5. ELINOR OSTROM, GOVERNING THE COMMONS: THE EVOLUTION OF INSTITUTIONS FOR COLLECTIVE ACTION 88-102, 212 (1990).

6. ["The discount rate tells us how to calculate present values. The discount rate is the rate that is earned from renting money out for one year in the market for money." WILLIAM T. ALLEN ET AL., COMMENTARIES AND CASES ON THE LAW OF BUSINESS ORGANIZATION 116 (2d ed., 2007). — EDS.]

Although the particular rules that are used within these various settings cannot provide the basis for an explanation of the institutional robustness and sustainability across these CPRs, part of the explanation that I offer is based on the fact that the particular rules differ. The differences in the particular rules take into account specific attributes of the related physical systems, cultural views of the world, and economic and political relationships that exist in the setting. Without different rules, appropriators could not take advantage of the positive features of a local CPR or avoid potential pitfalls that might be encountered in one setting but not others.

Instead of turning to the specific rules, I turn to a set of seven design principles that characterize all of these robust CPR institutions, plus an eighth principle used in the larger, more complex cases. . . . By "design principle" I mean an essential element of condition that helps to account for the success of these institutions in sustaining the CPRs and gaining the compliance of generation after generation of appropriators to the rules in use. . . .

For these design principles to constitute a credible explanation for the persistence of these CPRs and their related institutions, I need to show that they can affect incentives in such a way that appropriators will be willing to commit themselves to conform to operational rules devised in such systems, to monitor each other's conformance, and to replicate the CPR institutions across generational boundaries. I shall discuss each of the design principles in turn.

Clearly defined boundaries

1. Individuals or households who have rights to withdraw resource units from the CPR must be clearly defined, as must the boundaries of the CPR itself.

Defining the boundaries of the CPR and specifying those authorized to use it can be thought of as a first step in organizing for collective action. So long as the boundaries of the resource and/or the specification of individuals who can use the resource remain uncertain, no one knows what is being managed or for whom. Without defining the boundaries of the CPR and closing it to "outsiders," local appropriators face the risk that any benefits they produce by their efforts will be reaped by others who have not contributed to those efforts. At the least, those who invest in the CPR may not receive as high a return as they expected. At the worst, the actions of others could destroy the resource itself. Thus, for any appropriators to have a minimal interest in coordinating patterns of appropriation and provision, some set of appropriators must be able to exclude others from access and appropriation rights. . . .

Congruence between appropriation and provision rules and local conditions

2. Appropriation rules restricting time, place, technology, and/or quantity of resource units are related to local conditions and to provision rules requiring labor, materials, and/or money.

Adding well-tailored appropriation and provision rules helps to account for the perseverance of these CPRs. In all these cases, the rules reflect the specific attributes of the particular resource. . . . No single set of the rules defined for all irrigation systems in the region could deal with the particular problems in managing each of these broadly similar, but distinctly different, systems.

Collective-choice arrangements

3. Most individuals affected by the operational rules can participate in modifying the operational rules.

CPR institutions that use this principle are better able to tailor their rules to local circumstances, because the individuals who directly interact with one another and with the physical world can modify the rules over time so as to better fit them to the specific characteristics of their setting. Appropriators who design CPR institutions that are characterized by these first three principles — clearly defined boundaries, good-fitting rules, and appropriator participation in collective choice — should be able to devise a good set of rules if they keep the costs of changing the rules relatively low.

The presence of good rules, however, does not ensure that appropriators will follow them. . . . Actually following rules ex post, when strong temptations arise, is the significant accomplishment. . . .

Some recent theoretical models of repeated situations do predict that individuals will adopt contingent strategies to generate optimal equilibria without external enforcement, but with very specific information requirements rarely found in field settings. . . . In these models, participants adopt resolute strategies to cooperate so long as everyone else cooperates. If anyone deviates, the models posit that all others will deviate immediately and forever. Information about everyone's strategies in a previous round is assumed to be freely available. No monitoring activities are included in these models, because information is presumed to be already available.

It is obvious from our case studies, however, that even in repeated settings where reputation is important and where individuals share the norm of keeping agreements, reputation and shared norms are insufficient by themselves to produce stable cooperative behavior over the long run. If they had been sufficient, appropriators could have avoided investing resources in monitoring and sanctioning activities. In all of the long-enduring cases, however, active investments in monitoring and sanctioning activities are quite apparent. That leads us to consider the fourth and fifth design principles:

Monitoring

4. Monitors, who actively audit CPR conditions and appropriator behavior, are accountable to the appropriators or are the appropriators.

Graduated sanctions

5. Appropriators who violate operational rules are likely to be assessed graduated sanctions (depending on the seriousness and context of the offense) by other appropriators, by officials accountable to these appropriators, or by both.

. . . In these robust institutions, monitoring and sanctioning are undertaken not by external authorities but by the participants themselves. The initial sanctions used in these systems are also surprisingly low. Even though it is frequently presumed that participants will not spend the time and effort to monitor and sanction each other's performances, substantial evidence has been presented that they do both in these settings. The appropriators in these CPRs somehow have overcome the presumed problem of the second-order dilemma. . . .

. . . CPR appropriators create their own internal enforcement to (1) deter those who are tempted to break rules and thereby (2) assure quasi-voluntary compliers that others also comply. [H]owever, the normal presumption has been that participants themselves will not undertake mutual monitoring and enforcement because such actions involve relatively high personal costs and produce public goods available to everyone. . . . Given the evidence that individuals monitor, then the relative costs and benefits must have a different configuration than that posited in prior work. Either the costs of monitoring are lower or the benefits to an individual are higher, or both.

The costs of monitoring are low in many long-enduring CPRs as a result of the rules in use. Irrigation rotation systems, for example, usually place the two actors most concerned with cheating in direct contact with one another. . . . Monitoring is a by-product of their own strong motivations to use their water rotation turns to the fullest extent. . . .

[Likewise,] many of the ways that work teams are organized in the Swiss and Japanese mountain commons also have the result that monitoring is a natural by-product of using the commons. . . .

Similarly, it is apparent that personal rewards for doing a good job are given to appropriators who monitor. The individual who finds a rule-infractor gains status and prestige for being a good protector of the commons. The infractor loses status and prestige. Private benefits are allocated to those who monitor. When internal monitoring is accomplished as part of a specialized position accountable to the other appropriators, several mechanisms increase the rewards for doing a good job or exposing slackards to the risk of losing their positions. . . .

Consequently, the costs and benefits of monitoring a set of rules are not independent of the particular set of rules adopted. Nor are they uniform in all CPR settings. When appropriators design at least some of their own rules (design principle 3), they can learn from experience to craft enforceable rather than unenforceable rules. This means paying attention to the costs of monitoring and enforcing, as well as the benefits that accrue to those who monitor and enforce the rules. . . .

If the appropriators adopt contingent strategies — each agreeing to follow a set of rules, so long as most of the others follow the rules — each one needs to be sure that others comply and that their compliance produces the expected benefit. Thus, a previously unrecognized "private" benefit of monitoring in settings in which information is costly is that one obtains the information necessary to adopt a contingent strategy. If an appropriator who monitors finds someone who has violated a rule, the benefits of that discovery are shared by all who use the CPR, and the discoverer gains an indication of compliance rates. If the monitor does *not* find a violator, previously it has been presumed that private costs are involved without any benefit to the individual or the group. If information is not freely available about compliance rates, then an individual who monitors obtains valuable information from monitoring. The appropriator-monitor who watches how water is distributed to their appropriators not only provides a public good for all but also obtains information needed to make future strategic decision.

By monitoring the behavior of others, the appropriator-monitor learns about the level of quasi-voluntary compliance in the CPR. If no one is discovered breaking the rules, the appropriator-monitor learns that others comply and that no one is being taken for a sucker. It is then safe for the appropriator-monitor to continue to follow a strategy of quasi-voluntary compliance. If the appropriator-monitor discovers a rule infraction, it is possible to learn about the particular circumstances surrounding the infraction, to participate in deciding the appropriate level of sanctioning, and then to decide whether or not to continue compliance. If an appropriator-monitor finds an offender who normally follows the rules but in one instance happens to face a severe problem, the experience confirms what everyone already knows: There will always be instances in which those who are basically committed to following the set of rules may succumb to strong temptations to break them.

The appropriator-monitor may want to impose only a modest sanction in this circumstance. A small penalty may be sufficient to remind the infractor of the importance of compliance. The appropriator-monitor might be in a similar situation in the future and would want some understanding at that time. Everyone will hear about the incident, and the violator's reputation for reliability will depend on complying with the rules in the future. If the appropriator-monitor presumes that the violator will follow the rules most of the time in the future, the appropriator-monitor can safely continue a strategy of compliance. The incident will also confirm for the appropriator-monitor the importance of monitoring even when most others basically are following the rules.

A real threat to the continuance of quasi-voluntary compliance can occur, however, if an appropriator-monitor discovers individuals who break the rules repeatedly. If this occurs, one can expect the appropriator-monitor to escalate the imposed sanctions in an effort to halt future rule-breaking by such offenders and any others who might start to follow suit. In any case, the appropriator-monitor has up-to-date information about compliance and sanctioning behavior on which to base future decisions about personal compliance. . . .

. . . Let me summarize my argument to this point. When CPR appropriators design their own operational rules (design principle 3) to be enforced by individuals who are local appropriators or are accountable to them (design principle 4), using graduated sanctions (design principle 5) that define who has rights to withdraw units from the CPR (design principle 1) and that effectively restrict appropriation activities, given local conditions (design principle 2), the commitment and monitoring problems are solved in an interrelated manner. Individuals who think that a set of rules will be effective in producing higher joint benefits and that monitoring (including their own) will protect them against being suckered are willing to make a contingent self-commitment of the following type:

> I commit myself to follow the set of rules we have devised in all instances except dire emergencies if the rest of those affected make a similar commitment and act accordingly.

Once appropriators have made contingent self-commitments, they are then motivated to monitor other people's behaviors, at least from time to time, in order to assure themselves that others are following the rules most of the time. Contingent self-commitments and mutual monitoring reinforce one another, especially when appropriators have devised rules that tend to reduce monitoring costs. . . .

Conflict-resolution mechanisms

6.   Appropriators and their officials have rapid access to low-cost local arenas to resolve conflicts among appropriators or between appropriators and officials.

If individuals are going to follow rules over a long period of time, there must be some mechanism for discussing and resolving what constitutes an infraction. . . .

Although the presence of conflict-resolution mechanisms does not guarantee that appropriators will be able to maintain enduring institutions, it is difficult to imagine how any complex system of rules could be maintained over time without such mechanisms. . . .

Minimal recognition of rights to organize

7.   The rights of appropriators to devise their own institutions are not challenged by external governmental authorities.

Appropriators frequently devise their own rules without creating formal governmental jurisdictions for this purpose. . . . [I]f external governmental officials presume that only they have the authority to set the rules, then it will be very difficult for local appropriators to sustain a rule-governed CPR over the long run. . . .

Nested enterprises

8.   Appropriation, provision, monitoring, enforcement, conflict resolution, and governance activities are organized in multiple layers of nested enterprises.

All of the more complex, enduring CPRs meet this last design principle. . . . Establishing rules at one level, without rules at the other levels, will produce an incomplete system that may not endure over the long run. . . .

. . . In nonremote locations, the orientation of the ruling political regime can make a substantial difference in whether local appropriators supply their own institutions or are dependent on external authorities to solve their problems.

Individuals who are not able to supply new rules in an indifferent setting may succeed in adopting new rules under a political regime that allows substantial local autonomy, invests in enforcement agencies, and provides generalized institutional-choice and conflict-resolution arenas. In other words, regional and national governments can play a positive role in providing facilities to enhance the ability of local appropriators to engage in effective institutional design.

NOTES AND QUESTIONS

1.   *Between Open Access and CPRs.* Recall our discussion of Demsetz's account of the emergence of property rights in Chapter 5. As we have

indicated in Note 2, this theory addresses cases of *open access*, in which anyone at all may use a resource and no one may be excluded. A CPR or a commons property is a significantly different type of property, designating resources that are owned or controlled by a *finite* number of people who manage the resource together and exclude outsiders. In Chapter 5 we asked if you think that Demsetz's account can apply to commons property. Here we flip the question: Do you think that Ostrom's stories of successful CPRs can help address the dynamics of open access? Which is more relevant (in the sense that one is likely to encounter it) in modern society — an open-access or limited-access commons?

2. *Successful CPRs and Community Stability.* At the beginning of the excerpt, Ostrom mentions that the success stories she analyzes are typically enjoyed by stable communities with low discount rates. But how stable should these communities be? On one view, such successes come exclusively from factors within the group and are thus limited to strong, homogeneous cultural communities. *See* MICHAEL TAYLOR, COMMUNITY, ANARCHY AND LIBERTY 104-129 (1982); Sara Singleton & Michael Taylor, *Common Property, Collective Action and Community,* 4 J. THEORETICAL POL. 309, 311, 316 (1992). Ostrom, as you can guess, disagrees, claiming that strong community is neither sufficient nor *ex ante* necessary. Even heterogeneous sets of individuals may overcome the commons difficulties with the help of proper institutional innovation and design, such as the ones she identifies, although if they do not develop shared values, they will eventually fail. *See* Elinor Ostrom, *Community and the Endogenous Solution of Commons Problems,* 4 J. THEORETICAL POL. 343, 347-350 (1992). As Margaret McKean reports, most of these success stories include strong limitations on alienability (exit), which facilitate the commoners' cooperation. *See* Margaret A. McKean, *Success on the Commons: A Comparative Examination of Institutions for Common Property Resource Management,* 4 J. THEORETICAL POL. 247, 261-262 (1992). But is the price in terms of giving up the right to exit justified? Consult again in this respect the roles of exit in promoting autonomy and efficiency, discussed in Chapter 10.

3. *Liberal Commons?* Hanoch Dagan and Michael Heller argue that an important cluster of property institutions — which includes, for example, marital property, co-ownership, condominiums, partnerships, and close corporations — overcomes this dilemma, thus allowing commoners to capture both the economic gains from cooperation (notably economies of scale and risk-spreading) and the social benefits of interpersonal trust and cooperation. Each of these examples of what they call "the liberal commons" enables a limited group of owners to capture the economic and social benefits from cooperative use of a scarce resource, without sacrificing the liberal commitment to exit. This happy outcome can be achieved if the law provides the infrastructure of liberal commons institutions and further reassures prospective commoners that they will not be abused for cooperating. The former task is assigned to rules of property governance,

which promote well-tempered participation by setting up a majoritarian regime, limiting the majority's jurisdiction in order to protect minority rights, and prescribing procedural norms for the commoners' deliberation. The latter task — protection against opportunistic abuse — is further facilitated by rules that deter overuse and underinvestment, alongside alienation and dissolution rules that safeguard commoners from opportunistic abuses of the right to exit. Both types of rules function, in this view (and in line with Note 6 in Chapter 11), as background rules. *See* Hanoch Dagan & Michael A. Heller, *The Liberal Commons*, 110 Yale L.J. 549 (2001); *id.*, *Conflicts in Property*, 6 Theoretical Inq. L.197 (2005).

Consider against this view the idea that such facilitative law could be, at least in the long run, counterproductive. According to this view, such a legal regime induces people into making suboptimal investments in screening other potential cooperators and in learning how to cooperate better among themselves. Rather than facilitating cooperation, the argument goes, the law should channel people to agree up front on their governance structure by making its default commons regime unfriendly. If potential commoners could not opt out of such a regime by setting up their own constitution, they are better off not investing in a cooperative scheme that would then be doomed to fail. *See* James E. Krier & Stewart J. Schwab, *Property Rules and Liability Rules: The Cathedral in Another Light*, 70 N.Y.U. L. Rev. 440, 464, 478 (1995). Who do you think has the better argument in this debate? For Dagan and Heller's response, see *The Liberal Commons*, *supra*, at 580-881 (for ordinary, "mid-level" cooperators, Krier & Schwab's recommended regime discourages cooperation because learning to cooperate better is itself a second-order collective good for the commoners).

4. *Hybrids: The Semicommons.* Henry Smith identified a particularly interesting type of hybrid of private and common property rights, which he dubs "semicommon" ownership. "In a semicommons, a resource is owned and used in common for one major purpose, but, with respect to some other major purpose, individual economic units—individuals, families, or firms—have property rights to separate pieces of the commons." The example Smith gives of a semicommons comes from the European medieval and early modern open field system, where peasants owned the grain they grew on their individual strips, but were obligated during certain seasons to "throw their land open to all the landowners for grazing their animals (especially sheep) in common, under a common herdsman." The advantage of such a system is that it enjoys the economies of scale in grazing while preserving the benefits of private incentives regarding grain growing. This advantage, however, raises concerns of strategic behavior, as each commoner faces an incentive to impose costs on others' private plots. But as Smith demonstrated, such strategic behavior was efficiently prevented—so that the benefits from operating on multiple scales were materialized—by scattering peasant lots in a way that generated a physical layout that raised the costs of engaging in such strategic

behavior. *See* Henry E. Smith, *Semicommon Property Rights and Scattering in the Open Fields*, 29 J. LEGAL STUD. 131 (2000). Lee Anne Fennell helpfully generalizes this analysis, arguing that because "the problems associated with using resources on multiple scales" typify all types of commons property, the open fields case study demonstrates that "[i]ncentive compatible mechanisms not unlike those used in the spatial semicommons can help to build reversibility into property arrangements so that activities can be pursued at different scales [both] concurrently [and] consecutively." Lee Anne Fennell, *Commons, Anticommons, Semicommons, in* RESEARCH HANDBOOK ON THE ECONOMICS OF PROPERTY LAW 35, 50 (Kenneth Ayotte & Henry E. Smith eds., 2011). Is the semicommons concept useful in analyzing social institutions and practices existing in modern life? Can you think of examples of semicommons in the modern world?

5.   *Hybrids: Local Public Commons.* Amnon Lehavi analyzed another interesting hybrid — this time between public property and commons property — which is manifested in current urban settings such as local parks, playgrounds, and public squares, where "the otherwise unorganized users of local public goods . . . engage in grassroots, informal coordination and cooperation in the ongoing operation, maintenance, and improvement of the formally government-owned resource." As Lehavi reports, "local user coordination that starts out spontaneously and stabilizes into a long-enduring cooperative mode makes the public resource successful, endowing significant direct benefits as well as positive spillover effects." Amnon Lehavi, *Property Rights and Local Public Goods: Toward a Better Future for Urban Communities*, 36 URB. LAW. 1, 4 (2004). Lehavi argues that appreciating the significance of such forms of cooperation requires some attention to the predicament of the user group when the pertinent government decides to terminate the local public good. Local groups that can demonstrate sustainable value-enhancing cooperation should be entitled, he argues, by analogy to takings law, to a substitute facility. What positive spillover effects might such hybrids create? In cases where the government terminates the hybrid, say, by closing the park, cannot those who derive incidental benefits of the kind Lehavi describes provide substitutes for the government-owned resource themselves? And are there also negative effects to such local public commons that need to be taken into account? *See* Sheila R. Foster, *Collective Action and the Urban Commons*, 87 NOTRE DAME L. REV. 57, 91-133 (2012).

13 COMMODITY vs. PROPRIETY

1. HISTORICAL

Gregory S. Alexander, Commodity & Propriety: Competing Visions of Property in American Legal Thought 1776-1970[1]

For too long now, legal scholars, judges, historians, and political theorists have tended to accept uncritically the claim that there has been a single tradition of property throughout American history. Property, according to this mistaken view, has served one core purpose and has had a single constant meaning throughout American history: to define in material terms the legal and political sphere within which individuals are free to pursue their own private agendas and satisfy their own preferences, free from governmental coercion or other forms of external interference. Property, according to this understanding, is the foundation for the categorical separation of the realms of the private and public, individual and collectivity, the market and the polity.

The economic expression of this preference-satisfying conception of property is *market commodity*. Property satisfies individual preferences most effectively through the process of market exchange, or what lawyers call *market alienability*. The exchange function of property is so important in American society that property is often thought to be synonymous with the idea of market commodity.

The basic argument in this book is that this commodity theory of property is only half right. Property-as-commodity is one-half of a dialectic

---

1. Gregory S. Alexander, Commodity & Propriety: Competing Visions of Property in American Legal Thought, 1776-1970 1, 2, and 4-5 (1997).

187

that American legal writing has continuously expressed from the nation's beginning to the recent past. The other half of the dialectic is a conception that, following the lead of Carol Rose, I will call "property as propriety."[2] According to this view, property is the material foundation of creating and maintaining the proper social order, the private basis for the public good. . . .

Just what the proper social order is has been an enormously controversial issue throughout American history. The existence of different substantive conceptions of the proper social order means that there have been multiple versions of the proprietarian conception of property in American legal thought. Not only over time but also at any single moment, American legal writers have held sometimes radically different notions of the public good and its implications for property. All of these understandings of property share, however, a commitment to the basic idea that the core purpose of property is not to satisfy individual preferences or to increase wealth but to fulfill some prior normative vision of how society and the polity that governs it should be structured. . . .

As inhabitants of a modern, marketized society, we are so used to thinking of property as market commodity that it seems difficult to imagine that property might be intended to benefit anyone other than the owner. We are limited not only by the pervasiveness of market exchange in virtually every sector of modern life but also by the fact that the very notion of the public good seems anachronistic to modern sensibilities. That notion was more than familiar to our predecessors, however; it was an article of faith. So, too, was the idea that privately owned property is intended to serve the public good.

To many American lawyers in the generation of the Founders, the public good was whatever maintained a social structure within which each person and each institution had a proper role and position. The modern idea of a fluid society in which individuals readily move, either geographically or, more important, in the social hierarchy, was anathema to this mentality, which the Founders' generation inherited from premodern sources. The proper social order was by and large a static one. The public good was best served if everyone fulfilled a role in the natural hierarchy.

Property was central to this plan of social stability. It anchored the citizen to his (for in this premodern vision, the citizen-freeholder could only be a man) rightful place in the proper social hierarchy. Property, of which the only important form was the freehold estate in land, was more than wealth; it was authority, or at least a source of authority. Far from being looked on as a market commodity, land was, as Gordon Wood has put

---

2. See Carol M. Rose, *Property and Persuasion: Essays on the History, Theory, and Rhetoric of Ownership* (Boulder, Colo.: Westview Press, 1994), 58ff.

it, "a means of maintaining one's gentility and independence from the caprices of the market."[3]

The American Revolution effected some change in this proprietarian vision but did not eliminate it altogether from American legal thought or writing. A revised version of the proprietarian conception continued to be very much in evidence in the post-Revolutionary and Constitutional periods. The Revolutionary ideology of civic republicanism reshaped the old premodern understanding, to be sure, purging it of its most conspicuously hierarchical and aristocratic aspects. It is a mistake to suppose, however, that the civic republican understanding of property itself was neither hierarchical nor proprietarian. Nothing could be further from the truth. Republican property had its own hierarchy. Married women were legally incapacitated as autonomous property owners. Enslaved African Americans were non-owners in most respects. White males stood at the top of the property-owning hierarchy, and it was they to whom republican ideology looked to create and perpetuate the proper social order and the proper polity.

This is not to suggest that the idea of property as governance and order was the only way of thinking about property available to American lawyers in the eighteenth century. The opposing idea of property as commodity had always had some presence in eighteenth-century American legal discourse. It became increasingly conspicuous in the Constitutional era, as lawyers debated which interests merited special protection under the Constitution and what form of protection was appropriate. With the tremendous economic and social changes that characterized the decades after the War of 1812, the market seemed to Americans ever more important in their daily lives, and legal rhetoric reflected this growing market consciousness. This trend in legal writing about property hardly abated in the second half of the nineteenth century, characterized as it was by increasing accumulation and concentration of capital in the hands of a relatively small number of business firms. The idea of property as wealth loomed large in legal consciousness during this period, and it threatened to monopolize legal thought just as much as Standard Oil Company monopolized the oil industry. The threat never became reality, however. The old idea of property as propriety, although clearly weaker now than the commodity conception, still competed for attention.

The story is largely the same in the twentieth century. The language of the market has dominated American legal discourse about property, but the vision of property as the basis of proper order and the common good has remained viable. From the Progressive era through the New Deal and, later, the Great Society, property has undergone profound changes, both as a social institution and as a legal concept. But through all of these changes,

---

3. See Gordon S. Wood, *The Radicalism of the American Revolution* (New York: Vintage, 1991), 269.

one feature of American legal thought and writing about property has remained constant: its dialectical character.

Albert O. Hirschman, Rival Views of Market Society[4]

Once upon a time, not all that long ago, the social, political, and economic order under which men and women were living was taken for granted. Among the people of those idyllic times many of course were poor, sick, or oppressed, and consequently unhappy; no doubt, others managed to feel unhappy for seemingly less cogent reasons; but most tended to attribute their unhappiness either to concrete and fortuitous happenings — ill luck, ill health, the machinations of enemies, an unjust master, lord or ruler — or to remote, general, and unchangeable causes, such as human nature or the will of God. The idea that the social order — intermediate between the fortuitous and the unchangeable — may be an important cause of human unhappiness became widespread only in the modern age, particularly in the eighteenth century. Hence Saint-Just's famous phrase: "The idea of happiness is new in Europe" — it was then novel to think that happiness could be *engineered* by changing the social order, a task he and his Jacobin companions had so confidently undertaken. . . .

[T]he idea of a perfectible society was not to be nipped in the bud; to the contrary, it experienced a most vigorous development and, soon after the French Revolution, reappeared in the guise of powerful critiques of the social and economic order — capitalism — emerging at the beginning of the nineteenth century.

Here I am concerned with several such critiques and their interrelations. First I shall show the close relationship and direct contradiction between an early argument in *favor of* market society and a subsequent principal *critique* of capitalism. Next, I shall point to the contradictions between this critique and another diagnosis of the ills from which much of modern capitalist society is said to suffer. . . .

THE *DOUX-COMMERCE* THESIS

To begin, let me briefly evoke the complex of ideas and expectations that accompanied the expansion of commerce and the development of the market from the sixteenth to the eighteenth centuries. Here I must return to a principal theme of my book *The Passions and the Interests* (1977). . . . My book dwelt on the favorable side effects that the emerging economic system was imaginatively but confidently expected to have, with respect to both the character of citizens and the characteristics of statecraft. I stressed

---

4. ALBERT O. HIRSCHMAN, RIVAL VIEWS OF MARKET SOCIETY AND OTHER RECENT ESSAYS 105-124 (1986).

particularly the latter — the expectation, entertained by Montesquieu and Sir James Steuart, that the expansion of the market would restrain the arbitrary actions and excessive power plays of the sovereign, both in domestic and in international politics. Here I shall emphasize instead the expected effects of commerce on the *citizen* and *civil society*. At mid-eighteenth century it became the conventional wisdom — Rousseau of course rebelled against it — that commerce was a civilizing agent of considerable power and range. Let me again cite Montesquieu's key sentence, which he placed at the very beginning of his discussion of economic matters in the *Spirit of the Laws*: "it is almost a general rule that wherever manners are gentle *[moeurs douces]* there is commerce; and wherever there is commerce, manners are gentle." The relationship between "gentle manners" and commerce is presented as mutually reinforcing, but a few sentences later Montesquieu leaves no doubt about the predominant direction of the causal link: "Commerce . . . polishes and softens *[adoucit]* barbaric ways as we can see every day."[5]

This way of viewing the influence of expanding commerce on society was widely accepted throughout most of the eighteenth century. It is stressed in two outstanding histories of progress — then a popular genre — William Robertson's *View of the Progress of Society in Europe* (1769) and Condorcet's *Esquisse d'un tableau historique du proqres de l'esprit humain* (1793-94). . . .

One of the strongest statements comes in 1792, from Thomas Paine, in *The Rights of Man*,

> [Commerce] is a pacific system, operating to cordialise mankind, by rendering Nations, as well as individuals, useful to each other. . . . The invention of commerce . . . is the greatest approach towards universal civilization that has yet been made by any means not immediately flowing from moral principles.[6]

What was the concrete meaning of all this *douceur*, polish, gentleness, and even cordiality? Through what precise mechanisms was expanding commerce going to have such happy effects? The eighteenth-century literature is not very communicative in this regard, perhaps because it all seemed so obvious to contemporaries. The most detailed account I have been able to find appears in a technical book on commerce by one Samuel Ricard first published in 1704, which must have been highly successful as it was reprinted repeatedly through the next eighty years.

> Commerce attaches [men] one to another through mutual utility. Through commerce the moral and physical passions are superseded by interest. . . . Commerce has a special character which distinguishes it from all other professions. It affects the feelings of men so strongly that it makes him who was proud and haughty suddenly turn

5. See [Charles Louis] Montesquieu, *De l'esprit des lois* [(1748; Paris: Garnier, 1961)], p. 8.
6. See [Thomas] Paine[, *The Rights of Man* (1792; New York: E.P. Dutton, 1951)], p. 215.

supple, bending and serviceable. Through commerce, man learns to deliberate, to be honest, to acquire manners, to be prudent and reserved in both talk and action. Sensing the necessity to be wise and honest in order to succeed, he flees vice, or at least his demeanor exhibits decency and seriousness so as not to arouse any adverse judgment on the part of present and future acquaintances; he would not dare make a spectacle of himself for fear of damaging his credit standing and thus society may well avoid a scandal which it might otherwise have to deplore.[7]

Commerce is presented as a powerful moralizing agent which brings many nonmaterial improvements to society even though a bit of hypocrisy may have to be accepted into the bargain. Similar modifications of human behavior and perhaps even of human nature were later credited to the spread of commerce and industry by David Hume and Adam Smith: the virtues they specifically mention as being enhanced or brought into the world by commerce and manufacturing are industriousness and assiduity (the opposite of indolence), frugality, punctuality, and, most important perhaps for the functioning of market society, probity.

There is here, then, the insistent thought that a society where the market assumes a central position for the satisfaction of human wants will not only produce considerable new wealth because of the division of labor and consequent technical progress, but generate as a by-product, or external economy, a more "polished" human type — more honest, reliable, orderly, and disciplined, as well as more friendly and helpful, ever ready to find solutions to conflicts and a middle ground for opposed opinions. Such a type will in turn greatly facilitate the smooth functioning of the market. According to this line of reasoning, capitalism, which in its early phases led a rather shaky existence, having to contend with a host of precapitalist mentalities left behind by the feudal and other "rude and barbarous" epochs, will create, in the course of time and through the very practice of trade and industry, a set of compatible psychological attitudes and moral dispositions, that are both desirable in themselves and conducive to the further expansion of the system. And at certain epochs, the speed and vigor displayed by that expansion lent considerable plausibility to this conjecture.

THE SELF-DESTRUCTION THESIS

Whatever became of this brave eighteenth-century vision? I shall reserve this topic for later and turn now to a body of thought which is far more familiar to us than the *doux-commerce* thesis and happens to be its obverse. According to it, capitalist society, far from fostering *douceur* and other fine attitudes, exhibits a pronounced proclivity to undermining the moral foundations on which any society, including its own, must rest. I shall call this the self-destruction thesis.

---

7. See [Samuel] Ricard[, *Traitè gènèral du commerce* (Amsterdam: Chez E. van Harrevelt et Soeters, 1781)], p. 463.

. . . In his influential book *Social Limits to Growth,* Fred Hirsch dealt at length with what he called "The Depleting Moral Legacy" of capitalism. . . . He argues that the market *undermines* the moral values that are its own essential underpinnings, values that, so he asserts, have been inherited from *preceding* socioeconomic regimes, such as the feudal order. The idea that capitalism depletes or "erodes" the moral foundation needed for its functioning is put forward in the following terms:

> The social morality that has served as an understructure for economic individualism has been a legacy of the precapitalist and preindustrial past. This legacy has diminished with time and with the corrosive contact of the active capitalist values—and more generally with the greater anonymity and greater mobility of industrial society. The system has thereby lost outside support that was previously taken for granted by the individual. As individual behavior has been increasingly directed to individual advantage, habits and instincts based on communal attitudes and objectives have lost out. The weakening of traditional social values has made predominantly capitalist economies more difficult to manage.[8]

Once again, one would like to know in more detail how the market acts on values, this time in the direction of "depletion" or "erosion," rather than *douceur.* In developing his argument Hirsch makes the following principal points:

1. The emphasis on self-interest typical of capitalism makes it more difficult to secure the collective goods and cooperation increasingly needed for the proper functioning of the system in its later stages. . . .

2. With macromanagement, Keynesian or otherwise, assuming an important role in the functioning of the system, the macromanagers must be motivated by "the general interest" rather than by their self-interest, and the system, being based on self interest, has no way of generating the proper motivation; to the extent such motivation does exist, it is a residue of previous value systems that are likely to "erode."

3. Social virtues such as "truth, trust, acceptance, restraint, obligation," needed for the functioning of an "individualistic, contractual economy," are grounded, to a considerable extent, in religious belief, but "the individualistic, rationalistic base of the market undermines religious support."[9]

The last point stands in particularly stark contrast to the earlier conception of commerce and of its beneficial side effects. In the first place, thinkers of the seventeenth and eighteenth centuries took it for granted that they have to make do with "man as he really is" and that meant to them with someone who has been proven to be largely impervious to religious and moralistic precepts. With this realistic-pessimistic appraisal of human nature, those thinkers proceeded to discover in "interest" a

---

8. See [Fred] Hirsch[, *Social Limits to Growth* (Cambridge, MA: Harvard University Press, 1976)], pp. 117-18.

9. See Hirsch, p. 143.

principle that could replace "love" and "charity" as the basis for a well
ordered society. Second, and most important in the present context, to
the extent that society is in need of moral values such as "truth, trust,
etc." for its functioning, these values were confidently expected to be *generated*, rather than eroded, by the market, its practices and incentives.

Hirsch is only the latest representative of the idea that the market and
capitalism harbor self-destructive proclivities. . . .

The idea that capitalism as a socioeconomic order somehow carries
within itself the seed of its own destruction is of course a cornerstone of
Marxian thought. But for Marx, this familiar metaphor related to the social
and economic working of the system: some of its properties, such as the
tendency to concentration of capital, the falling rate of profit, the periodic
crises of overproduction, would bring about, with the help of an ever-more
numerous and more class-conscious and combative proletariat, the socialist
revolution. Thus Marx had little need to discover a more indirect and insidious mechanism that would operate as a sort of fifth column, undermining
the moral foundations of the capitalist system from within. Marx did,
however, help in forging one key link in the chain of reasoning that eventually led to that conception: in the *Communist Manifesto* and other early
writings, Marx and Engels make much of the way in which capitalism
corrodes all traditional values and institutions such as love, family, and
patriotism. Everything was passing into commerce; all social bonds were
dissolved through money. This perception is by no means original with
Marx. Over a century earlier it was the essence of the *conservative* reaction
to the advance of market society, voiced during the 1730s in England by the
opponents of Walpole and Whig rule, such as Bolingbroke and his circle.
The theme was taken up again, from the early nineteenth century on, by
romantic and conservative critics of the Industrial Revolution. Coleridge,
for example, wrote in 1817 that the "true seat and sources" of the "existing
distress" are to be found in the "Overbalance of the Commercial Spirit" in
relation to "natural counter-forces" such as the "ancient feelings of rank
and ancestry."[10]

This ability of capitalism to "overbalance" all traditional arid "higher"
values was not taken as a threat to capitalism itself, at least not right away.
The opposite is the case: even though the world shaped by it was often
thought to be spiritually and culturally much impoverished, capitalism was
viewed as an all-conquering, irresistible force, its rise widely expected to
lead to a thorough remaking of society: custom would be replaced by contract, gemeinschaft by gesellschaft, the traditional by the modern; all
spheres of social life, from the family to the state, from traditional hierarchy
to longtime cooperative arrangements, would be vitally affected. Meta-
phors often used to describe this action of capitalism on ancient social

---

10. See [Samuel Taylor] Coleridge[, *Collected Works*, vol. 6: *Lay Sermons* (Princeton, NJ: Princeton
University Press, 1972], pp. 169-70.

forms ranged from the outright "dissolving" to "erosion," "corrosion," "contamination," "penetration," and "intrusion" by what Karl Polanyi was to call the "juggernaut market."

But once capitalism was thus perceived as an unbridled force, terrifyingly successful in its relentless forward drive, the thought arose naturally enough that, like all great conquerors, it just might break its neck. Being a blind force . . . as well as a wild one, capitalism might corrode not only traditional society and its moral values, but even those essential to its own success and survival. To credit capitalism with extraordinary powers of expansion, penetration, and disintegration may in fact have been an adroit ideological maneuver for intimating that it was headed for disaster. The maneuver was especially effective in an age that had turned away from the idea of progress as a leading myth and was on the contrary much taken with various myths of self-destruction from the Nibelungen to Oedipus.

The simplest model for the self-destruction of capitalism might be called, in contrast to the self-reinforcing model of *doux commerce*, the *dolce vita* scenario. The advance of capitalism requires, so this story begins, that capitalists save and lead a frugal life so that accumulation can proceed apace. However, at some ill-defined point, increases in wealth resulting from successful accumulation will tend to enervate the spirit of frugality. Demands will be made for *dolce vita*, that is, for instant, rather than delayed, gratification, and when that happens capitalist progress will grind to a halt.

The idea that successful attainment of wealth will undermine the process of wealth generation is present throughout the eighteenth century from John Wesley to Montesquieu and Adam Smith. With Max Weber's essay on *The Protestant Ethic and the Spirit of Capitalism*, reasoning along such lines became fashionable once again: any evidence that the repressive ethic, alleged to be essential for the development of capitalism, may be faltering was then interpreted as a serious threat to the system's survival. Observers as diverse as Herbert Marcuse and Daniel Bell have written in this vein, unaware, it would appear, that they were merely refurbishing a well-known, much older morality tale: how the republican virtues of sobriety, civic pride, and bravery — in ancient Rome — led to victory and conquest which brought opulence and luxury, which in turn undermined those earlier virtues and destroyed the republic and eventually the empire.

While appealing in its simple dialectic, that tale has long been discredited as an explanation of Rome's decline and fall. The attempt to account for or to predict the present or future demise of capitalism in almost identical terms richly deserves a similar fate, and that for a number of reasons. Let me just point out one: the key role in this alleged process of capitalism's rise and decline is attributed first to the generation and then to the decline of personal savings so that changes in much more strategic variables, such as corporate savings, technical innovation, and entrepreneurial skill, not to speak of cultural and institutional factors, are totally left out of account.

There are less mechanical, more sophisticated forms of the self-destruction thesis. The best known is probably the one put forward by Joseph Schumpeter in *Capitalism, Socialism and Democracy*, whose second part is entitled *Can Capitalism Survive?* Schumpeter's answer to that question was rather negative, not so much, he argued, because of insuperable economic problems encountered or generated by capitalism as because of the growing hostility capitalism meets with on the part of many strata, particularly among intellectuals. It is in the course of arguing along these lines that Schumpeter writes:

> . . . capitalism creates a critical frame of mind which, after having destroyed the moral authority of so many other institutions, in the end turns against its own; the bourgeois finds to his amazement that the rationalist attitude does not stop at the credentials of kings and popes but goes on to attack private property and the whole scheme of bourgeois values.[11]

In comparison to the *dolce vita* scenario, this is a much more general argument on self-destruction. But is it more persuasive? Capitalism is here cast in the role of the sorcerer-apprentice who does not know how to stop a mechanism once set in motion so it demolishes itself along with its enemies. . . . [But] in addition to the mechanism of self-destruction, elementary forces of reproduction and *self-preservation* also ought to be taken into account. Such forces have certainly appeared repeatedly in the history of capitalism, from the first enactments of factory legislation to the introduction of social security schemes and the experimentation with countercyclical macroeconomic policies. . . .

What is surprising . . . is not that these somber ideas about self-destruction arose at the more difficult and somber moments of our century, but that there was a failure to connect them with earlier, more hopeful expectations of a market society bringing forth its own moral foundation, via the generation of *douceur*, probity, trust, and so on. One reason for this lack of contact is the low profile of the *doux-commerce* thesis in the nineteenth century, after its period of self-confidence in the preceding century. Another is the transfiguration of that thesis into one in which it was hard to recognize. The story of that low profile and that transfiguration must now be told.

ECLIPSE OF THE *DOUX-COMMERCE* THESIS AFTER THE EIGHTEENTH CENTURY

The most plausible explanation for the eclipse of the *doux commerce* thesis in the nineteenth century is that it became a victim of the Industrial Revolution. . . . As traditional products were subjected to competitive pressure from ever new "trinkets and baubles," as large groups of laborers were

---

11. See [Joseph A.] Schumpeter[, *Capitalism, Socialism, and Democracy* (New York: Harper, 1942)], p. 143.

displaced, and their skills became obsolete, and as all classes of society were seized by a sudden passion for enrichment, it was widely felt that a new revolutionary force had arisen in the very center of capitalist expansion.

As I have noted, that force was often characterized as wild, blind, relentless, unbridled—anything but *doux*. Only with regard to international trade was it still asserted from time to time, usually as an afterthought, that expanding transactions would bring, not only mutual material gains, but also some fine byproducts in the cultural and moral realms, such as intellectual cross-fertilization and mutual understanding and peace. Within the boundaries of the nation, the expansion of industry and commerce was widely viewed as contributing to the breakdown of traditional communities, and to the loosening and disintegration of social and affective ties, rather than to their consolidation.

To be sure, here and there one can still find echoes of the older idea that civil society is largely held together by the dense network of mutual relations and obligations arising from the market and from its expansion, which in turn is fueled by an increasingly fine division of labor. In fact, as soon as the matter is put this way one's thoughts travel to Emile Durkheim and his *Division of Labor in Society*. Durkheim argued, at least in part, that the advanced division of labor in modem society functions as a substitute for the "common consciousness" that so effectively bonded more primitive societies: "it is principally [the division of labor] which holds together social aggregates of the higher type." But in Durkheim's subtle thought, the transactions arising from the division of labor were not by themselves capable of this substitution. The decisive role was played by the many often *unintended* ties that people take on or fall into in the wake of market transactions and contractual commitments. Here are some formulations of this thought that recur throughout the book:

> We cooperate because we wanted to do so, but our voluntary cooperation creates duties which we did not intend to assume.
>
> The members [of societies with a fine division of labor] are united by ties that go well beyond the ever so brief moments during which exchange actually takes place . . . Because we exercise this or that domestic or social function, we are caught in a network of obligations which we do not have the right to forsake . . .
>
> If the division of labor produces solidarity, this is not only because it makes of each person an exchanger *[échangiste]* to speak the language of the economists; it is because the division of labor creates among men a comprehensive system of rights and duties which tie them to one another in a durable fashion.[12]

So Durkheim's construction is a great deal more complex and roundabout than Montesquieu's (or Sir James Steuart's): society is not held together directly nor is it made peaceful and *doux* by the network of

---

12. See [Émile] Durkheim[, *De la division du la travail social* (Paris: F. Alcan, 1892)], pp. 148, 192, 207, 402-3.

self-interested market transactions alone; for that sort of doctrine Durkheim has some harsh words that contrast sharply with the seventeenth
and eighteenth centuries' doctrine about interest:

> While interest brings people closer together, this is a matter of a few moments only; it
> can only create an external tie among them . . . The consciences are only in super-
> ficial contact; they do not penetrate one another . . . every harmony of interest con-
> tains a latent or delayed conflict for interest is what is least constant in the world.[13]

Durkheim was thus caught between the older view that interest-
oriented action provides a basis for social integration and the more
contemporary critique of market society as atomistic and corrosive of social
cohesion, He never spelled out in concrete detail how he conceived a
"solidary" society to emerge from the division of labor and eventually
moved on to a more activist view that no longer counted on this mechanism to achieve social cohesion and instead stressed moral education and
political action. But . . . there may be considerable virtue in his ambivalent
stance; and the idea that social bonds can be grafted onto economic transactions if conditions are favorable remains to be explored in depth. . . .

So much for sociology. What about the economists? After all, they had
a tradition of either outspokenly criticizing the capitalist system or defending and praising it. Should not the praisers, at least, have had an interest in
keeping alive the thought that the multiple acts of buying and selling
characteristic of advanced market societies forge all sorts of social ties of
trust, friendliness, sociability, and thus help to hold society together? In
actual fact, this sort of reasoning is conspicuously absent from professional
economics literature. . . .

. . . Economists who wish the market well have been *unable*, or rather
have tied their own hands and denied themselves the opportunity, to
exploit the argument about the integrative effect of markets. This is so
because the argument cannot be made for the ideal market with perfect
competition. The economists' claims of allocative efficiency and all-round
welfare maximization are strictly valid only for this market. Involving large
numbers of price-taking anonymous buyers and sellers supplied with perfect information, such markets function without any prolonged human or
social contact among or between the parties. Under perfect competition
there is no room for bargaining, negotiation, remonstration or mutual
adjustment, and the various operators that contract together need not
enter into recurrent or continuing relationships as a result of which they
would get to know each other well. Clearly this latter tie-forming effect of
markets can be important only when there are substantial departures or
"lapses" from the ideal competitive model. But the fact is that such lapses
are exceedingly frequent and important. Nonetheless, pro-market economists either have singled out ties among suppliers and, like Adam Smith,

13. See Durkheim, pp. 180-81. . . .

castigated them as "conspiracies against the public"; or, much more frequently, have belittled the various lapses in an attempt to present the reality of imperfect competition as coming close to the ideal. In this manner, they have endeavored to endow the market system with *economic* legitimacy. But, by the same token, they have sacrificed the *sociological* legitimacy that could rightfully have been claimed for the way, so unlike the perfect-competition model, most markets function in the real world.

Only in recent years have economists developed a number of approaches that do not look at departures from the competitive model as either sinful or negligible. To the contrary, with their stress on transaction costs, limited information and imperfect maximization, these approaches explain and justify the widespread existence of continuing relationships between buyers and sellers, the frequent establishment of hierarchies in preference to markets partly as a result of such "relational exchange," the use of "voice" rather than "exit" to correct mutual dissatisfaction, and similar phenomena that make for meaningful tie-forming interaction between parties to transactions. The stage could thus be set for a partial rehabilitation of the *doux-commerce* thesis. . . .

NOTES AND QUESTIONS

1. *Contrary Historical Views.* Not all historians share Alexander's account of the historical development of property in the United States. The distinguished historian Gordon Wood, for example, argues that by the end of the eighteenth century, the classical republican view of politics, and with it, what Alexander calls the "proprietarian" understanding of property, had ended, replaced by a view in which virtue played no role and the common good was replaced by self-interest and consent. *See* GORDON S. WOOD, THE CREATION OF THE AMERICAN REPUBLIC, 1776-1787 606-615 (1969). Within this new, post-revolutionary Republic, property was perceived to play a very different role, one far closer to what Alexander characterizes as "property-as-commodity." In Wood's view, then, the proprietarian conception of property was, by and large, lost by the end of the eighteenth century.

Jennifer Nedelsky finds even less evidence of competing conceptions of property in American history. In her view, American constitutional history from 1787 to 1937 has been one long story of property being privileged over all other interests and values. Property has meant the same thing to lawyers throughout these years: market property, property as commodity, property as the wall between private preference and the public weal. "[T]here were not," she contends, "two competing ideologies or rhetorics of property. The dominant image prevailed of property as a fundamental American value, a basic individual right secure against encroachment, even by the powers of government." JENNIFER NEDELSKY, PRIVATE PROPERTY AND THE LIMITS OF AMERICAN CONSTITUTIONALISM: THE MADISONIAN FRAMEWORK AND ITS LEGACY 227 (1990).

Nedelsky's argument echoes themes that we now associate with the so-called consensualist historians of the 1950s, notably Louis Hartz and Edward S. Corwin. Hartz's famous book *The Liberal Tradition in America* argued that since its founding, America has consistently had a single political tradition — liberalism. *See* Louis Hartz, The Liberal Tradition in America (1955). Corwin told a similar story about America's constitutional past. *See* Edward S. Corwin, The "Higher Law" Background of American Constitutional Law (1929). The implication of this consensualist history for property is that, *pace* Alexander, property has and has always had only one meaning in American political and legal thought, namely, property as market commodity.

2.   *The Political Valence of the Various Historical Views.* Although they agree on the history, Nedelsky, Hartz, and Corwin radically disagree about the political valence of that history. For consensualists like Hartz and Corwin, it was cause for celebration, a reason to take pride in America's past. Why would they think that?

For Nedelsky, it was a source of frustration and a reason for political and legal change. For the monopoly of the property-as-commodity conception of property and that conception's role in categorically separating the private and public realms were the bases, according to Nedelsky, for America's unequal and unjust distribution of wealth. "[T]he basic problem" of property, in Nedelsky's view, is that "the original focus on property placed inequality at the center of American constitutionalism." Nedelsky, *supra* Note 1, at 2. In her view, any serious attempt to deal with that problem using the concept of property as the tool for change is likely to fail because of the persistence of America's monolithic and mythic understanding of property as the foundation for a categorical separation between the public and private realms. Is Nedelsky's pessimism regarding the prospects of seriously addressing problems of wealth inequality through reform of property warranted? Can you think of examples of wealth redistributive measures that have been based on the concept of property? Consider this question in connection with the discussion of the so-called "New Property," discussed *infra* in Chapter 14.3.

Alexander states that "[t]he discovery that American legal thought and writing has understood property in a proprietarian sense as well as in a market sense means that there is no basis for historically privileging one conception over the other." Alexander, *supra*, at 7. As an example of unfounded historical privileging, Alexander cites Justice Scalia's opinion in the controversial Supreme Court takings case, Lucas v. South Carolina Coastal Council, 505 U.S. 1003 (1992), where the Court held that a South Carolina statute prohibiting construction of permanent inhabitable structures within a prescribed distance from the high tide line was *per se* a taking because affected land lost all market value as a result of the statute. Justice Scalia, writing for the Court, relied upon the supposed existence of a single American traditional understanding regarding the role of land and its legal protection. Alexander writes, "Had Justice Scalia been more historically informed, he would have understood that the legislature's determination itself [i.e., that the beachfront land was ecologically fragile and that building permanent habitations close to the ocean posed a serious risk to human life] was part of another tradition concerning the appropriate use of land — one that can be traced back to eighteenth-century republican roots." *Ibid.* Is the implication of Alexander's argument that historical traditions, or what one might call background traditions and culture, regarding property are irrelevant in resolving modern disputes over the appropriate uses of property?

3. *Commodity* as *Propriety?* Does the *doux-commerce* thesis that Hirschman reconstructs suggest that Alexander poses a false opposition, i.e., that commodity in the form of capitalism *is*, or at least can be, propriety, that is, a substantive conception of the properly ordered society? If that is the case, what might account for the perception by some observers, both legal and non-legal, that commodity and propriety, if not opposites, are in tension with each other?

4. *The Death — and Survival — of Capitalism?* The self-destruction thesis that Hirschman describes suggests that because capitalism sows the seeds of its own destruction by undermining its essential moral foundation, capitalism should have collapsed. But evidently it has not. (Or has it?) Assuming that capitalism still survives, does this necessarily indicate that the self-destruction thesis is wrong, or is it possible to reconcile that thesis with capitalism's survival?

Hirschman elaborated on the notion of economic and political orders sowing the seeds of their own destruction in his fascinating book, *Shifting Involvements* (1982). He argues there that popular interests tend to oscillate between periods of predominately public-mindedness and private interests. Each stage sows the seeds of its own destruction as it begins with unrealistic expectations that generate great enthusiasm and ends in disappointment as the expectations are inevitably not met. Widespread disappointment triggers a swing to the opposite pole, and the cycle goes on.

2. NORMATIVE

Elizabeth Anderson, Value in Ethics and Economics[1]

THE ETHICAL LIMITATIONS OF THE MARKET

7.1 Pluralism, Freedom, and Liberal Politics

Political theorists have often justified liberal practices by appealing to pluralism. My theory of value is pluralistic in two ways that are relevant

---

1. ELIZABETH ANDERSON, VALUE IN ETHICS AND ECONOMICS 141-146, 150-153, 163-167 (1993).

to political theory: it acknowledges a plurality of authentic but conflicting ideals and conceptions of the good, and it claims that different kinds of goods are rationally valued in different ways. Liberals appeal to the pluralism of ideals to justify individual rights to liberty against state interference in their personal choices. This grounds the liberal division between the public and private spheres. The second kind of pluralism supports a more robust system of social sphere differentiation that requires sharper limits on the scope of the market. Liberal theory has not yet come to grips with the full implications for human freedom and flourishing of this most expansionary institution of the modern world. In [what follows] I will focus on the limits of the market. I will show that an adequate grasp of liberal commitments to freedom, autonomy, and welfare supports more stringent limits on markets than most liberal theories have supposed.

The need to limit markets is based on a pluralistic theory of the social conditions for freedom and autonomy. Call a person free if she has access to a wide range of significant options through which she can express her diverse valuations. Individuals require social settings, governed by distinct social norms recognized and endorsed by others, to develop and express their different valuations. . . . Because people value different goods in different ways, their freedom requires the availability of a variety of social spheres that embody these different modes of valuation. Freedom thus requires *multiple sphere differentiation* — boundaries not just between the state and the market, but between these institutions and other domains of self-expression, such as family, friendship, clubs, professions, art, science, religion, and charitable and ideal-based associations. . . .

Call a person autonomous if she confidently governs herself by principles and valuations she reflectively endorses. Autonomy can be undermined internally by addictions, compulsions, phobias, and other neuroses, which motivate a person in ways she cannot reflectively endorse. It can be undermined externally by social stigmatization and relations of domination. Stigmatization undermines the self-respect a person needs to take her valuations seriously. Relations of domination give others the power to tell one what to do or to force one to do something without having to consult or respond to one's own judgments. Autonomy can be realized on a collective scale through democratic institutions. Collective autonomy consists in collective self-governance by principles and valuations that everyone, or the majority, reflectively endorses. It can be undermined by any non-democratic institution that controls political outcomes.

Autonomy, like freedom, requires social conditions for its realization that demand significant constraints on the scope of the market and private property rights. The discriminatory use of business property stigmatizes members of excluded groups and diminishes the range of significant options open to them. Liberals propose a differentiation within the private sphere between the personal sphere and civil society to solve this problem. While individuals are free not to befriend or marry members of groups they hate, they may not close their businesses to customers or job-seekers who belong to such groups. Protection of autonomy may sometimes require prohibiting the commodification of some things. Prohibiting the sale of addictive drugs can help preserve autonomy for individuals susceptible to drug abuse. Prohibiting the sale of votes helps preserve collective autonomy by blocking one way the wealthy may try to control political outcomes.

Most important to the preservation of autonomy are goods embodied in the person, such as freedom of action and the powers of productive and reproductive labor. To sell these goods to another person without retaining rights to consultation, self-judgment, and control over the conditions in which one acts is to reduce one's autonomy by subjecting oneself to another's domination. Liberal theorists recognize this as a reason for prohibiting the sale of persons into slavery, but they often fail to think through its implications for employment contracts and for contracts involving a person's sexual and reproductive powers. Autonomy requires that many rights in ourselves be inalienable.

The second kind of pluralism affirms the liberal commitment to freedom and autonomy but deepens its view of the social conditions under which they are realized. These conditions provide two grounds for constraining the scope of markets. Constraints may be needed to secure the robust sphere differentiation required to create a significant range of options through which people can express a wide range of valuations. And they may be needed to protect individual or collective autonomy. Although I focus on the uses of sphere differentiation to secure freedom and autonomy, "the art of separation" can be practiced to promote other liberal aims, such as equality, justice . . . , individuality, and neutrality. . . . These aims may require further constraints on the market.

My theory of sphere differentiation resembles Michael Walzer's. . . . But Walzer contends that the proper boundaries between social spheres can be derived only from a society's shared understandings of the meanings of goods, which are taken as an uncriticized given. This view encounters familiar difficulties: shared understandings, if they exist at all, are often riddled with contradictions and confusions, are established in relations of domination that silence the perspectives of some members of society, and fail to meet the pragmatic demands, such as the preservation of social order, that people ask of them. . . . Walzer is right in maintaining that shared understandings are the proper starting point of political argument. But justification need not be confined to such understandings. It allows for conceptual innovation in the space of reasons. . . . Justification also requires equality of the participants, so as to avoid a false consensus achieved by force or domination. With these qualifications in mind, let us consider in detail the ethical limitations of the market.

7.2 The Ideals and Social Relations of the Modern Market

Pluralism says that goods differ in kind if they are properly valued in different ways that are expressed by norms governing different social relations. Economic goods are goods that are properly valued as commodities and properly produced and exchanged in accordance with market norms. The proper limits of the market are partly defined by answering the following questions. First, do market norms do a better job of embodying the ways we properly value a particular good than norms of other spheres? If not, then we shouldn't treat them as commodities but rather locate them in non-market spheres. Second, do market norms, when they govern the circulation of a particular good, undermine important ideals such as freedom, autonomy, and equality, or important interests legitimately protected by the state? If so, the state may act to remove the good from control by market norms.

We can understand the nature of economic goods by investigating the ways we value commodities, the social relations within which we produce, distribute, and enjoy them, and the ideals these relations are supposed to embody. I call the mode of valuation appropriate to pure commodities "use." Use is a lower, impersonal, and exclusive mode of valuation. It is contrasted with higher modes of valuation, such as respect. To merely use something is to subordinate it to one's own ends, without regard for its intrinsic value. When owners of David Smith sculptures stripped the sculptures' paint to enhance their market value, they treated them as mere use-values, disregarding their intrinsic aesthetic worth in favor of their usefulness for independently defined ends. The impersonality of use is contrasted with valuing something for its personal attachments to oneself, as when one cherishes an heirloom. Mere use-values are fungible and are traded with equanimity for any other commodity at some price. But a cherished item is valued as unique and irreplaceable. It is often sold only under duress, and its loss is felt personally. . . . The exclusivity of use-values is contrasted with shared goods. Commodity values can be enjoyed in use by oneself or by private groups, excluding those with whom one exchanges the good. But the value to oneself of shared goods is dependent upon other people in civil society, or the people with whom one exchanges the good, also enjoying the same items according to shared understandings of what it means. For example, the site of a historical event may be valued as part of the national heritage, or the layout of a neighborhood valued as the locus of a community.

The most important ideal the modern market attempts to embody is an economic conception of freedom. Economic freedom consists in having both a large menu of choices in the marketplace and exclusive power to use what one buys there at will. It leaves one free from the constraints on use required to realize goods as higher, personal, or shared: it permits one to disregard or destroy the intrinsic value of what one owns; it gives one access to goods independent of one's personal characteristics or relations to others; and it leaves one free from uncontracted obligations to others, free to disregard their desires and value judgments, and free to exclude them from access to what one owns.

The norms structuring market relations that govern the production, circulation, and valuation of economic goods have five features that express the attitudes surrounding use and embody the economic ideal of freedom: they are impersonal, egoistic, exclusive, want-regarding, and oriented to "exit" rather than "voice." Norms with these features, though not governing all market transactions, are characteristic of the market. They express a shared understanding of the point and meaning of market relations recognized by every experienced participant. Consider these features in more detail.

The norms governing market relations are impersonal, suitable for regulating the interactions of strangers. Each party to a market transaction views his relation to the other as merely a means to the satisfaction of ends defined independent of the relationship and of the other party's ends. The parties have no pre-contractual obligations to provide each other with the goods they exchange. They deal with each other on an explicit, quid pro quo basis that serves to guarantee mobility. Because market transactions can be completed so as to leave no unpaid debts on either side, they leave the parties free to switch trading partners at any time. The impersonality of market relations thus defines a sphere of freedom from personal ties and obligations. Impersonal freedom also implies that one need not exhibit specific personal characteristics or invoke special relationships to gain access to the goods traded on the market. Money income, not one's social status, characteristics, or relationships, determines one's access to commodities. The impersonality of the market has been evolving for centuries, and, in some cases, notably regarding discrimination on the basis of race, ethnicity, gender, and sexual orientation, it still has a long way to go.

The market leaves its participants free to pursue their individual interests without considering others' interests. Each party to a market transaction is expected to take care of herself. Every extension of the market thus represents an extension of the domain of egoism, where each party defines and satisfies her interests independent of the other. But individuals' interests are independently definable and satisfiable only with respect to goods that are exclusive and are rivals in consumption. A good is exclusive if access to its benefits is limited to the purchaser. If there are no means of excluding people from enjoying a good, one cannot charge a market price for it. A good is a rival in consumption if the amount that one person consumes reduces the total amount of it available to others. . . . The use-value of commodities is rival, since it is tied to the distinct ends of the person who appropriates and uses it. One cannot give the value of a rival good to another without losing it oneself. Shared goods, by contrast, are not rival.

I do not lose, but rather enhance, my knowledge or my pleasure in a joke by conveying these goods to others.

The market is a want-regarding institution. It responds to "effective demand" — desires backed by the ability to pay for things. Commodities are exchanged without regard for the reasons people have for wanting them. The market does not draw any distinction between urgent needs and intense desires or between reflective desires, which can be backed by reasons, and mere tastes. Since it offers no means for discriminating among the reasons people have for wanting or providing things, it cannot function as a forum for the justification of principles about the things traded on it. Thus the market provides individual freedom from the value judgments of others. It does not regard any one individual's preferences as intrinsically less worthy of satisfaction than anyone else's. But it provides this freedom at the cost of reducing preferences, from the market's point of view, to mere matters of taste, about which it is pointless to dispute. . . .

Individuals influence the provision and exchange of commodities mainly through "exit," not "voice". . . . The counterpart to the customer's freedom to exit a trading relationship is the owner's freedom to say "take it or leave it." The customer has no voice, no right to directly participate in the design of the product or to determine how it is marketed. Where the good being sold is embodied in the person, voice may be alienated to the buyer. Employment contracts in capitalist firms that are unmediated by union negotiation or professional standards place the worker in the same voiceless position as the customer.

I shall say that a thing is a pure economic good if its production, distribution, and enjoyment are properly governed by the five norms above and its value can be fully realized through use. This defines what may be called the ideal type of an economic good, tied to an ideal typical account of market norms. . . .

7.4 Personal Relations and the Markets

The modern Western opposition of personal and market relationships is the product of historical processes that separated economic production from the household. . . . In this section I will focus on two of the many ideals distinctive to the sphere of personal relations: intimacy and commitment. Living on intimate terms with another person involves sharing private concerns and cherished emotions attuned to the other's personal characteristics. This is the romantic side of personal relations, involving passion, affection, and trust, but not necessarily devotion, as the romantic relationship may end as soon as the passions that animate it subside.

The deepest ideal of commitment involves dedicating oneself to permanently living a shared life with another person. The goodness of such a life for each partner is shared. It partially consists in the fact that the other partner also enjoys this life, that each partner realizes this, and that she knows that the other knows. One committed and loving partner cannot unequivocally rejoice in his life with his partner if he knows that the other finds the relationship oppressive in some way. Commitment to a shared life, such as a marriage, requires redefining one's interests as part of a *couple*. A person's committed interest in the aims of the marriage can be neither defined nor satisfied independent of her being joined with her partner in marriage.

These ideals inform the ways we value the people with whom we have personal relationships and the goods we exchange with them. The goods exchanged and jointly realized in friendship are not merely used but cherished and appreciated, for they are expressions of shared understandings, affections, and commitments. The goods proper to the personal sphere can be fully realized only through gift exchange. They cannot be procured by paying others to produce them, because the worth of these goods depends upon the motives people have in providing them. Among these goods are trust, loyalty, sympathy, affection, and companionship.

The norms of gift exchange differ from the norms of market exchange in several respects. . . . Gift exchange affirms and perpetuates the ties that bind the donor and the recipient. To refuse an appropriate gift is to insult a friend by failing to acknowledge or sustain a friendship. Gift exchange aims to realize a shared good in the relationship itself, whereas market exchange aims to realize distinct goods for each party. Although both forms of exchange involve reciprocity, the form and timing of the return of goods differ in the two cases. In market exchange, an uncontracted delay in reciprocation is cause for legal action. But the exchange of gifts among friends usually incorporates an informal understanding of reciprocity only in the long term. To be anxious to "settle accounts" of small sums, as when one person insists upon splitting a restaurant tab exactly in half, calculating sums to the penny, is to reject the logic of friendship. The delay in reciprocation expresses an intrinsic valuation of the recipient: gifts are given for the friend's sake, not merely for the sake of obtaining some good for oneself in return. The accounting mentality reflects an unwillingness to be in the debt of another and, hence, an unwillingness to enter into the longer term commitments such debts entail. The debts friends owe to one another are not of a kind that they can be repaid so as to leave nothing between them. (Debts involving large sums are another matter, since they threaten the relative financial self-sufficiency that is presupposed by modern friendship in market-based economies between equals who are not kin.)

Friendly gift exchange is responsive to the personal characteristics of friends and to the particular qualities of their relationship. We seek to give gifts to our friends that have more than a merely generic meaning. For gifts express friends' mutual understanding of how their relationship stands (or how the giver wishes it to be) and not merely a good of impersonal use-value to the receiver. . . . This is why cash is usually an inappropriate gift between friends: because it can be used by anyone to acquire any commodity, it expresses nothing of the giver's personality, of any particular thought the giver had for the receiver, or of the receiver's interests.

These differences between personal and market norms can help us explore how personal goods are undermined when market norms govern their circulation. The thought that authentic personal goods are undermined when this happens has been challenged by feminist theory, which locates a source of women's oppression in the personal sphere. Feminist critiques of the public/private split often focus on how the liberal state reinforces gender domination in the family by ignoring the violence against and coercion of women that takes place there and by structuring opportunities in civil society to the disadvantage of women, who have primary childcare responsibilities. . . . But some feminists have also criticized personal heterosexual relations for not conforming more to market norms. They attribute women's subordination in marriage to the fact that their roles are defined by status rather than by contract. Women can achieve full freedom and equality with men only when they acquire full property rights in their bodies — their sexual and reproductive capacities — and the freedom to remake the marriage contract at will. . . .

Against this critique, my account of personal goods may appear sentimental and naïve, because it seems to mask the gendered power relations that inform contemporary norms of intimacy and commitment. Where intimacy is taken to mean that a husband can force his wife to have sexual intercourse while immune from a charge of rape, and where commitment is enforced by women's economic dependency on their husbands, gravely compromising their powers of exit, there is much room to question how much women's sexual, emotional, and reproductive "gifts" to men are freely given, how much they express women's own valuations rather than men's valuations of them, and how much the gifts they receive in return reinforce their subordination. Where men's dignity and functioning in civil society is staked in their power to neglect the concerns of women's reproductive and household labor, the unexplicit basis of gift exchange in marriage leaves women performing labor indispensable to men's economic productivity, yet invisible or undervalued in the scheme of heterosexual reciprocity. This in turn puts women in a perpetual debt of asymmetrical gratitude for male "favors," which is discharged by submission to their wishes. . . .

These feminist criticisms of present embodiments of heterosexual intimacy and commitment are accessible within the standpoints of these ideals. They reinforce Mill's argument that true friendship in marriage can be fully realized only when the partners are related as equals. . . . Intimacy requires honesty and sensitivity to each other's needs. These are undermined by gendered power relations that impose penalties on women for revealing their dissatisfactions to their partners and that legitimate male contempt for housework and childcare. Commitment to a shared life requires dialogue on terms of mutual respect. These are undermined by gendered norms of conversation that represent women's conversational claims as less credible or less worthy of respect than men's, that permit men to decide that a woman's "no" means "yes," and that represent conversations directed toward sharing feelings as a threat to the autonomy and independence constitutive of masculinity. . . .

Far from presenting a sentimentalized representation of the goods proper to the personal sphere, the ideals of intimacy and commitment provide a perspective from which to radically criticize what currently goes on there. This provides grounds for wariness about proposals to free women from subordination in the personal sphere by using market norms to regulate the exchange of women's sexual and reproductive powers. These proposals draw their strength from an individualist view that regards all moves from "status" to "contract", from obligations determined internally to a socially defined form of relationship to obligations freely shaped by the will of the parties, as triumphs for freedom and equality. . . .

7.6 The Limitations of Market Ideologies

In this chapter I have explored several ways in which liberal commitments to freedom and human flourishing require stronger limitations on the market than most standard liberal theories recognize. Liberal theories of justice tend to criticize the way the market distributes income, while mostly ignoring its impact on the other goods it distributes. Libertarianism and welfare economics represent most expansions of the domain of market norms as gains for freedom and welfare. This is partly due to the fact that they represent freedom and welfare in the same limited terms to which the market is responsive. They take up the perspective of market relations on these goods and hence are blind to the ways markets fail to realize more adequate conceptions of them. This blindness can be traced to three fundamental errors in the theory of value. First, preference orientation: Libertarians and welfare economists tie freedom and welfare to the expression or satisfaction of given desires, rather than to the expression of rational attitudes. Second, individualism: they suppose that individuals are self-sufficient in their capacities to exercise freedom and to form and express their values, independent of their relations to others. Third, commodity fetishism: they tend to conceive of freedom or welfare in terms of the possession and use of exclusive goods, ignoring the expressive dimension of action and hence the meanings of the relations among people that we establish in governing our interactions by market norms.

Consider first freedom. Libertarians conceive of freedom as economic freedom. A person is free if she is free to express her preferences in using and exchanging her private property without having to respond to the values and preferences of others. . . . Preferences are seen as subjective "tastes" that an individual can have and rationally express independent of other people's preferences. Markets and contracts are seen as all-purpose mechanisms for satisfying preferences. They let individuals value commodities as much as they want, independent of others' preferences. Therefore, market relations seem to be generically appropriate relations through which to exercise freedom, because they appear to accommodate any preferences without passing judgment on them.

The attraction of the preference view of freedom is due to the thought that freedom is a matter of expressing one's valuations, plus the reduction of valuations to bare preferences or tastes. Pluralism accepts the first thought but rejects the second. Our valuations are expressed not just through preferences but through the whole range of rational attitudes. We can value goods in ways beyond use and bare liking only by participating in social practices governed by shared understandings of their value. Higher, shared, and personal ways of valuing goods require social constraints on use. We can express these valuations only in social spheres governed by non-market norms. So the market does not provide a sufficient domain for the expression of all our valuations, but must leave room for other social spheres to operate on non-market principles. The freedom to value a good as much as one wishes is not the freedom to value it in any *way* one wishes.

The individualistic preference model of freedom also masks the ways in which commodification can destroy autonomy. When autonomy is reduced to the expression of preferences and preferences are identified with actual market choices, theorists don't ask if these "revealed preferences" adequately express a person's own reflective attitudes, or whether they express irrational preferences or the preferences of others. When individuals are supposed to be the automatic and self-sufficient bearers of autonomy, theorists don't question the social relations of domination that exist prior to market transactions and that condition the choices individuals make there. Nor do they challenge the relations of domination the market creates when goods embodied in the person are commodified and alienated to others. These errors lead libertarians to argue that any constraints on people's freedom to alienate their property in themselves are paternalistic violations of liberty. . . . But in democratically prohibiting the market alienation of certain goods embodied in the person, people exercise collective autonomy over the background conditions of their interaction. They determine that the judgments that should control their actions are the judgments they make as fraternal citizens rather than as isolated laborers unable to protect themselves from competitively underbidding one another. Their collective self-protection, while limiting certain choices at any given time, makes available to all a broader range of significant choices over time than complete commodification would. Once autonomy is seen to be exercised collectively in democratic contexts and to require support by background social conditions, there is no reason to characterize these actions as paternalistic. . . .

Libertarianism conceives of freedom as a right to exclude others from participating in decisions over one's property, as if freedom were exercised only in one's dominion over things exclusively owned. Committed or involuntary relationships with other people that are governed by norms not freely defined in contracts are viewed as entangling constraints on freedom. This is a form of commodity fetishism. . . . We are not free to pursue the shared goods of deepest significance to human life within the terms of libertarian freedom alone. The personal and political spheres offer different ideals of freedom. In genuinely committed and intimate relationships we are free to reveal ourselves to others, without having our self-disclosure become the object of another's manipulations in egoistic market-oriented bargaining. In democratic societies we are free to partic-ipate in collective decisions that affect everyone. This is the freedom to be included, rather than to exclude others. When exit is impossible, when decisions concern shared goods, or when freedom can be effectively exercised by all only in public spaces of free and equal association, demo-cratic freedom supersedes market freedom.

Commodity fetishism also pervades the conception of human good embraced by welfare economics. It defines a person's welfare as the satis-faction of her given preferences, which it conceives as automatically expressed in her choices and as taking exclusively appropriated goods as their basic object. This conception of welfare is tailored to present markets in their best light, since markets deal only in exclusive goods and respond to given preferences. Hence welfare economics represents markets as gener-ically efficient providers of non-public goods. But the market can claim superior efficiency only when goods are unchanged by alternate means of provision. Gift values are undermined when they are produced and exchanged out of market motives, for their significance consists in part in their expression of non-market attitudes. Shared values can be realized only through nonexclusive distribution responsive to shared understand-ings of principles and needs arrived at through voice. In treating human relations as indifferently substitutable means for acquiring goods, welfare economics blinds itself to the ways markets undermine certain expressive relations with others.

The realization of some forms of freedom, autonomy, and welfare demands that certain goods be produced, exchanged, and enjoyed outside of market relations or in accordance with non-market norms. This conclu-sion does not mean that market institutions should not play a prominent role in a liberal society. Policy questions should focus more on the norms governing the production and circulation of goods than on the formal status of the institution, whether a governmental body or a private organization, that provides it. Governments can often act like markets, and private orga-nizations like public bodies. The prospect of developing hybrid social prac-tices that combine features of different spheres of life may help break through currently sterile debates which suppose that there is no "third way" between laissez-faire capitalism and comprehensive state planning of the economy. Some of these practices already exist, in the form of nonprofit and professional institutions of civil society. To argue that the market has limits is to acknowledge that it also has its proper place in human life. A wide range of goods are properly regarded as pure commodities. Among these are the conveniences, luxuries, delights, gadgets, and services found in most stores. The modern market produces and distributes these goods with unsurpassed efficiency and in unsurpassed abundance. It is beneficial not only to have these goods, but to be able to procure them freely through the anonymous, unencumbered channels the market provides. The difficult task for modern societies is to reap the advantages of the market while keeping its activities confined to the goods proper to it.

NOTES AND QUESTIONS

1. *Other Non-Market Realms.* Our excerpt discusses the constitutive characteristics of the market domain and those of the domain of intimate relations. But it also provides tools for analyzing the constitution of other non-market domains. Consider, for example, political goods. Anderson claims that the production, distribution, and enjoyment of political goods are governed by three norms diametrically opposite to the market norms: Citizens exercise their freedom in a democracy though voice (participating in self-government), not just exit; democratic governance distributes goods in accordance with public principles, rather than unexamined wants; and the goods provided by the public are provided on a non-exclusive basis. Anderson argues that to attempt to provide political goods through market mechanisms (which are exclusive, want-regarding, and regulated primarily through exit), is to undermine our capacity to value and realize ourselves as democratic citizens. Do you agree? Consider as test cases the two examples Anderson provides: the privatization of public areas such as streets and parks, and the conversion of public provision of goods in kind—such as education—to the provision of their cash equivalents. For the opposite view, in which politics is, and should be, governed by market norms, see generally ROBERT D. COOTER, THE STRATEGIC CONSTITUTION (2000). Can you think of a midway that allows both preferences and reason in the political realm?

2. *Incomplete Commodification.* Margaret Jane Radin argues that in many cases we should break away from the binarism of complete commodification versus complete noncommodification, which guides strategies of compartmentalization such as Anderson's. Radin urges policymakers to seek ways in which both market understandings and non-market understandings stably coexist in our polity. In our non-ideal world, such strategies of incomplete commodification—where money exchanges hands but the interactions retain a personal aspect—can offer a normatively

attractive substitute for a complete noncommodification that might accord with our ideals but cause too much harm. (Do you see why a regime of complete noncommodification may be harmful? Think, for example, of its implications in terms of efficiency and liberty. Consider also whether in certain contexts it might have distributive and expressive adverse effects.) Thus, Radin maintains that regulation of the distribution of the goods in work and in housing in an effort to take into account workers' and tenants' personhood can helpfully recognize and foster the non-market significance of their work and housing, thus preventing them from deteriorating into the status of completely monetizable and tangible objects of exchange. Although complete decommodification of work or housing is not now possible, these social incomplete commodifications can be seen as responses in our non-ideal world to the harm to personhood caused by complete commodification of work and housing. *See* Margaret Jane Radin, Contested Commodities ch.7 (1996).

3. *Commodification and The Law.* There are numerous contexts in which the law participates in commodifying, decommodifying, and stabilizing equilibria of incomplete commodification, as both Anderson's text and the previous Notes imply. Three classic contexts that have generated substantial debates are the commodification of body parts, of babies, and of sex. For the first, see Chapter 14.2 below; for the second and third, see Rethinking Commodification 46-76, 222-270 (Martha M. Ertman & Joan C. Williams eds., 2005). But these issues pervade more traditional legal doctrines as well. Can you think, for example, of the way our conceptualization of tort compensation can benefit from Radin's notion of incomplete commodification? *See* Radin, Contested Commodities, at ch.13. For an analysis of tax law through the commodification prism, see Tsilly Dagan, *Itemizing Personhood*, 29 Va. Tax Rev. 93 (2009).

Property law — the focus of this book — also participates in the construction of commodified, decommodified, and incompletely commodified realms of human interaction. Property law is obviously a major participant in the market domain. But as we have already seen in Chapters 6 and 12, property law can and oftentimes does participate in non-market domains. You may also find both Anderson's characterization of the market domain and Radin's notion of incomplete commodification useful in many of the chapters of Part III.

4. *Values in and of the Market Domain.* Notice that although Anderson and Radin warn against market imperialism, they both acknowledge that the market domain serves important human values. The market obviously provides helpful incentives for the efficient production and allocation of scarce resources, thus serving our aggregate welfare. (But notice that — due to the marginal utility of money — the market use of willingness to pay as a proxy to utility is systematically regressive. *See* Anthony T. Kronman, *Wealth Maximization as a Normative Principle*, 9 J. Legal Stud. 227, 240 (1980).) The market can also serve — as the Hirschman excerpt in Chapter 13.1

emphasizes — laudable (but not only laudable) human dispositions. Finally, the impersonality of the market can be, as Anderson implies, an important means for erasing the effects of prejudices. For a powerful example, see Ian Ayres & Joel Waldfogel, *A Market Test for Race Discrimination in Bail Setting,* 46 STAN. L. REV. 987 (1994), who demonstrate that — compared to bond dealers, who operate in competitive markets — courts set bail to minority defendants at unjustified high levels. But there are, as Anderson also observes, regrettable — and quite significant — remnants of market discrimination; one notable example for this is in the context of housing segregation, discussed in Chapter 16.4 below.

III PROPERTY IN CONTEXT

14 *THINGS (PROPERTY IN WHAT?)*

1. INFORMATION

Yochai Benkler, Freedom in the Commons: Towards a Political Economy of Information[1]

I. A MOMENT OF OPPORTUNITY

In 1999, George Lucas released a bloated and much maligned "prequel" to the Star Wars Trilogy, called The Phantom Menace. In 2001, a disappointed Star Wars fan made a more tightly cut version, which almost eliminated a main sidekick called Jar-Jar Binks and subtly changed the protagonist — rendering Anakin Skywalker, who was destined to become Darth Vader, a much more somber child than the movie had originally presented. The edited version was named "The Phantom Edit." Lucas was initially reported amused, but later clamped down on distribution. It was too late. The Phantom Edit had done something that would have been unimaginable a decade earlier. One creative individual took Hollywood's finished product as raw material and extracted from within it his own film. Some, at least, thought it was a better film. Passed from one person to another, the film became a samizdat cultural object in its own right.

The Phantom Edit epitomizes both the challenge and the promise of what has variously been called "the new economy," "the information economy," or, more closely tied to the recent technological perturbation, "the Internet economy." It tells us of a hugely successful company threatened by one creative individual — a fan, not an enemy. It tells us

1. Yochai Benkler, *Freedom in the Commons: Towards a Political Economy of Information*, 52 DUKE L.J. 1245, 1245-1254, 1260-1272 (2003).

of the tremendous potential of the Internet to liberate individual creativity and enrich social discourse by thoroughly democratizing the way we produce information and culture. And it tells us how powerful proprietors can weigh in to discipline this unruly creativity; to silence the many voices it makes possible.

In this Lecture, I want to outline two fundamental social aspects of the emerging economic-technological condition of the networked information economy: the economic — concerned with the organization of production and consumption in this economy, and the political — concerned with how we pursue autonomy, democracy, and social justice in this new condition. We have seen over the past few years glimpses of this emerging economy and of its emerging political implications. We have seen the surprising growth of free software, an oasis of anarchistic production that is beating some of the world's richest corporations at their own game — making reliable high-quality software. We have seen a Russian computer programmer jailed for weeks in the United States pending indictment for writing software that lets Americans read books that they are not allowed to read. These and many other stories sprinkled throughout the pages of the technology sections of our daily newspapers hint at a deep transformation that is taking place, and at an epic battle over how this transformation shall go and who will come out on top when the dust settles.

Let us, then, talk about this transformation. Let us explore the challenge that the confluence of technological and economic factors has presented for the liberal democratic societies of the world's most advanced market economies. Let us think about how we might understand the stakes of this transformation in terms of freedom and justice.

In a nutshell, in the networked information economy — an economy of information, knowledge, and culture that flow through society over a ubiquitous, decentralized network — productivity and growth can be sustained in a pattern that differs fundamentally from the industrial information economy of the twentieth century in two crucial characteristics. First, nonmarket production — like the Phantom Edit, produced by a fan for the fun of it — can play a much more important role than it could in the physical economy. Second, radically decentralized production and distribution, whether market-based or not, can similarly play a much more important role. Again, the Phantom Edit is an example of such decentralized production — produced by one person rather than by a corporation with a chain of command and an inventory of property and contract rights to retain labor, capital, finance, and distribution outlets. In both these ways, the networked information economy can be more open and admit of many more diverse possibilities for organizing production and consumption than could the physical economy. As free software has shown us, these modes of production are not a plaything. Most of what we do on the Internet runs on software produced by tens of thousands of volunteers, working together in a way that is fundamentally more closely related to the fan who wrote the Phantom Edit than to the LucasArts Entertainment Company.

None of this is to say that nonmarket and decentralized production will completely displace firms and markets. That is not the point. The point is that the networked information economy makes it possible for nonmarket and decentralized models of production to increase their presence alongside the more traditional models, causing some displacement, but increasing the diversity of ways of organizing production rather than replacing one with the other.

This diversity of ways of organizing production and consumption, in turn, opens a range of new opportunities for pursuing core political values of liberal societies — democracy, individual freedom, and social justice. . . .

The most advanced economies have now made two parallel shifts that attenuate the limitations that market-based production places on the pursuit of core liberal political values. The first move, in the making for over a century, is the move to the information economy — an economy centered on information (financial services, accounting, software, science) and cultural (films, music) production, and the manipulation of symbols (e.g., from making sneakers to branding them and manufacturing the cultural significance of the Swoosh). The second move, of more recent vintage, is the move to a communications environment built on cheap processors with high computation capabilities, interconnected in a pervasively networked environment — the phenomenon we associate with the Internet. This second shift allows nonmarket production to play an increasing role in the information and cultural production sector, organized in a radically more decentralized pattern than was true of this sector in the twentieth century. The first shift means that the surprising patterns of production made possible by the networked environment — both nonmarket and radically decentralized — will emerge, if permitted to emerge, at the core, rather than at the periphery, of the most advanced economies. Permitting these patterns to emerge could therefore have a profound effect on our conceptions of the ultimate limits on how social relations can be organized in productive, growth-oriented economies.

Together these shifts can move the boundaries of liberty along all three vectors of liberal political morality. They enable democratic discourse to flow among constituents, rather than primarily through controlled, concentrated, commercial media designed to sell advertising, rather than to facilitate discourse. They allow individuals to build their own windows on the world, rather than seeing it largely through blinders designed to keep their eyes on the designer's prize. They allow passive consumers to become active users of their cultural environment, and they allow employees, whose productive life is marked by following orders, to become peers in common productive enterprises. And they can ameliorate some of the inequalities that markets have often generated and amplified. . . .

II.   SOME ECONOMIC PARAMETERS OF THE MOMENT

. . . I will suggest that we call the combination of these two trends — the radical decentralization of intelligence in our communications network and the centrality of information, knowledge, culture, and ideas to advanced economic activity — the networked information economy. By "networked information economy," I mean to describe an emerging stage of what in the past has been called more generally "the information economy" or "the information society." I would use the term in contradistinction to the earlier stage of the information economy, which one could call the "industrial information economy."

Certain characteristics of information and culture lead us to understand them as "public goods" in the technical economic meaning of the term, rather than as pure "private goods" or standard "economic goods." Economists usually describe "information" as "nonrival." The analytic content of the term applies to all cultural forms, and it means that the marginal cost of producing information, knowledge, or culture is zero. Once a scientist has established a fact, or once Tolstoy has written War and Peace, neither the scientist nor Tolstoy need spend a single second on producing additional War and Peace manuscripts or studies for the one-hundredth, one-thousandth, or one-millionth user. Economists call such goods "public," because a market will never produce them if priced at their marginal cost — zero. Given that welfare economics claims that a market is producing a good efficiently only when it is pricing the good at its marginal cost, a good that can never be sold both at a positive price and at its marginal cost is fundamentally a candidate for substantial nonmarket production.[2]

Information has another quirky characteristic in the framework of mainstream welfare economics — it is both the input and the output of its own production process. This has important implications that make property rights and market-based production even less appealing as the exclusive mechanisms for information and cultural production than they would have been if the sole quirky characteristic of information were the public goods problem. These characteristics form the standard economic justification for the substantial role of government funding, nonprofit research, and other nonproprietary production in our information production system, and have been understood as such at least since Nobel Laureate Kenneth Arrow identified them in this context four decades ago.

The standard problems that economics reveals with purely market-based production of information and culture have now been coupled with a drastic decline in the physical capital costs associated with production and distribution of this public good. As I mentioned, one primary input into information or cultural production is pre-existing information, which is

---

2. Kenneth J. Arrow, *Economic Welfare and the Allocation of Resources for Invention, in* THE RATE AND DIRECTION OF INVENTIVE ACTIVITY: ECONOMIC AND SOCIAL FACTORS 609 (1962).

itself a public good. The other inputs are human creativity and the physical capital necessary to generate, fix, and communicate transmissible units of information and culture — like a recording studio or a television network. Ubiquitously available cheap processors have radically reduced the necessary capital input costs. What can be done now with a desktop computer would once have required a professional studio. This leaves individual human beings closer to the economic center of our information production system than they have been for over a century and a half. And what places human beings at the center is not something that is homogeneous and largely fungible among people — like their physical capacity to work or the number of hours they can stay awake. Those fungible attributes of labor were at the center of the industrial model that Fredrick Taylor's scientific management and Henry Ford's assembly line typified. Their centrality to industrial production in the physical economy was an important basis for concentration and the organization of production in managed firms. In contrast, human beings are central in the networked information economy because of attributes in which they differ widely — creativity, wisdom, taste, social experience — as well as their effort and attention. And human beings use these personal attributes not only in markets, but also in nonmarket relations. From our homes to our communities, from our friendships to our play, we live life and exchange knowledge and ideas in many more diverse relations than those mediated by the market. In the physical economy, these relationships were largely relegated to spaces outside of our production system. The promise of the networked information economy and the digitally networked environment is to bring this rich diversity of living smack into the middle of our economy and our productive lives. . . .

In all these communities of production, individuals band together, contributing small or large increments of their time and effort to produce things they care about. They do so for a wide range of reasons — from pleasure, through socially and psychologically rewarding experiences, to economic calculation aimed at receiving consulting contracts or similar monetary rewards. At this point, what is important to see is that these efforts mark the emergence of a new mode of production, one that was mostly unavailable to people in either the physical economy (barring barn raising and similar traditional collective efforts in tightly knit communities) or in the industrial information economy. In the physical world, capital costs and physical distance — with its attendant costs of communication and transportation — mean that most people cannot exercise much control over their productive capacities, at least to the extent that to be effective they must collaborate with others. The digitally networked environment enables more people to exercise a greater degree of control over their work and productive relationships. In doing so, they increase the productivity of our information and cultural production system beyond what an information production system based solely on the proprietary industrial model could produce.

III. SOME THOUGHTS ON THE POLITICAL MORALITY

. . . [I]f it is the case, as I suggest, that productivity can be sustained with nonproprietary and nonmarket production, and if it is the case, as I will suggest to you in the remainder of the talk, that (1) proprietary- and market-based production have systematic dampening effects on democracy, autonomy, and social justice, and (2) nonproprietary commons-based production, as well as other nonmarket production, alleviate these dampening effects, then two things follow. First, if the networked information economy is permitted to emerge from the institutional battle, it will enable an outward shift of the limits that productivity places on the political imagination. Second, a society committed to *any positive combination* of the three values needs to adopt robust policies to facilitate these modes of production, because facilitating these modes of production does not represent a choice between productivity and liberal values, but rather an opportunity actually to relax the efficient limit on the plausible set of political arrangements available given the constraints of productivity. . . .

A. Democracy

The industrial model of mass media communications that dominated the twentieth century suffers from two types of democratic deficits that could be alleviated by a greater role for commons-based production. The first deficit concerns effective political participation, the second deficit concerns cultural politics, or the question of who gets to decide the cultural meaning of social choices and conditions. . . .

The primary thrust of the first deficit is the observation that in the mass-mediated environment only a tiny minority of players gets to participate in political public discourse and to affect decisionmaking directly. . . . The high cost of mass media communications translates into a high cost of a seat at the table of public political debate, a cost that renders individual participation all but impossible. The digitally networked environment makes it possible for many individuals and groups of similar beliefs to band together, express their views, organize, and gain much wider recognition than they could at a time when gaining recognition required acceptance by the editors of the mass media.

This claim is the most familiar of the political economy claims that I will make here. It largely tracks the fairly well-known critique of mass media and democracy, in particular regarding media concentration, that has been part of academic and public discourse over media policy throughout at least the second half of the twentieth century. The primary difference represented in my position is that the solutions that the Internet makes possible are radically different from those that dominated the twentieth-century debate. In the second half of the twentieth century, concerns about the effects of mass media on political discourse resolved into support for government regulation of the mass media. In the United States, solutions took the form of limited regulation of media companies — such as the fairness doctrine in broadcast or various carriage requirements in cable. In Europe, they took the form of more extensive government ownership or control of these media. These regulatory solutions, however, created opportunities for government abuse and political manipulation, while at the end of the day providing a pale reflection of widespread participation in discourse.

The possibility of sustainable, widely accessible and effective communications by individuals or groups, organized on- or offline, makes possible direct democratic discourse. It creates direct means for the acquisition of information and opinion. It offers the tools for its production and dissemination to a degree unattainable in the mass-mediated environment, no matter how well regulated. . . .

. . . Maintaining a heavily market-based system requires definition and enforcement of property rights. These rights, in turn, usually take the form of burdening individual constituents and groups in their own exchanges, so that they may be made to pay the market-based provider. The core questions from the perspective of democratic theory are these: what are the respective roles of large, commercial media and smaller scale, nonmarket fora in democracy? Which is more valuable to democratic discourse? The strongest arguments in favor of strong media come from Sunstein and Netanel. Sunstein's core claim is that the mass media provide a common language, a common agenda, and a set of images with which to create a common discourse. Without these, he argues, we shall be a nation of political narcissists, incapable of true political discourse.[3] Netanel's most important claim is that the resources and market-based economic heft that the commercial mass media have is absolutely necessary, in the presence of powerful government and powerful business interests, to preserve the independence and critical force of the Fourth Estate as watchdog of our democratic system of governance.[4]

The relationship between democracy and the structure of information production cannot, however, be considered as though we were designing an ideal state. The beginning of the twenty-first century is not typified by a robust public sphere populated by newspaper readers debating the news of the day and commentary in the idealized coffeehouses of London. Today's society is a thoroughly unattractive system for democratic communication, where money talks and everybody who wants to speak must either raise vast sums of money or rely on a large endowment. The commercial mass

---

3. CASS SUNSTEIN, REPUBLIC.COM 99-103 (2001).

4. Neil Weinstock Netanel, *Market Hierarchy and Copyright in Our System of Free Expression*, 53 VAND. L. REV. 1879, 1919 (2000).

media that we actually have suffered from two major deficits—the Berlusconi effect (or, more charitably the Bloomberg effect), of powerful media owners using their media to achieve political power, and the Baywatch effect, the depoliticization of public conversation. . . . As against this backdrop, the shift to a networked information economy is a substantial improvement. The wealth of detailed information made possible through DemocracyNet, the richness of conversation on a site like Kuro5hin perhaps will not change the political world, but they will offer substantial outlets for more attractive democratic practices and information flows than we saw in the twentieth century.

What radical decentralization of information production promises is the correction of some of the main maladies of the electronic mass media—the centralization of power to make meaning, the increased power of corporate interest in influencing the agenda, and the inescapable sound-bite character of the discussion.

The second democratic deficit of the mass-mediated communications environment concerns what some, like Niva Elkin Koren[5] and William Fisher,[6] have called "semiotic democracy," a term originally developed by John Fiske to describe the extent to which a medium permits its users to participate in structuring its message.[7] In the mass media model, a small group of actors, focused on maintaining and shaping consumer demand, has tremendous sway over the definition of meaning in society—what symbols are used and what they signify. The democracy [deficit] implicated by this aspect is not political participation in formal governance, but rather the extent to which a society's constituents participate in making sense of their society and their lives. In the mass media environment, meaning is made centrally. Commercial mass media owners, and other professional makers of meaning who can buy time from them, largely define the terms with which we think about life and develop our values. Television sitcoms, Barbie dolls, and movies define the basic set of symbols with which most of us can work to understand our lives and our society. In the pervasively networked environment, to the contrary, meaning can be produced collaboratively, by anyone, for anyone. Again, as with public political discourse, this will result in a more complicated and variegated, perhaps less coherent, story about how we should live together as constituents of society. But it will be a picture that we made, not one largely made for us and given to us finished, prepackaged, and massively advertised as "way cool."

---

5. Niva Elkin-Koren, *Cyberlaw and Social Change: A Democratic Approach to Copyright Law in Cyberspace*, 14 Cardozo Arts & Ent. L.J. 215, 233 (1996).

6. William Fisher, *Theories of Intellectual Property, in* New Essays in the Legal and Political Theory of Property 193 (Stephen R. Munzer ed., 2001).

7. John Fiske, Television Culture 95 (1987).

B. Autonomy

Autonomy, or individual freedom, is the second value that I suggest can be substantially served by increasing the portion of our information environment that is a commons and by facilitating nonmarket production. Autonomy means many things to many people, and some of these conceptions are quite significantly opposed to others. Nonetheless, from an autonomy perspective the role of the individual in commons-based production is superior to property-based production almost regardless of the conception one has of that value.

First, the mass media model, and its core of an owned and controlled communications infrastructure, provides substantial opportunities for individuals to be manipulated by the owners of the media. . . .

. . . Conversely, policies that introduce into the network significant commons-based elements, over which no one exercises control and which are therefore open for any individual to use to build their own window on the world, represent an important mechanism for alleviating the autonomy deficit created by an exclusively proprietary communications system.

Second, decentralization of information production and distribution has the capacity qualitatively to increase both the range and diversity of information individuals can access. In particular, the commercial mass media model has generally presented a relatively narrow range of options about how to live, and these options have been mostly variations on the mainstream. This is so largely because the economies of that model require large audiences to pay attention to anything distributed, constraining the content to that which would fit and attract large audiences. Decentralization of information production, and in particular expansion of the role of nonmarket production, makes information available from sources not similarly constrained by the necessity of capturing economies of scale. This will not necessarily increase the number of different ways people will actually live, but it will increase the number of different ways of living that each one knows about, and thereby enhance their capacity to choose knowledgeably. . . .

C. Justice

There are a number of potential benefits — in terms of social justice — to organizing a substantial component of our communications and information environment as a commons, in which nonmarket production can take on a more important role. These gains fall into categories that might be understood as liberal — or concerned with equality of opportunity in some form or another — and social-democratic, or concerned with the universal provision of relatively substantial elements of welfare. . . .

. . . First, commons in infrastructure and information and cultural resources form a baseline equal endowment, available for all to use in pursuit of their goals. They form a resource set that somewhat ameliorates the real-world constraints on the attainment of justice in a liberal society — to wit, the inequality in wealth that meets us when we are born into society. Commons in information and communications facilities are no panacea for inequality in initial endowments, but they do provide a relatively simple and sustainable way of giving everyone equal access to one important set of resources. Second, commons in communications infrastructure provide a transactional setting that ameliorates some of the inequalities in transactional capabilities that [are] a focus for liberal redistribution. Differences in the capacity to acquire information about the world, to transmit one's own preferences or proposals, and to form and reform common enterprises with others can significantly disadvantage an individual's opportunities to go through life on equal footing with others . . . A ubiquitously available high-speed commons in the network, and open access to resources and outputs of the information production system, mute this effect.

Less clear is the contribution made by policies aimed at realizing the viability of commons-based nonmarket production to equality in the "social-democratic" sense of providing decent access to a substantial level of services to everyone, regardless of wealth . . . The expansion in scope and efficacy of the nonmarket sector suggests that in the domain of information, knowledge, and culture, a more substantial level of services and goods will be available from sources insensitive to the wealth of users, which relate instead to more evenly distributed attributes — some intangible, like desires or values shared with providers, others tangible, like time or attention. Insofar as this is true, increasing the role of commons-based nonmarket production will serve the social-democratic conception of equality. . . .

Building such a commons would [also] add a more competitive layer of goods and services from market-based sources, as well as nonmarket sources, thereby providing a wider range of information and cultural goods at lower cost. On the consumption side this has an unusual flavor as an argument within a social-democratic framework. Proposing a mechanism that will increase competition and decrease the role of government-granted and regulated monopolies is not exactly the traditional social-democratic way. But lower prices are a mechanism for increasing the welfare of those at the bottom of the economic ladder, and in particular, competition in the provision of a zero-marginal-cost good, to the extent it eventually drives the direct price of access and use to zero, will have this effect. More importantly, access to such resources, free of the usual capital constraints, will permit easier access to production opportunities for some in populations traditionally outside the core of the global economy — particularly in developing nations. Such access could provide, over the long term, somewhat greater equity in the distribution of wealth globally, as producers in peripheral economies take these opportunities to compete through a globally connected distribution medium, access to which is relatively unaided by wealth endowments.

NOTES AND QUESTIONS

1. *Celebrating the Public Domain.* Benkler argues that the networked information economy makes the informational public domain both viable and (at least potentially) normatively desirable. Lior Strahilevitz is much more skeptical. He believes that it is "premature to write about the success of social production without analyzing how social production networks can respond to the threats posed by early successes." More specifically, he argues that because these networks "tend to be open by nature," they become vulnerable to "malicious attacks and proprietary appropriation": "Whenever social production creates a valuable resource that large numbers of citizens want to use, that resource becomes an attractive target for the mischief-makers, proprietary competitors, free-riders, sketchy opportunists, and well-meaning dolts whose arrival can drive away the cooperators who built the successful network." Benkler's optimism is misplaced, Strahilevitz concludes, because he is "insufficiently sensitive to the way selection effects and competitive pressures will govern the rise and fall of social production." Lior Jacob Strahilevitz, *Wealth Without Markets?*, 116 YALE L.J. 1472, 1514-1515 (2007). Which of these views do you find more persuasive?

2. *On Positive Externalities and Free-riders.* Benkler implicitly seems to challenge the canonical economic injunction that the law should aim at internalizing externalities, both negative and positive. The law, on this view, should be cautious not to reduce participation in productive activities that yield beneficial spillovers. *See generally* Brett M. Frischmann & Mark A. Lemley, *Spillovers*, 107 COLUM. L. REV. 257 (2007). This also means, perhaps counter-intuitively, that free-riding is not always detrimental. As Wendy Gordon explains, no culture could exist "if all free-riding were prohibited within it" because culture "is interdependence, and requiring each act of deliberate dependency to render an accounting would destroy the synergy on which cultural life rests." Moreover, no community could exist because community is defined as interdependence: "persons learn from each other, sell complementary products, build on a common heritage." Wendy J. Gordon, *Of Harms and Benefits: Torts, Restitution, and Intellectual Property*, 21 J. LEGAL STUD. 449, 468 (1992); Wendy J. Gordon, *On Owning Information: Intellectual Property and the Restitutionary Impulse*, 78 VA. L. REV. 149, 167-68 (1992). Furthermore, not only a welfarist perspective at times justifies free-riding, but a distributive lens also may yield similar conclusions. Consider, for example, cases where the free-rider is able to receive a benefit free of charge because her stake in the collective enterprise is relatively small. In these circumstances the free-rider's nonparticipation may not frustrate the possibility of achieving the collective good when there is another single member of the group who is likely to derive sufficient benefits from the collective good to justify paying the entire cost of supplying it alone. *See* MANCUR OLSON, THE LOGIC OF COLLECTIVE ACTION: PUBLIC GOODS AND THE THEORY OF

GROUPS 41 (2d ed. 1971). Where the parties' stakes at the collective enterprise roughly correlate with their socio-economic predicament, the distributive consequences of many cases of this type may be rather happy, at least from an egalitarian point of view.

3. *Between Private Property and the Public Domain.* Property lawyers usually discuss information in the context of the various branches of intellectual property — copyright law, patent law, etc. — which prescribe the specific entitlements of authors and inventors as well as their transferees. Benkler belongs to a growing group of scholars who highlight the drawbacks of expanding these rights of private property and caution against shrinking the public domain. *See also* JAMES BOYLE, SHAMANS, SOFTWARE, AND SPLEENS: LAW AND THE CONSTRUCTION OF THE INFORMATION SOCIETY (1996); LAWRENCE LESSIG, FREE CULTURE (2004). These friends of the public domain typically seek to distance the discussion of information policy from the language of property, because it facilitates, so the argument goes, a social ecology that is *a priori* hostile to the public domain. *See, e.g.,* LESSIG, *id.,* at 83-84, 117-119, 172. This claim can be a good opportunity for reconsidering some of the materials of Parts I and II of this book.

Consider the relationship between some of the property values discussed in Part I and the proper boundary between the public domain and private rights in information. Does, for example, the notion that labor or workmanship justifies reward entail rigid private rights? (Recall in this respect Notes 2 and 3 at the end of Chapter 1.) Also, which types of information should, in your view, be affected by the personhood value of property, and in which ways? And what (if any) should be the consequences of the distributive implications of personhood theory, discussed in Note 5 of Chapter 2? Finally, does the notion that property is a means for maximizing aggregate well-being, explored in Chapter 5, indeed entail robust private rights in information? For an overview of the leading normative accounts of intellectual property law, see William Fisher, *Theories of Intellectual Property, in* NEW ESSAYS IN THE LEGAL AND POLITICAL THEORY OF PROPERTY 168 (Stephen R. Munzer ed., 2001). *See also* Abraham Drassinower, *Copyright Infringement as Compelled Speech, in* NEW FRONTIERS IN THE PHILOSOPHY OF INTELLECTUAL PROPERTY ___, ___ (Annabelle Lever ed., 2012) (arguing that "the purpose of copyright is . . . to affirm the inherent dignity of the author as a speaking being," and insisting that the most promising foundation of the public domain lies in such a neo-Kantian account because it "brings into relief the correlative autonomy of the members of her audience . . . as speaking beings").

If you end up concluding that there is no necessary cleavage between a commitment to the public domain and property discourse, reconsider Chapter 8, in which we have discussed the structure of property. Which of the competing positions explored there is supported by the example of property in information?

4. *The Evolution of Property Rights in Information.* One way to read Benkler's account is as an evolutionary process in which the property regime governing information shifts towards one that increases, rather than diminishes, the scope of open access (public domain). Can this shift be explicated in the economic terms discussed by Demsetz in Chapter 5 and the commentators mentioned in the following Notes?

Recall that in Note 1 of Chapter 5 we suggested that positive accounts of the development of property regimes must consider the effects of interest groups. In the context of information, commentators often emphasize the role of rent-seeking by the content industry in the legislative process (think, for example, of the repeated extensions of copyright's term and coverage of protection). *See generally* Lawrence Lessig, The Future of Ideas: The Fate of the Commons in a Connected World (2001); Neil Weinstock Netanel, Copyright's Paradox (2008); James Boyle, The Public Domain (2008).

5. *Property "Altlaws" and Intellectual Property.* Eduardo Peñalver and Sonia Katyal have coined the term "altlaws" to refer to persons whose use of intellectual assets may run afoul of the law but "at least arguably falls within the boundaries of legality and, at the same time, who do[] not reject out of hand the concept of intellectual property." Eduardo Moisés Peñalver & Sonia K. Katyal, Property Outlaws: How Squatters, Pirates, and Protesters Improve the Law of Ownership 77 (2010). The phenomenon results in part, they argue, from ambiguity in many areas of intellectual property law. One obvious example is the practice of some (many?) professors to reproduce and distribute to their students copyrighted material for classroom purposes without the copyright holder's authorization. The practice often falls within the scope of copyright law's fair use exception, but not always, in part because of uncertainty of the scope of that doctrine. Peñalver and Katyal argue that altlaws can generate important distributive and informational benefits and, therefore, that the law should not overreact to their activities, which constitute a path of legal change. *Id.* at 82. Can this effect counterbalance the impact of rent-seeking mentioned in the previous Note?

2. THE BODY AND BODY PARTS

Stephen R. Munzer, An Uneasy Case Against Property Rights in Body Parts[1]

This essay deals with property rights in body parts that can be exchanged in a market. The inquiry arises in the following context. With some

---

1. Stephen R. Munzer, *An Uneasy Case Against Property Rights in Body Parts,* 11 Soc. Phil. & Pol'y 259, 259, 260, 266-267, 269-270, 271-274, 284-285 (1994).

exceptions, the laws of many countries permit only the donation, not the sale, of body parts. Yet for some years there has existed a shortage of body parts for transplantation and other medical uses. It might then appear that if more sales were legally permitted, the supply of body parts would increase, because people would have more incentive to sell than they currently have to donate. To allow sales is to recognize property rights in body parts. To allow sales, however, makes body parts into "commodities" — that is, things that can be bought and sold in a market. And some view it as morally objectionable to treat body parts as commodities.

I present a qualified case against property rights in body parts that are transferable in a market. As used here, the term "body parts" includes any organs, tissues, fluids, cells, or genetic material on the contours of or within the human body, or removed from it, except for waste products such as urine and feces. The qualified case rests on a Kantian argument concerning human dignity. But the case is uneasy. There is no swift transition from the mere existence of a market in body parts to a sound objection in terms of commodities and Kantian dignity. . . .

I do not offer knockdown arguments for bold conclusions. I do contend that it is morally objectionable for persons to sell their body parts if they offend dignity by transferring them for a reason that is not strong enough in light of the nature of the parts sold. Furthermore, it is morally objectionable to participate in a market for body parts, as (say) a buyer or broker, if by doing so one offends the dignity of oneself or others. Lastly, it is morally objectionable for a market in body parts to exist if its workings offend the dignity of enough participants in the market. These contentions raise a moral objection based on dignity rather than the existence of a moral objection all things considered. That an action or institution is morally objectionable does not entail that one lacks a moral right to do it or participate in it, or that the state or others have a moral right to interfere with the action or institution. . . . [2]

III. A Kantian Starting Point

The works of Kant suggest several arguments against property rights in human body parts. One of them — the argument from dignity — runs as

---

2. Keith N. Hylton, "The Law and Ethics of Organ Sales," *Jahrbuch für Recht und Ethik*, vol. 4 (1996), pp. 115-36, discusses the full text of my paper. Most of the time he is careful to separate my highly qualified moral argument from the less cautious arguments of Ruth Chadwick, Leon Kass, and Margaret Radin (pp. 116-20). But occasionally he lumps all of us together as "Kantian writers" or "Kantian critics" (pp. 122, 124 n.23, 126, 134). In my judgment, Hylton's criticisms are ineffective against my arguments, no matter what force they might have against others. Because I was not discussing administrative issues, I need take no position on whether Hylton is correct to claim that the "serious grounds" against "a limited market in body parts are not on a moral level, but almost entirely on the level of administration" (p. 136). [This footnote did not appear in the original version of the article. We have added it at Professor Munzer's request. — Eds.]

follows. Human beings have dignity *(Würde)*. Dignity is an unconditioned and incomparable worth. Entities with dignity differ sharply from entities that have a price on a market.[3] If human beings had property rights in body parts and exercised those rights, they would treat parts of their bodies in ways that conflict with their dignity. They would move from the level of entities with dignity to the level of things with a price.

This argument, as just presented, is entirely too sketchy to be convincing. To fill it in, one must at least (1) unpack Kant's understanding of dignity, (2) explain his account of persons and their bodies, (3) clarify so far as possible the difference between sales and donations, and (4) articulate preliminarily the connection between selling a body part and being vulnerable to moral objection. I intend the resulting argument to be broadly Kantian in spirit. I do not claim that Kant scholars will find it faultless, or that it is consistent with everything that Kant says.

1. Persons have dignity just in virtue of being human.[4] This dignity is not lost even if a person acts immorally.[5] Moreover, dignity is "unconditioned"[6] — that is, it does not depend on needs, consequences, or other contingent facts. Dignity is also an "incomparable worth," for it is "exalted above all price" and "admits of no equivalent."[7] Thus, one cannot counterbalance an offense against dignity by any increase in price. Dignity is therefore priceless.

Dignity is an attribute not mainly of isolated individuals but of persons as "ends in themselves"[8] who are members of a "kingdom of ends."[9] Persons so understood belong to a moral community in which dignity and autonomy must be ascribed to every rational person with a will. Accordingly, the construction of a legal system for these persons must observe the dignity of each individual.

Let us now join these reflections on dignity with the idea of moral and legal rights. I suggest that Kant's understanding of dignity proceeds from an effort to wrestle with the question of how we must reciprocally recognize individuals in a moral and legal order that affords them equal rights. His answer is that we must ascribe to them the attribute of dignity if a practice of universal equal rights is to make sense. This attribute is transcendentally necessary. That is, ascribing dignity to oneself and others is a necessary condition of the possibility of universal equal rights. . . .

3. Immanuel Kant, *Groundwork of the Metaphysic of Morals* [1785], trans. H. J. Paton as *The Moral Law* (London: Hutchinson University Library, 1948), pp. 96-97.

4. See, for example, *ibid.*, pp. 96-97; Immanuel Kant, *The Metaphysics of Morals* [1797], trans. Mary Gregor (Cambridge: Cambridge University Press, 1991), pp. 216-17, 230-31, 254-55.

5. See, for example, Immanuel Kant, *Lectures on Ethics* [1775-1780], trans. Louis Infield and foreword by Lewis White Beck (Indianapolis and Cambridge: Hackett, 1963), pp. 196-97.

6. Kant, *Groundwork of the Metaphysic of Morals*, p. 97.

7. *Ibid.*, pp. 96, 97.

8. Kant, *Groundwork of the Metaphysic of Morals*, pp. 97-98.

9. *Ibid.*, pp. 98-100.

2. If these remarks help to explain Kant's understanding of dignity, they do little to elucidate the complicated, and not terribly clear, account of body parts, whole bodies, selves, and persons on which the argument seems to rest. Although Kant often makes stronger statements, his deepest objection, I think, is only to property rights in *some* body parts as defined in my introduction. He comments that the "body is part of the self; in its *togetherness* with the self it constitutes the person."[10] He also appears to distinguish between body parts that are organs, such as kidneys or testicles, and body parts that are not organs or otherwise integral to the functioning of the body, such as hair.[11] His emphasis, then, is on the integration or "togetherness" of the various parts that make up a human person. And the core of his protest is against the sale of any part that is integral to the normal biological functioning of that person.

One way to develop this Kantian argument is to distinguish between isolated sales and frequent exchanges in a market. Kant would have concerns about both. Even isolated transactions could offend the dignity of the few individuals involved. Yet frequent exchanges pose a graver risk to the dignity of many individuals. If a market is an arrangement in which sellers and buyers make exchanges, and if commodities are items that can be bought and sold in a market, then a market for those body parts integral to normal biological functioning, such as kidneys, would be quite worrisome for Kant. Specifically, the existence of such a market could transform attitudes that human beings have toward themselves and others. They might come to think of one another not so much as moral agents with inherent dignity, but more as repositories of organs, tissues, and other bodily substances. They might dwell heavily on the price that healthy organs would fetch on the market. In sum, a Kantian argument from dignity raises, at least prima facie, a concern about body parts as "commodities" that are exchangeable in a market. . . .

4. . . . [E]ven if the line between sales and donations is clear enough, it is necessary to articulate the connection between selling a body part and being vulnerable to moral objection. Recall that the core Kantian protest involves, in effect, two strands: selling body parts and losing body parts needed for normal biological functioning. A thought experiment can separate these strands and force consideration of what it is about *selling* that might be objectionable. Imagine that in the distant future artificial organs and other body parts are plentiful. Only a small subgroup of humans needs natural organs as replacements for organs that have become diseased or injured. A member of the larger group sells various natural organs to members of the subgroup, and immediately receives artificial organs in risk-free surgical procedures. He makes money in these transactions because the price for his natural organs far exceeds the cost of the artificial replacements

---

10. Kant, *Lectures on Ethics*, p. 166 (emphasis added); cf. *ibid.*, pp. 147-48.
11. Kant, *The Metaphysics of Morals*, p. 219.

and the surgeries. Hence, in this hypothetical example, the strand of losing a body part necessary to healthy functioning drops out as a pertinent consideration.

What, then, might be objectionable about selling as such? It will not do to say that the hypothetical seller should get a job rather than sell natural organs for a living. The seller may well be leading a shallow life and not fulfilling the possibilities of a genuinely human existence. Even if that is so, the objection appears to be, not to selling as such, but rather to leading a shallow and unfulfilling life. Nor will it do to say, in the case of some organs or body parts, that they are so bound up with the seller's personal identity that they should not be sold. Examples of such organs or parts might include the brain, face, genitals, hands, tongue, and larynx. Once again, if there is a sound objection, it relates, not to selling as such, but to the transfer of intensely personal parts of the body.

A better answer invokes the *strength of the reason* for selling the organ or body part. Getting money is a superficial reason for transferring a body part, at least when the seller has morally unproblematic ways of earning a decent living. Compare Kant's remark that it is objectionable "to have oneself castrated in order to get an easier livelihood as a singer."[12] Kant's thought here may be that if a somewhat less easy livelihood is still possible, one does violence to the humanity in one's person by becoming a castrato. The hypothetical seller's reason differs from deeper or nobler reasons, such as donating an organ to save the life of a member of the subgroup. Furthermore, receiving money would be an especially superficial reason for transferring an intensely personal part of the seller's body. For such parts, the reason could be deeper if the recipient were the seller's identical twin, though here donating betokens a nobler class of reasons and associated motives than selling. It is, of course, possible for a reason for donating a body part also to be insufficiently strong. . . .

As a first approximation, then, selling a body part might be morally objectionable if the strength of the reason for selling is insufficient in relation to the nature of the part sold. This preliminary result should be understood against the background of the following points. First, money is just a medium of exchange. Thus, receiving money in return for a body part is not inherently or always morally objectionable. One has to look at the reason for which the seller wants the money. Second, even if selling is morally objectionable, it does not follow that the seller lacks a moral right to sell. Here, as in other situations, persons sometimes have a moral right to do what is morally wrong, objectionable, base, ignoble, or degrading.[13] Third,

---

12. Kant, *The Metaphysics of Morals*, p. 219.

13. See Jeremy Waldron, "A Right to Do Wrong," *Ethics*, vol. 92 (October 1981), pp. 21-39. Any position worth stating in philosophy invites dispute, but Waldron's defense is stronger than Galston's criticisms of him. William A. Galston, "On the Alleged Right to Do Wrong: A Response to Waldron," *Ethics*, vol. 93 (January 1983), pp. 320-24; Jeremy Waldron, "Galston on Rights," *Ethics*, vol. 93 (January 1983), pp. 325-27. I do not claim that Kant would hold that there is a moral right to do

it is logically possible for an entity to have both a dignity-value and a market-value. Nevertheless, it may not be psychologically possible for someone to think of an entity as simultaneously having both and still retain the attitudes typically exhibited toward entities regarded as possessing dignity. And there can be a kind of social split-mindedness if many regard some persons — e.g., women or children — as simultaneously having both kinds of value. Fourth, even if a body part is salable and hence is a commodity, it does not follow that the body part is *only* a commodity. Fifth, this preliminary result has nothing to do with some familiar Marxian themes. The result does not suppose that anyone is exploiting the seller. Neither does it rest on the idea that exchange-value swamps or undercuts use-value. For instance, if kidneys can be bought and sold, then they have an exchange-value. But this fact does not interfere with their use-value, for sold kidneys, if successfully transplanted, will perform the same functions in the recipients that they did in the sellers. Sixth, so far only a possible objection to selling body parts has emerged. Lacking at the moment is any account of how buying body parts or the existence of a market for body parts could offend dignity.

IV.   THREE WAYS OF OFFENDING DIGNITY

The Kantian starting point has not got us far. It proposes a definitional connection between a market for body parts and a view of body parts as commodities. It suggests that the lack of a sufficiently strong reason is what can make selling body parts morally objectionable. And it introduces some speculative worries about the impact of a market for body parts on dignity. Yet the previous section does not explain how this market, or participating in it, can offend dignity. Providing such an explanation is the next order of business.

I shall describe three ways of offending dignity by buying or selling body parts. The classification is consistent with but does not stem from Kant's writings. The first way affronts, insults, or demeans dignity. The offense is direct. The second and third ways degrade the sense of dignity. Here the offenses are indirect. They relate proximally to the sense of dignity and only distally to dignity itself. I shall elaborate.

The first way of offending dignity occurs if and only if an action affronts, insults, or demeans dignity, but does not reduce it. Kantian dignity, it will be recalled, is an unconditioned and incomparable moral worth that all persons have *just* in virtue of being human. It relates to a transcendentally necessary attribute of human beings. Consequently, this first offense against dignity does not reduce the worth of a person. It cannot

---

what is morally wrong. [We have added the text following the citation to Jeremy Waldron's initial article at Professor Munzer's request. — Eds.]

do so. Unless the action kills the victim, or produces a mental disintegration that destroys the victim's capacity to act as a rational moral agent, the victim will survive as a person. And were the victim destroyed as a person, the dignity would be destroyed rather than merely reduced.

This first offense against dignity is significant because it is a specially disrespectful form of treatment. If one commits the offense against oneself, one exhibits a disregard for one's own inherent worth. However, I do not agree with those passages in Kant that suggest, for example, that by engaging in prostitution or selling oneself, one "jettison[s] [one's] person" and becomes a "thing" or a worm.[14] These actions, even if they are morally wrong, do not have a once-for-all effect. If others commit this offense against a person, indignation and resentment are appropriate. Suppose, for example, that a shop foreman upbraids a female employee, calls her a "typical stupid woman," and screams that her job "should be done by a man." The employee is entitled to protest and rebuke the wrongdoer and defiantly to reaffirm her worth in the face of such treatment. It is a tricky matter to say what sort of intention is necessary to offend dignity in this first way. The verb "affront" suggests that the intention selects dignity as its target. The verbs "insult" and "demean" probably require some less selective or precise intention to offend dignity.

Explaining the second and third offenses against dignity requires a pair of additional concepts. One is the *sense of dignity:* an awareness of unconditioned and incomparable worth. This awareness is connected to Kant's understanding of self-respect, which I take to be a sense of inner moral worth that comes from acting on principles rationally derived from the moral law. Unlike dignity, the sense of dignity is partly subjective, since it rests on a person's awareness of his or her moral worth. Furthermore, *unlike* dignity, the sense of dignity is susceptible of being reduced.

The possibility of a reduced sense of dignity brings into play the other concept: *degradation.* . . . [D]egradation is treating someone or something in such a way as to reduce, or to attempt to reduce, him, her, or it to a lower level or degree. There are many sorts of degradation. In the present context, a lower level or degree of sense of dignity is meant. So the thought is that to recognize and exercise property rights in body parts might sometimes be to lower a person's sense of dignity.

With these two concepts in hand, I return to the remaining offenses against dignity. The second way of offending dignity occurs if and only if an action has, and is intended to have, the outcome of degrading someone's sense of dignity. For instance, if an organ broker in a Third World country intended to make a prospective seller of a kidney feel of lesser moral worth, and if the broker succeeded, the broker would have degraded the prospective seller's sense of dignity. Of course, those who deal in body parts may

---

14. Kant, *Lectures on Ethics*, p. 124. But see *ibid*, pp. 196-97.

not have such refined intentions as to undermine a person's sense of moral worth. They are more likely to intend to make money by dealing in organs. But whenever the appropriate intention is present, and the intended outcome is achieved, the second offense against dignity arises.

The third way of offending dignity occurs if and only if an action has, but is not intended to have, the outcome of degrading someone's sense of dignity. Here the person who degrades does not intend to lower a person's awareness of moral worth, but lowers it through some lapse, fault, mistake, misjudgment, or the like. Suppose that you are a medical worker. Through insensitivity, you treat me as a repository of organs and tissues to be sold on the market. I am fragile and my sense of dignity declines. You have offended dignity in this last way.

The relevance to morality of this threefold classification of offenses against dignity is as follows. From the standpoint of consequences, the last two offenses are more serious than the first. From the perspective of the appraisal of intentions, the first two offenses are more serious than the third. Of course, the third offense may still exhibit a kind of moral fault that is distinct from consequences. It can be blameworthy to have allowed oneself to develop, say, the insensitivity to treat others badly without intending to lower their sense of dignity. . . .

The general payoff of this section is that participating in a market for body parts can sometimes undercut the distinction between dignity and price, and thus sometimes undermine the practice of mutual recognition as equal rights-bearing citizens. To appreciate this general point, one should, however, attend to the three different ways in which buying and selling body parts can offend dignity. Otherwise, one can fall into using such words as "demeaning" or "degrading" without noticing that they can apply to different situations requiring careful discrimination. In contrast to the previous section, we now have a tentative explanation of how market activities in addition to selling might sometimes offend dignity. . . .

VIII. The Uneasy Case Summarized

This essay contains a sufficiently intricate argument to be worth a summary. The argument starts from the Kantian premise that all human beings have dignity. Dignity is an unconditioned and incomparable worth. Human actions can offend dignity in at least three ways. They can do so directly by affronting, insulting, or demeaning the moral status of a human being. They can also do so indirectly by degrading, either intentionally or unintentionally, the sense of dignity of a human being. Offenses against dignity can be committed either by those whose dignity is offended, or by others, or by both.

Because Kantian dignity differs sharply from having a price on the market, sales of anything possessing such dignity may seem, at least prima facie, to be morally objectionable. Still, it is logically possible for an entity to have both a dignity-value and a market-value. Hence, the argument is not that having dignity precludes having a price on the market, or that exchange-value swamps use-value, or that if something can be bought and sold in a market it is *only* a commodity. Rather, the argument is that if an entity has dignity, then treating that entity or some part of it as a commodity is morally objectionable if the treatment offends dignity.

One now comes to the issue of *when* treating an entity having dignity in certain ways is morally objectionable. To grapple with this issue, we need to distinguish between whole persons and body parts. Most will readily agree that treating a *whole person* as a commodity—for example, as a slave to be bought and sold—offends dignity and thus is morally objectionable. But they might resist the claim that treating a *body part* as a commodity offends dignity. They might urge that any such claim rests on an illegitimate whole-to-part reasoning—the fallacy of division. This essay accepts that the fallacy of division really is a fallacy. And it rejects the idea that body parts *themselves* have dignity in Kant's sense.

How, then, can treating a *body part* as a commodity offend the dignity of a *person?* An answer lies in the pursuit of two complementary strategies. The integration strategy points to the fact that the unified organization of body parts, of various kinds, makes up a living human being. This strategy marks out a gradient of concerns about body parts as commodities. The derived-status strategy emphasizes that the status of any given body part is a function of the status of the whole organism and the role of that part in the whole. This strategy suggests a gradient of appropriate uses of body parts. Together these strategies keep one from falling in a blundering whole-to-part reasoning, while still enabling one to see how treating body parts as commodities *can* offend a person's dignity.

These strategies and gradients have theoretical implications. The implications vary among the participants in a market for body parts and the effects of the market on the participants' sense of dignity. It is morally objectionable for persons to sell their body parts if they offend dignity by selling for a reason that is insufficiently strong relative to the characteristics of the parts sold. It is also morally objectionable for others, such as buyers and brokers, to participate in a market for body parts if by doing so they offend the dignity of sellers or themselves. To say that these actions are "morally objectionable" is not to say that the agents have no moral right to do them, or that the state or other persons have a moral right to interfere with the agents. Finally, it is morally objectionable for a market in body parts to exist if its operation offends the dignity of enough participants in the market. This last implication is fragile. It is difficult to say how many participants are "enough." And even if such a market were morally objectionable on grounds of offense against dignity, it would hardly follow that people have no right to participate in the market, or that the state or other persons have a right to interfere with the market.

The practical payoff of these strategies and gradients is as follows. Worries about offenses against dignity are least serious if one sells body parts that are replenishable or naturally shed and whose removal involves virtually no risk. Examples include hair, blood, and, aside from specifically religious objections, sperm. The worries are not much more serious in the case of replenishable or naturally shed body parts whose removal involves some minor risk to the seller. Examples are ova and bone marrow. One reason that these last examples carry at least some extra concern is that, because of the risk and pain involved, financial considerations may exert more pressure than is desirable on the decision to sell.

Practical worries about offenses to dignity increase with the *inter vivos* sale of nonreplenishable solid organs, such as a kidney or a cornea, for transplantation. Removing the organ involves some risk to the seller especially in countries where the rate of mortality or morbidity is high. Even if the surgical removal is completely successful, a person with one remaining kidney has a slightly lower life expectancy than a person with two, and a person with one remaining intact eyeball has poorer vision than a person with two. Given these risks and consequences, only financial exigency is likely to spur someone to sell. Accordingly, the prospect of offenses against dignity, in any of the three forms described, looms larger than with sales of blood, sperm, ova, or even bone marrow.

NOTES AND QUESTIONS

1. *Legal Restrictions on the Sale of Human Body Parts.* Julia Mahoney and Pamela Clark point out that "[a]lthough the idea of property rights in solid organs, blood, gametes, and other human tissue triggers unease and even revulsion in many quarters, it is impossible to imagine a world devoid of such rights." Julia D. Mahoney & Pamela Clark, *Property Rights in Human Tissue, in* PROPERTY RIGHTS DYNAMICS: A LAW AND ECONOMICS PERSPECTIVE 138, 138 (Donatella Porrini & Giovanni Battista Ramello eds., 2007). Perhaps property rights in human tissue are all but inevitable in liberal societies, but legal systems closely regulate these rights nevertheless, reflecting societal concerns about them. In the United States, both federal and state statutes restrict what sticks are included in the bundle of rights that constitutes ownership of particular parts of the human body. These statutes are especially concerned with the transferability of human body parts. The National Organ Transplant Act, a federal statute enacted in 1984, for example, makes it "unlawful for any person to knowingly acquire, receive, or otherwise transfer any human organ for valuable consideration for use in human transplantation if the transfer affects interstate commerce." 42 U.S.C. §274(e). Similarly, the Uniform Anatomical Gift Act, which has been enacted into law in many states, makes it a felony for a person knowingly to purchase or sell a human body part for transplantation or therapy "if

removal of a part from an individual is intended to occur after the individual's death. . . . " Revised Uniform Anatomical Gift Act 2006 §16. What policy concerns underlie the restrictions on transactions in human body parts in these two statutes?

2. *A Right to Do Wrong.* At more than one point Munzer suggests that we may, at times, have a moral right to do some act that is morally wrong. How can this be? Munzer relies on an argument made in Jeremy Waldron, *A Right to Do Wrong*, 92 ETHICS 21 (1981). Waldron argues that it is one thing to say that some act a person does is morally wrong, and quite a different thing to say that it would be morally right or permissible to interfere with the person's performing that act. It may be morally wrong for *A* to give racist speeches, but the wrongness of *A*'s actions, Waldron argues, does not grant me moral license to stop *A* from continuing to give the racist speeches. Stating sincerely that giving racist speeches is morally wrong commits me to avoiding giving racist speeches in the sort of circumstances in which *A* is placed. But it does not, Waldron contends, commit me to interfering with *A*'s actions. Do you find this argument persuasive? If, because of my moral beliefs, I have a moral obligation not to commit a certain act, can I tolerate the same act when you commit it? If so, are there any principled limits to such a toleration?

3. *Paternalism?* Munzer states that given the consequences and risks of surgical removal of organs such as kidneys and corneas, which are non-replenishable, "only financial exigency is likely to spur someone to sell." Munzer, *supra*, at 285. Given the self-interested reasons not to sell, aren't legal restrictions on sale paternalistic? In many cases legal restrictions on sale may well be, in Joel Feinberg's terminology, strong paternalism, rather than weak paternalism, because they are not based on problems of information or on cognitive errors. As such, such restrictions are particularly difficult to justify in a liberal society, are they not? (On the distinction between strong and weak paternalism, see Joel Feinberg, *Legal Paternalism*, in PATERNALISM 3 (Rolf Sartorius ed., 1983).) To make matters even worse, the fact that the basis for the exigency of organ sales is poverty makes the state prohibition even more insulting, given that the state is frequently at least partly responsible for this harsh predicament.

4. *Commodification Redux and the Domino Theory.* Notice that the statutes restrict only commercial transactions. Gifts of human body parts are legal for all purposes under both acts. Part of the reason for this distinction is the concern with commodification, which we discussed previously in Chapter 13.2. The arguments that Margaret Jane Radin laid out in her book *Contested Commodities* are frequently provided as justifications for the legal distinction between sales and gifts of human body parts. We will not repeat those arguments here, but one concern bears special mention. Some moral theorists have worried that permitting sales will crowd out donations of body parts. This concern has been dubbed the "domino theory." *See* MARGARET JANE RADIN, CONTESTED COMMODITIES 95-101

(1996). As Radin states, "According to this [domino] argument, altruism is foreclosed if both donations and sales are permitted." Margaret Jane Radin, *Justice and the Market Domain, in* NOMOS XXXI: MARKETS AND JUSTICE 165, 170 (John W. Chapman & J. Roland Pennock eds., 1989). Richard Titmuss made a famous version of this argument with respect to human blood. *See* RICHARD M. TITMUSS, THE GIFT RELATIONSHIP: FROM HUMAN BLOOD TO SOCIAL POLICY (1971). Radin points out that the domino theory implicitly rests on two premises: one normative, and the other empirical. The normative premise is that it is morally valuable for non-market regimes to exist. The empirical premise is that a non-market regime cannot coexist with a market regime because market regimes tend to drive out their non-market rivals. Radin, *Justice and the Market Domain, supra,* at 173. Do you agree with either or both of these claims? For a critique of the domino theory, see Eric Mack, *Dominos and the Fear of Commodification, in* NOMOS XXXI: MARKETS AND JUSTICE 198, 209-219 (John W. Chapman & J. Roland Pennock eds., 1989) (distinguishing between internally valuable and motivated activities and activities that are instrumentally valuable and motivated, suggesting that this distinction requires abandonment of the simple consequentialist understanding of activities that underlies the domino theory).

    5.   Moore *and the Body-as-Property Metaphor.* A widely discussed case, Moore v. Regents of the University of California, 793 P.2d 479 (Cal. 1990), cert. denied, 499 U.S. 936 (1991), poses the question of how best to analyze legal disputes over control of human cells and assets made from human cells that have been excised from a person's body. In *Moore,* doctors removed Moore's spleen as part of his treatment for hairy-cell leukemia. Moore had consented to the operation, but the doctor did not tell him that the cells from his spleen had research and commercial value. The cells were later used to develop a patented cell line for which the potential market was estimated to be worth in the billions of dollars. When Moore learned what the doctor and his fellow researchers had done, he sued for damages. The issue was whether he had a cause of action. The court held that a cause of action existed for breach of the doctor's duty of disclosure but not for conversion. Moore had no continuing property interest in the cells from his spleen once they had been excised, a majority of the court concluded. The court's reasoning has been subject to scathing criticism from several scholars. Several of them have challenged judicial use of property as the central metaphor by which to analyze legal disputes over control and use of body parts. Alan Hyde, for example, writes:

> The *Moore* case well illustrates the impoverished nature of our legal discourse about the body, the indeterminacy of at least one key discursive construction, the body as property, and our foolishness in thinking that the deployment of these indeterminate constructions constitutes thinking about the problem. Moore's spleen is and is not property; calling it property makes Moore autonomous and degrades him; calling it property stakes out his autonomy from others yet does so only through a metaphor

that judges can bestow on things or not, as they see fit, guided by their notions of the greatest social good.

ALAN HYDE, BODIES OF LAW 73 (1997). Do you agree with Hyde that property is an unhelpful lens through which to look at problems such as that posed in cases like *Moore*? Is the perspective of property foolish even if we discard the Blackstonian conception of property and acknowledge property's pluralism (as discussed in Chapter 8.1 above)? Are there more illuminating lenses for such cases?

James Boyle approaches *Moore* in terms of information rather than in terms of property. Boyle argues that Moore's real claim was to the protection of his legal right to commodify the genetic information derived from his cells. From that perspective, the real question in the case was who is the "author" of that information. See JAMES BOYLE, SHAMANS, SOFTWARE & SPLEENS: LAW AND THE CONSTRUCTION OF THE INFORMATION AGE 105-106 (1996).

6. *Feminist Perspectives.* A number of feminist scholars in several disciplines have written on various questions involving the existence of property rights in human body parts and tissue. One prominent feminist scholar on the topic is the anthropologist Donna Dickenson. In her book, *Property in the Body*, Dickenson writes that there is a pervasive fear of "feminization" of the body, both male and female. By "feminization," she means a social phenomenon by which the human body is increasingly objectified and commodified as the result of the acquisition of property rights in human tissue and the human genome by researchers and biotechnology firms. She calls this phenomenon feminization because historically it was primarily the female body that was the subject of objectification. *See* DONNA DICKENSON, PROPERTY IN THE BODY: FEMINIST PERSPECTIVES 8 (2007).

Do you agree that both men's and women's bodies are now becoming "feminized"? Cécile Fabre adopts a quite different perspective of the sale of human body parts than that of most feminists. Arguing on the basis of what she calls a "sufficientist" theory of liberal egalitarian justice, she contends that the confiscation of both cadaveric and living body parts is justified on the ground that the preconditions for a minimally flourishing life can be realized only if people have a right to others' bodily organs they need, provided that there is no sacrifice of human flourishing to the donors as a consequence. Moreover, she argues that, as a consequence of their personal autonomy, people should be permitted to sell their body parts under strictly regulated conditions. *See* CÉCILE FABRE, WHOSE BODY IS IT ANYWAY? JUSTICE AND THE INTEGRITY OF THE PERSON 126-153 (2006).

7. *A Case Against Markets for Body Parts (and Bodies) Based on Equality?* None of the objections raised to markets in body parts or bodies themselves (as in the case of prostitution, for example) has considered the role of equality. Can a case against such a market be based on concerns with inequality? Debra Satz argues that inequality is precisely the reason why prostitution, surrogacy contracts, and similar forms of marketizing the

human body are objectionable. Prostitution, for example, "is a theatre of inequality: it displays for us a practice in which women are seen as objects of men's desires." Debra Satz, Why Some Things Should Not Be for Sale: The Moral Limits of Markets 133 (2010). This is a contingent argument, however, for what makes prostitution and surrogacy contracts objectionable is not an immutable condition or a condition that is intrinsic to women. Under other circumstances, presumably, such contracts would not be objectionable, according to Satz.

Anne Phillips has raised a non-contingent equality reason for objecting to markets in bodies. "[M]ore so, and more intrinsically than most markets," she argues, "markets in bodies rely on inequality." Anne Phillips, *It's My Body and I'll Do What I Like With It: Bodies as Objects and Property*, 39 Pol. Theory 724, 737 (2011). "It is hard to see why markets in body parts or services," she continues, "would arise except where there is inequality. The inequality that attends such markets is not just contingent; it is an intrinsic feature." *Id.* at 738. Are you persuaded that only conditions of inequality would lead a person to enter into, for example, a surrogacy contract?

8. *The Law-and-Economics of the Sale of Human Body Parts.* Under the current legal regime in the United States, demand for human organs for transplantation significantly exceeds legal supply. Not surprisingly, law-and-economics scholars have proposed solutions to adjust this imbalance between supply and demand. Henry Hansmann, for example, has suggested the creation of a futures market as a means of buying and selling cadaveric organs. As a central clearing mechanism for matching donors and recipients, Hansmann suggests, health insurance providers could be used as the primary purchasers of future rights in cadaveric organs. A policyholder can indicate on her annual premium statement that in case she dies during the coming period, the insurance company or its assignee may harvest the insured's transplantable organs. In return, she would receive a specified reduction in her insurance premium for that period.

With respect to living donors, Hansmann notes that one common argument against a market for organs is that the poor would be the principal sellers and that such a market would unacceptably exploit the poor for the benefit of wealthy recipients. Hansmann responds that concerns about exploitation and improvidently made agreements can be accommodated through regulation. For example, one might limit sales to federally licensed agencies. A cooling-off period of six months might also be required. "Moreover," Hansmann argues, "in considering distributive issues it is important to recognize that the poor and improvident are quite disproportionately represented among those who suffer from kidney failure. If commercial purchase of kidneys from living donors would substantially increase the supply available for transplantation, these groups would therefore gain much of the benefit. The net result might therefore be quite progressive." Henry Hansmann, *The Economics and Ethics of Markets for Human Organs*, 14 J. Health Pol.

POL'Y & L. 57 (1989). Are you persuaded by these arguments? Should existing legal restrictions on sales of human organs for transplantation be eliminated or at least substantially relaxed? *See also* Lloyd R. Cohen, *Increasing the Supply of Transplant Organs: The Virtues of a Futures Market,* 58 GEO. WASH. L. REV. 1 (1989).

3. THE "NEW PROPERTY"

Charles A. Reich, The New Property[1]

The institution called property guards the troubled boundary between individual man and the state. It is not the only guardian; many other institutions, laws, and practices serve as well. But in a society that chiefly values material well-being, the power to control a particular portion of that well-being is the very foundation of individuality.

One of the most important developments in the United States during the past decade has been the emergence of government as a major source of wealth. Government is a gigantic syphon. It draws in revenue and power, and pours forth wealth: money, benefits, services, contracts, franchises, and licenses. Government has always had this function. But while in early times it was minor, today's distribution of largess is on a vast, imperial scale.

The valuables dispensed by government take many forms, but they all share one characteristic. They are steadily taking the place of traditional forms of wealth—forms which are held as private property. Social insurance substitutes for savings; a government contract replaces a businessman's customers and goodwill. The wealth of more and more Americans depends upon a relationship to government. Increasingly, Americans live on government largess—allocated by government on its own terms, and held by recipients subject to conditions which express "the public interest."

The growth of government largess, accompanied by a distinctive system of law, is having profound consequences. It affects the underpinnings of individualism and independence. It influences the workings of the Bill of Rights. It has an impact on the power of private interests, in their relation to each other and to government. It is helping to create a new society. . . .

---

1. Charles A. Reich, *The New Property*, 73 YALE L.J. 733, 733, 734-738, 739-740, 744, 745, 756, 757, 768-771, 778-779, 785-787 (1964).

I. THE LARGESS OF GOVERNMENT

A. The Forms of Government-Created Wealth

The valuables which derive from relationships to government are of many kinds. Some primarily concern individuals; others flow to businesses and organizations. Some are obvious forms of wealth, such as direct payments of money, while others, like licenses and franchises, are indirectly valuable.

Income and benefits. For a large number of people, government is a direct source of income although they hold no public job. Their eligibility arises from legal status. Examples are Social Security benefits, unemployment compensation, aid to dependent children, veterans benefits, and the whole scheme of state and local welfare. These represent a principal source of income to a substantial segment of the community. . . .

Jobs. . . . The size of the publicly employed working force has increased steadily since the founding of the United States, and seems likely to keep on increasing. . . .

Occupational licenses. Licenses are required before one may engage in many kinds of work, from practicing medicine to guiding hunters through the woods. Even occupations which require little education or training, like that of longshoremen, often are subject to strict licensing. Such licenses, which are dispensed by government, make it possible for their holders to receive what is ordinarily their chief source of income.

Franchises. A franchise, which may be held by an individual or by a company, is a partial monopoly created and handed out by government. Its value depends largely upon governmental power; by limiting the number of franchises, government can make them extremely remunerative. A New York City taxi medallion, which costs very little when originally obtained from the city, can be sold for over twenty thousand dollars. The reason for this high price is that the city has not issued new transferable medallions despite the rise in population and traffic. A television channel, handed out free, can often be sold for many millions. Government distributes wealth when it dispenses route permits to truckers, charters to bus lines, routes to air carriers, certificates to oil and gas pipelines, licenses to liquor stores, allotments to growers of cotton or wheat, and concessions in national parks.

Contracts. Many individuals and many more businesses enjoy public generosity in the form of government contracts. Fifty billion dollars annually flows from the federal government in the form of defense spending. These contracts often resemble subsidies; it is virtually impossible to lose money on them. Businesses sometimes make the government their principal source of income, and many "free enterprises" are set up primarily to do business with the government.

Subsidies. Analogous to welfare payments for individuals who cannot manage independently in the economy are subsidies to business. . . . Government also supports many non-business activities, in such areas as scientific research, health, and education. . . .

B. The Importance of Government Largess

. . . [T]he proportion of governmental wealth is increasing. Hardly any citizen leads his life without at least partial dependence on wealth flowing through the giant government syphon.

In many cases, this dependence is not voluntary. Valuables that flow from government are often substitutes for, rather than supplements to, other forms of wealth. Social Security and other forms of public insurance and compensation are supported by taxes. This tax money is no longer available for individual savings or insurance. The taxpayer is a participant in public insurance by compulsion, and his ability to care for his own needs independently is correspondingly reduced. . . .

Dependence creates a vicious circle of dependence. It is as hard for a business to give up government help as it is for an individual to live on a reduced income. . . .

C. Largess and the Changing Forms of Wealth

The significance of government largess is increased by certain underlying changes in the forms of private wealth in the United States. Changes in the forms of wealth are not remarkable in themselves; the forms are constantly changing and differ in every culture. But today more and more of our wealth takes the form of rights or status rather than of tangible goods. An individual's profession or occupation is a prime example. To many others, a job with a particular employer is the principal form of wealth. A profession or a job is frequently far more valuable than a house or bank account, for a new house can be bought, and a new bank account created, once a profession or job is secure. For the jobless, their status as governmentally assisted or insured persons may be the main source of subsistence. . . .

II. The Emerging System of Law

Wealth or value is created by culture and by society; it is culture that makes a diamond valuable and a pebble worthless. Property, on the other hand, is the creation of law. A man who has property has certain legal rights with respect to an item of wealth; property represents a relationship between wealth and its "owner." Government largess is plainly "wealth," but it is not necessarily "property."

Government largess has given rise to a distinctive system of law. This system can be viewed from at least three perspectives; the rights of holders of largess, the powers of government over largess, and the procedure by which holders' rights and governmental power are adjusted. . . .

As government largess has grown in importance, quite naturally there has been pressure for the protection of individual interests in it. The holder of a broadcast license or a motor carrier permit or a grazing permit for the public lands tends to consider this wealth his "own," and to seek legal protection against interference with his enjoyment. The development of individual interests has been substantial, but it has not come easily. . . .

In all of the cases concerning individual rights in largess the exact nature of the government action which precipitates the controversy makes a great difference. A controversy over government largess may arise from such diverse situations as denial of the right to apply, denial of an application, attaching of conditions to a grant, modification of a grant already made, suspension or revocation of a grant, or some other sanction. In general, courts tend to afford the greatest measure of protection in revocation or suspension cases. The theory seems to be that here some sort of rights have "vested" which may not be taken away without proper procedure. On the other hand, an applicant for largess is thought to have less at stake, and is therefore entitled to less protection. The mere fact that a particular form of largess is protected in one context does not mean that it will be protected in all others.

While individual interests in largess have developed along the lines of procedural protection and restraint upon arbitrary official action, substantive rights to possess and use largess have remained very limited. In the first place, largess does not "vest" in a recipient; it almost always remains revocable. . . .

When the public interest demands that the government take over "property," the Constitution requires that just compensation be paid to the owner. But when largess is revoked in the public interest, the holder ordinarily receives no compensation. For example, if a television station's license were revoked, not for bad behavior on the part of the operator, but in order to provide a channel in another locality, or to provide an outlet for educational television, the holder would not be compensated for its loss. This principle applies to largess of all types.

In addition to being revocable without compensation, most forms of largess are subject to considerable limitations on their use. Social Security cannot be sold or transferred. A television license can be transferred only with FCC permission. The possessor of a grazing permit has no right to change, improve, or destroy the landscape. And use of most largess is limited to specified purposes. Some welfare grants, for example, must be applied to support dependent children. On the other hand, holders of government wealth usually do have a power to exclude others, and to realize income. . . .

III. The Public Interest State

What are the consequences of the rise of government largess and its attendant legal system? What is the impact on the recipient, on constitutional guaranties of liberty, on the structure of power in the nation? . . .

The recipient of largess, whether an organization or an individual, feels the government's power. The company that is heavily subsidized or dependent on government contracts is subjected to an added amount of regulation and inspection, sometimes to the point of having resident government officials in its plant. And it is subject to added government pressures. . . .

D. The New Feudalism

The characteristics of the public interest state are varied, but there is an underlying philosophy that unites them. This is the doctrine that the wealth that flows from government is held by its recipients conditionally, subject to confiscation in the interest of the paramount state. This philosophy is epitomized in the most important of all judicial decisions concerning government largess, the case of *Flemming v. Nestor*.[2]

Ephram Nestor, an alien, came to this country in 1913, and after a long working life became eligible in 1955 for old-age benefits under the Social Security Act. From 1936 to 1955 Nestor and his employers had contributed payments to the government which went into a special old-age and survivors insurance trust fund. From 1933 to 1939 Nestor was a member of the Communist Party. Long after his membership ceased, Congress passed a law retroactively making such membership cause for deportation, and a second law, also retroactive, making such deportation for having been a member of the Party grounds for loss of retirement benefits. In 1956 Nestor was deported, leaving his wife here. Soon after his deportation, payment of benefits to Nestor's wife was terminated.

In a five to four decision, the Supreme Court held that cutting off Nestor's retirement insurance, although based on conduct completely lawful at the time, was not unconstitutional. Specifically, it was not a taking of property without due process of law; Nestor's benefits were not an "accrued property right."[3] The Court recognized that each worker's benefits flow "from the contributions he made to the national economy while actively employed," but it held that his interest is "noncontractual" and "cannot be

2. 363 U.S. 603 (1960).
3. *Id.* at 608.

soundly analogized to that of the holder of an annuity."[4] The Court continued:

> To engraft upon the Social Security system a concept of "accrued property rights" would deprive it of the flexibility and boldness in adjustment of ever-changing conditions which it demands. . . . It was doubtless out of an awareness of the need for such flexibility that Congress included . . . a clause expressly reserving to it "[t]he right to alter, amend or repeal any provision" of the Act. . . . That provision makes express what is implicit in the institutional needs of the program.[5]

The Court stated further that, in any case where Congress "modified" social security rights, the Court should interfere only if the action is "utterly lacking in rational justification."[6] This, the Court said, "is not the case here." As the Court saw it, it might be deemed reasonable for Congress to limit payments to those living in this country; moreover, the Court thought it would not have been "irrational for Congress to have concluded that the public purse should not be utilized to contribute to the support of those deported on the grounds specified in the statute."[7]

The implications of *Flemming v. Nestor* are profound. No form of government largess is more personal or individual than an old age pension. No form is more clearly earned by the recipient, who, together with his employer, contributes to the Social Security fund during the years of his employment. No form is more obviously a compulsory substitute for private property; the tax on wage earner and employer might readily have gone to higher pay and higher private savings instead. No form is more relied on, and more often thought of as property. No form is more vital to the independence and dignity of the individual. Yet under the philosophy of Congress and the Court, a man or woman, after a lifetime of work, has no rights which may not be taken away to serve some public policy. The Court makes no effort to balance the interests at stake. The public policy that justifies cutting off benefits need not even be an important one or a wise one — so long as it is not utterly irrational, the Court will not interfere. In any clash between individual rights and public policy, the latter is automatically held to be superior.

The philosophy of *Flemming v. Nestor* . . . resembles the philosophy of feudal tenure. Wealth is not "owned," or "vested" in the holders. Instead, it is held conditionally, the conditions being ones which seek to ensure the fulfillment of obligations imposed by the state. Just as the feudal system linked lord and vassal through a system of mutual dependence, obligation, and loyalty, so government largess binds man to the state.[8] And, it may be

4. *Id.* at 609-10.
5. *Id.* at 610-11.
6. *Id.* at 611.
7. *Id.* at 612.
8. *See generally* [MARC] BLOCH, FEUDAL SOCIETY (1961). Personal dependence was a fundamental element of feudalism, expressed in the concept of being the "man" of another man. *Id.* at 145.

added, loyalty or fealty to the state is often one of the essential conditions of modern tenure. In the many decisions taking away government largess for refusal to sign loyalty oaths, belonging to "subversive" organizations, or other similar grounds, there is more than a suggestion of the condition of fealty demanded in older times.

The comparison to the general outlines of the feudal system may best be seen by recapitulating some of the chief features of government largess. (1) Increasingly we turn over wealth and rights to government, which reallocates and redistributes them in the many forms of largess; (2) there is a merging of public and private, in which lines of private ownership are blurred; (3) the administration of the system has given rise to special laws and special tribunals, outside the ordinary structure of government; (4) the right to possess and use government largess is bound up with the recipient's legal status; status is both the basis for receiving largess and a consequence of receiving it; hence the new wealth is not readily transferable; (5) individuals hold the wealth conditionally rather than absolutely; the conditions are usually obligations owed to the government or to the public, and may include the obligation of loyalty to the government; the obligations may be changed or increased at the will of the state; (6) for breach of condition the wealth may be forfeited or escheated back to the government; (7) the sovereign power is shared with large private interests; (8) the object of the whole system is to enforce "the public interest" — the interest of the state or society or the lord paramount — by means of the distribution and use of wealth in such a way as to create and maintain dependence.

This feudal philosophy of largess and tenure may well be a characteristic of collective societies, regardless of their political systems. According to one scholar, national socialism regarded property as contingent upon duties owed the state; Nazism denied the absolute character of property and imposed obligations conditioning property tenure: "In practice the development seems to have been toward a concept of property based on the superior right of the overlord."[9] . . .

The public interest state is not with us yet. But we are left with large questions. If the day comes when most private ownership is supplanted by government largess, how then will governmental power over individuals be contained? What will dependence do to the American character? What will happen to the Constitution, and particularly the Bill of Rights, if their limits may be bypassed by purchase, and if people lack an independent base from which to assert their individuality and claim their rights? Without the security of the person which individual wealth provides and which largess fails to provide, what, indeed, will we become? . . .

9. [Frieda] Wunderlich, *The National Socialist Conception of Landed Property*, 12 Social Research 60, 75 (1945).

V. TOWARD INDIVIDUAL STAKES IN THE COMMONWEALTH

There can be no retreat from the public interest state. It is the inevitable outgrowth of an interdependent world. An effort to return to an earlier economic order would merely transfer power to giant private governments which would rule not in the public interest, but in their own interest. If individualism and pluralism are to be preserved, this must be done not by marching backwards, but by building these values into today's society. If public and private are now blurred, it will be necessary to draw a new zone of privacy. If private property can no longer perform its protective functions, it will be necessary to establish institutions to carry on the work that private property once did but can no longer do.

In these efforts government largess must play a major role. As we move toward a welfare state, largess will be an ever more important form of wealth. And largess is a vital link in the relationship between the government and private sides of society. It is necessary, then, that largess begin to do the work of property.

The chief obstacle to the creation of private rights in largess has been the fact that it is originally public property, comes from the state, and may be withheld completely. But this need not be an obstacle. Traditional property also comes from the state, and in much the same way. Land, for example, traces back to grants from the sovereign. In the United States, some was the gift of the King of England, some that of the King of Spain. The sovereign extinguished Indian title by conquest, became the new owner, and then granted title to a private individual or group. Some land was the gift of the sovereign under laws such as the Homestead and Preemption Acts. . . . In America, land and resources all were originally government largess. In a less obvious sense, personal property also stems from government. Personal property is created by law; it owes its origin and continuance to laws supported by the people as a whole. These laws "give" the property to one who performs certain actions. . . .

Like largess, real and personal property were also originally dispensed on conditions, and were subject to forfeiture if the conditions failed. The conditions in the sovereign grants, such as colonization, were generally made explicit, and so was the forfeiture resulting from failure to fulfill them. In the case of the Preemption and Homestead Acts, there were also specific conditions.[10] Even now land is subject to forfeiture for neglect; if it is unused it may be deemed abandoned to the state or forfeited to an adverse possessor. In a very similar way, personal property may be forfeited by abandonment or loss. Hence, all property might be described as government largess, given on condition and subject to loss.

If all property is government largess, why is it not regulated to the same degree as present-day largess? Regulation of property has been

---

10. The Homestead Act had conditions of age, citizenship, intention to settle was cultivated [*sic*], and loyalty to the United States. 12 Stat. 392 (1862).

limited, not because society had no interest in property, but because it was in the interest of society that property be free. Once property is seen not as a natural right but as a construction designed to serve certain functions, then its origin ceases to be decisive in determining how much regulation should be imposed. The conditions that can be attached to receipt, ownership, and use depend not on where property came from, but on what job it should be expected to perform. Thus in the case of government largess, nothing turns on the fact that it originated in government. The real issue is how it functions and how it should function. . . .

The proposals discussed above, however salutary, are by themselves far from adequate to assure the status of individual man with respect to largess. The problems go deeper. First, the growth of government power based on the dispensing of wealth must be kept within bounds. Second, there must be a zone of privacy for each individual beyond which neither government nor private power can push — a hiding place from the all-pervasive system of regulation and control. Finally, it must be recognized that we are becoming a society based upon relationship and status — status deriving primarily from source of livelihood. Status is so closely linked to personality that destruction of one may well destroy the other. Status must therefore be surrounded with the kind of safeguards once reserved for personality.

Eventually those forms of largess which are closely linked to status must be deemed to be held as of right. Like property, such largess could be governed by a system of regulation plus civil or criminal sanctions, rather than a system based upon denial, suspension and revocation. As things now stand, violations lead to forfeitures — outright confiscation of wealth and status. But there is surely no need for these drastic results. Confiscation, if used at all, should be the ultimate, not the most common and convenient penalty. The presumption should be that the professional man will keep his license, and the welfare recipient his pension. These interests should be "vested." If revocation is necessary, not by reason of the fault of the individual holder, but by reason of overriding demands of public policy, perhaps payment of just compensation would be appropriate. The individual should not bear the entire loss for a remedy primarily intended to benefit the community.

The concept of right is most urgently needed with respect to benefits like unemployment compensation, public assistance, and old age insurance. These benefits are based upon a recognition that misfortune and deprivation are often caused by forces far beyond the control of the individual, such as technological change, variations in demand for goods, depressions, or wars. The aim of these benefits is to preserve the self-sufficiency of the individual, to rehabilitate him where necessary, and to allow him to be a valuable member of a family and a community; in theory they represent part of the individual's rightful share in the commonwealth. Only by making such benefits into rights can the welfare state achieve its goal of providing a secure minimum basis for individual well-being and dignity in a society where each man cannot be wholly the master of his own destiny.

CONCLUSION

This article is an attempt to offer perspective on the transformation of society as it bears on the economic basis of individualism. The effort has been to show relationships; to bring together drivers' licenses, unemployment insurance, membership in the bar, permits for using school auditoriums, and second class mail privileges, in order to see what we are becoming. . . .

At the very least, it is time to reconsider the theories under which new forms of wealth are regulated, and by which governmental power over them is measured. It is time to recognize that "the public interest" is all too often a reassuring platitude that covers up sharp clashes of conflicting values, and hides fundamental choices. . . .

Above all, the time has come for us to remember what the framers of the Constitution knew so well — that "a power over a man's subsistence amounts to a power over his will." We cannot safely entrust our livelihoods and our rights to the discretion of authorities, examiners, boards of control, character committees, regents, or license commissioners. We cannot permit any official or agency to pretend to sole knowledge of the public good. We cannot put the independence of any man . . . wholly in the power of other men.

If the individual is to survive in a collective society, he must have protection against its ruthless pressures. There must be sanctuaries or enclaves where no majority can reach. To shelter the solitary human spirit does not merely make possible the fulfillment of individuals; it also gives society the power to change, to grow, and to regenerate, and hence to endure. These were the objects which property sought to achieve, and can no longer achieve. The challenge of the future will be to construct, for the society that is coming, institutions and laws to carry on this work. Just as the Homestead Act was a deliberate effort to foster individual values at an earlier time, so we must try to build an economic basis for liberty today — a Homestead Act for rootless twentieth century man. We must create a new property.

NOTES AND QUESTIONS

1.   *Critiques of Reich, from the Left and the Right.* Reich's article has had many admirers over the years, but it has also attracted a fair amount of criticism from both ends of the political spectrum. From the Left, William Simon argues that "while Reich's argument is clearly designed to legitimate the redistributive activities of the welfare state, it has curiously conservative and anti-redistributive implications." Reich had argued, after

all, that all forms of wealth, the new property as well as the old, should be subject to constitutional protection, i.e., entitled to compensation in cases of governmental impairment. But in cases of such impairment, how could there be legitimate compensation? As Simon puts it, "Compensation for the impairment of one person's property could only be achieved by impairing someone else's. If all wealth is to be regarded as 'vested,' then there can be no coercive redistribution." William H. Simon, *The Invention and Reinvention of Welfare Rights*, 44 Md. L. Rev. 1, 31 (1985).

From the Right, critics like then-Professor (now Judge) Stephen Williams argue that the security that the New Property theory supposedly provides to the individual is illusory. Traditional property protects individual owners from the state in a variety of ways, both substantive and procedural in character. However, the protection provided under the New Property theory falls far short of this. The only form of protection is procedural due process. "Would judicially enforced procedural due process for entitlements," Williams asks rhetorically, "provide any serious balance against state power?" Stephen F. Williams, *Liberty and Property: The Problem of Government Benefits*, 12 J. Legal Stud. 3, 12 (1983). Moreover, Williams contends, Reich's theory sacrifices the special claims that liberty and traditional property have long had in our constitutional scheme. "Over the long pull, relinquishing those special claims may have a far more detrimental impact on individual independence from the state than denying due process protection for conditioned government benefits." *Id.* at 13.

Does either critique, Simon's or Williams's, persuade you? Are there compelling arguments in support of Reich's proposal even in the face of these critiques?

2.   *Conceptual Confusion?* James Harris has argued that the "new property" label is confusing and unnecessary. See J.W. Harris, Property & Justice 304 (1996). He states:

> None of [Reich's] claims warrants any shift in what property means. If the article had been entitled "[t]he need for a property substitute," and if it had not ended with the clarion call: "[we] must create a new property," there would have been no doubt about it. No expansive definition would have been proposed. As it is, the article can be understood as calling for an extension in the concept of property beyond its conventional use in the service of a justificatory analogy. *Id.* at 151.

Do you agree with Harris that the "new property" label extends the concept of property beyond its conventional boundaries? Assuming for the moment that you do, what harm, if any, is done by this conceptual extension? Would it cause conceptual confusion about the meaning of property? Or is Harris's critique rather dependent upon an understanding of property that should itself be criticized?

3.   *Property and Independence.* Reich argues that one of the central functions of property is and always has been to secure personal

independence by creating a bulwark against the depradations of society or the state. He argues further that the emergence and growth of governmental largesse in the welfare state has undermined this function, as individuals have grown more and more dependent on the state and vulnerable to its arbitrary actions. Reich implicitly assumes that the institution of property did at one time secure personal independence. Do you agree with that assumption? Apart from whether it did or did not once secure personal independence, do you think that today property, in comparison with other legal rights and institutions, plays a major role in maintaining citizen independence?

Recall the discussion of property in civic republican thought in Chapter 6. A core function of property in republican theory is to enable self-constitution. Is independence from the state necessary for self-constitution? Is it, as Reich assumes, the role of government to make self-constitution possible? What would Nozick likely think of Reich's "New Property" proposal and its theoretical underpinnings?

4. *Monism or Pluralism*? Reich's argument that government-derived largesse should be treated as, and be legally protected as, property is really an aspect of the question, "property in what?" To answer the question, "property in what," Reich relies on a single value — liberty — and argues from that value that government-derived largesse should be accorded the legal status of property. We have already seen, however, that property serves many values in addition to liberty (e.g., wealth-maximization, distributive justice, personhood, civic well-being). Reich does not mention any of those values. How would the "New Property" proposal fare under a more pluralistic approach, one that takes these other values into account?

One aspect that complicates a pluralistic analysis is the heterogeneity of the family of new properties. For example, there are varying degrees of personhood involved (e.g., taxicab medallions vs. aid for dependent children). There are also varying degrees of vulnerability of the recipient (e.g., pensioners vs. franchisors).

5. *The Reliance Interest in Property*. Contrast Reich's monist approach to the "property in what" question with the richly pluralist approach taken by Joseph William Singer in his article *The Reliance Interest in Property*, 40 STAN. L. REV. 611 (1988). Like Reich, Singer wishes to expand the conventional scope of interests that can be the objects of property rights based on the value(s) that property is supposed to serve. Unlike Reich, however, Singer bases his theory upon multiple values, no one of which can preempt the others. The setting for Singer's theory was an effort by a local labor union to prevent a steel firm from closing its plants, which had been in operation in the community for many years and upon which the community's economic health depended. Singer argued that the courts "should have recognized the workers' property rights arising out of their relationship with the company." *Id.* at 621. Such rights might have included a right of first refusal, giving the

workers an opportunity to buy the plant when the company plans to close it; a right of access to the firm's financial information so that the workers can determine the feasibility of plant modernization before it is too late; and a right of reasonable notice of mass dismissals and plant closings. *Id.* at 740-743. Singer acknowledged that this would have required the courts to recognize a new property interest, but he argued that such a new property interest was both necessary and appropriate to protect the workers' "reliance interest," an interest that Singer argued property law elsewhere has implicitly protected for many years under various doctrinal guises. Singer's normative foundation is pluralistic, appealing to notions of community, social relationships, sharing, and fairness, while also taking into account concerns about market freedom and economic efficiency.

Singer points out that property law grants property rights to adverse possessors, easement users, spouses, and others where reliance is part of the consideration for protecting them. But does property law protect reliance *per se*? Is reliance in and of itself an adequate foundation for justifying property entitlements?

7. *Blackstone or Hitler?* Reich states, "Nazism denied the absolute character of property and imposed obligations conditioning property tenure: 'In practice the development seems to have been toward a concept of property based on the superior right of the overlord.' (quoting, with apparent approval, WUNDERLICH, THE NATIONAL SOCIALIST CONCEPTION OF LANDED PROPERTY)." Reich seems to imply that only two choices are available — absolute property rights or a fascist property regime. Is this correct? Is there no alternative to these two regimes that provides a stable and normatively defensible equilibrium between these two extremes?

8. *Alienable Public Entitlements?* Reich notes that most forms of public entitlements are inalienable. He does not challenge this point, but perhaps it is worth challenging. Why are public entitlements legally inalienable? Is there an alternative to the binary choice between full alienability and inalienability that would be appropriate in the case of at least some public entitlements? Tsilly Dagan and Talia Fisher argue that there is a spectrum of alternative positions and the choice of which position to take should be guided by the values that are at stake. They offer the example of tax benefits applicable to charitable contributions, which under current law are personal and non-transferable. The current tax benefit (which takes the form of deduction) has been justified on various normative grounds, including redistribution, efficiency, democratic participations, and personhood. Dagan and Fisher argue that creating a legal secondary market for tax benefits for charitable contribution — which in their view should take the form of a tax credit — would improve the efficiency of the allocation of these tax benefits, reinforce distributive goals, facilitate personhood, and broaden participation. *See* Tsilly Dagan & Talia Fisher, *Rights for Sale*, 96 MINN. L. REV. 90 (2012).

4. ARTIFACTS OF CULTURAL PROPERTY

John Henry Merryman, The Public Interest in Cultural Property[1]

INTRODUCTION

Public questions affecting cultural property frequently arise: Should an old building be preserved? (Many are, pursuant to "historic preservation" laws.) Should the Crown of St. Stephen be returned to Hungary? (We did return it, over the protests of Hungarian emigres and a number of prominent public figures, including Senator Robert Dole.) Should the United States become a party to the 1970 UNESCO Convention[2] or the 1954 Hague Convention?[3] (We did join UNESCO 1970 but not, to our discredit, Hague 1954.) Should we attempt, as do most other nations, to control the export of cultural property? (Cultural objects, other than those illegally removed from federal or Indian lands, still are freely exportable from the United States.) Should "military necessity" justify the destruction of irreplaceable cultural monuments in time of war? (It does, under contemporary rules of international law.) How seriously should we take the practice of counterfeiting cultural objects? (At present we do not take it very seriously.) The answers to these and many other questions, taken together, express a policy toward cultural property.

Since the late 1960s, governments and international organizations have made an increasing number and variety of decisions about cultural property. As such decisions accumulate, assumptions harden, preferences achieve consensus, and policies are born. The various policies — local, national, and international — differ. Some have grown by accretion, guided by adventitious events and ad hoc interests. Others, like the 1970 UNESCO Convention, are the result of a deliberative process, one heavily conditioned by source-nation/market-nation, Third World/First World, and East Bloc/West Bloc politics. Differences in professional outlook further complicate matters; the attitudes and agenda of archaeologists and anthropologists, historians, museum professionals, dealers and collectors, and politicians often diverge. The resulting policies are both incomplete and incoherent, providing an inadequate, substantively dubious basis for public action. This Article is part of an effort to develop and clarify the bases for an appropriate public policy toward cultural property.

1. John Henry Merryman, *The Public Interest in Cultural Property*, 77 CAL. L. REV. 339, 339-341, 343, 344, 345-348, 349-352, 353, 355-364 (1989).
2. UNESCO Convention on the Means of Prohibiting and Preventing the Illicit Import, Export and Transfer of Ownership of Cultural Property, Nov. 14, 1970, 823 U.N.T.S. 231 [hereinafter UNESCO 1970].
3. UNESCO Convention for the Protection of Cultural Property in the Event of Armed Conflict, May 14, 1954, 249 U.N.T.S. 240 [hereinafter Hague 1954].

By "cultural property" I mean objects that embody the culture — principally archaeological, ethnographical and historical objects, works of art, and architecture; but the category can be expanded to include almost anything made or changed by man. . . .

The empirical evidence that people care about cultural objects is imposing: The existence of thousands of museums, tens of thousands of dealers, hundreds of thousands of collectors, millions of museum visitors; brisk markets in art and antiquities; university departments of art, archaeology, and ethnology; historic preservation laws; elaborate legislative schemes controlling cultural property in Italy, France, and most other source nations; public agencies with substantial budgets, like the National Endowment for the Arts in the United States and arts ministries in other nations; laws controlling archaeological excavations; laws limiting the export of cultural property; international conventions controlling the traffic in cultural property and protecting cultural property in war, all demonstrate that people care about cultural property. . . .

A great deal of public, corporate, and individual time, effort, and money are spent in making, finding, acquiring, preserving, studying, exhibiting, interpreting, and enjoying cultural objects, more in some times and places than in others, but imposing amounts in all. Human beings are the only animals that make, collect, preserve, study, and display such objects. The practice is very old, originating long before the modern state or earlier forms of political organization. . . .

We deal here with a basic human activity that goes on in all times and places, though with variations in style and prevalence from culture to culture. If we were to characterize the forces that hold groups of people together with such terms as "political," "social," or "economic," then "cultural" would chronologically precede the others (with the possible exception of the core family) and might, in the long run, outlast them all.

It is abundantly clear that people care a great deal about cultural property. The interesting question is "Why?" An answer to that question will help both to define the public interest in and to indicate the elements of a responsive public policy toward cultural property. In what follows, I first examine the sources of the public interest, dividing the discussion into three parts: the expressive value, the politics and religion, and the utility of cultural property. I then introduce three considerations that seem central to the development of cultural property policy: preservation, truth, and access.

I.   SOURCES OF THE PUBLIC INTEREST IN CULTURAL PROPERTY

A. *The Expressive Value of Cultural Property*

. . . *Truth and Certainty:* There is truth in objects. We yearn for the authentic, for the work as it left the hand of the artist or artisan. . . . Truth, certainty, and accuracy are closely related and may express the same fundamental need. When we stand before the authentic Domesday Book in the Public Record Office in London or the manuscript of Justinian's Digest in the Gregorian Library in Florence, we feel a sense of satisfaction. This is the real thing, speaking truly of its time. When we discover that the original of the Digest manuscript is kept elsewhere for protection and we have actually been looking at a reproduction, we feel cheated, no matter how accurate the reproduction might be. In part we resent having been fooled, but there is more: The magic that only the authentic object can work is dissipated. . . .

Morality: Cultural objects embody and express moral attitudes. This is most obviously true of religious objects. . . . But lay objects often display their own moral content. In the choice of materials, of methods of work, of subject-matter, of style, of care in execution and quality of finish, the artist or artisan or architect must make many decisions. Such choices are objectively conditioned to some extent by limitations of time and energy and by the realities of the market, but the market sets against them a sense of obligation to those who may use the object and the personal determination to make the thing "right." The maker chooses whether to settle for something that is "good enough" or strive for something better. Every such choice embodies a moral decision, and that morality is communicated, more or less perfectly, to the viewer who confronts or the scholar who studies the object. . . .

Memory: Cultural objects are the basis of cultural memory. . . . In a society characterized by mass production, mass media, and mass markets, we place a special value on hand-made objects: the painting that is the work of one artist's hand or the piece of furniture made by an artisan. But in the short time since the Industrial Revolution began, machine-made objects and the artifacts of mass merchandising have also become cultural property. Obvious examples of such treasured objects are stamps and coins, but what of vintage automobiles, the contents of railroad museums and of museums of science and industry? Consider the collectors of posters, of fruit box labels, of perfume bottles. Why do they care about such things? Although there are other explanations, at the center is the desire to remember, and to be remembered. . . .

Survival: Cultural objects are survivors. . . . Life may be short, but art is long. The object that endures is humanity's mark on eternity. We cherish cultural objects as intimations of immortality, of the defeat of time. The stone age cave paintings, the pyramids, the Dead Sea Scrolls, by their continued existence, encourage further human effort to create something that will endure, to hold back the night of oblivion. . . .

Identity: An art historian explains that works of art and, by extension, other cultural objects, "tell[ ] us who we are and where we came from."[4]

4. [Albert] Elsen, *Introduction: Why Do We Care About Art?*, 27 Hastings L.J. 951, 952 (1976); *see also* A[lbert] Elsen, Purposes of Art vi-vii (4th ed. 1981).

The need for cultural identity, for a sense of significance, for reassurance about one's place in the scheme of things, for a "legible" past, for answers to the great existential questions about our nature and our fate — for all these things, cultural objects provide partial answers. When war or natural disaster or vandalism destroys cultural objects, we feel a sense of loss. What is lost is the opportunity to connect with others and to find our place in the grand design.

Community: Cultural objects nourish a sense of community, of participation in a common human enterprise. Even a single object — a painting, say, or a lamp or a pot — illustrates humanity's social nature. The painting was made to be seen, the lamp and the pot to be used, by others. The social functions of objects testify to our common humanity. They illustrate one's connection with others, express a shared human sensibility and purpose, communicate across time and distance, dispel the feeling that one is lost and alone. . . .

B. The Politics . . . of Cultural Property

. . . Cultural property is put to a variety of political uses in a variety of political contexts — ethnic, regional, and national. The National Museum of Anthropology in Mexico City is an example of an extraordinarily sophisticated and effective use of cultural property to instill a sense of national identity and national pride. Like other culturally diverse nations, Mexico has found it difficult to resolve nation-building problems. Many Mexicans speak indigenous languages and relate more strongly to ethnic or regional identities than to the Mexican nation. Others are lost between cultures, confused about their identities. The Museum attempts to show the Mexican viewer that he is part of a great nation in which elements of native pre-Columbian and introduced European cultures have been combined to produce something important that is uniquely Mexican. . . .

Cultural property lends itself to many political uses. . . . The current movement for repatriation of cultural property to source nations probably derives most of its power from politics. The very term "repatriation" is political; it assumes that cultural objects have a *patria*, a national character and a national homeland. Each nation makes a special claim to cultural objects associated with its people or territory — to its "national cultural patrimony."

Cultural nationalism of this kind is a major force in shaping the international law of cultural property. The key instrument is the 1970 UNESCO Convention. Its primary purpose is to provide international enforcement of national cultural property retention laws, and the operative legal concept throughout the Convention is that of national cultural "heritage" or "patrimony". . . . A second major development was the establishment, again by UNESCO, of an Intergovernmental Committee for Promoting the Return of Cultural Property to Its Countries of Origin or

Its Restitution in Case of Illicit Appropriation. Cultural nationalism has also had an interesting, one-sided effect on United States policy. Most cultural property may be freely exported; we do not attempt to retain it. But in controlling imports, the U.S. is one of the strongest enforcers of foreign retention schemes.

C. The Utility of Cultural Property

. . . Cultural objects embody and preserve information. They are a source of knowledge and wisdom. This is most obviously true of manuscripts and inscriptions — for example, the Year Books or the Rosetta Stone — but is also the case with works of art and architecture and objects (furniture, apparel, implements) of daily or ceremonial use. They communicate to us directly, without the intervention of words. Their study tells us about how people lived their lives and ordered their values. Every human society manages to place its unique stamp on its artifacts and, in this way, to reveal something essential about itself. . . .

The museum is a place to learn about, and from, the past. Cultural property provides the base of much of what we know and believe. The study of newly discovered objects (such as the Dead Sea Scrolls) and the restudy of known objects (such as the work of the Rembrandt Study Project) constantly change the corpus of human knowledge and belief. . . .

II.   THE ELEMENTS OF A CULTURAL PROPERTY POLICY

All of the reasons why people care about cultural objects, taken together, imply a set of fundamental, related, yet sometimes conflicting, considerations that seem central to the development of cultural property policy. They can be considered under three headings: Preservation, Truth, and Access.

Preservation

The essential ingredient of any cultural property policy is that the object itself be physically preserved. The point is too obvious to need elaboration; if it is lost or destroyed, the Etruscan sarcophagus or the Peruvian textile or the Chinese pot cannot be studied, enjoyed, or used. . . .

The fundamental importance of preservation is clear, but it raises some problems. Some objects of the kind that Western collectors and museums preserve were created with the intention that they be consumed, or allowed to deteriorate through exposure, or deliberately destroyed after ceremonial use. Other objects are secret in nature, intended to be seen only by a restricted group of people at particular times or exposed only in a specific place. When a museum preserves and displays such objects, a clear culture conflict results. All of the reasons why we want to preserve and display such objects are present, but they conflict with the reasons why their creators want them to be consumed or destroyed or hidden.

This kind of conflict is common. Much of what remains to us from ancient cultures was found in graves and tombs, placed there with the intention that it remain with the dead. Every removal of such an object for a private collection, or even for a museum or for scholarly purposes, violates the source culture's intentions. Where that culture is itself dead, the conflict has been resolved . . . in favor of collection and preservation; but where the source culture is alive and aware, the matter is not so easily settled. To its maker, proper treatment of the object may be essential to life or status; to the culture, the violation may be a spiritual disaster that threatens drastic consequences for the group.

Physical preservation of discrete objects themselves may not be enough. Every cultural object is to some extent a part of a larger context from which it draws, and to which it adds, meaning. Separated from its context, "decontextualized," the object and the context both lose significance. At the extreme the object becomes anonymous, an orphan without reliable indication of its origin, its significance, its place and function as a part of something else. . . .

Although it would be wrong to dismiss such claims as insincere, they express values that seem marginal and ephemeral. In most cases they merely paraphrase Byronism—the sentimental notion that the object *belongs* somewhere because that is where it was made, or where it was first discovered, or where the cultural descendants of its makers now live.[5] Such an argument seems to stretch the notion of context too far. There must be a point at which the degree of decontextualization becomes too trivial to have significant policy consequences. That is particularly true of objects that are movable without significant damage or loss of explanatory power or aesthetic value: manuscripts, coins, pots, freestanding paintings and sculpture, articles of furniture, and many others.

Consider the Elgin Marbles. If atmospheric conditions permitted and the parties were willing, the Marbles might be recombined with the Parthenon, to their mutual benefit. Both would be more imposing and provide more enjoyment if they were recombined. . . . Atmospheric conditions in Athens, however, make such a project unacceptable because exposure would be fatal to the marbles. . . . The Greek government does not propose that the sculptures be returned to the Parthenon, but to a museum on the Acropolis, where they would be near the temple and protected in a controlled atmosphere. That clearly falls short of anything like full "recontextualization." The difference between installation on the temple and mere installation in an adjacent museum seems significant, perhaps critical.

---

5. Byronism, a product of early nineteenth Century Romanticism, is the unexamined premise that supports cultural nationalism today. . . .

True physical and contextual integrity, however, affect meaning and beauty, and their loss produces consequences analogous to those that follow from destruction. We care about context for the same reasons that we care about the objects themselves. The significant difference is that mere decontextualization may be reversible; destruction seldom is.

Truth

I use the term "truth" to sum up the shared concerns for accuracy, probity, and validity that, when combined with industry, insight, and imagination, produce good science and good scholarship. The basic concern is for authenticity and is fundamental to most of the reasons why we care about cultural property. Is this a genuine relic, speaking truly of its time? Does it embody the moral decisions made by its purported creator? Is it a true ingredient of cultural memory, genuinely evoking the pathos of a people whose works have largely vanished from the earth? Is it a reliable indicator of who we are and where we come from, an authentic survivor? And so on. Everything significant about cultural objects flows from authenticity.

Society makes a substantial investment in the quest for cultural truth: the thousands of museums and libraries in which cultural objects are preserved, studied, verified, attributed, and interpreted; the university departments of anthropology, archaeology, art and history, and the imposing body of scholarship that they produce about, or based on, cultural objects. Consider the market consequences of authenticity, where something deemed authentic may be worth millions but if found to be a fake, or merely reattributed to a different source or period, may have little market value. Truth about the culture is, in its way, as important to humanity as truth of other kinds—as scientific truth, for example. . . .

Access

The study of cultural objects requires that they be accessible to scholars; their enjoyment requires that they be accessible to the relevant public. These truisms conceal a number of interesting problems. Suppose the interests of scholars and the viewing public diverge, as they often do? What does "accessible" mean, and what is the "relevant public"? We have emphasized the importance of preservation, and preservation often is related to location. This creates interesting conflicts between the goals of preservation and access. . . . The Elgin Marbles have been better preserved in the British Museum than the sculptures left in place on the Parthenon, but moving them to London made them less accessible to Greeks. Examples could easily be multiplied.

Although legitimate concerns affecting access lead in different directions, the object in question can only be in one place. . . . That makes it necessary, and challenging, to deal in some way with the conflict, to establish criteria to guide access policy.

One plausible solution begins by arranging preservation, truth, and access in declining order of importance, with the corollary that where they conflict the higher controls. For example, although something important was lost, it was right for the Greeks to remove the Caryatids from the Erechtheion on the Acropolis, where they were under attack by the polluted atmosphere of Athens, and place them in a protected museum environment. The reproductions that replaced them at the site of the temple may be excellent, but they are not the real thing; the integrity of the temple has been compromised in the interest of preservation. Until something dramatic happens to the Athenian atmosphere, or until the structures on the Acropolis can be protected from it *in situ*, that seems to be the best solution. Few would question an art museum curator's decision to keep water colors and pastels, which are damaged by exposure to light, in cabinets or darkened rooms rather than on gallery walls, thereby limiting access in favor of preservation. Most would think it reasonable if extremely delicate works were made available only to scholars under controlled conditions, with access to them completely denied to the general public.

Cultural Nationalism

As a persuasive framework for policymaking about cultural property, the ordered triad of preservation, truth, and access is consistent with the reasons why people care about cultural objects, and it reflects the way informed people generally act toward them. But in the international arena, the claims of cultural nationalism become an important additional consideration. "National cultural heritage," broadly defined, is the basic legitimating concept. The *Grundnorm* is that objects forming part of the cultural heritage should remain in or be returned to the national territory. This principle dominates the policy process in contemporary international fora, such as the United Nations General Assembly, UNESCO, and the Council of Europe, and in the laws and policies of many nations. Ideally, there would be no conflict, but where it is necessary to choose, the national interest in retention routinely prevails over concerns about preservation, truth, and access.

News reports indicate, for example, that much cultural property retained in source nations is lost each year through inadequate protection and care. When a South American nation fails to care adequately for textiles from early Andean cultures, something irreplaceable is lost. In the prevailing nationalist view, however, the only acceptable remedy is to persuade and help that nation to improve its preservation facilities and correct its practices. The suggestion that neglect of cultural objects weakens a nation's claim to exclusive sovereignty over them does not arise in international cultural property discussions. . . . [A]lthough hard data are unavailable, few would doubt that the loss of the common cultural heritage through neglect far exceeds the damage done to it by the combined efforts of all the *huaqueros, tombaroli,* and their equivalents in other nations.

Cultural nationalism contrasts sharply with the idea of a "common cultural heritage" that has appeared in recent international legislation affecting cultural objects. . . . The striking prominence commonly given to the claims of cultural nationalism in international cultural property discussions, recommendations, and legislation clearly conflicts with this recent emphasis on a more general international interest. This situation invites further investigation. How can the appropriate balance be struck between national retention/repatriation claims, on one side, and the general interest in preservation of, truth about, and access to cultural property, on the other? How far can nations be permitted to control the "cultural heritage of all mankind"? Those are the major cultural property policy issues facing the international community as this is written. In my own view . . . contemporary cultural nationalism is (1) a relic of 19th century Romanticism that (2) has a superficial sentimental appeal that (3) gives it disproportionate influence in cultural policy determinations. . . .

NOTES AND QUESTIONS

1. *What is "Cultural Heritage" or "Cultural Property"?* In recent years lawyers and others have increasingly applied the term "heritage" to aspects of native and local cultures, as well as to biological species and the geographical location to which they are tied, that for various reasons are deemed significant and worthy of legal protection. The problem has been identifying the appropriate analytical framework within which to locate and evaluate claims to legal protection of cultural "heritage." As the anthropologist Michael Brown explains, "[D]ebate about heritage protection darts from one metaphor to another." For example, he further explains, "[s]ome indigenous advocates argue that 'control over one's culture' should be considered a basic human right. Others appeal to a supposed right of cultural privacy." Michael F. Brown, *Heritage as Property, in,* PROPERTY IN QUESTION 49, 50 (Katherine Verdery & Caroline Humphrey eds., 2004). Brown goes on to state that the current *lingua franca* for discussing legal protection of cultural heritage is property, specifically, "cultural property." *Ibid.*

Just what does this category of "cultural property" mean? On one view, the answer is straightforward: Cultural property is a property institution, like myriad other property institutions (e.g., marital property), that reflects multiple and sometimes conflicting values. (Recall here Dagan's conceptualization of property, discussed in Chapter 8.1.) The answer is not so straightforward, however, from the perspective of a monist theory, such as the exclusion theory that we considered in Chapter 9.1. Under exclusion theory, what value underlies cultural property? Consider also cultural property from the perspective of the bundle-of-rights conception, which we also examined in Chapter 8.1 *supra.* How does cultural property fit within that conception?

The specific issues covered by the debates over cultural heritage and cultural property range broadly, but all are highly controversial. They extend from the rights of modern nation-states to recover from museums antiquities that were plundered from the modern state's ancient predecessor to the rights of indigenous peoples to obtain intellectual property protection for traditional, or native, knowledge.

2. *Instrumental and Non-instrumental Values Underlying Cultural Property.* As Merryman points out, what policies we adopt for cultural property depend on what values we believe cultural property serves. Merryman identifies three categories of values—expressive, political, and utilitarian. Some of these are instrumental values, i.e., cultural heritage obtains legal protection as property just insofar as it serves certain social goods (scientific knowledge, public access, political legitimacy, etc.). Is this the only way or even the best way to understand what underlies claims to cultural heritage? Is the expressive value instrumental or non-instrumental? Is the personhood theory, which we considered in Chapter 2, related to the expressive function that Merryman describes?

Are there non-instrumental values at stake in controversies over repatriation of artifacts looted from aboriginal peoples' graves? Sarah Harding argues that at least some cultural heritage has intrinsic value insofar as it is constitutive of a flourishing human life. Important aspects of human flourishing are the unique aesthetic and cultural experiences that only cultural heritage makes possible. Hence, the best forms of cultural heritage should be preserved for reasons quite apart from their instrumental value. *See* Sarah Harding, *Value, Obligation and Cultural Heritage,* 31 ARIZ. ST. L.J. 291 (1999). What is your reaction to this argument? Would it justify, for example, preventing the private owner of a Rembrandt painting from destroying the painting? *See generally* JOSEPH L. SAX, PLAYING DARTS WITH A REMBRANDT: PUBLIC AND PRIVATE RIGHTS IN CULTURAL TREASURES 60-72 (1999). Does Harding's argument depend upon an extension of the personhood theory by invoking a *collective* constitutive claim?

3. *Traditional Knowledge as Intellectual Property.* Among the more controversial topics in the universe of cultural property is the question whether traditional knowledge should be protectable as intellectual property. "Traditional knowledge" refers to information or skills that indigenous peoples possess relating to their culture, folklore, or use of local flora for medical purposes. For example, the Rosy Periwinkle, a flower that is indigenous to Madagascar, has long been used by natives of that country for medicinal purposes and has now been patented for treatment of Hodgkins' disease. Efforts to privatize these forms of cultural information have largely come from two quite different sources. One source is of large corporations that

have discovered the potential for substantial profits to be reaped from, for example, patenting medicines derived from indigenous plants. Another source is aboriginal rights activists who, in an effort to promote the well-being of aboriginal peoples, seek legal recognition of novel forms of collective copyright.

Stringent legal protection of traditional knowledge as intellectual property has not escaped criticism. Michael Brown argues that "history suggests that the legal regulation of culture is at best a fruitless enterprise and at worst an invitation to new forms of manipulation by the powerful." MICHAEL F. BROWN, WHO OWNS NATIVE CULTURE? 252 (2003). Brown suggests that rather than legal regulation, civil society can be a more effective mode of protecting indigenous culture. Stephen Munzer and Kal Raustiala argue that the traditional justifications for property do not fit traditional knowledge and that significant legal protection of traditional knowledge requires major deviations from both established legal and theoretical doctrine. *See* Stephen R. Munzer & Kal Raustiala, *The Uneasy Case for Intellectual Property Rights in Traditional Knowledge*, 27 CARDOZO ARTS & ENT. L.J. 37 (2009). Based on your understanding of the justifications for property discussed in Part I of this book, do you agree?

4. *Repatriation and NAGPRA.* The disposition of cultural heritage has been an extraordinarily contentious issue in the past few decades, as objects of cultural property have been displaced through war, looting, vandalism, and other causes. Efforts to remedy displacement include repatriation laws. A notable example is the Native American Graves Protection and Repatriation Act (NAGPRA) of 1990, 25 U.S.C. §§3001-3013. The Act requires museums to inventory their holdings of Native American sacred objects and return them, upon request, to a "direct lineal descendant of an individual who owned the sacred object" or to a native tribe that "can show that the object was owned and controlled by the tribe." The museum must return the object unless it can show that it has a "right of possession" to the object. "Right of possession" is defined as "possession obtained with the voluntary consent of an individual or group that had the authority of alienation." NAGPRA has been controversial, especially among anthropologists. Professor Elizabeth Weiss, for example, asserts, "NAPRA and other repatriation laws obstruct the process of scientific endeavors; thereby, creating an ethical dilemma for scientists." Elizabeth Weiss, *NAGPRA: Before and After, available at* http://www.friendsofpast.org/nagpra/06 WeissNAGPRA.pdf. Weiss's statement follows from her empirical study of osteological research based on Native American remains, pre- and post-NAGPRA, finding that such research had significantly decreased after NAGPRA's enactment. Assuming for the moment that one can generalize from such studies to conclude that NAGPRA has impeded certain forms of scientific research, does it follow that repatriation measures such as NAGPRA are unwarranted? If not, is there any way to accommodate both NAGPRA's policy and such scientific concerns?

   5. *"Byronism" and the Parthenon (or Elgin) Marbles.* Merryman argues that repatriation often is based on cultural nationalism and that the premise of cultural nationalism is what he calls "Byronism," a "sentimental notion." He cites the Greek government's claim for repatriation of the Parthenon (or Elgin) Marbles as an example. The case of the Parthenon Marbles is one of the most controversial instances of repatriation, and Merryman is one of the foremost spokespersons opposing repatriation. What is your reaction to his argument? In thinking about Merryman's argument, some background is necessary. The Parthenon Marbles are a collection of classical Greek sculptures and architectural details from the Parthenon (portions of the frieze, metopes, and pediments) now on display in the British Museum in London. The term "Elgin Marbles" derives from Thomas Bruce, 7th Earl of Elgin and British Ambassador to the Ottoman Empire between 1799 and 1803, who removed them from the Parthenon and shipped them to England, where he sold them to the British Museum in 1816. In 1983, the Greek government formally requested that they be returned to Greece, but thus far the British government has declined. Both sides, British and Greek, claim legal ownership of the Marbles. The Greek government argues that even if the British are the legal owners, they nevertheless have a moral obligation to return the Marbles to their ancestral homeland. The British have refused on a variety of grounds, two of which Merryman discusses — preservation and access. The British government in the past has argued that keeping the Marbles on public display in the British Museum better preserves them and provides better access to them than any alternative that the Greeks would provide. Those reasons have now been significantly undermined by the opening of a state-of-the-art Acropolis Museum, which is devoted to the Parthenon and other temples. On the Parthenon Marbles debate, compare Christopher Hitchens, The Parthenon Marbles: The Case for Reunification (2008), with John Henry Merryman, *Thinking About the Elgin Marbles*, 83 Mich. L. Rev. 1881 (1985).

   What are the possible bases for the British Museum's having a moral obligation to return the Elgin Marbles to Greece? Suppose the British Museum had been a bona fide purchaser for value of the Elgin Marbles. How should that fact affect its moral obligations?

15 *FAMILY*

1. INHERITANCE AND INTERGENERATIONAL JUSTICE

D.W. Haslett, Is Inheritance Justified?[1]

Old ways die hard. A social practice may be taken for granted for centuries before humanity finally comes to realize it cannot be justified. Take, for example, slavery. Another example is the inheritance of political power. For many centuries, throughout most of the world, the suggestion that political power should be determined by democratic vote rather than heredity would have been met with scorn; today we realize just how unjustified determining political power by heredity really is.

Although we no longer believe in the inheritance of political power, most of us still believe in the inheritance of wealth, of *economic* power. But might not the inheritance of economic power be equally unjustified? This is the question to be examined here. Inheritance involves property rights; so another way of putting this question is: Should property rights incorporate the practice of inheritance as it exists today?

... I address only the justifiability of the practice (or institution) itself. ... I focus specifically upon whether it is justified in the *United States, today.* ... [F]or convenience also, I shall be using the word "inheritance" throughout to refer to any large amount one is *given* (as opposed to *earns*, or *wins*), whether it be, technically, a bequest or a gift. ...

... I examine what I take to be the most important objections to abolishing inheritance. I conclude that the practice of inheritance, as it exists today, should indeed be abolished. ...

1. D.W. Haslett, *Is Inheritance Justified?*, 15 Phil. & Pub. Aff. 122, 123, 137-138, 139, 140-142, 144-148 (1986).

In order to examine properly the objections to abolishing inheritance, we should have a definite proposal for abolishing inheritance before us, so that we know to what, exactly, these objections are meant to apply. I shall begin, therefore, by setting out a proposal that incorporates the main features I think any law abolishing inheritance should incorporate.

First, my proposal for abolishing inheritance includes the abolishment of all large gifts as well—gifts of the sort, that is, which might serve as alternatives to bequests. Obviously, if such gifts were not abolished as well, any law abolishing inheritance could be avoided all too easily. . . .

Next, according to my proposal, a person's estate would pass to the government, to be used for the general welfare. If, however, the government were to take over people's property upon their death then, obviously, after just a few generations the government would own virtually everything—which would certainly not be very compatible with capitalism. Since this proposal for abolishing inheritance is supposed to be compatible with capitalism, it must therefore include a requirement that the government sell on the open market, to the highest bidder, any real property, including any shares in a corporation, that it receives from anyone's estate, and that it do so within a certain period of time, within, say, one year from the decedent's death. This requirement is, however, to be subject to one qualification: any person specified by the decedent in his will shall be given a chance to *buy* any property specified by the decedent in his will before it is put on the market (a qualification designed to alleviate slightly the family heirloom/business/farm problem discussed below). . . .

Finally, the abolishment of inheritance proposed here is to be subject to three important exceptions. First, there shall be no limitations at all upon the amount a person can leave to his or her spouse. . . .

The second exception to be built into this proposal is one for children who are orphaned, and any other people who have been genuinely dependent upon the decedent, such as any who are mentally incompetent, or too elderly to have any significant earning power of their own. . . .

The third and final exception to be built into this proposal is one for charitable organizations—ones created not for purposes of making a profit, but for charitable, religious, scientific, or educational purposes. And, in order to prevent these organizations from eventually controlling the economy, they must, generally, be under the same constraint as is the government with respect to any real property they are given, such as an operating factory: they must, generally, sell it on the open market within a year. . . .

(1) With a specific proposal now before us, let us begin our survey of objections to abolishing inheritance with the one that is weakest: the objection that abolishing inheritance would be a violation of property rights. The trouble with this objection is, quite simply, that it begs the question. Property rights are not normally viewed as being unqualified, nor certainly should they be. On the contrary, property rights normally are, and certainly should be, viewed as having built into them a number of qualifications or

exceptions: an exception for taxes, an exception for uses which pose a danger of injury to others, an exception for eminent domain, and so on. As pointed out at the very beginning, the purpose of our investigation is precisely to determine whether we should recognize still another exception to property rights—an exception in the form of abolishing inheritance—or whether, instead, property rights should incorporate the practice of inheritance. . . .

(2) Let us turn next to the reason Milton Friedman supports inheritance. . . . [2] The argument upon which this objection is based proceeds somewhat as follows. Inheritance of property ("material" inheritance) is not the only source of unequal opportunity. Some people, for example, gain an unearned advantage over the rest of us by inheriting from their parents a beautiful singing voice, or keen intelligence, or striking good looks ("biological" inheritance). If we allow people to enjoy unearned advantages from biological inheritance, so the argument goes, it is only fair that we allow people to enjoy unearned advantages from material inheritance as well. We are told, in effect, that if we continue to allow one kind of unearned advantage to exist, we are, in all fairness, committed to allowing all other kinds of unearned advantages to continue to exist also.

The fallacy in this way of arguing should be apparent. One might just as well insist that racial discrimination is justified by arguing that, because we allow unearned advantages resulting from biological inheritance to continue to exist, we are, in all fairness, therefore committed to allowing unearned advantages resulting from racial discrimination to continue to exist also. To be sure, we do "allow" unearned advantages resulting from biological inheritance to continue to exist because, first of all, we cannot eliminate them and, second, even if we could, we would not want to since the costs of doing so would outweigh the benefits. Unearned advantages resulting from material inheritance, on the other hand, can be eliminated. Perhaps the costs of doing so outweigh the benefits here as well. But, once again, we can determine whether this is so only the hard way: by a careful and patient investigation into what the pros and cons actually are. We must not be dissuaded from this task by the above quick, but fallacious argument with which Friedman and others tempt us. . . .

(4) We turn next to what is, I suppose, the most common objection to abolishing inheritance: the objection that, if people were not allowed to leave their wealth to their children, they would lose their incentive to continue working hard, and national productivity would therefore fall. In spite of the popularity of this objection, all the available evidence seems to indicate the contrary. For example, people who do not intend to have children, and therefore are obviously not motivated by the desire to leave their children a fortune, do not seem to work any less hard than anyone else. And evidence of a more technical nature leads to the same conclusion: people,

2. [Milton] Friedman, *Capitalism & Freedom* [1962)], pp. 163-64; and [Milton & Rose Friedman,] *Freedom to Choose* [(1990)], p. 136.

typically, do not need to be motivated by a desire to leave their children (or someone else) great wealth in order to be motivated to work hard.

Common sense tells us the same thing. The prospect of being able to leave one's fortune to one's children is, no doubt, for some people one factor motivating them to be productive. But even for these people, this is only *one* factor; there are usually other factors motivating them as well, and motivating them to such an extent that, even if inheritance were abolished, their productivity would be unaffected. Take, for example, professional athletes. If inheritance were abolished, would they try any less hard to win? I doubt it. For one thing, abolishing inheritance would not, in any way, affect the amount of money they would be able to earn for use during their lives. So they would still have the prospect of a large income to motivate them. But there is something else which motivates them to do their best that is, I think, even more important, and is not dependent on money: the desire to win or, in other words, to achieve that which entitles them to the respect of their colleagues, the general public, and themselves. . . . Businessmen, doctors, lawyers, engineers, artists, researchers are not, with respect to what in the most general sense motivates them, really very different from professional athletes. Without inheritance, these people would still be motivated by the prospect of a sizable income for themselves and, probably even more so, by the prospect of "winning;" that is, by the prospect of achieving, or continuing to achieve, that which entitles them to the respect of their colleagues, the general public, and themselves.

But even if abolishing inheritance did lessen incentive by leaving people with no motivation to accumulate for their children, it would, in another respect, *increase* incentive. . . . Since abolishing inheritance would do much to equalize people's starting points, it should, in this way, increase people's incentives. And this increase, attributable to more equality of opportunity, would, I should think, more than make up for any decrease in incentive attributable to having no one to leave one's fortune to — if, indeed, there *were* any such decrease.[3]

(5) We come now to the most technical and, potentially, the most serious objection to abolishing inheritance: the objection that this would cause a substantial decrease in savings and investment, thus causing a serious reduction in capital which, in turn, would erode our standard of living. Abolishing inheritance, it is said, would reduce savings for two

3. Gordon Tullock claims that a better way to redistribute income and wealth than abolishing inheritance would be a direct tax on either income or wealth. See Tullock, "Inheritance Justified," *The Journal of Law and Economics* (October 1971). But, if I am right, abolishing inheritance would not, in general, decrease people's incentive to be productive (on the contrary, it would probably increase incentive); whereas the same cannot be said of Tullock's method of still greater income taxes, or of a substantial tax upon wealth. In any case, Tullock fails to realize that by no means is redistribution the only, or even the main, goal of abolishing inheritance; another goal, for example, is greater equality of opportunity (i.e., "starting places" that are more equal). Any tax upon income or wealth which still permitted vast sums to be inherited from various sources would not be as successful as abolishing inheritance, or as a modest quota (see below), in accomplishing *this* goal.

reasons. First, by breaking up large fortunes, it would reduce the number of 1)
people whose wealth far exceeded their capacity to consume, and who,
therefore, were able to sink vast amounts into savings and investment.
Without these vast amounts going into savings and investment, it is argued,
overall savings and investment, and thus capital, would go down. Sec- 2)
ondly, it is said that, not only would abolishing inheritance reduce people's
capacity to save by breaking up large fortunes, it would also reduce people's
incentive to save. Although, as we have seen, abolishing inheritance probably would not significantly affect people's incentive to produce, their
incentive to save might well be affected. If people could not leave their
wealth to their children, then rather than leave it to charity, or to the
government, they might well decide to consume it instead. In short: abolishing inheritance would shift people's consumption-savings pattern more
in the direction of consumption.

These points, although probably well taken, should not be exaggerated.
Abolishing inheritance would distribute wealth more evenly, the relatively
few enormous fortunes of today being replaced, in part, by a larger number
of moderate fortunes. Thus any slack in investment attributable to a decrease
in the *size* of the fortunes of those with enough to invest substantial amounts
would, to some extent, be taken up by an increase in the *number* of people
with fortunes large enough for them to invest substantial amounts. And
people's *motives* to save and invest would certainly not evaporate altogether
with the abolishment of inheritance. People would, of course, still want to
hold something back for a "rainy day." People would still want to save for
their retirement (and no one knows for how many years one will need to be
covered). Investments would still remain attractive aside from the savings
motive; they combine the excitement of a gamble with the satisfaction of
doing what is socially useful. And many people, especially the more wealthy,
would still want to save for charitable purposes; to have a scholarship or
perhaps a university building named after them, to support medical research,
or even to establish a charitable foundation to carry on with some project in
which they deeply believe. Another point to keep in mind is that most corporate investment — and corporate investment constitutes a large percent of
total investment — is generated by corporate income. Given the separation
between ownership and management in large corporations today, it is
unlikely that management would be influenced by the abolishment of inheritance to reduce the percentage of corporate income used for the replacement of capital and new investment. Indeed, if private funding became
increasingly scarce, funding from corporate income might well take up
some of the slack. In short, no one really knows for sure exactly how abolishing inheritance would affect savings and investment, but the effect might
turn out to be far less than some critics think.

However the most important reply to the investment objection is
this: even if abolishing inheritance significantly reduced investment,
countermeasures to increase investment — and to do so at relatively little

cost — are readily available. These countermeasures can be classified as either direct or indirect. Indirect methods include, for example, reducing the availability of consumer credit, requiring full funding of all pension plans, and taxing consumption. Direct methods, the more interesting of the two, take the form of some sort of direct government subsidy of investment. But, it should be emphasized, not even direct methods need be at the cost of any governmental *management* of investments, which would be the first step toward socialism. Indeed, they need not even be at the cost of any governmental *selection* of investments, something which most supporters of the free market would find objectionable also. . . .

. . . [C]apitalism['s] . . . enemies point to the extreme inequalities of wealth it generates, to the shameless inequalities of opportunity, and they ask if such a system deserves to survive. Frankly, I am not sure it does. Yet it is a system with virtues as striking as its deficiencies: it is extraordinarily productive, and it generates important freedoms. A system with so much going for it is worth trying to remedy from within. This will, I think, require major changes, not the least of which will be to unburden capitalism of an outmoded practice of inheritance.

NOTES AND QUESTIONS

1. *Inheritance and Capital Accumulation.* Haslett states that perhaps the most serious objection to abolishing inheritance is that doing so would cause a substantial decrease in capital accumulation. Economists also consider this to be the main reason not to abolish inheritance. *See* Gordon Tullock, *Inheritance Justified*, 14 J.L. & ECON. 465 (1971). Haslett believes that the objection has less bite than is usually believed. He makes three points: (1) The reduction of available capital due to breaking up large estates would be offset by increasing the amount of wealth in moderate estates; (2) people have strong incentives to accumulate capital independently of leaving it to their successors; (3) countermeasures to increase investment could be taken if abolishing inheritance did reduce investment. Are these responses persuasive? As Haslett notes, (Haslett, *supra*, footnote 3), Tullock argues that direct taxation of all forms of wealth is the most efficient means of equalizing wealth distribution. *See* Tullock, *supra*, at 470-472. Haslett responds that such a tax would probably reduce people's incentives to produce but that abolishing the institution of inheritance would not have that effect. Do you agree that these two methods — taxation vs. abolition — would affect incentives to accumulate capital so differently? Haslett says that because of other motives to be productive, if inheritance were abolished, people's productivity would be unaffected. Do you think this is true for most people?

2. *Egalitarianism, Inheritance, and Wealth Taxation.* The relationship between equality and inheritance of wealth has been a core topic of political and moral theory for many years. As Edward McCaffery states,

"Privately held wealth and its unequal distribution, and perhaps especially the transmission of such wealth across generations, have long been thought to pose particularly pernicious influences in a liberal democratic state." Edward J. McCaffery, *The Uneasy Case for Wealth Transfer Taxation*, 104 YALE L.J. 283, 284 (1994).

Policy analysts frequently fail to distinguish between two quite different forms of equality when discussing ideal taxation regimes. One is equality of opportunity, or what some scholars call, "resource equality." *See, e.g.*, Anne L. Alstott, *Equal Opportunity and Inheritance Taxation*, 121 HARV. L. REV. 470, 471 (2007). This form of equality focuses on the *ex ante* distribution of wealth and is individualistic. The other form is outcome equality. Unlike resource equality, it seeks to assure *ex post* equalization of wealth distribution. It is important to be clear about which form of equality is the ideal being pursued by any given wealth tax scheme because some schemes advance one form of equality but may be at odds with the other. For example, Anne Alstott argues that an inheritance tax designed to secure resource equality should tax gifts and bequests received by younger-generation beneficiaries at higher rates than those that older beneficiaries receive. Alstott, *supra*, at 473. What do you suppose is the logic behind this proposal?

3. *Bequests, Consumption, and the "Inflating Benefits Effects" Problem.* Are bequests of property more socially beneficial than lifetime consumption from an economic perspective? In thinking about this question, consider an argument made by Ariel Porat and Avraham Tabbach in a different context. Lifetime consumption of wealth reflects the value that the individual ascribes to his life in the sense of his ability to enjoy life through the consumption of his wealth. But this value—the value that the individual ascribes to his own life—does not represent his life's *social* value. This is because people commonly ascribe a higher value to their lives than the socially optimal level (e.g., overinvest in extending their lives relative to the socially efficient level of investment of life care). From society's point of view, any wealth that the individual consumes in order to increase his ability to consume his wealth over life (e.g., by having an expensive medical procedure that gives him a 50 percent chance of living 9 months longer) is social waste. In this situation individuals ascribe no value to their wealth after death, but society does. Once the individual dies, any unconsumed wealth passes to other people who will consume, invest, or enjoy the property. "Therefore," Porat and Tabbach conclude, "from a social perspective, it is inefficient to spend any resources on increasing the probability that that individual rather than others will enjoy the consumption of his wealth." Ariel Porat & Avraham Tabbach, *Willingness to Pay, Death, Wealth, and Damages*, 13 AM. LAW & ECON. REV. 45, 55 (2011).

What is your reaction to this argument? What are its implications vis-à-vis Haslett's attack on inheritance? If one accepts Porat and Tabbach's argument, what implications follow with respect to people's freedom to consume their wealth rather than passing it on to others? Are there mechanisms by which we might correct the inefficiency that Porat and Tabbach have identified? *See id.* at 60-65 (suggesting use of an "Improved Annuity," under which the individual undertakes to leave the annuity his wealth upon death in return for the annuity's promise to pay the individual, if he survives, an amount of money based on the expected value of his inheritance).

4. *Inheritance, Labor Theories, and Libertarianism.* The arguments in support of inheritance to which Haslett responds are primarily welfarist arguments. What about inheritance from the perspectives of the various forms of the labor theory? John Locke justified inheritance, but not on the basis of his labor theory. Rather, Locke's theory was that when a parent acquires a nut, say, by investment of labor, she acquires an interest that is subject to joint rights in her dependents. This is so because by bringing children into the world, the parent has a duty, as a matter of natural law, to preserve what she has begotten. *See* John Locke, Two Treatises of Government I, §88 (Peter Laslett ed., 1960). When the parent dies, then, her children acquire full ownership of the nut by survivorship. As Jeremy Waldron points out, Locke's account of inheritance is at odds with the familiar depiction of his political philosophy as that of "possessive individualism." Jeremy Waldron, *Locke's Account of Inheritance and Bequest*, 19 J. Hist. Ideas 39, 43 (1981).

Proponents of the labor-desert theory have contended that the theory justifies inheritance but only with substantial restrictions. Stephen Munzer, for example, uses the labor-desert theory to justify reducing wealth inequality through wealth transfer taxes and certain direct restrictions on the power to dispose of property. *See* Stephen R. Munzer, A Theory of Property 395-411 (1990).

Libertarianism is usually understood to justify not only the institution of inheritance but also a robust form of the principle of freedom of disposition. Recall that Robert Nozick, whose libertarian manifesto we have read in Chapter 3, argued that so long as the donor was entitled to the asset, he was free to transfer it, including by bequest or inheritance, as he wished. Efforts to secure patterns of wealth distribution through taxation or otherwise were, according to Nozick, illegitimate. Nozick appears to have had second thoughts about inheritance, however. In a later book, he indicated that his Entitlement Theory had problematic implications for the distribution of wealth through inheritance. He wrote:

> Bequeathing something to others is an expression of caring about them . . . yet bequests [are] sometimes passed on for generations to persons unknown to the original earner, . . . producing continuing inequalities of wealth and position. . . . The resulting inequalities seem unfair.
>
> One possible solution would be to restructure an institution of inheritance so that taxes will subtract from the possessions people can bequeath the value of what they themselves have received through bequests. People then could leave to others only the amount they themselves have added.

The simple subtraction rule does not perfectly disentangle what the next generation has managed itself to contribute—inheriting wealth may make it easier to amass more—but it is a serviceable rule of thumb.

ROBERT NOZICK, THE EXAMINED LIFE 30-31 (1989). Was Nozick right the first time, or did he get it right (or at least come closer to getting it right) in his later work?

5. *Is the Power of Bequest Inherent in Ownership?* Haslett denies that inheritance and the power of bequest are inherent in ownership, arguing that ownership is subject to a number of exceptions (among which he counts bequest as one). James Penner holds a quite different view. For him, the right to sell is not conceptually inherent in ownership, but the right to give is. Here is his argument:

> We understand gratuitous sharing and giving only when we understand how permitting someone else to use one's property counts as one's own disposition of that property as, in a sense, one's own use. First and foremost, when I permit someone to share property that is mine that permission is my decision. To that extent it appears obvious that I have adopted the shared use as 'mine' in some sense. But, of course, it is not my own use at all in another sense, as I am not the one who directly benefits from the use of the property; the person I permitted to use it is. Nevertheless, my claim is that this second person's use is my own use as well.
>
> In order to understand this, we need accept nothing more than the perhaps mysterious fact about humans that they may be better off simply because other persons they care about or love are better off; our lives are so connected. . . .
>
> The premiss underlying the view that the right to give property absolutely is a right entailed by the right of exclusive use is that, when we give something to someone, we treat the use of the donee *as our own use.* . . .
>
> . . . The reason the right to give is to be regarded as within the right of exclusive use, but contractual transfers without is that, on the view I have expressed, the interest underlying property rights encompasses the social uses of property like sharing and giving. In contrast, in general I could not care less what a contractual transferee does with the property he receives from me in an exchange, since his use does not implicate any of my interests. . . .

J.E. PENNER, THE IDEA OF PROPERTY IN LAW 88-90 (1997). Whose view do you find more persuasive? What do you make of Penner's distinction between the right to give and the right to sell, one inherent in ownership, the other not? At least for Fifth Amendment constitutional purposes, the U.S. Supreme Court agrees that the right to sell (or as the Court puts it, the right of commercial exploitation) is not inherent in ownership. *See* Andrus v. Allard, 444 U.S. 51 (1979) (federal Eagle Protection Act, prohibiting sale of eagle feathers and artifacts made with eagle feathers, not a taking of property under the Fifth Amendment Takings Clause).

6. *Milton Friedman, Bequest, and Social Stratification.* Haslett rather roundly rejects Milton Friedman's defense of freedom of bequest. He reads Friedman to say, "[I]f we continue to allow one kind of unearned advantage to exist, we are, in all fairness, committed to allowing all other

kinds of unearned advantages to continue to exist also." Haslett, *supra*, at 141. But can't Friedman be read differently? Perhaps he is arguing that allowing inheritance of earned benefits — as opposed to immutable ones as well as those that derive from better education of parents and similar factors — allows such "new money" to upset existing social stratification. What is your reaction to this argument?

7. *Inheritance and Intergenerational Justice.* The problem of justifying inheritance is closely related to the problem of intergenerational justice, i.e., justice between and/or among generations. It is an open (and controversial) question whether past and present generations owe duties, stemming from justice considerations, to future generations. *See, e.g.*, Douglas A. Kysar, *Discounting . . . on Stilts*, 74 U. Chi. L. Rev. 119 (2007). If they do, then some of the claims that future generations make of past and present generations almost invariably implicate considerations of distributive justice, and such considerations quickly lead to questions about the role of inheritance and bequest.

Some proponents of obligations to future generations have argued that what Bruce Ackerman and Anne Alstott call "old-fashioned inheritance" is "dysfunctional." Bruce Ackerman & Anne Alstott, The Stakeholder Society 36 (1999). Ackerman and Alstott write, "Although inheritances of substantial property occur only at the top of the socioeconomic pyramid, such bequests will [in the future] increasingly be divorced from one of their classic functions — to provide young adults with an initial stake." *Ibid.* (footnote omitted). Rather than relying on inheritance to this obligation to the next generation, Ackerman and Alstott propose giving each American citizen a stake in society: Upon reaching the age of maturity, each citizen will receive from the government a guaranteed stake of $80,000. This will be financed by an annual 2 percent tax levied on all of the nation's wealth. The stakeholders are free to use the money as they see fit, but they must repay it by the time they die. *Id.* at 3-5. What is your reaction to this proposal? Is this an effective means of satisfying each generation's distributive obligations to younger generations (assuming for the moment that such an obligation exists)? Are there more effective ways of satisfying whatever distributive obligations the ideal of intergenerational justice imposes on the present generation?

At the other end of the political spectrum, some scholars claim that no special measures are needed to respond to the demands of intergenerational justice. Richard Epstein, for example, argues that "if we continue to create sound institutions for the present, then the problem of future generations will pretty much take care of itself, even if we do not develop overarching policies of taxation or investment that target future generations for special considerations." Richard A. Epstein, *Justice across the Generations, in* Justice Between Age Groups and Generations 84-85 (Peter Laslett & James S. Fishkin eds., 1992). In Epstein's view, "A classical liberal regime of limited government, focused regulation, low taxation, personal liberty, and private property does better by future generations than any alternative regime that consciously enlists large government to restrain liberty and limit the present use of property for the benefit of future generations." *Ibid.* Is Epstein's point that limited government is the best means of meeting our obligations to future obligation, or is his point rather that we have no such obligation? Do you agree with either view?

8. *A Non-utilitarian Justification for Inheritance.* Most justifications for inheritance are based on utilitarian considerations, such as incentives to save. Are there any persuasive non-utilitarian justifications for the institution of inheritance? Shelly Kreiczer-Levy argues that inheritance is a property institution that "creates and maintains continuity through property." Shelly Kreiczer-Levy, The Riddle of Inheritance: Connecting Continuity and Property, *available at* http://papers.ssrn.com/sol3/papers.cfm?abstract_id=1789211. Kreiczer-Levy explains that inheritance creates:

> a particular form of continuity based on the significance of property as an important social and personal symbol. Accordingly, the law of inheritance today cannot be correctly characterized by reference to testamentary freedom alone. There is not just one central focal point, the owner of property, I contend, but actually *two* focal points. While they are hardly equal in their theoretical or practical strength, both are essential to establishing a conception of inheritance. Moreover, these two focal points are not independent interests that should be correctly balanced against each other. Rather, the interests of the owner and her receivers are intertwined, co-dependent, and guided by the same rationale.

Ibid. What is your reaction to this argument?

2. MARRIAGE

Carolyn J. Frantz & Hanoch Dagan, Properties of Marriage[1]

I. MARRIAGE AS AN EGALITARIAN LIBERAL COMMUNITY

Marriage as an egalitarian liberal community brings together three strands of marriage—community, autonomy, and equality. Though it is often assumed that they cannot coexist, this account of marriage accommodates particular conceptions of these three ideals to a remarkable degree. . . . By demonstrating that our account of marriage harmonizes conceptions of these values—and, indeed, shows how these values can be mutually supportive—this Part seeks to vindicate the viability and desirability of the ideal of marriage as an egalitarian liberal community. . . .

---

1. Carolyn J. Frantz & Hanoch Dagan, *Properties of Marriage*, 104 COLUM. L. REV. 75, 81-88, 91-94, 98-112 (2004).

1. Community

... There are many benefits to being married. Like any other pooling of resources, marriage provides advantages of economies of scale, specialization, and risk spreading. But these goods are hardly unique to marriage, and, more importantly, can be purchased on the market. The unique goods of "communal" marriage—intimacy, caring, and commitment—are collective in a crucially different way. A mercenary understanding of these goods is hopelessly misguided, corrupting the community ideal of marriage. A self-centered quest to capture these marital goods—cooperating to achieve solely individual ends—will not ultimately be successful. Rather, to secure these unique goods of marriage, what is good for one spouse must affect what is good for the other. This partial fusion, at the core of communal marriage, is achieved when spouses perceive themselves at least partially as a "we," a plural subject, that is in turn a constitutive feature of each spouse's identity as an "I."

It is not surprising that marriage is often a site for such communal life. Membership in a functioning marital community may be the best way to achieve one's communal goals. Spouses typically engage in a variety of collective projects, including child rearing, broader family relationships, friendships, and the common management of resources—a household, investments, and careers. This ever-increasing number of projects requires daily interactions that in turn produce an intensive, long-term fusion. It is this intensity (and its continuity) that stimulates closeness, interdependency, and mutual trust.

The association of marriage with the creation of plural identity is consistent with the move of divorce law from the title theory of property ownership—where each spouse individually owns property he or she has purchased with separate funds—to a regime that acknowledges the entitlements of both spouses in many marital goods. Sharing the advantages of life together as well as its difficulties is the linchpin of community. Sharing requires spouses to "infuse[] costs and benefits with an intersubjective character" and to reject any "strict accounting based on individual merit."[2] Realization of collective goods in marriage depends on each partner "carrying out the projects constitutive of his shared life in a spirit of trust and love rather than of the piecemeal calculation of individual advantage."[3] Communal marriage demands that spouses not ask for accountings or make individual claims of entitlement to marital goods. Rather, their cooperation should be based on an expectation of a lasting relationship that calls for mutual trust, support, and confident reliance on the other; sharing life and its projects requires spouses to pool their efforts and their rewards, "each operating on joint behalf of both."[4] ...

2. [Milton C.] Regan, [Jr., Family Law and the Pursuit of Intimacy] 147 [(1993)].
3. [Elizabeth] Anderson, [Value in Ethics and Economics] 157 [(1993)].
4. [Simon] Gardner, [*Rethinking Family Property*, 109 L.Q. Rev. 263], 283 [(1993)].

2. Autonomy

. . . Marriage as an egalitarian liberal community demands that spouses look beyond their narrow self-interest. But contrary to the belief of some traditional scholars, this vision does not require the negation of the self. . . .

A liberal conception of the marital community thus views the communal goods obtained through marriage as an aspect of individual self-fulfillment, with that "self" properly including the new plural self of marriage. Spouses' identification with and commitment to the marital community should be voluntarily chosen based in part on the value of the marital community to themselves—hence, the liberal qualifier. Thus, the plural identity constituted by marriage is only partial: Incorporating what is good for the other into the perception of what is good for oneself need not, and should not, erase each spouse's individual identity. In the ideal of marriage as an egalitarian liberal community, the community of marriage is good for the individual spouse, rather than simply good of her.

As we will see in discussing the scope of the marital estate, this core aspect of individual autonomy requires limits on the collectivization of projects individual spouses undertake during the tenure of their marriage. For now, it is important to note the implications of autonomy for exit. If the marital community is to be a good for each individual spouse, law should secure the ability of each spouse to decide whether or not, and for how long, to participate in the institution. While each spouse in a communal marriage is in part constituted by her relationship with the other, she should be able to choose to abandon, through divorce, this part of her identity. Liberal societies are accordingly committed to ensuring that the participation of individuals in marriages (and other social groups) is legally voluntary

. . . Meaningful self-identification and the goods it provides should be part of the good life for individuals, not a legal duty that they must bear regardless of its continuing appeal.

Social pressure may of course affect people's decisions to enter or exit marriage. Where this pressure takes the form of mere disapproval by friends, family, and religious communities, this is not necessarily illiberal because people can ultimately choose their own way. The law's power, however, cannot be escaped, and therefore a commitment to liberal values requires that the legal boundaries of marriage be open. Nonetheless, social pressure is at times institutionalized in a law-like fashion (consider, for instance, some close-knit and pervasive religious communities), making exit practically impossible. In these contexts, we hope that an exit-friendly law can begin to ameliorate those pressures. . . .

. . . [E]xit is not only passively compatible with marital community, but can actively support it. Part of what makes marriage meaningful as a community is that spouses know that it is entered into and maintained only by choice. Intimacy, caring, and commitment are particularly valuable if voluntarily chosen. The legal power to exit converts the daily life of marriage into a manifestation of a choice that positively reaffirms spouses' plural identity. . . .

We do not deny that the availability of exit poses a grave threat to the functioning of the marital community. As in other commons settings, exit tends to undermine sharing and trust by exacerbating the difficulty of collective action, inviting opportunism, and thus threatening cooperation, even in long-term relationships. This difficulty is particularly acute in marriage, where couples often make long-term, relationship-specific investments based on the assumption that their marriage will endure for a lifetime, thus creating asymmetric vulnerability as to the contingency of early termination by divorce. One particularly resonant example is the vulnerability created by "traditional" marriage, where one spouse (the wife) makes sacrifices early in hopes of reaping rewards later in life.

This does not mean that securing the communal goods of marriage in a liberal environment is impossible. Rather, as with other liberal commons institutions, the risks opened up by free exit should be taken as a challenge. Fortunately, there are quite a few things marriage law can do to mitigate these difficulties. First, entrenching the ideal of marriage as an egalitarian liberal community in marital property law can help to internalize these values, making opportunistic behavior even less likely. Moreover, guided by this ideal, marital property law can provide a safety net (as discussed below) that can ameliorate the vulnerability of spouses. And there is another possibility: making exit, though free, not necessarily easy. Cooperative relationships are particularly vulnerable to opportunistic behavior when the parties' horizon is only short term. Temporary time-limited restraints on exit — so-called "cooling-off periods" — can alleviate this problem, enabling parties to engage in longer-term cooperation and guarding against impulsive exit. Accordingly, state divorce schemes that provide for waiting periods before divorce may — if implemented carefully enough — partially counteract the difficulties exit poses for community.[5] . . .

3. Equality and Non-Subordination

People may engage in many joint enterprises where equality is not necessary. Joint owners in a business, for instance, may divide the ownership interest 70-30 without raising any alarm. But it would be perverse to conceive of a

---

5. Covenant marriage, first adopted in Louisiana, is one well-known institution integrating a cooling-off period. *See* LA. REV. STAT. ANN. tit. 9, §§272–275.1, 307–309 (West 2000) . . . ; *see also* Katherine Shaw Spaht, *What's Become of Louisiana Covenant Marriage Through the Eyes of Social Scientists*, 47 LOY. L. REV. 709, 711 (2001) (describing conditions on dissolution of covenant marriage, including mandatory premarital counseling, taking reasonable steps to preserve marriage, and various restrictive grounds for divorce). In a pervasive community, however, even such soft restrictions on exit must be viewed with caution. . . . To the extent that covenant marriage does not allow immediate exit from emotionally or psychologically abusive relationships, we obviously do not endorse it. . . .

marriage of this sort, where one spouse has a recognized controlling interest in the property that partially constitutes the marriage, and, correspondingly, in marital decisions. One reason for this difference is that marriage is a more pervasive engagement than any other enterprise. Disparity in the control of marital property moves beyond simple inequality — which an individual may rightly choose as a means to other ends — to subordination, which systematically denies the importance of whatever ends that individual chooses. As subordination in marriage is a threat to a spouse's basic personhood, the marital community must be bounded by a commitment to equality.

Equality as non-subordination is also crucial to the communal dimension of marriage. Spouses in an inegalitarian marriage cannot form a true plural self or enjoy the unique collective goods of marriage. This applies not only to the oppressed spouse, but also to the oppressor: "One committed and loving partner," Elizabeth Anderson explains, "cannot unequivocally rejoice in his life with his partner if he knows that the other finds the relationship oppressive in some way."[6] An oppressive marriage not only deprives the subordinated spouse of a voice, but also deprives the subordinating spouse of a partner, thus precluding realization of intimacy, caring, commitment, and emotional attachment.

Yet the history of equality in marriage is not promising. The marital community, a locus of sharing and trust, has been abused to shield subordinating patriarchal structures. Patriarchal marriages allow men to capture a disproportionately high share of the benefits (including decision-making power) of marriage and bear a disproportionately low share of its costs. "When we look seriously at the distribution between husbands and wives of such critical social goods as work (paid and unpaid), power, prestige, self-esteem, opportunities for self-development, and both physical and economic security, we find socially constructed inequalities between them, right down the list."[7]

The persistence of patriarchal marriages can be attributed to the enhanced leverage men have in their explicit and implicit bargaining with women. This is due to men's greater earning power, or, more precisely, the "cycle of power relations and decisions [that] pervades both family and workplace, and the [way in which the] inequalities of each reinforce those that already exist in the other."[8] It can also be attributed to "men's higher extramarital utility, better remarriage prospects, and longer reproductive life."[9] Finally, as Carol Rose explains, if women have a greater taste for cooperation than men or if they are perceived to

6. ANDERSON, *supra* note 3, at 151.

7. [SUSAN MOLLER] OKIN, [JUSTICE, GENDER, AND THE FAMILY] 136 [(1989)].

8. *Id.* at 147.

9. [Amy L.] Wax, [*Bargaining in the Shadow of the Market: Is There a Future for Egalitarian Marriage?*, 84 VA. L. REV. 509], 579 [(1998)].

have such a taste, over time men are likely to get the lion's share of the joint gains from marriage.[10]

Any subordination — whether based on gender or another feature — is problematic within marriage. However, exit and entry are sufficient for combating subordination that does not arise from gender inequality. If choice is otherwise unconstrained, spouses are unlikely to choose to enter into a marriage they find oppressive, and are likely to withdraw if it becomes oppressive over time. But with gender inequality, things are different. Heterosexual women cannot be expected to avoid marriage with those who have the power to subordinate them. Once they have married men, exit from a subordinating relationship will not necessarily be a tenable alternative. . . .

Because expecting women to protect themselves against marital subordination is both unrealistic and undesirable, the law must provide institutional guarantees of gender equality to support the marital community. This prescription is not only founded on the intrinsic value of gender equality, but is also entailed by the communal maxims of marriage. As Susan Moller Okin explains, men's ability to use the threat of exit as leverage affects the very functioning of the community by affecting women's voice within it.[11] With pervasive gender inequality, the fact that women remain in and cooperate during marriage may be due to social, economic, and cultural lack of choice. This is anathema to genuine community.

Admittedly, marital property law cannot completely free women or marriage from gender subordination. Fully compensating for all social gender discrimination is too great an obligation to put on marriage. In particular, expecting husbands to completely neutralize their wives' social disadvantages may jeopardize their own autonomy. Thus, the best we can hope for is a reasonable compromise between these competing goals. And yet there is hope that marital property law can help facilitate the egalitarian transformation. In Part II, we show that a commitment to the ideal of marriage as an egalitarian liberal community entails a significant legal reform: Spouses' claims to the marital estate, broadly defined, should be based on their joint and equal entitlement, rather than on a property redistribution theory. Through these and other reforms, we hope that a revitalized marital property law, consistent with the ideal of marriage as an egalitarian liberal community, will be one important — although by no means sufficient — step toward gender equality. . . .

II.   MARITAL PROPERTY LAW

Assessing the desirability of the egalitarian liberal community ideal for marriage requires not only abstract discussion of principles, but also an

---

10. *See* CAROL M. ROSE, *Women and Property: Gaining and Losing Ground, in* PROPERTY AND PERSUASION: ESSAYS ON THE HISTORY, THEORY, AND RHETORIC OF OWNERSHIP 233, 245-47 (1994).

11. *See* OKIN, *supra* note 6, at 137-38, 161, 167-68, 180.

analysis of the implications of these prescriptions for marital property law. Therefore, we now shift from theory to practice, to translate the ideal into a set of detailed rules. In Part I, we discussed the rules regarding exit. We endorsed no-fault divorce with perhaps a cooling-off period. Part II focuses on aspects of marriage and divorce law that address the property relationship between spouses: the rules regarding property division and alimony upon divorce, as well as those addressing the governance of property during marriage. We find that the law already reflects the ideal of the egalitarian liberal community to a significant degree. At the same time, we point to blemishes in the existing doctrine, some of which are very significant in their effects. In these contexts, we rely on the ideal of marriage as an egalitarian liberal community as a justification for important reforms.

A. Property Division

. . . The cornerstone of the contemporary law of marital property — the one rule that seems least disputed (at least as a theoretical matter) by courts, commentators, and lay people alike — is the rule of equal division upon divorce. Equal division is a relative latecomer to marital property law, but by now we can hardly think of the law without it.

Equal division of the marital estate has been endorsed as a rigid mandatory prescription in only three jurisdictions. Elsewhere equality typifies the law in softer ways. Many states have a presumption of equal division of property established either through statute or through common law rule. Several other states have adopted less powerful fifty-percent "starting points" for division. Even states that have failed to adopt an equality standard, or that explicitly reject the notion, presume equal ownership of jointly held property (typically the family home, the only significant existing marital asset in most cases), regardless of the origin of the purchase money. The "substantial evidence" needed to overcome such a presumption is rarely forthcoming — most couples do not discuss the ownership of the home in the event of divorce at the time of purchase — and, absent considerations involving housing of the couple's children, the value of the family home is frequently divided equally.

. . . While equality is the emerging norm in the law of property division, its underlying justification is far from settled. The American Law Institute's (ALI) Principles of Family Dissolution Law, which adopts the equal division rule, exemplifies the confusion. As the ALI notes, many have supported equal division on the basis of contribution theory, arguing that equal division accurately values the contributions of non-market work (typically expended disproportionately by women) to the joint marital enterprise. The ALI rightly rejects this argument because of its factual implausibility — there is little reason to believe that the non-market contributions of the spouse with less market power are sufficient to balance the other spouse's significant market power advantage. But then the ALI makes an inconsistent concession to contribution theory — that an equal division rule may in fact reflect contributions to the entire marital relationship, because "one spouse may have contributed more than the other in emotional stability, optimism, or social skills."[12] This, however, is no more factually defensible than the presumption of equal financial contribution. Are we to assume that women, with less market power, must necessarily have more interpersonal skills?

The problem with the ALI's explanation is that it ultimately depends on assigning an external value to each spouse's contribution, suggesting that on some meaningful external calculation, both spouses would inevitably come out equal. This is wrong not only because it is wishful thinking — assuming, to a certain extent, background gender equality — but also because it misunderstands the metric of marriage. As discussed above, spouses do keep some rough idea of the fairness of their marriage, but this is not based on the external value of their contributions, but rather on a rough assessment of mutual fairness that can only be internally measured and must be self-enforced. By relying on an external valuation of market and non-market contribution, the ALI fails to account for the communal character of marriage.

A similar response is appropriate for other dubious explanations for the equal division rule. Elizabeth and Robert Scott have argued that equal division of marital assets can be justified on grounds of efficiency — and is thus firmly grounded in spouses' hypothetical consent — as a means of preserving the incentive to share during marriage, as well as the incentive to exit the marital community at certain strategically valuable points. But even these authors admit that this contractual logic can only justify recovery to the extent of the opportunity costs of the non-propertied spouse.[13] Realistically, when parties enter the marriage with substantially differing degrees of market power, equal division is not necessary to secure the advantages of collective action.

. . . Instead of reference to contribution, efficiency, or hypothetical consent, we propose a justification for the equal division rule based on the ideal of marriage as an egalitarian liberal community. First, equal division performs a desirable expressive function. Equality stands against any investigation into the interior functioning of the marital community to determine individual desert, and best demonstrates that no party is any more entitled to marital resources than any other. Equal division also decreases parties' incentives to view their marriages individualistically. A fifty percent rule ensures that there is no advantage to keeping an accounting of individual investments in and returns from the marital relationship. The party who shows up in divorce court with a stack of receipts tracing

---

12. [AMERICAN LAW INSTITUTE, PRINCIPLES OF THE LAW OF FAMILY DISSOLUTION: ANALYSIS AND RECOMMENDATIONS] §4.09, at 732 & cmt. c, at 735 [(2000)].

13. [Elizabeth S.] Scott & [Robert E.] Scott, [*Marriage as Relational Contract*, 84 VA. L. REV. 1225,] 1271-74 [(1998)].

back to the beginning of the marriage has clearly not signed on to a communal understanding of the institution. A rule of equal property division on divorce discourages such behavior. Moreover, equal division makes it easier for spouses to engage in sharing behavior — investing in relationship-specific goods, specializing, and making individual sacrifices for the overall good of the community. Spreading the benefits and the risks of this kind of behavior equally between the parties transforms personal sacrifice into joint endeavor. . . .

Moreover, equal division can play a limited but significant role in achieving egalitarian marriage by partly ameliorating men's greater market advantages. We do not deny that women are still not on an economic par with men, even if granted half of the assets of the marriage. It is for this reason that we shortly turn to substantive [rehabilitative] alimony as a means to further address gender inequality. Still, even in terms of gender inequality, equal division has real advantages. Division of existing marital assets sends a powerful message of ownership — that the award is not a social welfare handout, but rather an entitlement. Unlike alimony, which carries the stigma of dependency and weakness, equal division promotes spouses' sense of personal dignity by signaling equal ownership of all marital property.

Identifying the most compelling justification for the equal division rule is not just a theoretical exercise. As usual, getting the theory right has important practical implications. Understanding the point of the central rule of marital property helps us understand and evaluate other less central rules, at times providing reasons to reform them. Moreover, even with respect to the equal division rule itself, understanding its justification suggests its proper application. If, as we argue, equal division is best explained as a rejection of contribution and an endorsement of egalitarian liberal community, then it is better applied as a presumption (and a strong one, at that) rather than a starting point. It should also apply to all marital property (the scope of which we discuss below) rather than simply the family home or any other subset. Furthermore, this presumption should never be rebutted by any factor relating to contribution, as this would undermine the very point of its existence.

B. The Assets Subject to Division

As important as the rules governing property division are the assets that are subject to these rules: the "scope" of marital property. The equal division rule cannot support an egalitarian liberal community if important marital assets are excluded from division.

We include the central cases, such as existing balances from wages earned during marriage, property purchased and investments made with these marital funds, as well as the slightly more controversial category of wage substitutes such as pensions. We exclude from the scope of marital property many of those things that have traditionally been excluded — for instance, the emotional trauma of divorce. We restrict our efforts to fungible goods, focusing on three controversial types: earning capacity, preexisting property, and gifts and inheritances. Remaining inequities on the interpersonal plane are properly beyond the scope of the law.

1. *Increased Earning Capacity.* — One of the most contested, and most important, issues in marital property law is the proper division of a spouse's future earning potential gained during marriage. This is commonly called the "professional degree" problem, based on one way this earning potential is generated. But there is no reason to so confine the category; instead, it should extend to future earning potential generated during the time of marriage, however derived.

Currently, most jurisdictions refuse to include increased earning capacity within the marital estate. In fact, only New York has a clearly established rule making at least some of this asset — professional degrees obtained during marriage — eligible for division.[14] Nor does the ALI recommend making such property divisible. Both state rules and the ALI compensate for this omission in other ways, primarily by making earning capacity changes relevant to alimony. But as we will show, these methods of dividing earning capacity are inadequate. A commitment to the ideal of marriage as an egalitarian liberal community requires treating spouses' increased earning capacity as marital property, while tailoring property division rules to address the unique features of this asset. Because in many marriages, increased earning capacity is the only asset of any significant value, this proposal may be the most important reform we recommend.

The joint creation of careers is often one of the most important projects of marriage. Therefore, excluding earning capacity from the marital estate "makes a mockery of the equal division rule."[15] It also exploits the spouse whose acceptance of burdens on behalf of the communal endeavor is transformed by the law into self-sacrifice. Additionally, where this spouse is the wife (the majority case), and a "traditional" wife at that, excluding increased earning capacity compounds the effects of pervasive gender inequality.

To a limited extent, existing alimony law already reflects these concerns. The ALI, echoing the rules of individual states, makes earning capacity relevant to the compensation spouses receive in some marriages of long duration. But compensation for individual expenditures or sacrifices is inappropriate for a marital community. Moreover, addressing the problem through the prism of alimony — even if cloaked under the name of compensation — is misguided. Alimony is associated with need and thus unjustifiably diminishes a spouse's entitlement to the other's

---

14. *See* O'Brien v. O'Brien, 489 N.E.2d 712, 713-14, 716 (N.Y. 1985). . . .

15. [Lenore J.] Weitzman, [The Divorce Revolution: The Unexpected Social and Economic Consequences for Women and Children in America] 388 [(1985)].

increased earning capacity. By associating the claim to this marital asset with dependency, this practice sends the wrong cultural message. More importantly, it has an undesirable material effect on the law. The ALI, for instance, makes entitlement to a portion of a spouse's future earning capacity dependent on differences in post-divorce income, adjusting it in the case of events such as remarriage. But if each spouse is entitled to the other's increased earning capacity, he or she should not forfeit these entitlements on remarriage, or because of hard work or simple good fortune.

Perhaps the most common objection to division of earning capacity on divorce is that it is not property. We, too, have limited the category of marital property to things that are fungible. But future earning capacity is not just a personal attribute: It is an income-generating asset. True, a spouse cannot sell her professional degree, but she certainly can sell a portion of her future earnings, even in advance. Future earning capacity is capable of treatment as property, and engaging in an essentialist inquiry into the nature of property simply masks the inherent normative choices.

The more serious objections to division of earning capacity are normative and arise from autonomy. Future earning capacity is seen as an individual accomplishment, indeed a constitutive component of the individual self. While we agree that career plays a role in individual autonomy and personhood, the development of careers during marriage is also centrally collective: Spouses move away from more desirable jobs, work fewer hours, sacrifice potential for advancement, and even give up careers entirely for the good of the community. Careers involve collective decision-making and collective action; they require a difficult accommodation of the wills of two individuals, and thus solidify spouses' collective commitments. Dividing increased earning capacity is therefore important to the marital community as well as to the individual spouse.

Fortunately, inclusion of career assets within the marital estate leaves room for their individual aspect. Dividing the financial component of one's career still leaves her with the features of her career most essential to individual autonomy and personhood. The rule we endorse does not, and should not, attempt to take away a spouse's sense of satisfaction or achievement, intellectual interest, or the friendships and other engagements that come from a career. This rule leaves the constitutive aspects of one's career as the accomplished individual's entitlement and "collectivizes" only the resulting income.

Another autonomy objection concerns the constraint that entitlement to a portion of a spouse's future earnings may pose on that spouse's ability to make future autonomous choices. Is a spouse who received a prestigious medical degree during the pendency of marriage obliged to practice as a physician in order to pay her former spouse half of the earning potential they together generated? This would constitute a serious intrusion on exit by placing a heavy and unjustified burden on future decisions concerning one's career.

This objection, while valid, need not be fatal. Designating that earning capacity is only subject to division once it is realized — that is, if and when the money is actually made — preserves each spouse's ability to make whatever career choices he or she wishes. If a spouse chooses to benefit from decisions made and advantages gained by the marital community, both spouses should benefit. This is not just a technical compromise; rather, a realization-based rule properly reflects the nature of the entitlement — the reason to divide increased earning capacity equally is not to reward individual investment but to share the rewards of a joint life. Even during marriage, spouses may choose not to realize their career potential, and that is not necessarily a wrong to the community or the other spouse.

How would earning capacity be valued as a marital asset? As both spouses will experience some change in earning capacity through the course of their marriage, differences in both spouses' earning capacities at the time of marriage and the time of divorce should be aggregated. All increases in earning capacity generated during marriage must be eligible for division; making inclusion dependant [*sic*] on contribution of the other spouse would be anathema to the equal sharing principle. Thus, in a traditional family, one spouse would likely have an earning capacity gain, while the other would have an earning capacity loss. When the aggregate of these is positive, the difference should be split between the parties. When the aggregate is negative — which may occur due to poor career choices, as well as when spouses give up careers to care for children or engage in other nonwage pursuits — the difference should be a debt to be divided. In both cases, the calculation should appropriately leave endowments like intelligence or creativity, which are intrinsic to the individual, out of the marital pool.

We do not deny that such valuations will be difficult. But it will likely be no more burdensome (and the calculations will be no more uncertain) than similar valuations that are currently done, particularly in tort actions. As in tort law, rough-and-ready estimates based on averages can be used, provided they can be adjusted in demonstrably unique cases. . . .

NOTES AND QUESTIONS

1. *Contribution Theory.* Frantz and Dagan celebrate a happy ideal of marriage, but aren't they discarding too quickly important property values? Thus, it has been claimed that each spouse deserves what are singularly the fruits of his or her contribution. *See* ALLEN M. PARKMAN, GOOD INTENTIONS GONE AWRY: NO-FAULT DIVORCE AND THE AMERICAN FAMILY 187 (2000). This view — contribution theory — seems to rely rather confidently on the desert for labor theory, discussed in Chapter 1. It also seems to follow the welfarist accounts of property, because it encourages spouses to efficiently invest in the marital estate. *See* Ira Mark Ellman, *The Theory of Alimony,* 77 CAL. L.

Rev. 3, 51 (1989). And thus, as Frantz and Dagan seem to admit while discussing the hypothetical contract theory of Elizabeth and Robert Scott, it may also follow the parties' hypothetical consent. Finally, contribution theory is also attractive to feminists, because it may force us to properly recognize women's contributions to marriage. *See* Katharine B. Silbaugh, *Gender and Nonfinancial Matters in the ALI Principles of the Law of Family Dissolution*, 8 Duke J. Gender L. & Pol'y 203, 205-211 (2001). So is contribution theory not superior to the one advanced by Frantz and Dagan? Can they reliably respond to these claims? For Frantz and Dagan's response, see Frantz & Dagan, *supra*, at 89-90, 96-97, 104-105 (arguing that the desert principle should apply to the marital unit; that spouses have other reasons to invest in their marriages; that equal sharing serves as a better default rule by forcing "Lockean spouses" to reveal their preferences; and that contribution theory tends to exacerbate gender inequality by reinforcing problematic gender roles).

2. *Other Assets.* Frantz and Dagan discuss in some detail the issue of increased earning capacity. (Are you convinced by their arguments?). But, as you may recall, they address (in parts that are not included in this chapter) two additional significant types of resources: preexisting property; and gifts and inheritances. The prevailing rule regarding the former is that premarital assets are not subject to division on divorce, but that (1) income generated during marriage by preexisting property is part of the marital estate, and (2) preexisting property may be transmuted into the marital community in cases of long marriages as well as if a spouse's name is added to the title of separate property. *See, e.g.,* J. Thomas Oldham, Divorce, Separation and the Distribution of Property §11.01[2], at 11-4 & n.11 (2003). Frantz and Dagan support these rules and only criticize courts that do not assume transmutation if a spouse can show an alternative benefit (such as a tax advantage) to be gained by placing title to property. *See* Frantz & Dagan, *supra*, at 113-117. Can you see how these rules are compatible with the ideal of marriage as an egalitarian liberal community? Can you understand why the alternative benefit rule is not?

Like preexisting assets, almost all states designate property acquired by one spouse by gift or inheritance during marriage as separate. Oldham, §6.02, at 6-3 & n.1 & §6-14.2 & n.1. Can you see how this rule is connected to contribution theory? Frantz and Dagan are dissatisfied with this rule, partly because they question the notion that both gifts and inheritances do not require spousal labor. If their claim that gifts and inheritances involve spousal labor is convincing (is it?), or if—as they claim—labor shouldn't matter anyway, isn't it the case that gifts and inheritances are often based on relationships with the donee that were cultivated during the marriage but may well have started long before the marriage? Can the law disentangle these different periods? *See* Frantz & Dagan, at 117-119 (recommending a bright-line rule for division of gifts and inheritances, based on the relative lengths of the marriage and the relationship between donor and donee).

3. *Property Governance.* There are two major regimes of marital property governance in the United States. The majority of states that, following the common law tradition, originally adopted title theory, allocating goods to individual spouses based on nonmarital ownership rules, have now shifted by statute to equitable division. And yet, in these states title still determines ownership during marriage, and therefore determines powers of management and alienation. Nine states (including California and Texas) are community property states, in which spouses are thus equal owners of all property acquired during marriage, regardless of how the property is nominally titled.[16] Community property designation is a default mode; couples may opt out of it for some or all of the assets that would otherwise be characterized as community assets. Which of these regimes seems to you more in line with the ideal of marriage as an egalitarian liberal community?

Community property states prescribe a tripartite governance regime: Decisions that have grave consequences, such as sales of community real estate, tend to require joint decision making; in some contexts, mostly regarding businesses, the exclusive management authority of one spouse is recognized; finally, a residual sphere of management includes those decisions that can be made by either spouse. Can you see the need for dividing decision-making authority along these lines? Can you trace the potential difficulties—both normative and practical—of each prong of this governance regime? Can you think of solutions? *See* Frantz & Dagan, *supra,* at 124-132.

4. *Domestic Partners.* Traditional law rejects the application of marital property law to unmarried domestic partners. A few states even invalidate explicit contracts between cohabitants as contrary to public policy. The modern trend, however, tends to narrow the gap between the economic aspects of marriage and cohabitation. *See, e.g.,* Marvin v. Marvin, 557 P.2d 106 (Cal. 1976). The *ALI Principles* (mentioned in footnote 12) take this trend to its logical conclusion, recommending equalizing them. *Id.* at §6. Modern proponents of the former view tend to validate explicit cohabitation contracts and—loyal to liberal principles of freedom of contracts— refuse to impose the rules of marital property where there is no such a contract; supporters of the latter approach tend to justify their position by reference to cohabitation's risk of exploitation due to gender differences or to relational commitments that may be embedded in long-term cohabitation. *See* Shahar Lifshitz, *Married Against Their Will? Toward a Pluralist Regulation of Spousal Relationship,* 66 Wash. & Lee L. Rev. 1565, 1574-1585 (2009). Lifshitz proposes a third alternative, in which cohabitation is regulated differently both from regular contracts and from marriage. His

---

16. Alaska—a common law jurisdiction—enacted a statute that enables spouses to proactively elect to hold their property as a community. *See* Alaska Stat. §34.77.030 (Michie 2002).

suggestion relies on "society's responsibility to provide a diversity of spousal institutions" and thus shapes cohabitation as a regime that "provides a screening mechanism" for spouses to express (and signal to each other) different levels of commitments (*id.* at 1569). The core characteristic of this regime is that it provides for regular cohabitants—as opposed to, for example, same-sex couples who are precluded from marriage—"a narrow contribution-based marital property regime. This regime categorizes only labor income that accumulates during marriage as marital property. It also deviates from the equal division rule in cases of asymmetry between cohabitants' contributions" (*id.* at 1572). Lifshitz's theory of cohabitation seems to provide one example for Dagan's conception of property as institutions discussed in Chapter 8.1; can you see why?

3. TRUSTS

Robert H. Sitkoff, An Agency Costs Theory of Trust Law[1]

. . . [T]he central feature of the private trust is that it "separate[s] the benefits of ownership from the burdens of ownership."[2] This implies that many of the analytical tools supplied by the agency cost theories of the firm, which are routinely applied in the economic analysis of corporate law, should be similarly applicable to the underdeveloped economic analysis of trust law. Indeed, problems of shirking and monitoring, the driving concerns of agency cost analysis, abound in trust administration. . . .

Consider a stylized example. In the prototypical donative trust, the settlor ("S") in effect contracts with the trustee ("T") to manage a portfolio of assets in the best interests of the beneficiaries ("B1" and "B2," collectively the "Bs"), subject to the ex ante restraints imposed by the settlor. Hence, using the vocabulary of agency in economic rather than legal parlance, T can be viewed as the agent of S; but T can also be viewed as the agent of B1 and B2. To the extent that T might slight or ignore what S would have wanted in the ongoing management of the trust, we have a problem of agency costs in the S/T relationship. But to the extent that T might slight or ignore what B1 and B2 want in the ongoing management of the trust, we have the usual agency problem when risk-bearing (here by B1 and B2) is separated from management (here by T). So where the corporate form

---

1. Robert H. Sitkoff, *An Agency Costs Theory of Trust Law*, 89 Cornell L. Rev. 621, 623, 624-625, 638-639, 640, 646-651, 652 (2004).

2. 1 Austin Wakeman Scott & William Franklin Fratcher, The Law of Trusts §11, at 2 (4th ed. 1987) [hereinafter Scott on Trusts].

presents one dominant source of agency costs (the shareholder/manager relationship), the trust presents two. . . .

That S saddled her transfer to B1 and B2 with the friction of competing principal-agent relationships is the core insight that animates the agency costs analysis. This Article's normative claim is that the law should minimize the agency costs inherent in locating managerial authority with the trustee (T) and the residual claim with the beneficiaries (B1 and B2), but only to the extent that doing so is consistent with the ex ante instructions of the settlor (S). This qualification gives priority to the settlor over the beneficiaries as the trustee's primary principal. The positive claim is that, at least with respect to traditional doctrines, the law conforms to the suggested normative approach. . . .

III. THE AGENCY COSTS MODEL

In comparison to the agency costs approach to corporate law,[3] the agency costs approach to trust law is both simpler and more complex. It is simpler because the trust is a less complicated organization. This makes the agency cost analysis and reckoning the hypothetical bargain of the principal parties easier. The analysis is more complicated, however, because the actions of those individuals interested in the trust are not metered by price signals from efficient capital markets. Moreover, the law regularly subordinates the interests of the beneficiaries as residual claimants to the dead-hand interests of the settlor, an outgrowth of the frequently paternalistic function of the donative trust.

A. The Contractarian Nexus

The trust is more than a simple contract between private parties. It is an organizational form with in rem as well as in personam dimensions. Thus, like the corporation and other organizational forms, the trust blends external in rem asset partitioning with internal in personam contractarian flexibility. The trust's internal relationships are contractarian not only because the law supplies default terms around which the parties may contract, but also because the underlying governance problems that stem from the asymmetric information of the parties are amenable to principal-agent modeling.

True, there is tension between the contractarian metaphor and the position of the beneficiary. Beneficiaries are not normally thought to give ex ante consent, and typically they are in no position to bargain. . . . But even if the beneficiaries do not literally contract with the other principal

---

3. The clearest example is the model of the corporation as a nexus of contracts, which was most notably advanced in the legal literature by Easterbrook and Fischel. *See* FRANK H. EASTERBROOK & DANIEL R. FISCHEL, THE ECONOMIC STRUCTURE OF CORPORATE LAW 1-39 (1991); Frank H. Easterbrook & Daniel R. Fischel, *The Corporate Contract*, 89 COLUM. L. REV. 1416 (1989).

parties, and even if the beneficiaries' stake is doctrinally more proprietary than contractarian, contractarian principal-agent modeling nonetheless illuminates the problems of governance relevant to the beneficiaries' welfare. From an economic perspective, hidden action (and possibly hidden information) abounds, so trust governance must confront both incentive and risk-sharing problems. . . .

Distilling the trust into its constituent relationships brings into view the applicability of hypothetical bargain analysis and the economics of the principal-agent problem. Both the relationship between S and T and the relationship between the Bs and T might be modeled on the principal-agent scheme. The former presents the temporal agency problem that helps distinguish the economic analysis of trust law from that of corporate law. The latter presents the traditional agency problem when risk-bearing is separated from management. This means that there is potential for considerable tension between T's loyalty to S and T's loyalty to the Bs. As we shall see in the next Part, American law resolves this tension by requiring T to maximize the welfare of the Bs within the ex ante constraints imposed by S. This is to say that, under the American approach (but not necessarily under the English approach) the donor's intent controls. . . .

D. Beneficiaries as Residual Claimants

The trustee and those who conduct business with the trustee as trustee have fixed claims on the trust corpus that generally have priority over the claims of the beneficiaries. Trustees are free to negotiate for their own fee schedules or other terms designed to protect their interests, and those who do business with the trustee over trust assets can likewise protect themselves by contract. Beneficiaries of donative trusts, however, are limited to taking so much as the trust instrument allows out of whatever is left of the trust's assets when all other claims are settled.[4] That is, as residual claimants, they bear the residual risk.

To say that the beneficiaries are the residual claimants is to say that managerial decisions are inframarginal[5] for all the relevant players except for the beneficiaries. This may provide an agency costs explanation for the rule in irrevocable trusts that only the beneficiaries may sue the trustee for a breach of trust. The same reasoning may also explain why the default fiduciary obligations of the trustee are designed to create incentives for the trustee to manage the trust from the beneficiaries' (and hence the marginal) perspective. Moreover, now that the trust form is used for more than

---

4. The limitation to donative trusts is necessary because in the commercial context, the beneficiaries are typically investors in trust certificates that, like debt, only entitle them to a return of their investment plus interest. Any surplus value goes back to the settlor, who is the residual claimant in such an arrangement. . . .

5. [The term "inframarginal" means inside of, rather than at the margin. So, if a firm is producing 100 widgets, the 101st is the marginal widget, and units 1 through 100 are *inframarginal.* — EDS.]

intergenerational conveyances and the preservation of ancestral land, status as a trust beneficiary brings both greater potential risk and greater potential reward.

Against the foregoing it might be argued that, because private trust beneficiaries are nothing more than passive recipients of a donative transfer, the analogy to Jensen and Meckling's nexus of contracts metaphor[6] is inappropriate. Indeed, even though acceptance (which can be implied) is a required element of every gift, trust beneficiaries do not give consent to their status as such in the same way that parties give consent to a literal contractual relationship. But the nexus of contracts model is just that, a model. The economics of agency provides a helpful framework for understanding the law's default solutions to problems of governance presented by the trust form of organization. . . .

IV. APPLICATIONS OF THE MODEL

By reference to illustrative applications, this Part demonstrates the positive and normative analytical power of the agency costs approach. The normative claim is that the law should minimize the agency costs inherent in locating managerial authority with the trustee and the residual claim with the beneficiaries, but only to the extent that doing so is consistent with the ex ante instructions of the settlor. This qualification gives priority to the settlor over the beneficiaries as the trustee's primary principal. To return to the exemplary trust settled by S for the benefit of B1 and B2 with T as trustee, the claim is that T should maximize the welfare of B1 and B2, subject to the ex ante limits imposed by S. Consequently, the optimal solution to the Bs-T principal-agent problem, which would be for the Bs to sell the residual claim to T (doing so would solve both the incentive and risk-sharing problems), is foreclosed by the settlor's choice of the trust over an outright transfer. Given the primacy of honoring the settlor's intentions, the best that the law of trust governance can hope for is a second-best solution to the Bs-T agency problem.[7]

The positive claim is that, at least with respect to traditional doctrines, the law conforms to the suggested normative approach. . . .

---

6. [The nexus of contracts metaphor owes to Michael C. Jensen & William H. Meckling, *Theory of the Firm: Managerial Behavior, Agency Costs and Ownership Structure*, 3 J. FIN. ECON. 305 (1976). Jensen and Meckling developed it to analyze corporations. — EDS.]

7. This solution is second best from the perspective of the beneficiaries ex post. American law, however, is more concerned with the ex ante perspective of the settlor. The normative analysis therefore assumes that the goal is to maximize the expected utility of the settlor. The settlor's expected utility, in turn, is assumed to depend on the settlor's (paternalistic) view of the beneficiaries' expected utility. Further exposition of this point, including development of a formal model, is beyond the scope of this Article. Note, however, that there are numerous complexities that surround this issue, including the relevance of the beneficiaries' own view of their utilities — something to which . . . English law gives greater attention. . . .

A. Donative Beneficiaries as Residual Claimants

Agency cost analysis prompts the classification of donative trust beneficiaries as residual claimants. Claims on the assets of the trust by all the other relevant parties—most notably the trustee and those with whom the trustee transacts as trustee—are usually set by express contract and have a higher priority than the beneficiaries' claims. Like the residual claimants in any other organizational form, donative trust beneficiaries therefore bear the residual risk of good or bad performance. Managerial decisions regarding the trust's assets are inframarginal to all but the beneficiaries. The emergence of the managerial trust, moreover, has enlarged the range of the beneficiaries' potential risk and reward. In this respect, modern trust beneficiaries are beginning more closely to resemble the residual claimants of other organizational forms than the trust beneficiaries of yore.

Yet today's prototypical donative trust beneficiaries have some interesting characteristics, relevant to reckoning the probable intent of the settlor, that distinguish them from the residual claimants of other organizational forms. . . .

1. The Duty of Impartiality

Trust law facilitates the creation of residual claimants with interests adverse to each other. The still classic example . . . is a trust for the lifetime income benefit of one party (B1) with the remainder principal benefit to another (B2). As residual claimants, the overall interests of B1 and B2 are grossly aligned on matters such as self-dealing or embezzlement by T. But often their specific interests in the day-to-day management of the trust will not be congruent. The most obvious example is that B1 should prefer income-producing investments while B2 should prefer capital appreciation. This creates "conflicts among the claim holders of different states because alternative decisions shift payoffs across states and benefit some claim holders at the expense of others."[8]

Trust law's amenability to residual claimants with adverse interests poses a challenge for crafting an effective governance regime, because the preference set of the residual claimants, in whose interests the trust should be managed, may not be coherent. Corporate law, by comparison, assumes that all shareholders share the basic aim of profit maximization (their preferences are said to be "single-peaked"). This assumption elides the problems of agenda manipulation and cycling.

Trust law's evolutionary response for aggregating the otherwise conflicting interests of different classes of beneficiaries is the fiduciary duty of impartiality. This duty requires the trustee to "act impartially in investing, managing, and distributing the trust property, giving due regard

---

8. Eugene F. Fama & Michael C. Jensen, *Agency Problems and Residual Claims*, 26 J.L. & ECON. 327, 329 (1983).

to the beneficiaries' respective interests."[9] Thus, under the default arrangement, T cannot justify an action as benefiting B1 or B2 exclusively. Instead, T must justify her decisions in relation to the aggregate welfare of B1 and B2 as a class. The trust's residual claimants' interests are made coherent in effect by directing the trustee to act with a view to their needs rather than their individual wants; balance is the overarching directive of the duty of impartiality. This appears consistent with the settlor's probable intent. True, in the foregoing example one might argue that S rated B1's position as superior to B2's because S gave B1 an immediate benefit but gave B2 only the remainder on the death of B1. But that seems a thin basis for concluding that S wanted T to prefer the interests of B1 over the interests of B2. If S had such a preference, it would have been simple enough to put something to that effect in the trust instrument. . . .

From this perspective the duty of impartiality is both a critical feature of trust governance and a salient distinguishing characteristic of trust law as organizational law. It is critical, because without it often there would be no coherent set of residual claimants in whose interests the trust's managers should operate. And it is a salient distinguishing characteristic, relevant to choice of form for commercial transactions, because the duty is not an explicit part of the default fiduciary obligation in most other organizational forms. . . .

B. The Settlor-Beneficiary Tension

In light of the agency cost considerations on both sides, this section explores four examples of how the law balances the ex post preferences of the beneficiaries with the ex ante wishes of the settlor. Consider once again the exemplary trust presented above, which was settled by S for the benefit of B1 and B2 (collectively the "Bs") with T as trustee. The nub of the problem is that the Bs bear the marginal costs and benefits of T's managerial decisions, but the ex ante preferences of S trump the later wishes of the Bs in guiding T's management. A variant of the well-known dead hand problem (which is perhaps a pejorative aphorism for the idea that the settlor's intent controls), this tension has been exacerbated by the modern trend toward the use of the trust as a vehicle for asset management by professionals. The modern managerial trust vests greater discretion in the hands of the trustee, which broadens the range of the trustee's hidden action. Moreover, the ongoing erosion of the Rule Against Perpetuities is expanding the temporal scope of the trustee's discretionary authority and hence the likelihood of later circumstances unanticipated by the settlor.

---

9. Unif. Trust Code §803, 7C U.L.A. 204 (Supp. 2003); *see also* Restatement (Second) of Trusts §§183, 232 (1959).

1. *Modification and Termination*

A useful example of the potential for divergent interests between the settlor and the beneficiaries involves the possibility of the beneficiaries seeking premature termination of the trust. This problem includes the issue of whether the beneficiaries can obtain judicial modification of the trust's terms, because the power to terminate subsumes the power to modify. The American rule, which originated with *Claflin v. Claflin*,[10] is unfriendly to termination and modification. Under the *Claflin* doctrine, a trust may be terminated prematurely only with the settlor's consent or, in the absence of the settlor's consent, if termination would not frustrate a "material purpose" of the trust.[11] Settlor's consent, however, is by definition unavailable when dealing with testamentary trusts, and courts have had little difficulty finding a "material purpose" that would be offended by a modification or termination. Thus, as a practical matter, unless the trustee consents,[12] American trusts are difficult to amend or terminate once established. Even if all the competent beneficiaries and the trustee were inclined to strike a deal, the frequency of unidentified or minor beneficiaries reduces the viability of this alternative.

The upshot of the *Claflin* doctrine is that it helps align the interests of the settlor and the trustee. The rule allows the trustee to preserve the settlor's original design, regardless of the beneficiaries' wishes, which is what the settlor likely would have wanted. . . . Thus the *Claflin* doctrine is consistent with the model of the settlor as the primary principal. Moreover, though a particular beneficiary might prefer the power to terminate the trust once it is established, the *Claflin* doctrine is advantageous to potential beneficiaries as a class because it increases the willingness of grantors to create a trust in the first place. The idea is that, in the aggregate, beneficiaries fare better with more trusts, and thus more gifting,[13] albeit with potentially greater managerial agency costs, than they would fare with fewer trusts, albeit with reduced potential for managerial agency costs.

The downside of the *Claflin* doctrine is that it entrenches the trustee and locks in a certain minimal level of beneficiary-trustee agency costs. Under the classic American approach, even if all the beneficiaries are identifiable adults who would be better off if the trust were terminated (perhaps because its consequent administrative expenses would be eliminated), the trustee need not assent to their wishes. Against the rule, therefore, it might

---

10. 20 N.E. 454 (Mass. 1889); *see* RESTATEMENT (THIRD) OF TRUSTS §65 cmt. a (2003).

11. *See* RESTATEMENT (THIRD) OF TRUSTS §65 & cmt. a (2003); Restatement (Second) of Trusts §337 (1959); 4 SCOTT ON TRUSTS, *supra* note 2, §§337-340.2.

12. *See* RESTATEMENT (SECOND) OF TRUSTS §342 (1959); ROGER W. ANDERSEN, UNDERSTANDING TRUSTS AND ESTATES 110-111 (3d ed. 2003); 4 SCOTT ON TRUSTS, *supra* note 2, §342, at 529-32.

13. The further assumption here is that in the absence of these rules, the overall volume of gifting would fall. If the level of overall gifting remained constant, then beneficiaries might fare better without the rule, provided that the alternative modes of transfer imposed fewer restrictions. But with fewer restrictions, these alternatives would be imperfect substitutes, so it is unlikely that the overall level of gifting would remain constant.

be argued that the fundamental decision whether or not to continue the trust is not in the hands of those who bear the marginal costs and benefits of that decision.

. . . [I]f we assume that settlors of today's managerial trusts ultimately want to maximize the welfare of the beneficiaries, then a different rule might be preferable — especially in view of the ongoing erosion of the Rule Against Perpetuities and hence the increasing temporal durability of modern trusts.[14] On this view, one-time settlors do not know to opt out of the default *Claflin* regime, perhaps because their advisors are failing to call this to their attention (an altogether different agency problem) or they did not obtain expert advice.

It is hardly surprising, therefore, that there is a strong academic and slowly emerging decisional trend toward liberalizing these rules.[15] [C]ourts are beginning to show a willingness to authorize deviation from the settlor's specific instructions that, over time, conflict with the settlor's assumed broader aim of benefiting the beneficiaries.[16] . . .

Note, however, that these liberalizations are designed to advance the settlors' probable intent. . . . All of these liberalizations, if understood as designed to effect a substituted judgment for what the settlor would have wanted, are consistent with a model of the trust in which the settlor is the primary principal. These liberalizing trends fulfill the beneficiaries' desires, but only when doing so would approximate what the settlor would have wanted. They add the nuance of a standard, as it were, to the hard-edged *Claflin* rule. . . .

C. Internal Governance and External Transactional Authority

By including creditors within its scope, the agency costs model of the trust as an organizational form highlights the interrelationship between internal governance and the scope of the authority of insiders to transact with outsiders. The agency cost considerations relevant to the substantive content of the rules of internal trust governance are a function of the scope of the authority of the principal parties to transact with outsiders. Similarly, the extent to which the trust insiders might safely be granted authority to transact over trust assets with outsiders is a function of the effectiveness of the internal governance structure. Thus the agency costs approach to the trust . . . should not be understood as embracing the sort of contractarian nihilism that leads to the conclusion that organizations have no

14. [Regarding this development, see Note 6 *infra* — EDS.]

15. *See* Edward C. Halbach, Jr., *Significant Trends [in the Trust Law of the United States]*, [32 VAND. J. TRANSNAT'L L. 531], 549 [(1999)]. . . .

16. *See, e.g., In re* Trusteeship Agreement with Mayo, 105 N.W.2d 900, 91 (Minn. 1960); Carnahan v. Johnson, 711 N.E.2d 1093, 1096-98 (Ohio Ct. App. 1998); RESTATEMENT (THIRD) OF TRUSTS rep. note §66 cmt. b (2003) . . . ; ROGER W. ANDERSEN & IRA MARK BLOOM, FUNDAMENTALS OF TRUSTS AND ESTATES §8.04, at 392 (2d ed. 2002).

boundaries. On the contrary, the approach recognizes that the existence of boundaries and asset partitioning (i.e., the de facto separate legal entity of the trust or its equivalent—the trustee as trustee) are crucial features of trust law.

This section advances the claim that the rules of internal governance are necessarily intertwined with the rules of external relations. Any change in one set of rules will have a ripple effect on the terms to which the relevant parties would have agreed concerning the other. Accordingly, agency cost analysis of trust law speaks not only to matters of internal governance and external relations, but it also brings into view the interrelationship between the two. . . .

2. The Spendthrift Trust

The spendthrift trust provides another example of the importance of the interrelationship between internal governance and the scope of the principal parties' external transactional authority. Spendthrift trusts, in comparison to ordinary trusts, shield the trust's assets from the beneficiaries' creditors.[17] This is true even if the trust instrument requires mandatory payouts, as such payments could be made directly to the beneficiaries' service providers. Not surprisingly, there is a substantial body of literature on the soundness of the policy behind the spendthrift trust.[18] There is also considerable divergence among the common law nations on the enforcement of spendthrift provisions. The majority of common law countries, most prominently England,[19] do not enforce them. In contrast, spendthrift provisions are valid throughout the United States, are included in customary American estate planning boilerplate, and by statute the spendthrift trust is even the default trust form in New York.[20]

The existing normative commentary on the spendthrift trust tends to present a tradeoff between paternalistic protection of feckless beneficiaries

---

17. *See* RESTATEMENT (THIRD) OF TRUSTS §58 (2003); RESTATEMENT (SECOND) OF TRUSTS §§152-53 (1959); UNIF. TRUST CODE §502, 7C U.L.A. 175 (Supp. 2003). State law restrictions on transfer are applicable in bankruptcy. *See* 11 U.S.C. §541(c)(2). A few privileged creditors, however, including children, spouses, and former spouses seeking support or maintenance, may sometimes reach the beneficiaries' interest despite a spendthrift clause. *See* RESTATEMENT (THIRD) OF TRUSTS §59 (2003); UNIF. TRUST CODE §503, 7C U.L.A. 176 (Supp. 2003); Carolyn L. Dessin, *Feed a Trust and Starve a Child: The Effectiveness of Trust Protective Techniques Against Claims for Support and Alimony*, 10 GA. ST. U. L. REV. 691, 699-720 (1994).

18. *See, e.g.*, JOHN CHIPMAN GRAY, RESTRAINTS ON THE ALIENATION OF PROPERTY (1883); ERWIN N. GRISWOLD, SPENDTHRIFT TRUSTS: RESTRAINTS ON THE ALIENATION OF EQUITABLE INTERESTS IMPOSED BY THE TERMS OF THE TRUST OR BY STATUTE (1936); Robert T. Danforth, *Rethinking the Law of Creditors' Rights in Trusts*, 53 HASTINGS L.J. 287, 291-306 (2002); Anne S. Emanuel, SPENDTHRIFT TRUSTS: IT'S TIME TO CODIFY THE COMPROMISE, 72 NEB. L. REV. 179 (1993); Mary Louise Fellows, *Spendthrift Trusts: Roots and Relevance for Twenty-First Century Planning*, 50 REC. ASS'N B. CITY N.Y. 140, 149-64 (1995); Adam J. Hirsch, *Spendthrift Trusts and Public Policy: Economic and Cognitive Perspectives*, 73 WASH. U. L.Q. 1 (1995); Alan Newman, *The Rights of Creditors of Beneficiaries Under the Uniform Trust Code: An Examination of the Compromise*, 69 TENN. L. REV. 771, 782-803 (2002).

19. The classic English case is Brandon v. Robinson, 34 Eng. Rep. 379 (Ch. 1811). . . .

20. N.Y. EST. POWERS & TRUSTS LAW §7-1.5 (McKinney 2002).

on the one hand and the protection of voluntary and, more clearly, involuntary creditors on the other. The usual focus, in other words, is on the soundness of limiting the scope of the beneficiaries' external transactional authority in view of how this limitation impacts both the beneficiaries and the outsiders with whom the beneficiaries might transact. This approach, however, overlooks the interrelationship between the ability of the trust insiders to transact with third parties and the details of the trust's internal governance regime. . . .

One governance benefit of enforcing spendthrift provisions is that payouts may safely be made mandatory. This reduces the trustee's discretion and so diminishes the potential for managerial agency costs. But the cost is that a potential check on agency costs — the theoretical possibility of the residual claimants' exit — is foreclosed as a matter of law. Although exit is, in theory, a powerful governance device, in practice its potential has not been realized in the context of donative trusts because there is no well-developed market for trust residual interests. Such a market, however, would provide price signals about the quality of the particular trust's management. Unlike the initial gratuitous transfer by the settlor, a subsequent sale by the beneficiary of her interest would indeed involve reckoning a price.

Moreover, alienable residual claims offer the possibility of welfare-improving secondary transactions. For example, if in the hands of the beneficiary the discounted present value of the future income stream from the trust is worth $10, but in the hands of someone who is more adept at monitoring and at fiduciary litigation the present value of the beneficiary's interest would be $15, then a spendthrift provision results in a $5 residual loss. This is the agency costs price of honoring the settlor's dead-hand interest in disabling the beneficiary from alienating her interest.

CONCLUSION

This Article's agency costs approach to the donative private trust not only helps to advance the ongoing debate over whether trust law is closer to property law or contract law, but also, and more importantly, it provides a rich positive and normative framework for further economic analysis of trust law. Principal-agent economics has great potential to offer further insights about the nature and function of the law of trusts. In particular, the agency costs analysis of this Article demonstrates how and why use of the private trust triggers a temporal agency problem (whether the trustee will remain loyal to the settlor's original wishes) in addition to the usual agency problem that arises when risk-bearing and management are separated (whether the trustee-manager will act in the best interests of the beneficiaries-residual claimants).

NOTES AND QUESTIONS

1. *Contrary Views.* Although highly influential, Sitkoff's article is not without its critics. Lee-ford Tritt, for example, argues that the agency theory of trusts is "fundamentally and fatally flawed if rigidly applied." Lee-ford Tritt, *The Limitations of an Agency Cost Theory of Trust Law*, 32 CARDOZO L. REV. 2579, 2582 (2011). He contends that "applying an agency cost analysis to trust law produces not only a positively inaccurate account of modern trusts but a normatively incoherent philosophy to guide the evolution of trust law." *Id.* at 2583 (footnote omitted). Specifically, Tritt argues that trusts are fundamentally different from corporations, the original institution that agency cost theorists analyzed. Trusts, at least family property trusts, are not market institutions; they are donative institutions. People create them for a wide variety of reasons, some of which are quite idiosyncratic, and it is very difficult, sometimes impossible, to determine just what the donors' preferences are. "The difficulty of ascertaining actual preferences and analyzing the decision making process of settlors," Tritt continues, "undermines the capability of forging a path that respects market preferences, which is the core of an economic project in the first place." *Id.* at 2599. What are your reactions to this argument? Does this mean that economic or welfare-maximizing analysis is never appropriate in the context of donative transfers? Are preferences more difficult to ascertain in the context of donative transactions than of exchanges?

2. *Is the Trust a Contract?* In a controversial article, John Langbein argues that although "[w]e are accustomed to think of the trust as a branch of property law[,] . . . [i]n truth, the trust is a deal, a bargain about how the trust assets are to be managed and distributed." John H. Langbein, *The Contractarian Basis of the Law of Trusts*, 105 YALE L.J. 625, 627 (1995). Henry Hansmann and Ugo Mattei take a different view, arguing that "it is precisely the property-like aspects of the trust that are the principal contributions of trust law." They continue, "[T]he essential purpose served by trust law . . . is to facilitate an accompanying reorganization of rights and responsibilities between the three principal parties [the donor, the trustee, and the beneficiary] and third parties, such as creditors, with whom the principal parties deal." Henry Hansmann & Ugo Mattei, *The Functions of Trust Law: A Comparative Legal and Economic Analysis*, 73 N.Y.U. L. REV. 434, 469-472 (1998). *See also* James Edelman, *When Do Fiduciary Duties Arise?*, 126 LAW Q. REV. 302 (2010).

3. *Trust Duties — Mandatory or Default?* One basis for the contractarian theory of trusts is the fact that nearly all of the trustee's fiduciary duties are default, rather than mandatory, in nature. That is, the donor ("settlor" in trust law parlance) may waive them in the trust instrument. *See* UNIF. TRUST CODE §105(b). Because the trustee's duties are, by and large, set by agreement between the settlor and trustee, it is easy to see why Langbein views the trust as a contract.

Notice, though, that we said "nearly" all. Certain fiduciary duties are deemed so essential to the existence of a trust that they are non-waivable. For example, the settlor may not waive the trustee's duty to act in good faith and in accordance with the terms and purpose of the trust. *See id.* at §105(b)(2). What is the reason for this restriction? Can it be explained in terms of the agency cost theory?

Trust contractarians seem to assume that mutability is alien to, or at least in tension with, property law? Do you agree with that view? On this point, compare Note 2 in Chapter 8.2.

4.   *The Beneficiary's Interest* — In Rem *or* In Personam? What is the nature of the trust beneficiary's interest? Is it *in rem*, like legal (i.e., non-trust) property interests, or is it *in personam*, like contract rights? The great English legal historian Sir Frederic Maitland took the view that the beneficiary had only an *in personam* right against the trustee: "[E]quitable estates and interests are not *jura in rem*. . . . [T]hey are essentially *jura in personam*, not rights against the world at large, but rights against certain persons. . . ." F.W. MAITLAND, EQUITY 107 (1936). That view has now been largely rejected in favor of the *in rem* view. First, it is important to distinguish between two different possible senses of the term *rights in rem*. One is that rights *in rem* are rights against the world at large; the other is that they are rights that exist in, to, and with respect to a thing. *See* 1 JOHN AUSTIN, JURISPRUDENCE 380, 392 (4th ed. 1879). It is now well accepted that trust beneficiaries have *in rem* rights in the first sense. The beneficiary certainly has more than claim against the trustee only. *See* III AUSTIN WAKEMAN SCOTT ET AL., SCOTT AND ASCHER ON TRUSTS §13.1, at 806-807 (5th ed. 2007).

Does the beneficiary have *in rem* rights in the second sense as well? That is, does she have a proprietary interest in the trust assets or only a mere chose in action? The generally accepted view is that she has a proprietary interest. A highly influential treatise states: "The beneficiary of a trust has a property interest in the subject matter of the trust. He has a form of ownership." *Id.* at 808. Why might it matter whether the beneficiary's interest is an *in rem* property right or an *in personam* right, akin to a contract right? If you were a trust beneficiary, why might you prefer that your interest be considered to be an *in rem* right?

5.   *Do Trust Settlors Always Have the Upper Hand (and Should They)?* At the beginning of his article, Sitkoff seems to suggest that trust law gives lexical priority to settlors over beneficiaries and that that is as it should be. The *Claflin* doctrine is consistent with this view insofar as it denies the beneficiaries the power to compel trustees to prematurely terminate the trust. However, Sitkoff criticizes the *Claflin* doctrine on the ground that settlors want to maximize the long-term welfare of trust beneficiaries and that a different rule would better achieve that objective. But suppose that a settlor creates a trust that puts the long-term security of the beneficiaries in jeopardy for the sake of the (now-deceased) settlor's personal whim. Suppose further that the settlor unambiguously states that his

personal (and whimsical) objective is not to be sacrificed regardless of the consequences for the beneficiaries. Does trust law in fact give settlor lexical priority over the beneficiaries' needs in all circumstances? The short answer is no. The Uniform Trust Code provides, for example, that although most trustee duties are waivable, certain ones are mandatory. Among these is the requirement "that a trust and its terms be for the benefit of its beneficiaries. . . . " UNIF. TRUST CODE §105 (b)(3). This means that a settlor may not act at the expense of the beneficiaries. As one commentator puts it, "When a settlor imposes manifestly value-impairing restrictions on the use or disposition of trust property, the requirement that the trust terms be for the benefit of the beneficiaries places an outside limit upon the normal rule of deference to the settlor's intent." John H. Langbein, *Mandatory Rules in the Law of Trusts*, 98 Nw. U. L. Rev. 1105, 1109 (2004).

6. *The Dead Hand Problem.* The excerpt from Sitkoff's article mentioned spendthrift trusts. Spendthrift trusts pose the "dead hand dilemma": "[i]ndividual freedom to dispose of [property] cannot simultaneously be allowed and fully maintained. If the donor of a property interest tries to restrict the donee's freedom to dispose of that interest, the legal system, in deciding whether to enforce or void that restriction, must resolve whose freedom it will protect, that of the donor or that of the done." Gregory S. Alexander, *The Dead Hand and the Law of Trusts in the Nineteenth Century*, 37 STAN. L. REV. 1189, 1189 (1985). "The dead hand problem," as it is commonly called, actually is a congery of discrete problems that freedom of disposition of property poses. One is the problem just mentioned, that created by direct restraints on subsequent transfers of interests given to beneficiaries. We shall discuss this more fully in Note 7. Another problem is that of public policy objections to conditions on gifts and bequests (in trusts and otherwise) that discriminate on the basis of race, religion, gender, and similar grounds. Finally, there is the problem that is perhaps most commonly associated with the term "the dead hand" — unanticipated, and costly, future changes of circumstances affecting property interests.

The last problem — unanticipated and costly changes of circumstances in the distant future — gave rise to what is perhaps the most (in)famous rule in all of Anglo-American property law, the Rule Against Perpetuities (RAP). The RAP, which is usually dated to the much-celebrated Duke of Norfolk's Case, 22 Eng. Rep. 931 (Ch. 1682), actually had a long gestation.[21] Its classical iteration was stated by John Chipman Gray: "No [contingent] interest is good unless it must vest, if at all, not later than 21 years after some life in being at the creation of the interest." J.C. GRAY, THE RULE AGAINST PERPETUITIES §201 (4th ed. 1942). This simple sentence is remarkably deceptive, for the RAP is highly complex. The bottom line, however, is that its effect on trusts historically has been to limit the duration of private

---

21. On the Duke of Norfolk's Case and the history of the RAP, see George L. Haskins, *Extending the Grasp of the Dead Hand: Reflections on the Origins of the Rule Against Perpetuities*, 126 U. PA. L. REV. 19 (1977).

(i.e., non-charitable) trusts to something around 100 years. A more recent statutory version of the RAP uses a flat 90-year outer limit. *See* UNIF. STATUTORY RULE AGAINST PERPETUITIES, 8B U.L.A. 223 (2001). The dead hand policy underlying the modern RAP is that "given that one can, to a limited extent only, foresee the future and the problems it will generate [property] owners should not be allowed to tie up [property] for periods outside the range of reasonable foresight." A.W.B. SIMPSON, LEGAL THEORY AND LEGAL HISTORY 159-160 (1987).

Times have changed. Nearly one-quarter of American jurisdictions have recently enacted legislation either completely abolishing the RAP in the case of interests in trusts or extending the duration of trusts very substantially (e.g., 1,000 years). The popularity of these so-called perpetual trusts has little to do with the desires of the wealthy to control the lives of their unknown descendants. Rather, it has to do with their desire to take advantage of major tax savings for long-term trusts available under a federal tax known as the generation-skipping tax. It also has to do with competition among states for trust business, as large trust companies have lobbied state legislatures to enact legislation permitting perpetual trusts. *See* Jesse Dukeminier & James Krier, *The Rise of the Perpetual Trust,* 50 UCLA L. REV. 1303 (2003).

7. *Spendthrift Trusts.* Spendthrift trusts are very common in the United States but not in the United Kingdom. They involve the use of so-called disabling restraints on alienation to prevent trust beneficiaries from transferring their trust interests (i.e., prior to the time when the trustee has paid it out to the beneficiary, free of the trust) and to prevent the beneficiaries' creditors from attaching the beneficiaries' interests while in the trust (i.e., immunize the beneficiaries' interests from creditor claims). Unlike English law and the law of the British Commonwealth, American trust law opts for the donor's freedom, the freedom of the dead hand of the past. So, in Broadway National Bank v. Adams, 133 Mass. 170 (Mass. 1882), the first American case squarely to hold that a restraint on alienation of a trust beneficiary's interest is valid, the court said, "The founder of this trust was the absolute owner of his property. He had the entire right to dispose of it . . . by a gift with such restrictions or limitations, not repugnant to law, as he saw fit to impose."

Apart from the agency cost considerations that Sitkoff raises, do you see any possible policy objections to spendthrift trusts? Bear in mind that the term "spendthrift trust" is a bit of a misnomer, as such trusts need not be limited for spendthrifts or persons who are unable to care for themselves. They can be created in favor of anyone.[22] Do spendthrift trusts create a moral hazard?

---

22. There are certain types of creditors, however, who are generally excepted from the effect of a spendthrift clause. Thus, a beneficiary's child seeking child-support payments can reach the beneficiary's trust interest. So, too, can the beneficiary's ex-spouse who seeks payment of alimony or support obligations from the trust interest. *See* UNIF. TRUST CODE §503(b)(1).

Was the court in *Broadway Bank* correct in saying that a creditor is always able to determine whether the interest of a trust beneficiary is subject to a restraint on alienation? If not, may spendthrift trusts sometimes have the perverse effect that honest debtors are subsidizing beneficiaries of spendthrift trusts?

The spendthrift trust is, in effect, only allowed for inherited wealth. In the vast majority of jurisdictions a person can create a spendthrift trust in favor of another person but not in favor of himself (i.e., no self-settled spendthrift trust).[23] Hence, persons with inherited wealth can be protected from creditors but persons who earn wealth cannot. Does this make sense?

Are there possible policy objections to spendthrift trusts other than the concern with creditor fraud? The influential nineteenth-century legal scholar John Chipman Gray argued that the real policy objection to spendthrift trusts is that "it is against public policy that a man 'should have an estate to live on, but not an estate to pay his debts with,' . . . and should have the benefits of wealth without the responsibilities." J.C. GRAY, RESTRAINTS ON THE ALIENATION OF PROPERTY 242-243 (2d ed. 1895). What is your reaction to this argument?

---

23. Approximately 12 states now have statutes authorizing self-settled spendthrift trusts, so-called "asset protection trusts." *See, e.g.,* Alaska Stat. §34.40.110. These statutes were prompted by competition for trust business from offshore asset protection trusts, which have become big business since they first appeared in the 1980s.

16 HOME

1. THE HOME

Stephanie M. Stern, Residential Protectionism and the Legal Mythology of the Home[1]

INTRODUCTION

Residential real estate has achieved an exalted status and privileged position in American property law. In the past century, there has been a proliferation of legislation that protects and privileges homeowners by reducing the risk of dislocation and extracting rents to the detriment of nonowners and lower-income owners. I term this movement "residential protectionism." The panoply of home-protective legislation includes bankruptcy protections, property tax relief, and most recently foreclosure reform and state eminent domain legislation. Residential protectionism has imposed social costs by encouraging excessive investment in residential real estate, raising the cost of credit, creating regressive tax subsidies, and frustrating land planning. Despite these costs, protective legislation has attained the stature of moral right. A compelling justification attributed to such legislation is that it safeguards one's (particular) home as a well-spring for psychological flourishing. Involuntary dislocation wreaks psychological devastation and imperils self and identity—one's very personhood.[2] The belief that ongoing control of one's home is a psychological imperative has become a tenet of American property law, discussed

---

1. Stephanie M. Stern, *Residential Protectionism and the Legal Mythology of the Home*, 107 MICH. L. REV. 1093, 1094-1096, 1097-1098, 1105-1007, 1109-1010, 1113, 1114-1015, 1127, 1128-1029, 1130, 1139-1040, 1142-1043, 1144 (2009).

2. *See, e.g.,* MINDY THOMPSON FULLILOVE, ROOT SHOCK 11-20 (2004). . . .

and conceded in every first-year property class and touted extensively in the legal scholarship. The legal academy has accepted this theoretical notion as fact and in doing so facilitated the home's illustrious and uncontested reign over American property law.

Property scholarship spins an alluring tale of how the force of law stands as a vigilant guardian over the personal and psychological values of the home. Few articles have enthralled property theorists as Margaret Radin's theory that certain kinds of property, including homes, are constitutive of personhood.[3] Radin argued that ongoing control over objects, such as homes, that are "bound up" with one's self is necessary for proper self-constitution and psychological flourishing. Personhood theory infused a generation of scholarship, engraining the notion that homes are special objects deeply intertwined with psychological functioning. Scholars have cited the personhood value of the home to support constraints on government takings, to justify property redistribution, and more generally to offer a long-awaited reprise to economic theory. . . . Astonishingly, no one has questioned whether empirical evidence exists to support these theories.

This Article offers a new perspective on these perennial debates in property law by distilling the empirical research on homes. The central claim of this Article is that the psychological and social benefits of remaining in a particular home do not warrant the vast apparatus of categorical protections that pervade American property law. We may opt to retain these protections for other reasons, but they cannot be justified on a theory of the home as psychologically vital. A corollary is that the legal academy has been unduly deferential to conjecture about homeowners' subjective preferences while neglecting entirely the data on objective psychological outcomes. In light of the psychological evidence, and absent compelling economic or other justifications, I advocate reducing the number and scope of home-protective laws. . . .

To clarify the scope of my analysis, I use the term "home" to refer to owner-occupied residential real estate. I focus on owners rather than renters because most home-protective legislation safeguards ownership interests; however, much of the psychological research applies with equal force to renters. My analysis targets the typical homeowner in the United States, not the comparatively rare instances of multigenerational family dynasty property, uniquely tight-knit enclaves, or extreme separatist communities. . . .

I.   RESIDENTIAL PROTECTIONISM: THE COSTLY MYTH OF HOME

B. The Legal Mythology of Home

The pervasiveness and variety of home protection in U.S. property law suggests that the law reflects (and encourages) a special ethos with respect

---

3. Margaret Jane Radin, *Property and Personhood,* 34 STAN. L. REV. 957, 958-59 (1982) [See Chapter 2, *supra*—EDS.].

to the home. The attribution of personal and social values to the home dates back to the nineteenth-century Romantic philosophy of the home as a paradise on earth and a refuge from the corruption and danger of urban life. The legal privileging of homes in the United States, however, did not begin in earnest until the New Deal's "modernized social compact" introduced government buyouts of defaulted mortgages, attractive direct lending programs, and lengthier mortgage amortization periods. Political rhetoric and business advertising broadcast visions of the "American dream," "home as castle," and "home is where the heart is." These ideological campaigns were disseminated most effectively by those with a financial interest in a robust housing market, such as banks, developers, and real estate companies. The marketing of the home as a powerful symbol, coupled with financial incentives, channeled wealth investment to residential real estate and encouraged attitudes glorifying homeownership.

A generation later, the concept of the home morphed from social recovery to personal self-development with Margaret Radin's theory of property for personhood. This legal theory of home spins a captivating tale of how the moral force of law safeguards the personal and psychological values of the home. The "personhood" character of one's home has become a tenet of property law, cited ubiquitously and accepted without challenge. Legal scholars, joined by legislators and judges, are the modern narrators of this myth. . . .

Following Radin's landmark article, a generation of legal scholars adopted the personhood perspective and focused in particular on the role of the home in human flourishing. The personhood perspective provided the normative basis for proposals to protect the "sanctity of home" from the alleged misuse of government eminent domain power, the greedy reach of creditors, and the wasteful excess of taxing authorities. Commentators noted that the home warrants enhanced protection as a psychologically vital and archetypal possession—the home is like "an extension of [owners'] selves, or like a part of their family."[4] In this view, the home is so critical to the maintenance of self and psychological well-being that displacement amounts to an emotional trauma. . . .

II. The Home as Property for Personhood: A Review of the Psychological Evidence

. . . [W]e can look to the research for evidentiary support for some of the logical distillations of Radin's theory. Specifically, the psychology research bears on the propositions of whether property is a primary constituent of self-concept and whether property loss is likely to impair or radically alter the self, as perceived by the dispossessed owner, or to harm long-term

4. [John] Fee, [*Eminent Domain and the Sanctity of Home*, 81 Notre Dame L. Rev. 783,] 788 [(2006)]. . . .

psychosocial functioning. In psychological terms, the self-constitution described by Radin and subsequent legal theorists implicates the concepts of identity and self. The psychological correlates of flourishing include development, psychosocial functioning, stress, adaptation, and life satisfaction. Personality and social psychologists have studied the formation and maintenance of self and identity extensively, while environmental psychologists have investigated the role of possessions as an "extended self" and dwelling as "place identity." Psychologists and sociologists have also researched the mental-health impacts of relocation and homeownership. . . . [C]ontrary to claims in the property scholarship, the home is not a primary construct of self and identity, residential dislocation does not typically harm mental health, and the relationship between homeownership and self-esteem is equivocal. Moreover, in contrast to the object focus of personhood theory, an enormous body of empirical work establishes that social interactions and ties — not possessions — are the bedrocks of psychological thriving.

A. The Nonprimacy of Home to Self-Constitution

Possessions, even subjectively important ones, do not form the principal tiers of self or identity. Instead, the empirical research shows that personality characteristics, values, social roles, and one's body parts are the conceptual categories most closely linked with self.[5] . . .

. . . The research indicates that residential real estate serves a primarily self-expressive, not self-constructive, function.[6] Homes and other possessions express attitudes, values, personal history, ethnic identity, and self-perceived status, or bolster an image of self we wish to convey to others.[7] There is evidence that self-expression through dwelling is effective. Subjects who rate perceived personality dimensions after viewing an owner's interior dwelling provide ratings that largely correspond to owner's self-ratings and that are more accurate than ratings based on behavioral information such as social activities of the owner. However, to conclude that homes deserve legal protection from creditors, taxing authorities, and

---

5. *See* Alan Page Fiske et al., *The Cultural Matrix of Social Psychology, in* 2 THE HANDBOOK OF SOCIAL PSYCHOLOGY, 915, 927 [(Daniel T. Gilbert et al. eds., 4th ed., 1998)]. . . .

6. Even researchers who have devoted their careers to elucidating the psychological function of possessions typically stop short of avowing that possessions construct identity. *See, e.g.,* HELGA DITTMAR, THE SOCIAL PSYCHOLOGY OF MATERIAL POSSESSIONS 155 (1992) ("[B]road social identity dimensions are reflected in, *and probably in part maintained by,* individuals' self-reported relationships with their personal possessions."). . . .

7. *See* [Russell W.] Belk, [*Attachment to Possessions, in* PLACE ATTACHMENT 37, 38 (Irwin Altman & Setha M. Low eds., 1992)]; [Clare] Cooper, [*The House as a Symbol of the Self, in* DESIGNING FOR HUMAN BEHAVIOR 130, 131 (Jon Lang et al. eds., 1974)] ("The house . . . reflects how man sees himself, with both an intimate interior . . . and a public exterior . . . or the self that we choose to display to others."). The expressive capacity of the housing structure varies depending on the degree to which the owner's housing choice was circumscribed by location, commuting time, or cost. *See* [Marsha L.] Richins, [*Valuing Things: The Public and Private Meanings of Possessions,* 21 J. CONSUMER RES. 504, 518 (1994)].

government because of their self-expressive capacity seems far-fetched. Citizens of capitalist nations have many ready substitutes for self-expression. Cars, clothes, and jewelry serve similar functions of announcing identity and benefit from broader visibility. Home decorations can be transferred to a new residence. Other alternatives for self-expression, such as group membership, religion, and speech do not depend on property at all. . . .

In summary, the weight of the psychological evidence does not support the idea that homes, or possessions in general, are strongly constitutive of psychological personhood. Specifically, the research fails to substantiate the theory that loss of "personhood" property impairs self-concept or self-development. At best, possessions and dwellings are lower-tier aspects of self and identity and serve a primarily self-expressive function.

B. Relocation and Psychological Flourishing

If homes are critical to human flourishing, as personhood theory suggests, we would expect to see psychological studies finding long-term mental health harms from involuntary relocation. The research suggests otherwise. . . . In general, people are highly adaptive to geographic change and typically return to premobility levels of satisfaction in relatively short order.[8] . . .

IV. RETHINKING RESIDENTIAL PROTECTIONISM

The notion that one's home is a psychological requisite has profoundly affected American property law. This mythology of home has cloaked rent seeking in the guise of moral compulsion and encouraged the overproduction of home-protective legislation. . . . In order to stem the tide of residential protectionism, and perhaps reverse some of the most abusive home protection shelters, it is time to change the way we think about the home.

A. Dismantling the Legal Mythology of Home: Implications for Property Theory

An evidence-based analysis has important implications for property scholarship. First, although the research cannot "disprove" personhood theory

---

8. Lee Cuba's study of 432 migrants to Cape Cod found that only twenty-five participants reported that they did not feel at home. *See* Lee Cuba & David M. Hummon, *Constructing a Sense of Home: Place Affiliation and Migration Across the Life Cycle* 8 Soc. F., 547, 552 (1993); *see also* PETER MARRIS, LOSS AND CHANGE 44 (2d ed. 1986) (discussing relocation of residents from the central districts of London to the Dagenham Estate in the London suburbs); Catherine Ward & Irene Styles, *Lost and Found: Reinvention of the Self Following Migration,* 5 J. APPLIED PSYCHOANALYTIC STUD. 349, 353 (2003) (majority of women surveyed about move from United Kingdom to Australia described their migration experience positively).

in the sense of direct hypothesis testing, the weight of the evidence does not support the psychological distillations of personhood theory with respect to self-constitution and human flourishing. The unsettling conclusion is that a theory of property protection, and specifically home protection, has dominated legal scholarship for almost three decades without empirical support. Abandoning personhood as the dominant noneconomic justification for legal safeguards promotes a healthy skepticism of protectionist laws and encourages more precise discourse on the values and preferences underlying property protection. It is likely that many people are primarily attached to the home not as a personhood or social asset, but as an economic asset — it is the potential loss of the home's financial value that provokes psychological distress. If this is true, it provides further evidence that homes are fungible property, no different from other economic assets. We may decide as a society, after weighing the costs and benefits, to protect economic assets or not — but presumably these assets should be treated equivalently.

Moving beyond the confines of personhood theory, there is no evidence of another form of compelling psychological interest or vital attachment to the physical home. Of course, the lack of evidence does not prove the point. . . . There may be a home interest as of yet unidentified in the research literature, or a heightened attachment based on race, income, or gender. For example, home protections may promote security (i.e., the ability to plan one's affairs without the threat of future dislocation) and thus reduce both psychological costs and transaction costs. However, security is neither an inevitable byproduct of ownership (as demonstrated by the recent foreclosure crisis) nor a universally positive attribute (as shown by the finding that homeownership often entraps lower-income owners in declining neighborhoods). Moreover, special protections for ownership are not the only way to provide reasonable security or respect psychological attachments — private contracting for longer rental terms or more favorable lease-renewal options can also provide long-term assurances.

This Article contends that legal theory and reform must move forward based on the best available evidence. In view of the current body of evidence, and the specific finding of benign long-term outcomes from relocation, it seems unlikely that attachment, security, or an alternative psychological interest justifies the degree of home protection in American property law. If subsequent psychological research proves otherwise, then an evidence-based approach not only encourages, but requires, further theoretical revision. . . .

Last, the research literature exposes the distinctly classist nature of the theories of property for personhood and residential communitarianism. Property theorists equate homeownership and "staying put" with liberty, dignity, and autonomy for poor residents. Sociologists view the same phenomenon as economic entrapment. If the positive effects of homeownership are not sufficient to reverse a declining neighborhood, then homeowners may end up entrapped by the high costs of exit (i.e., selling a house in a declining area or market). The groups most at risk for residential entrapment are black, low-income, and elderly owners.[9] In poor areas, there is evidence that residential stability increases depression and anxiety, despite the fact that it increases sociability and social ties.[10] Residential stability also has a weaker effect on decreasing perceived social disorder in poor neighborhoods compared to more affluent areas. Disturbingly, the evidence suggests that home-protective legislation is not only economically regressive but psychologically regressive as well. . . .

VI. APPLICATIONS

. . . By way of illustration of my evidence-based model, however, this Part offers some preliminary thoughts on how a revised theory of the home informs current debates in property law. . . .

B. Homestead Exemptions

Homestead exemptions impose high costs on society by raising the cost of credit and inviting abuse. As a categorical matter, there is little to recommend these laws. If the concern is that families have sufficient resources for starting over, there are other ways to meet that goal without offering blanket exclusions or hefty protection for homes (which are, after all, an expensive consumer good with ongoing costs to maintain). The modest psychological value of residential stability to individual owners and the high social costs of homestead exemptions, particularly in states such as Florida and Texas with unlimited exemptions, make these laws a classic example of residential protectionism.

The only potentially compelling justification for (limited) homestead exemptions is the needs of vulnerable demographic groups, such as school-age children and the elderly. The case for homestead exemptions for families with school-age children is relatively weak. . . . [T]he evidence of harm to children from normal levels of relocation is equivocal.

There is a stronger case for targeting limited homestead exemptions to the elderly, who experience heightened psychological costs from relocation. . . . [T]here may be justification for providing narrowly tailored protection to the elderly (or at least enhanced relocation assistance).

9. [William R.] Rohe, et al., [*The Social Benefits and Costs of Home Ownership: A Critical Assessment of the Research* 14-15 (Joint Ctr. for Hous. Studies of Harvard University, Working Paper No. LIHO-01.12, 2001) *available at* http://www.jchs.harvard.edu/publications/homeownership/liho01.12.pdf].

10. [Clare L. Twigger-Ross & Daniel L. Uzzell, *Place and Identity Processes*, 16 J. ENVTL. PSYCHOL. 205, 208 (1996)] ("[Neighborhood stability] does not benefit the mental health of residents of poor neighborhoods, and there is some evidence that it makes it worse.").

CONCLUSION

The notion of the home as a psychologically special object deserving heightened protection has dominated property law and theory. Scholars have argued that the home is a paradigmatic form of property for personhood — critical to an individual's very identity and ability to flourish in society. Other commentators have maintained a communitarian vision of the home rooting individuals in tightly knit communities. Contrary to the theoretical claims in property scholarship, the empirical evidence indicates that the psychological and social importance of the home has been vastly overstated. The psychological value attributed to the home has masked rent seeking as moral conviction and greased the wheels of the residential protectionism machine. To the extent we have premised protectionism on the psychological primacy of home, it is time to rethink the protection and privilege accorded to residential property.

D. Benjamin Barros, Home as a Legal Concept[11]

... The literature on the psychology of home provides a more detailed picture of people's relationships to their homes. Consistent with Radin's intuition, home is associated with a range of feelings related to a long-term tie to a physical location. Home is the physical center of everyday life and is a source of feelings of rootedness and belonging. Home is the locus of a person's immediate family and can be a source of emotional warmth and personal comfort. For people with long-term tenure in their homes, home is a source of feelings of continuity, stability, and permanence. . . .

   . . . Not all people relate to their homes in the same way, however, and dislocation can affect people in different ways. Additionally, many important psychological attachments to the home can move with an individual to a new home. . . .

   A closer examination suggests that Radin's intuitive view tends to overstate an individual's personal connection to a home in a particular location because many of the important personal values associated with a home are movable. Perhaps most importantly a person will also be able to move the personal belongings that are critical to making a new living space feel like home. Each of these movable values are [sic] critical components of people's psychological ties to their homes and would, therefore, be significant components of the intuitive notion that homes are special.

---

11. D. Benjamin Barros, *Home as a Legal Concept*, 46 SANTA CLARA L. REV. 255, 277, 278-281 (2006).

NOTES AND QUESTIONS

1. *Opposing Views*. Both Stern and Barros challenge the claim, propounded by Margaret Jane Radin, among others, that the home is a special form of property, one that is psychologically essential to development of a healthy sense of the personhood and to one's flourishing. In contrast, the English legal scholar Lorna Fox believes that the psychological and other non-economic dimensions of the home are legally underprotected. She argues, "[I]t remains evident that legal discourse has not developed a coherent concept of home that is capable of carrying weight against competing claims, such as the protection of commercial interests. When posited against such claims, home interests seem to evaporate into the ether." Lorna Fox, *The Idea of Home in Law*, 2 Home Cultures 25, 41 (2005). Fox advocates development of a legal concept of home that provides the basis for protecting the home's subjective, including psychological, aspects. *See generally* Lorna Fox, Conceptualising Home: Theories, Laws and Policies (2007).

What may account for the difference of viewpoints between Stern and Barros, on the one hand, and Fox, on the other, or is this just a simple disagreement? Is there any significance to the fact that Stern and Barros are both Americans and are writing about home in the American context, while Fox is English and is addressing the status of the home in English law? Might there be any underlying cultural differences between English and American attitudes toward the home that would affect their views?

Stern argues that "social interactions and ties — not possessions — are the bedrocks of psychological thriving." She states further, "Possessions, even subjectively important ones, do not form the principal tiers of self or identity." One psychologist, Helga Dittmar, whom Stern cites (see footnote 6), appears to disagree. Surveying several empirical studies, Dittmar concludes, "[S]ufficient empirical evidence exists to demonstrate that material possessions are regarded as part of the self . . . ." Helga Dittmar, The Social Psychology of Material Possessions 47 (1992). Specifically with respect to the home, Dittmar found that the empirical literature indicates that the home provides "a space to develop an identity," that the home is a "cultivator[]," and that homes are "symbols of the self." *Id.* at 113. *See also* E. Doyle McCarthy, *Toward a Sociology of the Physical World*, 5 Studies in Symbolic Interaction 105, 116-117 (1984) (analyzing the home as "an extension of personality"). Even if, as Stern claims, social ties, rather than possessions, predominate, does it follow that the home has little or no significance for psychological and emotional thriving?

The finding that homes symbolize the personalities of their inhabitants might seem to support Stern's argument that the home primarily serves a "self-expressive" function, which she distinguishes from self-construction. Are those two functions unrelated? Consider how Jeremy Waldron's notion of basing the value of personhood on notions of responsibility, a point that we considered in Note 2 of Chapter 2, might be helpful in establishing a conceptual connection between self-expression and self-construction. Moreover, to the extent that they are unrelated, why isn't self-expression in itself entitled to some legal privileges with respect to the home? Stern claims that many other assets, including cars and clothing, are equally substitutable modes of self-expression for the home. Do you agree?

Consider the public outcry that followed in the wake of the U.S. Supreme Court's decision in Kelo v. City of New London, 545 U.S. 469 (2005). *See* Janice Nadler & Shari Seidman Diamond, *Government Takings of Private Property: Kelo and the Perfect Storm, in* Public Opinion and Constitutional Controversy 287 (Nathaniel Persily et al. eds., 2008). Is this evidence that people have strong psychological attachments to their homes?

2.   *Is Personhood Empirically Contingent?* Stern's critique of Radin and of personhood arguments favoring the home is based on the premise that personhood theories must rest on empirical claims. Do you agree? Must the force of personhood arguments depend of empirical findings?

Stern's and Barros's critiques are based on empirical evidence concerning people's preferences. Their arguments tend to assume that law is exogenous to these preferences and is guided by them. But a well-developed body of literature has now made it clear that preferences are far from always being autonomous, but are rather sometimes a function of law. *See, e.g.,* Jon Elster, Sour Grapes (1983); Cass R. Sunstein, *Legal Interference with Private Preferences*, 53 U. Chi. L. Rev. 1129 (1986). To the extent that law is preference-shaping, then seemingly scientific arguments such as Stern's and Barros's may not be as strong as they present themselves.

Consider Jeremy Waldron's interpretation of Hegel's personality theory, which we briefly encountered in Chapter 2, Waldron interprets Hegel to argue:

> The importance of property to individual wills is this: the actions that an individual performs on or with this object now may constrain or determine the actions that he can perform on or with it later. This is how an object can embody a will — by registering the effects of willing at one point in time and forcing an individual's willing to become consistent and stable over a period.

Jeremy Waldron, The Right to Private Property 373 (1988). Is this argument premised on empirical assumptions?

3.   *A Non-Psychological Critique of the Home.* Like Stern and Barros, Stephen Schnably is also critical of Radin's defense of the home. His critique, however, is not based on psychological literature. Schnably contends that "people's involvement with their homes is nowhere near as

simple and uncontroversial as Radin's presentation suggests." Stephen J. Schnably, *Property and Pragmatism: A Critique of Radin's Theory of Property and Personhood,* 45 STAN. L. REV. 347, 364 (1993). He goes on to explain:

> [T]he home represents a whole set of assumptions and lived experiences. It is impossible to think about the home and its connection to personhood without thinking about its larger context. For example, the ideal of the home goes hand in hand with the assumption that fulfillment is primarily to be found in private life, rather than in communal activities. . . .
>
> Moreover, an essential part of our attachment to the home, suburban or otherwise, is grounded in its status as the privileged locale for intimate relationships. The home and family are practically inseparable not only in their conception, but also in their history: The rise of the home as an ideal and social practice was closely linked to the creation of women's role as homemakers.

Id. at 364-365 (footnotes omitted). For Radin's reply, see Margaret Jane Radin, *Lacking a Transformative Social Theory: A Response,* 45 STAN. L. REV. 409 (1993) (conceding that the traditional ideology of the home can reinforce oppressive understandings of women's roles and reinforce the isolation of suburbs, but insisting that these drawbacks are dwarfed by the significant benefits to relatively powerless groups, notably tenants and homeless people, from the view that people need a home for personhood).

4. *The Meaning(s) of Home.* As legal scholars of the home have observed, "One of the most pervasive clichés in the common law is that a man's home is his castle." Barros, *supra,* at 259. Yet the concept of home is not self-defining. Perhaps there is no improving on Robert Frost's definition: "Home is the place where, when you go there,/They have to take you in." Robert Frost, *The Death of the Hired Man, in* SELECTED POEMS OF ROBERT FROST 25, 28 (1963). Still, we need to know, is the home confined to owned dwellings, or does it include rental dwellings as well? Single-family houses are clearly included, but what about less conventional modes of group living, such as group homes for mentally disadvantaged persons? Can/should a dwelling be legally considered a home for some purposes but not for others? Scholars of the home are not always clear about their views on questions such as these. What interests and values might be implicated by these and other questions that raise the meaning of home in a concrete way? For a beginning to the answers to these questions, see Lorna Fox, *The Meaning of Home: A Chimerical Concept or a Legal Challenge?* 29 J.L. & Soc'y 580 (2002) (concept of "home" implicates several values that courts and legislatures should take into account when weighing the interests of occupants such as tenants and mortgagees against landlords and creditors; values include physical shelter, stability and security, personal identity, and cultural connection).

5. *Republicanism, Citizenship, and Homeownership.* Recall from Chapter 6 that landownership plays a critical role in republican political thought.

From the republican perspective, the purpose of land ownership is to secure the citizen's material independence so that he is free from sources of corruption and thereby able to act virtuously for the common good. Within the American version of republicanism, not land alone, but the home occupies a central place. In this context the home has a particular meaning: the single-family dwelling. As Joan Williams has observed, the version of republicanism that the modern American mythology surrounding home-ownership reflects is certainly not that of Jefferson's sturdy yeoman farmer. Rather, it is what she calls a hybrid form of republicanism, one that is blended with the "ideology of domesticity," by which she means a gender ideology in which the home signifies a haven from the world of the market, maintained by women for men. *See* Joan C. Williams, *The Rhetoric of Property*, 83 Iowa L. Rev. 277 (1998). As evidence of the strength of this ideology, Williams points to Village of Euclid v. Ambler Realty, 272 U.S. 365 (1926), in which the Supreme Court upheld the constitutional validity of zoning despite the fact that the court during the same period was striking down most other regulatory legislation. Is *Euclid* persuasive evidence in support of Williams' thesis?

As we saw in Chapter 6, citizenship is a core value in republicanism as well as other political theories. The link between citizenship and home-ownership has been a theme of many political theorists. *See, e.g.,* Hannah Arendt, The Human Condition 27-35 (1958). There is empirical evidence tending to support this linkage. *See* Eric J. Pido, *The Performance of Property: Suburban Homeownership as a Claim to Citizenship for Filipinos in Daly City*, (June 3, 2009), *Institute for the Study of Social Change*, ISSC Fellows Working Papers. Paper ISSC_WP_35, *available at* http://repositories.cdlib.org/issc/fwp/ISSC_WP_35.

6. *The Economics of the Household.* Another term sometimes used synonymously with "home" is "household" (although the two are not necessary identical in meaning). Robert Ellickson defines "household" as "a set of institutional arrangements, formal or informal, that governs relations among the owners and occupants of a dwelling space where occupants usually sleep and share meals." Robert C. Ellickson, *Unpacking the Household: Informal Property Rights Around the Hearth*, 116 Yale L.J. 226, 230 (2006). Ellickson's article focuses primarily on internal aspects of households, including their composition and governance. Regarding their governance his central thesis is that "in a liberal society, while law provides essential background rules that enable household formation, small-bore private law rules have little relevance to everyday domestic affairs." He goes on to argue, "[I]ntimate co-occupants and co-owners are able to coordinate mainly by means of gift exchange, a process that gives rise to household-specific norms." *Id.* at 234. Does this claim seem especially controversial to you? Is law's general irrelevance to the everyday regulation of the household surprising?

2. HOMELESSNESS AND A RIGHT TO HOUSING

Jeremy Waldron, Homelessness and the Issue of Freedom[1]

INTRODUCTION

There are many facets to the nightmare of homelessness. In this essay, I want to explore just one of them: the relation between homelessness, the rules of public and private property, and the underlying freedom of those who are condemned by poverty to walk the streets and sleep in the open. Unlike some recent discussions, my concern is not with the constitutionality of various restrictions on the homeless (though that, of course, is important). I want to address a prior question—a more fundamental question—of legal and moral philosophy: how should we think about homelessness, how should we conceive of it, in relation to a value like freedom?

The discussion that follows is, in some ways, an abstract one. This is intentional. The aim is to refute the view that, on abstract liberal principles, there is no reason to be troubled by the plight of the homeless, and that one has to come down to the more concrete principles of a communitarian ethic in order to find a focus for that concern. Against this view, I shall argue that homelessness is a matter of the utmost concern in relation to some of the most fundamental and abstract principles of liberal value. . . .

I. LOCATION AND PROPERTY

Some truisms to begin with. Everything that is done has to be done somewhere. No one is free to perform an action unless there is somewhere he is free to perform it. Since we are embodied beings, we always have a location. Moreover, though everyone has to be somewhere, a person cannot always choose any location he likes. Some locations are physically inaccessible. And, physical inaccessibility aside, there are some places one is simply not allowed to be.

One of the functions of property rules, particularly as far as land is concerned, is to provide a basis for determining who is allowed to be where. . . .

II. HOMELESSNESS

. . . One way of describing the plight of a homeless individual might be to say that there is no place governed by a private property rule where he is allowed to be. . . .

1. Jeremy Waldron, *Homelessness and the Issue of Freedom*, 39 UCLA L. REV. 295, 295-296, 299-300, 302, 304-307, 308, 310-313, 315, 318, 319-321, 322, 323, 324 (1991).

In fact, that is not quite correct. Any private proprietor may invite a homeless person into his house or onto his land, and if he does there will be some private place where the homeless person is allowed to be. A technically more accurate description of his plight is that there is no place governed by a private property rule where he is allowed to be whenever he chooses, no place governed by a private property rule from which he may not at any time be excluded as a result of someone else's say-so. As far as being on private property is concerned — in people's houses or gardens, on farms or in hotels, in offices or restaurants — the homeless person is utterly and at all times at the mercy of others. And we know enough about how this mercy is generally exercised to figure that the description in the previous paragraph is more or less accurate as a matter of fact, even if it is not strictly accurate as a matter of law.

For the most part the homeless are excluded from all of the places governed by private property rules, whereas the rest of us are, in the same sense, excluded from all but one (or maybe all but a few) of those places. That is another way of saying that each of us has at least one place to be in a country composed of private places, whereas the homeless person has none. . . .

III. LOCATIONS, ACTIONS AND FREEDOM

The points made so far can be restated in terms of freedom. Someone who is allowed to be in a place is, in a fairly straightforward sense, free to be there. A person who is not allowed to be in a place is unfree to be there. However, the concept of freedom usually applies to actions rather than locations: one is free or unfree to do X or to do Y. What is the connection, then, between freedom to be somewhere and freedom to do something?

At the outset I recited the truism that anything a person does has to be done somewhere. To that extent, all actions involve a spatial component (just as many actions involve, in addition, a material component like the use of tools, implements, or raw materials). It should be fairly obvious that, if one is not free to be in a certain place, one is not free to do anything at that place. . . . It follows, strikingly, that a person who is not free to be in any place is not free to do anything; such a person is comprehensively unfree. In [a] libertarian paradise we imagined . . . this would be the plight of the homeless. They would be simply without freedom (or, more accurately, any freedom they had would depend utterly on the forbearance of those who owned the places that made up the territory of the society in question). . . .

. . . [T]he homeless have freedom in our society only to the extent that our society is communist. . . .

A. *Negative Freedom*

Before going on, I want to say something about the conception of freedom I am using in this essay. Those who argue that the homeless (or the poor generally) have less freedom than the rest of us are often accused of appealing to a controversial, dangerous, and question-begging conception of "positive" freedom.[2] It is commonly thought that one has to step outside the traditional liberal idea of "negative" freedom in order to make these points.

However, there is no need to argue about that here. The definition of freedom with which I have been working so far is as "negative" as can be. There is nothing unfamiliar about it (except perhaps the consistency with which it is being deployed). I am saying that a person is free to be someplace just in case he is not legally liable to be physically removed from that place or penalized for being there. . . . In exactly this negative sense (absence of forcible interference), the homeless person is unfree to be in any place governed by a private property rule (unless the owner for some reason elects to give him his permission to be there). The familiar claim that, in the negative sense of "freedom," the poor are as free as the rest of us — and that you have to move to a positive definition in order to dispute that — is simply false.

That private property limits freedom seems obvious. If I own a piece of land, others have a duty not to use it (without my consent) and there is a battery of legal remedies which I can use to enforce this duty as I please. The right correlative to this duty is an essential incident of ownership, and any enforcement of the duty necessarily amounts to a deliberate interference with someone else's action. . . .

[One line of] objection is sometimes based on a distinction between freedom and ability. The homeless, it is said, are in the relevant sense free to perform the same activities as the rest of us; but the sad fact is that they do not have the means or the power or the ability to exercise these freedoms. This claim is almost always false. With the exception of a few who are so weakened by their plight that they are incapable of anything, the homeless are not unable to enter the privately-owned places from which they are banned. They can climb walls, open doors, cross thresholds, break windows, and so on, to gain entry to the premises from which the laws of property exclude them. What stands in their way is simply what stands in the way of anyone who is negatively unfree: the likelihood that someone else will forcibly prevent their action. Of course, the rich do try to make it impossible as well as illegal for the homeless to enter their gardens: they build their walls as high as possible and top them with broken glass. But that this does not constitute mere inability as opposed to unfreedom is indicated by the fact that the homeless are not permitted even to try to overcome these physical obstacles. They may be dragged away and penalized for attempting to scale the walls.

---

2. For the contrast between "positive" and "negative" conceptions of freedom, see I[SAIAH] BERLIN, *Two Concepts of Liberty, in* FOUR ESSAYS ON LIBERTY 118 (1969).

A second line that is sometimes taken is this: one should regard the homeless as less free than the rest of us only if one believes that some human agency (other than their own) is responsible for their plight. However, the idea of someone else's being responsible for the plight of the homeless is an ambiguous one. It may well be the case that people are homeless as a result of earlier deliberate and heartless actions by land-lords, employers, or officials, or as a result of a deliberate capitalist strategy to create and sustain a vast reserve industrial army of the unemployed. That may be the case. But even if it is not, even if their being homeless cannot be laid at anyone's door or attributed to anything over and above their own choices or the impersonal workings of the market, my point remains. Their homelessness consists in unfreedom. Though it may not be anyone's fault that there is no place they can go without being dragged away, still their being removed from the places they are not allowed to be is itself a dero-gation from their freedom, a derogation constituted by the deliberate human action of property-owners, security guards, and police officers. To repeat, their having nowhere to go is their being unfree (in a negative sense) to be anywhere; it is identical with the fact that others are authorized deliberately to drag them away from wherever they choose to be. We do not need any further account of the cause of this state of affairs to describe it as, in itself, a situation of unfreedom.

Thirdly, someone may object that a person is not made unfree if he is prevented from doing something wrong — something he has a duty not to do. Since entering others' property and abusing common property are wrong, it is not really a derogation from freedom to enforce a person's duties in these respects. . . .

[This objection] is confusing and question-begging in the present con-text. It elides the notions of a restriction on freedom and an unjustified restriction on freedom, closing off certain questions that common sense regards as open. It seems to rest on a sense — elsewhere repudiated by many liberals — that all our moral and political concerns fit together in a tidy package, so that we need not ever worry about trade-offs between freedom (properly understood) and other values, such as property and justice. . . .

B. General Prohibitions and Particular Freedoms

. . . [T]he conclusions about freedom that I have reached depend on taking the prohibitions relating to particular objects generated by property laws as seriously as we take the more general prohibitions imposed by the criminal law. No doubt these different types of prohibition are imposed for different reasons. But if freedom means simply the absence of deliberate interference with one's actions, we will not be in a position to say how free a person is until we know everything about the universe of legal restraints that may be applied to him. After all, it is not freedom in the abstract that people value, but freedom to perform particular actions. If the absence of a general prohibition tells us nothing about anyone's concrete freedom, then we should be wary of using only the checklist of general prohibitions to tell us how free or unfree a person or a society really is.

These points can readily be applied to the homeless. There are no general prohibitions in our society on actions like sleeping or washing. However, we cannot infer from this that anyone may sleep or wash wherever he chooses. In order to work out whether a particular person is free to sleep or wash, we must also ask whether there are any prohibitions of place that apply to his performance of actions of this type. As a matter of fact, all of us face a formidable battery of such prohibitions. Most private places, for example, are off-limits to us for these (or any other) activities. Though I am a well-paid professor, there are only a couple of private places where I am allowed to sleep or wash (without having someone's specific permission): my home, my office, and whatever restaurant I am patronizing. Most homeless people do not have jobs and few of them are allowed inside restaurants. ("Bathrooms for the use of customers only.") Above all, they have no homes. So there is literally no private place where they are free to sleep or wash.

For them, that is a desperately important fact about their freedom, one that must preoccupy much of every day. Unlike us, they have no private place where they can take it for granted that they will be allowed to sleep or wash. Since everyone needs to sleep and wash regularly, homeless people have to spend time searching for non-private places—like public restrooms (of which there are precious few in America, by the standards of most civilized countries) and shelters (available, if at all, only at night)—where these actions may be performed without fear of interference. If we regard freedom as simply the complement of the general prohibitions imposed by law, we are in danger of overlooking this fact about the freedom of the homeless. Most of us can afford to overlook it, because we have homes to go to. But without a home, a person's freedom is his freedom to act in public, in places governed by common property rules. That is the difference between our freedom and the freedom of the homeless.

C. Public Places

What then are we to say about public places? If there is anywhere the homeless are free to act, it is in the streets, the subways and the parks. These regions are governed by common property rules. Since these are the only places they are allowed to be, these are the only places they are free to act.

However, a person is not allowed to do just whatever he likes in a public place. There are at least three types of prohibition that one faces in a place governed by rules of common property.

(1) If there are any general prohibitions on types of action in a society, like the prohibition on murder or the prohibition on selling narcotics, then they apply to all tokens of those types performed anywhere, public or private. And these prohibitions apply to everyone: though it is only the homeless who have no choice but to be in public places, the law forbids the rich as well as the poor from selling narcotics, and a fortiori, from selling narcotics on the streets and in the parks.

(2) Typically, there are also prohibitions that are specific to public places and provide the basis of their commonality. Parks have curfews; streets and sidewalks have rules that govern the extent to which one person's use of these places may interfere with another's; there are rules about obstruction, jaywalking, and so on. Many of these rules can be characterized and justified as rules of fairness. If public places are to be available for everyone's use, then we must make sure that their use by some people does not preclude or obstruct their use by others.

(3) However, some of the rules that govern behavior in public places are more substantive than that: they concern particular forms of behavior that are not to be performed in public whether there is an issue of fairness involved or not. For example, many states and municipalities forbid the use of parks for making love. It is not that there is any general constraint on lovemaking as a type of action (though some states still have laws against fornication). Although sexual intercourse between a husband and wife is permitted and even encouraged by the law, it is usually forbidden in public places. The place for that sort of activity, we say, is the privacy of the home.

Other examples spring to mind. . . . [S]tates and municipalities are increasingly passing ordinances to prohibit sleeping in public places like streets and parks. The decision of the Transit Authority in New York to enforce prohibitions on sleeping in the subways attracted national attention [several years] ago. . . .

For a person who has no home, and has no expectation of being allowed into something like a private office building or a restaurant, prohibitions on things like sleeping that apply particularly to public places pose a special problem. For although there is no general prohibition on acts of these types, still they are effectively ruled out altogether for anyone who is homeless and who has no shelter to go to. The prohibition is comprehensive in effect because of the cumulation, in the case of the homeless, of a number of different bans, differently imposed. The rules of property prohibit the homeless person from doing any of these acts in private, since there is no private place that he has a right to be. And the rules governing public places prohibit him from doing any of these acts in public, since that is how we have decided to regulate the use of public places. So what is the result? Since private places and public places between them exhaust all the places that there are, there is nowhere that these actions may be performed by the homeless person. And since freedom to perform a concrete action requires freedom to perform it at some place, it follows that the homeless person does not have the freedom to perform them. If sleeping is prohibited in public places, then sleeping is comprehensively prohibited to the homeless. If urinating is prohibited in public places (and if there are no public lavatories) then the homeless are simply unfree to urinate. These are not altogether comfortable conclusions, and they are certainly not comfortable for those who have to live with them. . . .

V. FREEDOM AND IMPORTANT FREEDOMS

I have argued that a rule against performing an act in a public place amounts *in effect* to a *comprehensive* ban on that action so far as the homeless are concerned. If that argument is accepted, our next question should be: "How serious is this limitation on freedom?" . . .

On the whole, the actions specified by Bill of Rights are not what are at stake in the issue of homelessness. . . . They are significant in another way: they are actions basic to the sustenance of a decent or healthy life, in some cases basic to the sustenance of life itself. There may not seem anything particularly autonomous or self-assertive or civically republican or ethically ennobling about sleeping or cooking or urinating. You will not find them listed in any Charter. However, that does not mean it is a matter of slight concern when people are prohibited from performing such actions, a concern analogous to that aroused by a traffic regulation or the introduction of a commercial standard.

For one thing, the regular performance of such actions is a precondition for all other aspects of life and activity. It is a precondition for the sort of autonomous life that is celebrated and affirmed when Bills of Rights are proclaimed. I am not making the crude mistake of saying that if we value autonomy, we must value its preconditions in exactly the same way. But if we value autonomy we should regard the satisfaction of its preconditions as a matter of importance; otherwise, our values simply ring hollow so far as real people are concerned.

Moreover, though we say there is nothing particularly dignified about sleeping or urinating, there is certainly something deeply and inherently *un*dignified about being prevented from doing so. Every torturer knows this: to break the human spirit, focus the mind of the victim through petty restrictions pitilessly imposed on the banal necessities of human life. We should be ashamed that we have allowed our laws of public and private property to reduce a million or more citizens to something approaching this level of degradation.

Increasingly, in the way we organize common property, we have done all we can to prevent people from taking care of these elementary needs themselves, quietly, with dignity, as ordinary human beings. If someone needs to urinate, what he needs above all as a dignified person is the *freedom* to do so in privacy and relative independence of the arbitrary will of anyone else. . . .

VI.   HOMES AND OPPORTUNITIES

. . . Someone might object that I have so far said nothing at all about the fact that our society gives everyone the *opportunity* to acquire a home, and that we are all — the homeless and the housed — equal in *this* regard even if we are unequal in our actual ownership of real estate.

There is something to this objection, but not much. Certainly a society that denied a caste of persons the right (or judicial power) to own or lease property would be even worse than ours. The opportunity to acquire a home (even if it is just the juridical power) is surely worth having. But, to put it crudely, one cannot pee in an opportunity. Since the homeless, like us, are real people, they need some real place to be, not just the notional reflex of an Hohfeldian power. . . .

CONCLUSION

Perhaps the strongest argument for thinking about homelessness as an issue of freedom is that it forces us to see people in need as *agents*. Destitution is not necessarily passive; and public provision is not always a way of compounding passivity. By focusing on what we allow people to do to satisfy their own basic needs on their own initiative, and by scrutinizing the legal obstacles that we place in their way (the doors we lock, the ordinances we enforce, and the night-sticks we raise), we get a better sense that what we are dealing with here is not just "the problem of homelessness," but a million or more *persons* whose activity and dignity and freedom are at stake.

NOTES AND QUESTIONS

1. *Negative or Positive Freedom?* Most people who argue that homeless persons are unfree rely, implicitly if not explicitly, on a positive conception of freedom. Waldron's argument is different and more difficult to make. He argues that homelessness denies a person liberty in the classical, i.e., negative, sense of that term. One argument that might be made against his attempt to base the argument on the negative conception of liberty is that he assumes that the homeless have rights that they in fact do not have — either to trespass on private property or to abuse public property. Waldron's response is that this argument, which he terms the "moralization" of freedom, is question-begging in the sense that it "elides the notion of a restriction on freedom and an unjustified restriction on freedom." Waldron, *supra*, at 307. In thinking about this argument, particularly in connection with Waldron's discussion of opportunities, consider whether the argument is true of all homeless individuals. What about individuals who once had property and lost it because of choices they made? Does Waldron's analysis disregard their human agency?

2. *The "Geographies of Homelessness."* Waldron's analysis of homelessness focuses on space insofar as he is concerned with the absence of freedom of a *locus* to perform ordinary actions. Geographer Nicholas Blomley argues that Waldron is short-sighted. Nicholas Blomley, *Homelessness, Rights, and the Delusions of Property*, 30 URBAN GEOGRAPHY 577, 582 (2009). Blomley contends that although the "geographies of property" are important in Waldron's account, Waldron circumscribes them in ways that fail to take into account the full analytical and ethical significance of property to the homeless. The problem, from Blomley's perspective, involves the geographies of *private* property as well as public property. Thus, in today's global environment, cities compete for real estate investors, and this competition influences their planning and infrastructure decisions in ways that can directly affect the homeless. As an example, he cites a proposal to establish a "hygiene center" for the homeless in central Seattle. The planned center, which would have included showers, toilets, etc., ran afoul of a subsequent relocation of the Seattle Symphony, which became a catalyst for real estate investment. *Id.* at 545-585. Can you think of other ways in which the geographies of both private and public spaces can affect, indeed exacerbate, the problem of homelessness? How should society react to this insight?

3. *"Chronic Street Nuisances."* Robert Ellickson analyzes what he calls "chronic street nuisances" in cost-benefit terms, concluding that "a city's codes of conduct should be allowed to vary spatially — from street to street, from park to park, from sidewalk to sidewalk." Robert C. Ellickson, *Controlling Chronic Misconduct in City Spaces: Of Panhandlers, Skid Rows, and Public-Space Zoning*, 105 YALE L.J. 1165, 1171-1172 (1996). He defined "chronic street nuisances" to occur "when a person regularly behaves in a public space in a way that annoys — but no more than annoys — most others, and persists in doing so over a protracted period." *Id.* at 1169. The forms of urban conduct that Ellickson primarily had in mind were, as he called them, "protracted panhandling" and "bench squatting" — i.e., sleeping on public benches. *Ibid.* The result of Ellickson's analysis of these activities, in which homeless persons commonly participate, was that their costs greatly exceeded their benefits. Hence, in Ellickson's view, social welfare would be enhanced if courts permitted cities to create a system of zoning for public, especially urban land, just as they have done for private land.

Ellickson's proposal has attracted a number of critics. Waldron criticizes Ellickson's counting as a *cost* the offense and annoyance that panhandling and bench squatting causes other people. "Is this distress a *harm* to the citizen," Waldron asks, "something that in a utilitarian calculus should count *pro tanto* against his finding out about poverty and in favour of his being sheltered from this knowledge?" Waldron answers no, and he bases his answer on two arguments. The first, which he calls the "Appropriate Distress Argument," is based in J.S. Mill's argument that if we wish to progress as ethical agents, then it is important that we be confronted with ideas and lifestyles that challenge our comfortable presuppositions.

Waldron argues, "If the situation of some in society is distressing, then it is important that others be distressed by it; if the situation of some in society is discomforting, then it is important that others be discomforted." The second argument, first developed by Ronald Dworkin and called the "External Preference Argument," is this: "In cases where people feel vehemently about some matter of principle . . . it almost always misrepresents their view to say that the pleasure of vindication or the pain of offence are themselves grounds for the principle in question. From the point of view of the Principle's justification, these sorts of pains and pleasures are mere epiphenomena." So, Waldron suggests, a pedestrian's annoyance at repeatedly seeing homeless people sleeping on park benches does not count in and of itself as a cost of such street misconduct. Rather, it is simply the *effect* that the independent considerations regarding park-bench sleeping (e.g., effects on public health, tourism, etc.) have in the thinking of one who believes that these considerations warrant some sort of governmental action against park-bench sleeping. Eduardo M. Peñalver & Sonia K. Katyal, Property Outlaws 148-151 (2010). Is Waldron right that annoyance and irritation alone should not count as costs in a utilitarian calculation of the benefits and harms of "chronic street nuisances"? For another critique of Ellickson's argument, see Stephen R. Munzer, *Ellickson on "Chronic Misconduct" in Urban Spaces: Of Panhandlers, Bench Squatters, and Day Laborers*, 32 Harv. Civ. Rts.-Civ. Lib. L. Rev. 1 (1997).

4. *Squatters' Rights?* It is hardly uncommon around the world for those lacking legal housing accommodation to seek refuge from the streets by establishing residency on unoccupied land, publicly or privately owned, or in vacant buildings, often abandoned by private owners. Is it possible for such squatters to acquire some degree of legal protection against eviction, giving them, in effect, de facto property rights in their occupied spaces? Not surprisingly, the answer varies widely, not only across jurisdictions but also from context to context. In South Africa, for example, the Prevention of Illegal Eviction from and Unlawful Occupation of Land Act of 1998 fundamentally changed the apartheid-era policies and practices toward inhabitants of informal settlements. It decriminalized squatting and made eviction subject to a number of legal requirements that were designed to reverse the abuses of the old system. *See* Gregory S. Alexander, The Global Debate Over Constitutional Property 177-182 (2006). In the United States, responses to urban squatters have been mixed. Although many squatters are evicted, in some instances squatters of abandoned buildings whose titles came into the government's hands have been able to gain title. *See* Eduardo M. Peñalver & Sonia K. Katyal, *Property Outlaws*, 155 U. Pa. L. Rev. 1095, 1126-1128 (2007). For a careful discussion of squatters' legal positions under UK and EU jurisprudence, see Lorna Fox O'Mahony & Neil Cobb, *Taxonomies of Squatting: Unlawful Occupation in a New Legal Order*, 71 Mod. L. Rev. 878 (2008).

5. *A Right to Housing?* Should legal systems recognize a legal entitlement to housing? The national constitutions of some countries do

recognize positive welfare rights, including housing, but the United States is not one of them. In Lindsey v. Normet, 405 U.S. 56 (1972), the U.S. Supreme Court held that there is no right to housing in the U.S. Constitution. The Court stated, "[T]he Constitution does not provide judicial remedies for every social and economic ill. We are unable to perceive in that document any constitutional guarantee of access to dwellings of a particular quality." *Id.* at 74. Some state constitutions, however, do contain provisions recognizing positive rights. The New York State Constitution requires provision of welfare of those in need, but enforcement is subject to judicial discretion. N.Y. CONST. art. XVII, §1. Some New York cases have held that state statutes require the legislature to provide sufficient resources to permit families to live with their children rather than placing them in foster homes. Those provisions, however, are subject to legislative revision and discretion in determining how to meet those obligations. *See, e.g.,* Jiggetts v. Grinker, 553 N.E.2d 570 (N.Y. 1990); Morillo v. City of New York, 574 N.Y.S.2d 459 (Sup. Ct. 1991).

Some commentators, including Frank Michelman and Akhil Amar, have argued in favor of reading various provisions of the Bill of Rights of the U.S. Constitutions as guaranteeing basic welfare rights, including a right to housing. *See* Frank I. Michelman, *The Supreme Court, 1968 Term — Foreward: On Protecting the Poor Through the Fourteenth Amendment*, 83 HARV. L. REV. 7 (1969); Akhil R. Amar, *Forty Acres and a Mule: A Republican Theory of Minimal Entitlements*, 13 HARV. J.L. & PUB. POL'Y 37 (1990). *But see* Robert C. Ellickson, *The Untenable Case for an Unconditional Right to Shelter*, 15 Harv. J.L. & Pub. Pol'y 17 (1992). Curtis Berger proposed that "we guarantee to every American household a basic level of housing that meets current federal standards of quality and affordability." Curtis Berger, *Beyond Homelessness: An Entitlement to Housing*, 45 U. MIAMI L. REV. 315, 324 (1990-1991). His proposal envisioned legislative rather than constitutional provisions. It included several specific measures aimed at strengthening the supply of subsidized and low-cost housing and working with the private sector as well as the government.

South Africa's Constitution recognizes a right to housing, but qualifies that right in important ways. It states, in relevant part:

> 1. Everyone has the right to have access to adequate housing.
> 2. The state must take reasonable legislative and other measures, within its available resources, to achieve the progressive realisation of this right.

S. AFR. CONST. ch.2 §26. The leading case interpreting section 26 is Government of the Republic of South Africa v. Grootboom, 2001(1) SA 46 (CC) (SA). In *Grootboom*, the Constitutional Court held that the legislature's housing program violated section 26 because the program unreasonably failed to address the plight of 900 individuals, more than half of whom were children, in desperate need of legal housing after they were evicted from an illegal squatter settlement. Although the court interpreted section 26 as requiring the state to adopt a reasonable housing program that addresses both short- and long-term housing needs, it rejected the interpretation that section 26 imposes on the state a core obligation to supply a minimum essential level of housing. *Id.* at ¶¶ 30, 33, 43. This has made *Grootboom* a controversial decision. *See* ALEXANDER, THE GLOBAL DEBATE, *supra* Note 4, at 174-177.

3.   RESIDENTIAL COMMUNITIES

Evan McKenzie, Privatopia: Homeowner Associations and the Rise of Residential Private Government

CHAPTER 6 — HOMEOWNER ASSOCIATIONS AS PRIVATE GOVERNMENTS[1]

Like other corporations, homeowner associations have full legal rights, limited responsibility for the individuals who operate them, a potentially infinite lifespan, and a dedication to a narrow private purpose — in this case, protection of property values. In carrying out this purpose, home-owner associations function as private governments.

Private government is an idea with a long pedigree in political theory. References to private associations as governments within a government begin at least as early as the seventeenth century, when Thomas Hobbes wrote of private "systems" within the body politic — the commonwealth that are akin to the muscles of the body. Some of these systems, including those set up for business purposes, could bring about the disintegration of the commonwealth if there were too many of them or if they acquired too much power. "Another infirmity of a Common-wealth, is . . . the great number of Corporations; which are as it were many lesser Common-wealths in the bowels of a greater, like worms in the entrayles of a naturall man."[2]

In modern political science the same comparison of corporations to governments, in their internal workings, appears as early as the work of Arthur Bentley, who wrote in 1908 that "a corporation is government through and through."[3] . . .

---

1. EVAN MCKENZIE, PRIVATOPIA: HOMEOWNER ASSOCIATIONS AND THE RISE OF RESIDENTIAL PRIVATE GOVERN-MENT 122-123, 125-128, 140-142, 144-145, 146 (1994).

2. Thomas Hobbes, *Leviathan* (New York: J.M. Dent and Sons. 1976), 117-18.

3. Arthur F. Bentley, *The Process of Government: A Study of Social Pressures* (Bloomington, Ind.: Principia Press, 1908), 268.

More recently, John McDermott has argued that "the modern corporation is *the* central institution of contemporary society" and that the corporation has redefined the class structure and the meaning of property. "Liberal society," he argues, "is rapidly being supplanted by corporate society," with social classes now being based on position in the corporate hierarchy, and a new property system of "quasi-collective property" is emerging to replace the private property system.[4]

Of course, homeowner associations cannot rival corporations in financial resources. But many CIDs [common interest developments] are of comparable population, with tens or even hundreds of thousands of inhabitants. Residency in CIDs requires home buyers to become part of a corporation and live according to its rules, which reach into areas of people's lives that business corporations would leave alone. . . .

Homeowner Association Regimes

Although the precise names and legal descriptions vary slightly from state to state, there are four basic types of CIDs: condominiums, planned developments, stock cooperatives, and community apartments.

All four forms of ownership involve common ownership of common residential property coupled with individual use or ownership of a particular residential unit; mandatory membership of all property owners in an association that governs use of the commonly owned property and regulates the use of the individual unit; and a set of governing documents providing for the financing of the association, the procedures for its governance, and the rules that owners must follow with respect to common areas and individual areas. . . .

In a CID, everybody who buys a unit automatically becomes a member of the community association. So, although the decision to purchase may be voluntary, membership is mandatory. The association is founded on, and governed by, certain documents that are akin to a state's constitution and set of codes. Typically, these include some, or all, of the following: a set of covenants, conditions, and restrictions that run with the land and are legally binding on present and future owners of the property; articles of incorporation, if the association is incorporated; bylaws; and rules and regulations.

The CC&Rs are written by the developer and are normally only subject to modification by supermajority vote of all members, not just those who choose to vote. . . .

These documents are every bit as enforceable as the laws, charters, and constitutions of public governments, though new members often fail to

---

4. John McDermott, *Corporate Property: Class, Property, and Contemporary Capitalism* (Boulder, Colo.: Westview, 1991), 4–5.

recognize that fact. Taken together, they give a developer the power to create a distinct lifestyle in a development, which the developer can use as a powerful marketing tool. Moreover, they are the rules of the regime under which, ultimately, the residents will be living. . . .

Would Locke Have Lived in a Condominium?

One way to move toward understanding CID private government is to scrutinize it in the context of basic assumptions of liberal democracy. Government by homeowner associations departs in a number of ways from the liberal model but at the same time seems to carry some liberal assumptions to an extreme. . . .

First, the fact that only property owners are eligible to vote is reminiscent of Lockean principles. The CID concept is consistent with the notion that property ownership is at the heart of the social contract. Voting is based on a "one unit, one vote" principle, so owners of more than one unit have more than one vote. . . .

Second, it could be said that the CID corresponds in many respects to Nozick's "protective associations," libertarian utopias that are in some respects not far removed from Locke. Such associations, Nozick might say, are voluntarily entered into; have an explicitly defined relationship between association and individual; may be voluntarily left by selling; compete with each other for membership in the sense that owners can move from one to another; and offer due process rights but no substantive justice to members. Justice as fair procedures is consistent with Nozick's conception.

Third, it could be said that the ownership system that gives each owner an individual place to live, as well as shared ownership of the rest of the development, amounts to socialism by contract. Although there is no provision for redistribution of property on the basis of need, there is no initial inequality to correct, at least on the surface — everybody starts in relative equality, owning identical or similar units. This does not take into account the total economic picture of all residents but merely indicates that each has the basic necessity of a home, which implies the absence of poverty.

This socialism by contract analysis breaks down if a member can't make the mortgage payments, because there is no deeper commitment to social justice underlying the arrangement. There is no provision in CID documents for the association or other residents to help the family who is about to lose its home. . . .

Fourth, it could be said that CIDs have a communalistic, even cult-like, isolationist nature. They are deliberately cut off from the surrounding society and dedicated to living according to a specific set of rules. . . .

Residential isolation and the acceptance of seeming oppressive security measures (coupled with withdrawal from the work force, in the case of seniors) lends an eerie detachment to the atmosphere, not unlike what one might expect to encounter in a commune.

A children's book entitled *The Great Condominium Rebellion* describes the visit of a fictional thirteen-year-old girl and her brother to their grand-parents' condominium. The teenagers find themselves confronted with a bewildering array of behavioral restrictions that make adolescent life all but impossible and cause them to be the recipients of numerous disapproving stares and reproaches. To their horror, their grandparents fail to support them and instead accept the constraints as normal and necessary. In des-peration, the fictional teenagers write home, "Dear Mom and Dad: Who are these people living in Grandma and Grandpa's bodies? Love and tears, Stacy and Marc."[5]

Fifth, one could regard CIDs as the corporatization of the home. The vast majority of CIDs are incorporated, in most states as "mutual-benefit corporations," a status that gives them all the powers of a natural person. . . .

Another aspect of the corporate nature of CIDs is the increasing power of managers. . . . There is a pronounced tendency toward lack of involve-ment by the rank and file, who seem to turn things over to the board and management company. . . .

Once Upon a Time, There Was a Set of Rules

The CID, in a strange way, embodies bits and pieces of all these ideas—Lockean, libertarian, socialistic, . . . and corporatist. Rather than try to pigeonhole this new social and political entity, it is more important to examine it from the standpoint of its relative legitimacy and possible effects on the meaning of citizenship.

Some of the most troubling questions arise when we see CIDs as private governments and then attempt to find a legitimate basis for their rule. The classical liberal justifications used to legitimate American govern-ment tend to undermine, rather than support, this form of private govern-ment. CID regimes are inconsistent not only with political theories of legitimacy but with the normal process by which governments are created. . . .

The creators of CIDs—corporate developers and their lawyers—begin their projects on paper. They design the entire development on paper, including houses, streets, and recreational facilities, complete to the last detail. Using relatively standardized CC&Rs [covenants, conditions, and restrictions], articles of incorporation, and by-laws, they set up a sys-tem of government with a set of rules. . . .

This is a reversal of the Lockean belief that the right to own property arises in the state of nature, before the social contract is established, and is

5. Carol Snyder, *The Great Condominium Rebellion* (New York: Delacorte, 1981).

therefore largely outside the reach of government regulation, except for necessary taxation. The CID differs in other important respects from the classical liberal state-of-nature argument justifying government. . . .

In the theories of Hobbes and Locke we see the development of the distinction between private and public that, though often unclear, is with us today. The private sphere, for these theorists, is what we retain from the state of nature, and it remains ours by natural right. For Hobbes, the essential natural right is self-preservation. Locke adds to this the right to possess property. In the public sphere is the state, or government, along with the laws that regulate our behavior and are consistent with the ends of government — meaning, for Locke, that government would protect property rights and certainly not unduly interfere with them.

This order of events is turned on its head in the CID. At the outset there is nothing — a state of nature devoid of people except for the developer-creator, who begets the "community" and its social order to his liking and makes it unchangeable. After that is done, the people arrive at his invitation and are permitted to live there forever according to his rules, long after he has abandoned them to their own devices. This scenario is closer to Genesis than to Locke, resembling the early days of the Garden of Eden more than the Puritans' arrival in the New World. It also deviates significantly from the classical liberal justification for government.

In a variety of ways, CIDs elevate rules and legalisms above the social fabric of the subsociety. In essence, law, instead of serving the community, is elevated above it. There are three ways this priority of law over community manifests itself, all of which relate to what it means to be a citizen of these subsocieties, and these factors tend to undermine any claim to legitimacy under principles with which Americans are familiar:

1. There is a serious question regarding whether there is any meaningful consent to the rules of these subsocieties.
2. The concept of "rights" is replaced with the idea of "restrictions" as the guiding principle in the relationship of the individual to the community.
3. The concept of responsibility to the community is defined as nothing more than meeting one's economic obligations and conforming to the rules — all of which has the ultimate stated purpose of simply protecting property values.

The long-term effects of these departures from liberal assumptions may be significant. Students of politics have long recognized that people learn a great deal about the meaning of citizenship from day-to-day life in their communities. . . . The spread of common-interest housing means that different lessons are being learned and generations of children are "going to school" on the streets of a new kind of city.

NOTES AND QUESTIONS

1. *Solving Fragmentation Problems — Through Fragmentation.* Home-owner associations (or CIDs, as McKenzie also calls them) involve fragmentation of property rights or interests. CIDs involve land-use covenants that reciprocally bind all residents to forbear from certain activity (say, placing plastic pink flamingoes on the front lawn). As Lee Anne Fennell explains:

> The move of agreeing to such a reciprocal covenant effects a shift of property rights from the individual to the individual's neighbors, while delivering to the individual some of the property rights originally held by the neighbors. Even before the shift, some rights with respect to the use of an individual's land were already held by the community under background principles of nuisance law and, typically, zoning restrictions. As additional rights over the use of privately owned property are transferred from the individual to the community, the individual's rights over the use of her own property shrink accordingly. The compensation for this diminution comes in the form of additional rights over the property of others within the neighborhood. . . .
>
> Undoing the deal is obviously [difficult], at least in the absence of a governance structure capable of realigning rights without unanimous consent. Should [a home-owner] wish to recover an entitlement already alienated, such as the ability to display yard art, she must cobble the lost entitlement together by repurchasing the right to display yard art from each of the many community members to whom it was alienated. . . .
>
> Yet even as the covenant scheme in a private development creates a problem of fragmentation, it also solves another problem that could be similarly characterized as one of fragmentation, although it has not traditionally been thought of in those terms. When [a homeowner] disperses land use rights to her neighbors, she also collects rights over neighborhood aesthetics from each of them. That process of collection can be understood as bringing together in [the homeowner's] hands something that was previously fragmented among the neighbors — power to control certain aspects of neighborhood aesthetics.

Lee Anne Fennell, *Contracting Communities*, 2004 U. ILL. L. REV. 829, 844, 846-848 (2004). *See also* LEE ANNE FENNELL, THE UNBOUNDED HOME 75-80 (2009). For a comparative analysis that highlights the role of majority rule in solving such anticommons difficulties, see Emily Morris & Mark D. West, *The Tragedy of the Condominiums: Legal Responses to Collective Action Problems After the Kobe Earthquake*, 51 AM. J. COMP. L. 903 (2003). See also Note 10, *infra*.

2. *Homeowner Associations as Private Ordering?* McKenzie criticizes CIDs as inconsistent with classical liberal political theory in certain important respects. Do you agree with him? Defenders of CIDs have argued precisely the opposite. Robert Ellickson, for example, analyzed CIDs on the basis of an explicitly contractarian model. *See* Robert C. Ellickson, *Cities and Homeowners Associations*, 130 U. PA. L. REV. 1519 (1982). He argued that three features of homeowner associations make them contractarian:

> First, because a home purchase dwarfs a household's other expenditure decisions, households tend to shop carefully for housing units. Second, in some situations at

least, a market will work efficiently even for consumers who do *no* comparison shopping; a nonshopper can sometimes rationally decide to freeload on the shopping efforts of other households that have tastes similar to his. . . . Third, the contractarian model encourages individuals to improve their abilities to make decisions for themselves.

Id. at 1524-1525 n.24. Referring back to the discussion of Nozick in Chapter 3, are these factors sufficient to constitute CIDs as *contractarian* entities in Nozick's sense? Recalling our discussion of Locke in Chapter 1, are these factors sufficient to constitute CIDs as *Lockean* entities? Apart from Ellickson's factors, do the characteristics of CIDs as McKenzie describes them make them compatible with either Locke's or Nozick's versions of liberalism?

3.   *Contracts, Constitutions, . . . or Both?* While some scholars have analyzed CIDs in terms of contracts, others have done so in terms of constitutions. Uriel Reichman, for example, stated, "Although based on a mix of private law concepts of contract and property, [homeowner] associations are generally organized in a manner similar to the public law model of municipal government." Uriel Reichman, *Residential Private Governments: An Introductory Survey*, 43 U. Chi. L. Rev. 253, 253 (1976). On this view, the CC&Rs represent the CID's private constitution. What, if anything, does a model of CIDs as private residential governments, which we might call the private government model, add to the strictly contractarian perspective? Do you see any respects in which the private government model is deficient? One of the supposed similarities between residential private governments and public governments is that like its public counterpart, governance of the residential private government is conducted on the basis of democratic principles. Based on the excerpt from McKenzie's book, how democratic does the governance of CIDs appear to be? Based on your knowledge of the actual working of public government, at the federal, state, or local level, do CIDs appear to operate any more or less democratically than public governmental units? Various aspects of the private government model are analyzed and criticized in the essays included in Stephen E. Barton & Carol J. Silverman eds., Common Interest Communities: Private Governments and the Public Interest (1994).

Another commentator, Richard Epstein, analyzes CIDs from the perspective of *both* contract, or covenants, and constitutions. He writes, "Covenants and constitutions: strange bedfellows, but more than alliteration unites them." Richard A. Epstein, *Covenants and Covenants*, 73 Cornell L. Rev. 906, 906 (1988). He continues:

> The logic of contracting is the logic of unanimous consent. As the number of parties to a system of covenants becomes greater and the issues involved more complex, the polar differences between covenants and constitutions diminish.

Ibid. Epstein is surely right that the differences between the covenants in the CC&Rs of a CID and the terms of a constitution are not polar, but what about his claim regarding consent? Do you agree with him? Even if Epstein is correct that there is unanimous consent among the CID members regarding the original terms, what about subsequent amendments? Is it realistic to think that unanimous consent will prevail here too? Imagine a proposed amendment in a large, complex development with 50,000 owners. Are the differences between contracts and constitutions minimal or non-existent in this context?

4. *A "Norms-First" World?* McKenzie seems to suggest, particularly in the "Once Upon a Time" section of the excerpt, that one respect in which CIDs lack legitimacy is that within them law precedes norms. He seems to assume, that is, that the legitimacy of a social organization depends upon norms preceding law. Consider in this respect the points we raised earlier in the Notes in Chapter 11, especially Notes 3 and 6. Is McKenzie's analysis consistent with the points that were made there?

Aren't many of the problems with CIDs that McKenzie identifies also true of public land use controls? If so, is McKenzie relying on an idealized view of local governments?

5. *CIDs and Community.* Supporters of CIDs often tout the community benefits of living in CIDs. *See, e.g.,* http://www.caionline.org/info/readingroom-Pages/CommunityFirst.aspx. Some commentators have been skeptical about the community dimension of CID life, however. Two social scientists who have empirically studied CIDs observe:

> Since the writings of Jefferson and de Tocqueville, citizens of the United States have been extolled as [] natural joiners, working in voluntary associations to accomplish civic ends. It is misleading to consider the common interest development as another example of this. The CID highlights individual property interests rather than common purposes. The average owner does not participate and views the association as an expanded set of services purchased with the house. Disagreements typically are not over the best direction for the association as a whole but rather over what are perceived as individual private property rights.

Carol J. Silverman & Stephen E. Barton, *Community and Conflict in Common Interest Development, in* Common Interest Communities: Private Governments and the Public Interest 129, 140-141 (Stephen E. Barton & Carol J. Silverman eds., 1994). Another commentator has observed, "[A]s presently structured, CICs [common interest communities] — the promised land of connection and civility — are destined to disappoint." Paula A. Franzese, *Does It Take a Village? Privatization, Patterns of Restrictiveness and the Demise of Community,* 47 Vill. L. Rev. 553, 558 (2002). Franzese goes on to explain:

> [C]ommon interest communities, as presently configured, are hard-pressed to provide any genuine sense of community or connection. This fundamental default has allowed tension to mount and battles to escalate. . . .
>
> With increasing frequency, common interest community residents are balking at the restrictions to accompany association living. . . .

The trend toward litigation and state statutory intervention, coupled with erupting patterns of dissension, supports the premise that "something is rotten" in CIC-land. . . .

The problem in the common interest community setting . . . is that there are few incentives for residents to deal directly with each other. Instead, the system is set up to require dealings with a centralized medium — the board of directors or home-owners' association — who in turn enforce a formal code, in the form of the declaration of covenants, conditions and restrictions. At work is a rigid and abstract perception of what the community *should* be. This hinders the formation of real community.

Id. at 571-572, 573, 588 (footnotes omitted).

Are the criticisms of commentators like Franzese and Barton and Silverman based on idealized conceptions of community? Is it realistic to suppose that a 50,000-resident housing complex created by one developer could create the sense of community experienced by members of a small club who join for reasons of shared values and commitments and who meet and interact with each other on a regular basis? Even assuming that these criticisms accurately capture the experience of life in a CID, what conclusion follows from these critiques? Does it follow that CIDs are a failure and should be avoided?

6. *"Market Values."* McKenzie and other critics of CIDs have taken CIDs to task for their supposedly excessive focus on "market values." The notion of "market value" can be understood more benignly, however. As used by promoters of CIDs, it may be understood to refer not solely to economic values but to all the local goods that are bound to the home, goods that include safety, education, ambience, and other factors. *See generally* Fennell, *supra* Note 1, at 25-44.

7. *Social Obligations and CIDs.* In the last section of the excerpt, McKenzie criticizes CIDs for replacing "rights" with "restrictions" "as the guiding principle in the relationship of the individual to the community." Another way of looking at restrictions is as *social obligations* that the residents of CIDs owe to each other for their collective well-being as being the guiding principle underlying CIDs. Viewed this way, are CIDs so insidious? Consider the points that were raised in Chapter 9.2.

8. *CIDs, Exclusion, and Gated Communities.* Is community necessarily a positive social experience or moral value? Gregory Alexander argues, "One of the central dilemmas of community concerns the relationship between the group and the rest of society, . . . what I will call the paradox of exclusion. Communities by their very nature exclude." Gregory S. Alexander, *Dilemmas of Group Autonomy: Residential Associations and Community*, 75 Cornell L. Rev. 1, 52 (1989). Similarly, Jeremy Waldron writes, "'True community' in the sense of 'actually-existing community' — a real entity actually structured by a communitarian — is not always as nice as it looks. Actually-existing communities are often exclusionary and inauthentic . . . ." Jeremy Waldron, *Community and Property — For Those Who Have Neither,*

10 THEORETICAL INQ. L. 161, 188 (2009). Do you agree that communities are always, or at least usually, exclusionary? Is social exclusion always undesirable or harmful?

One type of CID that involves what some commentators consider a particularly objectionable form of exclusion is the gated community. Edward Blakely and Mary Gail Snyder, two social scientists who have studied gated communities, explain what they typically involve:

> Gated communities are residential areas with restricted access in which normally public spaces are privatized. They are security developments with designated perimeters, usually walls or fences, and controlled entrances that are intended to prevent penetration by nonresidents. They include new developments and older areas retrofitted with gates and fences, and they are found from the inner cities to the exurbs and from the richest neighborhoods to the poorest.

EDWARD BLAKELY & MARY GAIL SNYDER, FORTRESS AMERICA: GATED COMMUNITIES IN THE UNITED STATES 2 (1997). Blakely and Snyder go on to explain that one of the main motives behind the creation of all types of gated communities is fear of crime. *Id.* at 125. Indeed, they point out that "[m]uch of the growth in gated communities is created not by developers but by residents of existing neighborhoods who install gates and barricades in an attempt to defend their existing way of life. These are the security zone communities. . . ." *Id.* at 99. Residents of these neighborhoods commonly are poor or middle-class, and commentators have found them less objectionable than wealthy gated communities. If gating poor and middle-class neighborhoods for the purpose of keeping out crime is thought to be relatively unobjectionable, why is it objectionable when wealthy people do so?

9. *CIDs and Constitutional Rights.* Do/should fundamental constitutional rights apply to residents of CIDs? CIDs are private entities, and courts have generally held that provisions of state and federal constitutions do not apply to such private actors.[6] Nevertheless, several commentators have argued that the governing instruments of CIDs should be subject to a homeowner's bill of rights. Susan French, for example, states: "In drafting the constitution of private residential governments, developers should include a bill of rights to ensure future citizens of the community that the majority cannot unite to deprive them of the liberties they are not willing to sacrifice for the advantages of ownership in the community." Susan F. French, *The Constitution of a Private Residential Government Should*

---

6. In Community for a Better Twin Rivers v. Twin Rivers Homeowners' Assn, 929 A.2d 1060 (N.J. 2007), however, the New Jersey Supreme Court held that under some circumstances provisions of New Jersey's state constitution may apply when CIDs unreasonably restrict residents' free speech rights. Under New Jersey law, state action is not required for its constitutional rights to free speech and freedom of assembly to attach. For a discussion of the case, see Paula A. Franzese & Steven Siegel, *The* Twin Rivers *Case: Of Homeowners' Associations, Free Speech Rights, and Privatized Mini-Governments*, 5 RUTGERS J.L. & PUB. POL'Y 4 (2008).

Include a Bill of Rights, 27 WAKE FOREST L. REV. 345, 350 (1992). Among the provisions that French suggests for inclusion in this bill of rights are: *speech* (e.g., right to display political signs and symbols); *religion* (e.g., right to display religious signs, symbols, and decorations); and *pets* (unless pet-keeping is restricted at the time of sale of the first unit, no reasonable restriction on keeping pets is enforceable). *Id.* at 351-352. Do you agree with French? (It bears mention that French served as Reporter for the *Restatement (Third) of Property, Servitudes* (2000), a major project that substantially revised and reformed the law of covenants.) French suggests that developers include such provisions in the terms of their declarations of covenants with purchasers. Suppose that a developer does not do so. Should courts nevertheless impose such terms upon the parties as a matter of public policy, or should this be left to the parties themselves? If you believe that all residents in CIDs should be protected by such rights as a matter of public policy, then what about ordinary tenants? Should landlords be prohibited from, say, restricting tenants from displaying political signs in windows of their apartments? If not, how can you distinguish the two situations?

   10. *Optioning Entitlements.* CID covenants are usually enforced by injunctions. In the argot that was first introduced in a highly influential article by Guido Calabresi and Douglas Melamed, each resident's entitlement is protected by a "property rule," that is, cannot be taken from the owner except through voluntary transfer, rather than by a "liability rule," that is, can be taken from the owner upon payment of compensation (i.e., a forced sale). *See* Guido Calabresi & A. Douglas Melamed, *Property Rules, Liability Rules, and Inalienability: One View of the Cathedral,* 85 HARV. L. REV. 1089, 1090, 1092-1093 (1972). In the context of CIDs such a regime would lead to a great deal of rigidity, as holdouts could block any proposed changes regardless of how value-maximizing those changes would be for all other owners. As Lee Anne Fennell points out, the political apparatus of CIDs to some extent ameliorates the problem. The association's governing instruments usually allow changes to be made on the basis of less than unanimous consent, thereby avoiding the holdout problem. But, as Fennell notes, the price for this flexibility is that some homeowners may lose valuable entitlements without compensation. *See* FENNELL, *supra* Note 1, at 86.

   An alternative approach would be to substitute liability rules for property rules. That is, rather than banning the undesirable conduct (say, plastic pink flamingoes on front lawns), permit it but require the owner to pay the neighbors, through the CID, compensation for the costs suffered as a result of the conduct. But, as Fennell points out, there are problems with this approach, notably quantifying the damage inflicted on others. *Id.* at 87-88.

   Fennell has proposed an imaginative solution to the problem, one that involves tinkering with the bundle of rights in order to best serve the pertinent social values. She calls this tool an "entitlement subject to a self-made option." She explains:

> What is valuable about liability rules — their ability to side-step holdout behavior and other sources of high transaction costs — can be obtained without requiring one party to surrender all control over the terms of the transaction. The key to splitting up control over the transaction between the buyer and the seller lies in the use of self-assessed valuations to set transfer prices. . . . [T]he essential idea is to formulate self-executing penalties for both understatements and overstatements [of value]. . . .
>
> With such an information-forcing device in place, the seller . . . would have an incentive to name a value for her property that is close to its actual value to her. By doing so, she would effectively write an option for her property that the buyer could choose to exercise, or not. The seller's entitlement . . . would be protected neither by a traditional property rule nor by a traditional liability rule. Instead, it would be an "entitlement subject to a self-made option," or ESSMO. The ESSMO requires one party to package her subjective valuation in the form of an option, while allowing the other party to act unilaterally on that option. In this way, the ESSMO dodges the primary sources of inefficiency associated with property and ordinary liability rules — holdout problems and undercompensated transfers, respectively.

Id. at 104-105 (footnotes omitted). Fennell goes on to describe how the ESSMO device could be implemented in the context of CIDs.

> [W]e might . . . ask households to write options for the community, This approach would require homeowners in the first instance to undertake the work of specifying what they plan to do and placing a value on their right to do it. The community would then be given a choice between two alternatives: (1) allow the practice and collect a tax based on the valuation; and (2) stop the practice by paying the valuation. For example, suppose Hank wishes to spray herbicides on his front lawn every week. He could reveal the details of this lawn care regimen and state how much he valued the privilege of continuing with that preferred lawn care program for a particular temporal period, such as a season or a year. By doing so, he would effectively write an option that would permit a collective decision maker, such as a homeowners association, to buy back his lawn care privileges by paying the price set by Hank himself. In the meantime, he would be assessed a tax based on his own valuation.

Id. at 111-112. Fennell goes to explain that the owner (Hank) would receive a "customizable call option," a type of ESSMO, once he joined the CID and made his valuations. The call option would have two characteristics: First, it permits Hank to go forward with his lawn care program based on payment of the tax; second, it is reversible, or "callable." Hank can customize the callable feature in the sense that his own valuation would determine the strike price. Hence, the community would receive an option to call back Hank's lawn privileges upon payment of that price. *Id.* at 112.

Fennell claims that ESSMOs would respond to critiques such as McKenzie's by restoring a measure of autonomy to CIDs while simultaneously mitigating inefficiency and unfairness of restrictive covenant regimes. Are you persuaded that ESSMOs will have these effects?

Are there different or additional ways in which CIDs might experiment with entitlement forms so that CIDs live up to their normative promises?

4. HOUSING DISCRIMINATION

Abraham Bell & Gideon Parchomovsky, The Integration Game[1]

Several decades after *Brown v. Board of Education*[2] and the beginning of the civil rights movement, the legacy of racism and racial segregation remains a shameful mark on American society. Neither the invalidation of racially restrictive covenants in *Shelley v. Kraemer*,[3] nor the outlawing of private housing discrimination in the Fair Housing Act of 1968 have [*sic*] eradicated urban and suburban racial segregation. Recent studies show that urban America is only marginally less segregated today than it was in the 1960s and 1970s, during the height of racial rioting. Worse yet, other studies demonstrate that one's neighborhood largely determines one's achievements. Living in the wrong neighborhood often means a poor education, greater exposure to crime, fewer positive role models, and inadequate municipal services. Thus, the denial of housing opportunities on the basis of race inflicts additional harms on its victims beyond the already corrosive effect of racial discrimination. Paradoxically, still other studies show an increase in individual preferences of members of all ethnic groups for living in integrated communities. The incongruity of these two empirical findings — decreasing racial animus in the housing sphere and persistent racial segregation — has puzzled social scientists, legal scholars, and policymakers.

We argue that the solution to this puzzle lies in understanding the incentives that prompt individuals to take actions that strengthen racial segregation, even as these same individuals favor racial equality and integration. Traditional explanations of housing segregation have focused on the importance of the continuing pathology of racism. And indeed, we do not dispute that racism remains a persistent part of American life and plays a role in housing segregation. Yet, the traditional explanations fail to do justice to the complex web of motivations that make integration of the housing market such an elusive goal. In particular, they fail to take seriously the expressions of preference of most Americans for integration.

---

1. Abraham Bell & Gideon Parchomovsky, *The Integration Game*, 100 COLUM. L. REV. 1965, 1965-1970, 1972, 1973, 1974, 1989-1996, 2005-2008, 2009, 2011, 2014-2015 (2000).
   2. 347 U.S. 483 (1954).
   3. 334 U.S. 1 (1948).

We demonstrate the effects of these economic incentives by analyzing the case of dynamic resegregation, a primary obstacle to integration in recent decades. Dynamic resegregation is the commonly observed phenomenon of gradual departure of white homeowners from neighborhoods undergoing changes in racial composition. Scholars tend to attribute motives of racial animus to white homeowners fleeing from a neighborhood increasingly populated by racial minorities. But the true picture is much more complex.

Imagine a white homeowner in "Whiteacresville," a predominantly white, middle class neighborhood in a typically segregated American city. One day, she notices that an African-American family has moved into a house down the street. Several days later she observes several "for sale" signs in the neighborhood. She welcomes the opportunity, finally, to live in an integrated neighborhood, but several matters concern her. First, and most importantly, she has heard that other neighborhoods in the city that underwent racial change have not stabilized as integrated neighborhoods but, rather, have become resegregated minority neighborhoods. Second, in other neighborhoods where this resegregation has occurred, the value of real-estate dropped substantially and never recovered. She has been told that those who sold first received the best prices for their houses while those who waited received considerably lower prices. Third, in saying that she would prefer to live in an integrated neighborhood she means a neighborhood consisting of 80% whites and 20% blacks. The enjoyment she will derive from living in a neighborhood with a different racial composition is significantly lower. Finally, she suspects that her neighbors' preferences regarding the ideal mix for integration differ from hers.

That evening, she returns home to discuss her options with her spouse or partner. As long as the two of them believe that all the observations made earlier that day are correct, they will decide to sell their house immediately, unless their preference for integration—even as a member of a white minority in a majority black neighborhood—is sufficiently strong.

There are several things to note about this example. First, one may contribute to resegregation even though one places a positive value on living in an integrated neighborhood. Indeed, as in the example, even homeowners who harbor no racial animus may rationally decide to sell. Second, so long as one believes that an integrated neighborhood is not the expected outcome of the change in the neighborhood's racial composition, one's preference for an integrated neighborhood does not provide a sufficient motivation to stay. Third, even if it is possible for the neighborhood to become and remain integrated, one might nevertheless decide to sell in light of the failure to achieve the desired mix of integration, and the expected drop in one's house's market price. Thus, in the example, if she believes that the neighborhood will eventually stabilize with a white minority, she may still decide to sell. Fourth, the key presumption that underlies the homeowner's decision is the belief that irrespective of her decision, there will be rapid changes in the racial composition of her neighborhood that will lead to a neighborhood lacking the desired racial mix and to reductions in the value of her house. It makes no difference to the homeowner's decision to sell her house that the expected drop in housing values stems from racial animus or racial stereotyping. Although the stereotypes that lead to expectations of changes in housing prices may be unfounded, and, indeed, the expected price changes may never materialize, so long as these expectations are widespread, the homeowner will respect them in making her decision. Fifth, after minority group members — who are segregation's primary victims — the ones most likely to bear the cost of resegregation are those who value integration the most, that is, white integrationists who choose to stay despite the decrease in property value. While the segregated neighborhood satisfies the segregationist, it confounds the wishes of the integrationist, who never achieves her preferred living arrangement. . . .

. . . [T]he key to resolving the problem of residential segregation lies in mapping the complex interplay of homeowner motivations. We show that the housing market in many American cities displays the characteristics of three types of games: (1) the resegregation game (in which the dominant strategy of white homeowners is to sell as fast as possible); (2) the integration game (in which only some white homeowners depart and stable integration results); and (3) the assurance game (in which both selling and waiting are stable equilibria, but in which market signals of impending sales lead to mass exodus). Thus, to overcome the problem of dynamic resegregation it is necessary to alter the economic incentives presently operating in the housing market. In doing so it becomes possible to change the payoff matrix into one whose dominant strategy is staying in an integrated neighborhood, or to signal players in the assurance game that selling will not be the inevitable outcome. . . .

Hence, we propose the adoption of mechanisms in the housing market that neutralize the effects of panic and enhance social welfare. . . . [We] cannot submit that our proposed scheme will uproot racism completely. Yet, the game-theoretic perspective we develop offers two significant benefits over the existing situation. First, it is likely to reduce dramatically residential resegregation in the United States. Second, it leads to a separating equilibrium in which racially motivated homeowners will be forced to separate themselves from the rest of the public. By neutralizing the economic bias to resegregate, we make racially driven homeowners reveal their true colors and deal with the social consequences of their preferences. . . . This . . . will finally enable policymakers to combat effectively the racial roots of residential segregation [and] place the cost of dynamic resegregation on the parties who most strongly resent housing integration. . . .

[W]e present three different game models of the process of black entry, leading to three different outcomes. First, we present a model in which white reaction to black entry leads to a dominant strategy of resegregation as predicted by [Thomas] Schelling's basic model. Second, we present a model in which black entry leads to an assurance game, in which there is no dominant strategy, and, as a result, the neighborhood may become either integrated or resegregated. Finally, we present a third model in which white reaction leads to an intermediate separating equilibrium in which the neighborhood becomes stably integrated. This three-game model presents a far more accurate description of reality than does Schelling's single model in that it explains why some neighborhoods remain stably integrated, while others rush over the cliff of resegregation. Although our model is admittedly simplified, it represents the basic choice structure faced by homeowners in neighborhoods experiencing racial turnover: the choice between leaving and staying based upon one's expectation regarding her neighbors' choices. Furthermore, our model captures the central concerns of a homeowner in a potentially resegregating neighborhood: homeowners' preferences, the intensity of those preferences, and relative property values. . . .

All three of our models are designed around the same basic story. Extending Schelling's framework of analysis, we posit a neighborhood consisting of three houses, initially owned by three white homeowners — Alice, Beth, and Carol. As in Schelling's model, this simplified neighborhood allows us to examine the choices of a homeowner who looks only to her right and to her left — that is, to the two houses abutting her own. In our model, all three of the white homeowners favor integration (to varying degrees). One of the three white homeowners, Alice, sells her home to a black purchaser. This makes the racial composition of the neighborhood 33% black and 67% white. The remaining two white homeowners, Beth and Carol, must now choose whether to remain in the neighborhood or to sell their homes and leave. . . .

1. Resegregation Game. — In this first model, we presume that Beth prefers to live in a neighborhood that is 33% black, but that Carol prefers a neighborhood that is only 25% black (or any other percentage smaller than 33%). However, Beth's preferences are more [*sic?*] elastic than Carol's. That means that while Carol is mildly discomfited by each incremental divergence from her optimal integration preference, Beth's reaction is far more extreme.

Beth assigns a value of $100 to her continued residence in her home, so long as the current level of integration remains. Carol attaches less value to her continued residence in her current home, since her optimal level of integration has been exceeded. She assigns a value of $85 to remaining in her current home, and a higher value of $90 to relocating to a new predominantly white neighborhood. Beth assigns a value of only $70 to the option of relocating to a new predominantly white neighborhood, reflecting her more extremely gradated integration preferences. Finally, Beth assigns the even lower value of $60 to remaining in her home, should the neighborhood become 67% black. Should Beth leave while Carol remains, Carol would assign a higher value of $80 to living in a 67% black neighborhood, since her preferences are less gradated than Beth's.

The payoff matrix for this game is as follows:

Table 2: Resegregation Game

		Carol Stay	Carol Leave
Beth	Stay	100, 85	60, 90
	Leave	70, 80	70, 90

In this game, Beth has no dominant strategy. If Beth believes that Carol will leave, Beth will also choose to leave; if Beth believes that Carol will decide to stay, Beth will elect to stay. Carol, on the other hand, has a dominant strategy. No matter what Beth decides to do, Carol will decide to leave: Leaving guarantees Carol both the highest absolute payoff and the highest average payoff. Thus, the Nash equilibrium for this game is for both homeowners to sell their homes.[4] The result is the one predicted by Schelling: resegregation of the neighborhood.

2. Assurance Game: Segregation or Integration. — In this model, we assume that Beth and Carol now have the same preferences for integration at a level of 33% black. Both also have the same intensity in their preferences. Thus, both Beth and Carol assign a value of $100 to remaining in a 33% black neighborhood, but a value of only $60 to remaining in a 67% black neighborhood. Finally, both assign a value of $90 to moving to a different, predominantly white neighborhood.

The payoff matrix for this game is as follows:

Table 3: Assurance Game

		Carol Stay	Carol Leave
Beth	Stay	100, 100	60, 90
	Leave	90, 60	90, 90

In this game, there are two Nash equilibria: both players staying and both players leaving. For both Beth and Carol, then, the decision to stay or

4. This kind of game is known as the Boxed Pigs game. . . . This game differs from a classic prisoners' dilemma game in that only one of the players in this game has a dominant strategy. In a classic prisoners' dilemma game, both players have a dominant strategy.

leave is largely strategic. If Beth thinks that Carol is likely to leave, she too will decide to leave; if Carol thinks Beth will stay, Carol will stay as well. In this game, the outcome depends entirely on the parties' perception of the others' likely move. Thus, it is possible for either stable integration or resegregation to result. This game is known in the literature as an assurance game.[5]

3. *Weak Integration Game.*[6] — In the last model, we alter the assumptions of the previous game slightly. Beth is slightly less extreme in her opposition to living in a 67% black neighborhood and she assigns a value of $80 to this outcome. Otherwise the assumptions remain the same.

The payoff matrix for this game is as follows:

Table 4: Weak Integration Game

		Carol	
		Stay	Leave
Beth	Stay	100, 85	80, 90
	Leave	70, 80	70, 90

In this game, Carol retains her dominant strategy of leaving. However, due to the change in values, Beth now has a dominant strategy as well; irrespective of Carol's decision, Beth will decide to stay. This game thus has a dominant equilibrium outcome, meaning a single Nash equilibrium. Carol will leave and Beth will stay, meaning that the neighborhood will become stably integrated at 67% black.

4. *The Effect of Dropping Property Values.* — Finally, we must take note of the effect of changing property values on property owners' choices. Schelling's model predicts resegregation irrespective of changes in property values. In fact, Schelling's model omits reference to prices altogether. But, as we have seen, once prices are included in the model, resegregation is not the necessary result in the factual scenario predicted by Schelling. Consequently, changes in property values must be taken into account in predicting homeowner responses.

5. Assurance games are also known as Ranked Coordination games. Assurance games are characterized by a payoff structure in which (1) it is always better for the actors to make the same choice (A,A or B,B) than to make dissimilar choices (A,B or B,A); and (2) while both players would be better served by a certain choice (A,A over B,B), that choice is not the players' dominant strategy. While A,A is Pareto optimal, and therefore preferable to B,B, both A,A and B,B are Nash equilibria. . . .

6. We label this game the "weak" integration game in contrast with the later "strong" integration game in which the dominant strategy for both players is to stay.

We demonstrate here that while declines in property values do not change the outcomes of the resegregation and assurance games, they may change the outcome of the integration game. Specifically, declines in property values may transform the integration game into a resegregation game.

Returning to our hypothetical three-house neighborhood, let us presume that the utility of staying in the neighborhood drops by $10 for each 33% increase in black ownership. This drop reflects the decreased property values. For purposes of the game, we will assume that if both homeowners sell simultaneously, they split the loss for the next anticipated 33% change in racial makeup.

a. The Resegregation Game. — For the resegregation game, we use the same assumptions as in the previous resegregation game, and incorporate the expected property loss values.

Using these assumptions, the new payoff matrix becomes as follows:

Table 5: Resegregation Game, Modified to Reflect $10 Expected Loss in Property Value

		Carol	
		Stay	Leave
Beth	Stay	90, 75	40, 80
	Leave	60, 60	55, 75

The change in housing values does not change the players' strategies. Once again, Carol's dominant strategy is to leave, while Beth lacks a dominant strategy and would prefer to follow Carol. The result, once again, is resegregation.

Even if the change in values is more drastic, $30 rather than $10, the result is the same and neither player's strategy changes.

Table 6: Resegregation Game, Modified to Reflect $30 Expected Loss in Property Value

		Carol	
		Stay	Leave
Beth	Stay	70, 55	0, 60
	Leave	40, 20	40, 60

Indeed, we may generalize and say that in this game no reduction in value of any size can alter the players' strategy.

b. The Assurance Game.—In the assurance game, the playoff matrix becomes as follows:

Table 7: Assurance Game, Modified to Reflect $10 Expected Loss in Property Value

		Carol	
		Stay	Leave
Beth	Stay	90, 90	40, 80
	Leave	80, 40	75, 75

As in the case of the resegregation game, the change in values does not change the players' strategies. Neither Beth nor Carol has a dominant strategy, and, once again, there are two stable equilibria: for both to stay and for both to leave.

Also, as in the case of the resegregation game, even a more drastic reduction in property values fails to alter the underlying strategies.

Table 8: Assurance Game, Modified to Reflect $30 Expected Loss in Property Value

		Carol	
		Stay	Leave
Beth	Stay	70, 70	0, 60
	Leave	60, 0	45, 55

Indeed, as in the case of the resegregation game, no reduction in property values of any size can change the players' strategies.

c. The Weak Integration Game.—In the weak integration game, the playoff matrix changes to the following:

Table 9: Weak Integration Game, Modified to Reflect $10 Expected Loss in Property Value

		Carol	
		Stay	Leave
Beth	Stay	90, 75	60, 80
	Leave	60, 60	55, 75

Here, again, the players' strategies fail to change. Carol's dominant strategy is to leave, while Beth's is to stay, resulting in an equilibrium of stable integration.

However, if the drop in values is more drastic, the game will become like the resegregation game above, with an equilibrium result of both players leaving.

Table 10: Weak Integration Game, Modified to Reflect $30 Expected Loss in Property Value

		Carol	
		Stay	Leave
Beth	Stay	75, 55	20, 60
	Leave	40, 20	25, 45

Due to the reduction in property values, Beth now prefers to leave in the event that Carol leaves, so she no longer has a dominant strategy of staying. Carol's dominant strategy does not change; she will leave regardless. The game's equilibrium outcome, then, is for both players to leave.

Here, too, we may generalize the result. A small change in property values will not change the game's outcome, but a sufficiently large reduction in property values will change the game into a resegregation game.

The results of our analysis may be summarized as follows. First, black entry into predominantly white neighborhoods sets in motion a process that may lead to resegregation or to integration. The process may be mapped in three game-theoretic models—the resegregation game, the assurance game, and the weak integration game. Second, the particular game form that the process will take depends on white homeowners' integration preferences and their relative intensity, as well as changes in property values. Third, perceived declines in property values of sufficient magnitude drive white homeowners away from weak integration models, and accelerate the movement toward resegregation of racially changing neighborhoods. Fourth, and finally, perceptions (even inaccurate ones) are crucial in determining how white homeowners will respond to racial change. The likelihood that a white homeowner will abandon a racially changing neighborhood is dramatically enhanced by a perception that property values will decline or that one's white neighbors will leave the neighborhood. . . .

In [what follows] . . . we suggest the use of four major techniques: equity insurance, taxation of real-estate transactions, institutional subsidies, and growth controls, [which are aimed at eliminating] the panic accompanying black entry by neutralizing the economic incentive for whites to leave racially changing neighborhoods. . . .

A. *Equity Insurance*

Of the various techniques we present ... equity insurance is the only one that has been deliberately and systematically employed to counter white flight. A standard equity insurance scheme allows homeowners to purchase insurance against declines in the values of their homes. This insurance is intended to assure white homeowners that they will not suffer substantial losses from declining property values caused by changes in the racial makeup of their neighborhood. ...

Insufficient empirical evidence currently exists as to the effectiveness of home-equity insurance plans. In some neighborhoods, stable integration seems to have taken hold; in others, resegregation has not slowed significantly.

The mixed success record of equity insurance programs accords with our model's predictions. The standard home-equity insurance compensates homeowners for the decline in their homes' values to the extent that the decline is disproportionate to that which may be occurring in other neighborhoods that are not experiencing a significant change in racial composition. ... [O]ur model predicts that home-equity insurance programs will arrest resegregation only in two cases. First, insurance can effectively impede resegregation in neighborhoods in which most white homeowners would have elected integration but for the decline in real-estate prices. This is a case that was initially characterized by the payoff matrix of a weak integration game, but was transformed into a strong segregation game by a drop in real-estate value. By compensating homeowners for the reduction in property values, the insurance program reinstates the initial payoff matrix of the weak integration game. Second, insurance can prevent segregation in neighborhoods in which white homeowners are indifferent between leaving and staying — the underlying situation is an assurance game. In this case, insurance can signal to other homeowners an intention on the part of the insurance buyer to stay in the neighborhood.

Our model also predicts that home-equity insurance will fail to produce integration in the resegregation game that we outlined above. In that game ... only the prospect of a substantial gain associated with integration would transform the payoff matrix into that of an integration game. Existing insurance programs do not offer any such gain. Furthermore, insurance schemes will fail to produce integration if the underlying situation is one of an assurance game and other market signals drown out the signaling effect of the insurance program. The magnitude of the signal associated with insurance critically depends on the number of homeowners who decide to buy insurance. A strong enough signal will not be generated unless enough homeowners buy equity insurance. ...

For all these reasons, equity insurance is a less-than-ideal remedy to the problem of dynamic resegregation. It addresses only a limited subset of the choice structures that lead to resegregation and even in those cases it cannot be deemed a panacea. . . .

B. Taxes on Home Sales

A second way of adjusting the relative values of staying and leaving is the imposition of taxes on realty sales in neighborhoods with high turnover of real estate (a "sales tax"). In imposing this sales tax, policymakers should be cautious not to deter black entry altogether. Thus, we propose that the first 5% of the sales in every year should be tax-free and that all remaining transactions should be taxed substantially. The effect of this tax scheme would be to raise exit costs for all but the initial 5% of white homeowners who wished to sell. The combination of a tax-free set of transactions with a subsequent steep tax regime creates a mechanism akin to a "cooling-off" period. A neighborhood in which home sales have become "overheated" is placed in a tax regime designed to postpone most remaining sales to the subsequent year. . . .

. . . [T]he sales tax should be considered as one of the few means of introducing a time-related remedy to the distortions of choice that take place in situations of dynamic resegregation.

C. Institutional Subsidies

Our third proposed technique is less problematic and more far-reaching than equity insurance. We propose direct subsidization of community institutions in neighborhoods under threat of dynamic resegregation. Specifically, we propose creating a federal fund that will subsidize parks, schools, community centers, and basic infrastructure. The subsidies will be triggered by a certain level of turnover in realty ownership or by a certain level of neighborhood integration. . . .

. . . A less controversial way to trigger the subsidies would be to make them available any time a neighborhood experiences a turnover of a given percentage of its housing stock within a specified time period—for example, 20% within four years. As the subsidies would be available only after the requisite number of sales, one would hope that black entry into the neighborhood had already become sufficiently established to create an acceptable degree of integration. The magnitude of the subsidies should also be tailored to avoid creating too high an incentive for homeowners to stay in their homes. . . . [E]xaggeratedly large subsidies can deter even desirable transfers of control over the assets. Adjusting the subsidies to the proper level will therefore require continuous monitoring of neighborhood turnover.

Unlike equity insurance, the fund for subsidized community institutions is designed to disburse funds rather than merely to deter realty transactions. Consequently, a funding mechanism for the subsidies is of critical importance. . . .

D. Growth Control Measures

Our proposal to utilize growth controls to combat dynamic resegregation may seem, at first blush, counterintuitive. Growth controls on the local level are often attacked as exclusionary measures, designed to bar the entry of minorities and indigents into the community. . . . Nevertheless, we show that regional growth controls — as opposed to local growth controls — can have salutary effects on the housing market in periods of racial change. While growth controls may serve an exclusionary function when applied in small towns and individual suburbs, paradoxically, they can serve the opposite function when applied in large metropolitan areas.

The growth controls we propose do not seek to restrict the number of available residential units in the controlled area. Rather, they are intended to limit the development of new suburbs, thereby restricting the potential for resegregation. Admittedly, even our intended use will restrict housing supply at the margin. In contrast with traditional growth control, which aims to control the supply of all housing, our aim is to restrict the supply of segregated housing. Growth controls discourage resegregation by imposing the cost of undesired density on homeowners fleeing neighborhoods undergoing racial changes. . . .

NOTES AND QUESTIONS

1. *Schelling's Model.* Thomas Schelling's tipping model of housing segregation, which Bell and Parchomovsky critique, assumes that preferences among whites vary considerably with respect to their racial tolerance and their taste for racial integration. When the first African Americans move into a heavily Caucasian neighborhood, their presence "tips out" the least tolerant whites, leading them to leave for all-white neighborhoods, Schelling hypothesized. *See* THOMAS C. SCHELLING, MICROMOTIVES AND MACROBEHAVIOR 140-155 (1978). African Americans fill the resulting vacancies, leading more whites in turn to leave the neighborhood. In extreme cases the neighborhood becomes all-black, but in other cases the neighborhood ends up predominantly black with a minority white population. In any case, according to Schelling's analysis, the dynamic of black entry and white flight undermines the possibility of stable and sustainable integration.

Elsewhere in their article Bell and Parchomovsky identify three problems with Schelling's analysis. First, they argue, the preferences in Schelling's model are simple and absolute rather than complex and contextual. If a white homeowner prefers to live in a neighborhood that is up to

20 percent black, according to Schelling's model as soon as the percentage of black residents reaches 21 percent the homeowner will leave. In reality, Bell and Parchomovsky point out, the decision to leave is based on many other factors, including the cost of moving. *See* Bell & Parchomovsky, *supra*, at 1988.

The second flaw is that preferences in Schelling's model are isolated, meaning that white homeowners' choices whether to leave or stay in racially mixed neighborhoods are exogenous. But, Bell and Parchomovsky argue, a white homeowner's decision whether to move or stay is strategic, resting substantially on her prediction of her neighbors' behavior.

Third, Schelling treats preferences as given and immutable. Bell and Parchomovsky contend that this assumption is empirically unsupported. Preferences change over time in response to changes in external circumstances. Some people learn how to adapt to new circumstances, for example. The upshot of these flaws, Bell and Parchomovsky assert, is that resegregation is not as unavoidable as Schelling's model would lead one to believe. *Id.* at 1989.

2. *Changes in Housing Patterns and Preferences: An Apparent Paradox.* There is empirical evidence indicating that since 1970, black-white racial segregation has only modestly decreased in most U.S. metropolitan areas. *See* Douglas S. Massey & Nancy A. Denton, American Apartheid 222 (1993); David M. Cutler & Edward L. Glaeser, *The Rise and Decline of the American Ghetto*, 107 J. Pol. Econ. 455 (1999). Curiously, and somewhat incongruously, data indicate an increase in preferences for racial integration in housing. *See* Lawrence Bobo et al., *Changing Racial Attitudes Toward Racial Integration, in* Housing Desegregation and Federal Policy 152, 168 (John M. Goering ed., 1986); Gary Orfield, *The Movement for Housing Integration: Rationale and Nature of the Challenge, in id.* at 18, 27. What do you think explains these two findings? Does the analysis of Bell and Parchomovsky satisfactorily reconcile them? To what extent might racial disparities in income and wealth, which have steadily increased in America since the late twentieth century, contribute to persistent housing segregation?

Do Bell and Parchomovsky give sufficient weight to racism? Elsewhere in their article they acknowledge that racism remains "a persistent part of American life" and does play a role in housing segregation (*see* Bell & Parchomovsky, *supra*, at 1967), but they resist explanations of housing resegregation on that basis alone because such explanations, in their view, are inconsistent with the empirical findings of preferences for racial integration. Should those findings be substantially discounted on the ground that talk is cheap? For an argument to the contrary, see Daphna Lewinsohn-Zamir, *Consumer Preferences, Citizen Preferences, and the Provision of Public Goods*, 108 Yale L.J. 377, 391 (1998) ("talk is cheap" explanation is too simplistic and one-dimensional; insincerity may be part of the answer but people are also committed and responsible).

3.   *Residential Racial Segregation and the Construction of "Political Space."* Richard Ford explains the persistence of residential racial segregation, despite the elimination of legal racial segregation, on the basis of "political geography," which he defines as "the position and function of jurisdictional and quasi-jurisdictional boundaries." Richard T. Ford, *The Boundaries of Race: Political Geography in Legal Analysis,* 107 Harv. L. Rev. 1841, 1844 (1994). Specifically, Ford argues, local government law perpetuates historical patterns of racial segregation by granting suburbs, whose spatial definition often replicates racial and other sources of segregation, political autonomy to maintain homogeneity of class and, with it, race. Ford calls for moving away from "classic integrationism" in favor of "cultural desegregation." Concretely, this means removing those aspects of local government law that impose impediments to "fluid movement of persons and groups within and between political spaces." *Id.* at 1914. Residence, for example, should be eliminated "as a criterion for cultural-political affiliation." *Id.* at 1915 n.240. Granted that rapid mobility is an increasingly common feature of contemporary American life, has residence — space — disappeared as the basis for identity and affiliation? If so, what has replaced it? Even if the force of physical space has been diluted in this respect, does it necessarily imply that the autonomy of political subdivisions should likewise be diluted? What political entities might gain as a result of the suburbs' loss of political power? Would this be a politically healthy or unhealthy development?

4.   *Federal Housing Policy and Residential Racial Concentration.* In explaining the residential concentration of racial minorities, especially poor minorities, other scholars have focused on the federal government rather than local government. Michael Schill and Susan Wachter argue that throughout much of the twentieth century federal housing law and policy "have exhibited a locational bias that has promoted the growth of large concentrations of poor people in the inner city." Michael H. Schill & Susan M. Wachter, *The Spatial Bias of Federal Housing Law and Policy: Concentrated Poverty in Urban America,* 143 U. Pa. L. Rev. 1285, 1285 (1995). Specifically, Schill's and Wachter's findings suggest that the federal practice of concentrating public housing in inner-city neighborhoods is a main contributor to segregation along racial and class lines in urban America. They also find that federal mortgage assistance programs may have destabilized inner-city neighborhoods by redlining areas with high percentages of minority residents. *Id.* at 1308-1313. In light of findings such as these, what is your assessment of Bell and Parchomovsky's analysis? Do these findings suggest that they have missed the point?

5.   *Housing Discrimination Legislation and Its Effects.* Legislation enacted at all levels of government, federal, state, and local, seeks to prevent segregated housing and housing discrimination. The most important piece of such legislation is the federal Fair Housing Act, 42 U.S.C. §3601-3619, 3631, originally enacted in 1968 and amended several times since.

Although Schelling's model predicts that statutes such as the Fair Housing Act would have little to no impact, there is empirical evidence that it did in fact reduce somewhat discrimination against African Americans in housing. *See* Richard H. Sander, *Housing Segregation and Housing Integration: The Diverging Paths of Urban America*, 52 U. Miami L. Rev. 977 (1998). For more recent data, see Robert G. Schwemm, *Why Do Landlords Still Discriminate (and What Can Be Done About It)?*, 40 J. Marshall L. Rev. 463 (2007).

There is an additional reason, not mentioned in Schelling's analysis, why housing discrimination legislation has only limited impact. There is evidence that the agencies established to enforce anti-discrimination statutes are ineffective in carrying out their assigned tasks. When people of color file complaints to the agency responsible for enforcing anti-discrimination legislation, typically it takes several months, frequently more than a year, for the agency to resolve the matter. As Schill points out,

> Particularly with respect to housing, justice delayed may very well be justice denied. A person who brings a housing discrimination complaint to the [New York City Human Rights] Commission usually needs a place to live. Given the high transaction costs inherent in moving, when a remedy is not provided within weeks, it is likely that the complainant will no longer be interested in injunctive relief several months or, in some cases, years later. Furthermore, even in cases where the complainant has the ability to wait for a resolution, unless the Commission acts quickly, the landlord or seller, by renting the apartment or selling the house to someone else, may make it impossible for relief to be granted.

Michael H. Schill, *Local Enforcement of Laws Prohibiting Discrimination in Housing: The New York City Human Rights Commission*, 23 Fordham Urb. L.J. 991, 1023-1024 (1996).

6. *Racial Steering.* Explanations of housing segregation that point to racism often focus on the demand side of the market — white buyers looking at housing only in white-only neighborhoods. In contrast, Bell and Parchomovsky concentrate on the supply side. Another factor at work in housing segregation — racial steering — may be understood as affecting both the supply and the demand side. The term "racial steering" refers to the practice in which real estate brokers guide ("steer") prospective white buyers toward certain, i.e., white, neighborhoods and away from changing or primarily minority neighborhoods. It also includes the practice of failing to show black prospective buyers homes in heavily white neighborhoods. Steering affects the supply side by artificially limiting the range of homes made available to potential buyers. It affects the demand side by influencing the preferences of potential buyers.

The federal Fair Housing Act proscribes racial steering, but there is abundant evidence that real estate brokers have continued to engage in this practice. *See* Jan Ondrich et al., *Now You See It, Now You Don't: Why Do Real Estate Agents Withhold Available Houses from Black Customers?*, 85 Rev.

ECON. & STAT. 854 (2003); George Galster, *Racial Steering by Real Estate Agents: Mechanisms and Motives*, 19 REV. BLACK POL. ECON. 39 (1990).

7.   *LULUs and Residential Segregation.* Another aspect of racial discrimination in housing concerns the siting of locally undesirable land uses, commonly called LULUs. There is significant empirical evidence that LULUs are disproportionately located in neighborhoods predominately inhabited by people of color and the poor. *See* Vicki Been, *Locally Undesirable Land Uses in Minority Neighborhoods: Disproportionate Siting or Market Dynamics?*, 103 YALE L.J. 1383, 1392-1398 (1994). The cause(s) of this phenomenon, however, is not clear. Been's article shows that the data are unclear which came first—people of color and the poor or LULUs. She concludes that until more research about the origins of the problems is conducted, any solution will be premature.

17 *TRANSITIONS*

1. TAKINGS

Thomas W. Merrill, The Economics of Public Use[1]

The fifth amendment to the United States Constitution, as well as most state constitutions, provides that private property shall not be taken "for public use" unless just compensation is paid. American courts have long construed this to mean that some showing of "publicness" is a condition precedent to a legitimate exercise of the power of eminent domain. Thus, when a proposed condemnation of property lacks the appropriate public quality, the taking is deemed to be unconstitutional and can be enjoined. In practice, however, most observers today think the public use limitation is a dead letter. . . .

[Thus, in] *Hawaii Housing Authority v. Midkiff*[2] . . . the United States Supreme Court [considered] the constitutionality of the Hawaii Land Reform Act of 1967, which allows persons renting homes in development tracts of five or more acres to condemn their landlord's interest and thereby acquire an estate in fee simple. A unanimous Court, citing figures suggesting that land ownership in Hawaii is highly concentrated, sustained the Act as a constitutional means of "[r]egulating obligopoly and the evils associated with it," in particular the inability of renters to purchase homes at a "fair" price. Although declaring that courts play a role in enforcing the public use clause, and that a "purely private taking" would be unconstitutional, the Court nonetheless characterized the historical judicial posture as

1. Thomas W. Merrill, *The Economics of Public Use*, 72 CORNELL L. REV. 61, 61, 63-68, 74-78, 80-93 (1986).
2. 467 U.S. 229 (1984)

one of extreme deference: "where the exercise of the eminent domain power is rationally related to a conceivable public purpose, the Court has never held a compensated taking to be proscribed by the Public Use Clause."

[The cases] suggest several common themes. First, and most clearly, they suggest that modern courts will tolerate very wide-ranging uses of eminent domain. Legislatures may use eminent domain to promote the construction of a privately owned factory . . . ,[3] to force a favored tenant to remain in a government-owned facility . . . ,[4] or to engage in "land reform" *(Midkiff)*. Second, the cases suggest that modern courts are exceedingly deferential to legislative definitions of a permissible public use. Indeed, *Midkiff* hints that the public use analysis parallels the "minimum rationality" standard applied to equal protection and substantive due process challenges to economic legislation. Third, and perhaps most important, the cases suggest that courts have no theory or conceptual foundation from which meaningful standards for judicial review of public use issues might originate. Instead, the cases are filled with cliches regarding the "breadth" and "elasticity" of the "evolving" concept of public use, language indicating a dearth of theory — or perhaps a lack of any desire to develop one.

From an economic perspective, the extreme deference to legislative eminent domain decisions reflected in these cases is puzzling. After all, eminent domain entails coerced appropriation of private property by the state, and there is an important difference between coerced and consensual exchange. Consensual exchange is almost always beneficial to both parties in a transaction, while coerced exchange may or may not be, depending on whether the compensation is sufficient to make the coerced party indifferent to the loss. The distinction is equivalent to that drawn by Guido Calabresi and Douglas Melamed[5] between property rules, which allow an owner to protect a right or entitlement from an unconsented taking by securing injunctive relief, and liability rules, which afford protection only through an ex post award of damages. It seems peculiar that in the eminent domain area, which so often parallels private law doctrine, courts have effectively declared that liability rules alone shall protect all private property rights.

In . . . this article, I propose an explanation for the extreme judicial deference we see in public use cases. The underlying source of this deference, I suggest, is a historical focus on ends rather than means. Public use analysis has traditionally examined the ends of a government taking — the purpose or use to which property will be put once acquired. With the transition from the minimalist state to the activist state, however, courts have become increasingly uncomfortable defining the correct or "natural"

3. [Poletown Neighborhood Council v. City of Detroit, 304 N.W.2d 455 (Mich. 1981) — Eds.]
4. [City of Oakland v. Oakland Raiders, 646 P.2d 835 (Cal. 1982) — Eds.]
5. *See generally* Calabresi & Melamed, *Property Rules, Liability Rules, and Inalienability: One View of the Cathedral*, 85 Harv. L. Rev. 1089 (1972).

ends of government. Not surprisingly, therefore, courts have adopted a hands-off posture regarding questions of public use. In contrast, the property rule/liability rule distinction familiar to economists regards eminent domain as a *means* of achieving governmental ends. From this perspective, eminent domain offers just one of several possible means of acquiring resources, ranging from voluntary exchange at negotiated prices at one extreme to confiscation without compensation at the other. In this view, even if courts refuse to challenge legislative decisions about the ends to which property is put, they still might, and perhaps should, play some role in choosing the appropriate means to reach those ends.

. . . Drawing on economic analysis, I argue that eminent domain's purpose is to overcome barriers to voluntary exchange created when a seller of resources is in position to extract economic rents from a buyer. . . .

The two questions present sharply different inquiries. The ends questions asks what the government plans to do once the property is obtained. This inquiry, in turn, requires a clear conception of the legitimate functions or purposes of the state. May the state promote employment by subsidizing the construction of a privately owned factory? May it own a professional football team or undertake land reform? The answers to such questions demand an exercise in high political theory that most courts today are unwilling (or unable) to undertake. The means question, by contrast, is narrower. It asks where and how the government should get property, not what it may do with it. For example, the means approach accepts that a state may own a professional football team. It then asks: how should the state acquire the team? Must it purchase the team through voluntary negotiations? Or may the state coerce a transfer by condemning the team? Or may it simply commandeer the team under its police power? The means approach, of course, is also "political" in that it concerns state actions that will advance or retard conflicting interests. Nevertheless, the means approach demands a more narrowly focused and judicially manageable inquiry than the ends approach.

In deciding public use cases, courts nearly always pose the issue in terms of ends rather than in terms of means. Perhaps the constitutional language is responsible for this focus. The fifth amendment provides, "nor shall private property be taken *for public use,* without just compensation." This phrasing suggests that the government may exercise the power of eminent domain, but only if it puts the property acquired to a public use, that is, an end that is sufficiently "public" in nature. . . .

The distinction between ends and means . . . helps explain the emergence of language of extreme judicial deference in the last thirty years. Given that courts have understood the public use doctrine to refer to the ends of government, the question naturally arises: which institution is better suited to determine permissible ends — the courts or the legislature? In a society committed to majoritarian rule, not surprisingly the answer has been the legislature.

Here, as elsewhere, the crisis in democratic theory generated by judicial opposition to the New Deal provided the critical event. As late as 1930 the Supreme Court still clung to the position that legislative declarations of public use were subject to de novo judicial review. After a change in Court personnel produced a fundamental shift in judicial attitudes, however, the Court did an abrupt about-face and implied that the public use determination is exclusively for the legislature. This reversal ultimately produced Justice Douglas's formulation in *Berman v. Parker:* "Subject to specific constitutional limitations, when the legislature has spoken, the public interest has been declared in terms well-nigh conclusive."[6] As long as courts regard the public use doctrine as a limitation upon permissible government ends, this extreme rhetoric of deference to legislative judgments will no doubt persist. . . .

A. THE BASIC MODEL

The purpose of eminent domain is analogous to that of other liability rules, in that eminent domain applies where market exchange, if not impossible to achieve, is nevertheless subject to imperfections. To illustrate the point, consider the most common situation in which we see the exercise of eminent domain: a public or private project requiring the assembly of numerous parcels of land. Suppose, for example, that an oil refining company wants to construct an underground pipeline to transport crude oil from a producing field to a refinery several hundred miles away. Suppose further that only one feasible pipeline route exists. Without an exercise of eminent domain, the company must obtain an easement from each of hundreds of contiguous property owners. Each owner would have the power to hold out, should he choose to exercise it. If even a few owners held out, others might do the same. In this way, assembly of the needed parcels could become prohibitively expensive; in the end, the costs might well exceed the project's potential gains.

Some have described the above assembly problem in terms of monopoly-regulation. In the pipeline example, each owner is a monopolist, effectively dominating a resource needed to complete the project. Each owner can thereby engage in monopoly pricing, that is, can set his price well above the opportunity cost of the needed resource. The result: fewer oil pipelines will be constructed, and those few that are built will cost a higher than optimal price.

Alternatively, others have described the assembly problem in terms of transaction cost economics. Because each parcel owner has the power to hold out, each may be tempted to bargain strategically to appropriate some of the pipeline profit. On the other hand, the oil company — the sole buyer in the easement market — may also bargain strategically to appropriate

6. 348 U.S. 26, 32 (1954).

most of the pipeline's gains to itself. The problem thus is really one of bilateral monopoly. Such strategic bargaining in a bilateral monopoly situation increases the project's transaction costs, and if the transaction costs approach or exceed the project's gains, the pipeline may never be built.

In the final analysis, whether one describes the assembly problem in terms of antitrust economics or transaction cost economics does not matter. In either case, the underlying predicament is the same: market conditions allow the seller to seek economic rents, that is, to charge a price higher than the property's opportunity cost. The oil pipeline hypothetical illustrates the potential for rent seeking. The opportunity cost of any one landowner's interest is near zero. But when this interest combines with other similar interests to form a right of way for a pipeline, its potential value becomes considerable. The difference between these two sums — the property's negligible opportunity cost and its value as part of the pipeline project represents a potential economic rent to the seller.

Assembly projects, however, do not exhaust a seller's rent-seeking opportunities. For example, rent seeking can occur when a buyer wants access to land that he already owns, but which is surrounded by the seller's land. It can also arise when a buyer needs to expand an existing site by acquiring adjacent land; when the buyer will lose undepreciated improvements if he does not acquire certain property from the seller; or when the seller owns property uniquely suited for some undertaking by the buyer, such as promontory for a lighthouse or a narrows for a bridge. I will hereinafter refer to any situation where a seller can extract economic rents from a buyer as a "thin market." Conversely, I will call any situation where market conditions do not allow a seller to extract economic rents from a buyer a "thick market."

Whatever a thin market's source, its potential for engendering rent seeking may make it economically efficient to confer the power of eminent domain on a buyer. On the one hand, we know that eminent domain would transfer the resource to a higher-valued use, because its value in the new use exceeds its value in every existing possible use (its opportunity cost); otherwise the seller could not extract an economic rent. On the other hand, if this transaction were left to the market, monopoly pricing (or strategic bargaining) could lead to a suboptimal quantity of the resource being acquired, or could even prevent the transaction from taking place at all.

Before completing discussion of the basic model, however, we must consider another important factor. So far we have focused exclusively on what might broadly be termed the transaction costs of market exchange. But we must also consider the administrative costs of eminent domain, and compare these costs with the costs of market exchange in either thick or thin market settings.

There is reason to believe, at least in thick market settings, that eminent domain is more expensive than market exchange. First, and most important, legislatures must authorize the exercise of eminent domain. It is thus necessary to persuade a legislature to grant the power of eminent domain, or, if a general grant of the power already exists, to persuade officials to exercise it. Second, the due process clauses of the fifth and fourteenth amendments, as well as local statutes and rules, impose various procedural requirements upon the exercise of eminent domain. At a minimum, these include drafting and filing a formal judicial complaint and service of process on the owner. Third, nearly all jurisdictions require at least one professional appraisal of the condemned property, something generally not done (or not done as formally) in a private sale. Finally, both court-made and statutory law guarantee a person whose property is subject to condemnation some sort of hearing on the condemnation's legality and the amount of compensation due. . . .

Given what might collectively be called the "due process" costs of eminent domain — obtaining legislative authority, drafting and filing the complaint, serving process, securing a formal appraisal, the possibility of a trial and appeal, and so forth — it is safe to conclude that, in a thick market setting, eminent domain is a more expensive way of acquiring resources than market exchange. This conclusion has important implications for the basic model. In effect, it means that the decision whether to use eminent domain should be, from an economic perspective, self-regulating. In thick markets, where the model initially suggests that eminent domain is inappropriate, the acquiring party should in fact utilize market exchange because eminent domain would consume more resources. Conversely, in thin market settings, where the model suggests that it is appropriate to use eminent domain, the acquiring party should in fact use eminent domain, so long as the administrative costs are less than the costs of market exchange. . . .

If, as the basic model suggests, the decision to use the power of eminent domain is essentially self-regulating, this holds important implications for judicial review of public use issues. Most obviously, there would seem to be little point in courts second-guessing legislative and executive determinations of public use. Judicial review would add only uncertainty and expense. . . .

. . . Thus, the basic economic model reinforces the principle, enunciated in *Berman* and *Midkiff,* that courts should give virtually complete deference to legislative determinations of public use.

B. THE REFINED MODEL

Despite the basic model's appealing simplicity, with its thick market/thin market distinction and its modest conception of the judicial role, the model raises a number of troubling economic and noneconomic questions. To avoid unduly complicating the argument, I will discuss only the economic objections. . . .

... Each objection requires a partial modification of the basic model, and a corresponding refinement of the model's conception of the judicial role.

1. Uncompensated Subjective Losses

The basic model posits that eminent domain is designed to increase social wealth by facilitating certain transactions that otherwise would not take place, or that would take place only at an inefficiently high cost. Eminent domain, to use a familiar metaphor, is an instrument for increasing the size of the pie. But eminent domain also contains an implicit decisional rule for allocating the gains and losses associated with these forced transactions. This rule, manifested in eminent domain's compensation requirement, dictates that a condemnee is entitled to the fair market value of his property in its highest and best use *other than* the use proposed by the condemnor. In other words, the condemnee is entitled to an award equal to the opportunity cost of his contribution to the condemnor's project, no more and no less.

This opportunity cost compensation formula, however, fails to compensate the condemnee for all of his losses. The formula awards the condemnee what he would obtain in an arm's length transaction with a third party, but does not compensate him for the subjective "premium" he might attach to his property above its opportunity cost. In some cases, such as those involving undeveloped land, there may be no subjective premium. But in other cases, the premium may be quite large and may reflect several potential concerns: a condemnee may have a sentimental attachment to the property, or may have made improvements or modifications to accommodate his unique needs, or may simply wish to avoid the costs and inconvenience of relocation, other personal losses which do not "run" with the property, such as lost goodwill, consequential damages to other property, relocation costs, and attorney fees, are also not compensable.

This failure to compensate for subjective losses indicates that the basic model, which emphasizes the self-regulating character of eminent domain, may break down. If the subjective loss is large enough, the condemnee's loss may exceed the additional wealth generated when eminent domain is used to overcome barriers to exchange in thin markets. ...

One possible answer to the subjective loss problem is simply to construct a different compensation rule, one that approximates a Pareto-superior principle of full indemnification. However, although modifications in the current formula toward more complete indemnification may be possible, the indemnification principle can be taken only so far. A principle of full indemnification would pose difficult valuation problems, for subjective value is inherently difficult to measure. Furthermore, condemnees would have no incentive to limit their losses or economize on moving expenses, attorney fees, and the like. If these difficulties suggest that full indemnification is unrealistic, then we can no longer be confident that every exercise of eminent domain authorized by the basic model is in fact efficient.

The foregoing concerns counsel a qualification of the basic model's core conception of the judicial role. Specifically, they suggest that courts should closely scrutinize the decision to condemn whenever an owner's subjective losses are high. For example, courts might apply a cost-benefit analysis in these circumstances, upholding an exercise of eminent domain only if the taking's "surplus value," or the total value of the condemned resources to the condemnor net of compensation, exceeds the condemnee's uncompensated subjective loss. This approach, however, runs into all the difficulties of measurement and comparative institutional advantage associated with judicial cost-benefit analyses generally. More realistically, courts could simply scrutinize cases where subjective losses appear to be high to insure that these losses are not "excessive" relative to the project's probable surplus. In effect, courts would provide a condemnee faced with large subjective losses an additional "trump card," in the form of a higher probability that the project would be enjoined as failing the public use requirement. This additional leverage should induce the government to increase its settlement offer, thus offsetting, at least in part, the subjective losses.

2. Secondary Rent Seeking

A second objection to the opportunity cost compensation formula is that it encourages rent seeking by condemnors. Eminent domain almost always generates a surplus—a resource's value after condemnation is almost always higher than before. The present compensation formula allocates 100% of this surplus to the condemnor, and none to the condemnee. Commentators have questioned such a division on fairness grounds.

There are several conceivable justifications for awarding the entire surplus to the condemnor, rather than requiring restitution of all or part of the surplus to the condemnee. By giving the surplus to the condemnor, we provide an incentive to use eminent domain. In the case where the government directly undertakes public works projects that enjoy broad political support this additional incentive may be unnecessary, although a rule of restitution would put a higher price tag on government projects, and would probably reduce their number. In the case of profit-oriented entities, however, restitution could eliminate the use of eminent domain altogether. Profit-seeking condemnors would no longer be able to capture the added value from improvements brought about through condemnation. In effect, the surplus from eminent domain functions here much as profit does in the market. If we assume that in the long run citizens will be on both sides of eminent domain proceedings—either as condemnees or as taxpayers and ratepayers—then a rule that encourages value-maximizing exchanges through eminent domain may leave them better off than would a rule that provides for restitution or apportionment of the surplus.

In addition, a rule of restitution would require some method of measuring the surplus generated by an exercise of eminent domain. Gains from trade or surplus, like subjective values, are notoriously difficult to measure. Thus, under a rule of restitution, either the administrative costs of eminent domain would rise, or some arbitrary measurement rule would emerge that would almost certainly produce distorted incentives.

Finally, awarding all of the surplus to the condemnor is perhaps not as unfair as first appears. The surplus generated by a condemnation may be caused in a but-for sense by both the condemnor and the condemnee. But in most cases the condemnee is merely a passive participant, an involuntary supplier of capital. The active agent, the supplier of the idea and initiative, is the condemnor. The labor theory of property may be out of fashion, but as between a condemnor and a condemnee, the condemnor is typically more responsible for, and hence arguably deserving of, the surplus generated by the project.

Despite these justifications, there is legitimate reason for concern about allocating the condemnation's entire surplus to the condemnor. The present rule may produce a kind of secondary rent seeking of its own, as competing interest groups attempt to acquire or defeat a legislative grant of the power of eminent domain. In this way, eminent domain, an instrument designed to overcome rent-seeking behavior associated with thin markets, may inadvertently produce the very type of socially inefficient resource allocation it was designed to avoid. Indeed, in the extreme, the expenditures undertaken to obtain or defeat a grant of eminent domain could completely offset the expected surplus that would be generated by the use of eminent domain. . . .

. . . [O]ne must not overestimate the secondary rent-seeking problem. The incentive to capture the legislative process to secure the power of eminent domain is limited by the requirements that the condemnor award the condemnee compensation equal to the opportunity cost of his property and incur the due process costs associated with condemnation. For these reasons, eminent domain is considerably less attractive as a target for rent seeking than, for example, a government grant or a tax abatement, neither of which requires such offsetting expenditures. . . .

The danger of secondary rent seeking suggests that it may be appropriate to add a second qualification to the basic model. In cases where eminent domain is most likely to foster secondary rent-seeking behavior—where one or a small number of persons will capture a taking's surplus—courts should closely scrutinize a decision to confer the power of eminent domain. Cases involving delegation of eminent domain to one or a few private parties, or involving condemnation followed by retransfer of the property to one or a few private parties, present the primary situations where such secondary rent seeking is likely to occur.

3. *Market Bypass*

In addition to the foregoing limitations derived from eminent domain's compensation formula. . . . courts should at the very least closely scrutinize cases in which condemnors face thin markets as a result of their own intentional acts or negligence. . . .

C. THE EX ANTE/EX POST DILEMMA

The refined model suggests that heightened scrutiny is appropriate when one or more of three conditions is present: high subjective value, potential for secondary rent seeking, and intentional or negligent thick market bypass. But what does "heightened scrutiny" mean in this context? With respect to high subjective value, the model suggests a rough comparison of benefits and costs. Secondary rent seeking and market bypass, on the other hand, require a more complex analysis. In both cases, the objective is to discourage parties from engaging in secondary rent seeking or from intentionally or negligently bypassing exchange in thick markets — in short, to provide correct incentives for future behavior. But a rule that simply prohibits the use of eminent domain in these contexts would arguably sweep too broadly; it would sacrifice eminent domain's real value in overcoming barriers to exchange in thin markets. The quandary for a court, therefore, is to compare ex ante gains with ex post losses.

This quandary admits of no simple solution. Although in principle it would be possible to convert both ex ante gains and ex post losses into monetary values, in practice it is difficult to assign dollar values to ex post losses (surplus is hard to measure) and virtually impossible to compute ex ante gains (the deterrent effect of legal rules is hard to measure). A more practical solution might be to impose a pricing mechanism, analogous to the "due process tax" emphasized by the basic model, which would increase costs in those situations where we wish to discourage the use of eminent domain. Unlike a flat prohibition, imposition of a "surtax" would not altogether deny the use of eminent domain. It would simply make market exchange the medium of choice, and eminent domain a method of last resort. . . .

One might implement a surtax by adopting a limited version of the proposal . . . that would award condemnees 150% of fair market value in certain circumstances. Specifically, when one or more of the refined model's three suspect conditions is present — high subjective value, potential for secondary rent seeking, or market bypass — the condemnation could proceed only if the condemnor paid the condemnee 150% of the condemned property's opportunity cost. The bonus payment would have the effect of a surtax, discouraging the use of eminent domain in these three situations but not prohibiting it altogether.

There are, however, at least two problems with a surtax in the form of extra compensation. First, the bonus payment might not exactly measure the disutility from the exercise of eminent domain (lost subjective value and so on). In some cases it would undoubtedly provide the condemnee with a windfall, and could thus produce a kind of tertiary rent seeking; property owners might maneuver to get their property condemned in circumstances where they would receive bonus compensation.

Second, a judicially imposed bonus does not fit comfortably within a legal structure premised on constitutional rights. In particular, judicial enforcement of the public use requirement proceeds on an either/or basis: either a taking violates a condemnee's constitutional rights or it does not. In contrast, a pricing system entails no sharp differentiation between constitutional right and wrong, but implies instead that behavior ranges along a continuum, from less costly and more desirable to more costly and less desirable. The normative structure of constitutional adjudication seems to prohibit courts from declaring that the taking clause requires compensation equal to 100% of fair market value in some circumstances, and 150% of fair market value in others. In the hands of courts, the public use requirement is much cruder: courts either allow eminent domain because there is a public use or reject eminent domain because there is not a public use.

Because of the limited options available to courts in the adjudication of "rights" issues, the refined model does not predict a clearcut pattern of results as courts struggle to sort out ex ante costs and ex post gains. The refined model does, however, lead one to expect at least two patterns where one of the three limiting conditions is present. First, where the limiting conditions are present, one would expect a decline in the relative frequency of cases finding a valid public use. Second, where these conditions are present, one would expect to find a positive correlation between the public use decision and the size of the surplus generated by the condemnation. In particular, one would expect the relative frequency of holdings that a taking is for a public use to increase as the size of the surplus increases. . . .

NOTES AND QUESTIONS

1. Kelo *and Merrill's Theory.* In Kelo v. City of New London, 545 U.S. 469 (2005), a city approved an integrated development plan designed to revitalize its ailing economy. The plan called for construction of a waterfront hotel, restaurants, retail stores, residences, and office space, as well as marinas and support services. After the city purchased most of the property earmarked for the project from willing sellers, it initiated condemnation proceedings when the owners of the rest of the property refused to sell. Most parcels at issue were occupied by the owner or a family member; one petitioner lived in her condemned house her entire life. The U.S. Supreme

Court approved the condemnation in line with its "longstanding policy of deference to legislative judgments in this field." *Id.* at 480. This policy, the Court added, "has wisely eschewed rigid formulas and intrusive scrutiny in favor of affording legislatures broad latitude in determining what public needs justify the use of the takings power." *Id.* at 483. The Court acknowledged that the city's economic development plan may well benefit individual private parties, but sanctioned the plan nonetheless because this often happens when the government pursues a public purpose. The Court concluded that the plan "unquestionably serves a public purpose" given "the comprehensive character of the plan, the thorough deliberation that preceded its adoption," and the fact that the city believed that it "will provide appreciable benefits to the community, including—but by no means limited to—new jobs and increased tax revenue." *Id.* at 484-85. Does *Kelo* comply with Merrill's theory?

As Janice Nadler and Shari Seidman Diamond note, *Kelo* generated a "nearly uniform and extremely negative" public reaction: "a groundswell of popular outrage, a news frenzy, and immediate legislative reform." The experiments they conducted, aimed at exploring the causes underlying this reaction, indicate that "respondents reacting to the prospect of eminent domain are only moderately sensitive to the purpose of the public taking," whereas "the owner's relationship to the property exerted strong and consistent effects." Nadler and Diamond conclude that the latter factor was probably more responsible than the former to the post-*Kelo* public outrage, namely: that the *Kelo* backlash reflects "the power of the dignitary insult that a forced taking can engender by violating the homeowner's ability to exert control over this core personal possession." Janice Nadler & Shari Seidman Diamond, *Eminent Domain and the Psychology of Property Rights: Proposed Use, Subjective Attachment, and Taker Identity*, 4 J. Empirical L. Stud. 713, 714, 742-746 (2008). Can these findings be reconciled with Stephanie Stern's claims regarding the legal mythology of the home, discussed in Chapter 16.1? If not, which view do you find more persuasive?

2. *Land Assembly Districts.* Michael Heller and Rick Hills are unsatisfied with Merrill's discussion of secondary rent-seeking. On the one hand, it leaves them with an "uneasy impression that secondary rent-seeking could be ubiquitous enough to swallow Merrill's argument in favor of judicial deference to eminent domain." On the other hand, it forgets that landowners may be "politically effective," so that "[b]y giving them no incentive to promote a project, the market value measure of just compensation makes it likely that they will actively oppose it." Michael Heller & Roderick Hills, Jr., *Land Assembly Districts*, 121 Harv. L. Rev. 1465, 1482 (2008). Heller and Hills argue that in order to provide a satisfactory solution to the collective action problem inherent in land assembly cases (as opposed to the acquisition of sites impeded by target uniqueness), some institutional innovation is needed. They thus suggest creating a new form of special district: Land Assembly Districts (LAD). Such LADs will allow a

neighborhood's residents to collectively decide "by a majority vote, to approve or disapprove the sale of the neighborhood to a developer or municipality seeking to consolidate the land into a single parcel." This procedure will both solve the holdout problems and preserve the residents' *collective* veto power: "if the municipality or developer does not offer a price satisfactory to the LAD's constituents, then the assembly of land would not go forward." Such a mechanism gives "neighbors a chance to get a share of the land's assembly value," thus "enlist[ing] them to be supporters of land assembly whenever such an assembly really will have a higher value than the neighborhood that it will replace." And it does not harm the dissenters, because all residents can "have the right to opt out and receive the full, existing measure of constitutional protection (that is, condemnation based on fair market value) if they are dissatisfied with the bargain struck by the LAD." *Id.* at 1469-1470. LADs are an attractive idea, but given the possibility of heterogeneity among owners' valuations, it also might generate over- or under-assembly. Can you see why? *See* Daniel B. Kelly, *The Limitations of Majoritarian Land Assembly*, 122 HARV. L. REV. F. 7, 8-10 (2009) (discussing cases in which the median owner's valuation is lower or higher than the owners' average valuation).

3. *Just Compensation and Landowners' Subjective Value.* The conventional wisdom is that in eminent domain proceedings owners are systematically undercompensated because they receive only fair market value for their property rather than the owners' subjective value. *See, e.g.,* RICHARD A. EPSTEIN, TAKINGS: PRIVATE PROPERTY AND THE POWER OF EMINENT DOMAIN 183-184 (1985). Challenging this view, Nicole Stelle Garnett argues that the undercompensation problem is overstated. Takers have incentives to minimize the risk of undercompensation to avoid the negative publicity that often results when there are holdouts. Moreover, takers are usually legally required to provide substantial relocation assistance to displaced owners. Moreover, she points to evidence suggesting that takers often avoid taking property that has high subjective value. *See* Nicole Stelle Garnett, *The Neglected Political Economy of Eminent Domain*, 105 MICH. L. REV. 101 (2006).

4. *Regulatory Takings: Economic Accounts.* In addition to the law of eminent domain, takings law also covers regulatory takings, i.e., regulations that are deemed de facto takings and therefore valid only if accompanied by just compensation. The distinction between mere regulations and regulatory takings is one of the most difficult doctrinal questions in all of constitutional property jurisprudence and the subject of a vast scholarly literature. Consider first some of the insights offered by lawyer-economists regarding the incentive effects of different rules on the decisions of the pertinent actors and thus of their respective welfare consequences.

A conventional wisdom is that without a compensation requirement, public officials might suffer from a fiscal illusion as to the true social cost of government action. Compensation is required, on this view, to create a budgetary effect that forces governments to internalize the costs that their decisions impose on private resource holders. *See* Saul Levmore, *Takings, Torts, and Special Interests*, 77 VA. L. REV. 1333, 1344-1348 (1991). Turning from public officials to private individuals (landowners and potential land-owners), the case for compensation turns on isolating such risk-averse individuals from the risk that their land would be detrimentally affected by a public use in order to avoid suboptimal investment in land. *See* Lawrence Blume & Daniel L. Rubinfeld, *Compensation for Takings: An Economic Analysis*, 72 CALIF. L. REV. 569, 584-588, 593, 595 (1984).

Notice that both economic rationales for compensation rely on potentially controversial assumptions. The former assumes that democratic mechanisms make public officials accountable for budget management. *See* Daryl J. Levinson, *Making Government Pay: Markets, Politics, and the Allocation of Constitutional Costs*, 67 U. CHI. L. REV. 345 (2000). The latter rationale assumes that private insurance schemes are unlikely to effectively substitute for public compensation, and furthermore ignores the potential inefficiency of overinvestment in land that compensation may yield. See, respectively, Thomas W. Merrill, *Rent Seeking and the Compensation Principle*, 80 NW. U. L. REV. 1561, 1581-1582 (1987); Louis Kaplow, *An Economic Analysis of Legal Transitions*, 99 HARV. L. REV. 509, 528-532 (1986). Notice further that in both economic rationales the importance of awarding compensation is inversely correlated to the economic and political power of the landowner at hand. Can you see why? *See* HANOCH DAGAN, PROPERTY: VALUES AND INSTITUTIONS 90-95 (2011).

5. *Regulatory Takings: Other Perspectives.* The literature on regulatory takings law has obviously invoked not only the welfarist perspective mentioned above, but also many of the other property values discussed in Part I. Here we sample only three other seminal contributions.

Richard Epstein argued that compensation should be required every time the impact of a public action on the landowner is disproportionate to the burden (if any) carried by other beneficiaries of that public use. *See* RICHARD A. EPSTEIN, TAKINGS: PRIVATE PROPERTY AND THE POWER OF EMINENT DOMAIN 5, 204-209 (1985). Can you appreciate the implications of such a rule of strict proportionality in terms of the frequency of compensation award for land use regulations? How would you evaluate it in terms of liberty? And what would be its expected effects on social welfare, on our ideas of citizenship, and on distributive justice?

Frank Michelman claims that the answer to the question whether a regulation's redistributive effects should be canceled by compensation that spreads the loss among its beneficiaries requires a comparison between "the time, effort, and resources which would be required in order to reach [such] settlements" and the "demoralization costs" — in terms of impaired incentives, social unrest, and other forms of disutility — likely to be incurred by losers, their sympathizers, and other observers from the realization that no compensation is offered. In his attempt to ameliorate the practical difficulties of appraising demoralization costs, Michelman suggests that we resort to certain "supposed facts about human psychology and behavior." The key to demoralization, in his opinion, lies in the "risk of majoritarian exploitation," which—being "self-determining and purposive" and, therefore, systematic—is much more devastating "than the ever-present risk that accidents may happen." Frank I. Michelman, *Property, Utility, and Fairness: Comments on the Ethical Foundations of "Just Compensation" Law*, 80 HARV. L. REV. 1165, 1165, 1168-1169, 1214-1218 (1967). Do you agree with this account insofar as it aims to capture the pertinent utility costs and benefits? For example, do you think that systemic (and predictable?) harms indeed generate more disutility than randomized harm? Can Michelman's theory be read from the perspective of distributive justice, rather than utility? What are its lessons in this interpretation? *See* DAGAN, *supra* Note 4, at 98-101.

Joseph Sax distinguished between actions where the government is "enterpriser" and those where its role is "arbiter." In the first role government builds bridges and roads, operates airports, and the like. In the second role government decides disputes between private parties whose property uses conflict. In Sax's view, government should be compelled to pay compensation when it acquires property, directly or indirectly, to carry out entrepreneurial functions. But when acting in its second role government should not be under any compensation obligation, according to Sax. The purpose of drawing this distinction is to prevent arbitrary or unfair government action, which Sax views as the main purpose of the takings clause. *See* Joseph L. Sax, *Takings and the Police Power*, 74 YALE L.J. 36 (1964). Sax later refined his views, adopting the position that when government acts to control spillover effects, it should not be required to pay compensation. So, for example, government could, without paying compensation, prohibit mining near residential areas that would suffer drainage problems as a result of the mining. *See* Joseph L. Sax, *Private Property and Public Rights*, 81 YALE L.J. 149 (1971).

6. *Regulatory Takings: Historical Views*. Debates over the historical meaning of the Takings Clause and of the regulatory takings doctrine rage almost as furiously as those over normative questions. Among the more important contributions are the following: William M. Treanor, *The Original Understanding of the Takings Clause and the Political Process*, 95 COLUM. L. REV. 782 (1995) (original understanding of the Takings Clause was that it protects against government physical seizures of land but not regulations affecting value); John F. Hart, *Colonial Land Use Law and its Significance for Modern Takings Doctrine*, 109 HARV. L. REV. 1252 (1996) (colonial governments extensively regulated property for purposes other than preventing harm); Eric R. Claeys, *Takings, Regulations, and Natural Property Rights*, 88 CORNELL L. REV. 1549 (2003) (early nineteenth-century state cases used natural-rights theory to distinguish between proper regulations and "invasions" of property rights).

7. *Extra, Partial, and Varied Compensation.* Much of the existing literature on both eminent domain and regulatory takings assumes that whenever compensation is forthcoming it reflects only and all the fair market value of the claimant's loss. But there are some suggestions to open up the "black box" of compensation in order to better fine-tune takings law to its underlying normative commitments. Thus, for example, it has been suggested that whenever a community is uprooted a premium to compensate for its loss should be forthcoming. *See* Gideon Parchomovsky & Peter Siegelman, *Selling Mayberry: Communities and Individuals in Law and Economics*, 92 CAL. L. REV. 75 (2004) (describing how an entire Ohio town was voluntarily purchased from its residents, attributing the absence of holdouts to the way their sense of community unraveled as more residents agreed to sell). On the other hand, it has been noted that outside the American context, partial compensation is an alternative and a potentially desirable one as it provides a doctrinal space for reflecting the social dimension of the constitutional property right. *See* GREGORY S. ALEXANDER, THE GLOBAL DEBATE OVER CONSTITUTIONAL PROPERTY: LESSONS FOR AMERICAN TAKINGS JURISPRUDENCE 99, 235-243(2006). Finally, it has been noted that under the seemingly straightforward fair market value formula courts use rather diverse valuation mechanisms, which allow them to dissect the universe of takings and promote the proper goals of each subset. *See* Christopher Serkin, *The Meaning of Value: Assessing Just Compensation for Regulatory Takings*, 99 Nw. U. L. REV. 677 (2005).

Laura Underkuffler claims that takings law (both eminent domain and the regulatory takings doctrine) exhibits an even deeper differentiation. American property law, in her account, employs two different conceptions of property: one "protectionist" and the other "operative." The use of these competing conceptions is not chaotic or arbitrary; rather it can be explained by reference to the nature of rights, public interests, and the conflicts between them. More specifically, property rights are trumps — and should be trumps — whenever their core values differ from the core values of the competing public interests; the application of the power of eminent domain for a highway project is a classic example for this category. By contrast, when rights and competing public interests involve the same or similar core values, their conflict is — and should be — understood as internal to the right's definition, scope, and meaning. This, Underkuffler maintains, explains the deferential judicial stance in numerous cases of land-use control, zoning, environmental law, etc. *See* LAURA S. UNDERKUFFLER, THE IDEA OF PROPERTY: ITS MEANING AND POWER (2003). What are the efficiency and the distributive effects of such a broad deferential judicial stance? Can it be justified from the perspectives of the theories discussed in Notes 4 and 5?

8. *Judicial Takings.* Most of the takings jurisprudence deals with regulatory or legislative initiatives that harm landowners. In Stop the Beach Renourishment v. Florida Department of Environmental Protection,

130 S. Ct. 2592 (2010), a plurality of the U.S. Supreme Court held that the same rules may also apply in cases where "a court declares that what was once an established right of private property no longer exists." The crux of the plurality's reasoning for adding this category of judicial takings was that "[t]he Takings Clause bars *the State* from taking private property without paying for it, no matter which branch is the instrument of the taking." *Id.* at 2602. Indeed, from the landowner's perspective, the identity of the state actor seems irrelevant, doesn't it?

Is there any other reason to treat judges differently from legislators and regulators? For example, should courts be exempt from the takings protections because the judicial changes in the law are more objective, or less vulnerable to abuse, or because "subjecting the courts to the takings protections will prevent [them] from responding to societal and technological changes that call for shifts in property rights"? Barton H. Thompson, Jr., *Judicial Takings*, 76 Va. L. Rev. 1449, 1454 (1990). Thompson claims that these arguments are either "unconvincing" or "equally applicable to the legislative and executive branches of government." *Id.* Do you agree? Can you think of other possible reasons for differentiating the courts from these other branches? *See, e.g.,* Eduardo M. Peñalver & Lior Jacob Strahilevitz, *Judicial Takings or Due Process?*, 97 Cornell L. Rev. 305, 368 (2012) ("the nature of the adversarial process, and the pronounced underinvestment problem that can result from compulsory judicial takings insurance warrant significant restraint in identifying the proper scope of a judicial takings doctrine"); Laura S. Underkuffler, *Judicial Takings: A Medley of Misconceptions*, 61 Syracuse L. Rev. 203, 211 (2011) ("If a prior interpretation of the law by a court was later repudiated by that court, it is because the court believed that it was wrong; and it is theoretically impossible for a party to claim a protected right in a previously erroneous interpretation.").

2. ABORIGINAL LAND REGIMES AND COLONIALISM

Stuart Banner, Possessing the Pacific[1]

Conquest by Contract

In New Zealand, unlike in Australia, the British encountered an agricultural people, the Maori, with conspicuous rights to particular areas of land. And unlike in Australia, which was first settled by a well-armed government expedition, the earliest Britons in New Zealand were scattered

---

1. Stuart Banner, Possessing the Pacific 47-48, 49-51, 52, 53-54, 56, 57-58, 59, 60-61, 62-63, 68-71, 73, 75-76, 78-83, 84, 85,86, 87-88, 89, 91, 92, 93, 94-95, 96, 97, 98, 103, 125, 126-127 (2007).

individuals and private groups, who lacked the strength to seize land by force. By the time the British exercised sovereignty in 1840, white settlers had been purchasing land from the Maori for years. Practice turned into law upon colonization, as Britain formally recognized the Maori as owners of all the land in New Zealand, and the new colonial government began acquiring land through purchase. Over the next twenty years, much of New Zealand passed from Maori to British ownership, until by the late 1850s and early 1860s the Maori of the North Island succeeded in putting a near stop to land sales. At that point, the British were forced to change tactics.

Curious People

The earliest Europeans to reach New Zealand were astonished to discover that the Maori were farmers. . . . James Cook, whose 1769 visit was the second European encounter with New Zealand and the first since that of Abel Tasman over a century before, observed "a great deal of Cultivated lands."[2] . . . The Maoris did not just farm like the English; they also appeared to divide their farms much like the English. . . .

Such observations had strong implications for the colonizing venture the British assumed lay ahead. The Maori were evidently further along the path to civilization than some of the other peoples the British had encountered elsewhere. . . . Colonization promised to proceed more smoothly in New Zealand than it had in places with less advanced aboriginal populations. . . . But this same advancement simultaneously meant, on the other hand, that the process of acquiring land would not be as simple as it had been in Australia, where the absence of agriculture had implied the absence of any basis for recognizing any aboriginal rights to property in land. . . .

As both peoples would soon learn, the physical similarity of British and Maori agricultural methods masked some fundamental differences between British and Maori conceptions of property. The British tended to allocate property rights in land on a geographical basis. Land was divided into pieces, each piece was assigned to an owner, and the owner was ordinarily understood to command all the resources within that geographic space. . . . An owner of land was likewise understood to control the access of others. . . . These powers were understood to be unbounded in time. . . .

The reality of British landholding was often more complex than this ideal. A piece of land might be owned by several people at once. . . . Traces of old common rights had survived centuries of enclosure. . . . But these intrusions into the ideal of command over a geographic space were understood as just that — as exceptions to a rule, as overlays on a fundamental rule. . . .

---

2. J.C. Beaglehole, ed., *The Journals of Captain James Cook on His Voyages of Discovery* (Cambridge: Cambridge University Press, 1955-1974), 1:188, 183.

The Maori, by contrast, tended to allocate property rights among individuals and families on a functional rather than a geographical basis. That is, a person would not own a zone of space; one would instead own the right to use a particular resource in a particular way. One might possess the right to trap birds in a certain tree, or the right to fish in a certain spot in the water, or the right to cultivate certain plot of ground. Possession of such a right did not imply possession of other rights in the same geographic space. . . . Nor did possession of a use-right in one place preclude possession of use-rights in other places as well. A family might be understood to have the right to one place for sleeping, another for cultivating, another for catching eels, and others for various other activities. These rights were typically handed down from generation to generation within the family, so long as each new generation continued to use the right in question. . . .

Another fundamental difference between British and Maori conceptions of property involved the means used to remember the property rights already in existence. . . . The British had for centuries divided their land by written surveys and memorialized their land transactions in written agreements. The Maori, lacking writing, had developed a different method. Because property rights derived largely from one's ancestry, individuals trained themselves to remember their genealogy and the history of their kin group. The strategic use of landmarks, such as stones and marks in trees, served to aid the memory. . . .

The Maori system of property existed within political and economic contexts quite different from those to be found in Britain at the time, and these contexts had profound effects on the organization of property rights, effects that caused further divergence from British property arrangements.

The Maori were politically divided into *iwi*, or tribes, sets of interlocking kin groups with common genealogy and leadership. The *iwi* were composed of *hapu*, or subtribes, which were in turn made up of *whanau*, or extended families. The division into *hapu* and *whanau* was not clear-cut; because of intermarriage, the same individual might have ancestors from, and thus membership in, more than one. . . . Although individuals did not exert control over geographic space, *iwi* did, and *hapu* sometimes did as well, within the larger territory controlled by the *iwi*. Individual use-rights were located within this physical space. The tribal unit's relationship with its land accordingly corresponded more closely to the European conception of sovereignty than that of property ownership. It was the *iwi*, like the European state, that enforced the use-rights of individuals and families against encroachment from other tribe members, and that defended those use-rights against attack from other *iwi*. . . .

The precontact Maori economy provided very little occasion for the accumulation of personal wealth. There was no money, and few other durable goods, capable of being saved. . . . Land was . . . not understood as something that one might wish to sell. There existed little with which it could have been purchased, and had there been to exchange for it, the price at which land might have sold would have been extremely low. Any sale, moreover, would have had to have been within the tribal group that exercised control over the land. . . .

The British struggled for several decades to understand the Maori system of property rights. . . . Some of the difficulty can be attributed to simple prejudice, an unwillingness to accept the practices of savages as worthy of consideration. . . .

Much of the difficulty, however, stemmed from [the] circumstances for which the British cannot be as easily faulted. . . . [C]oming from a culture in which property rights were organized by geographic space, and observing many Maori exercising use-rights within the same zone of land, many colonists erroneously concluded that the land was held by all in common, and that property rights were therefore unknown. . . .

This view persisted in part because of its appeal to writers eager to contrast the equality associated with this supposedly Maori communism with the sharp wealth disparities to be found in nineteenth-century Britain. . . . But the view also persisted, ironically enough, because of the opposite sentiment. A world without property rights could also be understood as one in which "'might was right,' to all intents and purposes. . . . No right to land existed but in the pleasure of the most influential chief in the neighbourhood." . . .[3]

By the middle decades of the nineteenth century, however, as purchasing practices stabilized, colonists with a genuine interest in Maori practices seemed to have no trouble understanding Maori property in land. It was understood that although tribes controlled geographic spaces, individual property rights within those spaces were organized functionally rather than geographically. . . .

British perceptions of Maori property in land became crucial in the 1840s, when Britain assumed colonial authority over New Zealand and it became necessary to decide whether and to what extent the Crown should recognize Maori property rights. Three choices were in theory possible. Britain could, as in Australia, refuse to recognize any aboriginal property rights. It could, as in North America, recognize Maori rights in the whole of New Zealand. And third, between these two poles, it could recognize Maori ownership of the land the Maori were physically occupying when the British assumed sovereignty, but declare the rest of the land to be unowned.

The first possibility was precluded by prevailing British legal thought, which associated land ownership with cultivation. . . . New Zealand thus could not be treated like Australia, as terra nullius. . . .

The real choice accordingly lay between recognizing the Maori as owners of all of New Zealand or as owners only of the parts they were physically occupying at the time. On this question there was much division of opinion, both within the government and outside. The English text of the

---

3. *New Zealand Gazette*, 4 Oct. 1843, 2.

1840 Treaty of Waitangi, the document formally ceding sovereignty over New Zealand to Britain, was ambiguous on this point. . . .

In the end, the government chose to recognize Maori property rights in the entirety of New Zealand . . . in part because of the fear that any other course would involve Britain in a costly war against the Maori. . . .

Very Anxious to Sell

The recognition of Maori property rights meant that in the absence of war the British could acquire land only by purchase. Until 1865, land was purchased from tribes rather than from the Maori as individuals. The British were interested in acquiring geographic spaces, not individual rights to use particular resources, so they necessarily had to deal with the tribe as a whole, the only political unit with the authority to take action with respect to an entire zone of land. Before British assumption of sovereignty in 1840 . . . , the purchasers were individuals and private companies; afterward, the sole legal purchaser was the Crown. . . .

In the early years, the Maori were "very anxious to sell" their land, John Flatt reported. . . . This willingness arose because the Maori had so "much more than they seem to require for themselves," one 1821 observer concluded. In 1844-45, when the government briefly waived is right of preemption and allowed private purchasing, people came streaming into Auckland "in great numbers to hawk their lands for sale up and down the streets."[4]

The Maori, all agreed, seemed to welcome British colonists. . . .

British settlement was valued primarily as a means of engaging with the market economy the British brought; land sales earned European products or the means of acquiring them. Anglo-Maori trade had its darker side. The introduction of European weapons in the early nineteenth century created, in effect, an arms race, in which tribes hastened to acquire guns in order to defend themselves against other tribes who were making the same acquisitions. This would not be the last time that the fragmented and competitive nature of Maori political authority would produce insurmountable barriers to collective action. Even the more peaceful forms of trade could be viewed as an insidious fostering of dependence. . . .

But trade had its positive aspects as well. The early encounters between Maori and Europeans were an economist's dream: on one side was a group with an abundance of land and some agricultural products but few other assets, on the other was a group with surplus manufactured goods eager to obtain land. That there were enormous gains to be had from trade was evident to all. The Maori generally welcomed European products, technology, and agricultural methods. . . . [T]he Maori's dominant

---

4. BPPNZ [*British Parliamentary Papers: Colonies: New Zealand* (Shannon: Irish University Press, 1968-1970)], 1 Lords 48, 2:108; [George Augustus] Selwyn and [William] Martin, *England and the New Zealanders* [Auckland: College Press, 1847)], 53.

asset was land. Without selling land, participation in the new market economy would in most circumstances have been impossible.

Two aspects of the new colonial political order also had the effect of promoting land sales in the 1840s and 1850s. The colonial government conspicuously desired to purchase land, which may have made tribes, nervous that the government would favor sellers over nonsellers, quicker to offer land for sale. . . .

Early willingness to sell land also stemmed in large part from cultural misunderstandings as to the import of the transaction. The earliest European traders were, of necessity, bilingual. Without the presence of many other Europeans, traders learned the Maori language, married Maori women, and were effectively accepted as members of a tribe. The "sale" of land, in this context, was a way of bringing an outsider into the community, with the same privileges and responsibilities as other members. . . .

As the pace of settlement increased in the 1840s, and the British began living in communities of their own rather than among the Maori, they began more and more to interpret transactions within their own categories instead. They often believed themselves to have acquired the right to use every resource within a geographic space. This divergence in understanding caused each side to look upon the other's conduct as at variance with the agreement. . . . The mixture of two inconsistent systems of property rights produced mistrust on both sides. . . .

The date at which the Maori realized what the British meant by a sale most likely varied from place to place, as different tribes experienced purchases and their aftereffects at different times. By the 1860s at the latest, the British meaning of a land sale appears to have been understood throughout the colony. The Maori still owned a large majority of the North Island. . . .

[A]ll the[] circumstances — misunderstandings as to the meaning of a sale, Maori inexperience in selling land, Maori inability to predict the future course of prices — would have been much less important had the colonial government not been the sole legal land purchaser for all but one of the years 1840-1865. In a perfect market, where would-be land purchasers competed with one another to buy land, Maori beliefs as to the meaning of a sale would not have affected the price the Maoris received for the land. The purchasers would have bid up the prices to the level they would have been had the Maori possessed complete information as to the intentions of the British. . . .

No market is perfect, of course, and the high costs of transportation and communication probably made colonial land markets less perfect than most. Nevertheless, it seems likely that the government was able to exploit its informational advantage to a far greater extent than it could have in a competitive market. If an offer to buy land was misinterpreted as an offer to share use-rights, a low price might not seem as low as it really was, and there were no other purchasers legally entitled to offer a higher one. If the Maori wrongly believed that land prices would remain stable, they might accept an inadvisably low price, without the chance of being rescued by another prospective purchaser offering a better one. A competitive market is a powerful corrective for ignorance. . . . When there is only one lawful purchaser, on the other hand, a seller will pay very dearly for ignorance, as the purchaser can squeeze out the full disparity between what the asset is really worth and what the seller thinks it is worth. Between 1840 and 1865, that is in large measure what happened to the Maori. . . .

Preemption was possible only because the British were politically organized into a single unit capable of enforcing its monopoly over land. Had the Maori been able, they could have fought back with the same weapon, by forming a single organization to control the sale of land, and then either setting the price of land higher than that offered by the government or refusing to sell at all. Before the 1850s the Maori were simply too divided to organize in this way. Ancient tribal division could not be erased in a few years. Preemption demonstrated the importance of political organization in structuring the marketplace. Two peoples converged, and the well organized was able to take wealth from the poorly organized.

Make Fast the Land

Maori political fragmentation often caused difficulties for the colonial purchasing program, by adding to the costs of completing transactions. Government purchasers sometimes found themselves negotiating simultaneously with more than one tribe, each of which claimed the land the government sought to acquire. . . .

The situation grew even more acute from the British perspective in the 1850s, when the Maori were able to exploit these transaction costs in an effort to prevent future land sales. Individual Maori who opposed particular land sales had long tried various ad hoc ways of disrupting them. Small groups sometimes sabotaged surveys, by pulling out pegs or using force to prevent surveyors from entering an area. . . . Beginning in the late 1840s, however, these efforts grew larger and better organized, as more and more Maori came to perceive that land sales generally were contrary to their long-term collective interest. . . .

By the mid-1850s, the tribes inhabiting much of the North Island had succeeded in organizing so as to prevent further land sales. A Board of Inquiry examining land-purchasing practices reported in 1856 on the formation of "a league," the members of which "refuse to sell their lands. . . . This league embraces nearly the whole of the interior of the island, and extends from the east coast to the west coast." . . . The King movement, as the organization soon became known, was formally headed by a king, but the king lacked much true governmental authority, which remained with the tribes. He was instead largely a formal device for mutually agreeing not to sell land; each tribe would place its land under the king's authority, which gave the king the right to forbid sales. . . .

Agreements not to sell are usually very difficult to enforce, because of the opportunities for profit available to defectors. . . . The King movement succeeded in restricting sales in part because of the government's power of preemption. Unlike most sellers, Maori land sellers faced a single purchaser. A restriction on the supply of land would not cause the price of land to go up unless the government was willing to pay the higher price. Because the government would not pay a higher price, would-be defectors were not tempted by the prospect of land prices higher than normal. Without this incentive to cheat, there was little cheating.

The King movement also succeeded in restricting sales because the Maori were able to exploit the high transaction costs associated with purchasing land from the tribes. A rough tribal consensus was required to sell land, which meant that any sizeable contingent opposing a sale, even one short of a majority, would be able to block it. Once a contingent of that size sympathized with the King movement, *all* future sales would effectively be blocked. . . .

Resistance to land sales succeeded just as increased emigration was causing the British to anticipate a large rise in the demand for land. Government officials felt strong public pressure to ensure an adequate supply of land. They were accordingly alarmed by Maori efforts to restrict sales. . . .

. . . Under this pressure, government land purchasers cracked. In the 1850s they increasingly began to cut corners. The government began to receive more and more complaints that its land purchasers had not obtained the consent of an entire tribe or even a majority of the owners within a geographic space, but had negotiated quick, secret agreements with a secret faction willing to sell. . . .

By the early 1860s, conflict over ostensible land purchases from a mere handful of owners had erupted into full-scale war against the King movement. . . . At the war's end, the colonial government would accordingly devote considerable attention to transforming its method of purchasing Maori land. If purchases could no longer be made from tribes, perhaps they could be made from individuals.

Conquest by Land Tenure Reform

Long before the British encountered difficulty in purchasing land from tribes, the idea of reforming the Maori property system had been circulating among the settlers and the British humanitarians. Most perceived the British method of assigning property rights in land, in which rights were organized by geographic space and embodied in written records, to be a great advance over an unwritten system organized by use-rights. . . .

As the North Island tribes began refusing to sell in the 1850s, colonial officials, facing strong public pressure to acquire more land, started casting about for alternative methods of purchase. . . .

So the prospect of converting the Maori into the British system of property rights in land moved to the center of settler consciousness in the late 1850s and early 1860s, as a means of piercing Maori resistance to land sales. The project was often referred to as "individualizing title," a name that accurately enough conveyed the anticipated end result — individual Maori ownership of plots of land — but was misleading as applied to the process as a whole. . . .

The perceived need to break down Maori refusal to sell land was the catalyst that caused the colonial government to consider seriously the possibility of transforming the Maori system of property rights, but once the issue was on the public agenda it provoked an outpouring of a host of other British attitudes toward land ownership. These attitudes further strengthened the support for converting Maori property rights into British ones. All were longer term in nature; that is, they did not spring from the immediate situation with respect to land sales.

Civilization and Barbarism

Many colonists had an insight that would come readily to many today — that the Maori system of property rights was less efficient than the British system, in the sense that land could be more productive if divided spatially, because of the incentives provided by the ownership of geographic space. . . .

A second kind of productivity argument was also frequently made in support of transforming Maori land ownership. If any single proposition could have commanded near unanimity among the settlers, it was that, as the *Taranaki Herald* put it, "the want of land — open, available, accessible land — when hundreds of thousands of acres lie waste and unprofitable around, is the great misfortune under which we labor." . . . There was something intuitively wrong about letting perfectly good land sit uncultivated, especially when back in Britain there were millions of people with no land at all. . . .

But the Maori's failure to cultivate much of their land was, in the eyes of the British, much more than inefficient resource use. It was the violation of one of the most familiar — in fact, the very first — of the Lord's commands. As every settler knew well, just after creating Adam and Eve, God had instructed them in no uncertain terms to "replenish the earth and subdue it." Noah had received the same command, with the same priority, right after the end of the flood. Allowing fertile land to lie uncultivated was worse than a waste; it was a sin. . . .

Any means of bringing more land into cultivation, whether by the Maori or the British, would help fulfill the biblical injunction. If the Maori system of property rights was deterring cultivation, by preventing sales to the British or by giving the Maori a diminished incentive to farm on their own, then reforming the system would be a form of missionary work.

It would be a way of facilitating the salvation of the Maori, by turning them from a path that threatened to incur the Lord's anger. . . .

Property reform was also widely perceived to have important political implications. Converting to British titles, supporters argued, would simultaneously break down traditional Maori political structures and better integrate Maori individuals and the colonial government.

Maori tribes, to the dismay of many settlers, were effectively ministates within the larger colonial state. . . .

Property reform, it was hoped, would destroy traditional Maori collective political institutions, but it would simultaneously empower Maori individuals to exercise political rights in the colonial state, both directly and indirectly. In the most direct sense, voting required possessing freehold or leasehold land. . . .

Productivity, Christianity, and sound government were independent reasons to reform Maori land tenure, but reform promised benefits that were even more fundamental. Over and over again, the colonists associated "civilization" with property organized by geographic space. . . .

. . . "[C]ivilization" was less a single concept than a broad category of desirable characteristics [the British] found in themselves but absent in the Maori. One subset of these characteristics encompassed all the traits conventionally subsumed under the heading of morality. . . . But "civilization" was more than moral character. Sometimes it referred to simple neighborliness. . . . Whatever "civilization" was, it was always something the British had but the Maori did not, and it was something that could be promoted by helping the Maori "abandoned their communistic habits and ideas."

The ambiguity of "civilization" as it was used in these various contexts, and its elusive connection to any particular system of property rights, suggest it was a shorthand way of describing a vague feeling that the Maori ought in general to be more like the British. . . . Human history was understood as a progression toward civilization. In New Zealand, as in the other colonies, that meant progress from the native way of life to the British. . . .

A Native Land Court

The next several years . . . saw a flurry of proposed methods of instituting British-style land ownership among the Maori, a process that culminated in the Native Lands Act of 1865. The act created a new court, the Native Land Court. Upon receiving an application from Maori landowners, the court was to consider the claims of the applicants and anyone else alleging an interest in the land, and, after the land had been surveyed, to issue a certificate of title stating "the names of the persons or of the tribe who according to Native custom own or are interested in the land." A group receiving land could further petition to have the land subdivided among the group's members. Maori land to which certificates of title had been issued could be leased or sold; land not yet passed through the court could not. . . .

As for . . . the breaking down of Maori resistance to selling land, the Native Lands Act was in fact very successful, because of the way it transferred power from tribes acting collectively to individuals wishing to sell. Any single Maori person could start the machinery of the Native Land Court by filing an application to have title ascertained, even if every other tribe member wished to keep out of the court. Because rights to land were often the only significant asset a Maori person possessed, and because the steadily expanding market economy offered increasing opportunities for going into debt, the odds were good that at least one tribe member would need to sell. . . .

The Native Land Court was in this manner the conduit for the flow of a vast quantity of land from Maori to British owners over the rest of the century. This need not have been detrimental to the Maori, had they received a fair price for the land. In that case they would simply have been exchanging one asset for another of equal value. The opening up of Maori land to private purchasers in 1865 promised to create a competitive market that would give rise to prices much higher than those paid under the government monopsony in effect during the preceding decades. The Maori could have ended the century with less land but much more money. The actual operation of the court was extremely costly, however, and all those costs fell squarely on the Maori. In the end, the cost of selling land caused the Maori to receive much less than their land was actually worth. . . .

Power and Markets

Between 1840 and 1865, the colonial government established a market in Maori land with a single purchaser, the government itself. Whatever the degree of misunderstanding between buyer and seller as to the meaning of transactions, whatever the disparity in the parties' skill at negotiating or ability to predict future land values, the government as sole purchaser could exploit them to the fullest. After 1865 the government established a different kind of market in Maori land, one that imposed enormous costs on Maori sellers, costs that could not be passed through to land purchasers because the government itself offered a low-priced substitute. In both types of market, the Maori received much less for their land than they would have in a market constructed differently, in which buyers competed with one another to offer the best price, and in which administrative costs were lower and borne more equally. . . .

The British possessed two attributes the Maori did not, and those made all the difference. The first was the ability to organize themselves within the market as a single entity for the purpose of buying land at low prices. Had the British, like the Maori, been split into multiple political units, they would have been no more able to exercise monopsony power than multiple firms are able to cartelize for the same purpose. The second attribute possessed by the British but not the Maori is one that has implicitly lain beneath the entire discussion. The British had the power to set the rules of the game. The market looked the way it did because the British were powerful enough to design it and to rebuff Maori efforts to impose a different structure. That power rested on the military and technological superiority that allowed European states to colonize much of the world rather than vice versa. The British had the muscle to select exactly which property rights they would enforce and how they would be enforced. The transfer of land from the Maori to the British was thus a function of British power, as in Australia, but in New Zealand, more often than not, it was power exercised through the legal system rather than on the battlefield.

NOTES AND QUESTIONS

1. *New Zealand Sovereignty and the Treaty of Waitangi.* New Zealand's sovereignty was established by the 1840 Treaty of Waitangi. The distinguished historian J.G.A. Pocock further explains the significance of that treaty:

> New Zealand is exceptional for the reason that it is not a confederation but a unitary and sovereign state, whose sovereignty seems to rest upon a treaty—the *Treaty* or *te Tiriti* of Waitangi—which preceded and can be said to condition the declaration of the Crown's sovereignty in 1840. Alone among the cases I have been considering [Australia, Canada, and the United States], then, the political sovereignty which affirms and defines the national identity can be considered contingent or dependent on the performance or non-performance of a treaty between two cultures or discourses, whose meaning and history can be debated in two languages entailing two understandings of law, culture, sovereignty, and their existence in time.

J.G.A. Pocock, *Law, Sovereignty and History in a Divided Culture: The Case of New Zealand and the Treaty of Waitangi,* 43 McGill L.J. 481, 488 (1998). New Zealand's source of sovereignty in a treaty contrasts with the British experience in its other colonies, including North America, where no similar formal agreement resting upon Crown recognition of original sovereignty of the aboriginal peoples existed. The Treaty of Waitangi has been used as a foundational constitutional document, engendering narratives and counter-narratives about New Zealand's past as predicates for land claims and defenses to those claims. *See* P.G. McHugh, Aboriginal Societies and the Common Law: A History of Sovereignty, Status, and Self-determination 15 (2004). It also provided the basis for the creation in 1975 of the Waitangi Tribunal, which hears Maori claims, including historical claims, against the government. *Id.* at 349.

2. *Private Landownership, Commons, or Both?* Banner points out that the British system of landownership was actually more complex than simple private ownership. In fact, it contained elements of communal

ownership, making it in effect a hybrid system, which we discussed earlier in Chapter 12. Was the Maori land regime a commons, or was it, too, a hybrid?

Compare with the Maori land regime the land regime of the Bedouin in Israel's Negev desert. At present, more than 150 permanent Bedouin settlements dot the Negev. The Israeli government has tried to force the Bedouin out of the settlements into designated townships. Underlying this effort lie perceptions of the Bedouin as a rootless nomadic people with no land ownership system and of the Negev as empty. In fact, however, land plays a very strong role in constructing meaning in Bedouin lives. As the Bedouin see it, land contains the personality of its owner. Even after long periods of the owner's absence, land contains the owner's personality. Moreover, land ownership is the primary basis of Bedouin social distinction and hierarchy. Bedouin owners refuse to move to land that they consider to be owned already by other Bedouins. Historically, the Bedouin have had their own system for resolving land disputes and for acquiring, selling, and inheriting land, as well as for marking land boundaries. *See* Ronen Shamir, *Suspended in Space: Bedouins under the Law of Israel*, 30 Law & Soc'y Rev. 231, 232-236 (1996). Bedouin law recognizes individual ownership, but it is laced with communal concepts. For example, if a Bedouin wishes to sell his plot, the people of his clan have the right to interfere by exercising a right of preemption for the purpose of keeping the land in the clan. *See* Clinton Bailey, Bedouin Law from Sinai and the Negev 269 (2009). However, he is free to give part of it to whomever he wishes as a gift. *Id.* at 268. An owner may also give his land at will to discharge a legal obligation. *Ibid.*

The Bedouin land regime is a hybrid individual-communal ownership system. Yet it is different from both the Maori and the British systems. What are the salient differences among the three? Does the Bedouin system seem closer to the British system or to the Maori system, or is it simply *sui generis*?

3. *Meeting of the Minds, or Exercise of Power?* As Banner describes, the British and Maori had fundamentally different conceptions of land ownership. To the British, ownership was geographic, whereas to the Maori, it was functional. In Anglo-American law, of course, sales of land require agreement by seller and buyer, a "meeting of the minds." But how was a meeting of the minds possible given the fundamental difference between the British and Maori understandings of land ownership? What devices or mechanisms did the British use to facilitate land sale transactions in this environment? Do you think that the transfers of land that resulted were likely fair and consensual, or are you inclined to conclude that what happened in New Zealand was an acquiescence to power, with property law and government agencies serving as instruments of imperial expropriation?

In thinking about this question, recall the argument made in the famous article by Robert L. Hale, *Coercion and Distribution in a Supposedly Non-Coercive State*, 38 Pol. Sci. Q. 470 (1923), which we discussed in Note 2 of Chapter 7. Hale deconstructed the distinction between coercion and consent. He claimed that what we take to be free choice in transactions is just the result of coercion, or power, sanctioned by the state. Hale's claim provides a possible basis for denying enforcement of the land transactions between the British and the Maoris. But does Hale's claim stand up against further scrutiny? Recall Neil Duxbury's critique (mentioned in Note 2 of Chapter 7) in which Hale's conception of coercion rests upon "a wholly mechanistic image of the human individual." Do you agree? If so, and if, *pace* Hale, a coherent distinction between coercion and consent is still possible, how would you go about drawing that distinction? Were the land transactions between the British and the Maoris the result of coercion or mutual consent?

Assuming that these land transactions are properly analyzed as being the result of coercion, what are the policy implications of such historic injustice for contemporary decision makers? Do the facts that many years passed and circumstances changed make a difference? Should they? These are some of the questions we address in Chapter 17.3.

4. Terra Nullius *and the* Mabo *Decision.* Australia's past legal handling of aboriginal land holdings was quite different from that of New Zealand. Prior to the Australian High Court's famous 1992 decision in Mabo v. Queensland, (1992) 66 ALJR 408, Australian courts had considered that customary Australian Aboriginal land title was necessarily extinguished when the British Crown acquired the Australian colony in 1788. Until *Mabo*, the legal theory justifying colonization of Australia was that the Australian Aboriginal peoples were "barbarous or unsettled and without a settled law," *Id.* at 420, and that Australia itself was *terra nullius*, the land of no one. The *Mabo* decision squarely rejected both of these notions. The court held that customary native land title survived colonization. The majority concluded that although the Crown's sovereignty gave it "radical" (or "final") title, this radical title did not necessarily confer beneficial ownership. Sovereignty carried beneficial ownership only where no native title already existed. Radical title authorized the Crown to extinguish native title by appropriating land to itself or by alienating land to others. In the absence of such acts, however, native title continued.

In the wake of *Mabo*, the federal Parliament enacted the Native Title Act (1993). The Act gives native title the force of law and provides that native title may be extinguished only through compliance with specified federal procedures. It establishes a procedure for determining whether native title exists over particular land and, if so, what specific rights exist. The Act provoked a strongly hostile backlash, particularly in the large state of Western Australia, which unsuccessfully challenged the constitutional validity of the Act. *See* Western Australia v. Commonwealth, (1995) 69 ALJR 309. As one scholar has put it, "[The Act's process] necessitated the huge culture-change of the kind that the white Northern Territory and Western Australia authorities, too used to treating their huge landmass on their own terms, were loath to make." MᴄHᴜɢʜ, *supra* Note 1, at 582. McHugh goes on to observe, "White relations with the aboriginal peoples of North America and New Zealand had a history of such transacting (even if not a particularly honourable one), but to the Australian this change in mentality had no historical anchor or precedent." *Ibid. See also* Peter Butt, The Mabo *Case and Its Aftermath: Indigenous Land Title in Australia, in* PROPERTY LAW ON THE THRESHOLD OF THE 21ST CENTURY 495 (G.E. van Maanen & A.J. van der Walt eds., 1996).

5. *Uses and Misuses of History in Aboriginal Land Claims Disputes.* Not only have aboriginal land title claims been contested in several countries, the histories behind those claims have been contested. Indeed, some courts have challenged the relevance of history itself. As McHugh has observed, "In all common law jurisdictions . . . history became a legal battleground, as much used against as for aboriginal peoples." MCHUGH, *supra* Note 1, at 15. Courts have tended to be skeptical or even dismissive of indigenous histories used to support aboriginal claims. *See* James Clifford, *Identity in Mashpee, in* THE PREDICAMENT OF CULTURE: TWENTIETH CENTURY ETHNOGRAPHY, LITERATURE, AND ART 277 (1988).

An example of this dismissive attitude was the U.S. Supreme Court's refusal in Rice v. Cayetano, 528 U.S. 495 (2000), to recognize the native Hawaiians as a distinct tribal people. The case involved a civil rights claim brought by Hawaiian citizens challenging the eligibility requirements for voting for Office of Hawaiian Affairs. The Hawaiian Constitution restricted voter eligibility to persons whose ancestry qualified them as a "Hawaiian" or "native Hawaiian," as defined by statute. The Court held that by using ancestry as a proxy for race, the voting restrictions were race-based and therefore violated the Fifteenth Amendment of the U.S. Constitution. Providing a highly truncated history of native Hawaiians, the majority of the Court refused to recognize them as a distinct tribal people. The dissenting opinion opened with the statement, "The Court's holding today rests largely on the repetition of glittering generalities that have little, if any, application to the compelling history of the State of Hawaii." *Id.* at 528. For a good discussion of *Rice,* see Rose Cuizon Villazor, *Blood Quantum Land Laws and the Race versus Political Identity Dilemma,* 96 CAL. L. REV. 801 (2008).

6. *Historical Dispossession of Native American Land* — Johnson v. M'Intosh. The story of how Native Americans lost possession — and, ultimately, legal title — of their land following "discovery" of North America by the Europeans is surprisingly complex. The discovering European nations usually declared themselves sovereigns of huge stretches of land that were in fact inhabited by many thousands of natives. The European governments then succeeded in inducing or forcing the Indian nations to transfer sovereignty over specific tracts of land to them. These transfers were hardly "meeting of the minds." The colonists understood one thing — a transfer of what English land lawyers call fee simple title — while the Native Americans understood quite another — transfer of a temporary

and limited set of land use interests. *See* WILLIAM CRONON, CHANGES IN THE LAND (1983). The colonial powers and later the U.S. government acquired title to native land through a variety of means — conquest, coercion, voluntary agreement (contract), or judicial fiat.

According to the famous case of Johnson v. M'Intosh, 21 U.S. (8 Wheat.) 543 (1823), property and sovereignty of the Native American nations were first transferred to the appropriate colonial European nation (England, France, or Spain) and in time to the U.S. government upon independence. The federal government later distributed this land to individuals. Individuals who derived their titles from the previous colonial power were protected in their legal rights. But some individuals based their title on transfers directly from Native American nations. *Johnson v. M'Intosh* involved the legal enforceability of these titles against conflicting claimants who traced their title to the federal government.

In *Johnson,* the Supreme Court announced the so-called doctrine of discovery. According to this doctrine, when European sovereigns discovered portions of the North American continent, they acquired title to all discovered land, and indigenous peoples retained only a right of occupancy, which the discovering sovereign nation could terminate either through conquest or through contract. If a native nation decided to transfer this limited right, it could transfer it only to the discovering sovereign. Hence, the Court held, a land title derived from a transfer by an Indian tribe directly to an individual claimant was not enforceable under American law against one who derived his title from the federal government. Chief Justice John Marshall's famous opinion for the Court turns out to have been riddled with historical errors and inaccuracies. The full story on these is well-told in two books: STUART BANNER, HOW THE INDIANS LOST THEIR LAND (2005); LINDSAY G. ROBERTSON, CONQUEST BY LAW (2005). Another interesting discussion of *Johnson* is Eric Kades, *The Dark Side of Efficiency:* Johnson v. M'Intosh *and the Expropriation of American Indian Lands,* 148 U. PA. L. REV. 1065 (2000).

7.   *Current American Indian Land Claims.* Modern Native American land law is a large and complex topic. With regard to modern reparation claims, during the past 20 years or so, several eastern tribes have brought land claims against states based on state governments' takings of land. A number of the cases involve violations of the federal Non-Intercourse Act of 1790. The Act prohibits sales on tribal land to anyone other than the federal government. Despite the statute, several states entered into treaties with various Indian nations in order to cede tribal land to the states. Beginning in the late 1960s, eastern tribes brought lawsuits claiming that these transfers were void. In some of these cases the Supreme Court has held in favor of the tribes to the extent of recognizing that they have a federal common law right to sue the state under the Act. *See, e.g.,* Oneida Indian Nation v. County of Oneida, 414 U.S. 616 (1974). On the question of money damages, however, the Court has ruled that the Eleventh Amendment

of the Constitution bars tribes from recovery from states. *See* Blatchford v. Native Village of Noatak and Circle Village, 501 U.S. 775 (1991).

3. REPARATIONS

Jeremy Waldron, Superseding Historic Injustice[1]

I.   INJUSTICE AND HISTORY

The history of white settlers' dealings with the aboriginal peoples of Australia, New Zealand, and North America is largely a history of injustice. People, or whole peoples, were attacked, defrauded, and expropriated; their lands were stolen and their lives were ruined. What are we to do about these injustices? We know what we should think about them: they are to be studied and condemned, remembered and lamented. But morality is a practical matter, and judgments of 'just' and 'unjust' like all moral judgments have implications for action. To say that a future act open to us now would be unjust is to commit ourselves to avoiding it. But what of past injustice? What is the practical importance now of a judgment that injustice occurred in the past? . . .

[T]here is an importance to the historical recollection of injustice that has to do with identity and contingency. . . .

. . . Remembrance in this sense is [] important to communities—families, tribes, nations, parties—that is, to human entities that exist often for much longer than individual men and women. To neglect the historical record is to do violence to this identity and thus to the community that it sustains. And since communities help generate a deeper sense of identity for the individuals they comprise, neglecting or expunging the historical record is a way of undermining and insulting individuals as well. . . .

The topic of this article is reparation. But before I embark on my main discussion, I want to mention the role that the payment of money (or the return of lands or artifacts) may play in the embodiment of communal remembrance. Quite apart from any attempt genuinely to compensate victims or offset their losses, reparations may symbolize a society's undertaking not to forget or deny that a particular injustice took place, and to respect and help sustain a dignified sense of identity-in-memory for the people affected. A prominent recent example of this is the payment of token sums of compensation by the American government to the survivors of Japanese-American families uprooted, interned, and concentrated in

---

1. Jeremy Waldron, *Superseding Historic Injustice,*103 ETHICS 4, 4, 5, 6-10, 12-16, 20, 24-27 (1992).

1942. The point of these payments was not to make up for the loss of home, business, opportunity, and standing in the community which these people suffered at the hands of their fellow citizens, nor was it to make up for the discomfort and degradation of their internment. If that were the aim, much more would be necessary. The point was to mark—with something that counts in the United States—a clear public recognition that this injustice did happen, that it was the American people and their government that inflicted it, and that these people were among its victims. The payments give an earnest of good faith and sincerity to that acknowledgment. Like the gift I buy for someone I have stood up, the payment is a method of putting oneself out, or going out of one's way, to apologize. It is no objection to this that the payments are purely symbolic. Since identity is bound up with symbolism, a symbolic gesture may be as important to people as any material compensation.

II. THE COUNTERFACTUAL APPROACH TO REPARATION

I turn now to the view that a judgment about past injustice generates a demand for full and not merely symbolic reparation—a demand not just for remembrance but for substantial transfers of land, wealth, and resources in an effort actually to rectify past wrongs. I want to examine the difficulties that these demands give rise to, particularly when they conflict with other claims that may be made in the name of justice on the land, wealth, and resources in question.

It may seem as though the demand is hopeless from the start. What is it to correct an injustice? How can we reverse the past? If we are talking about injustice that took place several generations ago, surely there is nothing we can do now to heal the lives of the actual victims, to make them less miserable or to reduce their suffering. The only experiences we can affect are those of people living now and those who will live in the future. . . .

. . . [T]here is a sense in which we can affect the moral significance of past action. Even if we cannot alter the action itself we may be able to interfere with the normal course of its consequences. The present surely looks different now from the way the present would look if a given injustice of the past had not occurred. Why not therefore change the present so that it looks more like the present that would have obtained in the absence of the injustice? Why not make it now as though the injustice had not happened, for all that its occurrence in the past is immutable and undeniable?

This is the approach taken by Robert Nozick in his account of the role played by a principle of rectification in a theory of historic entitlement:

> This principle uses historical information about previous situations and injustices done in them (as defined by the first two principles of justice [namely, justice in acquisition and justice in transfer] and rights against interference), and information about the actual course of events that flowed from these injustices, until the present,

and it yields a description (or descriptions) of holdings in the society. The principle of rectification presumably will make use of its best estimate of subjunctive information about what would have occurred (or a probability distribution over what might have occurred, using the expected value) if the injustice had not taken place. If the actual description of holdings turns out to be one of the descriptions yielded by the principle, then one of the descriptions yielded must be realized.[2]

The trouble with this approach is the difficulty we have in saying what would have happened if some event (which did occur) had not taken place. To a certain extent we can appeal to causal laws or, more crudely, the normal course of events. We take a description of the actual world, with its history and natural laws intact, up until the problematic event of injustice (which we shall call event 'E'). In the actual course of events, what followed E (events F, G, and H) is simply what results from applying natural laws to E as an initial condition. . . . [I]n our counterfactual reasoning, we replace E with its closest just counterpart, $E+$ . . . and we apply the laws of nature to that to see what would have happened next. . . . The same laws of nature that yield F given E, yield a different sequel $F+$ given the just alternative $E+$ and further sequels $G+$ and $H+$ on the basis of that. The task of rectification then is to take some present event or situation over which we do have control (e.g., H, a distribution of resources obtaining now) and alter it so that it conforms as closely as possible to its counterpart $H+$ — the situation that would obtain now if $E+$ rather than E had occurred.

But what if some of the events in the sequel to $E+$ are exercises of human choice rather than the inexorable working out of natural laws? Is it possible to say counterfactually how choices subsequent to $E+$ would have been made, so that we can determine what state of affairs ($H+$) would obtain now in a society of autonomous choosers, but for the problematic injustice? . . .

. . . The problem quickly becomes intractable particularly where the counterfactual sequence $E+$, $F+$, $G+$, $H+$ is imagined to extend over several generations, and where the range of choices available at a given stage depends on the choices that would have been taken at some earlier stage. . . .

Part of our difficulty in answering these questions is our uncertainty about what we are doing when we try to make guesses about the way in which free will would have been exercised. The status of counterfactual reasoning about the exercise of human freedom is unclear. I do not mean that the exercise of human choice is necessarily unpredictable. We make predictions all the time about how people will exercise their freedom. But it is not clear why our best prediction on such a matter should have moral authority in the sort of speculations we are considering. . . .

2. Robert Nozick, *Anarchy, State, and Utopia*, pp. 152-53 [in Chapter 3 of this volume — Eds].

A . . . general difficulty has to do with our application of rational choice in counterfactual reconstruction. People can and often do act freely to their own disadvantage, and usually when they do, they are held to the result. A man who actually loses his land in a reckless though voluntary wager and who accepts the justice of the outcome may be entitled to wonder why, in the attention we pay to aboriginal reparations, we insulate people from the possibility of similar vicissitudes. He may say, "If we are going to reconstruct a history of rational choice, let us do so for all holdings, giving everyone what they would have had if they had never acted voluntarily to their own disadvantage. Maybe that will lead to a more just world. But if we are not prepared to do that, if we insist that it is alright, from the point of view of justice, to leave a person like me stuck with the results of his actual choices, it may be more consistent to admit that we simply can't say what (by the same token) justice now requires in the case of those whose ancestors were wrongfully dispossessed."

The dilemma is a difficult one. On the one hand, there is nothing normatively conclusive about rational choice predictions. Why should the exaction of specific reparation in the real world be oriented to what the idealized agents of rational choice would have secured for themselves in a hypothetical world? On the other hand, hypothetical rational choice is essential to our normative thinking about justice. . . .

Ultimately, what is raised here is the question of whether it is possible to rectify particular injustices without undertaking a comprehensive redistribution that addresses all claims of justice that may be made. . . . Quite apart from particular frauds and expropriations, things were not marvelous in the nineteenth century. Many people lacked access to any significant resources, and many people had much more than what one might regard as a fair share. Why take all that as the baseline for our present reconstruction?

III. THE PERPETUATION AND REMISSION OF INJUSTICE

So far we have focused on the effects of isolated acts of injustice . . . , events that took place firmly in the past. But we are seldom so fortunate as to confront injustice in discrete doses. The world we know is characterized by patterns of injustice, by standing arrangements — rules, laws, regimes, and other institutions — that operate unjustly day after day. . . .

. . . Instead of regarding the expropriation of aboriginal lands as an isolated act of injustice that took place at a certain time now relegated firmly to the past, we may think of it as a persisting injustice. The injustice persists, and it is perpetuated by the legal system as long as the land that was expropriated is not returned to those from whom it was taken. On this model, the rectification of injustice is a much simpler matter than the approach we discussed in the previous section. We do not have to engage in any counterfactual speculation. We simply give the property back to the person or group from whom it was taken and thus put an end to what would otherwise be its continued expropriation.

Difficulties arise of course if the original owner has died, for then there is no one to whom the property can be restored. We could give it to her heirs and successors, but in doing so we are already setting off down the counterfactual road, reckoning that this is what the proprietor's wish would have been had she had control of her property. Fortunately, that difficulty is obviated in the case of many aboriginal claims: usually the property is owned by a tribe, a nation, or a community — some entity that endures over time in spite of mortality of its individual members. It is this enduring entity that has been dispossessed, and the same entity is on hand now more than a hundred years later to claim its heritage.

. . . Are we sure that the entitlement that was originally violated all those years ago is an entitlement that survives into the present? The approach we are considering depends on the claim that the right that was violated when white settlers first seized the land can be identified as a right that is still being violated today by settlers' successors in title. Their possession of the land today is said to be as wrongful vis-à-vis the present tribal owners as the original expropriation. Can this view be justified?

It is widely believed that some rights are capable of "fading" in their moral importance by virtue of the passage of time and by the sheer persistence of what was originally a wrongful infringement. In the law of property, we recognize doctrines of prescription and adverse possession. In criminal procedure and in torts, we think it important to have statutes of limitations. The familiarity of these doctrines no doubt contributes to the widespread belief that, after several generations have passed, certain wrongs are simply not worth correcting. Think of [an] example of the theft of my automobile. Certainly, the car should be returned if the thief is discovered within weeks or months of the incident. But what if she is never caught? What if the stolen car remains in her family for decades and is eventually passed down as an heirloom to her children and grandchildren? Are we so sure that when the circumstances of its acquisition eventually come to light, it should be returned without further ado to me or my estate?

The view that a violated entitlement can "fade" with time may seem unfair. The injustice complained of is precisely that the rightful owner has been dispossessed. It seems harsh if the fact of her dispossession is used as a way of weakening her claim. It may also seem to involve some moral hazard by providing an incentive for wrongdoers to cling to their ill-gotten gains, in the hope that the entitlement they violated will fade away because of their adverse possession.

Still, the view that certain rights are prescriptable has a number of things to be said in its favor. Some are simply pragmatic. Statutes of limitations are inspired as much by procedural difficulties about evidence and memory, as by any doctrine about rights. It is hard to establish what happened if we are enquiring into the events that occurred decades or generations ago. There are nonprocedural pragmatic arguments also. For better or worse, people build up structures of expectation around the resources that are actually under their control. If a person controls a resource over a long enough period, then she and others may organize their lives and their economic activity around the premise that that resource is "hers," without much regard to the distant provenance of her entitlement. Upsetting these expectations in the name of restitutive justice is bound to be costly and disruptive.

There may be reasons of principle as well. One set of reasons has to do with changes in background social and economic circumstances. If the requirements of justice are sensitive to circumstances such as the size of the population or the incidence of scarcity, then there is no guarantee that those requirements (and the rights that they constitute) will remain constant in relation to a given resource or piece of land as the decades and generations go by. I shall deal with this in detail in the next section of this article. . . .

IV. CIRCUMSTANCES AND SUPERSESSION

It is difficult to resist the conclusion that entitlements are sensitive to circumstances. Certainly, the level of our concern for various human predicaments is sensitive to the circumstances that constitute those predicaments. One's concern about poverty, for example, varies depending on the extent of the opportunities available to the poor: to be poor but to have some opportunity for amelioration is to be in a better predicament than to be poor with no opportunities at all. . . . Now, the (appropriate) level of our concern about such predicaments is directly related to the burden of justification that must be shouldered by those who defend property rights. If an individual makes a claim to the exclusive use or possession of some resources in our territory, then the difficulty of sustaining that claim will clearly have some relation to the level of our concern about the plight of other persons who will have to be excluded from the resources if the claim is recognized. The only theory of property entitlement that would be totally immune to variations in background circumstances would be one that did not accept any burden of justification in relation to our real concerns. . . .

. . . [T]he burden of justifying an exclusive entitlement depends (in part) on the impact of others' interests of being excluded from the resources in question and [] that impact is likely to vary as circumstances change. Similarly an acquisition which is legitimate in one set of circumstances may not be legitimate in another set of circumstances. From this I infer[] that an initially legitimate acquisition may become illegitimate or have its legitimacy restricted (as the basis of an ongoing entitlement) at a later time on account of a change in circumstances. By exactly similar reasoning, it seems possible that an act which counted as an injustice when it was committed in circumstances C_1 may be transformed, so far as its ongoing effect is concerned, into a just situation if circumstances change in the meantime from C_1 to C_2. When this happens, I shall say the injustice has been *superseded*.

Consider the following example.[3] On the savanna, a number of groups appropriate water holes, in conditions where it is known that there are enough water holes for each group. So long as these conditions obtain, it seems reasonable for the members of given group, P, to use the water hole they have appropriated without asking permission of other groups with whom they share the plains; and it may even seem reasonable for them to exclude members of other groups from the casual use of their water holes, saying to them, "You have your own water hole. Go off and use that, and leave ours alone." But suppose there is an ecological disaster, and all the water holes dry up except the one that the members of P are using. Then in these changed circumstances, notwithstanding the legitimacy of their original appropriation, it is no longer in order for P to exclude others from their water hole. Indeed it may no longer be in order for members of P to casually use "their own" water hole in the way they did before. In the new circumstances, it may be incumbent on them to draw up a rationing scheme that allows for the needs of everyone in the territory to be satisfied from this one resource. Changing circumstances can have an effect on ownership rights notwithstanding the moral legitimacy of the original appropriation.

Next, suppose as before that in circumstances of plenty various groups on the savanna are legitimately in possession of their respective water holes. One day, motivated purely by greed, members of group Q descend on the water hole possessed by group P and insist on sharing that with them. (What's more they do not allow reciprocity; they do not allow members of P to share any water hole that was legitimately in the possession of Q.) That is an injustice. But then circumstances change, and all the water holes of the territory dry up except the one that originally belonged to P. The members of group Q are already sharing that water hole on the basis of their earlier incursion. But now that circumstances have changed, they are entitled to share that water hole; it no longer counts as an injustice. It is in fact part of what justice now requires. The initial injustice by Q against P has been superseded by circumstances.

... [I]t may be objected that this reasoning generates a moral hazard—an incentive for wrongdoers to seize others' lands confident in the knowledge that if they hang on to them wrongfully for long enough their possession may eventually become rightful. But the argument of this section is not that the passage of time per se supersedes all claims of injustice. Rather, the argument is that claims about justice and injustice must be

---

3. The example is suggested by David Lyons, "The New Indian Claims and Original Rights to Land," in *Reading Nozick*, ed. J. Paul (Oxford: Blackwell, 1982), p. 371.

responsive to changes in circumstances. Suppose there had been no injustice: still, a change in circumstances (such as a great increase in world population) might justify our forcing the aboriginal inhabitants of some territory to share their land with others. If this is so, then the same change in circumstances in the real world can justify our saying that the others' occupation of some of their lands, which was previously wrongful, may become morally permissible. There is no moral hazard in this supersession because the aboriginal inhabitants would have had to share their lands, whether the original injustice had taken place or not. . . .

Of course, from the fact that supersession is a possibility, it does not follow that it always happens. Everything depends on which circumstances are taken to be morally significant and how as matter of fact circumstances have changed. It may be that some of the historic injustices that concern us have not been superseded and that, even under modern circumstances, the possession of certain aboriginal lands by the descendants of those who expropriated their original owners remains a crying injustice. My argument is not intended to rule that out. But there have been huge changes since North America and Australia were settled by white colonists. The population has increased manyfold, and most of the descendants of the colonists, unlike their ancestors, have nowhere else to go. We cannot be sure that these changes in circumstances supersede the injustice of their continued possession of aboriginal lands, but it would not be surprising if they did. The facts that have changed are exactly the sort of facts one would expect to make a difference to the justice of a set of entitlements over resources.

V. CONCLUSION

It is important that defenders of aboriginal claims face up to the possibility of the supersession of historic injustice. Even if this particular thesis about supersession is mistaken, some account has to be given of the impact on aboriginal claims and on the reparation of generations-old injustices of the demographic and ecological changes that have taken place.

Apart from anything else, the changes that have taken place over the past two hundred years mean that the costs of respecting primeval entitlements are much greater now than they were in 1800. Two hundred years ago, a small aboriginal group could have exclusive domination of "a large and fruitful Territory"[4] without much prejudice to the needs and interests of very many other human beings. Today, such exclusive rights would mean many people going hungry who might otherwise be fed and many people living in poverty who might otherwise have an opportunity to make a decent life. Irrespective of the occurrence of past injustice, this imbalance

4. The phrase is from Locke, *Two Treatises*, bk. 2, sec. 41.

would have to be rectified sooner or later. That is the basis for my argument that claims about historic injustice predicated on the status quo ante may be superseded by our determination to distribute the resources of the world in a way that is fair to all of its existing inhabitants.

Behind the thesis of supersession lies a determination to focus upon present and prospective costs—the suffering and the deprivation over which we still have some control. The idea is that any conception of justice which is to be made practically relevant for the way we act now must be a scheme that takes into account modern circumstances and the way those affect the conditions under which people presently live their lives. Arguments for reparation take as conclusive claims of entitlement oriented toward circumstances that are radically different from those we actually face: claims of entitlement based on the habitation of a territory by a small fraction of its present population, and claims of entitlement based on the determination to ignore the present dispersal of persons and peoples on the face of the earth, simply because the historic mechanisms of such dispersal were savagely implicated in injustice. And yet, here we all are. The present circumstances are the ones that are real: it is in the actual world that people starve or are hurt or degraded if the demands of justice in relation to their circumstances are not met. Justice, we say, is a matter of the greatest importance. But the importance to be accorded it is relative to what may actually happen if justice is not done, not to what might have happened if injustice in the past had been avoided. . . .

NOTES AND QUESTIONS

1. *Reparatory Justice.* Reparatory justice is a complex topic of study and a more complex political policy that many transitional regimes have pursued. In her review of reparatory practices, Ruti Teitel suggests that most transitional regimes—regimes following the end of war, military dictatorships, or totalitarianism—have pursued some form of reparatory justice, despite considerable differences in their legal cultures. *See* RUTI G. TEITEL, TRANSITIONAL JUSTICE 119 (2000). Teitel points out that reparatory justice debates raise "conflicts between the backward-looking purposes of compensating victims of past state abuses and the state's forward-looking political interests." *Id.* In post-communist transitions, for example, new regimes have tried simultaneously to repair past state wrongs (e.g., through wrongful state confiscations) and to promote transformation to a market economy through state privatization programs. These two objectives are often in tension with each other, and states must decide how much and what forms of repair for past injustice are compatible with the needs for successful economic transformation.

2. *The Supersession Thesis.* Waldron's supersession thesis has been quite controversial. It is important to be accurate about what it says and,

just as important, what it does not. Supersession involves two components: a change factor(s) and an effect that the change factor(s) produce(s) concerning some historical injustice. Regarding the first, does Waldron argue that time alone is the operative factor? If not, just what is? Concerning the second component, is the thesis that the effect of the change factor, whatever it is, is to cleanse or expunge a historical injustice? If so, does this mean that the extant distribution of holdings is just? What are your reactions to Waldron's arguments regarding the two components? In addition to the article that we have excerpted, Waldron further elaborates his supersession thesis in two other articles, Jeremy Waldron, *Redressing Historic Injustice*, 52 U. TORONTO L.J. 135 (2002); *id.*, *Settlement, Return, and the Supersession Thesis*, 5 THEORETICAL INQ. L. 237 (2004). Commentators have raised a number of objections to Waldron's supersession thesis. One objection is that the only injustice that changed circumstances have possibly superseded is the present holdings of the territory in question, *not* the historic injustice itself. *See* TAMAR MEISELS, TERRITORIAL RIGHTS 48-50, 53-61 (2005). Another objection is that Waldron's point that the descendants of colonists have nowhere else to go can support only modest claims of colonists' descendants to rights to residency and access to resources, but not to territorial sovereignty. *See* Cara Nine, *Superseding Historical Injustice*, 11 CRITICAL REV. INT'L SOC. & POL. PHIL. 79 (2008). Are these objections persuasive?

3. *No Reparations or Only Some Reparations?* Is Waldron's argument that because of change in context the victims of historic injustices are entitled to *no* reparations or just that they are not entitled to full reparations, i.e., their original holdings? The latter claim leaves open the possibility of returning *some* of the victims' original holdings. Does historic supersession negate even this weaker claim? Do forms of reparations that do not involve transfers of land (say, money compensation) suffer from the same problems that Waldron discusses?

4. *Counterfactual Reasoning.* As Waldron points out, arguments in favor of reparations for historic injustices often rely on counterfactual reasoning. (A counterfactual is simply an alternative version of past or present worlds, based on one or a few deliberately falsified antecedent features of the actual world. *See* WHAT MIGHT HAVE BEEN: THE SOCIAL PSYCHOLOGY OF COUNTERFACTUAL THINKING 3 (Neal J. Roese & James M. Olson eds., 1995).) Waldron states, "The status of counterfactual reasoning about the exercise of human freedom is unclear. . . . [I]t is not clear why our best prediction on [how people would have acted under different conditions] should have moral authority in the sort of speculations we are considering." *Should* counterfactual reasoning be given moral weight? One problem is that counterfactual thinking is subject to cognitive biases that may lead one to draw the wrong causal inference. For example, social psychologists have found that the ability to generate counterfactual

alternatives to reality is intimately tied to emotional responses. *See* Steven J. Sherman & Allen R. McConnell, *Dysfunctional Implications of Counterfactual Thinking: When Alternatives to Reality Fail Us, in* WHAT MIGHT HAVE BEEN, *id.*, at 199, 217. Thus, people tend to react more emotionally to specific instances than to abstract cases, and as their emotional responses are triggered, they may readily generate counterfactual alternatives to reality. *Id.* at 216.

Recall Waldron's discussion of Robert Nozick's principle of rectification, which represents a moral demand for historic reparations in certain circumstances. What implications do the cognitive insights regarding problems with counterfactual thinking have for Nozick's principle?

5. *Historical Rights and the Effect of Time.* Nozick's theory, which we discussed in Chapter 3, is a theory of historical rights rather than an end-state theory of distributive justice. Is it possible to reconcile a historical approach to entitlements with sensitivity to the effects of passing time and changed circumstances? Waldron doesn't believe so. John Simmons disagrees. He argues that, although the mere passage of time, considered solely by itself, cannot affect the substance of our moral rights, including rights to rectification for past injustices, the passage of time and changed circumstances *can* affect the content of those rights. *Pace* Nozick, Simmons argues that historical rights are not rights to particular things; rather, they are rights to "certain-sized share[s] of . . . particular set[s] of holdings — namely, to a share of the holdings of the wrongdoer." A. John Simmons, *Historical Rights and Fair Shares*, 14 LAW & PHIL. 149, 162 (1995). Does this approach remain faithful to the principles of a historical approach to entitlements?

6. *Reparations for Slavery.* One of the more controversial reparations topics in recent years concerns demands for reparations for slavery of African Americans. Scholars and public commentators have engaged in protracted debates over whether and under what circumstances reparations should be paid to African Americans for harms perpetrated upon them as a result of slavery and other acts of racism. *See, e.g.,* ROY L. BROOKS, ATONEMENT AND FORGIVENESS: A NEW MODEL FOR BLACK REPARATIONS (2004); RANDALL ROBINSON, THE DEBT: WHAT AMERICA OWES TO BLACKS (2000); Symposium, *The Jurisprudence of Slavery Reparations*, 84 B.U. L. REV. 1135 (2004). The issue has not been confined to journals and newspapers. African Americans have filed legal claims for damages against various firms that were allegedly involved in the slave trade in some capacity or that were allegedly involved in discrete acts of racially motivated violence against African American victims. *See* Anthony J. Sebok, *A Brief History of Mass Restitution Litigation in the United States, in* CALLING POWER TO ACCOUNT: LAW'S RESPONSE TO PAST INJUSTICE 341 (David Dyzenhaus & Mayo Moran eds., 2004); Keith N. Hylton, *A Framework for Reparations Claims*, 24 B.C. THIRD WORLD L.J. 31 (2004). Generally, these claims seek damages as compensation for the present-day harmful effects of injustices perpetuated in the past. These

claims, however, have largely been unsuccessful. *See, e.g.,* In re African American Slave Descendants Litigation, 471 F.3d 754 (7th Cir. 2006), *cert. denied sub nom.* Farmer-Paellman v. Brown & Williamson Tobacco Co., 552 U.S. 941 (2007). Does Waldron's supersession theory undermine the case for such claims? How might supporters of these claims respond to the supersession theory?

Commentators have raised a host of problems with these claims. Reparation claims may rest on individualist or collectivist (group) premises. Both types of claims pose problems. With respect to individualist claims, a question often asked is how can reparation claims made by persons who are not themselves the victims of past injustices but rather the descendants of the victims be justified? One response is that the claim seeks damages not for the past injustice in and of itself but instead for the continuing harmful effects of past injustices. Another response rests on the present-day descendants' right of inheritance from their ancestors. As one commentator puts it, "[the descendants'] right to receive an inheritance does not follow from a theory of historical title that includes an unquestionable right of bequest. It is underwritten [instead] by lifetime-transcending interests of individuals, the importance to individuals of family and friendships, and, most of all, by the role that families play in the lives of individuals." Janna Thompson, Taking Responsibility for the Past 145 (2002). Are these arguments persuasive?

Where the claim rests on moral collectivist premises, other problems arise. Collectivist-based claims involve two assertions: first, that one group—whites—harmed another group—Blacks—by enslaving them; second, responsibility for the present-day harms resulting from that injustice to the descendants of the original members of the group of victims properly rests with the descendants of the original members of the group of the perpetrators. Commentators have contested both assertions. One problem is that had the injustice of slavery not been perpetrated, the members of one group—the African American claimants—would not have existed. *See* James S. Fishkin, *Justice between Generations: Compensation, Identity, and Group Membership, in* Nomos XXXIII: Compensatory Justice 85, 93 (John W. Chapman ed., 1991). Is there any response to this problem? *See id.* at 93-94 (group non-existence provides a possible compensable benchmark in a way that individual non-existence does not). Another problem concerns the identity of members of both groups. *See* Eric A. Posner & Adrian Vermeule, *Reparations for Slavery and Other Historical Injustices,* 103 Colum. L. Rev. 689 (2003). In American society, perhaps more than any other in the world, racial differences quickly blur. Many African Americans are descendants of whites (and perhaps members of other races) as well as African slaves, and by the same token, white Americans very often have members of other races in their ancestral bloodlines. Given this racial ambiguity, can the relevant group memberships be adequately defined?

7. *Reparations in the European Court of Human Rights.* In Demopoulos and Others v. Turkey [GC], nos. 46113/99, 3843/02, 3751/02, 13466/03, 10200/04, 14163/04, 19993/04, 21819/04 §70, Eur. Ct. H.R. 2010-IV, the European Court of Human Rights addressed reparations claims brought by dispossessed Greek Cypriot owners of property, including land, in the northern part of Cyprus currently under the control of the "Turkish Republic of Northern Cyprus" ("TRNC"). The proclamation of the TRNC occurred in 1983 following the continuing division of the island of Cyprus in the aftermath of the 1974 conflict on that island between Turkey and Greece. Although the United Nations Security Council declared the proclamation to be legally invalid, the government of Turkey recognized TRNC as a democratic and constitutional state, politically independent of all other sovereign states, including Turkey. At the same time, TRNC had the status of "a subordinate local administration" under Turkish jurisdiction. UN peacekeeping forces have maintained a buffer zone between TRNC and the southern part of the island (the Republic of Cyprus), to which many Greek Cypriot residents fled from the north.

A TRNC compensation law enacted in 2005 provides that persons may bring claims for "compensation, exchange and restitution" of movable and immovable property before the Immovable Property Commission ("IPC"), which was established under the legislation for this purpose, until the end of 2009 (the deadline was later extended to 2011). Under this law, an applicant must prove beyond a reasonable doubt that the claimed property was registered in his name prior to 1974 (or that he is the legal heir of such a person), that he was forced to abandon it due to conditions beyond his volition, and that there are no other claimants to the property.

In *Demopoulos*, several Greek Cypriots filed claims against the government of Turkey asserting that following Turkey's invasion of northern Cyprus in 1974, they had been prevented from enjoying their homes and property in violation of several provisions of the European Convention on Human Rights and Protocol No. 1 to the Convention. Specifically, they claimed violations of Articles 8 ("Everyone has the right to respect for . . . his home. . . .") and 14 (the non-discrimination provision) and Article 1 of Protocol No. 1 ("Every natural or legal person is entitled to the peaceful enjoyment of his possessions. . . .").

The court stated the background context of the claims in terms that echoed Waldron's argument:

84. . . . [S]ome thirty-five years have elapsed since the applicants lost possession of their property in northern Cyprus in 1974. Generations have passed. The local population has not remained static. Turkish Cypriots who inhabited the north have migrated elsewhere; Turkish-Cypriot refugees from the south have settled in the north; Turkish settlers from Turkey have arrived in large numbers and established their homes. Much Greek-Cypriot property has changed hands at least once, whether by sale, donation or inheritance.

85. Thus, the Court finds itself faced with cases burdened with a political, historical and factual complexity flowing from a problem that should have been resolved by all parties assuming full responsibility for finding a solution on a political level. This reality, as well as the passage of time and the continuing evolution of the broader political dispute must inform the Court's interpretation and application of the Convention which cannot, if it is to be coherent and meaningful, be either static or blind to concrete factual circumstances.

_Id._ at ___.

The claimants challenged the IPC remedy as being inadequate. Since it began functioning in 2006, the IPC had concluded 85 applications by the time this litigation reached the ECHR (300 claims remained pending before the IPC). Of those applications concluded, four resulted in restitution, exchange of property in several others, and substantial amounts of money had been paid in compensation. Claimants had argued that restitution should be the primary remedy. The court responded that at the present time, many decades after the loss of possession by the original owners, in many cases property has changed hands several times through gift, inheritance, or other means. So, it is open to question, the court suggested, whether the notion of title is realistic in practice. "The losses . . . claimed become increasingly speculative and hypothetical."

> . . . [I]t would be unrealistic to expect that as a result of these cases the Court should, or could, directly order the Turkish Government to ensure that these applicants obtain access to, and full possession of, their properties, irrespective of who is now living there or whether the property is allegedly in a militarily sensitive zone or used for vital public purposes.
>
> 113. The Court can only conclude that the attenuation over time of the link between the holding of title and the possession and use of the property in question must have consequences on the nature of the redress that can be regarded as fulfilling the requirements of Article 35 §1 of the Convention.

_Id._ at ___. The court went on to observe that the contracting parties to the case are free to choose the means by which they will implement redress for violations of property rights, noting that from a Convention standpoint, "property is a material commodity which can be valued and compensated for in monetary terms." _Id._ at ___. Unsurprisingly, then, the court unambiguously ruled out the possibility of ordering across-the-board restitution. The court stated, "[S]ome thirty-five years after the applicants, or their predecessors in title, left their property, it would risk being arbitrary and injudicious for [the court] to attempt to impose an obligation on the respondent State to effect restitution in all cases, or even in all cases save those in which there is a material impossibility." _Id._ at ___.

What are your reactions to this decision and the court's reasoning? Are the parameters that the court drew sufficient to enable Greek Cypriot claimants to obtain fair relief?

4. "FROM MARX TO MARKETS"[1]

Claus Offe, Disqualification, Retribution, Restitution: Dilemmas of Justice in Post-Communist Transitions[2]

A thick layer of fog, containing traces of . . . intuitions and arguments . . . both *pro* retroactive justice and *con*, has been hanging over the post-Communist world since 1989. Neither clear, universally accepted, consistent principles nor legislative nor judicial practices have emerged from this fog. A persistent sense of "something must be done, but nothing really can in good conscience be done" dominates the scene. I do not pretend to have sufficient breath to blow the fog away. My ambition in this paper is limited to explaining why it is so hard to come up with a consistent and clear-cut solution, and why, at the same time, it would be so desirable to have one. My task is thus to provide an overview of problems, solutions of problems, and the attendant problems of solutions. . . .

Here, I shall concentrate on the dilemmas of post-Communist retroactive justice as they appear in the German case, with occasional glances at other cases. That obviously is the case I know best and have had the opportunity to study continuously over the last three years. But the German case also has an interesting systematic relevance. If a solution to the problem of retroactive justice can be designed and implemented anywhere, it should be in Germany. Needless to say, my reason for believing so has nothing to do with national character or the like but derives instead from two peculiarities of the German case. First, Germany is the country with the greatest experience in addressing, and debating the proper way to address, the crimes of its recent past due to the unique nature and volume of these crimes.

My second reason requires more elaboration. The German case of post-Communist retrospective justice is unique, as compared to all other post-Communist transitions, in that the state by which and in which these crimes have been committed—namely, the German Democratic Republic—has ceased to exist. Its component parts have become parts of the new Federal Republic of Germany, and as such are largely governed by the legal and institutional structure (as well as, for the most part, the political elite) that had evolved in the former West German state. Thus, seen from the point of view of the old GDR and its population a "foreign" regime has been imposed upon its territory, while in all other post-Communist states the

---

1. We borrow the phrase from Michael Heller. *See* Michael A. Heller, *The Tragedy of the Anticommons: Property in the Transition from Marx to Markets*, 111 Harv. L. Rev. 621 (1998).—Eds.

2. Claus Offe, *Disqualification, Retribution, Restitution: Dilemmas of Justice in Post-Communist Transitions*, 1 J. Pol. Phil. 17, 19-23, 40-44 (1993).

regime change amounts to a giant bootstrapping act of self-extrication. This peculiarity had the predictable and intended consequence of a much more abrupt, rapid and comprehensive regime change, made feasible by the fact that the former West German state offered itself as the "Archimedean point" at which the required leverage could be generated. Due to its size and resources being much greater than that of the old GDR, the former West German state came to serve as the functional equivalent to post-World War II occupation regimes which were able similarly to impose upon the defeated territories virtually any concept of social and political order they saw fit. In contrast, one may locate the structural problem of the other post-Communist states precisely in the fact that there is no "occupation regime" or equivalent. Hence they do not yet have collective agencies exercising the kind of "governing capacity" needed for coming to terms with the past according to strictly imposed rules and procedures.

Only Germany, therefore, is in command of the political resources to *enforce effectively* whatever rules and principles derive from the *intense theoretical and moral debate* about how to come to terms with the past—a debate which has, for good reasons and with relentless force, been prominent in the German public sphere for the better part of the past forty years. No other country has seen an equally intense debate, and none has autonomous political control over the remnants of the past comparable to that of the new German state that came into being with the inclusion of the former GDR. From all this, it is safe to conclude that if even the Germans do not find a consistent and practicable solution to the problem, or if even the Germans fail to implement it, then no other country will be capable even of coming close to a satisfactory way out of the dilemmas involved in coming to terms with its Communist past. Germany must therefore be the case chosen for a "most favorable case" analysis.

To say that the German public has developed a sharp awareness of the problems of retrospective justice through being exposed, for more than a generation, to the experience of the Nazi regime and its repercussions in time and space is not to say that the two pasts to be dealt with are similar or strictly comparable. There are probably no definite lessons from the past to be drawn about how to draw lessons from the past. The only general lesson that can be drawn is the need for, and the practice of, fair deliberation. Treating the former GDR elites and their criminal elements with the same kind of benign neglect that many Nazi leaders and activists enjoyed in the early years of the West German state would raise the objection that the German elites are unwilling or unable to learn from their previous failures to face the past. But treating them more severely, and prosecuting their acts more thoroughly, would raise the objection that by implication the GDR regime is taken as *more* criminal and objectionable than the Nazi regime, which is an obvious absurdity.

The three most important differences between the situations after 1945 and after 1989 are clear enough. First, the earlier case involved unparalleled charges of genocide, war crimes and crimes against international law, none of which applies to the latter case. Second, the earlier case was processed by the victorious powers after a total military defeat of the German Reich, whereas the latter case involves a relatively robust liberal democracy being established in the now unified Federal Republic of Germany which has the legitimate authority to deal with injustices perpetrated in the former German Democratic Republic. Third, the task is made somewhat easier by the fact that, in stark contrast to the Nazi regime, the former GDR had at least nominally adopted (through legislation, in its constitution and through its ratification of international laws and agreements such as the Helsinki documents) certain principles against which to measure the acts that its political elites committed, ordered, condoned or tolerated.

In consequence of these vast differences, both the option of "adopting the same approach as before" and the option of "doing better this time" are out of the question. The only remaining option is to approach the new case independently and on its own terms, keeping in mind that the only thing it has in common with the earlier case is that it poses once again a formidable challenge to our moral, political, and legal capacities. The challenge is that "something must be done" — even if . . . this "something" may perhaps consist in a well-reasoned decision to limit the kind and scope of action, even to the point of "doing nothing."

II. THE OPTIONS AVAILABLE

If something must be done, three principal options are available, which admit of any number of different combinations. There are *perpetrators* and *victims*; and there are the means of *civil law* (regulating allocation of property rights, income and status) as well as the means of *criminal law* (dispensing negative sanctions, such as fines and imprisonment). Combining these two distinctions yields three options: *disqualification, retribution* and *restitution*.

(1) *Disqualification*, or proscription, refers to legally-mandated acts designed to deprive categories of perpetrators, be they natural or legal persons, of (some measure of) their material possessions and civil status. Disqualification deprives people of possessions or status on the grounds either that they are deemed to have been wrongfully obtained under the old regime or else that they have been derived from the function, which as such is not liable to criminal prosecution, which those persons have performed under and in active support of the old regime. This type of measure can also be aimed against the property of corporate actors, such as the Party or parties, state-controlled trade unions, newspapers, publishing houses and so on.

(2) By *retribution* I mean criminal sanctions dispensed against individual perpetrators for criminal acts, proven in a formal court proceeding and on the basis of a criminal code.

(3) *Restitution* refers to legally-mandated acts designed to compensate victims, in cash or kind, for that of which the old regime has deprived them.

The first empirical generalization I wish to draw is that none of the post-Communist regimes can rely on either [*sic*] of the three main options to the exclusion of the other two. All three strategies will probably be used in all cases. . . .

V. RESTITUTION: COMPENSATING VICTIMS

A strong preference for this option may result from the thought that it is generally much easier to identify victims than to identify the actors who deprived them unrightfully of their lives, health, property, incomes, careers or freedom. This priority might also do more to heal wounds and to further political integration. Upon closer inspection, however, it turns out that being a "victim" is not a self-evident and easily recognized fact but is, instead, a thoroughly political construct. And even after the quality of being a "victim" is established, it depends upon which legal doctrine legislators wish to follow whether compensation is granted at all, and, if so, on the basis of rights, needs, or desirable consequences.

First of all, compensation for losses presupposes proof of loss. Such proof is much easier to provide in some categories of loss (expropriation of immovables, confiscation, imprisonment) than in others (movable property, health, lost opportunities). Even in the former case, access to the official documents which are required as proof of former property titles and inheritance may be difficult as these documents are often incomplete, contested or hard to locate. These conditions give rise to questions of fairness — not only between proprietors and other victims of the old regime but also among proprietors.

Next, compensation can take place in a variety of modes, some of which can be implemented with or without quantitative or temporal restrictions on the right of the owners to alienate property thus restituted. These modes are, in a decreasing order of "tangibility":

- natural restitution of the identical piece of land, etc.;
- restitution in kind, but of some non-identical piece of property having roughly equal value;
- restitution in cash, the amount being determined through some shadow-pricing procedure;
- restitution in vouchers or coupons, that is, shares in the national property that is to be privatized (the relative attraction of this method being that it helps to alleviate fiscal burdens and perhaps also to accelerate future privatization of state enterprises);
- rehabilitation, usually applied in cases other than through the confiscation of property, such as the loss of freedom through criminal prosecution or discrimination.

On a collective level, symbolic restitution consists in giving back their old names to streets, places, and cities. Also, the relocation of institutions such as federal courts of justice, federal administrative agencies or major research institutes to East German cities has been suggested and partly implemented as a means to provide some symbolic (as well as material) compensation to local and regional communities.

Finally, even if it were agreed that compensation should take place only to owners of immovables and only as natural restitution, the universe of legitimate claimants still needs to be determined. Distinctions might turn on: the past and present nationality of owners/heirs; the willingness to return in the case of claimants who currently live abroad; family status, in the case of heirs (close versus distant relatives); the time of property losses; the size of the property in question; natural persons' versus corporate (for example, church) property; the willingness and financial ability to invest in the reprivatized property or to accept liabilities that stem from ecological damages or damages resulting from past negligence; their criminal record; and the prehistory of the property in question and the reasons for its expropriation by the old regime.

The major difference between restitution and retribution is that the former involves massive transfers of material resources. By definition, such resources have "alternative uses," and their transfer thus involves opportunity costs, measured as the costs of forgoing alternative uses. Creating owners through restitution is an act that correlatively creates non-owners. For instance, must the tenants—who so far have enjoyed considerable security as they were protected from eviction and rent increases—now be compensated for the rent increases that fall upon them as a direct consequence of restoring property titles to the former owners? As restitution is a political act, rather than an act of "original appropriation," the prospective nonowners must consent to restitution and tolerate its consequences, particularly if they constitute a majority, since the transfer of property to former owners precludes other conceivable uses of these assets and imposes very tangible material burdens upon them.

That past injustices call for compensation may meet with a widely shared moral intuition of backward-looking justice. It is good up to a point, but ought [to] cease at that point at which the opportunity costs of such compensation begin to be felt. Beyond that point, restitution will only be supported if the burden of perceived opportunity costs is mitigated by considerations of forward-looking justice. In order to catalyze this shift of perspective, a proposition of the following kind needs to be made and accepted: restitution is just not only because the *former* owners deserve it, but also because *all of us* deserve the fruits of a more efficient economy which is most easily and reliably established through restitution.

This proposition, however, is open to three kinds of objections. First, it may be argued that other forms of privatization (as opposed to reprivatization) may be more conducive to those anticipated collective benefits, and at least some of the individual interests of former owners ought therefore rightly [to] be ignored. The sheer quantity of restitution claims (estimated to number 1.5 million in East Germany) and the time necessary to process them may delay the process of economic reconstruction to an intolerable extent. Restitution will also put the property into the hands of persons who may lack the talent, interest or financial means to maintain or develop it; or they may simply default on their stated commitments to do so. To be sure, restitution is less costly in fiscal terms than any reasonably adequate level of compensation payment would be. But that may hold true only in the short run, while in the long run the delay in economic reconstruction caused by restitution will involve heavy fiscal losses as well.

Second, it is objected that the "valley of transition" that separates the present condition from the supposedly bright future is too deep and wide (in terms of unemployment and large-scale societal disorganization) to make the above proposition credible. The special problem of the German case consists in the fact that, if and when a dynamic of self-sustained growth eventually takes hold in the economy of the former GDR, it will be due to massive transfers that the citizens of the old *Länder* will have contributed to make this recovery possible. These contributions, currently estimated to amount to more than 2000 billion Deutschmarks over the next half decade, are needed for the reconstruction of the East German infrastructure (including the repair of its worst ecological damage), as well as subsidies for investment, employment and consumption. These sacrifices and their volume now begin to raise the question of "secondary compensation," namely, the question concerning the compensation that *West German citizens* can and will request in return for their contribution (as being paid in terms of higher taxes, higher prices, higher social security contributions, higher interest rates, as well as increases in the public debt) to the East German recovery.

Third, the moral objection may be raised that it is unfair that, within the universe of victims of the old regime, the subset of *expropriated owners of productive assets alone* can rely on the subsidiary force of consequentialist considerations to defend their claims, whereas all others (including, for instance, those having served long prison terms for convictions in political trials) must depend on nothing but the vulnerable and conceivably transient political will to implement standards of backward-looking compensatory justice. Suppose, on the other hand, it is firmly agreed that those who have suffered damages of a kind unrelated to the loss of property (spoiled careers, imprisonment, damaged health, impossibility of travel to the Mediterranean) from the old regime must also be compensated, strict restitution being logically impossible in their case. What then is the schedule according to which such compensation should be granted? Recently adopted legislation in Germany provides for a payment of DM 300 to DM 600 per month in prison, which is by necessity an arbitrary range of figures. So far there have been no proposals for compensation for losses in terms of careers or health, as has partly been the case with the so-called *Wiedergutmachung* paid to the victims of Nazi crimes.

The problems with such monetary compensation are, first, that it cannot really reverse the damages from which victims have suffered and, second, that in each individual case a relevant counterfactual must be established by the administration and eventually in court. For instance, if compensation for a prison term is claimed, some proof must be provided that the case would not have led to imprisonment (or would have led to fewer years of imprisonment) had the defendant been given a fair trial, according to rule-of-law principles. In practise, [*sic*] such proof must largely rely on very rough proxies and potentially controversial indicators, such as whether the presiding judge has been a communist party activist or not. Any conceivable legal regulation of restitution is bound to be open to the objection of arbitrariness and unfairness, since such regulation concerns the *level* of compensation in cash and the forward and backward *time boundaries* of restitution, as well as the thorny problem which types of property should be *exempt* from restitution, in the interest of promoting investment and growth.

NOTES AND QUESTIONS

1. *Post-Communist Reparations in Central and Eastern Europe.* In the wake of the fall of soviet-style socialist regimes throughout Central and Eastern Europe in 1989, many of the new political regimes instituted programs of property reparations as part of their larger programs aimed at achieving both privatization of the economy and transitional justice. As Jon Elster has observed, the extent of the efforts to provide transitional justice varied widely throughout the region. Such efforts were most extensive in the Czech Republic and least important in Romania. JON ELSTER, CLOSING THE BOOKS: TRANSITIONAL JUSTICE IN HISTORICAL PERSPECTIVE 67 (2004).

Specifically with respect to restitution, the spectrum ranged from the Czech Republic, whose restitutionary plan was among the most ambitious, to Hungary, where the new regime put into effect a much less ambitious plan of restitution, according to Michael Heller and Christopher Serkin. *See* Michael Heller & Christopher Serkin, *Revaluing Restitution: From the Talmud to Postsocialism*, 97 MICH. L. REV. 1385, 1399-1405 (1999). Summarizing the results of the restitution efforts in the two countries as of 1999, Heller and Serkin write:

> Restitution in the Czech Republic is one of the largest such programs in Eastern Europe. Favoring a policy of "natural" restitution . . . , the Czech government is restoring a still inestimable amount of property to its precommunist owners or their heirs. Truck drivers, shoe moguls, western bankers, human rights activists, elderly men and women with distant memories of expropriated properties, and

heirs to ancient estates are among the many people repossessing property in the former Czechoslovakia. . . .

Three Czech laws together create a comprehensive program of restitution. All three laws codify a preference for "natural restitution," which gives property back to its "original" owner. When the property's value increased significantly during communist possession, however, monetary compensation is sometimes awarded, equivalent to fair market value at the time of expropriation. This alternative is subject to strict monetary caps on the cash any single claimant can receive, the balance being paid in riskier state securities. . . .

Id. at 1399-1400.

As Heller and Serkin describe, Hungary adopted a significantly different approach from that of the Czech Republic. Hungarian restitution is frequently described as "limited" compensation. It does not provide natural (i.e., in-kind) restitution but instead pays compensation at fixed rates for property taken by the communists. The fixed rates applied to property commonly provide only a token percentage of the property's actual value. Claims up to $2,300 are compensated in full; the next $1,150 are compensated at 50 percent; the next $2,300 get 30 percent; and amounts above these totals get 10 percent up to a maximum compensation of about $57,000.

Hungarian restitution is "limited" not only because of the undervaluation of restorable property. The Hungarian approach also restricts the form of the compensation. Rather than cash, the Hungarian government pays original owners compensation in the form of state-created coupons. Although these coupons are freely tradable securities, they are not fully liquid for five years and are intended to be used to repurchase state-owned property. The goal of the Hungarian approach is modest. Rather than reprivatization or full compensation, it is partial indemnification. *See id.* at 1402.

Declaring these policies was one thing; implementing them was quite another. The Czech restitution program became embroiled in a number of controversies. As Istvan Pogany explains, "[The] problems stem[med] largely from the difficulty of neatly separating the Communist period, in moral, historical or constitutional terms, from the two preceding historical phases, i.e., the war years and the immediate post-war period." Istvan Pogany, Europe in Change: Righting Wrongs in Eastern Europe 150 (1997). The Czech restitution laws limited claims to those for property that the state acquired between 1948 and 1990. As Pogany notes, this limitation "excluded consideration of the massive takings of private property which were focused on Czechoslovakia's former Jewish minority between 1939 and 1945 and, after the war, on Czechoslovakia's then-substantial *Volksdeutsche* community." *Id.* at 152.

With respect to Hungary's program, Pogany observes that "the partiality of Hungarian restitution schemes was not dictated by pragmatism alone; it also had clear ideological roots." *Id.* at 156. He continues, "restitution schemes were often intended not merely to rectify past injustices, but to serve as an aid to social regeneration of a very specific type." *Ibid*. For example, one clear objective of restitution legislation was to return land to former owners of small plots of agricultural land who were dispossessed by communist rule in 1949. This was the result of interest-group politics, as the political party representing small landholders exerted considerable power in the coalition government. *See id.* at 156-165.

2. *Why Restitution at All?* Was restitution in post-communist Europe warranted at all? In a controversial article, Jon Elster argues that "one should target everybody or nobody" and that because it is impossible to reach everyone who suffered under communist rule "nobody should be punished and nobody compensated." Jon Elster, *On Doing What One Can: Against Post-Communist Restitution and Retribution*, 1 E. EUR. CONST. REV. 15 (1992). More fully, Elster argues that with respect to restitution, "the main issue . . . is that of equal treatment. It is important to keep in mind that essentially everybody suffered under Communism." *Id.* at 16. Because everyone experienced some sort of material loss under communist rule, he contends, compensating one group of victims—those who lost tangible property—but not others would be arbitrary and wrong. "Doing what one can," by compensating as far as is feasible, is, Elster asserts, "incoherent." *Id.* at 17. Do you agree? Is partial justice unreasonable or irrational? Will no restitution give those who would not have received any compensation or restitution under a policy aimed at protecting only those who lost tangible property a greater sense of fairness or justice than a policy of partial restitution?

3. *"Natural" Restitution and Partial Restitution: A Common Rationale?* As we have seen, the Czech and Hungarian restitutionary programs embody two different approaches, one providing for so-called "natural" (i.e., in-kind) restitution, the other only partial restitution. One might suppose that these two different approaches reflect two different policies. Michael Heller and Christopher Serkin, however, argue that this is not so, at least not necessarily. Drawing upon Hanoch Dagan's general theory of restitution (*see* HANOCH DAGAN, UNJUST ENRICHMENT: A STUDY OF PRIVATE LAW AND PUBLIC VALUES (1998)), Heller and Serkin argue that both programs provide limited *ex post* property protection that may create a perverse *ex ante* incentive for the government to expropriate. "Natural restitution," they contend, "sends a message: not of the vindication of personhood through protection of property, but nearly the opposite, that the communists could gamble with your land and then, when they lost, return it to you in shambles." Heller & Serkin, *supra* Note 1, at 1408. Like the Czech program, Hungary's restitution program was based on a rationale of protecting well-being rather than personhood, Heller and Serkin argue. Moreover, they suggest, Hungary's program sent a similar message to expropriators. "Expropriators have effectively been granted an entitlement to use the property, while being called upon to restitute only a fixed and minimal percentage of its

actual value." *Ibid.* If Heller and Serkin are correct, why in the wake of communism would newly democratic regimes set out to promote their own programs of well-being rather than to vindicate personhood? *See id.* at 1406 (restitution is part of national myth-making, linking current citizens with "natural" owners of resources; programs provide insight into national ethoses).

4. *Transitional Justice vs. Distributive Justice.* A concern similar to the one Waldron discussed in Chapter 17.3 is that transitional justice, whether in the form of in-kind reparations or cash payments, does not occur in a vacuum. Resources used to pay reparations are unavailable for other social purposes. Some commentators have objected to all but symbolic reparations on precisely this ground, arguing that particularly in new democracies, such as in post-communist Europe, the demands for distributive justice are greater than those for corrective justice. *See* Christopher Kutz, *Justice in Reparations: The Cost of Memory and the Value of Cheap Talk*, 32 PHIL. & PUB. AFF. 277 (2004). On what basis can we compare the needs for these two forms of justice against each other?

18 ENVIRONMENTAL LAW AND POLICY

J.B. Ruhl, Climate Change Adaption and the Structural Transformation of Environmental Law[1]

INTRODUCTION

The path of environmental law has come to a cliff called climate change, and there is no turning around. Someday . . . the federal government will take the big leap and enact new legislation designed to curb our nation's greenhouse gas emissions. Whether it is through a carbon tax, a cap-and-trade program, or some new regulatory innovation, the measure will be hailed by many and derided by many others. The supporters will throw a big party, and the opponents will hold a wake. When the hangovers wear off the next day, however, one thing will still be soberingly true no matter how aggressive the newly-minted legislation: Humans and our fellow species are looking into a future of climate change that will last a century or more, and we've done very little in the United States to prepare ourselves for it.

Indeed, the policy world's fixation on achieving, or blocking, federal greenhouse gas emission legislation as part of our national strategy for

---

1. J.B. Ruhl, *Climate Change Adaptation and the Structural Transformation of Environmental Law*, 40 ENVTL. L. 363, 365-366, 392, 394-395, 397, 398, 400-401, 402, 406-407, 408, 409-410, 412, 413, 414-416, 417-418, 423, 425, 426, 427, 428, 429, 431, 432-434 (2010).

climate change mitigation[2] has contributed to our neglect of national policy for climate change adaptation. . . . [3]

III. TEN STRUCTURAL TRENDS IN ENVIRONMENTAL LAW

. . . [N]o one could reasonably accuse environmental law of being static; indeed, the forty-year story of modern statutory environmental law is one largely of change. But it has been a story primarily of goal-oriented change motivated from within environmental law to address discrete pollution media and conservation objectives. Those days are over. Environmental law does not "own" climate change adaptation policy. Rather, it may be just the reverse, as national, state, and local adaptation priorities place tremendous pressure on environmental law to partner with other fields of law in facilitation of adaptation. I am not sure where this leads, but I have some ideas about how climate change adaptation policy will most profoundly transform environmental law — ten of them to be exact.

A. Trend One: Shift in Emphasis from Preservationism to Transitionalism in Natural Resources Conservation Policy

The development of environmental law has taken many of its cues from environmental and ecological sciences . . . . [T]he "dynamic equilibrium" model that is now firmly in place in ecology is based on the assumption of "stationarity," which as Milly et al. explains is "the idea that natural systems fluctuate within an unchanging envelope of variability." . . . [4]

The stationarity premise and all on which it is based, however, are going to fall to pieces in the era of climate change. . . .

---

2. Climate change mitigation "refers to options for limiting climate change by, for example, reducing heat-trapping emissions such as carbon dioxide, methane, nitrous oxide, and halocarbons, or removing some of the heat-trapping gases from the atmosphere." U.S. GLOBAL CHANGE RESEARCH PROGRAM, GLOBAL CLIMATE CHANGE IMPACTS IN THE UNITED STATES 10-11 (2009), *available at* http://downloads.globalchange.gov/usimpacts/pdfs/climate-impacts-report.pdf; see also INTERGOVERNMENTAL PANEL ON CLIMATE CHANGE, CLIMATE CHANGE 2001: MITIGATION app. at 716 (Bert Metz et al. eds., 2001), *available at* http:// www.grida.no/climate/ipcc_tar/wg3/pdf/app.pdf (mitigation strategies involve "an anthropogenic intervention to reduce the sources or enhance the sinks of greenhouse gases").

3. Climate change adaptation "refers to changes made to better respond to present or future climatic and other environmental conditions, thereby reducing harm or taking advantage of opportunity. Effective mitigation measures reduce the need for adaptation." U.S. GLOBAL CHANGE RESEARCH PROGRAM, *supra* note 2, at 11; see also INTERGOVERNMENTAL PANEL ON CLIMATE CHANGE, CLIMATE CHANGE 2007: IMPACTS, ADAPTATION AND VULNERABILITY app. at 869 (M.L. Perry et al. eds., 2007) ("Adjustment in natural or human systems in response to actual or expected climatic stimuli or their effects, which moderates harm or exploits beneficial opportunities."), *available at* http://www.ipcc.ch/pdf/assessment-report/ar4/wg2/ar4-wg2-app.pdf. Climate change adaptation is also known as "climate proofing," see Paul Stanton Kibel, *Climate Adaptation Policy at the Continental Level: Natural Resources in North America and Europe*, 27 PACE ENVTL. L. REV. 473 (2010), and as "coping," see U.S. Envtl. Prot. Agency, Adaptation, http://www.epa.gov/climatechange/effects/adaptation.html (last visited Apr. 18, 2010).

4. P.C.D. Milly, et al., *Stationarity is Dead: Whither Water Management*, 319 SCI. 573, 573 (2008).

So, what is the successor for conservation policy? Clearly, the preservationist foundations of the habitat reserve strategy, whether applied in the form of a wildlife refuge, a habitat mitigation set aside for an endangered species, a wilderness area, or a wetlands mitigation bank, are on shaky ground. What is it that the reserve is preserving if "natural" and "native" no longer have the same meaning as they do under the stationarity premise? Is a species migrating from a now inhospitable climate-altered ecosystem "invasive" in its new ecosystem, or is it to be commended and protected for its "natural" adaptation? Is a wildlife refuge established for waterfowl a failure if it dries up, and if so should we import water to keep it "natural" so the "native" species can remain there? We could debate these questions, of course, but my point is that the prevailing model of conservation has no answers. These questions only exist because we are entering a whole different ballgame. . . .

[T]he successor, managing for change, must embrace the transform and move modes, looking toward a transition to the future for its reference points rather than to the past as preservationism does. The transition, to put it bluntly, is from the nature we once knew to the nature that we expect to find around us on the other side of climate change. Only when we get there, however, can we begin to talk again about what belongs where under the new set of natural conditions. . . .

B. Trend Two: Rapid Evolution of Property Rights and Liability Rules Associated with Natural Capital Adaptation Resources

. . . Climate change adaptation will inextricably and fundamentally link people in ways they have not experienced before, and new controversies are bound to surface in connection with their property and their safety. Put simply, some people are going to take actions with their property and personal behaviors, or fail to take actions, that put the property and safety of other people at significant risk of injury. It is inevitable that those injured will pursue remedies, and the courts will have to determine who should pay. . . .

. . . Climate change adaptation strategies are even more likely to trigger property rights disputes in need of new judicial examination given mounting knowledge about ecosystem services. As natural capital resources that provide ecosystem services such as storm surge mitigation factor increasingly into climate change adaptation policy — which will happen precisely because of the ecosystem services provided — it is likely that the common law will grab hold of this new knowledge even more aggressively. Indeed, whereas the public nuisance and other common law claims that states and other interests have lodged against large sources of greenhouse gas emissions as part of a mitigation litigation strategy are high profile media stories notwithstanding limited success, it is likely to be in the more discrete, small-scale context of adaptation in which the common law will have reason to evolve. . . .

C. Trend Three: Accelerated Merger of Water Law, Land-Use Law, and Environmental Law

. . . .

D. Trend Four: Incorporation of a Human Rights Dimension in Climate Change Adaptation Policy

Just as climate change impacts will be felt unevenly across the globe, so too is the capacity to adapt unevenly distributed. In both cases, unfortunately, it is the least developed countries that drew the short straw — they will feel climate change more severely and have the least capacity to reduce vulnerability and boost resilience. This double whammy effect has led the international law community to characterize global adaptation policy as a human rights issue. Indeed, the vast majority of legal scholarship on climate change adaptation focuses on international law and international relations addressing four principal facets of this human rights dimension — the responsibilities of developed nations to 1) assist the adaptation efforts of least developed nations, 2) assist the adaptation efforts of small island nations, 3) assist the adaptation efforts of indigenous people, and 4) assist the migration efforts of people from these three communities who are displaced by climate change notwithstanding adaptation assistance. . . .

Only a few legal scholars have addressed even the tip of the iceberg of this looming question of *domestic* climate justice policy, and in general "the national debate on climate change policies has given insufficient attention to their environmental justice implications." . . .

What lessons come out of this emerging theme of *domestic* human rights for *domestic* environmental law? One seems inevitable and critical to bear in mind — that it will be important to define the human right of climate justice and distinguish it from the concept that there is a human right to a certain level of environmental quality. With respect to the adaptation side of climate policy, climate justice articulates not a right to environmental quality, but rather a right to equitable distribution of the benefits of climate change adaptation, which may or may not align with environmentalist norms of minimum conditions of environmental quality. Equitable distribution of climate adaptation resources and protections may not always fulfill conventional environmental protection norms such as conserving ecosystems and imperiled species, as, for example, when seawalls or beach renourishment may be needed to protect human communities unable to transform or move, or when water may need to be transferred to sustain urban populations of poor and people of color who have no options. This is not to say that climate justice will not promote environmental protection, but primarily when doing so serves climate justice interests. Climate justice, in other words, is first and foremost about protecting the poor and people of color, not the environment.

E. Trend Five: Catastrophe and Crisis Avoidance and Response as an Overarching Adaptation Policy Priority

[T]he synergistic effects of changes in variability of storm, flood, drought, and fire events with absolute changes in sea level, temperature, and other climate features will lead to higher risks of catastrophic events and pandemic crises. People will demand protection. . . .

[T]he United States has complies close to zero in the way of coordinated anticipatory adaptation policy for managing the risk in the United States of climate change catastrophe and crisis. . . . This is a direct result of the adaptation deficit, not some rationalized decision to adopt a wait-and-see reactive adaptation orientation. . . .

I am headed here in much the same direction as with climate justice policy, which is a form of risk management for particular populations: Environmental law will be one among many players in the design of climate change catastrophe and crisis risk management. . . .

F. Trend Six: Frequent Reconfigurations of Transpolicy Linkages and Tradeoffs at All Scales and Across Scale

[A] complex of policy linkages will take place over three broad, interconnected dynamics that will challenge the ability of law to continue to operate on the premise of "stationarity" in social and economic affairs. The first will involve feedback between various fronts of climate change adaptation policy as local, state, federal, and private institutions attempt to mainstream adaptation strategies as a flow of coordinated decisions linking environmental policy with national security, immigration, trade, public health, finance, foreign aid, tax, social welfare, business policy, and housing policies, to name just a few, and do so across all governance scales. . . .

The second major dynamic will be the interaction of climate change adaptation policy holistically with other major global change drivers. Chief among these, according to an interdisciplinary team of researchers, will be increasing antibiotic resistance; increasing economic, social, and ecological connectivity; rising human numbers and urbanization; increasing per capita resources use; nuclear proliferation; international terrorism; energy, food, and water crises; declining fisheries; increasing ocean acidification; and emerging diseases. These "intertwined global-scale challenges spawned by the accelerating scale of human activity" are "outpacing the development of institutions to deal with them and their many interactive effects." . . .

The third major dynamic integrates the international dimension of climate change adaptation into national policy, as the United States loses its global hegemonic position and thus increasingly must set its national adaptation policy with other nations' adaptation strategies taken into account. . . .

My ultimate message in this may be unsettling to environmentalists: Climate change adaptation policy is going to transcend environmental law quickly and decisively. Environmental law will be competing with a shifting array of other adaptation policy demands possessing potentially greater urgency and importance. . . .

G. Trend Seven: Shift from "Front-End" Decision Methods Relying on Robust Predictive Capacity to "Back-End" Decision Methods Relying on Active Adaptive Management

For purposes of climate change adaptation policy, the demand for predictive capacity will be the Achilles' heel for the application of conventional environmental impact assessment and cost-benefit analysis. As previously discussed, the impacts of climate change necessitating human and environmental adaptation will be excruciatingly difficult to predict. Nonlinearities in change dynamics, environmental feedback properties, and the interactions of social and ecological responses will soon exceed the boundaries of environmental stationarity that have allowed environmental impact assessment and cost-benefit analysis to maintain what reliability and credibility they have. . . .

H. Trend Eight: Greater Variety and Flexibility in Regulatory Instruments

If adaptive management will be environmental law's methodology for climate change adaptation, what will be its instruments for adaptation decision implementation? . . .

In this regard, a growing number of environmental law scholars have gravitated to what has been dubbed New Governance theory, which turns "away from the familiar model of command-style, fixed-rule regulation by administrative fiat, and toward a new model of collaborative, multiparty, multi-level, adaptive, problem-solving" governance. The central organizing principles of New Governance theory are stakeholder participation, collaboration among interests, diversity of and competition between instruments, decentralization of governance structures, integration of policy domains, flexibility, and an emphasis on noncoerciveness and adaptation. Rigidly relying on fixed, uniform regulatory instruments, such as technology standards and regulatory prescriptions, forecloses adaptation to the kind of evolving, complex problems climate change adaptation will present. Governance institutions will need a broader array of instruments, ranging from "hard" prescriptive mandates to "soft" incentive- and information-based tools, to test for leverage over the more tractable attributes of climate change adaptation problems over time. . . .

I. Trend Nine: Increased Reliance on Multiscalar Governance Networks

In the mitigation context, debate over the federalism question is reminiscent of the well-known "Matching Principle," which claims that "regulatory authority should go to the political jurisdiction that comes closest to matching the geographic area affected by a particular externality." Yet it is difficult enough to conceive of which scale best does so for mitigation policy; searching for the right scale in adaptation policy is an even more complex undertaking. . . .

. . . Although it has not been focused on climate change adaptation policy, the emerging theory of Dynamic Federalism has captured the attention of environmental law scholars for how it could address the multiscalar attributes of other large-scale environmental problems, and it is likely to gain credence in the adaptation context as well. Under Dynamic Federalism, "federal and state governments function as alternative centers of power and any matter is presumptively within the authority of both the federal and the state governments." The theory is not radical—it does not suggest overhauling the basic federal-state-local structure of governance. Rather, it explicitly calls for overlapping federal and state (and, through states, local) jurisdictions. . . .

Proponents of Dynamic Federalism have primarily focused on its advantages of plurality, dialogue, redundancy, accountability, and economies of scale. The key point relating to the federalism question in climate change adaptation policy is the theory's overlapping, flexible distribution of authority between federal, state, and local agencies. . . .

J. Trend Ten: Conciliation

Environmental law is not omnipotent, though one would not gather so from the rhetoric of environmental law on climate change mitigation policy. . . . But some strident proponents of emissions regulation have described their agenda as far broader and deeper in scope and intensity. As they put it, "we must launch a thousand arrows immediately," and the arrows they have in mind are lawsuits under existing federal environmental laws such as the ESA [Endangered Species Act], CWA [Clean Water Act], and NEPA [National Environmental Policy Act]. . . .

My fear is that the "thousand arrows" strategy will creep into environmental law's approach to climate change adaptation as well. . . . Climate change adaptation thus presents an opportunity for environmental law to break free from its culture of litigation and contestation and build back what that culture has eroded most—trust. Trust generally does not come about through threats to sue.

[E]nvironmental law has a choice to make and the luxury of making it early in the formulation of climate change adaptation policy—is it going to be about conflict or conciliation?

The other trends I have predicted suggest that it should be about conciliation. . . .

IV.   CONCLUSION

Climate change adaptation is profoundly about the environment, but it is not profoundly about environmental law. Indeed, environmental law has a debt to repay to the nation's adaptation deficit. . . . [W]hile environmental law now recognizes mitigation and adaptation as being joined at the hip, adaptation policy dialogue has thus far not allowed environmental law to stake adaptation as its domain.

NOTES AND QUESTIONS

1. *Is Environmental Law Irrelevant?* Prior to the emergence of the problem of climate change, lawmakers, policy analysts, and scholars widely believed that environmental problems could be solved through the tools of environmental law. Is Ruhl arguing that with growing understanding of the nature of climate change, environmental law is no longer relevant because its tools are inadequate to cope with the types of problems that climate change creates? If that is his claim, do you agree?

Richard Lazarus, while not arguing that the tools of environmental legislation are conceptually incapable of coping with the problems of climate change, worries about the risk of shortsightedness when it comes to lawmaking in the context of climate change. "Climate change legislation is peculiarly vulnerable to being unraveled over time for a variety of reasons," he contends, "but especially because of the extent to which it imposes costs on the short term for the realization of benefits many decades and sometimes centuries later." Richard J. Lazarus, *Super Wicked Problems and Climate Change: Restraining the Present to Liberate the Future*, 94 CORNELL L. REV. 1153, 1157 (2009). In his view, successful climate change legislation requires institutional design features that make it asymmetric, in the sense that it is easier to change the law in one substantive direction rather than another. Is the problem that Lazarus identifies — the ease with which lawmakers can undermine legislation through subsequent amendments or non-enforcement — unique to the problem of climate change, or is it endemic to legislation in all areas, not just environmental law? Consider tax legislation, for example. A familiar pattern of tax legislation is that Congress periodically enacts a major tax reform act, only to undermine its own effort a few years later by reinstating many of the old tax system's features that it sought to reform. *See* Jason S. Oh, *The Social Cost of Fundamental Tax Reform*, 65 TAX L. REV. ___ (forthcoming 2012).

2. *Collaboration, Cooperation, and "New Governance" Theory.* One of the future trends that Ruhl identifies is a shift away from state coercion toward

more flexible and more collaborative forms of regulation (Trend Seven). In this regard he refers to the so-called "new governance" theory. That theory is "a variety of alternative approaches to regulation that eschew government mandated rules, norms and directives that are issued from the top down and are implemented primarily by governmental actors." Lisa T. Alexander, *Stakeholder Participation in New Governance: Lessons from Chicago's Public Housing Reform Experiment,* 16 Geo. J. on Poverty L. & Pol'y 117, 120 (2009). New governance theorists argue that "positive long-term outcomes are possible for traditionally marginalized stakeholders who participate in substantially deregulated public-private collaborations." *Id.* at 121.

Does the new governance approach bear any resemblance to Ostrom's theory of successful common-pool resource management, which we examined in Chapter 12? Recall that Ostrom there described seven design principles of robust common-pool resources. Among these was the principle that individuals affected by the institutional rules governing use and management of common-pool resources have the authority to participate in changing those rules. Bear in mind that Ostrom's theory concerns the internal regulation of groups, whereas the new governance theory is concerned with external effects.

3.   *Commodification or Decommodification in Environmental Law.* One approach that lawmakers have taken to deal with the problem of pollution and other environmental problems is through the creation of environmental trading markets (ETMs). The twin goals of ETMs are environmental protection and efficient resource allocation.

Although ETMs have been used in a wide variety of contexts, ranging from air pollution to endangered species, they all share a common feature — exchangeable units of trade that are fungible. *See* James Salzman & J.B. Ruhl, *Currencies and the Commodification of Environmental Law,* 53 Stan. L. Rev. 607 (2000). Some commentators have challenged the assumption underlying that feature — the belief that a common currency exists within each environmental system such that apples are being traded for apples. These commentators argue that in many cases ETMs involve trading the wrong things, trading apples for oranges, even apples for automobiles. *Id.* at 613. ETMs sometimes exhibit non-fungibilities across space, type, and time, creating a problem with respect to the need for a common currency that enables exchange. For example, wetlands mitigation banking programs permit real estate developers to compensate for wetlands that will be destroyed as a result of development by ensuring restoration of wetlands in a different location. The programs require trades that ensure equivalent values and functions between the destroyed and restored wetland. The standard currency used for such trading is acreage: Restored wetlands must be exchanged for destroyed wetlands on an acre-for-acre basis. But critics have argued that this currency is inadequate because it fails to account for the social value of habitat. *Id.* at 648-665. They argue that many ETM programs need redesigning to accommodate problems of non-fungibility and inadequate currencies.

Specifically, they argue, "[t]he commodity model of trading cannot . . . sufficiently satisfy the demands posed by the trading of nonfungible environmental amenities." *Id.* at 693. The more appropriate model, they contend, is a barter model, in which the goods exchanged are not generic. *Id.* at 669. This model favors rigorous *ex post* review of trades to assure equivalence in trading, especially with respect to values that a simple common currency, such as acreage, ignores (e.g., the ecological functions and services of wetlands). Can the market mechanism of ETMs accommodate such *ex post* review of trades? Or would the substitution of a thicker, more fine-grained currency effectively decommodify the units of trade, thereby undermining the overall market mechanism?

4. *Non-Regulatory Approaches to Controlling Carbon Emissions.* Despite the fact that individuals and households account for approximately 30 to 40 percent of all carbon emissions in the United States, relatively little attention has been paid to ways in which these sources of carbon emissions might be reduced. Policy analysts commonly assume that controlling carbon emissions means government regulation, but this assumption may not hold true. Michael Vandenbergh and his co-authors have argued that large emission reductions can be achieved with limited governmental expenditures through non-regulatory means. Specifically, they argue that "information provision may be an effective and politically viable measure to reduce individual and household emissions in some cases, and in other cases combinations of information provision, economic incentives, and modest legal requirements may succeed, even in the antiregulatory environment prevailing in the United States." *See* Michael P. Vandenbergh et al., *Individual Carbon Emissions: The Low-Hanging Fruit*, 55 UCLA L. Rev. 1701, 1705 (2008). They identify seven "potential low-hanging fruit [carbon emission] reductions" — voluntary individual actions "that have the potential to generate prompt, large reductions at lower cost than many of the measures adopted or proposed to date." *Id.* at 1706.

The actions they recommend are: "Reduce the component of motor vehicle idling that has net costs to the driver"; "Reduce standby power electricity use"; "Accelerate the substitution of compact fluorescent light bulbs (CFLs) for incandescent bulbs"; "Adjust temperature settings two degrees in both summer and winter"; "Decrease household thermostat settings on water heaters"; "Maintain the recommended tire pressure in personal motor vehicles"; and "Change air filters in personal motor vehicles at recommended intervals." *Id.* at 1720. The overall target of these actions is to reduce individual and household carbon emissions by 7 percent in five years.

Most (all?) of these actions may seem easy enough, but do you think that most people will take them voluntary? Consider, for example, reducing the thermostat setting on household water heaters. Even if you are willing to do this (or have already done so), do you think most people are willing, especially in winter?

5. *Two Competing Paradigms of Environmental Risk Regulation.* In the world of risk regulation, which includes not only environmental risk but also health and safety risk, two basic paradigms compete for attention. One is cost-benefit analysis (CBA), which "strives to enhance social welfare by predicting, weighing, and aggregating all relevant consequences of policy proposals in order to identify those choices that represent welfare-maximizing uses of public resources . . . ." Douglas A. Kysar, *It Might Have Been: Risk, Precaution and Opportunity Costs*, 22 J. LAND USE & ENVTL. L. 1, 3-4 (2006). The other is the precautionary principle (PP), which "eschews optimization in favor of more pragmatic forms of decisionmaking." *Id.* at 4. A familiar statement of PP is: "When an activity raises threats of harm to human health or the environment, precautionary measures should be taken even if some cause and effect relationships are not fully established scientifically." Peter Montague, *The Precautionary Principle in the Real World, available at* http://www.rachel.org/lib/pp_def.htm (describing and quoting the 1998 Wingspread Declaration).

Although CBA is currently the reigning paradigm in the United States, it has its share of critics. They have attacked its use of discounting to compare intertemporal costs and benefits. *See, e.g.,* Douglas A. Kysar, *Discounting . . . On Stilts*, 74 U. CHI. L. REV. 119 (2007). They have also attacked its reliance on aggregate, monetized benefits as excluding issues of fairness and morality. *See* Frank Ackerman & Lisa Heinzerling, *Pricing the Priceless: Cost-Benefit Analysis of Environmental Protection*, 150 U. PA. L. REV. 1553, 1563 (2002).

Defenders of CBA argue that the PP is indeterminate and offers no guidance for future action, whereas CBA is objective and provides socially optimal solutions to environmental problems. *See, e.g.,* CASS R. SUNSTEIN, LAWS OF FEAR: BEYOND THE PRECAUTIONARY PRINCIPLE (2005); CASS R. SUNSTEIN, RISK & REASON: SAFETY, LAW, AND THE ENVIRONMENT (2002); Cass R. Sunstein, *Beyond the Precautionary Principle*, 151 U. PA. L. REV. 1003 (2003). Critics of CBA, such as Douglas Kysar, contend that "the precautionary principle's requirement that we pause to consider the environmental consequences of our actions is at bottom a reminder that social choices express a collective moral identity—*our* identity, an identity that cannot be located within the freestanding optimization logic of [welfare] economics . . . ." DOUGLAS A. KYSAR, REGULATION FROM NOWHERE: ENVIRONMENTAL LAW AND THE SEARCH FOR OBJECTIVITY 22 (2010). Rather than aiming at optimal results, as CBA analysts do, PP proponents suggest that heuristic decision-making procedures should be used, especially where realistic but unquantifiable threats such as climate change exist. For example, in the case of air pollution, such a heuristic might be the precautionary practice of using the best available abatement technology. *See* Kysar, *It Might Have Been, supra,* at 24-25.

Kysar's critique of CBA rests on a more fundamental critique of CBA's philosophical foundations, namely, welfarism and utilitarianism. He argues that these theories "suffer[] from a fundamental conceptual difficulty, in that its command of impartial causal optimization serves to erode the very basis on which individuals have come to think of themselves as agents whose choices and actions somehow matter." *Id.* at 13. Recall the materials in Chapter 5 and our discussion there. Do you agree that welfarism, as an offspring of utilitarianism, sublimates human agency in such a way that individuals over time lose a strong sense that their actions warrant moral evaluation and, where appropriate, condemnation? Even if human agency retains some sense of integrity under welfarism, does it follow that environmental problems are best approached in terms of a model that claims to be morally objective and whose objective is optimization? In view of Ruhl's observations regarding the nature of climate change, is that problem one that lends itself to optimization?

AUTHOR INDEX

Principal authors are in italics.

Ackerman, Bruce A., 41, 102, 278
Ackerman, Frank, 427
Adams, John, 74, 77
Alexander, Gregory S., 71, 79, 80, 101, 109, 122, 131, *134*, 137, 138, 143, 144, 145, 146, 175, *187*, 199, 200, 201, 305, 330, 332, 340, 376
Alexander, Lisa T., 425
Allen, William T., 176
Alstott, Anne L., 275, 278
Amar, Akhil R., 331
American Law Institute, 286
Andersen, Roger W., 299, 300
Anderson, Elizabeth, 40, *201*, 212, 213, 214, 280, 283
Anderson, Terry L., 64, 68
Appleby, Joyce, 74, 80
Arendt, Hannah, 320
Aristotle, 63, 71, 78, 79
Arrow, Kenneth J., 220
Austin, John, 170, 304
Avi-Yonah, Reuven S., 40
Axelrod, Robert, 165, 168
Ayres, Ian, 214

Bailey, Clinton, 389
Baker, C. Edwin, 41
Bakija, Jon, 69
Banner, Stuart, 377, 388, 389, 390, 392
Barnett, Randy, 40-41
Barros, D. Benjamin, *316*, 317, 318, 319
Barton, Stephen E., 338, 339, 340
Been, Vicki, 359

Beiner, Ronald, 79
Belk, Russell W., 25, 312
Bell, Abraham, 69, *344*, 355, 356, 357, 358
Bell, Daniel, 195
Benkler, Yochai, 93, *217*, 227, 229
Bentham, Jeremy, 19, 88, 102, 170
Bentley, Arthur F., 332
Berger, Curtis J., 111, 331
Berlin, Isaiah, 125, 323
Black, Donald, 165
Blackstone, William, 97, 100-101, 102, 105, 135, 146, 170, 241, 255
Blakely, Edward, 341
Bloch, Marc, 248
Blomley, Nicholas, 329
Bloom, Ira Mark, 300
Blume, Lawrence, 374
Bobo, Lawrence, 356
Bolingbroke, Henry St. John, 194
Boyle, James, 228, 229, 241
Brandeis, Louis, 23
Brooks, Roy L., 403
Brown, Michael F., 264, 266
Brudner, Alan, 25, 55-56
Buckle, Stephen, 13
Butt, Peter, 391

Calabresi, Guido, 101, 162, 163, 342, 362
Carpenter, Kristen A., 26
Chadwick, Ruth, 230
Christman, John, 39
Claeys, Eric R., 375

Clark, Pamela, 238
Clay, Karen, 170
Clifford, James, 391
Coase, Ronald, 162, 164
Cobb, Neil, 330
Cohen, Felix S., 108, 132
Cohen, G.A., 40
Cohen, Lloyd R., 243
Cohen, Morris, 92
Coleridge, Samuel Taylor, 194
Cook, James, 378
Cooper, Clare, 312
Cooter, Robert D., 212
Corwin, Edward S., 200
Cronon, William, 392
Cuba, Lee, 313
Curran, Barbara, 166
Cutler, David M., 356

Dagan, Hanoch, 14, 26, 55, 79, 102, *103*,
    108, 109, 120, 121, 122, 131, 133,
    136, 137, 144, 145-146, 159, 160,
    183, 184, 264, *279*, 290, 291, 292,
    293, 374, 375, 415
Dagan, Tsilly, 40, 213, 255
Dan-Cohen, Meir, 24
Danforth, Robert T., 301
Davidson, Nestor M., 121
de Tocqueville, Alexis, 339
Demsetz, Harold, 57, 62, 63, 64, 68,
    161, 182, 183, 229
Denton, Nancy A., 356
Desan, Christine, 10
Dessin, Carolyn L., 301
Diamond, Shari Seidman, 318, 372
Dickenson, Donna, 241
Dittmar, Helga, 24, 312, 317
Donahue, Charles, Jr., 121
Dorfman, Avihay, 121
Drassinower, Abraham, 228
Dukeminier, Jesse, 306
Durkheim, Émile, 197, 198
Duxbury, Neil, 93, 108, 390
Dworkin, Ronald, 108, 330

Easterbrook, Frank H., 294
Edelman, James, 303
Eggertsson, Thráinn, 68

Eisenberg, Rebecca S., 65
Elkin-Koren, Niva, 224
Ellickson, Robert C., 64, *161*, 167,
    168, 169, 170, 320, 329, 330, 331,
    337, 338
Ellman, Ira Mark, 290
Elsen, Albert, 258
Elster, Jon, 318, 413, 415
Emanuel, Anne S., 301
Engels, Friedrich, 84, 194
Epstein, Richard A., 73, 136, 278, 279,
    338, 339, 373, 374

Fabre, Cécile, 241
Fama, Eugene F., 297
Fee, John, 311
Feinberg, Joel, 13, 239
Feldman, Yuval, 170
Fellows, Mary Louise, 301
Fennell, Lee Anne, 68, 185, 337, 340,
    342-343
Field, Barry C., 64
Fischel, Daniel R., 294
Fisher, Talia, 255
Fisher, William, 11, 224, 228
Fishkin, James S., 404
Fiske, Alan Page, 312
Fiske, John, 224
Fitzpatrick, Daniel, 63
Ford, Richard T., 357
Foster, Sheila R., 185
Fox, Lorna, 317, 319
Frantz, Carolyn J., *279*, 290, 291, 292
Franzese, Paula A., 339, 340, 341
Fratcher, William Franklin, 293
French, Susan F., 341, 342
Freyfogle, Eric T., 144, 145, 146
Friedman, Milton, 41, 271, 277, 278
Friedman, Rose, 271
Frischmann, Brett M., 227
Frost, Robert, 319
Fullilove, Mindy Thompson, 309

Galster, George, 359
Galston, William A., 233
Gans, Chaim, 26
Gardbaum, Stephen A., 81
Gardner, Simon, 280

Garnett, Nicole Stelle, 373
Geertz, Clifford, 81
Glaeser, Edward L., 356
Goodman, Paul, 80
Gordon, Wendy J. 227
Gray, John Chipman, 301, 305, 307
Gray, Kevin, 143, 145
Gray, Susan Francis, 143, 145
Green, Leslie, 147, 158, 160
Griswold, Erwin N., 301

Halbach, Edward C., Jr., 300
Hale, Robert L., 92, 389
Hampton, Jean, 79
Hansmann, Henry, 120, 242, 303
Hardin, Garrett, 63
Harding, Sarah, 265
Harrington, James, 73, 77
Harris, J.W., 128-129, 253
Hart, H.L.A., 40
Hart, John F., 375
Hartz, Louis, 200
Haskins, George L., 305
Haslett, D.W., 269, 274, 275, 277, 278
Hayek, 170
Hegel, G.W.F., 20, 21, 22, 25, 56, 87, 318
Heinzerling, Lisa, 427
Heller, Michael A., 65, 121, 183, 184,
    372, 407, 413-414, 415
Herzog, Don, 106
Hettinger, Edwin C., 14
Hill, P.J., 64, 68
Hills, Roderick, Jr., 372
Hirsch, Adam J., 301
Hirsch, Fred, 193, 194
Hirschman, Albert O., 149, 158, 160,
    165, *190*, 201, 213
Hitchens, Christopher, 267
Hobbes, Thomas, 161-162, 164, 175,
    332, 336
Hoffman, Elizabeth, 164, 165
Hohfeld, Wesley Newcomb, 97, 101, 102,
    103, 106, 108, 328
Honoré, Tony, 101
Hume, David, 63, 149, 192
Hummon, David M., 313
Hyde, Alan, 240-241
Hylton, Keith N., 230, 403

Jaffe, Louis L., 168
Jefferson, Thomas, 73, 74, 75-77,
    320, 339
Jensen, Michael C., 296, 297

Kades, Eric, 392
Kant, Immanuel, 38, 40, 43, 44, 45, 46,
    47, 49, 50, 51, 53, 54, 54, 55, 56, 79,
    228, 230, 231, 232, 233, 234, 235,
    236, 237
Kaplow, Louis, 55, 374
Kass, Leon, 230
Katyal, Sonia K., 26, 229, 330
Katz, Larissa, 132
Katz, Stanley N., 77, 80, 133, 159
Kearns, Thomas R., 169, 170
Kelly, Daniel B., 373
Kibel, Paul Stanton, 418
Knowles, Dudley, 25
Korobkin, Russell, 25
Kraakman, Reinier, 120
Kramer, Matthew H., 14
Kraut, Richard, 78
Kreiczer-Levy, Shelly, 279
Krier, James E., 63, 184, 306
Kronman, Anthony T., 55, 213
Kukathas, Chandran, 148, 150
Kutz, Christopher, 416
Kymlicka, Will, 11, 39, 40
Kysar, Douglas A., 278, 427

Lametti, David, 103, 145
Langbein, John H., 303, 305
Lazarus, Richard J., 424
Leacock, Eleanor, 58, 59
Lehavi, Amnon, 185
Lemley, Mark A., 227
Lessig, Lawrence, 228, 229
Levinson, Daryl J., 374
Levmore, Saul, 374
Lewinsohn-Zamir, Daphna, 55,
    69-70, 356
Lifshitz, Shahar, 292, 293
Lindblom, Charles E., 41
Llewellyn, Karl N., 102, 108
Locke, John, 3, 9, 10, 11, 13, 15, 44, 54,
    150-151, 164, 276, 291, 334, 335,
    336, 338, 400

Lovett, John A., 143
Luce, R. Duncan, 169
Lyons, David, 399

Macaulay, Stewart, 164, 168, 169
Mack, Eric, 240
Macpherson, C.B., 73
Mahoney, Julia, 238
Maine, Sir Henry Sumner, 170
Maitland, Sir Frederic W., 304
Marcuse, Herbert, 195
Marris, Peter, 313
Martin, William, 381
Marx, Karl, 20, 40, 84, 85, 86, 194, 407
Marx, Leo, 75
Massey, Douglas S., 356
Mattei, Ugo, 303
McAdams, Richard H., 167
McCaffery, Edward J., 274-275
McCarthy, E. Doyle, 317
McConnell, Allen R., 403
McDermott, John, 333
McHugh, P.G., 388, 390-391
McKean, Margaret A., 65, 183
McKenzie, Evan, 332, 337, 338, 339, 340
Meckling, William H., 296
Meisels, Tamar, 402
Melamed, A. Douglas, 101, 162, 163,
    342, 362
Merrill, Thomas W., 110, 120, 121,
    122, 131, 132, 133, 159, *361*, 371,
    372, 374
Merryman, John Henry, 256, 265, 267
Michelman, Frank I., 41, 69, 80, 81, 92,
    135-136, 331, 374-375
Mill, John Stuart, 208
Mills, J.S., 329
Milly, P.C.D., 418
Montague, Peter, 427
Montesquieu, Charles Louis, 191,
    195, 197
Moore, Underhill, 168
Morris, Emily, 337
Mossoff, Adam, 13, 132
Munzer, Stephen R., 12, 13, 14, *229*, 230,
    234, 239, 266, 276, 330
Murphy, Liam, 40

Nadler, Janice, 318, 372
Nagel, Thomas, 40
Nedelsky, Jennifer, 199, 200
Netanel, Neil Weinstock, 223, 229
Newman, Alan, 301
Nine, Cara, 402
Novak, William J., 71
Nozick, Robert, 10, 11, *29*, 38, 39,
    40, 41, 44, 54, 55, 78, 86, 88,
    146, 254, 276-277, 334, 338,
    394-395, 403
Nussbaum, Martha, 138, 141

Offe, Claus, 407
Oh, Jason S., 424
Okin, Susan Moller, 283, 284
Oldham, J. Thomas, 291
Olmsted, Frederick Law, 141, 175
Olson, Mancur, 227
O'Mahony, Lorna Fox, 330
Ondrich, Jan, 358
Orfield, Gary, 356
Ostrom, Elinor, 64, *176*, 183, 425
Otsuka, Michael, 40

Paine, Thomas, 191
Parchomovsky, Gideon, 69, *344*, 355, 356,
    357, 358, 376
Parkman, Allen M., 290
Peñalver, Eduardo M., 134, 137, 138,
    145, 158, 160, 229, 330, 377
Penner, J.E., 39, 54, 102, *123*, 131, 132,
    133, 159, 277
Pettit, Philip, 78-79
Phillips, Anne, 242
Pido, Eric J., 320
Plott, Charles R., 25
Pocock, J.G.A., 72, 73, 74, 79, 388
Pogany, Istvan, 414
Polanyi, Karl, 195
Porat, Ariel, 275, 276
Posner, Eric A., 169, 404
Posner, Richard A., 65, 68, 69, 161
Pound, Roscoe, 163
Proudhon, Pierre-Joseph, 86,
    89, 90
Purdy, Jedediah, 133, 134

Radin, Margaret Jane, 17, 24, 25, 26, 27, 212, 213, 230, 239-240, 310, 311, 312, 316, 317, 318, 319
Raiffa, Howard, 169
Rasmussen, Eric B., 167
Raustiala, Kal, 266
Rawls, John, 41, 93, 94, 147
Regan, Milton C., 280
Reich, Charles A., 243, 252, 253, 254, 255
Reichman, Uriel, 338
Reid, John Phillip, 164
Ricard, Samuel, 191, 192
Richins, Marsha L., 312
Riley, Angela R., 26
Ripstein, Arthur, 54
Robertson, Lindsay G., 392
Robertson, William, 191
Robinson, Randall, 403
Rohe, William R., 315
Rose, Carol M., 63, 101, 122, 141, 159, *171*, 188, 283, 284
Rothman, Jennifer E., 170
Rousseau, Jean-Jacques, 191
Rubinfeld, Daniel L., 374
Rudden, Bernard, 111
Ruhl, J.B., 417, 424, 425, 428
Ryan, Alan, 11, 78

Salzman, James, 425
Sander, Richard H., 358
Sarat, Austin, 169, 170
Satz, Debra, 241-242
Savigny, Friedrich Carl von, 170
Sax, Joseph L., 265, 375
Schelling, Thomas C., 347, 348, 349, 355, 356, 358
Schill, Michael H., 357, 358
Schnably, Stephen J., 25, 318
Schorr, David B., 101
Schumpeter, Joseph A., 196
Schwab, Stewart J., 184
Schwemm, Robert G., 358
Scott, Austin Wakeman, 293, 304
Scott, Elizabeth S., 286
Scott, Robert E., 169, 286
Sebok, Anthony J., 403
Selwyn, George Augustus, 381

Sen, Amartya, 138
Serkin, Christopher, 376, 413-414, 415
Shamir, Ronen, 389
Shavell, Steven, 55, 69
Sherman, Steven J., 403
Shiffrin, Seana Valentine, 15
Siegel, Steven, 341
Siegelman, Peter, 376
Silbaugh, Katharine B., 291
Silverman, Carol J., 338, 339, 340
Simmons, A. John, 403
Simon, William H., 81, 252, 253
Simpson, A.W.B., 306
Singer, Joseph William, 101, 103, 105, 109, 135, 144, 146, *153*, 158, 159, 160, 254, 255
Singleton, Sara, 183
Sitkoff, Robert H., 293, 303, 304, 305, 306
Slemrod, Joel, 69
Smith, Adam, 173, 192, 195, 199
Smith, Henry E., 110, 120, 121, 122, 131, 132, 133, 159, 170, 184, 185
Smith, Henry Nash, 75
Smith, Stephen A., 102
Snyder, Carol, 335
Snyder, Mary Gail, 341
Spaht, Katherine Shaw, 282
Speck, Frank G., 59, 60
Spitzer, Matthew, 164, 165
Sreenivasan, Gopal, 10
Stern, Stephanie M., 309, 317, 318, 372
Steuart, Sir James, 191, 197
Strahilevitz, Lior Jacob, 132, 227, 377
Styles, Irene, 313
Sunstein, Cass R., 80-81, 223, 318, 427

Tabbach, Avraham, 275, 276
Taylor, Michael, 183
Teitel, Ruti G., 401
Thompson, Barton H., Jr., 377
Thompson, Janna, 404
Titmuss, Richard M., 240
Tolstoy, Leo, 220
Treanor, William M., 375
Tritt, Lee-ford, 303
Tullock, Gordon, 272, 274

Twigger-Ross, Clare L., 315
Tyler, Tom R., 170

Underkuffler, Laura S., 376, 377
U.S. Envtl. Prot. Agency, 418
U.S. Global Change Research
    Program, 418
Uzzell, Daniel L., 315

Vandenbergh, Michael P., 426
Vandevelde, Kenneth J., 102
Vermeule, Adrian, 404
Villazor, Rose Cuizon, 391

Wachter, Susan M., 357
Waldfogel, Joel, 214
Waldron, Jeremy, 10, 11, 25, 26, 80, _83_,
    91, 92, 93, 94, 130, 132, 233, 234,
    239, 276, 317, 318, _321_, 328, 329,
    330, 340, _393_, 401, 402, 403, 404,
    405, 416
Walzer, Michael, 80, 158, 203
Ward, Catherine, 313

Warren, Samuel, 23
Wax, Amy L., 283
Weber, Max, 163, 195
Weinrib, Ernest J., 25, _43_, 54, 55, 93
Weiss, Elizabeth, 266
Weitzman, Lenore J., 288
Wesley, John, 195
West, Mark D., 337
Williams, Joan C., 111, 320
Williams, Stephen F., 253
Williamson, Oliver, 161
Wolff, Jonathan, 38
Wood, Gordon S., 72, 79, 188,
    189, 199
Wright, Gavin, 170
Wunderlich, Frieda, 249, 255
Wyman, Katrina Miriam, 63

Yadlin, Omri, 168
Yen, Alfred, 14
Yngvesson, Barbara, 170

Zeiler, Kathryn, 25

SUBJECT INDEX

Aboriginal peoples
  in Australia, 393
  colonialism and, 377-393
  expropriation of lands of, 377-383
  land claims disputes, uses/misuses of
    history in, 391
  in New Zealand, 377-388, 393
  in North America, 393
  private ownership of land,
    generally, 58
  sovereignty of, 388
Absolute self-ownership, right of,
  11, 40
Access, right of, 153-158, 158-159
Acquisition of holdings, 29. *See also*
  Justice in holdings
Acropolis, 261, 263
Adverse possession, 26, 255
African Americans
  racist acts against, reparations for,
    403-404. *See also* Discrimination;
    Racism
  slavery of, reparations for, 403-404.
    See also Slavery
Aid to dependent children, 244
Air pollution
  ETMs, use of, 425
Air space, taking of, 143
ALI. *See* American Law Institute (ALI)
Alienability as incident of ownership,
  39, 130
Alimony or support, 287, 288
  spendthrift trust exception, 306
Allocation of resources, 103-104
"Altlaws," 103-229

American Law Institute (ALI),
  285-286, 288, 289
American Revolution, 72, 80, 189
Animals
  cattle trespass, 161, 163-164,
    165, 170
  domestic vs. wild, 67-68
  fur trade, 58-60
Anticommons property, theory of, 65
Anti-fragmentation principle, 121-122
Appropriation of property, 5-7, 10
  spoilage proviso, 5, 10
  sufficiency proviso, 5, 10, 11
Artifacts. *See* Cultural property
Asset protection trusts, 307. *See also*
  Trusts
Associative freedom, 150
Assurance game, 346, 347, 348-349,
  351, 352
Atomism, 81, 105
Australia, 393
  aboriginal land holdings, legal
    handling of, 390-391
Autonomy, 54, 56, 74, 77, 109, 131,
  136, 137, 148, 201
  collective, 152-153, 202, 203
  exit and, 150-152
  of groups, 152-153, 202, 203

Babies, commodification of, 213
Bail setting, race discrimination in, 214
Balance of power, 77
Bankruptcy, property exemptions
  in, 70
Beach access, 139-142, 172, 174

Bedouin land regime, 389
Belief and behavior, restrictions on, 147
Bench squatting, 329-330
Beneficiaries of trusts
   in rem vs. *in personam* right of
      beneficiary, 304
   interest of, 304
   as residual claimants, 295, 297
Bequest
   freedom of, 275, 277-278
   social stratification, 277-278
Bill of Rights, 249, 327, 331
Body parts
   cells made from cells, 240-241
   commodification of, 213, 230, 237
   defined, 230
   dignity and, 230-238
   domino theory, 239-240
   donation of, 229, 232
   economics of markets in, 242-243
   equality, role of, 241-242
   exploitation, concerns about, 242
   feminist perspectives on property
      rights in, 241
   futures markets in, 242
   gifts of, 239
   law-and-economics of sale of,
      242-243
   legal restrictions on sale of, 238
   markets for, 241-243
   poor, exploitation of, 242
   property rights in, 229-238
   regulation of sale, 242
   sale of, 229-238, 242
   supply and demand, 242
   transferability of, 238
Bright-line rules, resort to, 122
British landholding in New Zealand,
   377-388
British Museum, 267
British system of landownership,
   388-389
Bruce, Thomas, 267
Bundle of rights, 97-100, 101,
   102-103, 104, 108, 123, 131, 145,
   153, 157-158, 174, 238, 265, 342
Business property, discriminatory use
   of, 202

Byronism, 261, 267

Capitalism, 84-85, 190, 192, 194, 195,
   196, 201, 212
Capitalist market relations, 20
Carbon emissions. *See also* Climate
   change adaptation policy;
   Greenhouse gas emissions
   non-regulatory approaches to
      reduction of, 426
   voluntary actions to reduce
      emissions, 426
Caryatids, 263
Cattle trespass, 161, 163-164,
   165, 170
CBA. *See* Cost-benefit analysis (CBA)
Chamberlain, Wilt, 34-35, 39
Charitable contributions, tax benefits
   for 255
Child-support payments
   spendthrift trust exception, 306
Chronic street nuisances, 329-330
CIDs. *See* Common interest
   developments (CIDs)
Citizenship, 71-81
   home ownership and, 320
Civic republicanism, 72, 73-74, 78,
   79-80, 146, 189, 254
Civic solidarity, 14
Civil Liability Research Project (CLRP),
   166-167
Civil responsibility, 145
Civil Rights Act of 1866, 155
Civil rights movement, 344
Claflin doctrine, 299-300, 304
Classic integrationism, 357
Clean Water Act, 423
Climate change, 428
   environmental law, relevance of,
      424. *See also* Environmental law
      and policy
   legislation, requirements for
      success, 424
Climate change adaptation policy,
   417-424
   adaptive management, 422
   back-end decision methods, shift
      to, 422

catastrophe and crisis avoidance and response, 421
conciliation, 423-424
dynamic federalism theory, 423
equitable distribution of resources and protections, 420
federalism question, 423
global change drivers, interaction with, 421
human rights dimension, incorporation of, 420
land-use law, 420
liability rules, evolution of, 419
mitigation policy, 418, 423, 424
natural capital adaptation resources, 419
new governance theory, 422, 424-425
policy linkages, reconfigurations of, 421-422
predictive capacity, 422
property rights, evolution of, 419
stationarity and, 418, 421
water law, 420
Climate justice, 420, 421
Close corporations, 183
CLRP. *See* Civil Liability Research Project (CLRP)
CLS. *See* Critical Legal Studies (CLS)
Coercion, land transactions as result of, 389-390
Cohabitation
contracts, 292
marital property and, 293
regulation of, 292-293
Collaboration. *See* New governance theory
Collective ownership, 125
Commerce, 190-192. *See also* Market domain
Commodification
of babies, 213
of body parts, 213, 239-240
complete, 212-213
of environmental law, 425-426
incomplete, 212-213
of sex, 213
Commodity fetishism, 209, 211

Commodity theory of property, 187-190
property as commodity, 199, 200
propriety and, 187-190, 201
Common interest communities, 339-340. *See also* Common interest developments; Homeowner associations
Common interest developments (CIDs), 333-336, 337-339. *See also* Homeowner associations
community benefits of, 339-340
constitutional rights and, 341342
enforcement of covenants, 342
entitlement subject to a self-made option, 343
exclusion, 340-341
gated communities, 341
market values, focus on, 340
optioning entitlements, 342
property rules vs. liability rules, 342
social obligations and, 340
Common law states, marital property in, 292
Common ownership, 125
Common-pool resources. *See* CPR institutions
Commons property
anticommons, 65
governance of, 176-185. *See also* CPR institutions
hybrids, 185
liberal, 183-184
local public commons, 185
property regimes, 63-65
semicommons, 184-185
tragedy of, 63, 64, 65, 68, 171
urban, 185
Communal property, 3-4, 10, 60-62, 63-65
Communism
post-Communist transitions, 407-416
Communitarianism, 79-80, 81, 105
Community, 131, 138
Community apartments, 333
Community-based social-obligation norm, 136-142
Community property states, marital property in, 292

Conciliation
  environmental law and policy,
    423-424
Concurrent ownership, 103
Condominiums, 183, 333, 334-335
Consensualist history for property, 200
Constitution, 249. *See also* specific
    amendments
Constitutive resources, 24-25, 26
Contract law
  property law vs., 110, 124, 303
Contractarian theory
  community-based social-obligation
    norm, 136-142
  trusts and, 294-295, 296, 303-304
Contribution theory
  marital property, 285-286, 290-291
Cook, James, 378
Cooperation, voluntary, 168-169.
    See also New governance theory
Co-ownership, 183
Copyright law, 26, 229. *See also*
    Intellectual property
  fair use exception, 229
  protection of copyright, 14-15
Corrective justice, 43-44, 416. *See also*
    Transitional justice
Costs
  administrative costs of eminent
    domain, 365, 366
  agency costs model, trusts and,
    294-296, 296-302, 303
  cost-benefit analysis (CBA), 427-428
  demoralization costs of regulatory
    takings, 374-375
  due process costs of eminent
    domain, 366
  of exit, 158
  frustration costs, 116-117
  information costs, 118
  of measuring attributes of property
    rights, 113-116
  of privatization, 64, 68
Council of Europe, 263
Countryside and Rights of Way Act
    2000 (England and Wales), 142
Covenants, 111

Covenants, conditions, and restrictions
    (CC&Rs), 333, 335, 338. *See also*
    Homeowner associations
CPR institutions, 176-183
  appropriation rules, 178, 179
  boundaries, clearly defined, 177
  collective-choice arrangements, 178
  conflict-resolution mechanisms,
    181-182
  contingent self-commitments, 181
  enforcement of rules, 179, 180
  modification of operational rules,
    participation in, 178
  monitoring, 179-180
  nested enterprises, 182
  open access and, 182-183
  operational rules, 178-179
  organize, rights to, 182
  provision rules, 178
  resource management, 425
  rewards for doing good job, 179-180
  sanctions, graduated, 179-181
  stability of community, 183
  successful CPRs, 183
  violation of operational rules, 179
Critical Legal Studies (CLS), 111
Crown of St. Stephen, 256
Cultivation of property, 6
Cultural desegregation, 357
Cultural heritage, 14, 264-265
  disposition of, 266
  property. *See* Cultural property
Cultural property, 26, 256-267
  accessibility of, 262-263
  Byronism, 267
  cultural nationalism, 263-264
  defined, 257, 264
  displacement of, 266
  expressive value of, 257-259, 265
  instrumental values, 265
  non-instrumental values, 265
  policy, elements of, 260-264
  politics of, 259-260, 265
  preservation, importance of, 260-262
  public questions concerning, 256
  repatriation laws, 266, 267
  sources of public interest in, 257-260

traditional knowledge as intellectual property, 265-266
truth, concern for, 262
utility of, 260, 265
values underlying, 257-260, 265
Custom, role of, in law, 170
Cyprus, Republic of, 405
Czech Republic, restitution in, 413-414, 415

Dead hand problem, in trusts, 294, 298, 302, 305-306
Dead Sea Scrolls, 258, 260
Death, restrictions on owners' power to control property after, 70
Decentralization, 40
Decommodification, 213
Defeasible estates, 103
Defeasible fee simple, 110
Demoralization costs of regulatory takings, 374-375
Dependency, 74, 76, 78, 137
Dephysicalization of property rights, 102
Desert-for-labor theory of property, 11-12, 12-13
Despotic dominion, 97, 100-101, 102, 105, 135
Destroy, right to, 132
Difference principle, 94
Discovery, doctrine of, 392
Discrimination. *See also* Racism; Residential resegregation
  business property, in use of, 202
  in housing. *See* Housing discrimination
  price discrimination, 117
  prohibition against, 153-157, 159
  public accommodation laws. *See* Public accommodation laws
  in sale or rental of residential dwellings, 159. *See also* Housing discrimination
Disintegration of property, 102-103
Dispute-resolution practices, 166-167
Disqualification, defined, 409
Distributive conception of property, 81
Distributive justice, 14, 30, 31, 32-38, 39, 43-44, 46-47, 83-94, 122, 130, 131, 152, 254, 278, 374, 375, 403

transitional justice vs., 416
Divorce, 282, 285. *See also* Marital property
Domesday Book, 258
Domestic partners, 292
Doux-commerce thesis, 190-192, 195, 196-199, 201
Dropping property values, effect of, 349-352
Dynamic analysis, 65, 66, 69
Dynamic federalism theory, 423
Dynamic property, 74-76
Dynamic resegregation, 345, 354, 355. *See also* Residential resegregation

Eagle Protection Act, 277
Easements, 111, 154, 172, 255
Economic determinism, 93
Economic dynamism, 76
Economic freedom, 204
Economic theory of property rights, 65-68
Egalitarian theory of ownership, 39, 40
Eleventh Amendment, 392
Elgin Marbles, 261, 262, 267
Eminent domain, 26, 361-371, 371-376. *See also* Takings
  administrative costs, 365, 366
  compensation requirement, 361-376
  due process costs of, 366
  heightened scrutiny, 370
  market bypass, 370
  market exchange and, 364, 365, 366
  public use analysis, 361-371, 371-372
  secondary rent seeking, 368-368, 370, 372
  subjective losses, uncompensated, 367-368, 370, 371-372, 373
  surtax proposal, 370
  uses of, 362
Enclosure of land, 6
Endangered species
  Endangered Species Act, 423
ETMs, use of, 425
Endowment effect, 25
Endowment taxation, 40
England, right to roam in, 142-143

Entitlement theory, 31, 33, 35, 276
Entry
 exit and, 159-160
 property as entrance, 158
 right to, 159
 values of property and, 159
Environmental law and policy,
  417-428
 adaptation policy, 424. *See also*
  Climate change adaptation policy
 climate change. *See* Climate change;
  Climate change adaptation policy
 commodification, 425-426
 conciliation, 423-424
 conservation policy, 14, 419
 cost-benefit analysis of protection,
  427-428
 decommodification, 425-426
 domestic, 420
 dynamic equilibrium, 418
 dynamic federalism theory, 423
 mitigation, 424
 natural resources conservation
  policy, 418
 new governance theory, 422, 424-425
 precautionary principle, 427
 preservationism, 418-419
 relevance of, 424
 risk regulation, 427
 transitionalism, 418-419
Environmental trading markets
  (ETMs), 425-426
 air pollution, 425
 endangered species, 425
Equality
 marital property division. *See* Marital
  property
 outcome, 275
 resource, 275
Equity insurance, 352, 353-354
Erechtheion on the Acropolis, 263
Escheat, 88
Estoppel, 10-11
Ethical limitations of market, 201-212
ETMs. *See* Environmental trading
  markets (ETMs)
European Convention on Human
  Rights, 405-406

European Court of Human Rights,
  reparations in, 405-406
Evolutionary theory of property rights,
  57-62, 63-64
Exchange function of property, 187
Exclusion, 123
 right of, 153-158, 159, 171
 theory, 128, 131, 264-265
Exclusivity, 133
Exit, 206, 211, 212
 costs of, 158
 entry and, 159-160
 harms of, 158
 marriage and, 281-282, 284, 285
 right of, 147-153
 taxes, 152
 voice and, 149, 158, 199
Expropriation of lands
 from aboriginal peoples, 377-383
Externalities, 57-62

Fair housing, 159
Fair Housing Act, 159, 344, 357, 358
Fair share of common resources, 152
Fair use of copyrighted works, 159, 229
Family property, 21
 inheritance. *See* Inheritance
 marriage. *See* Marital property;
  Marriage
 trusts. *See* Trusts
Federal land programs, 80
Federal Republic of Germany, 407, 409
Federalism, and climate change
  adaptation policy, 423
Fee simple absolute ownership, 103,
  108
Fee simple ownership, 75, 78, 80, 110,
  116
Fee tail estate, 80, 103, 107
Fetishism, 18, 19, 20, 209, 211
Feudal vision of property relationships,
  80, 111, 247-249
Fiduciary duties of trustee, 295,
  297-298
Fifteenth Amendment, 391
Fifth Amendment, 277, 361, 366
First come, first served, 126
Flatt, John, 381

Forced labor, 36-37. *See also* Labor
Forms of property
   limit on. *See Numerus clausus*
     principle; Standardization
   substance of property vs. form, 104
Fourteenth Amendment, 366
Fragmentation of property, 121-122
Franchises, 244
Free-riders, 135, 227-228
Free software, 218
Freedom, 201-203, 209
   of association, 150, 152
   of dissociation, 151
   economic, 204
   of expression, 152
   homelessness and. *See* Homelessness
   individualistic preference model, 210
   moralization of, 328
   negative, 322-324, 328
   positive, 323, 328
Frustration costs, 116-117
Fungible property, 18, 23-24, 26
Fur trade, 58-60
Future interests, 103, 111

Game theory, 165, 167, 346-352
Garden of Eden, 336
Gated communities, 341
Generation-skipping tax, 306
Genesis, 336
Geographies of property, 329
German Democratic Republic, 407,
   408, 409
German Reich, 409
Germany
   post-Communist retroactive justice,
     407-413
Gifts, 124
   exchange, norms of, 207-208
   as separate property, 291-292
   transfer through, 44, 87, 88
Global change drivers, interaction
   with, 421
God-given property, 3-6, 11
Gossip, role of, 165
Government largesse
   alienability of public entitlements,
     246, 255

   benefits, 244
   confiscation, 251
   contracts, 244-245
   features of, 249
   feudalism, 247-249
   franchises, 244
   growth of, 243-255
   heterogeneity of types, 254
   impact of rise of, 247-249
   income and benefits, 244
   jobs, 244
   licenses, 244, 246
   limitation on use, 246
   occupational licenses, 244
   permits, 245, 246
   private rights in, 250
   private wealth, changes in forms
     of, 245
   procedural protection, 246, 253
   proposals, 250-252
   public interest state, 247-249, 250
   regulation of, 250-251, 252
   revocability of, 246
   Social Security benefits, 244, 245,
     247, 256
   subsidies, 245
   substantive rights to possess and
     use, 246
   system of law, 246-247
   tax benefits for charitable
     contributions, 255
   wealth created by, 243-255
Great Society, 189
Greece
   Acropolis Museum, 267
   Cypriot owners of property,
     reparations claims by, 405-406
   Parthenon Marbles, 267
Greenhouse gas emissions, 417, 419.
    See also Climate change adaptation
    policy
Growth control measures, 355

Hague Convention 1954, 256
Harm principle, 135
Hawaii
   Hawaii Land Reform Act of 1967, 361
   native Hawaiians, 391

Helsinki documents, 409
Historical views of property in United
    States, 187-190, 190-199,
    199-201
Hodgkins' disease, 265
Holdouts, 135
Home. *See also* Housing discrimination;
    Residential resegregation
  citizenship and home-ownership,
    320
  equity insurance, 353-354
  homestead exemptions, 315
  "household" distinguished, 320
  as legal concept, 316
  meanings of, 319, 320
  non-psychological critique of,
    318-319
  psychological evidence, 309-316,
    317-318
  relocation, 312, 313, 314, 315, 316
  revised theory of, 315
  self-constitution, nonprimacy
    to, 312
  self-expressive function of, 317
  single-family, 319, 320
  social evidence, 309-316, 317-318
Homelessness
  freedom, 327
  general prohibitions, 324-325
  geographies of, 329
  housing, right to, 330-332
  important freedoms, 327
  indignity and degradation, 327
  negative freedom, 322-324, 328
  opportunity to acquire home, 328
  particular freedoms, 324-325
  public places, 325-327
  right to housing, 330-332
  squatters' rights, 330
Homeowner associations. *See also*
    Common interest developments
    (CIDs)
  as contractarian, 337-338
  fragmentation problems, 337
  as private governments, 332-336
Home-protective legislation,
    309-316
Homestead Act, 80, 250, 252

Household, defined, 320
Housing discrimination, 344-359
  enforcement of laws, 358
  legislation, effect of, 357-358
  locally undesirable land uses
    (LULUs), 359
Housing segregation, 214. *See also*
    Residential resegregation;
    Residential segregation
Housing right, 330-332
Human body parts, sale of. *See* Body
    parts
Human flourishing, 137-142, 145
Hungary, restitution in, 413, 414-415
Hybrid public property/commons
    property, 185

Idiosyncratic property rights, 113-116
Implied covenant to deliver
    possession, 70
Implied warranty of habitability, 70
Improvement of property, 5-7
In personam right, 97-100, 304
In rem right, 97-100, 127, 128, 129,
    130, 131, 304
"Income effect," 69
Incomplete commodification, 212-213
Independence
  personal, 54
  property and, 253-254
Indeterminacy, 109
Individualism, 209
Industrial Revolution, 194, 196, 258
Information costs, 118
Information economy, 217-226,
    227-229
  autonomy, 225
  commons, benefits of, 217-226
  decentralization of information
    production, 225
  democracy deficit, 222-224
  evolution of property rights in
    information, 229
  justice, 225-226
  nonmarket production, 217-226
Information, property in. *See*
    Information economy
Inframarginal, defined, 295, 297

Inheritance
  abolishment of, proposal for, 269-274
  bequest power and ownership, 277
  bequests vs. lifetime
      consumption, 275
  biological, 271
  capital accumulation and, 274
  egalitarianism and, 274-275
  entitlement theory and, 276
  inflating benefits effects, 275
  intergenerational justice, 278-279
  labor theories, 276
  law of, 77
  libertarianism, 276
  non-utilitarian justification for, 279
  as separate property, 291-292
  taxation of wealth, 275
Innate right, 48
Institutional subsidies, 352, 354-355
Institutions, property, 104-107,
      120-121, 159, 183
  for common property resource
      management, 183
Integration, 344-355
  changing racial attitudes, 356
  dynamic resegregation as obstacle,
      345. *See also* Residential
      resegregation
  partial, 134
  property values, drop in, 349-352
  weak, 349, 351
Intellectual property, 11, 14-15, 65,
      111, 132, 134
  "altlaws," 229
  custom, role of, 170
  private property vs. public
      domain, 228
  traditional knowledge as, 265-266
  Inter vivos arrangements, 88
Interdependency, 137, 141
Intergenerational justice, 278-279
Internalization, 57-62
Internet economy, 217-219. *See also*
      Information economy
Intimacy, 206, 208
Intuitive view of property, 17-24
Israel
  Bedouin land regime, 389

Japanese-American families, symbolic
      payments to, 393-394
Jobs, government largesse, 244
Joint tenancy, 106
Justice in holdings. *See also* Corrective
      justice; Distributive justice;
      Transitional justice
  current time-slice principles, 31-32
  end-result principles, 32-38
  historical principles, 32
  patterning, 32-38
  theory of, 29-38
Justinian's Digest, 258

Kantian right, property as, 43-56

Labor, 3-15
  background conditions, 12-13
  cultivation of property, 6
  defined, 12
  desert-for-labor theory of property,
      11-12, 12-13
  effects of, 4
  enclosure of property, 6
  evaluative or normative features of
      effects of laboring, 12-13
  features of laboring situation, 12-13
  forced, 36-37
  improvement of property, 5-7
  individual property right to, 4-9
  labor-desert theory of property,
      11-12, 12-13, 276
  mixture of labor with commonly
      owned object, 4, 11, 13
  modifications to labor-desert
      theory, 14
  physical effects of laboring, 12-13
  psychological effects of laboring,
      12-13
  revised labor theory, 14
  reward for, 13-14
  taxation of earnings, 36-38, 40
  as workmanship, 13
Labor-desert theory of property, 11-12,
      12-13, 276
Laissez-faire capitalism, 212
Land assembly districts (LADs),
      372-373

Land Reform (Scotland) Act 2003, 142
Länder, 412
Landlords, 135
Landlord-tenant, 111
Landmarks preservation, 26
Land-use law, 420
Law-and-economics theory, 161-167
Law-making by private groups, 168
Leasehold, 107, 110
Legal centralism, 161-163, 163, 165,
   167-168
Legal knowledge, scantiness of, 165-166
Legal peripheralism, 168
Liability rules, 101-102
   vs. property rules, 362, 363
Liberal commons, 183-184
Liberal politics, 201-203
Liberal property theory, 134-136
Liberal theories of justice, 202, 209
Liberalism, 158, 200
   classical, 134-136
Libertarianism, 78-79, 209, 276
   libertarian property regime, 40-41
Liberty, 18, 29-41. *See also* Freedom
Licenses, 244, 246
Life estate, 103, 110
Local public commons, 185
Locally undesirable land uses
   (LULUs), 359

Madagascar, 265
Maori property rights, 377-388, 389
Marital property, 26, 105, 183,
   284-293. *See also* Divorce;
   Marriage
   assets subject to division, 287-290
   cohabitants, 293
   common law states, 292
   community property states, 292
   contribution theory, 285-286,
      290-291
   decision-making authority, 292
   division of, 285-287
   equal division, 285-287
   gifts as separate property, 291-292
   governance regimes, 292
   increased earning capacity,
      288-290, 291

inheritances as separate property,
   291-292
non-market contributions, 285
premarital assets, treatment of, 291
professional degree problem, 288
scope of, 287-290
title theory, 292
Market domain
   alienability, 187
   commodity, 187
   discrimination in, 214
   exchange, norms of, 207-208
   limitations of market ideologies,
      209-212
   market society, 190-199
   norms governing relations, 205-206,
      207, 212
   personal relations and, 206-209
   property law participation in, 213
   social relations of, 204-206
   values in and of, 213-214
Marriage
   autonomy, 281-282
   benefits of, 280
   communal, 280
   community, 280
   cooling-off periods, 282, 285
   covenant, 282
   divorce and, 282, 285
   as egalitarian liberal community,
      279-284, 286, 287, 288, 292
   equality, 282-284
   exit, 281-282, 284, 285
   marital property law. *See* Marital
      property
   non-subordination, 282-284
   oppressive, 283
   patriarchal, 283
   property of. *See* Marital property
Marxists, 40, 407. *See also* Communism
Mass media communications,
   222-224, 225
Measurement-cost externalities,
   113-116
Minimal state, 38-39
Minimum rationality, 362
Mobility. *See also* Relocation
   political, 158

of property, 74-75
right to, 151
Money, invention of, 8-9, 10
Monist theory, 254, 264
Moral development, 25
Moral merit, distribution according
    to, 33
Moral obligations, 239
Multiple sphere differentiation,
    202, 203
Multital right, 97-100

NAGPRA. *See* Native American Graves
    Protection and Repatriation Act
    (NAGPRA)
National cultural heritage, 263-264.
    See also Cultural heritage
National Endowment for the Arts, 257
National Environmental Policy
    Act, 423
National Museum of Anthropology
    (Mexico City), 259
National Organ Transplant Act, 238
Native American Graves Protection
    and Repatriation Act (NAGPRA),
    266
Native Americans
    expropriation of land of, 391-392
    graves, protection of, 266
    modern land law, 392-393
Native Lands Act of 1865 (New
    Zealand), 386
Native Title Act (Australia), 390
Natural resources, responsibilities of
    ownership, 144
Natural right, 44
Nazi regime, 408, 409, 412
Negative freedom, 18, 322-324, 328
Negev desert
    Bedouin settlements in, 389
Neighborliness, 167, 169
Networked information economy, 93,
    217-226, 227-229. *See also*
    Information economy
New Deal, 189, 311, 364
New governance theory, 422, 424-425
New property, 200. *See also*
    Government largesse

New World, 336
New Zealand
    aboriginal land regime,
        377-388, 393
    British land holding in, 377-388
    Maori property rights, 377-388
    sovereignty of, 388
Noise in neighborhood, disclosure of
    problems, 135
Noncommodification, 212-213. *See also*
    Commodification
Non-domination, 79
Non-Intercourse Act of 1790, 392
Nonlegal systems
    social order, role in, 161
Non-market realms, 212
Norms, 167, 169
    conflict with law, 170
    custom and, 170
    limitations of, 169
    market relations, 205-206,
        207, 212
North America
    aboriginal peoples, 393
No-transfer conception of property, 87
Nuisances
    chronic street nuisances, 329-330
    negative obligation to avoid
        committing nuisance, 135
Numerus clausus principle, 70,
    110-122

Occupational licenses, 244
Open access, 63, 68
    CPR and, 182-183
Ostracism, role of, 165
Ownership, 97-122
    exclusion and. *See* Exclusion
    forms of, 103
    give vs. sell, right to, 277
    responsibility and,133, 134-146

Panhandling, 329
Parthenon, 261, 262, 267
Parthenon Marbles, 267
Partnerships, 183
Paternalism, 239
Patterning, 32-38

Paucital right, 97-100
Permits, 245, 246
Perpetual trusts, 306. *See also* Trusts
Personal property, 18, 23-24, 26
Personal relations
  cohabitation. *See* Cohabitation
  commitment, 206-207
  domestic partners, 292
  feminist criticisms of intimacy and
    commitment, 208
  intimacy, 206, 208
  markets and, 206-209
  marriage. *See* Marriage
Personality theory of property, 25, 318
Personhood perspective of property,
  17-27
  home, and personhood theory, 310,
    311-313, 314, 318
Petit-bourgeois, 84, 85
Planned developments, 333
Pluralism, 106, 109, 133, 146, 159,
  201-203, 204, 210, 241, 250,
  254, 255
Political geography, 357
Political goods, 212
Political relativism, doctrine of, 76
Polycentric governance, 40
Poor people. *See* Homelessness; Poverty
Positive externalities, 227-228
Possession of property, 9
"Possessive individualism," 73
"Possessive" conception of property
  rights, 135-136
Post mortem arrangements, 88
Poverty
  public duty to support the poor,
    43-47, 51-54, 55
  taxes to support the poor, 43-47,
    51-54, 55
Precautionary principle (PP), 427
Preemption Act, 250
Preference satisfaction, well-being
  and, 69-70
Pre-political property, 54
Prevention of Illegal Eviction from and
  Unlawful Occupation of Land Act
  of 1998 (South Africa), 330
Price discrimination, 117

Primary right, 100, 101
Primogeniture, 80
Principles of Family Dissolution Law,
  ALI's, 285
Prisoner's dilemma, 168
Private law libertarianism, 54-55
Private property
  criticism of, 84-92
  freedom, limitation on, 321-322,
    323
  general-right-based argument for,
    83-92
  homelessness and, 321-322
  rights, legitimacy of, 9
  special-right-based argument for,
    83-91, 92
Privatization, 411
  costs of, 64, 68
  public areas, 212
Professional degree problem
  marital property, 288
Progressive era, 189
Property rules vs. liability rules, 362,
  363
Property values, drop in, 349-352
Proprietarian understanding of
  property, 71, 199
Propriety
  commodity and, 187-190, 201
  property as, 71, 188
Prospect theory, 25
Prostitution, 241, 242
Protective associations, 334
Protocol No. 1 to European Convention
  on Human Rights, 405
Public accommodation laws, 153-157,
  158, 159
Public areas, privatization of, 212
Public domain, 227, 228. *See also*
  Intellectual property
Public good, 71-72
Public property, 171-175
Public provision of goods, 212
Public trust doctrine, 68, 140, 172
Public use doctrine, 361-371,
  371-372
  economics of public use, 361-377
Puritans, 336

Quality constraints on property
  rights, 70

Racial and other minorities
  federal housing policy and housing
    for, 357
Racial steering, 358-359
Racial stereotyping, 346
Racially restrictive covenants, 344
Racism, 344, 356
  bail setting, discrimination in, 214
  reparations for racist acts, 403-404
  resegregation and, 356. *See also*
    Residential resegregation
  segregation and, 344, 356, 357.
    See also Residential segregation
Ranked coordination games, 349
Realist approach to property, 104-109
Realist legacy, 93
Reciprocity, 133, 145
  long-term reciprocity theory,
    143-144
Reconciliation, 133-134
Recreation, 140-142, 172, 174-175
  social relationships, role in,
    141-142
Rectification of injustice in holdings,
  30, 31, 403
Redistribution, 36, 135
Regulatory measures, 136, 145
Regulatory takings, 373-375, 376.
  See also Eminent domain
  demoralization costs, 374-375
  historical views, 375
Reliance interest in property, 105,
  254-255
Relocation, 312, 313, 314, 315, 316
Rembrandt Study Project, 260
Remedies, 101-102
Rent control, 26
Rent seeking, 229, 365, 368-369,
  370, 372
Reparations, 393-406
  cash payments, 416
  Central and Eastern Europe, post-
    communist, 413-415
  circumstances and supersession,
    398-400, 400-401

counterfactual approach to,
  394-396, 402-403
entitlement, claims of, 401
in European Court of Human Rights,
  405-406
historical rights, 403
individualist- vs. collectivist-based
  claims, 404
injustice and history, 393-394,
  400-401
in-kind, 416
none vs. some, 402
perpetuation of injustice, 396-398
post-communist transitions, 401,
  413-415
remission of injustice, 396-398
reparatory justice, 401
restitution. *See* Restitution
for slavery, 403-404
socialist regimes, in wake of fall of,
  413-415
supersession of historic injustice,
  400-401, 401-402, 404
symbolic, 416
time, effect of, 403
transitional regimes and, 401
Reprivatization, 411
Republicanism, 72-74, 76-81, 319-320
Resegregation, 344-355. *See also*
  Residential resegregation;
  Residential segregation
Residential communities, 332-344
Residential entrapment, 314-315
Residential protectionism, 309,
  310-316
Residential real estate, 309
Residential resegregation, 344-355
  assurance game, 346, 347, 348-349,
    351
  countering white flight, 352-355
  dropping property values, effect of,
    349-352
  growth control measures, regional,
    355
  home equity insurance, 353-354
  institutional subsidies, 354-355
  integration game, 346, 347, 349,
    351-352

key to resolve problem, 346
motivations of homeowners, 346
racism and, 356
resegregation game, 346, 347-348, 350
subsidized community institutions,
    354-355
taxes on home sales, 354
techniques to neutralize economic
    incentive to leave, 352-355
Residential segregation, 344-355
    changes in housing patterns and
        preferences, 356
    concentration of poor racial
        minorities, federal housing policy
        and, 357
    federal housing policy, 357
    locally undesirable land uses
        (LULUs), 359
    political geography, 357
    racial steering, 358-359
    tipping model, critique of, 355-356
Responsibility-focused approaches to
    property, 134-146
Restitution, 14, 406
    backward- vs. forward-looking
        justice, 411, 413
    cash, 410
    claimants, determination of
        universe of, 411
    Czech Republic, 413-414, 415
        defined, 409
        exempt properties, 413
    Hungary, 413, 414-415
        identification of victims, 410
        in kind, 410
        loss, proof of, 410
        modes of compensation, 410
        natural, 410, 411, 415
        objections to, 411-413, 415
        partial, 413, 414-415
        rehabilitation, 410
        relocation of institutions, 410-411
        retribution compared, 411
        symbolic, 410-411
        victims, identification of, 410
        vouchers or coupons, 410, 414
        well-being vs. personhood,
            protection of, 415

Retaliatory action, 165
Retribution
    defined, 409
    restitution compared, 411
Revised Uniform Anatomical Gift Act
    2006, 239
Right-based account of property, 55-57
Risk regulation
    cost-benefit analysis, 427
    precautionary principle, 427
Roam, right to, 142-143
Romania, 413
Rosetta Stone, 260
Rosy Periwinkle, 265
Rotating credit associations, 81
Rule Against Perpetuities, 298,
    305-306. *See also* Trusts

Sacrifice, ethic of, 79
Same-sex couples, 293
Scotland, right to roam in, 142, 143
Seattle Symphony, 329
Secondary right, 100, 101
Segregation, 344-355. *See also*
    Residential resegregation;
    Residential segregation
Self-constitution, 254
Self-destruction thesis, 192-196, 201
Self-determination, 22, 48
Self-direction, 151
Self-help enforcement of entitlements,
    165
Self-identification through
    property, 19
Self-ownership, right of, 11, 40
Self-realization, 133
Self-sacrifice, 146
Self-settled spendthrift trusts, 307
Semicommons, 184-185
Semiotic democracy, 224
Servitudes, 111
    "Several property," 40-41
Sex, commodification of, 213
Single-family homes, 319, 320
Slavery, 80, 189, 203
    reparations for, 403-404
Sociability, 141
Social contract, 51

Social groups' control over members, 147-149
Social norms
  evolution of, 169
  law, interaction with, 169
Social obligation theory, 134-143, 145, 146
Social order, proper, 188
Social Security Act, 247
Social Security benefits, 244, 245, 247, 256
Social transformation, 78
Socialism, 32, 85, 194
  by contract, 334
Socializing, recreation's role in, 174-175
South Africa
  housing, right to, 331
  squatters' rights, 330
Sovereignty of aboriginal peoples, 388
Speech and conduct codes, 147
Spendthrift trust, 301-302, 305, 306-307
  alimony or support, exception for, 306
  child-support payments, exception for, 306
  policy objections to, 307
  self-settled, 307
Sphere differentiation, 202, 203
Spoilage of property, 5, 10
Squatters' rights, 330
Stability in ownership, 69
Standardization, 107, 110-122
Static analysis, 65-66, 68
Static property, 74-76, 78
Stationarity, 418, 421
Stereotyping, 346
Stigmatization, 202
Stock cooperatives, 333
Street nuisances, 329-330
Structural pluralism, 109
Subsidies, 245
  institutional, 352, 354-355
"Substitution effect," 69

Takings Clause, 277
Takings law, 143-144, 145, 361-377.
  See also Eminent domain

compensation requirement, 361-376
  deferential judicial stance, 376
  eminent domain. *See* Eminent domain
  extra compensation, 376
  historical views, 375
  judicial, 376-377
  partial compensation, 376
  regulatory, 373-375
  varied compensation, 376
Tasman, Abel, 378
Taxes, 69, 88-90, 92, 135
  charitable contributions, tax benefits for, 255
  on earnings, 36-38, 40
  endowment taxation, 40
  exit, 152
  on home sales, 352, 354
  the poor, support of, 43-47, 51-54, 55
  reform, 424
Tipping model, critique of residential segregation, 355-356
Tit-for-Tat strategy, 165, 168
Transfer of holdings, 29
  justice in transfer, 30
Transitional justice, 407-416
  disqualification, 407, 409
  distributive justice vs., 416
  restitution. *See* Restitution
  retribution, 407, 409, 411
Transitions, 361-416
  aboriginal land regimes. *See* Aboriginal land regimes and colonialism
  justice in. *See* Transitional justice
  takings. *See* Takings
Treaty of Waitangi, 381, 388
Trespassory rules, 128, 132
  cattle trespass, 161, 163-164, 165, 170
Trusts, 293-307
  agency costs model, 294-296, 296-302, 303
  beneficiaries as residual claimants, 295, 297-298
  beneficiary, interest of, 304
  Claflin doctrine, 299-300, 304

contract vs. property law, 303
contractarian theory of, 294-295,
    296, 303-304
dead hand problem, 294, 298, 302,
    305-306
default duties, 303
donative, 295-296
external transactional authority,
    300-302
fiduciary duties of trustee, 295,
    297-298
in rem vs. *in personam* right of
    beneficiary, 304
internal governance, 300-302
mandatory duties, 303, 305
material purpose, 299
modification, 299-300
perpetual, 306
private, 293, 296
prototypical example, 293-294
residual claimants, 295, 297-298
Rule Against Perpetuities, 298,
    305-306
settlor-beneficiary tension, 298-300
spendthrift trust, 301-302, 305,
    306-307
termination, 299-300
waiver of fiduciary duties, 303, 305
Turkey, 405
Turkish-Cypriots, 405
Turkish Republic of Northern Cyprus
    (TRNC), 405

Unemployment compensation, 244
Unequal distribution, dilemma of,
    76-78
UNESCO, 263
UNESCO Convention 1970, 256, 259
Uniform Anatomical Gift Act, 238-239
Uniform Trust Code, 305
United Nations
    Educational, Scientific, and Cultural
        Organization. *See* UNESCO
    General Assembly, 263
    Security Council, 405

Urban commons, 185
Use, right to, 125-131, 132
Utilitarianism, 427-428

Value
    changes in value of property,
        349-352
    commodity values, 204
    in ethics, 201
    indeterminacy, 109-110
    shared goods, 204
    use value, 204
Veterans benefits, 244
Victims
    compensation of, 410. *See also*
        Reparation; Restitution
    identification of, 410
Virtue
    civic, 78
    defined, 72, 137
    ethics, 145
    private ownership of land and, 78
    social, 193
Voice, 206, 212
    exit and, 149, 158, 199. *See also* Exit

Waitangi Tribunal, 388
Waiver of fiduciary duties, 303, 305
Wales, right to roam in, 142-143
War of 1812, 189
Water law, 420
Welfare
    state and local, 244, 246-247
Welfare economics, 209
Welfare state, 14, 55, 250, 251, 252
Welfarism, 427-428
Well-being, 57-70
    objective understanding of, 69-70
    preference satisfaction, 69-70
Wetlands mitigation banking
    programs, 425
White flight, 352-355. *See also*
    Residential resegregation
World War II, 408
Year Books, 260

CPSIA information can be obtained at www.ICGtesting.com
Printed in the USA
BVOW04s1811180814

363304BV00004B/13/P